THOMAS CROMWELL

*From a picture in the Bodleian Library*

# LIFE AND LETTERS

## OF

# Thomas Cromwell

BY

ROGER BIGELOW MERRIMAN

*With a Portrait and Facsimile*

VOLUME I

LIFE, LETTERS TO 1535

OXFORD
AT THE CLARENDON PRESS

*Oxford University Press, Ely House, London W. 1*

GLASGOW NEW YORK TORONTO MELBOURNE WELLINGTON
CAPE TOWN SALISBURY IBADAN NAIROBI LUSAKA ADDIS ABABA
BOMBAY CALCUTTA MADRAS KARACHI LAHORE DACCA
KUALA LUMPUR HONG KONG TOKYO

FIRST PUBLISHED 1902
REPRINTED LITHOGRAPHICALLY IN GREAT BRITAIN
AT THE UNIVERSITY PRESS, OXFORD
BY VIVIAN RIDLER
PRINTER TO THE UNIVERSITY
1968

# PREFACE

THIS book is an attempt to present the life of Thomas Cromwell as a statesman, and to estimate his work without religious bias. Though it would certainly be difficult to overrate his importance in the history of the Church of England, I maintain that the motives that inspired his actions were invariably political, and that the many ecclesiastical changes carried through under his guidance were but incidents of his administration, not ends in themselves. Consequently any attempt to judge him from a distinctively religious standpoint, whether Catholic or Protestant, can hardly fail, it seems to me, to mislead the student and obscure the truth. I cannot agree, on the other hand, with those who have represented Cromwell as a purely selfish political adventurer, the subservient instrument of a wicked master, bent only on his own gain. It seems to me as idle to disparage his patriotism and statesmanship, as it is to try to make him out a hero of the Reformation. He merits a place far higher than that of most men of his type, a type essentially characteristic of the sixteenth century, a type of which the Earl of Warwick in England and Maurice of Saxony on the Continent are striking examples, a type that profoundly influenced the destinies of Protestantism, but to which theological issues were either a mere nothing, or else totally subordinate to political considerations.

It has been justly said that Cromwell's correspondence is our chief source of information for the period
immediately following the breach with Rome. To
transcribe *in extenso* the letters he received would be
almost the task of a lifetime; for they form the bulk
of the enormous mass of material with which the
editors of the Calendars of State Papers for the years
1533–40 have had to deal. But the number of extant
letters he wrote is, comparatively speaking, extremely
small; it has therefore been possible to make full
copies of them in every case, and I trust that the
many advantages—linguistic as well as historical—
that can only be secured by complete, and as far as
possible accurate transcriptions of the originals, will be
accepted as sufficient reason for editing this collection
of documents, twenty-one of which have neither been
printed nor calendared before. The rules that have
been observed in transcription will be found in the
Prefatory Note (vol. i. p. 311). The Calendar refer-
ences to the more important letters received by
Cromwell, where they bear directly on those he wrote,
are given in the notes at the end of the second
volume.

My warmest thanks are due to Mr. F. York Powell,
Regius Professor of Modern History in the University of Oxford, who has guided me throughout in
matter, form, and style; and to my friend and master
Mr. A. L. Smith, Fellow of Balliol College, whose
advice and encouragement have been an inspiration
from first to last. It is not easy for me to express
how much I have depended on their suggestions and
criticism. I am indebted to Mr. Owen Edwards,
Fellow of Lincoln College, for indispensable help in
the early stages of my work. The main plan of this

book is in many respects similar to that of his Lothian Essay for the year 1887, which I regret that he has never published. My grateful acknowledgements are also due to Mr. James Gairdner of the Public Record Office for information about Cromwell's early life; to Professor Dr. Max Lenz, of the University of Berlin, for helpful suggestions in connexion with the Anglo-German negotiations in the years 1537–40; and to Mr. G. T. Lapsley, of the University of California, for similar services in regard to the Pilgrimage of Grace, and the reorganization of the North after the suppression of the rebellion.

I beg to express my appreciation of the kindness of the Duke of Rutland, the Marquess of Salisbury, Earl Spencer, Lord Calthorpe, William Berington, Esq., and Alfred Henry Huth, Esq., in giving me access to the manuscripts in their private collections.

In conclusion, I wish to thank the officials of the Public Record Office, British Museum, Heralds' College of Arms, and Bodleian Library, for facilitating my work in every way; more especially Messrs. Hubert Hall, R. H. Brodie, E. Salisbury, and F. B. Bickley, who have repeatedly aided me in my search for uncalendared letters and continental documents, and in deciphering the most difficult manuscripts I have had to consult.

R. B. M.

BALLIOL COLLEGE, OXFORD.
*February*, 1902.

# CONTENTS

## VOLUME I

## VOLUME II

## ILLUSTRATIONS

# LIFE OF THOMAS CROMWELL

## CHAPTER I

THE manor of Wimbledon comprises the parishes of Wimbledon, Putney, Roehampton, Mortlake, and East Sheen, and parts of Wandsworth and Barnes [1].  In West Saxon times it was one of the estates of the see of Canterbury, but after the Conquest it was seized by Odo, the high-handed Bishop of Bayeux: in 1071, however, it was recovered by Lanfranc, and with one trifling interruption in the reign of Richard II, it remained in the possession of the archbishopric until 1535. In that year Cranmer surrendered it to Henry VIII in exchange for the priory of St. Rhadegund in Dover, and a little later the King granted it to Thomas Cromwell [2], who was born there some fifty years before, the son of a well-to-do blacksmith, brewer, and fuller.  The early history of the manor of Wimbledon is almost unknown, for we do not possess its Court Rolls prior to the year 1461: they were probably lost or destroyed during the Wars of the Roses. After 1461, however, they are continuous, with the exception of the years 1473 and 1474.

An entry in these rolls, written in the year 1475, states that 'Walter Smyth and his father keep thirty sheep on Putney Common, where they have no common [3].'  A number of subsequent mentions of this same Walter Smyth shows that he

---

[1] Antiquarian Magazine, Aug. 1882, vol. ii. p. 57.

[2] Manning and Bray, History and Antiquities of the County of Surrey, vol. iii. p. 268.

[3] Court Rolls of Wimbledon Manor, 15 Edw. IV. These rolls are now in the possession of Earl Spencer, lord of the manor. They were made accessible to me through the courtesy of his steward, Mr. Joseph Plaskitt.

was also called Walter Cromwell. The name Walter Cromwell occurs more than ninety times in the rolls, and the name Walter Smyth at least forty times. That both these names stand for the same person is proved by one entry written, 'Walter Cromwell alias Walter Smyth,' by two written, 'Walter Smyth alias Cromwell,' and by five written, 'Walter Cromwell alias Smyth.' Who then was this Walter Cromwell, whence did he come, and how did he acquire this double name?

The Cromwell family did not originate in Wimbledon. An entry in the Close Roll of Edward IV states that in the year 1461 John Cromwell, son of William Cromwell, late of Norwell in Nottinghamshire, surrendered his right in Parkersplace, Kendalsland and other property there to Master John Porter, prebendary of Palishall[1]. Mr. John Phillips of Putney further informs us that nine years before John Cromwell gave up his lands in Norwell, he was granted the twenty-one years' lease of a fulling-mill and house in Wimbledon by Archbishop Kempe, lord of the manor, and had moved there with his family[2]. It would be interesting to know what Mr. Phillips' authority for this statement is: unfortunately he has given no reference for it. But whatever the precise date and circumstances of their change of home, there can be little doubt that the Cromwells migrated to Wimbledon from Norwell some time before 1461. There is plenty of evidence in the Court Rolls to show that Walter Smyth alias Cromwell was the son of John Cromwell, and the entry of 1475 proves that they were both in Wimbledon in that year. The family in Nottinghamshire from which they sprung was well-known

---

[1] The original entry reads: 'Johannes Cromwell filius et heres Wilelmi Cromwell nuper de Northwell in comitatu Nottingham remisit totum jus &c. in quodam messuagio vocato Parkersplace et in quodam tofto et v acris terrae et in uno tofto cum crofto et vii acris terrae dudum nuper vocatis Kendalisland et in viii acris terrae et dimidio jacentibus in villa et campis de Northwell magistro Johanni Porter prebendario prebende de Northwell vocato prebende de Palishall in ecclesia collegii beatae Mariae Suthwell et successoribus suis' (Dods. MSS. in Bibl. Bodl., vol. xxxvi. p. 97, 1 Edw. IV).

[2] Antiquarian Magazine for August, 1882, vol. ii. p. 59.

and well-off; both John Cromwell's father William and his grandfather Ralph were persons of wealth and position there [1].

Several entries in the Court Rolls indicate that John Cromwell's wife was the sister of a certain William Smyth, who is often mentioned as 'William Smyth armourer,' and sometimes as 'William Armourer.' It seems probable that this William Smyth came with John Cromwell to Wimbledon from Norwell, and the entries in the manorial records show that he lived there with his brother-in-law. There is also reason to believe that the latter's son Walter was apprenticed to him during his younger days, and so acquired the name Smyth.

Walter Cromwell grew up as a brewer, smith, and fuller in Putney. He had an elder brother named John, who moved to Lambeth and settled down there to a quiet and prosperous life as a brewer, later, according to Chapuys, becoming cook to the Archbishop of Canterbury [2]. Walter, however, remained in Wimbledon, and appears to have been a most quarrelsome and riotous character. Most of the entries in the Court Rolls concerning him are records of small fines incurred for petty offences. Forty-eight times between 1475 and 1501 was he forced to pay sixpence for breaking the assize of ale. In order to prevent the sale of bad beer in those days, an ale-taster was appointed to pass, or condemn as unfit, all brewing in the parish. Walter Cromwell did not go to the ale-taster before he drew and sold his beer, and for failing so to do was fined as aforesaid. There is also record that he was not seldom drunk. In 1477 a penalty of twenty pence was inflicted on him for assaulting and drawing blood from William Michell, and he and his father were very often brought before the court on the charge of 'overburthening' the public land in Putney with their cattle, and cutting more than their share of the furze and thorns there [3]. But in spite

---

[1] Dods. MSS., vol. xi. pp. 193 a, 248 a; vol. xxxvi. p. 103. Thorold Rogers, in his History of Agriculture and Prices, vol. iv. p. 3, refers to Ralph Lord Cromwell as 'one of the richest men of the fifteenth century.'

[2] Cf. Appendix I at the end of this chapter.

[3] The following are some of the more common entries concerning Walter Cromwell :—

'*Presenta*nt  qu*o*d  Gualterus

of all these petty misdemeanours, Walter Cromwell appears to have been a man of property and influence in Wimbledon, and the Court Rolls in 1480 show that he then possessed two virgates of land in Putney parish. To these were added six more virgates in 1500 by grant of Archbishop Morton[1]. Walter Cromwell was also made Constable of Putney in 1495[2], and his name constantly occurs in the Court Rolls as decenarius and juryman[3]. Towards the end of his life, however, his character appears to have become so bad that he forfeited all his position and property in Wimbledon. In 1514 he 'falsely and fraudulently erased the evidences and terrures of the lord,' so that the bedell was commanded 'to seize into the lord's hands all his copyholds held of the lord and to answer the lord of the issue[4].' This is the last mention of the name of Walter Cromwell in the Wimbledon Manor Rolls.

Walter Cromwell's wife was the aunt of a man named Nicholas Glossop, of Wirksworth in Derbyshire[5]. Mr. Phillips gives no reference for his statements that she was the daughter of a yeoman named Glossop, and that she was residing

Cromwell est communis braciator de bere et fregit assisam' and 'quod Gualterus Cromwell et . . . sunt communes tipellarii seruisie et fregerunt assisam ideo ipsi in misericordia vi d.' (Court Rolls, 17 Nov., 10 Hen. VII ; 17 Oct., 15 Hen. VII ; 28 Oct., 17 Hen. VII).

'Item presentant quod Gualterus Smyth alias Crumwell nimis excessive suponunt communam pasturam domini . . . cum aviis suis ad commune nocumentum ideo ipse in misericordia vi d.

'Item presentant quod { Gualterus { Johannes Smyth de Puttenhith succidunt spinas in communa pastura domini apud Puttenhith. Ideo ipsi in misericordia iiii d.' (Court Rolls, 28 Oct., 17 Hen. VII).

[1] Court Rolls, 20 Edw. IV and 16 Hen. VII.

[2] According to the record of 20 May, 11 Hen. VII : 'Elegerunt in officio constabularii de Puttenhith Gualterum Smyth qui juratus est in eodem officio.'

[3] As by an entry of 20 May, 19 Hen. VII : 'Gualterus Smyth et . . . ibidem jurati presentant omnia bene.'

[4] The entry in full reads : 'Item presentant quod W . . . Crumwell alias Smyth false et fraudulenter rasuravit evidences et terrures domini in diversis parcellis ad perturbacionem et exheredacionem domini et tenencium ejus ut plenius apparet in eisdem. Ideo consolendum est cum domino et medio tempore prefatum est bidello seisire in manus domini omnia terras et tenementa sua tenta de domino per copiam, et de exitu eorum domini respondere' (Court Rolls, 10 Oct., 6 Hen. VIII ; also Extracts, p. 74).

[5] Cal. vi. 696.

in Putney at the house of an attorney named John Welbeck, at the time of her marriage with Walter Cromwell in 1474[1]; but we have no evidence that these assertions are incorrect. At least two daughters and one son were born to Walter Cromwell. He may have had other children, but as there was no registration of births, marriages, or deaths in England until 1538, we can only be certain of these three, of whom there are mentions in the Court Rolls and in other contemporary records. The eldest daughter Katherine, who was probably born about the year 1477, grew up and married a young Welshman named Morgan Williams[2], whose family had come to Putney from Llanishen in Glamorganshire. The Williamses were a very important family in Putney, and John, the eldest of them, was a successful lawyer and accountant, and steward to Lord Scales, who was then in possession of a residence and some land in Putney parish. The youngest daughter of Walter Cromwell was named Elizabeth. She married a sheep-farmer named Wellyfed, who later joined his business to that of his father-in-law[3]. Christopher, the son of Elizabeth Cromwell and Wellyfed, grew up and was later sent to school with his cousin Gregory, son of his mother's brother Thomas[4]. We are now in a position to examine the many conflicting statements concerning the son of Walter Cromwell, the subject of this essay.

The traditional sources of information about Thomas Cromwell's early life are the characteristic but somewhat confusing stories of the martyrologist Foxe, founded to some extent upon a novel of the Italian author Bandello, the meagre though probably trustworthy accounts contained in Cardinal Pole's 'Apologia ad Carolum Quintum,' a letter of Chapuys to Granvelle written November 21, 1535, and a few scattered

[1] Antiquarian Magazine, vol. ii. p. 178.

[2] Cal. iv. 5772. Cf. also Noble, Memoirs, vol. i. pp. 4-5, 238-241. The statements in Noble about the Williamses and Cromwells are most confusing and contradictory. Except for the information afforded concerning Morgan Williams, they are without value, and for the most part have been superseded by documentary evidence, discovered at a later date.

[3] Court Rolls, 10 Oct., 5 Hen. VII, and Cal. iv. 5772.

[4] Cal. iv. 5757.

statements in the chroniclers of the period. To these were added in 1880 and 1882 the results of the researches of Mr. John Phillips in the Wimbledon Manor Rolls[1]. Mr. Phillips has certainly brought to light a large number of interesting facts about the ancestry and family of Thomas Cromwell : it is the more unfortunate that he should have gone so far astray in some of his statements concerning the man himself. He is surely correct in assuming Thomas to be the son of Walter Cromwell ; the evidence afforded by the State Papers leaves no doubt of this. He is also right in stating that the name Thomas Cromwell does not occur in the Court Rolls. But it is more difficult to believe the theory which Mr. Phillips has evolved from these data. As he finds no entry concerning Thomas Cromwell in the manorial records, he seeks for some mention of him under another appellation, and hits upon that of Thomas Smyth as the most likely, owing to the fact that his father was called by both surnames. He finds two entries in the Court Rolls concerning Thomas Smyth, and assumes that they refer to Thomas Cromwell. These entries occur in the records of Feb. 26, 1504, and of May 20 in the same year. The first states that ' Richard Williams came to the court and surrendered into the hands of the lord two whole virgates of land in ⟨Roe⟩-hampton, one called Purycroft and the other called Williams, to the use of Thomas Smyth, his heirs and assigns ' ; the second, that ' Richard Williams assaulted Thomas [Smyth] and beat the same Thomas against the peace of the lord the King,' and further that ' Thomas Smyth came to the court and surrendered into the hands of the lord two whole virgates of land in Roehampton, one called Purycroft and the other called Williams, to the use of David Doby, his heirs and assigns[2].' Mr. Phillips has made these entries the basis

---

[1] Antiquary for October, 1880, vol. ii, p. 164. Antiquarian Magazine for August and October, 1882, vol. ii. pp. 56 and 178.

[2] The original entries read as follows :—

1. 'Ad hanc cur*iam* venit Ricard-us Williams et surs*um* red*idit* in

man*us* dom*i*ni duas *i*ntegras virgatas terrae in Hamptone . . . quarum una vocata Purycroft . . . et alia virgata vocata Williams ad op*us* Thomae Smyth hered*um* et assign*atorum*' (Court Rolls, 26 Feb., 19 Hen. VII).

2. ' Ricard*u*s Williams fecit in*s*ul-

for an attack on the veracity of many of the best-known stories of Bandello and Foxe concerning the early life of our subject, but his whole case hangs on the assumption that Thomas Smyth and Thomas Cromwell were one and the same man, and until he can prove this ingenious but somewhat improbable theory his arguments cannot be supported. He discusses at length the two entries in the Court Rolls, adducing them as a proof of the falsity of the accounts which assert Cromwell to have been in Italy previous to 1504, but concluding that the record that Thomas Smyth disposed of his lands in Putney in May of that year indicates that Thomas Cromwell left England at that time. To corroborate this last theory he refers to the story of Chapuys that Cromwell was ill-behaved when young, and was forced after an imprisonment to leave the country, and also asserts, in order still further to strengthen his case, that 'the Court Rolls contain nothing more respecting Thomas Cromwell than what we have already stated [1].'

It seems very extraordinary that Mr. Phillips should make this last statement in view of his readiness to jump at the conclusion that Thomas Smyth and Thomas Cromwell are identical. 'Thomas Smyth,' as a very cursory examination of the Court Rolls will show, is mentioned therein every year from 1493 to 1529 (inclusive), except in 1494 and 1516. As there is certain evidence that Thomas Cromwell was in other places during many of the years that Thomas Smyth was in Wimbledon, it is clear that the two names cannot always stand for the same man. The question which now arises is this: were there two Thomas Smyths, one of them Thomas Cromwell and the other some other member of the Smyth family, perhaps a descendant of William Smyth, armourer?

---

*tum* Thomae [Smyth] et eundem Thomam verberavit con*tra* pac*em* d*omi*ni Regis' . . . 'Ad hanc cur*iam* venit Thomas Smyth et surs*um* redidit in man*us* domi*ni* duas i*n*tegras virgatas terrae in Rokhamptone . . . quar*um* una virgata vocata Purycroft · et alia virgata vocata Williams ad op*us* Davidii Doby hered*um* et as-sign*atorum*' (Court Rolls, 20 May, 19 Hen. VII).

[1] Antiquarian Magazine for October, 1882, vol. ii. p. 183.

Or is the Thomas Smyth mentioned in the Court Rolls one man, and not Thomas Cromwell at all? 

The second theory seems on the whole more probable than the first. There are no contradictory statements about Thomas Smyth in the rolls, nor is the name mentioned twice in any of the lists of the Homage or Frank Pledge. Moreover had there been two Thomas Smyths, one of whom was entitled to the name Cromwell, he would almost certainly have been called so, in order to avoid confusion. On the other hand, it scarcely seems likely that the son of Walter Cromwell should not be mentioned at all in the Court Rolls. But this may be partially explained by Chapuys' account of his youthful wildness and early imprisonment; it seems quite probable that he was a mere boy when he left his home. The evidence which we possess certainly seems to strengthen the conclusion that there was but one Thomas Smyth: the man mentioned in the Court Rolls by that name was probably a descendant of William Smyth, armourer [1]. Surely none of the entries in the manorial records concerning Thomas Smyth can be said to prove anything conclusive concerning the early life of the subject of this essay. It has been the fashion to decry Bandello and Foxe and to disbelieve all their stories, because of the undoubted confusion of dates

---

[1] It is possible that the Thomas Smyth, whose name occurs so frequently in the Court Rolls, was identical with a certain 'tryumphant trollynge Thomas Smyth,' who, in 1541, wrote several ballads 'declaring the despyte of a secrete sedycyous person,' by name William Graye, who had composed certain verses very derogatory to the memory of Thomas Cromwell. This Thomas Smyth describes himself as 'servaunt to the Kynges. royall Majestye, and clerke of the Quenes Graces Counsell, though most unworthy'; he had perhaps obtained his position through the influence of the King's minister. He was supported in his tirade against Graye by 'the ryght redolent and rotunde rethorician R. Smyth . . . in an Artificiall apologie articulerlye answerynge to the obstreperous obgannynges of one W. G. evometyd to the vituperacyon of the tryumphant trollynge Thomas Smyth . . . to thende that the imprudent lector shulde not tytubate or hallucinate in the labyrinthes of this lucubratiuncle.' 'R. Smyth' was probably another member of the Smyth-Cromwell tribe. The name 'Ricardus Smyth' occurs frequently in the Court Rolls (Cal. xvi. 423).

which vitiates their testimony. But if no reliance can be placed on them, or on Pole, Chapuys, and the chronicles of the period, must we not confess that our knowledge of the early years of our subject's life must reduce itself to an interrogation point? Let us guard ourselves against accepting with implicit faith the statements of these authors, but let us not cast them aside as utterly worthless. Let us rather recognize that they still remain our most trustworthy sources of information concerning the early life of Thomas Cromwell, and therefore make a careful attempt to glean from their very confusing statements the more probable facts concerning him.

None of the different accounts sheds any light upon the date of Cromwell's birth, but it is doubtful if it occurred later than 1485, in view of his probable age at the time of his sojourn abroad. That he had a quarrel with his father seems very likely: Bandello's statement that he came to Italy, 'fleeing from his father,' and Chapuys' assertion that he was ill-behaved when young, together with the many entries in the rolls concerning the tempestuous and disorderly conduct of Walter Cromwell, all point to the truth of this story [1]. Foxe moreover asserts that Cromwell told Cranmer in later years 'what a ruffian he was in his younger days.' Pole informs us that he soon became a roving soldier in Italy, a statement which is borne out by the tales of Bandello and Foxe that he was at the battle on the Garigliano (Dec. 28–29, 1503), in the service of the French army [2]. The well-known story of the Italian novelist about Cromwell and Frescobaldo the Florentine merchant, may well have some foundation in fact: there are several mentions of Frescobaldo in the State Papers of the years 1530–1540, which prove that Cromwell was intimate with an Italian of that name [3]. Some

[1] See Appendices I and III at the end of this chapter.

[2] See Appendices II and IV at the end of this chapter. The suggestion of Mr. Galton (The Character and Times of Thomas Cromwell, p. 22) that 'Garigliano' may be a mistake for 'Marignano' is scarcely plausible. The great victory of Francis I occurred in 1515, when there is every reason to suppose that Cromwell was in England.

[3] Cal. v. 1197; vii. 923.

scholars have gone so far as to refuse to believe that Cromwell ever went to Italy at all ; but this must be the incredulity of madness in face of the fact that all our contemporary witnesses agree that he went there, and of the evidence afforded by his wide acquaintance with Italians, and by his knowledge of their language and literature.

From the date of the tale of Bandello up to 1512, the most probable story concerning Cromwell's life is that contained in Pole's Apologia.  It is there stated that after his brief military career he became a merchant, but did not remain a merchant long ; and that he later attached himself as accountant to a Venetian, whom Pole knew very well. Bandello informs us that Cromwell returned to England after his stay in Florence ; it seems more probable, however, that he first went to Antwerp and engaged in trade there ; for Foxe and Chapuys both agree that he was in Flanders, and the former asserts that he was in the service of English dealers in the Flemish marts.  Another singular but character-istic and not improbable story of the martyrologist strengthens the theory that Cromwell was in Antwerp some time after the battle on the Garigliano.  One Geoffrey Chambers was sent to Rome as a representative of the Gild of Our Lady in St. Botolph's Church in Boston, to obtain from the Pope certain pardons or indulgences by which the severe rules concerning Lenten observances might be relaxed ; and passing through Antwerp he fell in with Cromwell, whom he persuaded to accompany him.  The latter entered into the spirit of the enterprise ; arrived at Rome, he procured some choice sweet-meats and jellies, and armed with these lay in wait for the Pope on his return from hunting.  The delicacies were offered, Julius was delighted with them, and granted the desired indulgences without delay.  Foxe states that this episode took place about the year 1510[1].

---

[1] The fact that this tale concerns itself with Foxe's native town of Boston increases the pro-bability of its authenticity.  It was probably this same Geoffrey Chambers who in later years was so active as Cromwell's agent, and as Surveyor-General of the King's purchased lands. Cf. Cal. xii. (ii), 490, 783, 835, 852, 857, and Ellis, 3rd Series, vol. iii. p. 168.

This story seems to indicate that Cromwell went to Italy a second time. It fits in well with Pole's statement that after his military experience he became first a merchant, and then a clerk to a Venetian trader. The absence of any trustworthy chronology, however, prevents us from regarding any of the accounts of these different writers as really historical ; and when at last we meet with a date on which we can rely, it is most tantalizing to find that the evidence which is afforded us in connexion with it is of such a nature as to leave us almost as much in the dark as before. In a letter written in June, 1536, a certain mercer, by name George Elyot, addresses Cromwell as follows [1] : ' Ryght onourabyll sir my dewty Consethered as to youre Masterscheppe apertayneth that hyt may plece your Masterscheppe For the love off god to Exceppe my Rewd Maneres in thes behalf of wrytyng vnto you butt hyt ys onely to schowe yowre Masterscheppe my pore mynd furste for the onour of god & secondly For the god love & trew hartt that ⟨I⟩ have howtt vnto you sensse the syngsson Martt at medelborow in anno 1512.' This quotation does not prove that Cromwell was at the Syngsson Mart at Middelburg in 1512, nor does it shed much light on the position he occupied at that time ; still the probabilities strongly favour the conclusion that he was either a merchant or a clerk to a merchant in the Low Countries in 1512 : the accounts of Foxe and Chapuys agree that he was in the Netherlands in his younger days, and the letter of the mercer seems to fix the date. We have also reason to believe that he was in London soon after this practising as a solicitor. There exists in the Record Office a document dated November, 1512, and endorsed, in a hand which certainly resembles that of Cromwell's later correspondence, ' The tytle of the manour Whityngham for Mr. Empson [2].' The endorsement may of course be of a very different date from that of the document itself ; still the evidence which it affords is not utterly valueless, especially as another reason for supposing that Cromwell returned to England in 1512, or soon after, is afforded by the fact that his marriage must have taken place about this time :

---

[1] Cal. x. 1218.                    [2] Cal. i. 3556.

the age of his son Gregory being such that it could scarcely
have occurred much later. The State Papers of 1512 give
us more information concerning the early life of Thomas
Cromwell than those of any other year up to 1523. The
sum total of the evidence which they afford seems to indicate
that he was in England and in the Netherlands, that he was
occupied both as a merchant and as a solicitor, and that he
was married in that year or soon afterwards.

Cromwell's wife, to whom Chapuys refers as the daughter
of a shearman, was Elizabeth Wykys, descended from one of
an ancient family of esquires, who was gentleman-usher to
Henry VII[1]. A reference in Cromwell's will of July 12,
1529, to one 'Mercye Pryo*ur*' as his mother-in-law[2] has led
some writers to suppose that he married Elizabeth, daughter
of Sir John Pryor, and widow of Thomas Williams, a Welsh
gentleman; but a letter to Cromwell from one Harry Wykys
of Thorpe, near Chertsey, dated November 2, 1523[3], disproves
this theory, and corroborates the other. The most probable
explanation of the entry in the will is that Mercy Pryor
married twice, and that she was the mother of Elizabeth
Wykys by her first husband[4]. Cromwell's wife was probably
a woman of some property. He was exactly the sort of man
who would seek a wife with an eye to the financial advantages
of the match, and the theory that Elizabeth Wykys was rich
fits in well with the evidence that her mother was married
a second time. Moreover Cromwell's property increased so
fast during his years of service under Wolsey, that even his
notorious accessibility to bribes could not account for it, had
it not been augmented from some outside source.

Chapuys goes on to say that for some time after his
marriage Cromwell kept servants in his house, carrying on the
business of his father-in-law; a statement corroborated by
his correspondence, which shows that he plied his trade as

[1] Appendix I to this chapter;
Antiquary for Oct. 1880, vol. ii.
p. 164.

[2] Appendix to chapter iii. p. 59.

[3] Cal. iii. 3502.

[4] 'Mr. Pryor' and 'Mistress
Pryor' both had rooms in Cromwell's house, at Austin Friars Gate,
where he lived after the year
1524. Before that date he resided
near Fenchurch (Cal. iii. 2624;
iv. 3197).

a cloth and wool merchant at least as late as 1524. There can be little doubt, however, that he continued his business as a solicitor at the same time, for it would be impossible to explain his sudden advance in legal prominence in the years 1520 to 1525, if he had not had long practice in the law beforehand. The strange combination of employments in which Cromwell was engaged fitted in well with the peculiar versatility of the man, and brought him into close contact with diverse sorts of men, in diverse conditions of life. A more detailed account of his career during the seven or eight years which followed his probable return to England it is impossible to give, for between 1512 and 1520 there occurs another extraordinary gap in the life of Thomas Cromwell, during which we do not possess a single trustworthy contemporary record concerning him. In 1520 there is certainly evidence that he was known to Wolsey, but precisely how or when his connexion with the Cardinal began, it is impossible to tell.

The statement in the Dictionary of National Biography that Wolsey appointed Cromwell collector of his revenues in 1514 is apparently unfounded [1], and no reference is given for the assertion in Singer's Cavendish [2] that the Cardinal first met his future servant in France. Another unverified story is that Lord Henry Percy, who had been an intimate of the Cardinal's household in his early years, borrowed money from Cromwell, and conceiving a high opinion of his creditor, introduced him to Wolsey [3]; while Mr. Phillips informs us that Robert Cromwell (the son of Walter Cromwell's brother John), who was vicar of Battersea under the Cardinal, gave to his cousin Thomas the stewardship of the archiepiscopal estate of York House, after Wolsey had been made archbishop there. Though Mr. Phillips has again failed to cite his authority for this last statement, it is but fair to say that the probabilities are strongly in its favour: the theory that Cromwell owed his appointment as Wolsey's servant to his cousin Robert seems particularly plausible, as

[1] Mr. Gairdner kindly informs me that he was misled by a record concerning Robert Cromwell (Cal. ii. (i) 1369).

[2] Singer's Cavendish, vol. i. p. 193 *n*.

[3] Ellis, Thomas Cromwell, p. 12.

the latter was certainly well known to the Cardinal. It is possible that the origin of the connexion had something to do with the young Marquis of Dorset, who later became Cromwell's patron. Wolsey had long been acquainted with the Marquis; he had been the friend and tutor of his father when he was principal of Magdalen School, and had been given the living of Limington in Somerset by a still older member of the family in 1500 [1]. The date of the origin of Cromwell's connexion with Wolsey must remain as much a matter of conjecture as its cause. It seems probable that those historians who have placed it as far back as 1513 or 1514 have been at fault, for had Cromwell entered the Cardinal's service as early as that there would almost certainly have been more entries in the State Papers to show it. As it is, we possess only one piece of evidence in contemporary records to show that he was known to Wolsey before October, 1520, and that is of such a nature that little reliance can be placed on it. On the back of a letter, written in August, 1514, by the Abbot of Winchcomb to Wolsey [2], are some lines in a hand which bears some resemblance to Cromwell's, apparently intended as an exercise in penmanship; the similarity of the handwritings, however, is not so striking that it can be regarded as affording any very conclusive proof: moreover as the words on the back have no connexion with the letter itself, it is quite likely that they were written at a much later date. It is safe to say that the lack of information on the subject in the State Papers makes it probable that if Cromwell's connexion with Wolsey began much before 1520, it was certainly of very minor importance.

In the autumn of that year, however, we possess a record which leaves little doubt that Cromwell had at least become known to the Cardinal. An appeal had been made to the Papal Court at Rome against the sentence of the Prerogative Court of Canterbury, in a suit between the vicar of Cheshunt and the Prioress of the nunnery there. Wolsey, as Papal Legate, soon afterwards received a copy of the citation and

---

[1] Life of Wolsey, Dictionary of National Biography, vol. lxii. p. 325.
[2] Cal. i. 5355.

inhibition 'with other information by the letters of Thomas Cromwell,' making clear the rights and wrongs of the case, and the best method of handling it [1]. No other mention of Cromwell in connexion with the Cardinal occurs until 1523, when he drafted a petition to Wolsey in Chancery for a certain John Palsgrave [2]. But these two records are enough to prove that he was known to the Cardinal in the capacity of a solicitor and clerk from a period at least as early as 1520. The gap between that date and 1512 is more difficult to fill. The supposition that Cromwell was in Wolsey's service as early as 1513 is perhaps the easiest method of disposing of these years, but it certainly cannot be regarded as more than a theory, unless some new document is found which corroborates it.

Most of the letters addressed to Cromwell during this period from 1520 to 1524 concern themselves with legal business, and request his aid as a practised lawyer in some suit for the collection of debts or the decision of a title to lands [3]. In August, 1522, he acted as an 'indifferent person' in a dispute between Richard Chauffer, alderman of Calais, and Lord Mountjoy. In December, 1523, he served on the inquest of wardmote in the ward of Bread Street. But it is also evident from his correspondence that he had by no means lost interest in his business as a cloth merchant and wool-dyer [4]. It may have been in this capacity that he first became known to the family of the Marquis of Dorset. The 'old lady Marques' writes to him in August, 1522, as her 'sonne marquys *servau*nt,' and desires him to send in haste 'the trussynn bed of cloth of tyssewe and the fether bed wyth the fustyons, and amateras longyng to the same wyth the cownterpoynt . . . . tentes pauylyons & hales [5].' There is also record that Cromwell was a great lender of money at high

---

[1] In the original document (Cal. iii. 1026) the name of the Cardinal is not expressly mentioned. The copy of the citation, however, was sent by his chaplain, Clerk, and can scarcely have been intended for any one but Wolsey, since the case had already reached the Papal Court.

[2] Cal. iii. 3681.

[3] Cal. iii. 1026, 1940, 1963, 2441, 3657.

[4] Cal. iii. 2624.

[5] Cal. iii. 2437.

rates of interest.  His friendship and reputation with foreign merchants brought him an enormous amount of business, and his property increased to a great extent.  The training he received during and after his journey on the Continent was probably the best that he could have had to fit him for the difficult life-work that was given him to perform.  The spirit of the Italy of Machiavelli and Caesar Borgia stamped itself deeply upon his youthful character. It gave him his ideas, his theories.  The hard school of adversity (at first almost a struggle for existence), through which he passed during his early years, afforded him the intimate knowledge of men and things, the wonderful insight into human nature, and the ability to turn every event to the advancement of his own purposes, that enabled him at a later day to mould the destinies of the English nation.

> ' And my experience happily me taught
>   Into the secrets of those times to see,
> From whence to England afterward I brought
>   Those slights of state deliu'red vnto mee,
> In t'which were then but very few that sought,
>   Nor did with th'umour of that age agree,
>     After did great and fearful things effect,
>     Whose secret working few did then suspect.'
>
> Michael Drayton.  The Legend of Great Cromwell, p. 13.

# APPENDIX TO CHAPTER I

## I

### PASSAGE FROM A LETTER OF CHAPUYS TO GRANVELLE, NOV. 21, 1535[1]

'Mᵉ Cremuel . . . est filz dung poure marechal lequel en son vivant se tenoit en vng petit villaige pres dici dune lieue et demye et est sepulture au cemetiere de lad. parroiche dud. villaige de plus pouurement que soient la son oncle[2] pere dung syen cousin qui⟨l⟩a desia fait fort riche estoit cousinier du feu euesque de Conturberi led. Cremuel en sa jeunesse fust assez mal condicionner, et apres quelque emprisonnement il fut contrainct vuider le pays et senpasser en flandres et dois la en rome ou et ailleurs en italie il demeura quelque temps, estant de retour il se maria a la fille dung tondeur de draps, et tint quelque temps en sa maison seruiteurs exercent led. art apres il devint solliciteur de causes et par ce moyen se feit congnoistre au cardinal de york, lequel congnoissant la vigilance et diligence dud. Cremuel et habilite et promptitude tant a mal que a bien, il le tint on nombre de ses serviteurs, et l'employa principalement quant il fut question de ruyner et demoler cinq du[3] six bons monasteres. Venant a descherir led. cardinal il ny eust personne que saquittast myeulx enuers led. cardinal que luy. Apres le decez dud. cardinal maistre valloup a present ambassadeur en france le poursuyuant de injures et menasses le plus fort du monde, et non voyant autre reffuge ne remede que de recourir au roy, il fait tant par prieres et presens quil eust audience dud. roy auquel il deust promettre de le faire le plus riche que oncques fut en angleterre, et luy parla si bien et beaul qui le retint des lors de son conseil, sans autre aduis et ne le decouurit led. roy a personne des siens deans quatre moys apres Maintenant il a empiete de telle sorte quil a baille le bout a toute la reste ⟨si⟩ ce nest a la dame, et le tient

---

[1] The original is in the Vienna Archives. This copy was made from the official Record Office transcript. Cf. Cal. ix. 862, and

Thomas, The Pilgrim, p. 107.

[2] John Cromwell of Lambeth.

[3] *sic*, read 'ou.'

tout le monde auoir plus de credit auprez de son maistre, que neust
oncques le cardinal du temps duquel en y auoit questoient en con-
currence de credit comme maistre Conton[1] et le duc de suffocq et
autres, mais maintenant il n'y a personne que face riens que luy, et
ne sert le chancellier synon pour mynistre et organe dud. Cremuel,
lequel jusques yci na voulu accepter led. office de chancellier, mais
lon pense bien tost il se layra persuader de lempoigner.   Il est
home bien parlant en sa langue et mediocrement en la latyne
francoyse et italyenne, home de bonne chiere liberal et de ses
biens et de bonnes et gracieuses parolles, home manifique en trayn
et batissement . . .'

## II

PASSAGE FROM CARDINAL POLE'S APOLOGIA AD CAROLUM
QUINTUM.   Pars I. p. 126, c. xxviii.

' Sic ergo, si tale nomen quaeratur, Cromvellum eum appellant,
si genus, de nullo quidem ante eum, qui id nomen gereret, audivi.
Dicunt tamen, viculum esse prope Londinum, ubi natus erat, & ubi
pater ejus pannis verrendis victum quaeritabat, sed de hoc parum
refert.   Nunc si conditio quaeratur, sic quidem de eo intellexi,
aliquem in Italia fuisse gregarium militem, fuisse etiam mercatorem,
nec tamen longius progressum in mercatura fuisse, quam ut scriba
esset mercatoris, & libros rationum servaret, optime vero novi illum
mercatorem, qui Venetus erat natione, cui operas suas locabat.
Tandem hujus conditionis pertaesus, domum reversus, causidicis se
immiscuit, his qui jura Regni profitentur.   In quo eo magis se
proficere sperabat, quod versuti & callidi ingenii sibi conscius esset
ad defendendum tam iniquum, quam aequum, quod ex externorum
commercio valde acuerat, cum nostrorum hominum ingeniorum
simplicitatem semper contemneret.   Nec tamen in hoc genere valde
crevit, antequam ad Monasteriorum ruinam perventum est.   Quod
incoepit vivente adhuc Cardinali Eboracense, dum Monasteria quaedam pene a suis deserta, & illorum bona ac praedia in subsidium
pauperum, qui in Gymnasiis literis operam dabant, essent conversa.
Hic vero notus esse coepit, idque ostendit ad hanc artem solam se
natum fuisse, ad ruinam & vastationem, id quod crebra aliarum
artium mutatio declaravit, in quibus nihil crevit, in hac vero statim

---

[1] Sir William Compton.   See Dictionary of National Biography, vol. xi.
p. 453.

celebris esse coepit, & pluribus notus, ita tamen in illis initiis hujus suae artis notus, ut cum Cardinalis, cujus assecla fuit, & ex cujus authoritate et imperio illam suam artem exercebat, ab administratione Reipublicae remotus esset, et dignitate privatus, ipse omnium voce, qui aliquid de eo intellexerant, ad supplicium posceretur. Hoc enim affirmare possum, qui Londini tum adfui, & voces audivi, adeo etiam ut per civitatem universam rumor circumferretur, eum in carcerem fuisse detrusum, & propediem productum iri ad supplicium. Nec vero populus ullum spectaculum libentius expectabat, nec ille rumor ex alia re nascebatur, nisi quod omnes eum sciebant omni supplicio dignum . . .'

## III

NOVELLA XXXIV DELLA SECONDA PARTE DE LE NOVELLE DEL BANDELLO, Tomo quinto, p. 251.

'Francesco Frescobaldi fa cortesia ad uno straniero, e n' è ben rimeritato, essendo colui divenuto Contestabile d'Inghilterra.'

'Ne la famiglia nobile et antica de i Frescobaldi in Firenze fu, non sono molti anni, un Francesco, mercadante molto leale et onorevole, il quale, secondo la costuma de la patria, essendo assai ricco, trafficava in diversi luoghi e faceva di gran faccende, e quasi per l'ordinario dimorava in Ponente, in Inghilterra, e teneva la stanza in Londra, ove viveva splendidissimamente et usava cortesia assai; non la veggendo sì per minuto come molti mercadanti fanno, che la contano fin a un picciolo quattrino, come intendo dire che fa Ansaldo Grimaldo Genovese, che tien conto fin d'un minimo foglio di carta e d'un palmo di cordella da legar i pacchetti de le lettere. Avvenne un giorno che essendo Francesco Frescobaldi in Firenze, se gli parò dinanzi un povero giovine, e gli domandò elemosina per l'amor di Dio. Veggendolo il Frescobaldo sì mal in arnese e che in viso mostrava aver del gentile, si mosse in pietà, e tanto più, quanto che lo conobbe esser Inglese; onde gli domandò di che contrada di Oltramontani fosse. Egli gli rispose che era Inglese; e chiedendogli alcune particolarità, il Frescobaldo, d'Inghilterra, come colui che assai pratico n'era, il giovine molto accomodatamente al tutto sodisfece, dicendogli: Io mi chiamo Tomaso

Cremonello, figliuolo di un povero cimatore di panni, che fuggendo
da mio padre son venuto in Italia col campo de i Francesi, che
è stato rotto al Garigliano, e stavo con un fante a piedi, portandoli
dietro la picca. Il Frescobaldo la menò in casa molto domestica-
mente, e quivi alcun dì se lo tenne per amor de la nazione Inglese,
de la quale egli aveva ricevuti di molti piaceri ; lo trattò umana-
mente, lo vestì, e quando volse partirsi per ritornar ne la patria, gli
diede sedici ducati d' oro in oro fiorentini et un buon ronzino. Il
giovine veggendosi esser stato messo in arnese sì bene, rese al
Frescobaldo quelle grazie che seppe le maggiori, e se n' andò ne
l' isola a casa.'

   .   .   .   .   .   .   .   .   .   .

[The next four pages are devoted to a more or less accurate account
of Cromwell's life in London, his connexion with Wolsey, and his
entrance into the King's service. The events narrated in the following passage may be supposed to have taken place about 1535
or 1536.]

   .   .   .   .   .   .   .   .   .   .

... 'Dico adunque che in quei dì che il Cremonello era padrone
e governatore de l' isola, che Francesco Frescobaldo si ritrovava in
Italia, ove, ᴄ ome spesso a mercadanti interviene, avendo patiti molti
disastri e di gran danni ne la perdita de le sue mercadanzie, restò
molto povero ; perciò che essendo uomo leale e da bene, pagò tutti
quelli a cui era debitore, e non puotè ricuperar ciò che da gli altri gli
era dovuto. Veggendosi egli ridutto a così povero stato, e fatto i suoi
conti e benissimo calculati, trovò che in Inghilterra aveva crediti per
più di quindici migliaia di ducati ; onde si deliberò passar quindi,
e veder di ricuperar più che gli fosse possibile, e mettersi a viver
il rimanente de la sua vita quietamente. Così con questo pensiero
passò d' Italia in Francia, e di Francia in Inghilterra, e si fermò in
Londra, non gli sovvenendo perciò mai del beneficio che egli fatto
già in Firenze aveva al Cremonello ; cosa veramente degna d' un vero
liberale, che de le cortesie che altrui fa, memoria mai non tiene,
scolpendo in marmo quelle che riceve, per pagarle ogni volta che
l' occasione se gli offerisce. Attendendo adunque in Londra a
negoziar i fatti suoi, e caminando un giorno in una contrada,
avvenne che il Contestabile passava anch' egli per la strada mede-
sima, venendo a l' incontro del Frescobaldo. Così subito che il
Contestabile lo vide e gli ebbe gli occhi fermati nel viso, si ricordò
costui certamente esser quello, dal quale così gran cortesia aveva in
Firenze ricevuta, et essendo a cavallo, dismontò, e con meraviglia

grandissima di quelli che seco erano, chi v'erano più di cento
a cavallo de i primi del regno che gli facevano coda, l'abbracciò con
grande amorevolezza, e quasi lagrimando gli disse : Non sete voi
Francesco Frescobaldo Fiorentino ?    Sì sono, signor mio, rispose
egli, e vostro umil servidore.    Mio servidore, disse il Contestabile,
non sete già voi nè per tal vi voglio, ma bene per mio grande amico,
avvisandovi che di voi ho giusta ragione di molto dolermi, perchè
sapendo voi ciò che io sono e dove era, devevate farmi saper la
venuta vostra qui ; che certamente io averei pagato qualche parte
del debito che confesso aver con voi.    Ora lodato Iddio che ancor
sono a tempo ; voi siate il benissimo venuto.    Io vado ora per affari
del mio Re, e non posso far più lunga dimora vosco, e m'averete per
iscusato ; ma fate per ogni modo, che in questa mattina vegnate
a desinar meco, e non fate fallo.    Così rimontò il Contestabile
a cavallo e se n'andò in Corte al Re.    Il Frescobaldo, partito che
fu il Contestabile, s'andò ricordando che cotestui era quel giovine
Inglese che egli già in Firenze in casa sua raccolse, e cominciò
a sperar bene, pensando che il mezzo di così grand' uomo molto gli
giovarebbe a ricuperar i suoi danari.    Essendo poi l'ora di desinare,
se n'andò al palazzo del Contestabile, e quivi nel cortile poco attese
che egli rivenne.    Il quale smontato che fu, di nuovo amicabilmente
riabbracciò il Frescobaldo, e volto a l' armiraglio, et ad altri prencipi
e signori che con lui erano venuti a desinare, disse : Signori, non vi
meravigliate de le amorevoli dimostrazioni che io faccio a questo
gentiluomo Fiorentino, perchè queste sono parte di pagamento
d' infiniti obblighi che io conosco e confesso di avergli, essendo nel
grado che sono per mezzo suo, et udite come.    A l' ora, a la presenza
di tutti, tenendo sempre per mano il gentiluomo Fiorentino, narrò
loro in che modo era capitato a Firenze, e le carezze che da lui
aveva ricevute ; e così tenendolo sempre per mano, se ne salirono le
scale, e giunti in sala si misero a tavola.    Volle il Contestabile
che il Frescobaldo gli stesse appresso, e sempre l' accarezzò amore-
volissimamente.    Desinato che si fu e quei signori partiti, volle il
Contestabile saper la cagione, per la quale era il Frescobaldo ritornato a Londra.    Narrogli a l' ora tutta la sua disgrazia il Frescobaldo,
e che non gli essendo rimaso, de la casa in fuori in Firenze et un
podere in contado, quasi niente, se non quei quindeci mila ducati
che in Inghilterra deveva avere, e forse duo mila in Ispagna, che per
ricuperargli s' era ne l' Isola trasferito.    Or bene sta, disse il Contestabile.    A le cose passate, che fatte non sieno, non si può trovar
rimedio ; ben mi posso con voi dolere de gl' infortunii vostri, come

con il core faccio ; al rimanente si darà tal ordine, che voi ricupera-
rete tutti i vostri danari che qui devete avere, e non vi si mancherà
di quello che io potrò, assicurandovi, che la cortesia che m' usate, non
mi conoscendo altramente, mi vi rende di modo ubbligato che
sempre sarò vostro, e di me e de le mie facultà potrete disporre
come io proprio, e non lo facendo, il danno sarà vostro, nè più farò
offerta alcuna, parendomi che sarebbe superflua. Basti che questo
vi sia ora per sempre detto. Ma leviamoci et andiamo in camera,
ove il Contestabile serrato l' uscio, aperse un gran coffano pieno di
ducati, e pigliandone sedeci gli diede al Frescobaldi, e gli disse :
Eccovi, amico mio, i sedeci ducati che mi donaste al partir di
Firenze, eccovi gli altri dieci che vi costò il ronzino che per me
comperaste, et eccovene altri dieci che spendeste in vestirmi. Ma
perchè essendo voi mercadante, non mi par onesto che i vostri
danari debbiano esser stati tanto tempo morti, ma s'abbiano gua-
dagnato, come è il costume vostro, eccovi quattro sacchetti di ducati,
in ciascuno de i quali sono quattro mila ducati. Voi in ricompensa
de i vostri ve gli pigliarete, godendogli per amor mio. Il Frescobaldo, ancor che da grandissime ricchezze fosse caduto in gran
povertà, nondimeno non aveva perduto la sua generosità d' animo,
e non gli voleva accettare, ringraziandolo tutta via di tanta sua cortesia ; ma a la fine astretto per viva forza dal Contestabile, che gli
desse tutti i nomi in nota de i suoi debitori ; il che Frescobaldo fece
molto volentieri, mettendo il nome dei debitori e la somma che gli
devevano. Avuta questa cedula, chiamò il Cremonello un suo uomo
di casa, e gli disse : Guarda chi sono costoro, che su questa lista
sono scritti, e fa che gli ritrovi tutti, siano dove si vogliano in questa
isola, e farai loro intendere che se fra quindici giorni non hanno
pagato tutto il lor debito, che io ci porrò la mano con lor dispia-
cere e danno, e che facciano pensiero, che io sia il creditore. Fece
l' uomo il comandamento del suo padrone molto diligentemente, di
maniera che al termine statuito furono ricuperati circa quindici mila
ducati. E se il Frescobaldo avesse voluto gl' interessi, che in così
lungo tempo erano corsi, tutti gli averebbe avuti, fin ad un minimo
denaio ; ma egli si contentò del capitale, nè volse interesse alcuno,
che di più in più gli acquistò credito e riputazione appresso tutti,
massimamente sapendosi già da ciascuno de l' isola il favore che egli
aveva appresso la persona del Contestabile. In questo mezzo, fu di
continovo esso Frescobaldo commensale del Cremonello, il quale di
giorno in giorno si sforzava d' onorarlo quanto più poteva. E deside-
rando che di continovo egli rimanesse in Londra, piacendogli molto

la pratica sua, gli offerse di prestargli per quattro anni sessanta mila ducati, a ciò che mettesse casa e banco in Londra e gli trafficasse, senza volerne profitto d' un soldo, promettendogli oltra questo ogni favore ne le cose de la mercadanzia. Ma il Frescobaldo che desiderava di ritirarsi a casa, e viver il resto de la sua vita in quiete et attender solamente a se stesso, infinitamente lo ringraziò di tanta suprema cortesia, e con buona grazia del Contestabile, rimessi tutti i suoi danari in Firenze, a la desiderata patria se ne ritornò, dove essendo ritornato assai ricco, si mise a viver una vita quietissima. Ma poco tempo visse in quiete, perchè quell' anno istesso che da Londra era partito, in Firenze se ne morì.'

.  .  .  .  .  .  .  .  .  .  .

## IV

PASSAGES FROM THE LIFE OF LORD CROMWELL AS CON-
TAINED IN FOXE'S ECCLESIASTICAL HISTORY, vol. ii.
pp. 419–434.

'Thomas Cromwell although born of a simple Parentage and House obscure, through the singular excellency of Wisdom and dexterity of Wit wrought in him by God, coupled with like industry of mind, and deserts of life, rose to high preferment and authority;'

.  .  .  .  .  .  .  .  .  .

'First as touching his Birth, he was born at Putney or there-about, being a Smiths Son, whose Mother married after to a sheerman.'

.  .  .  .  .  .  .  .  .  .

'As touching the order and manner of his coming up, it would be superfluous to discourse what may be said at large: only by way of story it may suffice to give a touch of certain particulars and so to proceed.' . . . 'Nothing was so hard which with wit and industery he could not compass. Neither was his capacity so good but his memory was as great in retaining whatsoever he had attained. Which well appeareth in canning the text of the whole new Testament of Erasmus Translation without Boqk, in his journey going and coming from Rome, whereof you shall hear anon.'

'Thus in his growing years, as he shot up in age and ripeness, a great delight came in his mind to stray into forreign Countries to see the World abroad, and to learn experience, whereby he learned such Tongues and Languages as might better serve for his use hereafter.'

'And thus passing over his youth being at Antwerp, he was there retained of the English Merchants to be their Clerk or Secretary, or in some such like condition placed pertaining to their affairs.'

'It happened the same time that the Town of Boston thought good to send up to Rome for renewing of their two pardons, one called the great pardon and the other the lesser pardon. Which thing although it should stand them in great expences of money (for the Popes Merchandise is always dear ware) yet notwithstanding such sweetness they had felt thereof, and such gain to come to their town by that Romish Merchandise (as all Superstition is commonly gainful) that they like good Catholick Merchants and the Popes good customers, thought to spare for no cost, to have their leases again of their pardons renewed, whatsoever they paid for the fine. And yet was all this good Religion then, such was the lamentable blindness of that time.'

'This then being so determined and decreed among my Countrymen of Boston to have their pardons needs repaired and renewed from Rome, one Geffery Chambers, with another Champion was sent for the messengers, with writings and money, no small quantity, well furnished, and with all other things appointed necessary for so chargeable and costly exploit. Who coming in his journey to Antwerp, and misdoubting to be too weak for the compassing of such a weighty piece of work, conferred and perswaded with T. Cromwel to associat him in that legacy, and to assist him in the contriving thereof. Cromwel although perceiving the enterprise to be of no small difficulty to traverse the Popes Court, for the unreasonable expences amongst those greedy Cormorants, yet having some skill of the Italian Tongue, and as yet not grounded in the judgement of Religion in those his youthful days, was at length obtained and content to give the adventure, and so took his journey towards Rome. Cromwel loth to spend much time, and more loth to spend his money; and again perceiving that the Popes greedy humour must needs be served with some present or other (for without rewards there is no doing at Rome) began to cast with himself what thing best to devise wherein he might best serve the Popes devotion.'

'At length having knowledge how that the Popes holy tooth greatly delighted to new fangled strange delicates and dainty dishes, it came in his mind to prepare certain fine dishes of gelly, after the best fashion, made after our Countrey manner here in England, which to them of Rome was not known nor seen before.'

'This done, Cromwell observing his time accordingly, as the Pope was newly come from hunting into his pavillion, he with his companions approached with his English presents brought in with a three mans song (as we call it) in the English tongue and after the English fashion. The Pope suddenly marvelling at the strangeness of the song, and understanding that they were English men, and that they came not empty handed, willed them to be called in. Cromwel there shewing his obedience, and offering his jolly junkets, such as Kings and Princes only, said he, in the Realm of England use to feed upon, desired the same to be accepted in benevolent part, which he and his companions, as poor suters unto his Holiness had there brought and presented, as novelties meet for his recreation etc.'

'Pope Julius, seeing the strangeness of the dishes, commanded by and by his Cardinal to take the assay. Who in tasting thereof liked it so well, and so likewise the Pope after him, that knowing of them what their sutes were, and riquiring them to make known the making of that meat, he incontinent, without any more adoe, stamped both their pardons as well the greater as the lesser: . . . it seemeth that Cromwell obtained this Pardon aforesaid about the year of our Lord, 1510.' . . .

[The rest of the story deals for the most part with Cromwell's career in the service of the Cardinal and of the King. Historically it is almost worthless—nearly every paragraph contains statements which the more trustworthy sources prove to be impossible. A curious legend of Cromwell's saving the life of the Earl of Bedford at Bologna is followed by a more plausible account of the latter afterward commending his preserver to the King. Foxe also states that Sir Christopher Hales, a violent papist, but a friend of Cromwell's, took an opportunity to say a good word for him to Henry after Wolsey's fall, that the King at last had an interview with his future minister in Westminster Gardens, and was advised by him to shake off the yoke of Rome. The latter part of this story follows closely the account of Cardinal Pole (see chapter vi. p. 92). Foxe goes on to an exhaustive defence of Cromwell's actions during his ministry, especially the suppression of the monasteries and the measures adopted for the promotion of the new religion. The story of the loss of Cranmer's Book Against the Six Articles at the bear-baiting on the Thames (see chapter xiii. p. 255) and the account of Frescobaldo's kindness to Cromwell in Florence are related at length. Many other minor incidents of Cromwell's life are also recorded: we are told how he stopped a skirmish in Paternoster Row, how he prevented a friar from wearing his cowl in the streets, how he imprisoned a ruffian with long hair, and how he aided a poor man whose father had once befriended him in distress. The story closes with an account of Cromwell's fall, sentence and execution, and gives the speech and prayer he is supposed to have made on the scaffold. (See Appendix at the end of chapter xiv.)]

# CHAPTER II

## THE PARLIAMENT OF 1523

THE heavy veil that shrouds in mystery the early life of Thomas Cromwell is not completely lifted until after he becomes counsellor to the King, but even before and during his service with Wolsey, we catch several interesting glimpses of him. Especially important is the information we possess concerning the part he played in the Parliament of 1523. We have no means of knowing how he obtained a seat there, but there are fortunately preserved two documents of undoubted authenticity that shed much light on the attitude he assumed towards the problems which came up for discussion. The first is a speech which exists to-day at the Public Record Office in the hand of one of Cromwell's clerks, and contains a distinct and careful enunciation of the policy which the future minister actually pursued in after years. The second is a letter from Cromwell to a friend, John Creke, in Biscay, in which he tells how he 'amongyst other indured a parlyament[1].' This epistle is in itself an excellent index to the character and political ideals of its author. Cromwell's ill-concealed contempt for the vague discussions and fruitless arguments of the Commons, who finally in disgust left off where they began, his evident disappointment that the 'right large subsydye' had been granted in spite of his disapproval, and his sneering statement that this Parliament had failed as signally as its predecessors had, to do anything of real practical value to King or realm, but had wasted its time in foolish theorizing and useless debate—all are perfectly consistent with the characteristics revealed by his later policy and actions.

In order to understand the speech which Cromwell wrote to deliver in this Parliament, a preliminary survey of some of

---

[1] Letters, I.

the business that lay before the House may be helpful. The period immediately previous to the session of 1523 had been occupied by Henry and Wolsey in sending messages to the powerful and traitorous Duke of Bourbon, to obtain from him a recognition of the King's title to the throne of France. The breach between England and Francis was becoming wider every day. Charles V had of course seized the favourable opportunity to ally himself with Bourbon and Henry, and had as usual succeeded in making the latter do the lion's share of the work, and pay practically all the bills. Loans to the Emperor and to the Duke, and the expense of keeping up the defences in the north, where Scotland daily threatened to break out into open war, had drained the country's resources to their lowest ebb.

Under these circumstances Henry thought it fit to summon a Parliament, the first since December, 1515. The policy of Wolsey, in regard to the great legislative body of the kingdom, had up to this time been very closely followed. He had not reached the point which Cromwell at a later day was destined to attain; that is, he had not so completely obtained the upper hand of the Commons that he could use them as a tool to accomplish his will. He rather regarded Parliament as a dangerous power to be suppressed at all costs, than as a means to attain his own ends. Consequently it had not met for nearly eight years. But the present crisis was one which called for more than the ordinary resources of the nation; nothing could be accomplished against France unless an enormous subsidy was granted; that subsidy could only be granted by Parliament, and Wolsey, rather unwillingly, was forced to consent to the King's summoning it, relying on Henry's great personal popularity, and the peculiarly bitter national hatred of France, to make it accomplish for him what he could not do for himself[1].

Sir Thomas More was chosen Speaker, probably because of his high favour with Henry, who did not scruple to give Parliament broad hints of his pleasure in all matters in which he was interested, and though, as Roper says,

[1] On this paragraph cf. Creighton's Wolsey, pp. 128–130.

More was 'very loath to take this room upon him[1],' yet the King would not consent to his resignation. And the story goes on to tell how Wolsey 'found himself much grieved with the burgesses of this Parliament, for that nothing was so soon done or spoken therein but that it was immediately blown abroad in every ale-house[2],' and how, fearing that the subsidy bill might not pass, he determined to be present at the debate himself, and was received, at Sir Thomas More's suggestion, 'with all his pomp, with his maces, his pillars, his poleaxes, his crosses, his hat, and his great seal too.' But Wolsey need not have been so anxious about the passage of his bill. Though at first the House would not deign to consider the subsidy in his presence, alleging that 'there was not so much money out of the King's hands in the whole realm,' it had been out of practice too long to realize its own power, and after a great deal of haggling and fruitless endeavours by the members to beg off for less than the £800,000 at first demanded, Wolsey carried his point[3], and by the end of June was able to announce to Henry that there was no further hindrance to the proposed invasion of France.

While the debate was in progress, however, Cromwell was

---

[1] Roper, Life of More, pp. 34–35.

[2] Ibid. pp. 35–38.

[3] On the 29th of April Wolsey entered the House and proposed a subsidy 'which he thought should not fall short of £800,000, to be raised by a tax of four shillings in the pound on all men's goods and lands.' The principal provisions of the Act to which the Commons were finally induced to give their consent were as follows : for two years 'a rate of 5 per cent. was imposed on all lands and goods of the value of £20 and upwards ; 2½ per cent. on goods between £20 and £2 ; 1⅔ per cent. on goods of 40s., or on yearly wages averaging 20s. In the third year 5 per cent. on all lands of £50 and upwards ; and in the fourth and last year, 5 per cent. on personal property of £50 and upwards. These rates were doubled in cases of aliens. The Act was not to extend to Ireland, Wales, Calais, to the counties of Northumberland, Cumberland, or Westmoreland, to Chester, to the bishopric of Durham, or to Brighton in Sussex.' (Cf. Introduction to vol. iii of the Calendar, pp. 243, 253, 270.) Brewer informs us that 'it had been computed that the subsidy granted by the Commons would produce £800,000,' though he confesses that we are ignorant of the data on which this estimate was based. Lingard does not discuss the amount of the subsidy, but lays stress on the fact that the Commons asserted their right to debate on the measure alone. (Hist. of England, vol. vi. pp. 91–92.)

one of the strongest opponents of the Cardinal's scheme. The following speech, which he wrote to deliver on this occasion [1], clearly reveals his attitude on the questions before the House.

' To recouer agayne by the sworde the Realme of Fraunce, belongyng to our most Redowbtid Souerayne by good and iuste tytle, and to chaunge the Sums of monay whiche we haue in sundrey yeres Receyued from thens into the hole and iust Reuenues that myght there from yere to yere be Leuyed yf we did peasibly enioye the same, who ys here present that wold not gladly dispend not oonly all his goodys but also his lyffe yf euery of vs had ten thowsand lyues to help to obtayne vnto our most benygne souerayne and his most noble Succession besydys the high honour and wyde spredyng of his most glorious fame, whiche while this world endured shuld euer be had in memory, suche yerely reuenues and wellyng spryngges as [2] treasure as shuld by thyse means contynually be browght into this Realme, Whereoff there were no dowte but that ryght haboundant stremys shuld from his most liberall magnyfysence be dereuyed into euery parte of this his Realme to the grete Inryching and enprosperyng of vs and all suche as hereafter showld lyue vnder hys obeysaunce and subieccion. And that this high and Magnanyme enterpryse ys at this present by our saide Souerayne not only in secret wyse in his high cowrage conceyued, but also vttred to his most prudent counsayll, and at sundrey tymes by his grace and them rypely dygested debated ye and fynally concluded as the thyng by his most high wysdome and thens thowght not only possible but also very apparaunt and lykely, all reasonable dowtes auoyded, we All haue clerely persayued as well by the mowth and reporte of my lorde legattes good grace as by the Recapitulacion of the Right worshipfull best Assuryd and discrete Speker, in so moche that we haue bene aduertised of the

---

[1] Cal. iii. 2958. There can be no reasonable doubt concerning the authorship of this speech. Neither Brewer nor Gairdner question it, and Pauli, in an article on Wolsey and the Parliament of 1523 (Historische Zeitschrift for 1889, p. 52), says, ' Die Rede selbst kann schlechterdings keinen anderen Urheber haben, und ist späterhin bei der Confiscation der Papiere Cromwell's in das Staatsarchiv gekommen.'

[2] *sic*, for ' of.'

Indentures all reddy passed bytwene our said most noble
Souerayne and the Emparours Magesty, conteynyng not
oonly the nombre of horsemen and Fotemen, estemed
sufficient for the saide enterpryse, but also the day prefixid
for the Arryuall beyond the see of the saide Army.  Whyche
thyng sythyns our most Redowbted Souerayne hathe so
depely myndyd, that for the more effectuall puttyng in
execucion of the same, his high enterpryze, he hathe promysed
in the saide endentures, to goo ouer in his owne noble persone
Whoo ys here present in this ryght worshipfull assemble, or
any other his subiet Whatsoeuer he be whiche to the vtterest
of his power wold not payne and endeuer hymself, that this so
glorious, so profyttable and so wysshefull an enterpryse myght
properously be atcheuyd and our souerayne with assuryd
honour to Retourne agayne after this grete acte well and
victoryously perfynysshed.  But for somoche As yt hathe
pleased our most Redowbtid Souuerayne of his most high
and haboundant goodnes, to declare vnto vs by the mowthe
of my saide Lorde Cardinallis grace, not only this his purpose,
but also the manyfold prouocacions and hainous iniures done
aswell to his noble highnes, as to his most dere sister the
quene Douriere of Fraunce, in wrongus [1] withholding of her
Dowre, and also the grete vexacion of his subiectes by
robbyng and spoylyng of them, to theire vtter vndoyng, by
Francoys now raynyng there, and on the other side the
manyfold policies and gracious meanes studied by our saide
most noble Souuerayne, and hys Counsayll, to establysshe
a generall peace amongyst all Crysten Prynces and to stay
the saide Frauncoys yf yt had bene possible by mannys
industry from his synyster wayes and disturbyng of all
Regions abowte hym.  Me semyth that his highnes hathe
heryn Declared vnto vs the grettest loue that euer did noble
prynce vnto his humble and obeysaunt subiectes, seyng that
his high wysdome doth not disdayne to communicate and
declare vnto vs his waighty entrepases and affayres, in this
autentyk maner assemblyd by the mowthe of so notable
a personage, beseching god of his haboundant goodnes and

---

[1] *sic*, for 'wrongous' or 'wrong.'

ynfynyte mercye whiche withdrawyth not his lyght from the
poore and low estate but vnto humble harttes departyth of his
grace, that this notable benygnete of our saide Souerayne be
not amongyst vs all frustrate, but that sum of vs here present
may say in this weyghty matier the thyng vaylable and
worthye in his most highe Juggement to be regarded whiche
by the Mowthe and report of the ryght wyse dyscrete and
excellently lettred speker may be benyng Interpretacion And
as we meane cum vnto his most gracious Erys.    Whiche my
perfyte trust ys that his noble grace wyll not so vtterly regecte,
but that yt may oons entre into his noble harte byfore the
tyme come that he shall put hys high entrepryse in execucion
seyng yt ys yet oon hole yere therunto and all thowgh
I reckyn myselff of all other the most vnworthy to haue in
the awdience of so many sauge and notable persons, any
manner saiyngges, especially in this weighty mattier whiche
makyth me to tremble, for fere, whan I thyncke upon hyt and
represent vnto my fantasy How the thre gouernours of
Crystendom, accompanyed with so grete nombre of prynces
noble men and other their Subgiettes shuld after so manyfold
prouocacions of dedely hattred encounter togyder with theire
Swordys in theire handes, to trye where the pleasure of god
shalbe to stryke, and shew his indignacion, Of whiche slawghter,
most nedis ensue, the moste Lamentable cryes, and sorowfull
wryngyng of handys, that hath happened in Cristendome
many yeres.    Neuerthelesse after my symple and yngnorant
maner, I shall humbly beseche yow all of your benygne
Supportacion that I may here with your fauours vtter my
poore mynde whose intent ys none other but to geue vnto
yow, whiche be of far more assuryd Wysdom, Lernyng and
experience then I, occasion to vtter your wyse counsaylles, for
yn myself I know well ys nought elles but the intent of good
wyll, and entier desyre, of the Contenuaunce yn prosperite of my
most redowtyd souerayne, with the most frutefull conseruacion
of the polytyk weall of this his noble Realme, and the good
fertheryng of all the enterprysys and affayres in any wyse
belongyng to the same.

'To speke of peace certeynly as now hit ys no tyme, Albe

hit that I doo in my hart therfore ryght sore lament, but want
of trowth ys so depely in the Frenche Nacion enrotid, and theire
insaciable apetite to extent theire bond*es* and to accroche from
other their Domynyons and possessions to the grete molestyng
and trowbelyng of all the nacions abowte theym, ys so manyfest
and notorys to all the word [1], w*ith*oute any regarde hauyng
ether to godde or Justyce, that thowgh we Hadde for o*ur*
owne *p*articuler causes no mann*er* quarell*es* vnto them, yet
cowld we not but haue in detestacion their false and fleyghty
Dealyng Wherw*ith* other Cristened prync*es* be by them so
sore molestyd.   But now ys hyt soo that our most Drad
Souerayne ys soo notably prouoked by the manyfold Iniuryes
done aswell to hymself as to his most derest Syster, and
sundrey his Subiect*es* that me thynckyth, there be none, his
true and faythefull Subiett*es*, that can refrayne to bere toward*es*
them a worthy haatred and fast inpryntyd groutche, as vnto
the nacion, whiche eu*er* ys onrestful, And of suche malicious
nature that there ys no remedy, but other they most be
skowrgyd or ellys they wyll suerly be a skowrge to other, and
other their possessions must be ruffilled and dymynysshed or
ellys they wyll not cesse to Dymynysshe and take away from
other their possessions, of whiche Arogant Nacion thowgh we
haue of o*ur* self*es* by goddys Ayde and suffer*au*nce ben the
Chastners and terryble stronge yet at this p*r*esent tyme All-
myghty god ys so benygne vnto vs that we haue now a muche
grete aduauntage to compell them not oonly to syt in rest but
also gladly to com*e* to Reason seyng that by theyre sayde
mysprowde arregancy the [2] Haue in so sundry Wayes prouoked
the saide Emparo*ur*s magestye vnto iust hatered and dyspleasure agaynst them w*ith* whome o*ur* most Redowbted
Souerayne ys most assurydly co*n*federate and alied, Whose
high and myghty power ys so great that Joyned vnto owers
they be enverouned on eu*er*y syde wyth the nacions, whiche
by goddes grace shall afflycte them and abate their pryde.
Whiche thyng the emparo*ur*s maiesty hath full well for his
partie shewyd in Recoueryng agayne of Nauerne Where they
had no smale ou*er*throw and also by Wynnyng from theym

---

[1] *sic*, for 'world.'                    [2] *sic*, for 'they.'

the Cytte of Tourney and the hole Countrey Tornasyes
adiacent therunto, and farthermore to the more sorar encresyng
of their Anguysshefull abasshement and shame haue dryuen
them quyte owte of Ittaly and dispossessed them of the noble
Dowchye of Millayne, the gettyng and defendyng wherof
hath bene so maruaylous chargeable vnto theym and also to
the Cyttyes of Genes with the Terretoryes therunto belongyng.
And we for our partye haue spoyled and brent Morkesse,
Destroyed also a grete Contrey with sundry villages and
Townes therin, and to the grete and high honour of our
soueraigne and his valiaunt nacion, and the grete Lawde and
Prayse of the well fortunate and sawge Capetayn, the yerle of
Surrey, whiche taryed in the Domynyons of the saide
Francoyse with a smale Nombre of men in comparyson by the
space or vj or vij wekys where all the power of Fraunce durst
not geue hym battayll whiche sayde valiant Capeteyne, I trust
by goddes help, shall ouerthrow and subdue also the Skottes,
whome the Frenche men haue so custuously intertayned,
and of so long tyme mayntayned agaynst vs, whiche thingges,
yf almyghty god of his goodnes, wyll suffre to contynue this
a while, there ys no dowte but that their hawlte and mysprowde Cowrage shall or owght long abate, and that we shall
constrayne theym to be glad to entret for pease as men dryuen
in to grete and extreme Dyspayre, seing their peces whiche
they haue bene so long in gettyng bene so valiauntly and
withowt any hardynesse in theym to make Resystance
pullid away from theym, and they dare not trye hyt by the
sworde, nother with vs, nor with the saide Emparours Subiectes
for whan soeuer they so doo, they wyn nowght ellys but
a shamefull overthrow, as we all know, by good experyence.
But now myght yt be in questyon whyther hyt showld be for
the more aduaunsyng of our most Rodowtyd Souerayns
Honour and the Emperours Mageste also, and more vayllable
for the spedy acheuyng of bothe their desiryd purposys other
to contynew styll thys kynde of warre whyche hytherto god
be thancked hathe so prosperously succedyd or ellys to chaunge
our warre in to another kynde, more sharper, more violent and
also more terable, that is to say, where he hathe not bene so

hardy as to mete A meane Armyee, other of owers or of the
Emperours, to conuey now in to hys Realme on eyther of
our sydys, so grete and myghty a puyssaunce as shalbe able
by goddys ayde, clerely to vanquysshe hym vtterly and to
subdue hym.

' To this question I beseche god that sum sauge and well
experte man here amongyst vs present may say the thyng
that may be honorable to our most Redowted souerayne and
proffyttable this to his noble Realme, As for myne owne partye
knowyng my most redowtyd Souerayns high pleasure Whereof
we haue all by my saide lorde Cardinalles grace bene so clerely
enfourmed, I am at a poynt suche as dothe become an humble
and obeysant subiect to be, beyng aduertisid of his Souerayns
most redowtyd pleasure, especially by the mowthe of hys
most nere and cheffest Counsaylour, declaryd, oonly oon
thyng there ys whiche puttyth me in no small agonye, me
thowght I harde my lorde Cardynalles grace say that our
most gracious Souuerayne, more derer vnto any of hys Subiectes
that hathe any maner zele to our commen welthe then hys
owne propre lyfe, indendyth to go ouer in his Royall persone,
Whyche thyng I pray god for my partie I neuer lyue to see,
Most humbly beseching hys haboundant and tendre benygnyte
of mercy and pardone of this my saiyng, for the humble and
obeysant loue I ow vnto his noble person, causyth me in this
case to forget obeysance, and I cannot consent to obey vnto
this hys pleasure wheryn lyith the hazardyng of this his
noble Realme, and apon the whiche myght follow (whiche
god defend) the grettyst Calamyte and afflation[1] that euer
happynned ther vnto by cause I am desyrous to be owte of
all dowttes that I may all my lyfe dayes hereafter be his
humble and obeisant subiet, and see with the prosperite and
suretye of his noble parson, his Realme and power subiectes
to lyue assuryd in tranquylyte and to be reconforttid with his
noble presence, whose welthe and prosperyte ys so vrgently
necessary vnto vs all that I am sure their ys no good Englysshe
man whiche can be mery the day whan he happenyth to thynk
that his grace myght perchaunce be dystemperid of his helthe

---

[1] *sic*, for ' affliction.'

so that albe hyt I say for my partie, I stomak as a sory
Subiect may doo, the high Iniures done by the saide Francoys,
vnto his most dere souerayne, yet rather then the thyng shuld
goo so ferre forth I cowld for my partie be contented to forget
altogyther soo that I may know the parson of my souerayne
to be yn helthe, and suretye owte of the thowsand Daungiers
whiche chaunce in warre, and lyue at his high Pleasure and
assuryd myrth for yf the Frenche men haue establysshed an
ordenaunce amongyst theym that their kyng in hys owne
persone shall neuer come in Raungyd Battayll agaynst our
nacion bycawse of the sundry hazardys that their saide prynces
haue suffred in their owne parsons, notwithstandyng their
maruelous pollecy deuysed amongest them for the certayn and
the establysshid succession of their Crowne, how neidfull ys
hyt for us consideryng in what case we be to make the
humblest sewyt that euer did pore Subiectes to theyre Souuerayne, that he wyll for our sakes and specially for the tendre
and Fathyrly loue he beryth to his most dere and oonly
dowghter upon whose wele and sircumspecte bestowyng next
his noble parson dependyth all our welthis somethyng to
Reffrayne his high magnanyme Courage and for our assuryd
welthe and quyet and specially of her noble person desyst
from that Dawngerows entrepryse, And whereas his highnes
hath the Renoum to be the most faythefull and substauncyall
prynce, Crystayned yn the trew perfourmyng of all his pro-
myses that hyt may lyke his grace to lay the wyte on vs his
poore Subiectes thowgh that he breke in that poynt the tenour
of his Indenture, For yf his highnes wold so farre presse vs by
our allegence that he wold nedys cary ouer with hym the
Armay in the same Endentures expressed, I am suer there
showld not be oon amongest them all that had any reason in
his hed but he shuld be more metar to wayle and wryng hys
handes than assuryd to fyght, whan he consydered that yf
otherwyse then well showld fortune to that prescious Juell
whiche he had for hys partye, in custody, yt were more
metar for hym to departe in to Turkey than to Retourne
agayne in to his naturall Contray to hys wyffe and chyldren.
And now as yt fortunyth naturally where as a man ys fully

perswadyd in any matter as I am trewly that our most
Redowtid soueraygne showld in no wyse passe the Sees in his
owne noble person consideryng the thynges aforsaide to fayne
Reasons to make for His purpose, soo doo I now Fantasye
syns I am so extremely desyrows that the noble parson yf[1]
my saide Prynce showlde tarry withyn Hys Realme that hit
were better to trayne owre warre and by lyttyll and lyttyll to
attempte wery the saide Francoys then at oons to send ouer
agaynst hym the power Royall of this noble Royalme.

'In the reasonyng of whiche matter I shall but vtter myne
ygnoraunce afore Hanyball as our ryght wyse spekar rehersid
now of late, but syns I am wadyd thus far vnder your benygne
supportacion I shall here vtter my pore mynde yf thys grete
and puysaunt armaye of xxx Thowsand fotemen and ten
Thowsand horsemen showld be conueyed in to the partyes of
beyond see I ymagyn with myself whiche wayes they myght
take to noy our enemyes most Consideracion fyrst had vnto
their owne saufegarde, How they myght suerly be victualled
and thus I reason yf they shuld so invade Fraunce that they
myght euer with suretye haue victayles owte of the Archedukedome, than put I no dowbtes but they showld saufely
Retourne agayne, for any daungyer that showld come vnto
theym by their enemyes, for synse they durst not this yere
last past set vpon the Hardy and valiaunt Capetayn the
Yerle of Surrey notwithstandyng any prouocacions that he
Cowld by hys experte wysedome in the Feattes of warre
Imagyn to bryng them thervnto how moche more wold they
beware to mete with so howge an Armye whose bruit
I suppose god beyng indyfferent the poore of Fraunce were
not hable to susteyne, but by this meanes lyke as our saide
Armye shuld be in saftye soo showld the harme whiche they
showld doo to the Realme of Fraunce be nothyng so moche
as the harmys whiche we ourselffes showld susteyn in
sowldyng of so great an army which were hable or iii
Somers were expyred to exhawste and vtterly consume all
the Cogne and bolyon withyn this Realme whiche I coniecture can not passe moche aboue a Million For yf all the

---

[1] *sic*, for 'of' ?

valew of the hole Realme excede not iiii Millions as my lorde
Cardinalles grace Declaryth playnly vnto vs all of whiche
the possessions were estemyd to amount to oone Hole
Million, me thynkyth that there ys no dowbte but that the
Cornes, Cattalles our owne Commodeties vtensilles Apparayll
for man and women whiche was neuer soo sumptuous and
also the wares not oonly made of our owne commodetyes
but also conveyed from the partyes of beyond the see Hyther
wherof was neuer so grete Haboundaunce Dothe amount at
the lest vnto other ij Millions This yf we showld take thys
way or euer we showld doo to our enemy any hurt that were
worthy to be regardid we showld be brought in to that case
that we showld neuer be hable neuer to hurt hym ne none
other, nor to help our Prynce, nor this his noble Realme
What aduersyte soeuer shuld fortune to Hap ye and what
showld we then Doo, but sit in peace with the highest
ignomine and Desperat confusion that euer did nacion and
be constraynyd for the mayntenaunce of commutacion and
biyng and sellyng amongyst ourselffes to koyne lether agayne,
lyke as we oons haue done, whiche as for me I could well
ynowgh be content with but yf yt showld fortune our most
Redowtyd Souerayne, yf he wold nyedys go ouer yn hys
owne persone to happyn by any aduerse fortune, whiche
almyghty god defend to cum into the handes of our enemyes,
how shuld we then be hable to Redeme hym agayne yf they
wyll nought for their wynes but golde they wold thynck
grete skorne, to take lether for our prynce, ye and how moche
the Inhabitauntes of the saide Archedukedome be desirows to
haue moche of our monaye for Lytyll of their victuaylis
whiche showld the sonner bryng this inconuenyence to passe,
we haue hadde ryght good experyence aswell whan our
moste Redowbtid Souerayne last went ouer in His owne
Royall parson as in the last yere, whan my lorde of Surrey
was sent by our saide Souerayne in to those parties whose
Soldyers at their Rettourne made of the raryte and high
prysed victuales no lytyll complaynt.  But yf we nedys wold
conuaye our armye by their possessions and to make our
way as short as myght be, to goo the most nere and dyrect

way to Parrys where vndowbtyd were no small spoylle to
be gotten and in manner the place self not hable in strength
to kepe vs owte Assone as euer we were Departyd owte of
the Marchys of the saide Archedukedome, we showld then
clerely persayue whatt manner warre the Frenche men wold
vse ayenst vs whiche neuer wyll offer to medyll with our
Armye, but lye yn wayte yf any of our saide Armye
happened to straye or stragle abrode or to destroye the
Conductours of our victuayle.   And as for victuaylys in our
waye we shuld be sure none to fynde that other hadde legges
to convey hyt sylf from vs or elles by the diligence of the
paysans myght convaide[1] to the next strong holdys and then
myght we perchaunce (whiche god defend) persayue what
high daunger to leue any strong holdys behynde vs,
whiche the most Saugge and Poletyke Prynce Kyng Henry
the vij[th] of gracious memory thowght not best to doo.
For when he passed the Sees to wyn the ryght in Fraunce
he began fyrst to lay Seige to Bolayn, or euer he wold enter
anye farther in to the land.   And our most Redowtyd
souerayne now raynyng beyng in purpose as I harde reportid
goo as farre as Parres after the occupacion of his sawge
Counsayle began Fyrst at Tyrouenne and the Emperours
mageste Imployed A whosoeuer be in Tournay bycawse yt
was thowght to his high wysedome and hys noble councellers
euydently dawngerous yf he wold at any tyme hereafter
passe any farder by that way in to Fraunce, to leue suche
strong hold in the possession of his enemyes behynde hym
at hys bakke, and soo yf we showld for any dyspleasure
done vnto vs ammuse our Coscions armye abowte the
wynnyng of any those holdys, what maruelous Inconueny-
ences Let of purpose and Importable Charges we showld
sustayn therbye our most drad souerayne lorde hathe theryn
to good experyence in the wynnyng of Tyrouen which cost
his highnes more then xx[ti] suche vngracious Dogholes
cowld be worthe vnto hym But yf we wold vtterlye leue
this waye, and Determyn to Invade Normandie Bretayn or
sum other Contraye in the possession of his enemye vpon

---

[1] *sic*, for 'be conveyed.'

the Ryvage of the see and make *our* preparacions here
wit*h*yn this noble Realme suche as showld be thowght
conuenable for suche an armye Royall Thys thyng passith
the streche of my pore wyt to speke for oon*e* thing
I suppose, besid*es* the Inestymable molestacion and charge
whiche I ymagyn this noble Realme showld sustayne for
theyr p*r*eparacion for ware I can se nothyng but manyfest
dawngier on eu*er*y syde to be toward*es* the saide Armaye
not onely at their Arryvall amongest their enemyes at all
tymes and so long as they shall there tarry Whiche to shew
theym their saide enemyes showld have no smale aduauntage,
and that in sundry wyse, but also how they should surely
be victayled for thowgh we made here neu*er* so good
dylygence to prepare victailes for them in due tyme yet
stode bothe we and they in daungier of the wynde in whose
oncerteynte god defend that the Flower, nay in mann*er* the
hole Chyualry of this noble Realme showld so be hazardid
for thereby myght Chaunce the most lamentable losse ye
and wit*h*out Recou*er*y that eu*er* heretofore to me happenyd
For thowgh we be indowtyd ryght sore dymynysshed of
*our* Treasure, We haue yet a farr gretar want of defensable
men whiche to any good Englysshe man that ys not
affeccionat to his owne pryuat lucre but w*i*t*h* good harte and
true zele louyth the Commen wele ys to moche manyfest at
the yee, and hyt pleasid god of the contrary Wherby Supposid
that Almyghty god sent *our* souerayne his desiryd purpose
how showld we be Able to possede the large Cuntreye of
Fraunce whiche haue *our* owne Realme so meruelous rarely
storyd of inhabytaunt*es* and hable men, but there paraad-
venture yt myght be saide vnto me Why puttyst thow so
many dowtt*es* ayenst this my most redowtyd souerayns
enterpryse, he beyng so high in courage of maruelous
wysdome and well tryed experyence in all m*a*rciall Condutt*es*
seyng other his progenito*ur*s of farre lesse graces w*i*t*h* an
handfull of men in comparyson to his armye haue geuyn
them soo notable oue*r*throwes To thys question breuely to
show my pore mynde Trewly the manyfold victoryes that we
haue had ayenst theym bryngyth theym in playne dyspayre

to trye hyt anye more with vs In raunged battayll and to the
experyence that they haue of our Condicions bothe in warre
and pease hathe geuyn the saide Francoys hardynes thus
haynowsly to prouoke our Souerayne as he doyth for lyke
as he knowyth that in Armys our nacion ys ynvincible so
knowyth he our Impacience to Contynew in warre many
yeres and in especiall in wynter for we desier nowght elles
but to trye hyt with our handes at ones and that the
Maruelous charge far aboue any other nacion that we most
nedys continually be at for victuayles and other necessaryes
ys so grete that at the length we most nedys wery ourself
as oftyn as we be assemblyd to fyght yf We soo togyther
assemblyd long contynew thowgh none other nacion fyght
with vs I cowld here also towche what polecye we haue to
kepe thinges when we haue gottyn theym, but I let that
passe and wyll now shew the notable aduauntages that our
souerayns progenitours had ouer that we haue now, the
mean warre ayenst Fraunce yn tymes past we had euer
places surlye to Lond in other of our owne, or of our assured
confederattes and alies as Gascoyne Gwyen Bretayn and
sumtyme Normandie and at the lest we had Sum assuryd
freyndes there whiche wern grete men of power and furthermore their Townes and holdes were nothyng of the meruelous
strength that they be of at this present but now all thyse
thynges be chaunged places.   We haue none to lond in any
of the saide Countrays but suche as we may be sure to haue
allemanner dyspleasure shewyd vnto vs that they dare or
may doo and as for any frendes We haue that I dare not
presume to speke in, but as ferre as my pore coniecture
ledyth me there was neuer nacion more maruaylusly Lynkyd
togyder then they be amongyst theymselfes nor more sundry
prouysyons found how suche A[1] nature hath made of high
courage beyng borne amongyst them myght be prouyded
of welthful lyuynges vnder their obeysaunce to consent to
any Dysturbyng of their Commen Welth thowgh he showld
for that intent be offeryd a great and notable Treasoure
But how by[2] Coruptable all the worlde with the meruelows

---

[1] sic, for ' as.'          [2] sic, for ' be,' possibly meaning ' very.'

sleyght*es* in excessyff gyft*es* the Emper*ours* maiestye hathe
for his partie had of late ryght euydent experyence, For whyle
he was here in thise parties occupied abowte the wynnyng
of To*u*rney and other his affayres they had corrupted iij or
iiij of the grettest nobles of Spayne, apon whiche parsonages
for their euydent ontrewth the Emper*ours* Magestye was
constraynyd to do Justyce at his Reto*u*rnyng thyther,
whiche was no small losse onto hym yf they had lyke trew
subgiett*es* accordyngly regarded their allegiaunce and that
is to be m*er*uayled at my lorde of Sheuerys [1] the most
bounden creature of the sayde Emparo*urs* Maieste that eu*er*
was subiect to his Souuerayne, me thowght I harde my lorde
Cardinall*es* grace reporte, that he was also by their m*er*uelous
subtyle pollice and gyft*es* corrupt, and also yt ys euyde*n*t
that synse the saide Emper*ours* Maiestie Reto*u*rnyd in to
Spayne agayne the gou*er*no*ur*s of his Archedukedome haue
grauntyd dyu*er*s of safecondut vnto m*er*ch*au*nt*es* of the
Frenche nacion ye and for their Sakys vnto Skott*es* also,
whiche ys a maruelous hyndraunce after my pore Jugeme*n*t
to o*u*r souueraynes and the saide Emper*ours* warres. For
yf o*u*r co*m*modeties had aswell ben*e* kepte from theim as
their co*m*modeties be from vs many a thowsand artyfycer
lyuyng vnder the saide Francoys Domynyon whiche hathe
none other lyuyng but by workyng of o*u*r wollys haue
ben*e* constrayned to haue made to their kyng lamentable
sute for peace, as people browght to extreme distresse and
not wottyng how to lyue.

‘ Thus haue I here vttred my pore and symple mynde ryght
hartylly thanckyng yow all of yo*u*r benygne Supportacion
and how that yow haue Wytsaufe to here so pacientlie my
ignorance most humbly beseching the tender benygnyte of
my most dere and most redowtyd souuerayn whiche w*ith*-
drawyth hys m*er*cifull yee from Wylfull offenders yf they
humbly make sute vnto his grace for pardon, that he wyll of
his haboundaunt goodnes wytsaufe to take me as I meane
whiche am as desyrous that all his most noble entrepases
should prosperously go forward as any symple creature that

---

[1] William de Croy, Lord Chievres.

euer was borne vnder his obeisaunce thinckyng after my
Ignorant Jugement that yf yt wold please his magnanime
Courage to conuert Fyrst and chief his hole intent and
purpose not only to the ouer ronnyng and subduyng of
Skotland but also to Joyne the same Realme vnto his,
Soo that both they and we myght lyue vnder oone
Bessaunce Law and Pollecy for euer.  He shold therby
wyn the highest honour that euer dyd any noble progenitours synse thys Iland was fyrst Inhabyt to Joyne
vnto his noble Realme so populus a Cuntray wherby his
strength shold be of no small parte encresid and of this acte
should follow the highest abasshement to the saide Francoys
that euer happened to hym or any his progenetours afore
hym not oonly for that he Left the saide Skottes his auncient
allies and which haue for hys and their Sakes prouokyd our
nacion so notably heretofore at thys tyme vndefended by
reason of our souerayns naiuye whiche he dare not encounter
with nor neuer dare send theim socour so long as he shall
know the narrow sees substansially to be kept, but also for
somoche as he shall vnderstand that we haue chaunged our
manner of warre, whiche were wont nought else to doo but
to skore the nacions abowt, but whan he shall persayue that
by the hygh and pollytyk wysdome our saide most redowtid
Souerayne they be Joyned vnto vs in oone politik boddye
what fere shall we then stand in to Lose his possessions
without any hope of Recouere agayne, and thowgh hit be
a commen sayng that yn Skotland ys nought to wyn but
strokes, for that I alledge another commen sayng, who that
entendyth Fraunce to wyn with Skotland let hym begyn,
Whiche enterpret thus truely hyt ys But a Symplenesse for
vs to thyncke to kepe possessions in Fraunce, ⟨which⟩ ys
seuowryd from vs by the ocean see, and suffre Skotland
Joyne⟨d⟩ vnto vs by nature all in oon Iland, vnto which
we may haue Recourse at all tymes whan we woll, whiche
also to subdue, god beyng indifferent lyeth euer in our hand
to lyue vnder a nother pollecy and to Recognyse another
Prynce send god that our most Redowty Souuerayne ⟨may
conquer Scotland⟩ whiche whan we haue ones Joyned vnto

*our* polecy as a memb*re* by nature dyscendyng apon the hole, than shall we therby have the experyence how to wyn and kepe other possessions of *our* most redowtyd souerayne of due ryght and enherytaunce belonging to his noble Crowne whiche we ⟨have⟩ in the parties of beyond the see in whyche entrepryses I beseche god send *our* most dere and most redowtyd souuerayn prosperous Succession and fortunat atcheuyng of all this his noble entrepryse.'

There is no record that this speech was ever delivered; even if it was, it certainly had no effect in this unwieldy and unpractical session of Parliament. But the accuracy and force of the speaker's reasoning were destined to be proved by the subsequent course of events. For the student of the present day, who is enabled to glance at the whole picture from a distance, so that the various facts assume more or less their proper proportion and perspective, Cromwell's words on this occasion will always remain as one of the strongest proofs of his political wisdom and foresight.

After touching on the subject of the war, and assuring the House of his conviction that any one present would give goods and life ten thousand times over to recover France for the King (a shrewd beginning, for if Henry was not present in person, no one knew better than Cromwell how accurately every word spoken in the Parliament would be reported to him, and how important it was for one who would gain the royal favour to put his loyalty to the Crown first of all), he goes on, after a few commonplace remarks about the war's being waged with energy, to crave the pardon of the House for addressing so noble an assembly. This preface is eminently characteristic of the speaker. When not perfectly certain of his ground, and in the presence of those whom he wished to conciliate, none could be a more adroit flatterer than he; it was only when he was completely master of the situation (and he had a peculiar gift of discovering just what his position was in relation to other people) that he became contemptuous, overbearing, and cruel.

But not even yet had he said enough to prove his loyalty to the King. He agrees that war is inevitable, and that the question now is how it may be most effectually carried on, but when he foresees that the King will go in person, he is greatly distressed. He talks loudly about the danger of the King being killed, hints that Henry possessed a courage and a self-sacrifice to the interests of England which would render him impervious to any argument about personal risk, and then launches himself into the heart of his discourse. The King is an absolute necessity to the welfare and progress of the State. If the King were removed, the country would probably be brought face to face with the horrors of a civil war. Cromwell thus brings his hearers to the first great principle of the policy that he was destined later to pursue, namely, concentration of power in the hands of the Crown, as a *sine qua non* of unity at home and safety abroad. This principle he enforces with many other arguments. The danger from the hostility of Scotland was enormous ; let the King 'Reffrayne his high magnanyme Courage' and remaining at home, so direct the movements of his forces, that England and Scotland may together move as a unit. France has bought off many who may seem to be England's allies on the Continent. The consequence of an invasion of France would be the scattering of the army ; it might be cut off in an attempt to capture Paris, and England would be left to the mercy of its first invader. The country must make sure of its own safety, before entering upon a war of aggression.

He brings up other points to prove his case, and here speaks against the proposed subsidy. He saw, as a merchant, that the amount proposed was excessive ; his fear was that all the coin and bullion in the realm would be exhausted by three summers of fruitless warring, so that the nation would be forced 'to koyne lether agayne,' as it had done once before. His appreciation of the importance of sound finance, and the evils of a depreciated currency show a knowledge of economic principles far in advance of his time. 'Yf yt showld fortune o*ur* most Redowtyd Souerayne, yf he wold nyedys go ou*er* yn hys owne p*er*sone to happyn by any adu*er*se fortune, whiche almyghty god defend to cum into the hand*es* of o*ur* enemyes,' says Cromwell, 'how shuld we then be hable to Redeme hym agayne yf they wyll nought for their wynes but golde they wold thynck grete skorne, to take lether for *our* prynce.' Cromwell had early learned the lesson that money and brains were rapidly becoming far more important factors in winning battles, than mere superiority in brute strength or numbers. In his ingenious argument against the subsidy, he had pleaded the cause of the poor people, on whom the taxes fell most heavily, and had at the same time avoided arousing the opposition of the other party, by his adroit flattery at the outset.

His appreciation of the increased difficulty of waging war abroad compared with that in previous ages, because of lack of bases of supplies and friendly towns on the Continent, which before had been numerous, betokens great foresight and knowledge of details. Though he expressly declares, at the beginning of his speech, his intention to leave to 'sage persons' the task of deciding how the war should be carried on, he hints that it would be better to play a waiting game and weary the French, while things were consolidated at home, than to try to conquer France by invasion. His attitude about Scotland is repeated with great vigour at the close of his speech. For the King to unify England and Scotland would secure him greater honour than his predecessors had ever attained, and would in the end prove a much more telling blow against France, than a direct invasion. The question of gaining possessions across the sea is of secondary importance: the first thing is to obtain control of a country which belongs to the same island.

Thus Cromwell succeeded in clearly enunciating the main principles of the policy by which he was so soon to guide the affairs of England, while he so flattered King, nobles, and people, that he made many friends, and avoided the enmity of those opposed to him. The man who could make such a speech as this, would not be likely to escape the notice of such an astute man as Henry VIII. It was probably within the walls of this Parliament, that Cromwell laid the first stone of his future greatness as servant and counsellor of the King.

# CHAPTER III

AFTER the year 1524, there is no further mention of Thomas Cromwell as the cloth-merchant and wool-dyer. He probably realized that his business as a lawyer brought him into much more prominence as a public man, but his term in Parliament doubtless aroused in him a desire for even greater things than the life of a successful solicitor. His advance in legal prominence, however, is marked by his admittance in 1524 as a member of Gray's Inn, and by his appointment in the same year as one of the Subsidy Commissioners for the Hundred of Ossulton in Middlesex[1] ; but such petty distinctions fade into the background in the face of a matter of far more absorbing interest, that is, his rapidly growing favour and intimacy with Cardinal Wolsey.

During the years 1524-5 he was actively engaged in the Cardinal's service, and received many letters on legal business which he transacted for his master[2]. Seekers for Wolsey's mercy or patronage invariably came to him, as a likely means of getting their wishes granted. In several cases requests to the Cardinal are addressed directly to the 'right worshipful Mr. Cromwell.' It is evident from the tone of the letters which he received, that to obtain his favour was the first and most important step towards gaining that of his master. He was usually spoken of as ' Councillor to my Lord Legate,' and was pre-eminent above all the rest of Wolsey's advisers. It has been thought by some that the Cardinal employed him in connexion with his political schemes, but this is an error. Cromwell began modestly, as befitted his lowly birth and humble origin, and at this time, at any rate, was employed

---

[1] Cal. iv. 969 ; Doyle's Baronage, vol. i. p. 689.

[2] Cal. iv. 294, 388, 979, 1385-6, 1620, 2347-8, 2379.

merely as an agent, chosen for his wonderful knowledge of human nature and his great capacity for business.

In the beginning of 1525, however, Wolsey felt that he had in Cromwell a servant sufficiently capable to be trusted with the performance of a work which was nearest the Cardinal's heart, namely the destruction of some of the smaller monasteries to furnish funds for the building of his college at Oxford. So on the 4th of January of that year, he commissioned Sir William Gascoigne, William Burbank, and Thomas Cromwell, to survey the monasteries of Tykford, Raveneston, Poghley, Medmenham, Wallingford, and Fynchingbroke and their possessions, and on the same day he appointed Thomas Cromwell and John Smyth as attorneys for the site and circuit of Thoby, Blakamore, Stanesgate, and Tiptree, which had been granted to John Higden, Dean of Cardinal's College [1].

It may seem strange that Wolsey's suppression of the smaller religious houses brought him so much unpopularity. It was certainly true that the monasteries had long since ceased to observe the strict traditions of religious asceticism, which had been the watchword of their foundation. Some of them had become resorts of the idle and worthless, who were permitted by supine or indulgent superiors to exchange a life of monastic discipline for one of luxury and indolence, if not of downright vice. But there were a few, seemingly unimportant facts, which outweighed all these charges. In the first place the monks were the easiest of landlords. In their practically defenceless state, it was surely for their advantage to conciliate their fellow men in every way, and to avoid disputes at any cost. They consequently suffered themselves to be imposed upon by their neighbours and tenants, in preference to risking their popularity by asserting themselves. So Wolsey's measures, which brought in stricter landlords, increased rents, and did away with the good old slipshod management of so many years' standing, met with ill-concealed dislike. The monks, moreover, were the most hospitable of people ; the poor were never turned away unfed, the traveller

---

[1] Cal. iv. 989, 990.

could always find shelter beneath their roof, and this fact, coupled with the rooted opposition of the less educated class to any sweeping measure of reform adopted apparently without reason, while the old system appeared to all intents and purposes to work well, explained the rest. Wolsey's measures to suppress the smaller monasteries, and confiscate their possessions to the use of his own colleges, may justly be described as universally unpopular[1].

The first requisites for the accomplishment of such a design as the suppression of the monasteries were an intimate knowledge of law, especially as related to lands and property, and a far-seeing, harsh, and rather unscrupulous nature. These qualities Cromwell possessed in the very highest degree, and as he had been eminently successful in carrying on all Wolsey's legal business up to this time, and as the Cardinal was too busy with his foreign policy to give his own attention to this favourite scheme, it is no wonder that he chose Cromwell to supervise it for him. The work consisted in surveying and estimating the value of the property of the condemned monasteries, making careful inventories thereof, and finally in stripping them of all their transportable riches, which usually meant altars, furnishings, bells, and tapestry, while their lands and permanent possessions were sold or leased on the spot. The transfer of property, settlements with tenants, and adjustment of claims were a task of far greater intricacy than Wolsey had expected, and Cromwell's success in carrying it out was little short of marvellous. He was usually present in person at the surrenders and dissolutions; when this was impossible one of his many and faithful agents sent him an exact account of the proceedings in his absence. The number of monks and nuns that were suddenly turned out upon the world with small and irregularly paid pensions was not the least evil feature of the ruthless way in which the suppressions were carried on; but it was nothing to what was to follow a decade later[2].

In addition to surveying and confiscating monastic property,

---

[1] Cf. Preface to volume iv of the Calendar, pp. 368-9.
[2] Cal. iv. 1833-4, 2365, 5117, 5145.

Cromwell was employed directly in connexion with the new buildings at Oxford and Ipswich. He drew up all the necessary deeds for both foundations, and was appointed receiver-general of Cardinal's College by Wolsey in 1527. He kept account of all the incomes from the suppressed houses and all the expenses incident to the building of both colleges. He was continually superintending the workmen at Oxford and Ipswich, and reported their progress to his master. The Dean of the college at Ipswich wrote to the Cardinal, Sept. 26, 1528, how Cromwell came thither with copes, vestments, and plate, and took great pains to see all the stuff carried in safely, and to prepare hangings and benches for the Hall. Long lists of the manors and monasteries, the incomes of which were devoted to the building and establishment of the two colleges, are to be seen to-day at the Record Office, and attest the gigantic amount of labour that he performed [1].

Cromwell's efficiency in carrying on this work was only equalled by his notorious accessibility to bribes and presents in the disposal of monastic leases. Adding to this the fact that the measure was radically unpopular in itself, and that when no bribes were offered, Cromwell and most of Wolsey's other agents were harsh and overbearing in the extreme, the reader ceases to wonder at the outburst of popular indignation. The minute Wolsey's back was turned Cromwell and his companion Dr. Alen, a hard and grasping man equally well trained in business, proceeded to use the power given into their hands to enrich themselves by every possible means, some of which were utterly unjustifiable. The monastery which could pay a large bribe was often left untouched; of those that were suppressed, probably a certain proportion of the spoils was never employed at Oxford or Ipswich, but went straight into the pockets of the suppressors [2]. Petitions to save farms for poor people, or to get benefices for those whose property was gone, were answered by Cromwell favourably, if granting them meant a substantial reward for him;

[1] Cal. iv. 3461, 4778, 5330; Letters, 6, 8.
[2] Cal. iv. 3360.

unfavourably, if the reverse. He became so generally hated that in August, 1527, it was said that a 'sanctuary man' lay in wait to slay him, and Cardinal Pole, who was then in London and knew him well, informs us that it was commonly reported that he had been sent to prison, and would be punished for his crimes as Wolsey's agent [1].

But in spite of all this, instead of being removed from his important post, Cromwell kept on rising to higher favour and more importance. In April, 1527, Henry Lacy writes to congratulate him on his promotion through Wolsey's favour. In May of the same year he is mentioned as a granter of annuities. His position brought him a great amount of patronage. In 1528 Richard Bellyssis promises him a good gelding, if he will prefer a friend to the position of mint-master in Durham. A merchant requests him to get his son a promotion from the Cardinal. He received many petitions from poor men, who feared they would lose house and home through the dissolution of the monastery from which they were held. But the noble and great, as well as the lowly and humble, were his correspondents and suitors. The Abbot of York writes his heartfelt thanks for his kindness in speaking well of him and his monastery to Wolsey, and Lord Berners begs for his aid in his dealings with the Cardinal [2].

By far the greater portion of Cromwell's correspondence during the years 1525–1529 is connected with the suppression of the monasteries or the foundation of Wolsey's colleges. Reports and receipts of money from his agents who visited the religious houses in various parts of the country at his orders, or who superintended the works at Ipswich and Oxford, crowd in upon him with great frequency. Deeds of the sale of castles and manors, valuations and inventories of the property of various monasteries, are received by him in large numbers [3]. In these letters we frequently meet with the names of William Brabazon and Ralph Sadler, who were

---

[1] Cal. iv. 3334, and Appendix II at the end of chapter i, p. 19.
[2] Cal. iv. 3079, 3119, 4201, 5169, 5365, 5456.
[3] Cal. iv. 3198, 3475, 3535, 3676, 4117, 4275, 4570, 4573, 5399, 5411.

destined in the near future to become so well known as his
agents and commissioners when he entered the King's service.
Before this period he had made the acquaintance of Stephen
Vaughan, his friend and correspondent in later years, who
figured in connexion with Tyndale in the Low Countries.
Vaughan was certainly known to Cromwell at least as early
as 1523[1]; and in 1526 was employed by the Cardinal's servant
in connexion with the college at Oxford. In April, 1527, we
find Cromwell helping his friend in the recovery of certain
goods lost on the sea, and in the following year Vaughan
addresses a cordial letter to his benefactor, reporting various
things of interest in London, and announcing that he has
found so strong a chain for the wicket of Cromwell's house
at Austin Friars Gate, that it will be impossible for any one
to enter by force[2]. A year later he was employed as Cromwell's agent in the Netherlands.

Though mainly occupied with Wolsey's affairs, Cromwell's
correspondence during the years 1524–1529 shows that he
still kept up his business as a lawyer independently. William
Bareth writes in November, 1525, that he trusts he will
solicit his matter to Mr. Rowe, and sends his wife six plovers
'for to drynke a quart of wyn wit*h*all[3]'; in August, 1526,
George Monoux, alderman, promises Cromwell that if his
'grete matier' is brought to a safe conclusion, he shall have
twenty marks[4]. A 'lovyng le*tte*re' from the Aldermen of our
Lady's Gild in Boston, in Dec. 1528, shows that Cromwell
still retained the friendship which he probably made years
before by obtaining for them the indulgences from the Pope
by the offer of choice sweetmeats. It was doubtless through
him that the Gild gained the privilege of supplying rare and
delicate fowls for the Cardinal's sumptuous table[5]. Cromwell
also found time to correspond with Miles Coverdale, who was
then at Cambridge, and who writes with enthusiasm of the
pleasures of a visit to his friend in London[6].

It is probable that the terrible sweating sickness which

---

[1] Letters, i.
[2] Cal. iv. 2538, 3053, 4107.
[3] Cal. iv. 1768.
[4] Cal. iv. 2387.
[5] Cal. iv. 5080, 5141.
[6] Cal. iv. 3388.

ravaged England from 1527 to 1528 carried off Cromwell's wife Elizabeth, as there is no further mention of her in his later papers and correspondence, except in his will of July, 1529, where she is referred to as his ' late Wyff [1].' She left him one son, Gregory, who appears to have been a dull and plodding lad, and who, after his mother's death, was sent with his very precocious cousin, Christopher Wellyfed, and several other boys, to be put under the care of a tutor at Cambridge, John Chekyng by name, whose correspondence with Cromwell about the progress of ' his scolers ' is very interesting and entertaining [2]. Chekyng seems at the very outset to have been unfavourably impressed with Gregory's talents, declares that he has been so badly taught that he could hardly conjugate three verbs when committed to his care, and reports that he is now studying ' the things most conducive to the reading of authors,' and spends the rest of the day in forming letters; while Christopher does not require ' much stirring up.' A little later he sends word that Gregory is getting on well in learning under his care, and desires his father to send five yards of ' marble frieze,' for his winter ' galberdyne '; and again, in 1530, he declares that he has been so successful in his teaching, that Gregory will be 'loadyd with Latyne' before he comes home again; but it is evident throughout that Chekyng considers every step in advance to have been due to the excellence of his own tuition, rather than to the aptitude of his pupil. If the tone of Gregory's letters to his father be taken as a criterion of the boy's character, he must indeed have been stupid and slow beyond belief [3]. But Cromwell was too much occupied with his own affairs, to pay much attention to the remarks of honest John Chekyng. Indeed there is reason to think that his grasping disposition showed itself in small ways to such an extent that he did not always pay the very moderate bills that the tutor sent in for Gregory's board, lodging, and tuition ; but instead taunted Chekyng with not having done well with his ' folks.' To these insults Chekyng replied that he had brought up six

---

[1] Cf. Appendix at the end of this chapter, p. 58.

[2] Cal. iv. 4560, 4837, 4916.

[3] Cal. iv. 4561.

M.A.'s and fellows of colleges, and that the least Cromwell could do was to pay for the furniture which his scholars had ruined ; he then goes on to tell how Christopher 'dyd hynge a candel in a playt to loyk apone hys boyk and so fell ascleype and the candell fell into the bed strawe' and there were burnt the bed, bolster, 'three overleydes and a sparver[1].'

In spite of his niggardly treatment of John Chekyng, it is certain that Cromwell was in very comfortable circumstances during his years of service under Wolsey. An inventory of his goods at his house at Austin Friars, dated June 26, 1527[2], which exists to-day at the Public Record Office, proves that his dwelling was furnished handsomely if not luxuriously, while a draft of his will, written July 12, 1529[3], indicates that his property at that time was by no means inconsiderable. It is to this document that we owe the greater part of our present information concerning Cromwell's family.  It is written in the hand of Cromwell's chief clerk, and was altered at a later date by Cromwell himself[4].  The document is for the most part self-explanatory, but there are a few interesting facts to be especially noted in connexion with it.  The bequests to Cromwell's daughters 'Anne and Grace' and to his 'litill Doughter Grace' are our only proof that he had other children than Gregory ; and the fact that both these items were crossed out after the year 1529 possibly indicates that the daughters died when young.  We also learn that Cromwell's nephew Richard, the son of Katherine Cromwell and Morgan Williams, had followed in his uncle's footsteps, and was 'seruaunt with my lorde Marques Dorssett' at the time that the will was first composed; but he certainly received other employment soon afterwards, for the name

---

[1] Cal. iv. 4433, 5757, 6219.

[2] Cal. iv. 3197.

[3] Appendix at the end of this chapter. The will is also printed in Froude, Appendix to chapter vi. The statement in a footnote that the names Williams and Williamson are used interchangeably is scarcely credible.

[4] Cf. footnote 1 in the Appendix,

p. 56.  The will was originally mis-dated, owing to an obviously careless error by the clerk, which was corrected by him at the time.  The other corrections, by Cromwell, are written in a different-coloured ink ; and the handwriting according to the Calendar (cf. footnote to vol. iv. no. 5772) indicates that they were made at a later date.

of his master was scored through in the will by Cromwell
at a later date, and we also know from other sources that
Richard Williams entered his uncle's service and was active
in suppressing the monasteries and in subduing the Pilgrimage
of Grace, during the year 1536 and afterwards[1]. Before this
date he had changed his name to Cromwell, and later became
great-grandfather to the Protector[2]. His mother died before
1529, for Cromwell in his will refers to Elizabeth Wellyfed
as his 'onlye Suster.' Cromwell's wife, as we have already
seen, had also died before the will was made; her sister
Joan married a certain John Williamson, an old friend of
Cromwell's, who later figured prominently in the latter's
service. We also meet with many of the other names
mentioned in this will, in Cromwell's later correspondence.
Nearly all the friends of his earlier days were employed by
him in one capacity or another as spies, agents, or even minor
ambassadors to foreign Courts, after he had entered the King's
service.

[1] Cal. xi. 1016; xii. (ii) 646.
[2] Cf. the genealogy in the Antiquary, vol. ii. pp. 164 ff.

# APPENDIX TO CHAPTER III

## THE WILL OF THOMAS CROMWELL

### R. O. Cal. iv. 5772 (1)

In the name of god Amen The xij[th] Daye of Iulie in the yere of our lorde god mccccxxxix[ti] [1] and in the xxj[ti] yere of the Reigne of our Souereigne Lorde king Henry the viij[th] I Thomas Crumwell of london gentilman being hole in bodie and in good and parfyte memorye Lauded be the holie Trynytee make ordeyn and Declare this my present testament conteyning my last will in maner and ⟨fourme⟩ Folowing. Furste I bequethe my Sowle to the grete god of heuen my maker Creatour and Redemer beseching the most gloryous virgyn our blessed ladie Saynct Mary the vyrgyn and Mother with all the holie companye of heuen to be Medyatours and Intercessours for me to the holie trynytee So that I may be able when it shall please Almightie god to call me out of this miserable worlde and transitorie lif to inherite the kingdome of heuen amongst the nomber of good christen people. And whan so euer I shall departe this present lif, I bequethe my bodie to be buryed where it shall please god to ordeyn me to die and to be ordered after the discression of myn executours vndernamed And for my goodes which our lorde hathe lent me in this Worlde I will shalbe ordered and disposed in maner and fourme as hereafter shall insue. Furst I gyue and bequethe vnto my Soon Gregory Crumwell Syx hundreth threscore Syx poundes thirten shelynges foure pens [2] of lawfull money of Englonde With the Whiche Syx hundreth three-score Syx powndes xiij[s] foure pens [3] I will myn executours vnder-named ymediatlye or assone as they conuenyently may after my Decesse shall purchase londes tenementes and hereditamentes to the clere yerelye value of xxxiij[li] vj[s] viij[d] [4] by the yere aboue all charges

---

[1] Altered at the time from:— 'mccccc xx viij[ti]' by the clerk. All the other changes are in Cromwell's hand, and were probably made at a later date. Cf. footnote in the Calendar, vol. iv. pt. iii. p. 2573.

[2] Altered from:—'Foure hundreth powndes.'

[3] Altered from:—'ccccc[li].'

[4] Altered from:—'xx[li].'

*and* reprysys to thuse of my saide Soon Gregorye for terme of his
lif And after the Decesse of the saide Gregorye to the heyres Males
of his bodie lawfully to be begotten And for lacke of heires Males
of the bodie of the saide Gregory lawfully to be begotten to the
heires generall of his bodie lawfully begotten. And for lacke of
suche heires to the right heires of me the saide Thomas Crumwell
in Fee. I will also that ymedyatly and assone as the saide lond*es*
tene*mentes* and hereditamen*tes* shalbe so purchased after my deth
as is aforsaide by myn executours that the yerelie proffyt*es* thereof
shalbe hollie spent and imployed in and about*es* the educacyon and
fynding honestly of my saide Soon Gregory in vertue good lerning
and Maners vntill such tyme as he shall cu*m* to the full age of xxij
yeres. During Which tyme I hertely desir *and* require my saide
executours to be good vnto my saide Son Gregory and to see he
do lose no tyme but to se him ve*r*teously ordered & brought vp
according to my trust Item I gyue and bequethe to my saide Soon
Gregorie When he shall cu*m* to his full age of xxiiij yeres Twoo [1]
Hundreth pound*es* of lawfull ynglissh money to order then as *our*
lorde shall gyue hym grace and discression Which cc$^{li}$ I will shalbe
put in suertie to thintent the same may cu*m* to his hand*es* at his
saide age of xxiiij$^{ti}$ yeres. Item I gyue and bequethe to my saide
Soon Gregory of such houseold stuf as god hathe lent me Three [2]
of my best Fetherbedd*es* wi*th* thayr bolsters ij$^o$ the best [3] payre of
blankett*es* of Fustyan my best Couerlet of Tapistrye and my Quylte
of yelow Turquye Saten, x payre of my best Shet*es* foure [4] pillowes
of downe wi*th* iiij payre of the best pillowe beres foure [5] of my best
table clothes, foure of my best towell*es* Twoo dosen [6] of my Fynest
Naptkynnes and ij$^o$ dozen of my other Naptkynnes, ij$^o$ [7] garnyssh
of my best vessell, iij of my best brasse pott*es*, iij of my best brasse
pannes, ij$^o$ of my best kettill*es*, ij$^o$ of my best Spitt*es*, My best ioyned
bed of Flaunders wo*ur*ke wi*th* the best Syler and tester and other
thapp*ur*tena*unces* therto belonging My best presse caruen of Flaunders
wo*ur*ke and my best Cupbourde caruen of Flaunders wo*ur*k wi*th*
also vj Joyned Stoles of Flaunders wo*ur*ke and vj of my best
Cusshyns Item I gyue and bequethe to my saide Soon Gregorye
A Bason wi*th* a Lewer p*ar*cell gilte my best Salt gilt my best Cup

---

[1] Altered from :—'one.'

[2] Altered from :—'twoo.'

[3] These last six words are altered
from :—'a Bolster the best.'

[4] Altered from :—'two.'

[5] Altered from :—'ij$^o$.'

[6] Altered from :—'One Dozen.'

[7] Altered from :—'A.'

gilt, Three[1] of my best goblettes gilt three other of my best goblettes parcell gylt, Twelue of[2] my best Syluer spones, Three of[3] my best Drynking ale potes gilt.   All the which parcelles of plate and house-old stuf I will shalbe savelye kept to thuse of my saide Soonne Gregorye till he shall cum to his saide full age of xxij[ti] yeres and all the which plate  household  stuf  Naperye  and  other  the  premisses I will myn executours do put in saufe keping vntill my saide Soon shall cum to the saide yeres or age of xxij[ti].  And if he die before the age of xxij[ti][4] Then I will all the saide plate vessell and houseold stuf shalbe sold by myn executours And the money thereof cum-myng to be gyuen and equallie Deuyded amongst my poure kynnes-folkes.   That is to say amongst the children as well of myn owne Susters Elizabeth and  Katheryn as of my late Wyffes Suster Johane Wif to John Willyamson, And if it happen that all the children of my saide Susters and Suster in law Do dye before the particyon and deuysion be made and none of them to be lyuyng Then I will that all the saide plate vessell and houseold stuf shalbe solde and yeuen to other my poure kynnesfolkes then being on lyue and other poure and indigent people in Deades of charytee for my Sowle my Father and Mother their Sowles, and all Christen Sowles[5] Item I gyue and bequethe vnto my Suster  Elizabeth Wellyfed Wif to Wyllyam Welly-

---

[1] Altered from :—' iij.'

[2] Altered from :—' vj of.'

[3] These last two words are altered from :—' and.'

[4] Altered from :—' xxiiij[ti].'

[5] Crossed out :—' Item I gyue and bequethe to my Doughter Anne one hundreth Markes of lawfull money of Englond when she shall cum to her lawfull age or happen to be maryed And xl[li] towardes her Fynd-ing vntill the tyme that she shalbe of lawfull age or be maryed.  Which xl[li] I will shalbe Delyuered to my Frend John Croke on of the Six clerkes of the king his Chauncerie to thintent he may order the same and cause the same to be imployed in the best wise he can deuyse about the vertewous educacyon and bring-ing vp of my saide Doughter till she shall cum to her lawfull age or

maryage.  And if it happen my saide Doughter to Dye before she cum to her saide lawfull age or be maryed Then I will that the said c Markes and so moche of the said xl[li] as then shalbe vnspent and vnim-ployed at the Day of the deth of my said Doughter Anne, I will it shall remayne to Gregory my Soon if he then be on lyue, And if he be Dede the same c Markes and also so moche of the saide xl[li] as then shalbe vnspent to be departed amongst my Sustres children in maner and fourme forsaid And if it happen my saide Sustres children then to be all Dede, Then I will the saide c Markes and so moche of the saide xl[li] as then shalbe vnspent shalbe deuyded amongst my kynsfolkes such as then shalbe on lyue.'

fed xl$^{li}$ [1] iij Goblett*es* w*ith*out a Cou*er* [2] a Macer, And A Nutt Item
I gyue and bequethe to my nephew Rycharde Wyllyams [3] lxvj$^{li}$ xiij$^s$
iiij$^d$ [4] sterling*es* my best [5] gowne Doblett and Jaquet It*em* I gyue and
bequethe to my nepue *Christ*ofer Wellyfed my nephe xl$^{li}$ [6] my v$^{th}$
gowne doblett and Jaquett It*em* I gyue and bequethe to my nephew
Wyllyam Wellyfed the Yonger xx$^{li}$ [7] Item I gyue and bequethe to my
nece Alice Wellyfed to her Maryage xx$^{li}$ And if it happen her to
Dye before maryage then I will the saide xx$^{li}$ shall remayne to her
brother *Christ*ofer And if it happen him to Dye the same xx$^{li}$ to
remayne to Willyam Wellyfed the yonger his brother. And if it
happen them all to Dye before their lawfull age or maryage, then
I will that their part*es* shall remayne to Gregory my Soon. And
if it happen him to Dye before them then I will all the said p*artes*
shall remayn to Rychard Wyll*i*ams and Water Will*i*ams my nephews [8]
And if it happen them to Dye then I will that all the said part*es*
shalbe Distributed in Dead*es* of charytee for my Sowle my Father
and Mothers Sowles and all christen Sowles. Item I gyue and
bequethe to my Mother in law Mercye Pryo*ur* xl$^{li}$ of lawfull ynglissh money and her ch*a*umber w*ith* certen houseold stuf, That is
to saye A Fetherbed, a Bolster ij pillowes w*ith* their beres vj payre
of Shet*es* A payre of blankettes, A garnyssh of vessell, ij$^o$ pott*es*,
ij$^o$ pannes, ij$^o$ Spytt*es* w*ith* such other of my houseold stuf as shalbe
thought mete for her by the Discression of myn executours And
suche as she will reasonablye Desire not being bequethed to other
vses in this my p*res*ent testament and last will. Item I gyue and
bequethe to my said mother in law a lytill Salt of Syluer a Maser,
vj Silu*er* Spones and a drinking pot of Syluer And also I charge
myn executours to be good vnto her duryng her lyffe. Item I gyue
and bequethe to my brother in law Willya*m* Wellyfed xx$^{li}$ my thurde
gown Jaquet and Doblet. Item I gyue and bequethe to John
Wyllyamson my brother in law c m*a*rkes [9] a gown a Doblet and
a Jaquet, A Fetherbed, A bolster vj payre of Shet*es* ij$^o$ table clothes,
ij$^o$ Dozen Naptkynnes, ij$^o$ towell*es* ij$^o$ brasse pott*es*, ij$^o$ brasse pannes,

---

[1] Altered from:—' xx$^{li}$ I Saye
Twentye pound*es* st*er*ling': and
this is altered from:—' xxx$^{li}$ which
she oweth me.'

  [2] Crossed out:—' and.'

  [3] Crossed out:—' s*er*ua*u*nt w*ith*
my lorde Marques Dorssett.'

  [4] Altered from:—' xl$^{li}$.'

[5] Altered from:—' Fourth.'

  [6] Altered from:—' xx$^{li}$.'

  [7] Altered from:—' x$^{li}$.'

  [8] Altered from:—' shall remayne
to Anne and Grace my doughters.'

  [9] Altered from:—' xl$^{li}$': and this
is altered from:—' xx$^{li}$.'

a Syluer pott A Nutte parcell gilt, and to Iohane his wyf x$^{li}$ [1]. Item I gyue and bequethe to Johane Wyllyamson their Doughter to her maryage xx$^{li}$ and to euery other of their children vj$^{li}$ xiij$^s$ iiij$^d$ [2]. Item I bequethe to Walter Wyllyams my nephue [3] xx$^{li}$ Item I gyue and bequethe to Rafe Sadleyer my seruaunte cc [4] Markes of lawfull ynglissh money my Seconde [5] gowne Jaquet and Doblet and all my bokes Item I gyue and bequethe to Hugh Whalley my Seruaunt vj$^{li}$ xiij$^s$ iiij$^d$. Item I gyue and bequethe to Stephen Vaughan sumtyme my seruaunte c markes [6] a gowne Jaquet and Doblet. Item I gyue and bequethe to Page my Seruaunte otherwise called John du Pount vj$^{li}$ xiij$^s$ iiij$^d$ [7] and also to Thomas Auerey my seruauntt vj$^{li}$ xiij$^s$ iiij$^d$ [8]. Item I gyue and bequethe to John Horwood vj$^{li}$ xiij$^s$ iiij$^d$ [9] Item that the rest of myn apparell before not gyuen ne bequethed in this my testament and last will shalbe yeuen and equally Departed amongst my Seruauntes after the order and discression of myn executours Item I will also that myn executours shall take the yerely profyttes aboue the charges of my Ferme of Canberye

---

[1] Altered from :—' vj$^{li}$ xiij$^s$ iiij$^d$.'

[2] Altered from :—' iiij$^{li}$ vj$^s$ viij$^d$.'

[3] Altered from :—' Cosyn.'

[4] Altered from :—' c.'

[5] Altered from :—' Best.'

[6] Altered from :—' x$^{li}$.'

[7] Crossed out :—' Item I gyue and bequethe to Elizabeth Gregory sumtyme my Seruaunt xx$^{li}$ vj payre of Shetes A Fetherbed A payre of blankettes A Couerlet ij$^o$ table clothes, One Dozen Naptkynnes ij$^o$ brasse pottes, ij$^o$ pannes, ij$^o$ Spyttes.'

[8] Crossed out :—' Item I gyue and bequethe to John Croke one of the vj clerkes of the Chauncerye x$^{li}$ my Second gowne Doblet and Jaquet. Item I gyue and bequethe to Roger More Seruaunt of the king his bakehouse vj$^{li}$ xiij$^s$ iiij$^d$ iij yardes Saten and to Maudelyn his wyf iij$^{li}$ vj$^s$ viij$^d$.'

[9] Crossed out :—' Item I gyue and bequethe to my litill Doughter Grace c Markes of lawfull ynglissh money when she shall cum to her lawfull age or maryage and also

xl$^{li}$ towardes her exhibucyon and Fynding vntill suche tyme ⟨as⟩ she shalbe of lawfull age or be maryed Which xl$^{li}$ I will shalbe delyuered to my brother in law John Willyamson to thintent he may order and cause the same to be imployed in and aboutes the vertewous educacyon and brynging vp of my saide Doughter till she shall cum to her lawfull age or Maryage. And if it happen my saide Doughter to Dye before she cum to her lawfull age or maryage then I will that the saide c markes and so moche of the saide xl$^{li}$ as then shalbe vnspent and vnimployed aboutes the fynding of my saide Doughter at the Day of the Deth of my saide Doughter shall remayne and be Delyuered to Gregory my Soon if he then shall happen to be on lyue. And if he be Dede then the saide c Markes and the saide residue of the saide xl$^{li}$ to be euenlye Departed amongst my poure kynnesfolkes, that is to say my Susters children forsaide.'

and all other thing*es* Conteynyd wi*th*in my sayd lease of Canberye
in the Cowntye of Middelsex [1] And wi*th* the proffyt*es* thereof [2] shall
yerelie paye vnto my brother in law Will*i*am Wellffe⟨d⟩ and Elysa-
bethe his wyffe myn onlye Suster Twentye pownd*es* duryng thayr lyves
and the longer of them and after the discease of the sayd Will*i*am
and Elysabeth the proffett*es* of the sayd Ferme ou*er and* aboue the
yerlye Rentt to be kept to the vse of my Son gregorye tyll he Cu*m*
to the age of xxij[ti] and at the yeres of xxij[th] the sayd lease *and*
Ferme of Canberye I do gyue and bequethe to my sayd Son gregorye
to haue the same to hym his executors and assignes [3] and if it
Fortune the saide Gregorye my Soon to dye before he shall cu*m*
to the age of xxij [4] yeres My sayd bruthur*en* in lawe and syster being
dede Then I will my Cosyn Rychard Will*i*ams shall ⟨haue⟩ the
Ferme wi*th* the appurtena*un*c*es* to hym and his executors *and* assignes and yf it happen my sayd Brother in law my Suster [5] my
Son gregorye *and* my sayd Cosyn Rycharde to dye before the
accoumplyshement of this my wyll touching*e* the sayd Ferme then
I wyll myn executors shall Sell the sayd ferme and the moneye
therof Cummyng to Imploye in ded*es* of charyte to praye [6] for my
Sowle and all *Christe*n Sowles.    Item I will that myn executours
shall conducte and hyre a pryest being an honest p*er*son of contynent
and good lyuyng to Syng for my Sowle by the space of vij [7] yeres
next after my deth and to gyue him for the same Fortye Syx pownd*es*
thertene sheling*es* Foure pens that ys to saye vj[li] xiij[s] iiij[d] yerlye for
his stypend [8].    Item I gyue and bequethe toward*es* the making of high
wayes in this Realme where it shalbe thought most necessary [9] xx[li]

---

[1] The last seventeen words are
altered from:—'Sutton at Hone
and Temple Dartford in the Countie
of Kent And shall take the p*r*offyte
of my Ferme of the p*ar*sonage of
Sutton.'

[2] Crossed out:—'cu*m*myng.'

[3] Crossed out:—'in Dead*es* of
charytee ou*er* and aboue the charges
and reparac*i*ons gyue and Distry-
bute for my Soule quarterly xl[s]
among*st* poure people vntill my
Soon Gregorye shall cu*m* to the
age of xxv yeres if he so long do
Lyue And then my saide Soon
to haue my said Fermes During

the yeres conteyned wi*th*in my
leases.'

[4] Altered from:—'xxv.'

[5] Crossed out:—'and.'

[6] Crossed out:—'my saide executours shall sell my said Fermes
to the most proffyte and adua*un*tage
And the money thereof growing
to bestowe in Dead*es* of charytee
vppon my poure kynnesfolk*es* and
other charytable Dead*es* to pray.'

[7] Altered from:—'iij.'

[8] The last eighteen words are
altered from:—'iij yeres xx[li].'

[9] Added and crossed out:—'by
the discression of myn executors.'

to be Disposed by the Discression of myn executours. Item I gyue
and bequethe to euery of the v orders of Freers within the Cytee
of London to pray for my Soule xx$^s$ [1]. Item I gyue and bequethe
to lx poure Maydens Maryages xl$^{li}$ [2] That is to saye xiij$^s$ iiij$^d$ [3] to
euerye of the saide poure Maydens to be gyuen and Distributed
by the Discression of myn executours. Item I will that there shalbe
Delt and yeuen after my decesse amongst poure people howseholders
to pray for my Sowle xx$^{li}$ [4]. Item I gyue and bequeth to the poure
parochians Suche as by myn executors shalbe thowght most needffull
of the paroche Where god shall ordeyn me to haue my dwelling
place at the tyme of my Deth x$^{li}$ [5] to be trewlye Distributed amongst
them by the Discression of myn executours [6] Item I gyue and
bequethe to the poure prysoners of Newgate Ludgate Kynges benche
and Marshall See to be equallye Distributed amongst them x$^{li}$ Wylling
charging and desiring myn executours vnderwrytten that they shall
See this my Will perfourmed in euery poynte according to my trew
meaning and intente as they will answer to god and discharge their
consciences.

[7] Item I gyue and bequeth to William brabason my seruaunt xx$^{li}$
sterling A gowne A dublett A Jaquet and my second gelding.

Item I gyue and bequeth to John averey yoman of the bottell with
the kynges highnes vj$^{li}$ xiij$^s$ iiij$^d$, and doublet of Saten.

Item I bequeth to thurston my Coke vj$^{li}$ xiij$^s$ iiij$^d$.

Item I gyue and bequethe to William bodye my seruauntt vj$^{li}$
xiij$^s$ iiij$^d$.

Item I gyue and bequeth to Peter mewtes my seruauntt vj$^{li}$
xiij$^s$ iiij$^d$.

Item I gyue and bequeth to Rychard Swyft my seruauntt vj$^{li}$
xiij$^s$ iiij$^d$.

Item I gyue and bequeth to george Wylkynson my seruauntt
vj$^{li}$ xiij$^s$ iiij$^d$.

Item I gyue and bequeth to my Frend Thomas alvard x$^{li}$ and my
best gelding.

Item I gyue and bequeth to my frend Thomas Russhe x$^{li}$.

Item I gyue and bequeth to my seruauntt John Hynde my horse-
keper iij$^{li}$ vj$^s$ viij$^d$.

---

[1] Altered from :—'xiij$^s$ iiij$^d$.

[2] Altered from :—'xx$^{li}$.'

[3] Altered from :—'vj$^s$ viij$^d$.'

[4] Altered from :—'x$^{li}$.'

[5] Altered from :—'v$^{li}$.'

[6] Crossed out :—'Item I gyue and
bequethe to my paroche churche
for my tithes forgotten xx$^s$.'

[7] The last eleven bequests are
added in Cromwell's hand.

Item I wyll that myn executors shall Saluelye kepe the patentt of the Manour of Rompney to the vse of my Son gregorye and the money growing therof tyll he shall Cum to his lawfull Age to be yerely Retayned to the vse of my sayd Son and the hole revenew therof Cumyng to be trewlye payd vnto hym at suche tyme as he shall Cum to the age of xxj yeres.

The residue of all my goodes catalles and debttes not bequethed my Funeralles and buryall perfourmed which I will shalbe Don without any erthelye pompe and my Dettes payed, I will shalbe sold And the money thereof cummyng to be Distributed in wourkes of charytee and pytee after the good Discression of myn executours vndernamed whom I make and Ordeyn Stephyn Vaughan ¹ Rafe Sadleyer my seruaunttes and John ² Wyllyamson my brother in law. Prayeng and Desiring the same myn executours to be good vnto my Soon Gregorye ³ and to all other my Frendes poore kynsfolkes and Seruaunttes before named in this my testament And of this my present testament and last Will I make Roger More myn Ouerseer Vnto whom and also to euery of the other myn executours I gyue and bequethe vjˡⁱ xiijˢ iiijᵈ ⁴ for their paynes to be taken in the execucyon of this my last will and testament ouer and aboue suche legacies as herebefore I haue bequethed them in this same my testament and last will.   In Wytnes Wherof to this my present testament and last will I haue sett my hand in euery lefe conteyned in this Boke the day and yere before lymyted

per me Thomam Crumwell ⁵

*Endorsed.* Thomas Crumwell a Copy of my Master his Will And bookes of debtes owinge to him.

---

¹ Altered from :—' John Croke one of the vj clerkes of the king his Chauncerye.'

² The last four words are altered from :—' my Seruaunt Iohn Smyth and John.'

³ Crossed out :—' and to my litill Doughters Anne and Grace.'

⁴ Added and crossed out :—' ouer and aboue thayr legacyes beforsayd.'

⁵ Every page, except the last two, is also signed by Cromwell.

# CHAPTER IV

## THE FALL OF THE CARDINAL

In October, 1529, Cardinal Wolsey lost the King's favour, and fell into disgrace. He was forced to give up the Great Seal, sign an indenture acknowledging that he had incurred the guilt of Praemunire, forfeit most of his lands, possessions, and offices, and retire to his seat at Esher[1]. His faithful biographer, Cavendish, gives a very touching account of the Cardinal's surrender of his goods, his removal from the scene of his labours, and his enforced living in 'estraunge estate[2].' Few fallen ministers have ever been in a more pitiful position. To have incurred the ill-will of his master, as he had done, meant certain ruin in those days; and besides this he had turned the people against him by the part he had taken in the divorce. Anne Boleyn, whose influence at the Court was at its height, detested him for his failure to bring it about; the clergy and common people hated him for attempting it. The few friends who retained their fidelity to him in his trouble were prevented from showing it by their consciousness of the royal and popular displeasure.

As Wolsey's servant, counsellor, and friend, Cromwell naturally felt the keenest anxiety lest he should be involved in his master's ruin. It has been already shown that his action in suppressing the monasteries had made him very generally hated; and now that the prop that had supported him in his difficult and unpopular task was gone, he had great need to look to himself, if he did not wish to fall with the Cardinal. That he was perfectly well informed of the position in which he was placed is proved by a letter which he received from his friend Stephen Vaughan, written at Antwerp, October 30, 1529, which tells him that he is more hated for

---

[1] Cal. iv. 6017.　　　　　　　　　　[2] Cavendish, pp. 160-6.

his master's sake than for anything which he has wrongfully done to any man[1]. Another letter from his companion in Wolsey's service, Sir Thomas Rush, who was employed with him at Ipswich, gave him further warning of the evil reports that were circulated about him[2]. It is no wonder that he was seriously alarmed.

Modern investigation has made it certain that there is but little historical foundation for the touching pictures drawn by Cavendish, Shakespeare, and, at a later day, Froude, which represent Cromwell as the faithful servant of his fallen master, unselfish, and exclusively devoted to his interests[3]. There is no reason to think that Cavendish, whose testimony is most valuable as that of an eye-witness of the scenes he describes, wilfully distorted the facts, but it is certain that his directness and simplicity often prevented him from drawing just conclusions from them, when he had to do with such astute men as Wolsey and Cromwell. By comparing his story with the events which followed, we shall see that while Cromwell kept up the appearance of spending all his time in helping Wolsey in his disgrace, he really was occupied in serving his own ends, and in regaining the favour he had lost as the Cardinal's agent. Though he carefully abstained from doing or saying anything prejudicial to Wolsey's cause, for fear of alienating people by laying himself open to the accusation of faithlessness to his master, he really did nothing to the Cardinal's advantage that did not redound, in an infinitely greater degree, to his own profit and advancement. Let us follow the letters of Cromwell, the narrative of Cavendish, and the records of the Parliament of 1529, for our facts, but let us draw our own conclusions from them.

'It chanced me upon All-hallowne day,' says Cavendish, 'to come into the Great Chamber at Assher in the morning, to give mine attendance, where I found Mr. Cromwell leaning in the great windowe with a Primer in his hand, saying our

---

[1] Cal. iv. 6036.  [2] Cal. iv. 6110.
[3] Cavendish, pp. 175 ff.; Shakespeare, Henry VIII, iii. 2 ; Froude, vol. ii. pp. 112 ff.

Lady mattens : which had bine a strange sight in him afore.
—Well, what will you have more? He prayed no more earnestly, than he distilled teares as fast from his eyes. Whom
I saluted and bad good-morrowe. And with that I perceived
his moist chekes, the which he wiped with his napkine. To
whom I saide, "Why, Mr. Cromwell, what meaneth this dole?
Is my lord in any danger that ye doe lament for him? or is
it for any other losse, that ye have sustained by misfortune?"
"Nay," quoth he, "it is for my unhappy adventure. For I am
like to lose all that I have laboured for, all the daies of my
life, for doing of my master true and diligent service." "Why
Sir," quoth I, "I trust that you be too wise to do anything
by my lord's commaundement otherwise than ye might doe,
whereof you ought to be in doubt or daunger for losse of
your goods." "Well, well," quoth he, "I cannot tell; but this
I see before mine eyes, that everything is as it is taken; and
this I knowe well, that I am disdained withal for my master's
sake; and yet I am sure there is no cause, why they should
do soe. An evill name once gotten will not lightly be put
away. I never had promotion by my lord to the encrease
of my living. But this much I will saye to you, that I will
this afternoone, when my lord hath dined, ride to London,
and to the courte, when I will either make or marre, or ever
I come againe. I will put myself in prease, to see what they
will be able to lay to my charge." "Mary," quoth I, "then in
so doing you shall doe wisely, beseeching God to send you
good lucke, as I would myselfe [1]." '

Cromwell performed his promise well. He dined with
Wolsey on that All-hallowne Day, and later helped him to
discharge his servants, causing his chaplains to pay part of
the yeomen's wages, in return for the benefices and livings
which they had received from the Cardinal; setting an
example himself, with unusual liberality, by a contribution
of five pounds to this end. He then desired of Wolsey leave
to go to London, which was granted, and he departed immediately with Ralph Sadler, his clerk.

No one knew better than Cromwell that the best place for

---

[1] Cavendish, pp. 169, 170.

him to 'make or marre' the Cardinal's fortunes and his
own, was in the Parliament which was to meet November 3
(two days later), and, 'being in London, he devised with
himself to be one of the burgesses[1].' He sat as a member
from Taunton, as the records of Parliament attest[2], but there
are very contradictory reports about the way in which he
obtained his seat. According to Cavendish 'he chaunced to
meete with one Sir Thomas Rush, knighte, a speciall friend
of his, whose son was appointed to be a burgess, of whome
he obtained his rome, and so put his fete into the parliament
house.' This may possibly be true, but it is not the whole
truth, for a letter of November 1, from Sadler to Cromwell,
the genuineness of which it is impossible to doubt, hints at
a good deal more than is to be found in Cavendish's account,
which must have been made from Cromwell's own story about
his proceedings[3]. This letter reads as follows :—

'Wourshipfull Sir it may please you to be aduertised that
a litle before the receipte of your lettere I cam from the courte
where I spake with Mr. Gage and according to your commaundement moved him to speke vnto my lorde of Norffolk
for the burgeses Rowme of the parlyament on your behalf
And he accordingly so dyd without delay lyke a faythfull
Frende, wherevppon my saide lorde of Norffolk answered
the saide Mr. Gage that he had spoken with the king his
highnes and that his highnes was veray well contented ye
should be a Burges So that ye wolde order yourself in the
saide Rowme according to suche instructions as the saide
Duke of Norffolk shall gyue you from the king Aduertesing
you ferther that the saide Duke in any wise willeth that ye
do speke with his grace to morow for th[at] purpose. In
token whereof his grace sent you by mr. Ga[ge] your Ryng
with the turques, Whiche I do now sende you by this berer.
As touching mr. Russhe I spake with him also at [the] courte
if I then had knowen your pleasure I could now haue sent
you answere of the same. Howbeit I will speke with him
this night god willing and know whether ye shalbe Burges

---

[1] Cavendish, p. 179.          [2] Parliamentary Papers, vol. lxii. pt. i. p. 370.
[3] Cal. iv. App. 238.

of Oxforde or not And if ye be not elect there I will then
according to your ferther commaundement repayre vnto
Mr. paulet and requiere him to name you to be one of the
Burgeses of one of my lordes townes of his busshopriche of
Wynchester accordingly.  Sir me thinketh it were good, So
it may stonde with your pleasure, that ye did repayre hither
to morowe assone as ye conuenyently may for to speke with
the Duke of Norffolk by whom ye shall knowe the king his
pleasure how ye shall order yourself in the parliament house
Assuring you that your Frendes wolde haue you to tary with
my lorde there as litle as might be for many consideracions
as Mr. Gage will Shew you who moche desireth to speke with
you.  the king his grace wilbe to morow at night at yorke
place.  Other newes at the courte I here none but dyuers
of my lorde his seruauntes as Mr. Aluarde Mr. Sayntclere
Mr. Forest, Humfrey lisle Mr. Mores & other ben elect and
sworne the king his seruauntes.  Mr. Gifforde & I cam from
the courte togither but when we cam into london he departed
from me I knowe not whither.  Newes I inquiered of him
but he sayed he knew none other then as I haue wrytten
you here, which Mr. Gage also shewed him.  Humblie beseching you, if it be your pleasure, to make spede hither.
And thus I most hertely beseche our lorde god to sende you
your hertes Desire and to induce and bring all your good
purposes and affairees to good effecte.  From london in
haste this present all Saynctes Day at iiij of the clocke after
none by

Your most humble Seruaunte

RAFE SADLEYER.'

From this letter then it seems probable that Cromwell obtained his seat in the Parliament of 1529 through the influence
of the Duke of Norfolk.  He was keen-sighted enough to see
that at Wolsey's fall all the royal favour had been transferred
to this man and to Gardiner.  Both of these were Wolsey's
enemies, and Cromwell, whose name was coupled everywhere
with that of the Cardinal, saw that to gain influence at
Court, it was necessary at all costs to do away with their
hostility, which he must have incurred as Wolsey's agent.

Thus Cromwell's first move at the time of his master's disgrace was to take steps to get himself into favour with Norfolk. Cavendish's account is explained by the fact that Cromwell would not have been very likely to tell Wolsey how he had gone straight over to his bitterest enemy, but far more probably sent back to Esher the incomplete tale about Rush and his son, which the honest and simple-minded biographer probably never suspected for an instant. One can hardly doubt that Cromwell would not have been elected to this Parliament had he not secured the consent of the Cardinal's worst foe. He had thus killed two birds with one stone; he had gained his position in the House of Commons where his influence would be felt, and he had successfully escaped the odium of the chief person at the Court, which would have naturally fallen upon him as Wolsey's servant, and turned it into at least a temporary friendship.

From the contents of the letter above quoted, we may also suppose that Cromwell's doings in the Parliament of 1529 were 'ordered' by the King. The bill of attainder or 'boke of artikels' against the Cardinal was the first business that lay before the House. It had passed the Lords and was sent down to the Commons, but it was so violent and so false, that even Henry and Norfolk relented. It had probably been very clearly hinted to the Parliament that the King did not wish it to pass, and royal 'hints' at this period of English history were generally respected and obeyed. Cavendish tells us that when Cromwell had obtained his seat in Parliament, and the attainder was brought forward, he consulted with Wolsey ' to know what answer he might make in his behalf; insomuch that there was nothing alleadged against my lord but that he was ready to make answer thereto,' and he inveighed against the bill ' so discreetly and with such witty persuasions and depe resons that the same could take none effect,' so that ' at length his honest estimation and earnest behaviour in his master's cause grewe so in every man's opinion, that he was reputed the most faithful servant to his master of all other, wherein he was greatly of all men commended [1].'

[1] Cavendish, pp. 179 ff.

This is all doubtless true, but whether or not he was alone in the stand he made against the bill is quite another question. Henry was perfectly satisfied with humbling the Cardinal to the extent that he had already done, and did not wish him to suffer any more ; in fact the opposition, consisting of most of the nobles led by Norfolk and Anne Boleyn, were in constant fear up to the day of Wolsey's death, lest he should regain the King's favour. If Cromwell had gone openly over to the other side at this juncture, he would have gained nothing, and incurred the odium due to a deserter. He took the only generous and right side, but in serving his master he served himself far more [1]. Wolsey, as we have seen, had made a written confession of all his misdeeds as soon as the first blow had been struck against him [2]. This confession was produced by Cromwell, and it gave the proposers of the bill of attainder an excuse for dropping it. Cromwell supplied the pretext for abandoning a measure displeasing to the King, and consequently impossible to carry through this very subservient Parliament ; by so doing he gained the praise of a saviour of his master in his extremity.

This was the first step : the second was to win the favour of other nobles, while still preserving the appearance of loyally serving his fallen master. It was scarcely less important than the first, and was carried through by Cromwell with the greatest rapidity and success. His method of accomplishing it, however simple, was eminently characteristic, and merits description.

It has already been shown how thoroughly Cromwell realized the importance of money as a political force. Though the traditional reproach of parsimony and stinginess so often cast at Henry VII [3] is in great measure unmerited, it is undeniable that his careful financial management and accurate audits had served to surround his government with an atmosphere of ostensible frugality. Henry VIII, on the contrary, delighted in outward splendour and magni-

---

[1] Cal. iv. 6098, 6203, 6249. Cf. also Dixon, vol. i. pp. 48-9 n. Stubbs' Lectures, p. 315, and the Life of Cromwell in the Dictionary of National Biography, vol. xiii. p. 197.

[2] Cal. iv. 6017.

[3] Busch, pp. 288, 289.

ficence; his Court was by far the most brilliant that England
had ever beheld, and nobody could play his part there who
was not prepared to lavish vast sums upon his outfit.
But the greater part of the nobles were quite unable to do
this. It had been an important part of the plan of Henry VII
for establishing a strong kingship to keep all possible rivals
of the Crown in a state of financial dependence. Many
items in the State Papers of his son's reign bear witness
to the complete success of these schemes of impoverishing
the nobility[1]. Only by pawning and selling lands, estates,
goods and chattels could the nobility obtain sufficient
sums to make a good appearance at the brilliant Court of
Henry VIII.

Such a state of affairs was a golden opportunity to a man
in Cromwell's position and of Cromwell's talents. To Wolsey,
whose mind had been intent on the larger schemes of his
foreign policy, the notion of staving off the hatred of the
influential people about the King by gifts of money, would
never have occurred. Cromwell hit upon the scheme in a
moment, as the only sure road to favour at the Court[2]. Now
that Wolsey had surrendered himself almost wholly to the
counsels of his painstaking, watchful, close and wholly unscrupulous adviser, Cromwell immediately persuaded him to
grant annuities to the Court favourites. The casual reader
must not deceive himself into thinking that this was done
at Wolsey's own suggestion; the measure was too evidently
Cromwellian to leave any room to doubt its originator, and
if any further proof be needed, it is furnished by evidence in
the Cardinal's papers. In a letter to Cromwell written in
December, 1529, Wolsey says, ' Yf the desspleasure of my lady
Anne be [some]what asswagyd, as I praye God the same
maye be, then yt shuld [be devised t]hat by sume convenyent
meane she be further laboryd [for th]ys ys the only helpe
and remedy. All possyble meanes [must be used for] at-
teynyng of hyr favor . . . . . . . . . I comyt me to yower wyse
handling[3].' In the same month Cromwell made out the

---

[1] Cal. iii. 3694, and iv. 6216, 6792.

[2] Cf. Introduction to vol. iv of the Calendar, pp. 549, 550.

[3] State Papers, vol. i. p. 351

draft of a grant by Wolsey to George Boleyn, Knight, Viscount Rochford, son and heir apparent of Thomas Earl of Wiltshire and Ormond, bestowing on him an annuity of £200 out of the lands of the bishopric of Winchester, and a similar gift of £200 out of the abbey lands of St. Albans [1]. Another letter from Wolsey to Cromwell in January, 1530, says that, according to his servant's advice, he has had Mr. Norris's fee increased from £100 to £200, and would like to have Sir John Russell's annuity of £20 made 40 or 50, if Cromwell thinks it expedient [2].

It is thus clear that these and other similar gifts were bestowed at Cromwell's advice and suggestion, and that the inevitable consequence was that the advantage resulting from them accrued to a far greater extent to the Cardinal's agent than to the Cardinal himself. Wolsey, in his confinement at Esher, was forced to trust himself implicitly to the shrewd and selfish counsellor, who moved about among those whom it was most important for him to propitiate, and soon found means to make it appear that Wolsey's favours in reality emanated from him. Cromwell's selection of those to whom the presents were made seems also to hint that he was working in his own interest more than in his master's. He must have known that the members of the Boleyn party, to whom the greater part of the grants were made, hated Wolsey himself too thoroughly to permit them to forget their grudge for the sake of a few hundred pounds, but the sums bestowed were sufficiently large to make the recipients of them very friendly to the Cardinal's agent, who to all intents and purposes appeared to be the real giver. Hints of all this must indeed have reached Wolsey's ears. Though throughout all the period of the attainder his gratitude, as expressed in his many letters, was, in view of the real facts, most unnecessarily effusive [3], he later writes to Cromwell that he hears ' he has not done him as good offices as he might, in connexion with his colleges and his archbishopric.' But Cromwell had by this time got everything into his own

<hr />

[1] Cal. iv. 6115.  [2] Cal. iv. 6181.
[3] Cal. iv. 6098, 6181, 6204, 6249.

hands, so that Wolsey was forced to do exactly as he was bidden. Whenever the Cardinal undertook anything on his own responsibility, without asking his servant's advice, it was greatly resented. If Wolsey dared to hint that Cromwell was not wholly devoted to his interests, the latter sent back a complaining and half-threatening reply[1]. The Cardinal was even forced to write a humble apology to his agent for sending Edmund Bonner on some mission without his advice[2]. The less able Wolsey became to help himself, the more harsh and imperious was his all-powerful counsellor. With the whole control of his master's interests at the Court in his own hands, it was exceedingly simple for a man of Cromwell's peculiar talents to dispose the funds committed to his care in such ways as tallied best with his own interests, while casual onlookers simply regarded him as an honest servant of his fallen master ; and Wolsey, unable to learn the true state of affairs at Court, was kept practically ignorant of his real designs. Cromwell had thus succeeded in attaining a most enviable position, which was aptly described in a letter which he received from Stephen Vaughan, who took the opportunity to congratulate him, and also to warn him against over-confidence in the following words :—' A mery semblance of wether often thrustithe men into the Daungerous sees, not thinking to be sodaynly opprest wythe tempest when vnwares they be preuented and brought in great ieopardie. The Wyndes arn mutable vnsure and will not be caryed in mennys handes to blow at a becke. Parell euerywhere followithe men, from the birthe to the Dethe, And more thretenethe them whiche entreprise Difficult and vrgent matters, then those whiche only sekethe easy and light matters ye thoughe they have great apparance of vertue, such is thinstabilitie of the worlde, wher we find undique miseriam[3].'

A final opportunity was given to Cromwell to ingratiate himself with King and nobles when Henry took into his hands the revenues of St. Albans and Winchester, and of the colleges at Oxford and Ipswich. In this, even honest Cavendish could see that ' Cromewell perceyved an occasion

---

[1] Letters, 13.       [2] Cal. iv. 6203.       [3] Cal. iv. 6196.

given him by time to helpe himselfe.' The intricacies of the law of the period were such that annuities and fees out of the revenues of these colleges, granted by the King, after he had seized them, could only be good while Wolsey was living, because the King, having obtained his right to them by Wolsey's attainder in the praemunire, could not retain that right after the Cardinal's death[1]. Thus, to have the grants secure during the lifetimes of the recipients, 'there was none other shifte but to obtaine my lord's confirmation of their patents. Then began every man both noble and gentleman who had any patents out of Winchester and St. Albans to make suite to Mr. Cromwell to solicit their cause to my lorde to get therin his confirmation, and for his paines therin bothe worthily to reward him and every man to shewe him such pleasures as should be at all times in their small powers, whereof they assured him. . . . Now began matters to worke to bringe Master Cromwell into estimation in suche sorte as was muche hereafter to his increase of dignity; . . . and having the ordering and disposition of the landes of these colleges he had a great occasion of suitors, besides the continual access to the King, by meanes whereof and through his witty demeanour he grewe continually into the King's favour[2].'

It is hard to realize how deeply Wolsey felt the seizure of his two colleges. They had been the pride and joy of his declining years. Instead of working earnestly to avert their surrender into the King's hands, as a true servant would have done, Cromwell permitted and almost welcomed it, as a means to give him a chance to further his own ends, and wrote empty, and, it would seem, almost contemptuous letters of consolation to the Cardinal, of which that of August 18 is an excellent example[3]. Instead of going to his master in his sorrow and disgrace, as Wolsey repeatedly requested him to do, he held himself aloof, and under the pretext of looking after the Cardinal's interests at Court, contrived for his own rise and advancement. It is true that he stood by Wolsey in

---

[1] Introduction to vol. iv of the Calendar, pp. 584, 585.
[2] Cavendish, p. 198.      [3] Letters, 18.

the parliamentary crisis in 1529, and that it was largely through his efforts that Wolsey obtained his temporary pardon in February, 1530 ; but when, at the last, the Cardinal's enemies turned against him a second time and secured his complete downfall, there is no record of Cromwell's saying a word or doing a thing in his behalf. On November 29, 1530, Wolsey died, shattered and disgraced.

It is very unfortunate that there still exist so few of Cromwell's letters during the last two years of Wolsey's life. There are preserved at present only twelve letters from him during this period [1], seven of which are addressed to Wolsey. In none of them does he give evidence of a sincere desire to serve his master at all costs ; the dominant note of the greater part of them is one of selfish and rather supercilious advice ; of a morality easy and cheap, because the preacher of it evidently felt himself beyond the possibility of its ever being applicable in his own case. There is also very little trust-worthy information about the means he employed to introduce himself to the King, except what has already been mentioned in connexion with Wolsey's fall. Foxe asserts that Sir Christopher Hales, Master of the Rolls, commended him to Henry, and further affirms that Sir John Russell said a good word for him, in return for Cromwell's saving his life at Bologna, so that the latter was enabled to have a private conversation with the King in Westminster Gardens [2]. Part of this story is obviously false ; Cromwell could not have been at Bologna when Sir John Russell was (between 1524 and 1528), because he was occupied in England at that time, as his correspondence shows. To judge from this, little reliance can be placed on the rest of Foxe's tale ; and there are no con-temporary documents that bear out his statements. Another story, which is perhaps more probable, is that of Chapuys [3], who states that at Wolsey's death Sir John Wallop attacked Cromwell with insults and threats, so that the latter for pro-tection procured an audience with Henry, whom he promised to make the richest king that ever was in England. Henry,

---

[1] Letters, 9-20.
[2] Foxe, vol. ii. pp. 419 ff.
[3] See Appendix I at the end of chapter i. p. 17.

it appears, was so struck with this offer, that he immediately
made Cromwell a member of his Council, but told nobody
about it for four months.  This tale is in many respects
similar to the account contained in Pole's Apologia : but the
story of the Cardinal does not mention the quarrel with
Wallop, and the report of Chapuys does not say a word about
the plan for the solution of Henry's 'grete matier' by which
Cromwell, according to Pole, completely fascinated the King.
All the accounts, however, seem to agree that by some means
he managed to secure an interview with Henry soon after
Wolsey's death, at which he clinched everything that he had
already gained, and obtained the favour of the King by one
master-stroke.  Pole's story of this interview contains information which leads us into the thick of Cromwell's political
career.  Before we proceed to examine it in detail a brief
chapter must be devoted to a description of the actors and
past events of the great political drama in which Cromwell
was to play a part, and to a further analysis of his own
character and ideals.

# CHAPTER V

## THE CHARACTER AND OPPORTUNITY OF THOMAS CROMWELL

THE condition of England at the time of Wolsey's death was in many ways an extraordinary one. At home and abroad she had already begun to reap glorious fruits from the untiring efforts and masterful policy of the first Tudor. United under a powerful monarchy, which had strengthened itself at the expense of every other institution in the realm, she rested secure in the enjoyment of internal peace and of a high degree of estimation and respect in foreign lands. That she had lost nearly all those continental possessions which had been the proudest boast of Edward III and Henry V now proved an inestimable advantage. The wise Cardinal had made use of England's insular position to such good advantage, that she had been able, at least up to the time when the political situation had been complicated by the question of the divorce, to keep the Emperor and the King of France in a state of constant anxiety concerning her real attitude, and often to force the two rivals to bid against each other for her alliance. In 1521 Henry had dedicated to Leo X a treatise which he had written against the heresies of Luther, and had been rewarded with the proud title of 'Defensor Fidei.' Success abroad meant popularity at home, at least for the King, whose enthusiasm and winning manners endeared him to his subjects, and who usually contrived to shift the blame for the unwelcome measures of his government on to the shoulders of the Cardinal. As long as the national honour was upheld on the Continent without draining too deeply the resources of the people at home, the country seemed quite willing to trust the King to the full and to allow him to rule as well as govern.

Such was the bright side of the picture, the side which first claims the attention of the casual observer. A more critical examination of the state of the country, however, reveals an undercurrent of discontent, which was almost lost in the crowning years of Wolsey's greatness, but which did not fail to make itself felt at a later day, when the allegiance of so large a part of the people had been alienated by the affair of the divorce. The surest proof that Henry and Wolsey were aware of this latent hostility is afforded by the infrequent assemblings of Parliament. Seldom did the King dare to face the representatives of the nation with the demand for a subsidy; he preferred to veil his oppressive financial exactions under the name of an Amicable Loan. The poverty of the nobles was notorious; and the distress of the poor people daily increased owing to a succession of bad seasons, thin harvests, and a few outbreaks of a devastating plague. Economic and agrarian changes contributed to swell the universal discontent[1]. The break-up of the old manorial system, the increase of enclosures for pasturage, and the substitution of convertible husbandry for the old three-field system all served to displace labour, and so temporarily to diminish the demand for it. Great distress among the agricultural poor was necessarily the first result of these changes: unfortunately economic science was not sufficiently advanced to enable men to discern that it was but a passing phase, and that as soon as labour had adjusted itself to the new conditions permanent advantages to it were bound to ensue. The country-folk contrasted their own wretched condition with the many reports which reached them of Henry's sumptuous and luxurious Court: small wonder if the government was wrongly blamed for a large share of the misery which was inevitably the first consequence of sudden and great economic development. Finally all malcontents were united in opposition to the King's attempts to gain a divorce from his first wife, during the closing years of Wolsey's ministry; so that the maintenance and further strengthening of the powerful monarchy established at the accession of the House of Tudor promised

---

[1] Cf. Ashley, Economic History, vol. ii. pp. 259-304.

in the near future to afford a problem of even greater difficulty than before.

To turn for a moment to the situation on the Continent. The House of Hapsburg, under Charles V, seemed to have attained the acme of its greatness, but its power was not by any means as real as it appeared. The Emperor's insatiable desire for foreign conquest had caused him to neglect affairs in Spain and in the Empire, and to overtax his powers and drain his resources by continual struggles with his great rival the King of France. The bone of contention was ostensibly Italy; perhaps a truer cause of the struggles of the two sovereigns is to be found in the geographical position of the countries over which they ruled. The newly-consolidated realm of France divided the dominions of the Emperor into two parts: the dream of Charles was to connect them; the object of Francis was to forestall him. Northern Italy belonged to neither, but it was a rich prize and a fighting-ground easily accessible to both the combatants, and so it very naturally became the field of war. Soon after the Imperial election of 1519 the tide began to set slowly but surely against Francis; he was a true soldier, and was not a man to submit to any encroachment without a struggle; still he fought at a terrible disadvantage, betrayed as he was by the Duke of Bourbon, and in 1525 he was forced to acknowledge a thorough defeat, at the fatal battle of Pavia[1].

Although the first idea that occurred to Henry and Wolsey after the news of Charles' great victory had reached them was a plan for the conquest and subdivision of the kingdom of Francis, they soon came to the conclusion that such a scheme would render the Emperor far too powerful. Charles himself, moreover, had received with little favour the extravagant proposals for an invasion of France which England had sent him as soon as the result of Pavia was known, and had consistently refused to allow Henry any share in his triumph. The Pope also, who had watched with terror the victorious march of the Imperial army, ventured for

[1] On this and the succeeding pages, cf. Creighton's Papacy, vol. vi. pp. 296–362, and Mignet, vol. ii. pp. 340–358.

the last time to present himself as the centre of the opposition to Charles V, and strove in every way to reconcile
England and France. The obstinate resistance that the
Commissioners for the collection of the Amicable Loan had
encountered in the spring of 1525 was certainly no encouragement for undertaking a war of aggression, and Henry and
Wolsey soon determined to abandon all plans of invasion, and
to pursue the wiser policy of maintaining neutrality between
the two great continental powers. With this thought in
mind a treaty of peace was made with Francis in August,
and after the escape of the French King from captivity in
January, 1526, the two continental rivals were once more
placed on an even footing. With this restoration of equality
Henry was perfectly satisfied, and he took good care to avoid
committing himself permanently to Francis, by refusing
openly to join the League of Cognac in the following spring.
At this juncture the matter of the divorce began to occupy
his exclusive attention, and the foreign affairs of the next
three years were left almost entirely in Wolsey's hands.

Circumstances now drove the Cardinal temporarily to lose
sight of the policy which he had pursued for the most part
up to this time—that of strict neutrality—and to attempt to
convert the peace with France into a permanent alliance.
And certainly the events of 1527 seemed to give him every
justification for this new departure. The sack of Rome
appeared to put Italy at the mercy of the Imperialists, and
now the difficulties connected with Henry's matrimonial affairs
pointed to the need of securing a firm ally who would aid him
in persuading the captive Pontiff to consent to the divorce in
opposition to the wishes of his jailor the Emperor. With all
his experience the Cardinal had hardly learned how rapidly the
diplomatic combinations of Europe could change. The last
great venture of his foreign policy resulted in disaster: the
French alliance utterly failed to accomplish what was expected
of it. At first indeed it seemed that the matrimonial projects
which formed the basis of it would succeed, but the crafty
policy of Francis ruined all. His war with the Emperor broke
out again, as was to be expected, immediately after his release

from captivity, but secret negotiations for peace were soon
set on foot, and finally, in 1529, took shape in the treaty of
Cambray—the news of which came as a stunning blow to
Wolsey's dearest hopes. The lesson which the Cardinal
learned at the expense of his office was by no means lost on
his master. Absorbed in the attempt to obtain a divorce
from Katherine, Henry possibly had not been able to foresee
the course of events abroad any better than his minister;
but when, in 1529, the news of the treaty of Cambray aroused
him to a true appreciation of the state of affairs, he at once
realized how dangerous any permanent alliance with either
Francis or Charles would be, as long as the situation on the
Continent remained so uncertain. He resolved that, as soon
as he could rectify the Cardinal's false step, nothing should
tempt him again to abandon the only safe policy—that of
strict neutrality between the two great European powers—
as long as the two rivals remained nearly equal. This point
has been purposely dwelt upon here as a foreshadowing of
what was to happen to Cromwell a few years later. Departure
from the policy of neutrality between France and Spain helped
to ruin Wolsey: a similar blunder in foreign affairs was
destined to lead his successor to destruction.

The entire attention of England was now turned to the
absorbing question of the divorce. The history of Wolsey's
failure to bring about the separation of Henry and Katherine
of Aragon, does not belong to the ground covered by this
essay. Suffice it to say that the Cardinal's ineffectual
attempts to satisfy Henry's chief desire, coupled with the
obvious error in his foreign policy, sealed his doom and
gave Cromwell his opportunity. There is little need to dwell
upon the way in which the attempt to divorce the Queen was
regarded abroad. Henry was looked upon as the disturber
of Christian unity, not only by the Emperor, but also by all
continental Europe [1]. Charles, of course, was the obvious
person to avenge the wrongs of his aunt, but he was far
too busy just then with his schemes for suppressing the Protestants in Germany and of checking the advance of the

---

[1] Cal. iv. 6521, 6691.

Turk into the borders of Christendom, seriously to contemplate an invasion of Henry's dominions. It was not the only time that England's fortunes were saved by the turn of affairs in distant lands.

It now remains only to say a few words about the chief persons at the Court of Henry VIII, preliminary to a description of Cromwell himself. Foremost among these was of course Anne Boleyn. Born probably in 1507 of a good English family, a niece of the Earl of Surrey, she had spent a good part of her early life in France, as 'one of the French queen's women,' and returned to England in the latter part of the year 1521 [1]. At Henry's exceedingly corrupt Court she did not want for admirers and suitors, foremost among whom was the King himself, who had formerly been in intimate relations with her sister Mary. Henry's passion for her is sufficiently attested by a succession of royal grants and favours to her father, beginning only two months after her arrival in England, and continuing for over three years [2]. How far Anne was responsible for causing Henry to take steps to divorce Katherine, and how far he was moved thereto by a conscience that became over-sensitive at suspiciously short notice, or by more legitimate political considerations, it is not our business now to inquire ; our best sources of information are the grants to her father, above mentioned, and a most remarkable series of love-letters [3]. Though she temporarily had the King at her feet, no woman of Henry's Court was really to be less envied. Katherine and Mary, and, in consequence, the majority of the people, were her bitter foes ; to protect herself against the popular odium, she gathered round her a following, known at Court as the Boleyn faction, the chief person of which was her uncle, now Duke of Norfolk.

Norfolk was fifty-seven years old when Cromwell came into power. He was a Catholic and against the New Faith. He had received in his younger days a thorough military

---

[1] For the date of the birth of Anne Boleyn see Friedmann, chap. i, and Note A in the Appendix; Round, The Early Life of Anne Boleyn ; and Gairdner in the English Historical Review, vol. viii. p. 58, and vol. x. p. 104.

[2] Cal. iv. 1431 (8), 6083, 6163.

[3] Cal. iv. 4477, 4383, 4410, 3325, 3326, 3218-21.

and diplomatic training, and in 1531 was characterized by the Venetian ambassador, Falieri, as 'prudent, liberal, affable, and astute; associating with everybody . . . and desirous of greater elevation.' This is a very flattering description of this crafty and ambitious statesman. The chief traits that characterized him were a cringing subservience to the will of the King, and a bitter hatred of any rival to his influence with Henry; a hatred which first directed itself against Wolsey, for whose downfall he laboured incessantly, and later against Cromwell, whose opponent he was during the decade of the former's greatness. He was the equal of neither of these two as a statesman; but his utter lack of honour and consistency, and his willingness to break promises in order to please the King, rendered him an invaluable servant of the Crown at a period when one startling change followed on the heels of another. He threw himself heart and soul into the interests of his niece when Henry's love for her was increasing; and yet when the royal passion waned, and Anne was accused in 1536, he was not ashamed to preside at her trial and sentence her to death [1].

The other important person at the Court was Stephen Gardiner, who in 1531 became Bishop of Winchester. Ten years Norfolk's junior, he was introduced into political and diplomatic life by the Duke, and spent a large part of his early life as Wolsey's servant and ambassador. He did not cherish any lasting friendship for the Cardinal, however, and he seems to have been an adherent of the Boleyn faction at Wolsey's fall; we find Anne writing to him when the struggle between the two parties was at its hottest, to thank him for his 'wylling and faythefull mynde [2].' Still he took more or less a middle course on the divorce question, and pleaded warmly, though vainly, for the restitution of Wolsey's colleges. But when the Cardinal's fate was settled he certainly expected that his old master's favour with the King would be transferred to himself, and when he was disappointed in this by Cromwell's stepping in, he developed a hatred for him which he never

---

[1] Cf. the Life of Norfolk in the Dictionary of National Biography, vol. xxviii. p. 65.        [2] Cal. iv. 5422.

abandoned. He was less active than Norfolk in his opposition to Rome, and though he lacked the Duke's subserviency, he was fully as able a diplomat. Neither of the two men could have played the rôle of Cromwell: the scope of their talents was more limited; they were merely exceedingly able politicians, but as such they were by no means to be despised. When, however, they united to procure their rival's ruin it was difficult to resist them [1].

Thus when at Wolsey's fall Cromwell entered the King's service, the situation of England both at home and abroad was critical in the extreme. The relations of the government with Rome were strained, owing to Henry's proceedings in the divorce; his 'grete matier' was unpopular with the country at large; France and Spain were both of them very doubtful quantities, and might become friends or foes at any moment. At the Court, various factions with different aims were disputing for the precedence, and the best course to be steered by one who was about to enter the King's service, after leaving that of a fallen minister, was not an easy thing to decide. Before inquiring into Cromwell's action at this crisis, a brief description of the person and of the character of the man himself at this time will not be out of place.

Cromwell was a short, strongly-built man, with a large dull face. He was smooth-shaven, with close-cropped hair, and had a heavy double chin. His mouth was small and cruel, and was surmounted by an extraordinarily long upper lip, while a pair of grey eyes, set closely together, moved restlessly under his light eyebrows. He had an awkward, uncouth gait which lent itself well to the other peculiarities of his personal appearance, and gave one the idea that he was a patient, plodding, and, if anything, a rather stupid sort of man. But this was all merely external. According to Chapuys, who knew him well, he possessed the most extraordinary mobility of countenance, so that when engaged in an interesting conversation, his face would suddenly light up, and the dull, drudging, commonplace expression give way to a subtle,

---

[1] Cf. the Life of Gardiner in the Dictionary of National Biography, vol. xx. p. 419.

cunning, and intelligent aspect, quite at variance with his
ordinary appearance.  His conversation at such moments was
witty and entertaining to the last degree, and the Spanish
ambassador notes that he had the habit of giving a roguish
oblique glance whenever he made a striking remark.  This
extraordinary power of facial control, according to the circumstances in which he was placed, merely reflects one of
the dominant characteristics of the man.  He obviously had
remarkable power of quickly adapting himself to his sur-
roundings.  He rarely failed to realize immediately his relation
to those with whom he came in contact, and his manner,
behaviour, and expression varied accordingly.  No one knew
better how or when to flatter than Thomas Cromwell ; on
the other hand no one could be more harsh and cruel than
he, when he was in a position to dictate.  He had thoroughly
learned the lesson

> 'To beguile the time
> Look like the time.'

There are many evidences of his good taste and love of
beautiful things [1].  A long and complicated correspondence
with his friend Stephen Vaughan about an iron chest of very
curious workmanship, which he wanted for his house at Austin
Friars, of such expense that Vaughan was almost afraid to
buy it, is not without interest.  There is record of his purchasing a globe, with a set of explanatory notes, and the only
two 'Cronica Cronicarum cum figuris' that could be found in
all Antwerp [2].  Especially great was his love of Italian things.
His stay in Italy was of sufficient duration to steep him in the
spirit of the Renaissance ; he read and studied his Machiavelli,
so that it was a guide to his future political career ; we can
well imagine him repeating to himself the sentence in chapter
xviii of The Prince which begins 'Ma è necessario questa
natura saperla bene colorire, ed essere gran simulatore e
dissimulatore [3],' or the passage in chapter xvii of the same,
'Deve pertanto un principe non si curare dell' infamia di cru-
dele per tenere i sudditi suoi uniti ed in fede [4].'  He doubtless

---

[1] Cf. Pauli, Thomas Cromwell, p. 301.
[2] Cal. iv. 4613, 4884, 5034, 6429, 6744.
[3] Il Principe, chap. xviii, p. 304.    [4] Ibid., chap. xvii, p. 291.

possessed many of the important Italian books in print at that time. In April, 1530, Edmund Bonner writes to him to remind him of his promise to lend him the Triumphs of Petrarch and the Cortigiano, and to make him a good Italian [1].

Of his social gifts and of his charm as a host there is no room to doubt. There are many proofs that he was a most magnificent entertainer, and that his personal attraction, when he wished to make himself agreeable, was such that no one could resist it. The letters of Chapuys inform us that even the most careful and experienced politicians were often completely put off their guard by Cromwell's pleasing presence and address; and more than once were induced to say things which should not have escaped them.

But all these manners and externals were simply disguises to hide the real inward character of the man. The whole essence of Cromwell's personality consists of different manifestations of one fundamental, underlying trait, which may perhaps be best expressed by the common phrase 'a strict attention to business.' Cromwell worshipped and sought after the practical and the useful only, and utterly disregarded everything else. The first evidence of this quality has been already noticed, as coming in the shape of a contempt for the vague generalizations of the Parliament of 1523, which beat about the bush for an entire session without ever coming to the point [2]. Here it assumes a somewhat negative form. Another striking instance of it occurs in the conversation which Pole relates as having taken place between himself and Cromwell, at Wolsey's house, concerning the proper duty of a true servant of a Prince [3]. Pole as usual began theorizing about the best way to bring honour to one's master, when he was rudely interrupted by Cromwell, who advised him in few words to forsake the remote learning of the schools, and devote himself to reading a new book which took a practical view of the case, and which Pole later found was the adviser's favourite Prince of Machiavelli. Cromwell

[1] Cal. iv. 6346.　　　　　　　　　　　　　[2] Letters, I.
[3] Pole, Apologia ad Carolum Quintum, chap. xxix.

at the same time took occasion to tell Pole that the great art of the politician was to penetrate through the disguise which sovereigns are accustomed to throw over their real inclinations, and to devise the most specious expedients by which they may gratify their appetites without appearing to outrage morality or religion[1]. It is not astonishing that Pole realized that it was dangerous for him to remain in England, when Cromwell came into power.

Another more positive and striking way in which this characteristic stood forth, was in his utter lack of emotion. It was this quality which enabled Cromwell to tick off in his memoranda the lives of human beings, as if they were items in an account; or to send people to trials, of which the verdicts had been determined beforehand, as 'the Abbott of Redyng to be Sent Down to be tryed & excecutyd at Reding[2].' He totally disregarded the justness or morality of any action; its utility was for him its morality, and created its justification. He never struck at his victims in a moment of passion, uselessly or capriciously; no personal feeling of hatred mingled with his crime. On the other hand, had the sacrifice of one of his nearest or dearest friends been necessary to the accomplishment of his purposes, he would hardly have hesitated a moment. Any means that could bring about the ends he sought were *ipso facto* for him justifiable. Whether his desires were attained by fair means or foul, mattered little to him: he kept his eyes steadily fixed upon the goal; the smoothness or roughness of the road to it was of no consequence in his eyes[3].

---

[1] This account was drawn up by Pole in 1538. Canon Dixon (History of the Church of England, vol. i. p. 41) questions the truth of the story on the ground that The Prince was not published until 1532, several years after the reported conversation took place. The book, however, was written in 1513, as Canon Dixon admits, and there is every probability, especially in view of his early experiences in Italy, that Cromwell possessed a manuscript copy. Pole, moreover, expressly states that Cromwell offered to lend him the work, provided he would promise to read it.

[2] Cal. xiv. (ii) 399.

[3] The chronicler, John Stow, in his Survey of London, p. 180, gives the following anecdote, which proves that Cromwell was no less arbitrary as a man than as a minister:—

Finally, and perhaps most important of all, Cromwell never lost anything that might be turned to good account. It has been shown how he not only succeeded in freeing himself from any ill-name at Wolsey's fall, but also actually used his master's overthrow to further his own ends, and make himself known and popular at Court. But this is only a slender hint of what was to follow. It was precisely from this same practical utilitarian standpoint, that he regarded and made use of to his own ends the King's amours, the suppression of the monasteries, the Reformation. Catholicism and Protestantism passed over his head; he was not touched by either of them. He simply used them as pieces in the great game which he was playing.

Such was the man who, for the next ten years, was to have almost the sole guidance of the course of English history. As was his purpose when he rode on the afternoon of All Hallows Day to London to look after his own interests and those of his master, so was his mission as minister and counsellor of the King, ' to make or to marre.'

' On the south side and at the west end of this church (the Austin Friars) many fayre houses are builded, namely in Throgmorton streete, one very large and spacious, builded in the place of olde and small Tenementes by Thomas Cromwell ... This house being finished, and hauing some reasonable plot of ground left for a Garden, he caused the pales of the Gardens adioyning to the north parte thereof on a sodaine to be taken downe, 22 foot to bee measured forth right into the north of euery man's ground, a line there to bee drawen, a trench to bee cast, a foundation laid, and a highe bricke wall to bee builded. My father had a Garden there, and an house standing close to his south pale, this house they lowsed from the ground & bare vpon Rowlers into my Father's Garden 22 foot, ere my Father heard thereof: no warning was given him, nor any other answere when hee spake to the surueyers of that worke but that their Mayster Sir Thomas commaunded them so to doe, no man durst go to argue the matter, but each man lost his land, and my Father payde his whole rent, which was vi$^s$. viii$^d$. the yeare, for that halfe which was left. Thus much of mine owne knowledge haue I thought good to note, that the suddaine rising of some men, causeth them to forget themselves.'

# CHAPTER VI

## IN THE KING'S SERVICE

THE decade which followed Cromwell's appointment as counsellor to Henry VIII, witnessed some of the most striking changes that have ever taken place in England. The question which must obviously occur to every student of the period, is whether the King himself, or his new minister, was the real cause of the secular and religious revolution of the years 1530 to 1540. The difficulty of the problem is increased by the fact that Henry and Cromwell made every effort to conceal their traces; scarcely any information can be gleaned from their correspondence. We are therefore forced to draw our conclusions for the most part from external evidence and the reports of contemporary writers.

It may be justly said that in general the probabilities point to Cromwell as the true originator of the startling changes which occurred soon after his accession to power. The fact that the ultimate object of all these changes was the concentration of power in the hands of the Crown is not in itself of great value in determining the identity of their originator; for the strengthening of the monarchy was an end which both King and minister always kept in view: in the methods by which this object was attained, however, we have a most valuable clue to aid us in the solution of our problem. These methods were all intensely Cromwellian: their directness and efficiency are essentially and distinctively characteristic of the King's new minister. In the contrast between the dawdling ineffectiveness of Wolsey's device for solving the problem of the King's divorce, and the summary, revolutionary process by which it was finally secured after the Cardinal's fall, lies our strongest ground for supposing that it was at Cromwell's instance that the decisive step was taken. It seems almost impossible that Henry, after having suffered himself to be guided so long by Wolsey, in the management of his 'grete matier' should have adopted at the Cardinal's death a plan to secure his wishes, so thoroughly repugnant to the principles of his old adviser, unless the idea had been put into his head by another. When the King had once determined to break with Rome, it followed as a matter of course that the advice of the minister who had suggested the first step, should be adopted in devising measures to secure the King in the new position which he had assumed. The means employed to attain this end—the intimidation of the clergy and the suppression of the monasteries, the attacks on the independence of Parliament, the ruthless execution of those who opposed the late innovations—all bear the stamp of the sinister genius of Cromwell as unmistakably as the great revolution that rendered them necessary. Documentary evidence too comes in to help us here; scarcely an important Act was passed in Parliament between the years 1533 and 1540, of which there is not some previous mention in Cromwell's papers and memoranda. Against these reasons it may be urged that none of the foreign ambassadors at the English Court mentions Cromwell as an important factor in the government until three years after he entered the King's service, and that the country in general certainly regarded the events of the years 1530 to 1533 as the work of Henry alone; and that these facts are strong testimony that the King's new minister did not attain any high degree of prominence until the crucial period of the struggle with Rome had passed. But this paucity of contemporary information concerning Cromwell's earlier years in the King's service may be better explained in another way. If Henry's new minister was the true author of all the revolutionary measures of this period, it was certainly most unlikely that he should be paraded before the eyes of the people as such; it was, on the contrary, to his own interest, and also to the King's, that he should be kept in the background. By permitting the people to think that Henry was the real originator of all the new schemes for establishing the Royal Supremacy in Church and State, the suddenness of the transition between

Wolsey's ministry and that of his successor was disguised. Moreover, had the people known that Cromwell was at the bottom of these changes, which were universally unpopular, nothing would have saved him from their revenge. As long as the new measures were attributed to the King, respect for the royal name was enough to prevent a revolt. Cromwell, on the contrary, who was not even of noble birth, could not have struck a blow in his own defence, had the people fastened upon him as the cause of the hated innovations. It was necessary to keep him concealed until his position was so secure that the popular odium could not shake him from it. When, in 1533, the mask was finally thrown off, Chapuys and the other foreign ambassadors realized all at once that Cromwell's sudden burst into prominence would have been quite impossible, had not the ground been thoroughly prepared for it by important services rendered during the first years of his ministry.

Such, then, are the general reasons for thinking that Cromwell was the man who planned out and carried through the various measures which have rendered famous the period of his ministry. In examining separately the different events which took place, we shall meet with other evidence which points to the same conclusion. Most important is the account contained in Pole's Apologia ad Carolum Quintum, which describes at length Cromwell's first measure, his plan to secure Henry's divorce from Katherine of Aragon ; a scheme by which he won the confidence of the King and irrevocably committed himself and his master to the policy which he followed to the end of his days. Henry, it seems from Pole's story, had become utterly discouraged at the time of Wolsey's death concerning the prospect of ever obtaining a separation from his first wife. He had vainly attempted to get an encouraging reply from the English clergy, and his failure in this added to his despondency ; his council, which lacked all initiative, could only rejoice that he intended to abandon his efforts. At this juncture the *Satanae Nuncius*, as Pole names Cromwell, solicited and obtained an audience with the King, and proposed a plan by which Henry could free himself from

Papal restrictions, marry Anne, divorce Katherine, and yet
ostensibly remain true to the Catholic Faith.

Cromwell introduced himself with his usual tact and skill.
In a few modest and carefully selected sentences he excused
himself for daring to offer an opinion on a subject of which he
felt himself to be so very ignorant—but, he continued, his
loyalty to the King would not permit him to be silent when
there was the smallest chance of his being able to serve his
sovereign at this momentous crisis.   He was certain, he said,
that the King's troubles were solely due to the weakness of
his advisers, who listened to the opinions of the common herd,
and did not dare to act upon their own responsibility.   All
the wise and learned were in favour of the divorce ;  the only
thing lacking was the Papal sanction ;  was the King to hesitate
because this could not be obtained ?   It would be better to
follow the example of the Lutherans, who had renounced the
authority of Rome.   Let the King, with the consent of Parliament, declare himself Head of the Church in England, and
all his difficulties would vanish.   England was at present
a monster with two heads.   If the King should take to himself
the supreme power, religious as well as secular, every in-
congruity would cease ;  the clergy would immediately realize
that they were responsible to the King and not to the Pope,
and would forthwith become subservient to the royal will.
Henry may have been surprised by the audacity of Cromwell's
scheme, but he was also much pleased, as it promised to
satisfy all his dearest wishes.   The *Satanae Nuncius* received
his hearty thanks, and was further rewarded by a seat in the
Privy Council [1].

Cromwell must have realized from the first, that the adop-

---

[1] Pole, Apologia ad Carolum Quintum, chap. xxix, and Lingard, vol. vi.
p. 233.   There is every reason
to believe in the veracity of this
report.   Pole was in London at
the time, and knew Cromwell intimately.   He reiterates the truth of
his tale in the following words :—
' Hoc possum affirmare nihil in illa
oratione positum alicujus momenti

quod non vel ab eodem nuncio
(Cromwell himself) eo narrante intellexi, vel ab illis qui ejus consilii
fuerunt participes.'   This interview
was doubtless the one which Chapuys describes as due to the quarrel
with Sir John Wallop.   According
to both accounts it ended by Cromwell's becoming a Privy Councillor.

tion of his scheme to throw off the Papal authority in England would encounter the greatest opposition from the clergy, but he had already devised a plan by which every objection could be silenced and the refractory ecclesiastics overawed. His whole policy in this crisis was based on the knowledge that the position of the clergy since Wolsey's fall was completely altered. They were no longer in any sense popular. The State Papers of the period contain many lists of the grievances of the Commons against them [1]. They had received a severe lesson from the Parliament of 1529 ; they were now isolated, timid and demoralized. Cromwell was the first to perceive and make use of their changed condition. At the same time he realized how completely the House of Austria had possessed itself of the Papacy ; the failure of Wiltshire's embassy to the Emperor in Bologna, in 1530 [2], assured him, if he needed any assurance, that the day of compromise with the Pope was passed, and that no divorce would ever come from the Vatican ; he saw that if a separation of Henry and Katherine was to be secured at all, the battleground on which it was to be won was not the Papal Curia at Rome, but the Houses of Convocation and Parliament.

So it was conveniently discovered that Wolsey's guilt was shared by Convocation, the Privy Council and the Lords and Commons, and indirectly by the nation itself; as all these had recognized the Cardinal in his capacity of legate, and so had become, by language of the statute, his 'fautors and abettors.' Again conveniently, but also most unreasonably, while the laity, who had eagerly availed themselves of the Cardinal's jurisdiction, were tacitly passed over, the clergy who had been the only ones to make a stand in opposition to the legatine authority, were included in the Praemunire. So in December, 1530, as Holinshed quaintly puts it, ' the kings learned councell said plainlie' that the ' whole cleargie of England . . . . . . were all in the premunire [3],' and the Attorney-General was instructed to file a brief against the entire body in the Court of King's Bench. The clergy then

[1] As Cal. iv. 6183.                    [2] Cal. iv. 6111, 6154-5.
[3] Holinshed's Chronicle, p. 766.

assembled in Convocation, 'and offered the King 100,000 pounds to be their good lord, and also to give them a pardon of all offences touching the Praemunire, by act of Parliament.' To their surprise and dismay, however, Henry refused the bribe, unless, in the preamble to the grant, a clause were introduced making him 'to be the Protector and only Supreme Head of the Church and clergy of England[1].' The whole plot on the part of the King and the Privy Council was conducted with the greatest possible secrecy, and their real motives were probably not guessed at by the world outside. Even the astute Chapuys was completely deceived respecting the King's actual intention. In his letters of the 23rd and 31st of January, 1531, he informs the Emperor that 'when the King has bled the clergy, he will restore to them their liberties, and take them back into his favour,' and later declares that 'the whole thing was done to bring about a union between the clergy and the nobles[2].' It was not until the 14th of February, when the entire affair had been carried through, that the Spanish ambassador really understood what was happening, and discovered that it was all something more than a striking exhibition of Tudor avarice[3].

In the meantime a number of Latin manifestoes appeared favouring the King's divorce, and inveighing against the Papal Supremacy[4]. But in spite of all these intimidations, the clergy though weak did not intend to surrender without a struggle. We are told that 'ille de suprematu regis conceptus haud bene placuit praelatis et clero, inde eum modificari voluerunt. Per tres itaque sessiones cum consiliariis regiis (among whom Cromwell doubtless was most prominent) ratio inita fuit quomodo regis animum flectere possent ad mollioribus verbis exprimendum articulum illum[5].' At first Henry announced to the clergy through Rochford that the only alteration he would accept would be the insertion of the

---

[1] There were to be in all five concessions, the first of which was the really important and crucial one—'Ecclesiae et cleri Anglicani, cujus protector et supremum caput is solus est.' Wilkins, vol. iii. p. 725.

[2] Cal. v. 62, 70.

[3] Cal. v. 105.

[4] Cal. v. 7, 9; vi. 416.

[5] Wilkins, vol. iii. p. 725.

words 'post Deum.' In the end, however, he yielded in this point, and consented to an amendment moved by Archbishop Warham, so that in its final form the clause read 'Ecclesiae et cleri Anglicani, cujus singularem protectorem, unicum et supremum dominicum, et quantum per Christi legem licet etiam supremum caput ipsius majestatem recognoscimus.' Both the Canterbury and York Convocations hastened to accept this compromise, and the latter voted an additional grant of £18,000. The only bishop who raised the slightest objection to the royal demand was Cuthbert Tunstall, of Durham. It is obvious that if the famous 'quantum per Christi legem licet' was really enforced, the victory which the King's party had gained was but an empty one: the amendment has been characterized as 'a clause by which all practical value was taken out of the act[1].' But Henry certainly had no idea of permitting a restriction as vague as this seriously to interfere with his schemes; if the qualification became really troublesome he was quite prepared to have it expunged. For the moment he had been willing tacitly to acknowledge that there was some force in the clause in order to overcome the obstinacy of his opponents, but Chapuys was certainly not far wrong in saying that it was 'all the same as far as the King is concerned as if they had made no reservation, for no one will now be so bold as to contest with his lord the importance of this reservation[2].' The long-deferred pardon was at last granted: though when it was first sent down from the Lords, the Commons discovered that the laity were not mentioned and so were still in the Praemunire: a deputation from the Lower House, however, waited upon the King and expressed their doubts, and though at first Henry treated them harshly, he finally succumbed, and the laity were included in the pardon[3].

But the struggle was not yet over. The following year witnessed a continuation of the attacks on the independence of the clergy. This time, however, Henry and Cromwell had determined that the brunt of the battle should be borne by

[1] Friedmann, vol. i. p. 142.          [2] Cal. v. 105.
[3] Cal. v. 171.

Parliament, which responded to the mandates of the King and his minister with gratifying celerity. Shortly after the opening of the session, in January, 1532, there appeared in the Lower House that famous document, which is usually known as the 'Supplication of the Commons against the Ordinaries [1].' The designation is certainly misleading: so preponderant was the part played by one of the Commons in the preparation of this memorable petition, that it cannot be fairly regarded as the work of them all. The nature of the charges of which the 'Supplication' was composed, its phraseology and the handwritings in the various drafts of it which are preserved to us to-day [2] leave little doubt that it was originally devised by the genius of Cromwell. It was in fact the first of a number of measures ostensibly emanating from Parliament, but in reality prepared by the King's minister and forced by him upon the very tractable Lords and Commons. The purport of the supplication was, in brief, to accuse the clergy of making laws and ordinances without the assent of the King or his lay subjects, of demanding excessive fees, of dealing corruptly and unfairly, especially with cases of heresy, and to request the King to take measures for the remedy of these abuses. The Ordinaries, to whom the petition was delivered from the King on April 12, at once composed a temperate and dignified reply, in which the injustice and unreasonableness of the charges preferred against them were courteously but plainly pointed out [3]. Parliament in the meantime had been prorogued for three months, but as soon as it had reassembled it was forced to take up the cudgels again [4]. The clergy had stated their case so well that Henry, in dread lest the faint-hearted Commons should abandon too soon a quarrel into which his minister had led them, thought it advisable to intervene himself in the dispute. A short interview between the King and the Speaker was enough to reanimate the drooping spirits of the House: Henry was even spared the trouble

---

[1] Hall, p. 784.
[2] See Appendix at the end of this chapter, p. 104.
[3] Wilkins, vol. iii. pp. 748, 750.
[4] Hall, p. 788; Cal. v. 989.

of a frank avowal of his attitude in words—a gracious promise to be 'indifferent' between the disputants was quite sufficient to ensure the continuance of the struggle. The Ordinaries were not slow to discover that their first reply had been totally ineffectual, and hastened to compose a second which, though maintaining in general the position which had originally been assumed, contained a concession that no new laws should be published without the royal consent [1]. A good deal more haggling, however, was necessary before the final compromise was reached [2]. In fact matters moved so slowly that the King was obliged to make (or let Cromwell make for him) another of his suspiciously timely discoveries to the effect that his sovereign rights as Supreme Head were not clear, because every bishop at his consecration had made an oath of allegiance to the Pope. The Commons were asked to rectify this, and were about to pass severe censure on the bishops, when they were prorogued once more on account of the ragings of the plague. Before he let them go, however, the King had probably ascertained that the clergy intended to submit. Threatened on all sides, Convocation on the 16th of May finally agreed not to pass any more new regulations without the King's licence, and to examine and revise, according to the royal wishes, the canons already made [3]. The most important result of the controversy for us to notice is that the King, acting (as he evidently did) on the advice of Cromwell, had succeeded in reducing Convocation to complete subjugation, and in making Parliament pliant to his will, as it had never been before. The scheme of controlling the clergy is doubly significant, first, as the cause of a great change in itself; second, as the first step of the dominant policy of the next ten years, for establishing the Royal Supremacy in Church and State. It must not be forgotten however that Cromwell's action, in defiance of Papal authority at this juncture, arose from no hate of the Romish dogmas nor from any love of the new religion. He carried out all his schemes solely from political motives; the religious, the emotional side

[1] Cal. v. 1018.      [2] Cf. Dixon, vol. i. pp. 74–111.

[3] Cal. v. 1023.

left him absolutely untouched; the practical, the politically serviceable aspect of the case, alone appealed to him.

Popular as Henry doubtless was, Cromwell must have realized, when he thus threw himself heart and soul on the King's side in the divorce case, that he had staked everything on the continuance of the royal favour. The best of the clergy were strongly against the cause of Anne Boleyn, and there were but few who disagreed with them. The general sympathy of the nation for Katherine was greater than ever. Chapuys tells us that Henry was urged by the crowd in the streets to take back the Queen, and that Anne Boleyn was not infrequently publicly insulted [1]. The mob, and still more the friars, spoke of her openly as a common prostitute, who 'ruled the King and beggared spiritualty and temporalty also.' A letter of the imperial ambassador tells us that the provincial of the Friars Observants at Greenwich (better known as Friar Peto) preached before the King, and told him that 'the unbounded affection of princes and their false counsellors deprived them of their knowledge of the truth, and that Henry was endangering his crown by his marriage, for great and little were murmuring at it.' The King concealed his vexation as best he could, but later ordered one of his chaplains to preach there in his presence, and contradict all that Peto had said. At the end of this sermon the warden arose, and answering for his minister in his absence, dared to say in Henry's presence that the royal chaplain had lied. The King was very angry and had the warden and preacher both arrested [2]. Most of the Greenwich friars were eager to stand by their brethren, but some proved less incorruptible, and gave secret information against the steadfast ones.

The result of all these murmurings among commons and friars was that Cromwell was kept very busy in finding out and extirpating 'sedycyous opynyons' as they were termed. In order to clinch the advantages that were to accrue to Henry as a result of his newly-assumed ecclesiastical position, it was as necessary to discover and either destroy or convert

---

[1] Cal. v. 1202.　　　　　[2] Cal. v. 941.

the laymen opposed to it, as it was to keep in submission the clergy from whose hands it had been snatched. Henry could have probably found no abler man in the realm to accomplish this purpose than his new minister. Early in 1532 Cromwell began to create a system of espionage, the most effective that England had ever seen, that in a short time was to render unsafe the most guarded expression of dissent in politics or religion. The success which this organized method of reporting treason later obtained, is one of the most striking proofs of the relentless energy of its originator. But Cromwell's efforts to extirpate sedition, and to encourage the new ecclesiastical system, were not confined to England alone during these first years of his ministry. The years 1531 and 1532 must not be passed over without some slight reference to his connexion with William Tyndale. There was no counsellor about the King, upon whom Cromwell could rely as an intelligent and consistent ally, to help him carry out his schemes of 'political Protestantism.' In this dilemma he turned to William Tyndale, who was at that time in the Low Countries. The theory of 'one King, one law in the realm; no class of men exempt from the temporal sword, no law except the law of the land' advocated in 'The Obedience of a Christian Man,' doubtless struck Cromwell, if he read the book. It was perhaps the nearest approach he had yet found in writing to the policy he was steadily pursuing; he immediately desired to induce the reformer to return to England and to enlist him in the defence of his great cause. The fact that Cromwell was able to persuade the King to permit him to attempt this is a good proof of his influence with Henry. In May, 1530, Tyndale had been denounced as a perverter of God's word[1]; but so great was the change which the new minister's accession to power had wrought in the royal policy, that Henry now allowed Cromwell to write to his old friend Stephen Vaughan in the Netherlands[2], and commission him to try and discover where Tyndale was, and induce him to return to England. To this request Vaughan sent a double reply to Henry and

[1] Demaus, p. 257.　　　[2] Demaus, p. 274.

Cromwell, informing them that he had written to the reformer (three separate letters to different places, not knowing where he was) and had received his answer, in which Tyndale said that the news of what had lately happened in England made him afraid to go there[1]. In a confidential postscript to the letter to Cromwell, Vaughan writes in most glowing terms about the reformer, saying that he was of far greater knowledge than the King's Highness took him for, as plainly appeared by his works. 'Would God he were in England.' As usual Vaughan's enthusiasm had run away with his discretion. He was the exact opposite of Cromwell in this respect; he was ever full of emotion and feeling, while his master was to the last degree practical and calculating.

In spite of his first rebuff, Vaughan persevered in his attempts, and on the 25th of March sent Cromwell another letter, in which he expressed a little more hope of getting Tyndale to go to England[2]. Three weeks later his efforts received some more substantial reward, for on the 18th of April he wrote to Henry[3], that he had at last obtained an interview with the reformer, and that though the latter still refused to comply with his request, his words had been such as to arouse the enthusiasm of Cromwell's agent more than ever. With this letter Vaughan sent to Henry the manuscript of Tyndale's new book against Sir Thomas More, called the Answer, which the reformer did not wish to put in print till Henry had seen it, because the latter had been displeased at the hasty and unlicensed printing of his former work, The Practise of Prelates. The letter and the book were not destined, however, to have the desired effect on the King. The Answer was sufficiently plain to indicate that Tyndale's religious beliefs were not of the sort that would ever be serviceable to Henry; the reformer was altogether too full of Protestantism for its own sake, to suit either the King or

---

[1] Cal. v. 65. Doubtless Vaughan referred to the steps taken by Bishop Stokesley and others to punish those who favoured the new religion. It was at this time that Tyndale's brother John had been arrested in London for selling New Testaments received from abroad.

[2] Cal. v. 153.

[3] Cal. v. 201.

his counsellor. For once Cromwell had mistaken his man. To say that the King was thoroughly vexed and annoyed, when he had perused Vaughan's letter, and the enclosed work, is a mild statement of the facts. The original letter which Vaughan wrote is not extant, but there is a copy of it in the British Museum which ends most abruptly with the words 'To declare to your Magyste what In my pore Judgement I thynke of the man, I asserteyne your grace I haue not communyd with A man[1]'; a fact which suggests the possibility that the irritable King vented his anger on the unoffending sheet of paper, and tore it in two. The letter with which Cromwell, at the King's direction, replied to Vaughan, is a still surer index to the impression which the latter's report had produced on the King. What with the precipitation of his emotional, enthusiastic, and unpractical friend, Cromwell must have been placed in a very awkward position. The many corrections and interlineations in the draft of the letter he wrote in reply to Vaughan, sufficiently reveal his great perplexity and bewilderment[2]. The subject-matter of the letter will speak for itself. The rage of the King is vividly described, and Vaughan is repeatedly warned to abandon the reformer: but in spite of everything he continued to attempt to persuade Tyndale to return. He had two more fruitless interviews with the latter, described in his letters to Henry of the 20th of May, and to Cromwell on the 19th of June[3], and after that came back to England for the summer. In November he returned to the Netherlands, and wrote again to Cromwell warmly on Tyndale's behalf, but not a word did he receive in reply[4]. In the meantime Henry and Cromwell had dispatched Sir Thomas Elyot to arrest the reformer and bring him home[5]. Vaughan finally saw the danger he ran in advocating the cause of the author of the 'venemous and pestiferous workes,' and dared say no more. The rest of his letters during these two years do not even once mention him. The whole Tyndale episode is noteworthy as the nearest

---

[1] British Museum, Titus B, vol. i. p. 67.

[2] Letters, 21.

[3] Cal. v. 246, 303.

[4] Cal. v. 533, 574, 618.

[5] Demaus, p. 307.

approach to a mistake in Cromwell's internal policy. Henry's anger probably gave him a clear warning that many more such would bring him to certain ruin. He was saved from serious consequences in this case, only because he had amply atoned for it by his brilliant success in obtaining the submission of the clergy.

Cromwell was also occupied, during these two years, in re-establishing Wolsey's foundation at Oxford, under the new name of King Henry the Eighth's College. He was appointed receiver-general and supervisor of all the lands belonging to it; and the adjustment of claims, transfer of property, new foundation and charter kept him very busy, and gave him an excellent opportunity to display his legal talent. He also superintended the building of a new palace at Westminster, regulated the wages of the men working on the fortifications at Calais, and was also busy with minor duties in the King's own household—the care of the royal plate and jewels, and even the drawing of patterns for Henry's robes of state[1]. From the close of the year 1529 until his fall, the best index to the various occupations in which he was engaged is afforded by his famous 'remembrances.' These consist largely of short and usually incomplete sentences, sometimes even single words, jotted down at odd moments by Cromwell or his chief clerk, on loose sheets of paper—often on the backs of letters and drafts of important documents. They are for the most part absolutely disjointed and unconnected in matter, form, and handwriting. Sandwiched in between apparently careless phrases which later expand into the most drastic of parliamentary enactments, we find minute details concerning the wages of labourers, the cost of New Year's presents at the Court, or even matters of a private nature: next to a memorandum for the signing of a letter for some Spaniards occur the significant words, 'To Remember the Auncyent Cronycle of magna Carta and how *libera sit* Cam into the Statute[2].' The less important items are of course by far the more numerous, especially in the first

---

[1] Cal. v. 701, 1548, 1600, 1728;     [2] British Museum, Titus B, vol. i.
Letters, 36, 39.                        p. 422.

six years when the King loaded his new minister with details of the greatest variety and complexity. Towards the last the 'remembrances' are fewer in number, and deal less extensively with minor matters ; but even up to the very end we find ample evidence that the King's minister carried in his head an amount of detail of a comparatively unimportant nature, which would have been quite impossible for a man like his predecessor. The Cardinal, absorbed in studying the great diplomatic combinations of continental Europe, had shamefully neglected minor affairs at home. Cromwell, in his ten years of power, not only atoned for the errors of Wolsey, but also familiarized himself with every detail of domestic administration to an extent that no King or minister had ever done in England before. It would have been almost impossible to carry through the tremendous changes which had followed the divorce, without the aid of a counsellor of the peculiar talents of Thomas Cromwell.

The thread of our narrative now becomes so complicated, when the new minister is at last fully installed in the King's service, that it will be necessary to depart from the chronological order of events hitherto followed, and to treat separately each phase of Cromwell's policy, up to the reaction of 1539. The Internal and Foreign Administration, Suppression of the Monasteries, of the Pilgrimage of Grace, &c., all move on hand in hand, and in order to understand their bearing on one another, it is only needful to remember that they were all the work of one man, and were proceeding in general at the same time.

# APPENDIX TO CHAPTER VI

## THE SUPPLICATION OF THE COMMONS AGAINST THE ORDINARIES

Four drafts of this petition exist to-day in the Public Record Office. One of them is written in a hand which may be recognized in the greater part of Cromwell's correspondence of the time, and which is probably that of his chief clerk; it is corrected and revised by Cromwell himself. Of the other three, one, which is uncorrected and probably a final draft, is also written by the clerk—and the other two, chiefly in a strange handwriting, are filled with interlineations by Cromwell. The following copy was made from the first of these drafts (Cal. v, 1016 (4)). The words in brackets are crossed out in the original manuscript: the words in italics are inserted between the lines. All the corrections are in Cromwell's hand.

### 'To the King our Sovereigne Lorde

In most humble Wise Shewen vnto y*our* excellent highnes and most prudent wisedom your faithfull louyng and most humble and obedient Subiect*es* The Co*m*mons in this your p*r*esente parliament assembled That where of late aswell thorough new fantasticall and erronyous opynyons growen by occasion of Frantike sedycious and oue*r*thwartly Framed bokes compiled imprynted publisshed and made in the englishe tong contrarie and ayenst the veray trew catholique and Cristen Faith as also by the {vnreasonable and} extreme {rygour vndiscrete} *and vncharytable* behaueour and dealing of dyuers ordynaries *Ther Co*mmyssaryes and Substytutt*es* which haue heretofore had and yet have thexamynacion in and vppon the saide errours and hereticall opynyons moche discorde varyaunce and debate hathe rysen and more and more daylie is like to encrease and insue emonges the vniu*er*sall sorte of your saide Subiect*es* aswell sp*iri*tuall as temporall either ayenst other in most vncharitable man*er* to the grete inquietacion vexacion and breche of your peax w*ith*in this your most catholik realme. The speciall perticuler greues whereof which most principally concerne your saide Co*m*mons and lay Subiect*es* and whiche ar (as they vndoubtedlie suppose) the veray chief Founteyns occasions and causes that daylie bredeth Fostereth Norissheth and maynteneth the saide sedycions factyons dedelie hatered and most vncharitable parte taking*es* either parte and sorte of your saide Subiect*es* spirituall and temporall ayenst thother hereafter Folowinglye Do ensue.

Furst where the prelat*es* and sp*iri*tuall Ordynaries of this your most excellent Realme of Englonde and the clergie of the same haue in their conuocac*i*ons heretofore made and caused to be made and also daylie do make dyuers and manye *Facyons of* lawes constytuc*i*ons and ordena*uu*nc*es* w*it*hout your knowlege or most royall assente and w*it*hout the assent and consent of any your lay Subiect*es* vnto the whiche lawes your saide lay Subiect*es* haue not onelie heretofore and daylie be {boundene} *constraynyd to obbeye* aswell in their bodies goodes and possessions But also ben compelled daylie to incurre into the censures of the same and ben contynuallie put to importable charges and expens*es* ayenst all equytee right and good conscience. And yet your saide humble subiect*es* ne their predecessours coulde eu*er* be pryuey to the saide lawes Ne any of the saide lawes haue ben declared vnto them in thinglisshe tong or otherwise *publysshed* By knowlege whereof they might haue extued the daungiers censures and penaltees of the same Which lawes so made yo*ur* saide most humble and obedyent subiect*es* vnder the supportacion of your Maiestee Suppose to be not onelie to the dymynucyon and derogacion of your imperyall iurisdiction and prerogatif royall But also to the grete preiudice inquietacion and damage of all your saide Subiect*es* And also where now of late there hathe ben deuysed by the most Reuerende father in god Wyllyam Archebusshop of Caunterburie that in the Court*es* whiche he callith his Courtes of the Arches and Audience shalbe but onelie Ten proctours at his deputacion which be sworn to p*re*ferre and promote the onelie iurisdiction {and preferrement} of the saide Court*es*. By reason whereof if any of your lay Subiect*es* shoulde haue any lawfull cause ayenst the Judge of the saide Court*es* or ayenst any docto*ur* or proctour of the same or any of their Frend*es* or adherent*es* they can ne may in any wise haue indifferent counsaill. And also all the causes depending in any of the saide court*es* may by the confederacie of the saide Few proctours be in suche wise tracted and delayed as your Subiect*es* suing in the same shalbe put to importable charges costes and expenc*es*. And in case that any matiers there being p*re*ferred shoulde touche Your Crowne Regallie Jurisdiction and p*re*rogatif royall yet the same shall not be disclosed by any of the saide procto*ur*s for fere of losse of their offices. Wherefore your saide most

obedient Subiect*es* vnder the protexion of yo*ur* maiestee Suppose
that your highnes should haue the nomynacion of som conuenyent
nombre of proctours to be alwayes attendaunt in the saide court*es*
of tharches and audience there to be sworne aswell to the preferrement of your iurisdiction and prerogatif royall as to thexpedyc*i*on
of all the causes of your Lay Subiectes repayring and suing to the
same.

And Where also many of your saide most humble and obedient
subiect*es* and specyallie those that be of the pourest sorte w*ith*in
this your Realme ben daylie conuented and called before the saide
sp*iri*tuall Ordynaries their Co*m*missaries and Substytut*es* ex officio
somtyme at the pleasures of the saide Ordynaries and Substytut*es*
for malice w*ith*out any cause and sumtyme at the onelie p*ro*mocyon
and accusement of their {false} Somoners and apparitours being
veray light and vndiscrete persons w*ith*out any lawfull cause of
accusacion or credible fame proued ayenst them and w*ith*out any
presentement in the vysitacion ben inquieted distou*r*bed vexed
troubeled and put to excessiue and importable charges for them to
bere and many tymes be suspended and exco*m*munycate for small
and light causes vppon thonelie certificat of the proctours of the
adue*r*saries made vnder a fayned Seale which eu*er*y procto*ur* hathe
in his keping where as the partie suspended and exco*m*munycate
many tymes neu*er* had any warning and yet when he shalbe absouled
if it be out of the courte he shalbe compelled to pay to his owne
procto*ur* xxd and to the procto*ur* which is ayenst him other xxd
and xxd to the Scribe besid*es* a pryuey rewarde that the Judge
shall haue to the grete impouerysshing of your saide poure Lay
Subiect*es*.

Also Your saide most humble and obedient subiect*es* Fynde them
greued w*ith* the grete and excessyue Fees taken in the said sp*iri*tuall
court*es* and in especiall in the saide Court*es* of tharches and audience
where they take for eu*er*y Cytacyon ii*s* vi*d* for eu*er*y Inhibycyon
vj*s* viij*d*, for euerie proxie xvj*d* for eu*er*y certificat xvj*d*, for eu*er*y Libell
iij*s*. iiij*d*., for eu*er*y answer to any Lybell iij*s* iiij*d*, for eu*er*y acte if it
be but two woord*es* to the Register iiij*d*, for eu*er*y personall Cytacion
or decree iij*s* iiij*d*. for euery sentence or iudgement to the Judge
xxvi*s*. viij*d*, for eu*er*y testi*m*onyall vppon any suche sentence or iudgement xxvj*s*. viii*d* for eu*er*y significauit xij*s*. for eu*er*y co*m*myssion to
examyn wytnes xij*s* Which is thought to be importable to be borne
by your saide Subiect*es* and veray necessarie to be refo*ur*med.

And Furthermore Where the saide spyrytuall Ordynaries {many

tymes purposedlie to revenge their inwarde greves and displeasures and to put their saide lawes in execucion} *theyr Commyssaryes & Substytuttes* sumtyme *for thayr own pleasures Sumtyme* by the Synister procurement of other spirituall persons vse to make out proces ayenst dyuers of your saide Subiectes and thereby compell them to appere before themselffes to answer at a certen day and place to suche articles as by them shalbe of office afore themselffes then purposed *and that Secretlye and not in oppen places* and fourthwith vppon their apparaunce without cause or any declaracion then made or shewed commytt and sende them to warde Where they remayne without bayle or mayneprise sumtyme half a yere and somtyme a hole yere and more or they may in any wise knowe either the cause of their imprysonement or any name of their accuser and fynallie their grete costes charges and expences therin when all is examyned and nothing can be proued ayenst them but they clerelie Innocente for any Faute or cryme that can be layed vnto them in that parte ben set ayen at large without any recompence or amendes in that behalf to be towardes them adiudged.

And also if percase vppon the saide proces and apparaunce any partie be vppon the saide matier cause or examynacion brought Fourth and named either as partie or wytnes and then vppon the proffe and tryall thereof not able to prove and verefie his saide accusacion or testymonye ayenst the partie so accused to be trew then the person so causeles accused is {clerely} *for the more parte* without any remedie for his charges and wrongful vexacyon to be {in that parte} towardes him adiuged and recouered.

Also vppon thexamynacion of the saide accusacion if heresie be ordynarylie layed vnto the charge of the partie so accused then the saide ordynaries or their ministres vse to put to them suche subtile interrogatories concerning the high misteries of our feith as ar able quyckelye to trappe a simple vnlerned or yet a well wytted lay man without lerning and bryng them by suche sinyster introduction sone to his owne confusion And Fourthwith if there chaunce any heresie to be by suche subtill polycie by him confessed in wourdes and yet neuer commytted nor thought in dede, then put they without ferther fauour the saide person either to make his purgacion and so thereby to lose his honestie and credence for euer orelles as som simple sely Sowle precyselie stonding to the clere testymonye of his owne well knowen conscience rather then to confesse his innocent trouth to abyde {thextreme examynacion of deth by the Fyer} *thextremyte in that behalf* and so is vtterly distroyed.

And if it fortune the saide partie so accused to denye the saide
accusacion and so put his aduersarie to proue the {false} same
vntrewlie forged and ymagened ayenst him then for the more parte
suche wytnesses as ben brought fourth for the same be they but
ij in nombre neuer so sore diffamed of litle trouth or credence
aduersaries or enemies to the partie yet they shalbe allowed and
enabeled *onlye by Discrecyon of the sayd ordenaryes ther Commyssaryes
& Substytuttes* and therevppon sufficient cause to procede to iudgement to delyuer the partie so accused either to the seculer handes
{and so to be burned} after abiuracion without remedie and afore
if he Submytte himself to compell him when best happeneth to make
his purgacion and bere a Fagotte to his extreme shame and vtter
vndoing.

In Consideracyon whereof most gracious Souereigne Lorde And
Forasmoche as there is at this present tyme and by a Few yeres past
hathe ben outrageous vyolens on thone parte and moche defaulte
and lacke of pacyent sufferaunce charitee and good will on thother
parte, A meruelous Disorder of the godlie quyet peax and tran-
quillyte that this your realme heretofore euer hitherto hathe ben
in thorough your poletique wisedom in most honourable fame and
catholik feith invyolablye preserued. It may therefore most benigne
Souereigne lorde lyke your excellent goodnes for the tender and
vnyuersallye indyfferent zele benigne loue and fauour that your
highnes berith towarde both the saide parties, the saide articles if
they shalbe by your most clere and perfite iudgement thought any
instrumentes or causes of the saide variaunce and disorder or those
and all other occasions whatsoeuer accompted by your highnes to
make towardes the saide factions depelie and weightylie after your
accustomed weyes and maner serched weyed and considered gra-
ciouslie to prouyde all vyolence on both sides vtterlye and clerelie
set a parte some suche necessarie and behofull remedies as may
effectuallie reconsile and bryng in perpetuall vnytee your saide
Subiectes spirituall and temporall. And for thestablisshing thereof
to make and ordcyn on both sides suche straite lawes ayenst the
brekers transgressours and offendours as shalbe to hevye daungerous
and weightie for them or any of them to bere suffer and susteyne.
Whereunto Your saide Comons most humblie hertelie and entierlie
beseche your grace as the onely hed Souereigne lorde protectour and
Defendour of bothe the saide parties in whom and by whom the
onelie and sole redresse reformacion and remedie herein absolutely
restith and remayneth. By occasion whereof all your saide Comons

in their conscience surelye accompt that beside the meruelous Feruent loue that your highnes shall thereby ⟨gain⟩ and engendre in their hartes towardes Your grace Ye shall do the most pryncelie Feate and shew the most honourable and charitable president and Mirrour that euer did Souereigne lorde vppon his subiectes and therewithall merite and deserue of our mercyfull lorde eternall blisse Whose goodnes graunt your grace in most godlie pryncelie and honourable astate long to reigne prosper and contynew as the Souereigne lorde ouer all your saide most humble and most obedyent Subiectes.

*[Two blank pages here.]*

And Where *also* the said prelatis and ordinaries daily do permytte and suffer the parsons vicars Curates parishe prestes and other spirituall parsons hauing Cure of soule within this your Realme Ministring {vnto your said loving subgiettes} *to exact and take of your humble & obedyent Subiectes dyuers Summys of money for* the Sacramentes & sacramentalles of holy churche {as the holy sacrament of the Aulter Baptyme, Matrimonye Confession, buriall weddyng churchinges and suche other} *Sumtyme denying the same without they Fyrst be payd the sayd Summys of money* {& *to take* for the ministracion of the same of your said Subiectes diuers and certen sommes of money allegging the same to be their dueties.} Whiche sacramentes and sacramentalles your saide most humble & obedient subiectes vnder the protection of your highnes doo suppose & think ought to be in most Reuerent charitable & goodlie wise freely mynystred vnto them at all tymes requisite withoute denyall or {any maner somme or} *exaccyon of any maner* sommes of money {or other duetie or contribucion to be asked demaunded or required for the same} *to be demaundyd or askyd for the same* And also where in the spirituall courtes of the said Prelatis & ordinaries ben lymyted and appoynted for many Judges Scribes Apparitours Somoners praysours and other ministres for the approbacion of testamentes Whiche coveting somoche theire owne priuate Lucres and satisfaccion of the appetites of the said prelates and Ordinaries that when any of your said loving subiectes do Repaire to any of the said Courtis for the probate of any testamentes they do in suche wise {extorte and} *make long delays or* excessively take of theym so large fees and Rewardes for the same as is Importible for theym to beare directly against all Justice lawe equite and goode conscience

{And also where most gracious soueraigne the Judges Constituted and appoynted by the said spirituall Ordinaries in their said Courtes

to here and determyne causes there, do in likewise daily take many
grete and excessive fees and rewardes of your said pore subiect*es*
having any cause or matier depending before theym as is aforsaid
And ou*er* that when any Judgement or sentence by the said Judge
shalbe yeven before them wille also have grete so*m*mes of money
for the same. So that no thing is or can be obteyned in any of the
said Court*es* wit*h*oute money. }

*Wherfor* Your said most humble and obedient subiect*es* do
therfore vnder yo*ur* gracious correction and supportacion suppose
it were veray necessary that the said ordinaries in the deputacion of
suche Judges shulde be bounde to appoynte and assigne suche
discrete gravous and honest p*er*sons having sufficient Lernyng witte
discrecion & vnderstonding and also being indewed w*ith* such
sp*iri*tuall promocions stipend and salarye as they being Judges in
their said Court*es* myght and may mynystre to eu*er*y parson repairing
to the same Justice wit*h*oute taking any man*er* fee or Rewarde for
any maner sentence or Judgement to be yoven before theym.
And also where as diu*er*se sp*iri*tuall p*er*sons being p*re*sented aswell
by yo*ur* highnes and by other patrons wit*h*in this yo*ur* Realme to
{any} *dyuers* benefices or other sp*iri*tuall promocion. The said
ordinaries and there mynystres do not onely take of theym for theyr
L*ett*eres of Institucion and Induction many grete and {excessive}
*large* so*m*mes of money & Reward*es* But also do pact and couena*u*nte w*ith* the same, taking sure bond*es* for their indempnite to
aunswer to the said ordinaries the first frutes of the said benefices
after their Institucion so as they being ones p*re*sented or promoted
as is aforesaid ben by the said ordinaries veray {extremely} *vncharyt-*
*ablye* handled to their no litle hynderaunce & impoue*ris*shement
whiche yo*ur* said subgiett*es* suppose not onely to be against all lawes
right & good consciens but also to be Symony and contrary to the
Lawes of god.

And also where as the said sp*iri*tuall Ordinaries do daily conferre
and geve sundry benefices vnto certen yong folkes calling them their
Nephews *or Kynsfolk*es being in their mynorite and wit*h*in age not
apt ne able to S*er*ue the Cure of any suche benefice Wherby the said
ordinaries do kepe and deteyn the frutes & p*ro*fittes of the same
benefices in their owne handes and therby accumulate to themsel*ffes*
right grete and large so*m*mes of money & yerely p*ro*fitt*es* to the most
p*er*nicious exsample of all yo*ur* said lay subiect*es* and so the Cures
& other promocions youen vnto suche Infant*es* ben onely {youen
but} *Imployed* to {enriche} *thenryching of* the said ordinaries & the

pore sely soules of your people and subiectes whiche shulde be taught in the paroches yoven as aforsaid for lak of good curates do perisshe withoute doctrine or any good teaching.

And also where a grete nombre of holy daies whiche nowe at this present tyme with veray smalle Devocion be solempnised and kept thorough oute this your Realme vppon the whiche many grete abhomynable and execrable vices idle and wanton sportes ben vsed and exercised whiche holy daies if it may stond with your gracious pleasure *and specyall suche as Fall in the heruest* myght by your maiestie by thadvice of your most honourable counseill prelates and ordinaries be made fewer in nombre and those that shall herafter be ordeyned to stond & contynue myght and may be the more Devoutely religiously & reuerently obserued to the Laude of almyghty god and to thencrease of your high honour & fame.'

*Endd.* ' A boke ayenst the clergy for takyng excessyve Fees'

# CHAPTER VII

FROM the close of the year 1532 until his fall, the entire domestic administration of England was in Cromwell's hands. From the moment that he entered the King's service he had definitely committed himself to the policy which he was to follow till the end of his days. His own theories of internal government, the traditions of the Tudor monarchy, and the situation of the realm at the time of his accession to power, combined to convince him that the maintenance of an all-powerful kingship was indispensable to England's safety ; the nature of the proposal by which he first won Henry's confidence was tantamount to an irrevocable declaration of that principle, and a promise that it should be the guiding thought of his entire administration. The revolt from Rome was an incident rather than an aim of his policy. He had suggested it at first as offering the only possible solution of the immediate difficulties of the Crown, and as affording golden opportunities for the increase of the power of the monarchy ; but as soon as the decisive step had been taken, he saw that the security of his own position had become conditional upon the permanence of the new ecclesiastical system, which in turn could only be ensured if the King, for whose sake it had been created, was rendered supreme in Church and State. Cromwell's very existence had thus become dependent on the success of his endeavours to maintain and carry further the policy initiated by Henry VII, and to elevate the Crown to sovereign power above every other institution in the realm. Perhaps no minister has ever had more varied problems to confront him, than those which Cromwell had to deal with during these eight years ; and yet his action in every case is a logical, intelligent application of the theory of internal government, which he believed was the only sure road to national greatness. With this great principle firmly borne in mind, the history of Cromwell's domestic administration becomes comparatively simple.

A further assertion of the Supremacy of the Crown in ecclesiastical affairs was necessary, before Cromwell could attempt to strengthen its already predominant position in the State. The chief object of the more important measures of the years 1533 and 1534 was to utilize the consequences of the breach with Rome for the benefit of the monarchy, and to provide that none of the power of which the Pope had been deprived should be permitted to escape the King. During the year 1532 Henry had deluded himself with hopes that his first attack on the liberties of the English clergy might frighten Clement into acquiescence in the divorce, but at last his patience came to an end, and he surrendered himself entirely to the guidance of Cromwell, who had been persuaded from the first that nothing further was to be obtained from the Pope. In January, 1533, the King was secretly married to Anne Boleyn; on the 10th of May Cranmer, who had lately been raised to the see of Canterbury, opened his archiepiscopal court at Dunstable [1]. With a promptitude which must have been highly satisfactory to Henry after the delays of the previous proceedings at Rome, the sentence of divorce was pronounced. There can be little doubt that Cromwell gave efficient aid in hastening the verdict [2]; but what is far more important, he took effective measures, even before it was rendered, to prevent its revocation. Parliament had been in session during the three months previous to the assembling of the court at Dunstable: in anticipation of the coming sentence, it had been induced to pass an Act [3] to deprive Katherine of the only hope that remained to her by forbidding appeals to Rome, and by ordaining that the decision of an archiepiscopal court should be final, except in cases where the King was concerned, when appeal might be made to the Upper House of Convocation.

---

[1] Cal. vi. 180, 461.  [2] Cal. vi. 461, 469, 496, 525, 526, 527.
[3] 24 Hen. VIII, c. 12.

A notable effort was made to conceal the obvious and immediate purpose of this statute under a shroud of pious and patriotic verbiage. The life of the Act, however, was but short. Though it had dealt the death blow to the jurisdiction of the Pope in England, it had not made adequate provision for the maintenance of the Supremacy of the Crown ; so in 1534 the statute of the previous year was superseded by a new one[1], which enacted that an appeal might always be made from an archbishop's court to the King's Court of Chancery, the decision of which was to be final. The abolition of the Annates (which will be considered in another place) occurred at the same time. The effect of these two measures was to complete the work begun in 1530, and to sever the last links of the chain which bound the Church of England to Rome.

In the meantime the famous Act of Succession[2], bastardizing the Princess Mary and establishing the offspring of Anne Boleyn as lawful heirs to the throne of England, had also been passed in Parliament, and before the year had closed a new statute[3] had formally recognized the King's ecclesiastical supremacy for the third time ; for Henry was not satisfied with the acknowledgements he had wrung from the clergy in 1531 and 1532, nor with the express assertion that the King was on earth Supreme Head of the Church of England, contained in the oath to the new succession, which Cromwell's commissioners began to administer throughout the realm in the summer of 1534. The last vestige of the independence of the English bishops was also removed in the course of this memorable year, by certain provisions of the final Act for the restraint of Annates[4]. It had not been necessary, however, to

---

[1] 25 Hen. VIII, c. 19.

[2] 25 Hen. VIII, c. 22. Mendez Silva, pp. 14 and 15, asserts that Cromwell was responsible for the passage of this statute. The King's minister appeared in Convocation and Parliament, and made a speech in which he said that his master desired that Mary be excluded from the succession and Elizabeth received in her place, and that he was sure that they all loved His Majesty so much that they would not refuse to do his will. Clergy, Lords, and Commons, ' al peligro de la conciencia . . . se reduxeron facilmente.'

[3] 26 Hen. VIII, c. 1.

[4] 25 Hen. VIII, c. 20.

introduce any very radical innovation here. The bishops
were already virtually in the King's hands, for the elections by
chapters had long been a mere farce, and the royal nominee
had been almost invariably chosen. So the Act had aimed at
a legalization of the *status quo*—merely adding a few new
provisions to strengthen the King's hold on the Church. All
relations with the Pope were of course to cease; the bishops
were to be consecrated by virtue of a royal commission; and
if the chapter failed to elect within twelve days, the King
was empowered to fill the vacancy by letters patent. But
even this does not seem to have been enough to satisfy
Cromwell. A letter of Chapuys in the early part of 1535
informs us that the King's Secretary called some of the
bishops before the Council to ask them if the King could
not make and unmake them at pleasure: ' they were obliged
to say yes, else they should have been deprived of their
dignities: as the said Cromwell told a person, who reported
it to me, and said that the Council had been summoned only
to entrap the bishops[1].' Cromwell followed this up, later in
the year, by causing a Prohibitory Letter to be sent out in
the King's name, forbidding the bishops to visit any monastery
or to exercise any right of jurisdiction during the visitation of
the religious houses then in progress[2]. It appears that even
Cromwell, with all his audacity, was at a loss to devise a
means to silence the objections which were raised against this
high-handed measure. He was not ashamed to take a hint
from the fertile brains of his two blood-hounds, Legh and
Ap-Rice, who suggested an ingenious argument to crush all
opposition, the gist of which is contained in the following
quotation from a letter which they wrote to Cromwell,
Sept. 24, 1535[3]:—

'Yf they (the bishops) had any Jurisdiction, they muste
ned*es* haue receued ⟨it⟩ either by the lawe of god or by the
busshop of Romes Authoritie or els by the King*es* grace
permission. Which is no sufficient discharge ageinst the
statute.

[1] Cal. viii. 121.
[2] Cal. ix. 517.
[3] British Museum, Cleop. E. vi.

254; and Strype, Ecclesiastical
Memorials, vol. i. pt. ii. p. 216.

' Yf they saye by the Lawe of god, Lett theym bring foorth scr*i*ptur but I thinke theym not so impudent as to saye so.

' Yf they saye by the busshop of Romes Authoritie. Lett theym exercise it still, yf they thinke it mete.

' Yf they saye by the Kinges permission why be they more discontent that the king shuld call agein nowe to his hand*es* that which came from hym to theym, than they wolde haue ben*e* yf he had never graunted it theym. And surely they are not able to iustifie thexercise of their iurisdiction hetherto.' Fortified by such reasoning as this did the Royal Supremacy pass into effect.

Having thus obtained the complete submission of the greater lights of the Church, Cromwell consistently pursued his relentless policy with the humbler orders of friars and monks. His method of dealing with the latter did not differ materially from his policy with the former, except that it was perhaps more sanguinary. Priors Lawrence and Webster, two Carthusians who denied the validity of the King's new title, were examined by Cromwell, and when they stubbornly refused to retract their assertions, they were promptly sentenced and executed[1]. Three others, Houghton, Hale, and Reynolds, suffered death a little later, and the latter dared to tell Cromwell that in spite of the terror he had caused by his late proceedings, all good men in the kingdom really held the same opinion, that the Headship of the Church was not the King's[2]. But notwithstanding the wide popular dissatisfaction at the new measures, most malcontents, both lay and spiritual, kept their thoughts to themselves. Men were beginning to discover how dangerous it was to criticize the doings of the King and his minister. The elaborate system of espionage and the commissions to seek out and punish treason, which Cromwell had so laboriously established all over the country in 1532, had now begun to bear fruit. It was impossible to tell who the government spies were : impossible to know when or against whom the next accusation would be made. The words which men spoke in the bosom of their families or to their most intimate friends and neighbours were

---

[1] Cal. viii. 565, 895.     [2] Cal. viii. 609, 661.

as likely to be laid to their charge as their utterances in public: harmless, obscure and ignorant country folk were brought before the magistrates as often as those of higher degree. Edmond Brocke, husbandman, eighty years of age, of Crowle in Worcestershire, was walking home in the rain from Worcester market on the Saturday before St. Thomas' Day, in company with Margaret Higons. 'Yt ys long of the Kyng that this wedre is so troblous or vnstable,' he said, 'and I wene we shall nevir haue better wedre whillis the Kinge Reigneth, and therefore it makith no matter if he were knocked or patted on the heed[1].' These facts were declared on August 12, 1535, before John Russell Esq., Justice of the Peace, by Richard Fulke, husbandman, and Joan Danyell of Crowle. Brocke confessed that he had said 'that it was a hevy and grevous wether and that there was neuyr good wedringes sithins the King began this busines,' but what he meant by 'busines' he could not tell: as to the rest of his words, he said, he was mad or drunk if he spoke them—more than this he would not answer. William Ferrall, of Eastbourne in Sussex, deposed before Sir John Gage on August 14, 1536, that Sir William Hoo, vicar of Eastbourne, and suffragan of the diocese of Chichester, walking with him in the church-yard, said that 'they that rule about the King make him great bankettes and geve him swete wynes and make him dronke,' and that then 'they bring him byllis and he puttyth his sign to them whereby they doo what they will and no man may Correcte them[2].' Margaret Chanseler, of Senklers Bradfeld in Suffolk, spinster, was forced to confess before Sir Robert Drury in February, 1535, that, when drunk and under the influence of an evil spirit, she had said, in presence of Edmond Tyllet and Anthony Harward, 'that the quenes grace had one child by our souereigne lorde the Kynge, which the seid ⟨child⟩ was ded borne, & she prayed god that she myght neuer haue other; also that the quenes grace was a noughtty hoore & that the Kynges grace ought not to mary within his realme.' Tyllet and Harward, when summoned, made the matter somewhat worse. They declared

---

[1] Cal. ix. 74.     [2] Cal. xi. 300 (2).

that the spinster had called the Queen 'a goggyll yed hoore,' and that she had added 'God save queen Katteryn for she was ryghtuous queen, & that she trusted to see her queen Ageyn & that she should warrant the same[1].' All the magistrates before whom these depositions were laid, received ample instructions from Cromwell how to deal with every case; if the accusation was very heavy, the offender was usually sent up to the minister himself, to answer for his misdeeds at head quarters. The punishments in these cases were very severe: there are almost no records of the penalties inflicted on those against whom the depositions were brought, but there is reason to believe that comparatively slight misdemeanours were not seldom rewarded with death.

But of all the devices 'For the putting the Kyng*es* subiect*es* and other in more terroure,' as Cromwell once expressed it[2], the most ruthless remains to be mentioned. The execution of the Carthusians had had its effect, but Cromwell was persuaded that more blood would have to be spilled before his victory could be considered complete. As was usual with him, he laid the axe at the root of the tree, and chose as his victims the noblest and foremost in the land. The opinions of Bishop Fisher and Sir Thomas More were well known to be opposed to the Royal Supremacy, and as such they carried enormous weight. Cromwell must have seen that it would be impossible to establish the King in his new position with any security, until these two men were either converted or destroyed. So, never once swerving from his purpose, nor letting the rank and position of these distinguished men change or deter him, he set about the business of 'making or marring,' with his usual directness and method. If he knew More and Fisher at all well, he must have been reasonably certain that he could never alter their convictions, so it became necessary for him to look for some adequate pretext for getting rid of them. Such a pretext soon presented itself.

In July, 1533, occurs the first mention of serious disturbance due to the visions and prophecies of Elizabeth Barton, better

---

[1] Cal. viii. 196.    [2] Letters, 107.

known as the Nun of Kent[1]. Her reputation for holiness and for divine inspiration was so high throughout the land, that her mad follies were everywhere regarded with almost superstitious reverence. Cromwell, at the King's command, caused her to be examined by Cranmer, but apparently did not succeed in eliciting the information he desired, for the investigation was continued by other interrogators who were less leniently disposed than the Archbishop[2]. The Nun was finally obliged to confess that ' she never Hadd Vision in all her Lyff, but all that ever she said was fayned of her owne ymagynacion, only to satisfie the Myndeis of theym Whiche Resorted vnto her, and to obtayn worldly prayse[3].' She and her accomplices were forced to read their public confessions on a scaffold erected at Paul's Cross, while a sermon was preached in denunciation of the fraud. In the following spring she was condemned to death in Parliament, and in April she was executed with some of her accomplices at Tyburn[4].

But the destruction of the Nun was only of secondary importance for Cromwell's plans; he was mainly looking for some mesh in which he could entrap others of whom he was in much more fear than Elizabeth Barton. Every effort appears to have been made to elicit from her a confession of communication with the divorced Queen, but without success. More and Fisher, however, were not destined to escape so easily. Because the Bishop of Rochester, after several interviews with the unhappy woman, had not reported to Henry her disloyal prophecies (which the Nun had already made in presence of the King himself), it was taken as a sign of treason and neglect of duty to the sovereign. The long letter which Cromwell wrote to Fisher in February, 1534, gives a detailed account of the numerous and unfounded charges against him[5]. This letter impresses the reader as having been written *pro forma* only. Cromwell must have realized that he could never hope to overcome two men who were so

---

[1] Cal. vi. 835.   [2] Letters, 52; Cal. vi. 967, 1445.
[3] British Museum, Harl. MSS. 6, 148 f, 40 a.
[4] Cal. vii. 54 (31), 522.   [5] Letters, 68.

much his intellectual superiors as More and Fisher, in an argument. He therefore carefully avoided having any conversation with them, and wrote to them only in order to have some slight outward justification for his arbitrary action. Fisher sent pathetic letters to the King and the Lords, when Cromwell refused to accept his excuses or listen to his arguments, but in vain. His name was included in the Act of attainder of Elizabeth Barton and her accomplices which was passed in March, 1534, but his life was spared until the King could find a more valid pretext for actually destroying him [1].

The accusations in the case of Sir Thomas More were even more groundless than in Fisher's. The only charges that could be proved against him were an unimportant interview with the Nun herself, a letter which he confessed to have written to her, warning her to leave political subjects entirely alone, and an insignificant conversation about her with a certain father Resbye, Friar Observant of Canterbury [2]. So much was made of these slight accusations, however, that More was forced to write a long letter of excuse to Cromwell. His explanations about the Nun and about his attitude on the Papal Supremacy appear to have been satisfactory; when he was examined by Cromwell and Audeley, all the inventiveness of his accusers seemed to be used to no purpose. 'As the King did not find,' says Chapuys, 'as it seems he hoped, an occasion for doing him more harm, he has taken away his salary [3].' But this unfortunately was not destined to be the end of the affair; if the King was not determined on the ex-Chancellor's destruction, his Privy Councillor was; but Cromwell was forced to bide his time and wait for a better opportunity, so that further proceedings were stayed until the following April.

In the meantime the new Act of Succession had been passed in Parliament, and the oath of allegiance which it required was promptly tendered to More and Fisher, who finally consented to swear to the statute itself but not the preamble [4]. They were unwilling to give their reasons for

---

[1] Cf. Lewis, chap. xxxii.
[2] Cal. vii. 287.
[3] Cal. vii. 296.
[4] Cal. vii. 499, and Letters, 71.

rejecting the latter, but Cranmer cannot have been far wrong when he wrote to Cromwell that the cause of their refusal to accept it lay in its attacks on the authority of the Pope and the validity of the King's first marriage [1]. The Archbishop, ever on the side of humanity, urged the King's minister to accept the compromise which More and Fisher offered, but in vain. The ex-Chancellor and the aged bishop were committed to the Tower, which they never quitted again. For more than a year they remained there subjected to every sort of indignity, until on May 5, 1535, they were summoned by the King, and told that unless they swore to the Act of Succession and the Royal Supremacy, they would be treated no better than the Carthusian monks who had lately been executed [2]. They were allowed six weeks for reflection, but they replied that they would not change their opinion in six hundred years, if they lived so long. So strong was the popular feeling however, that it is doubtful if Henry would have dared to execute Fisher, simply because he said that 'the King, our sovereign Lord, is not Supreme Head of the Church of England'; but when it was announced that the Pope, at a consistory held May 20, had created him a Cardinal, the King was so enraged that he threw all caution to the winds. He declared in his fury that 'he would give Fisher another hat, and send his head to Rome for the Cardinal's hat afterwards,' and ordered both his prisoners to swear to his ecclesiastical headship before St. John's Day, or suffer punishment as traitors [3]. Cromwell had endeavoured from the beginning to keep up the appearance of being reluctant to punish the aged bishop and his noble companion, and there is record that when he heard of the latter's first refusal to abandon his beliefs, 'he sware a great oath [4].' But in spite of this there is every reason to think that he was the true cause of the ex-Chancellor's death. It is not likely that Henry would have consented to the execution of a man whom he

[1] Strype, Cranmer, vol. i. p. 39; vol. ii. p. 693.
[2] Cal. viii. 666.
[3] Cal. viii. 742, 876. Cf. also

Lewis, chaps. xxxiv, xxxv, and xxxvi.
[4] Cal. vii. 575.

had formerly loved and respected as much as More, unless his counsellor had poisoned his heart against him. Moreover, the mentions of More and Fisher in Cromwell's 'remembrances' are so frequent and of such a character, as to leave little doubt that he had determined to ruin them from the first. They both suffered death by beheading in the summer of 1535[1]. It was a terrible evidence of the ruthlessness of the forward policy to which Henry had now committed himself by the advice of his new minister. The most brilliant and cultivated Englishman of the time had been brought to the block to bear testimony to the King's relentless anger; the gentleness and humility of the oldest prelate in the realm had not shielded him from Henry's wrath and the swift, passionless blow of his all-powerful agent. Terror had mastered the country, and men wondered what the end would be[2].

But though Cromwell's truculent measures had gained the day in England, they excited the anger and horror of continental Europe. Sentence of excommunication had been passed on Henry in the summer of 1534; public opinion would not have permitted the Pope longer to postpone the final blow, even if he had wished to do so. It now became more than ever necessary to defend the position of the King, and Cromwell was busily occupied in filling the pulpit at Paul's Cross with preachers who were willing and able to expound the word of God to Henry's profit and advantage[3]. In this he was greatly helped by Bishop Rowland Lee of Coventry and Lichfield, who later played such an important part in connexion with the subjugation of Wales. In seeking means to defend the Royal Supremacy Cromwell's knowledge of the law stood him in good stead. In a letter written in the year 1538, Sir Thomas Denys tells how Cromwell three years earlier had advised him to 'rede in a boke called Bratton[4] nott vnwrittyn this cccc yer*es* where he doth call the

---

[1] Lewis, chap. xxxvii; Roper, 55.

[2] 'Obraua Cromuel, estas, y otras atrocidades libremente, dando á entender ser conueniencia del Principe, para la estabilidad de su Corona, sujecion, y terror en los vassallos.' Mendez Silva, p. 13.

[3] Letters, 197.

[4] Henry de Bracton's De Legibus et Consuetudinibus Angliae.

Kinge*s* Grace *Vicarius Christi*, . . . . wherfor,' he continues,
' I do rekyn a papiste and a traito*ur* to be one thing [1].'   But
the most drastic of the measures which Cromwell adopted to
strengthen the power of the Crown was the famous Act
about Proclamations, which he was able to force the Lords
and Commons to pass in 1539.   By this statute, all Proclamations made by the King and Council were given the force
of Acts passed in Parliament, save when they touched the
subject's lives, lands, goods, or liberties, or infringed the established laws ; and these exceptions were expressly declared
inapplicable to those who should disobey proclamations concerning heresy.   Cromwell had planned for the passage of this
statute from a period at least as early as 1535.   A letter [2]
which he wrote to Norfolk in July of that year affords us
interesting information concerning the origin of the measure.
In a controversy about the best means of preventing the
export of coin from the realm, the Chief Justice had delivered
the opinion that ' For the avoyding of any suche daungers . . .
proclamacyons and polyces so deuysyd by the King & his
cownsayll for any such purpose sholde be of as good effect as
Any law made by parlyament or otherwyse [3].'   The Chief

---

[1] Cal. xiii. (i) 120.

[2] Letters, 107.

[3] The following passage from a
letter which Gardiner wrote to the
Protector Somerset in the reign of
Edward VI gives a slightly dif-
ferent account of the origin of the
Act about Proclamations :—

' Whether the King may command against the Common Law
or an Act of Parliament there is
never a Judge, or other man in the
realm, ought to know more by experience of that the Lawyers have
said, than I . . . being of the Council, when many Proclamations were
devised against the Carriers out of
Corn ; when it came to punishing
the Offenders the Judges would
answer, it might not be by the Laws,
because the Act of Parliament gave

liberty, Wheat being under a price :
wherupon at the last followed the
Act of Proclamations, in the passing
whereof were many large words.'

It will be noticed that this account of the origin of the Act is
in many ways similar to that contained in Cromwell's letter : the
chief difference being that according to the latter the measure was
adopted to prevent the export of
*coin*, while Gardiner informs us that
the statute was devised to prevent
the export of *corn*.   It is possible
that the Bishop of Winchester,
writing so many years later, had
forgotten the exact circumstances,
and was really referring to the
same incident as that described
by Cromwell.   Burnet has printed
Gardiner's letter in full (Collection

Justice probably came to this decision at a hint from Cromwell ; in any case the latter saw that the good work which had been already begun could not be considered complete until the opinion expressed had been given legal form. From this time onward there occur in his ' remembrances ' frequent mentions of an Act to be passed in Parliament to this effect, but the measure proposed was so radical, that with all his energy and unscrupulousness, it was four years before he was able to carry it through [1].

of Records and Original Papers, &c., part ii, book i, no. 14), but he does not seem to have made use of the information it contains ; for in another part of his work (part i, book iii, p. 423) he asserts that the Act about Proclamations was the result of the great exceptions made to the legality of the King's proceedings in the articles about religion and other injunctions published by his authority, which were complained of as contrary to law. Hallam (vol. i. p. 35 n.) apparently agrees with Burnet in this last statement, and ignores the evidence supplied by the letter of the Bishop of Winchester. It is probable that both writers have gone astray in this matter. The opposition aroused by the King's ecclesiastical proclamations may have hastened the passage of the Act, but they can scarcely be regarded as its origin in the face of the testimony of Cromwell and Gardiner. Burnet and Hallam were perhaps led to ascribe the source of the statute to religious matters, by the fact that the Act was passed almost simultaneously with the Six Articles, and by the special provision which it contained concerning heretics.

[1] Canon Dixon (History of the Church of England, vol. ii. p. 129) sees in the Act about Proclamations ' a timid attempt to draw the prerogative within the limits of regular legislation,' and seeks to show that its true intent was to curtail, while legalizing, a power which the Crown had exercised hitherto illegally and without any restraint. It is doubtless true that the King had issued proclamations before, and had enforced obedience to them, without the sanction of law ; and it is equally certain that the intent of this Act (like that of so many others which Cromwell devised) was to legalize a privilege of which the Crown had already made use. But it is more difficult to agree with the reasoning by which Canon Dixon attempts to show that the true purpose of this process of legalization was to restrict and not to confirm the power of the King. It is pretty certain that the practical value of these limitations was in reality far less than at first appeared ; for, as Hallam and Burnet justly remark, the immediate effect of them was to confer great power on the judges, upon whom the duty of interpreting the statute devolved ; and the judges—mere puppets in the hands of Henry and Cromwell —were sure to render every verdict

It is scarcely necessary to state that a legislative body which could be forced to consent to such a statute as this retained in practice but few traces of that independence of the Crown which it theoretically possessed. The passage of the Act about Proclamations marks the culmination of a process begun long before Cromwell came into power, but only perfected at the close of his ministry, by which the subserviency of Parliament to the royal will was secured. But though the system did not reach its highest development until 1539, the earlier years of Cromwell's administration show such an advance over that of his predecessor in this particular, that we are justified in regarding the entire period of his ministry as the golden age of Tudor despotism. From the time that the Commons permitted the King and his counsellor to force on them the petition against the clergy in 1532, it is scarcely too much to say that the sole function of Parliament was to register the decrees which emanated from the royal council chamber.

Of course in order to render Parliament as 'tractable' as it was, it became necessary for Cromwell to regulate the choice of members for the King's profit, and the success of his endeavours in this direction is little short of marvellous. Royal interference in elections was certainly not unknown

in favour of the Crown. The exceptions in the Act about Proclamations may well be compared to the *Quantum per Christi legem licet*, which had been tacked on to the recognition of the King's Supremacy. Both were concessions granted merely as a sop to the popular feeling : both were so guarded that they could easily be rendered nugatory. Finally, the fact that Cromwell himself was so active in assisting the passage of this statute should be a conclusive proof that its real aim was not to legalize and limit, but to legalize and confirm the power of the Crown. The straightforward verdicts of Hume and Hallam on the true significance of the Act are certainly correct : 'The prerogative could not soar to the heights it aimed at, till thus imped by the perfidious hand of Parliament.' The fact that the statute was repealed in the first year of Edward VI simply proves that it was so unpopular that it was impossible to renew it, when the strong hand of Henry VIII had been removed. Cf. Hume, vol. iii. pp. 255, 256 ; Hallam, vol. i. p. 35 ; and Blackstone, vol. i. p. 269. There is a curious passage in Beowulf (ll. 67-73), in which the King rules as he wills, saving his subjects' lives and heritages, that is in striking congruence with this Act.

before his time, but it had not attained the proportions which it was destined to assume under Cromwell, and it was often strongly resented by the people. It was only with 'much difficulty,' that Henry VII, in the year 1506, succeeded in forcing the citizens of London to abandon the right to elect their own sheriff, which had been granted them by the charter of Henry I [1], and to accept the royal nominee to that office [2]. But thirty years later, the Crown had carried its encroachment on the popular liberties so far that it seemed to be usually regarded as a matter of course that a royal nomination should take the place of a fair election. If any protest was raised against Henry's palpable infringement of ancient rights—and this was very rarely the case—the King and his minister affected to regard the complaint with a sort of indignant amazement. Let us examine the details of an election in Canterbury, which took place when Cromwell was at the height of his power. Writs had been issued for the choice of two members to Parliament from that city in early May, 1536. Between eight and nine in the morning of the eleventh of that month, the sheriff, John Hobbys, caused the commonalty of Canterbury to assemble in the accustomed place, where John Starky and Christopher Levyns were duly elected burgesses. After the voters had dispersed, about noon-time, John Alcok, the mayor of Canterbury, came to Sheriff Hobbys in great perplexity, with a letter from Cromwell and Audeley, which desired, on the King's behalf, that Robert Derknall and John Bryges 'shulde fulfill the seid

---

[1] Stubbs, Const. Hist., vol. i. p. 439.

[2] 'William Copingar, Thomas Johnson, Sherifes. These Sherifes being on the morrow after Michaelmas day by the Maior and Aldermen presented before the Barons of the Exchequer, only William Copingar was admitted and sworne, but Thomas Johnson they woulde not admitte till they knew farther of the Kings pleasure. The x of October a commandment was brought from the King to the Lord Maior that he should cause an election to bee made for a new Sheriffe, at which day, came into the Guild Hall Mayster Edmond Dudley the Kings President, and there shewed the King's letters, that his commons shoulde name for the Kings pleasure, William Fitz William, to bee Sheriffe for the peace ensuing, which with much difficulty at length was granted, which William Fitz William kept his feast the Sixteenth day of October.' Stow's Chronicle, p. 879.

rom*es*.' On the following morning the sheriff directed a humble
letter to Cromwell[1], stating the facts, and begging that the
election of Starky and Levyns might be allowed to stand, as
the King's wishes were not known until too late; 'if your seid
l*ette*re had come to me byfore the seid eleccion,' he pleaded,
'I wolde haue done the best that had been in my powr to
⟨have⟩ Accomplished our Souereigne lord the King*es* pleasure
and y*our*s in the pr*e*mysses.'   But the King's minister gave
no heed to the representations of John Hobbys: the fact that
an election had already been held did not trouble him in the
least: the King's will was to be accomplished at all costs.
On May 18 he addressed a significant letter to the Mayor
and Burgesses of Canterbury, which was quite sufficient
to induce the recipients to nullify their former proceedings.
The phraseology of the letter is noteworthy: the King's
minister did not discuss the fact that his first message had
arrived too late.   He simply reminded the burgesses that the
King's pleasure had been signified to them, and that they
'the same litle or nothynge regardynge but rather co*n*temn-
y*n*g' had elected their own candidates, according to their
'owne wylles and myndes co*n*trarie to the king*es* plesure and
comandeme*n*t in that behalfe.'   This of course was a thing
whereat the King did 'not a lytell marvell,' and the burgesses
were admonished 'notwythstondynge the seyd elecc*i*on' to
'pr*o*cede to a new and electe thosse other, accordyng to the
tenure of the former l*ette*res': they were also desired to notify
Cromwell at once 'if any p*er*sone wyll obstynatly gaynsay
the same,' so that the King's minister might deal with the
refractory burgess according to his master's pleasure.   Two
days later Mayor Alcok replied with the following dutiful
letter.   'In humble Wise certefie you that the xx[th] Day
of this pr*e*sent monyth of Maye at vi of the Clok in the
mornyng I John Alcok mayre of Cauntebury receyved your
lett*e*re Dyrected to me the seid mayre Sheryf and Comynaltie
of the seid Citie sygnyfying to vs therby the kyng*es* plesure
and co*m*maundement is that Robert Darknall and John
Bryges shoulde be burgesses of the P*a*rlyament for thesame

---

[1] Cal. x. 852.

Citie of Cauntebury by Vertue wherof accordyng to our bounde Dutye immedyatly vppon the syght of your seid *lette*re and conten*tes* thereof *per*ceyved caused the Comynaltye of the seid Citie to Assemble in the Court Hall ther wher appered the nombre of Fower score and xvii *per*sones Citizens and Inhabit*au*ntes of theseid Citie And accordyng to the Kyng*es* plesure and Co*m*maundement frely with one voyce and wi*th*out any contradiccon haue elected and chosen the fore-seid Robert Darkenall and John Bryges to be burgesses of the *par*lyament for thesame Citie which shalbe duly certefied by Indenture vnder the seales of the seid Citizens and Inhabytaun*tes* by the grace of the blyssyd Trynyte Who *preser*ue you . . .[1].' Such was the calm way in which parliamentary suffrage rights were made of no effect and the King's pleasure enforced. It is important to notice in this connexion how careful Henry and Cromwell were to cloak their most unwarrantable proceedings by the preservation of ostensible constitutionalism. Never was the now farcical form of a fair election abandoned ; never did the King fail outwardly to observe those legal restrictions by which the Crown was supposedly fettered, and the liberties of the nation theoretically preserved. The autocracy which Cromwell had done so much to establish was carried on 'within and upon the already existing constitution,' and the public protest was thus in great measure disarmed.

It is no wonder that the invaluable services which Cromwell rendered to the Crown were rewarded by an almost exclusive

---

[1] The letter of Cromwell to the Mayor and Burgesses of Canterbury (Letters, 148) is now in the British Museum ; it was put into my hands by the kindness of Mr. Brodie of the Public Record Office. It was overlooked at the time of the compilation of the tenth volume of the Calendar, and escaped the search of Froude and Friedmann, both of whom discuss the details of this election at some length. Its discovery throws much fresh light on the history of one of the most famous cases of arbitrary interference in the choice of members to Parliament that has come down to us from Tudor times. The reply of the Mayor (Cal. x. 929) is comparatively well known. Froude has printed it in full (vol. iii. p. 347), but has misread the name of one of the burgesses, which is 'Darkenall' or 'Derknall,' not 'Sacknell.'

enjoyment of the royal confidence, which enabled him soon
to do almost what he pleased with his two great rivals,
Norfolk and Gardiner. At first he had cautiously held himself aloof from these men, but now that he had outstripped
them in the King's favour, his bearing towards them altered
accordingly. It is a very significant fact that in his ten years
of service, he never left the King for any considerable length
of time, but often contrived to get Norfolk and Gardiner sent
away—the one to cope with internal troubles, the other to act
as ambassador to France. Cromwell succeeded in harassing
them both while they were at Court, and in making them
abandon every pretence to consistency. Chapuys, in a letter
of December 9, 1533, tells us that Norfolk, hitherto the most
pronounced of Catholics, uttered 'a thousand blasphemies'
against the Pope, even more shocking than those of the King,
calling him 'an unhappy whoreson, a liar, and a wicked man;
and that it should cost him (Norfolk) wife and children . . . . .
and all that he possessed, or that he would be revenged on him.
He has a good deal changed his tune, for it was he . . . . who
favoured most the authority of the Pope ; but he must act in
this way not to lose his remaining influence, which apparently
does not extend much further than Cromwell wishes ; for which
reason, I understand, he is wonderfully sick of the Court[1].'
In the spring of 1535 the Duke was forced to surrender
entirely, and retire to his estate at Kenninghall. Gardiner
had to abandon the Secretaryship in 1534 in Cromwell's
favour. The new minister tantalized him in much the same
way as he did Norfolk, and doubtless increased the enmity
of the Bishop of Winchester, which he had first incurred
at the time of Wolsey's fall, and which five years later
was to be such an important factor in effecting his own
destruction.

Cromwell was perhaps the only man at the Court who, in
the early days of his ministry, had the least suspicion that
Anne Boleyn might sometime lose the royal favour. He
was able to comprehend the King's love for her better than
anyone else, and to discern that when the royal passion had

[1] Cal. vi. 1510.

been satisfied, Henry's affection for his second wife would be a thing of the past. The King's chagrin that Anne had not brought him a male child, and the rage awakened by her subsequent miscarriage could not have escaped him. From thenceforth he must have become convinced that her ruin was ultimately certain, and he began to throw out hints that he no longer wished to be reckoned among her adherents. In April, 1536, it was notorious that there was a marked coolness between them, and a month later a very unexpected turn in foreign affairs brought matters to a head and forced him to take active measures against her, in order to save his own reputation with the King [1]. There is reason to think that he was the prime mover in the plot which led to her arrest. He certainly worked against her at her trial, and was present at her execution; in fact he took every possible step to forestall all chances of being included in her fall. His sudden abandonment of one whom a few years before he had done so much to support, should be enough to confute those who have seen in his previous devotion to the cause of Anne Boleyn an evidence that he favoured the Reformed faith. Anne was certainly a professed Protestant; she possessed the English Bible and read it; but it was only because her Protestantism was temporarily useful to Cromwell's designs, which were to obtain for his master a divorce from Katherine, that he identified himself with her party during the first years of his ministry. When the divorce had been secured, and Henry had been declared Supreme Head of the Church of England; when the love which Anne had once enjoyed had been transferred to Jane Seymour, and Cromwell saw that to favour the cause of the unhappy Queen in opposition to the King might mean ruin and disgrace, he deserted her at once.

Nor can the fact that Cromwell's name figures prominently in connexion with the publication of the Ten Articles of 1536 be justly urged as a reason for ascribing to him any real devotion to the cause of Protestantism. Now that the

---

[1] Cal. x. 351, 601, 1069, and footnote to page 232. Cf. also Froude, The Divorce of Catherine of Aragon, pp. 413-5.

severance from Rome was complete, the King and his minister saw that a definition of the faith of the Church of England had become necessary, in order that the unity of the new ecclesiastical system might be preserved. The Ten Articles of 1536 were adopted to make good this deficiency. Circumstances had rendered them inevitable, and the fact that Cromwell presented them to Convocation, and signed them first of all the members proves nothing, except perhaps the importance of his ecclesiastical office. The Ten Articles declared the Bible and the three Creeds to be the only Rule of Faith : Penance, Baptism, and the Eucharist were kept as sacraments : the veneration of saints, soliciting of their intercession, use of images, and the usual ceremonies in the service, though still held to be highly profitable, and as such worthy to be retained, were pronounced in themselves powerless to justify the soul[1]. But though the main aim of these Articles was doubtless to preserve the integrity of the Church of England at home, the time and circumstances under which they were published seem to indicate that they were also intended to serve a purpose abroad. We shall hear of them in this connexion in another chapter.

Cromwell's zeal for the publication of the Bible in English, and also his injunctions to the clergy[2], must in the same way be attributed to political rather than to religious motives. He saw what a powerful weapon the Bible had become in the hands of the German Reformers, and soon succeeded in forcing Convocation, on December 19, 1534, to present a petition to the King for the suppression of treasonable books in the vulgar tongue, and for a translation of the Scriptures into English[3]. Less than two years later Cromwell's efforts were rewarded by the appearance of an edition of the Scriptures patched together ' out of Douche[4] and Latyn' by his friend Miles Coverdale. There seems to have been a very general impression current that all passages which might have been interpreted in favour of Katherine, had purposely been rendered in the opposite

---

[1] Wilkins, vol. iii. p. 817.
[2] Letters, 159, 266, 273.
[3] Cal. vii. 1555.
[4] ' High Dutch' not ' Low Dutch.'

sense [1]. But this version was soon destined to be superseded. The following year witnessed the appearance of the edition which is usually known as Matthew's Bible, and which consisted of a combination of the translations of Tyndale and Coverdale. It received the official sanction of Cromwell and Cranmer, but its life was almost as short as that of its predecessor. In the autumn of 1537 Grafton and Whitchurch, two London printers whose names had been connected with the previous editions, received a licence from the King to publish a new version of the Bible at Paris, where the facilities for carrying on their trade were better than in England [2]. At first the work seems to have progressed with great success, and in September, 1538, the King's minister, in anticipation of its speedy completion, issued injunctions that a copy of it should be placed in every church at the cost of the parson and the parishioners, and that no one was to be discouraged from reading it: he advised, however, that 'the explication of obscure plac*es*' be referred 'to men of higher iugement in scripture [3].' But Cromwell was a little premature with his injunctions. An unforeseen event occurred, which made the immediate publication of the new edition impossible. The Royal Inquisition had apparently got wind of the doings of Grafton and Whitchurch at Paris, and just as the task was approaching completion, they and all their subordinates, and the French printer at whose house the work was being carried on, were suddenly cited to appear before the Inquisitor-General for the realm of France [4]. The Englishmen made haste to escape, without even waiting to collect the implements of their trade or the Bibles that had already been printed. Cromwell, on hearing of the disaster, went with a piteous tale to the French ambassador, telling him that he himself had contributed 600 marks towards the publication of the Bible in Paris, and begging him to ask his master to permit the work to be continued there, or at least to allow the copies already

---

[1] Cal. x. 352, 698; xiv. (i) 186(v).
[2] Cal. xii (ii), Appendix 35, and xii. (ii) 593.
[3] Letters, 273.          [4] Cal. xiii. (ii) 1085.

finished to be sent to England safely, and not to suffer the Inquisition to confiscate them. But Francis replied that good things might be printed in England as well as in France, but that bad things should never be permitted to be printed in Paris, and he further refused to deliver up the copies already completed. He was unable, however, to prevent the final accomplishment of the work in London in 1539 [1]. The new version, commonly known as the Great Bible, was the last authorized translation completed in the reign of Henry VIII, but apparently great efforts had to be made to prevent the publication of unlicensed editions. It was not long before a royal commission was issued to Cromwell, commanding him, in order to avoid diversity of translations, to see that no man printed any English Bible during the next five years except persons deputed by himself [2].

Perhaps the strongest point of Cromwell's domestic administration was his financial policy. He never forgot the promise he had made on entering the King's service to make Henry 'the richest king that ever was in England,' for he was shrewd enough to see that a full treasury was the first essential to the attainment of the larger aim of his policy, the establishment of a royal despotism. He skilfully contrived that many of the measures of the earlier years of his ministry, primarily intended to cut the bonds which held England to Rome, should also serve to increase the wealth of the Crown. The most noteworthy and successful of these measures was the abolition of the Annates. There can be little doubt that it was through Cromwell's agency that a supplication was addressed to the King early in the year 1532 [3] urging him to arrest the payment of First Fruits to the Papacy: 'bokes of annates' and remembrances concerning

---

[1] Cal. xiii. (ii) 1163; xiv. (i) 37, 371. Dixon, vol. ii. p. 77, and Eadie, vol. i. p. 360.

[2] Rymer, vol. xiv. p. 659.

[3] Wilkins, vol. iii. p. 760. It is not clear whether this petition was put forth in the name of Convo-cation or of Parliament. But the question is of minor importance: it is safe to say that neither body originated the Supplication, but that it was forced upon the Commons or the clergy by the King or his minister.

them are to be found in large numbers among the minister's letters and papers[1], and the petition by which the measure to abolish the First Fruits was initiated was a method especially characteristic of him, reminding us in many respects of the way in which the independence of the clergy had been attacked but a short time before. But the King was very cautious in granting the request, which had thus been laid before him. He had not yet given up all hope of a peaceful solution of his difficulty with the Pope, and was not yet prepared, as Cromwell was, openly to defy the Holy See. So at first he determined to try the effect of a threat. The immediate result of Cromwell's efforts was the passage in Parliament of an Act[2] which abolished Annates, but preserved to the Holy See certain payments on bulls obtained for the election of bishops : the ratification of this statute by the Crown, however, was expressly withheld, and the Act consequently remained inoperative, while a post was sent to Rome ' to frighten the Pope about the Annates[3].' But this plan failed : Clement refused to be terrorized into submission ; the King became convinced that a complete break was inevitable, and, in July, 1533, the Act was ratified and declared in force by letters patent[4]. The following year saw the passage of another statute, which abolished all the payments preserved by the exceptions to the Act of 1532[5], and a little later Parliament completed the work which Cromwell had forced it to undertake by annexing the Annates to the Crown[6]. Supplementary to these statutes was the Act concerning Peter's Pence and Dispensations[7], by which the Pope was deprived of all contributions that had not already been arrested by the Acts about Annates. The use to which the rescued funds were put is aptly described by a significant ' remembrance ' of Cromwell's to the effect that ' thenhabitauntes and peple of this realme shall pay yerely vnto the

---

[1] Cal. vi. 299 (ix. x), 1381. In one place occurs the significant item ' To Remembre to make a byll for the parlyament touching the augmentacyon of the Annattes.' British Museum, Titus B. i. 421.

[2] 23 Hen. VIII, c. 20.
[3] Cal. v. 879.
[4] Cal. vi. 793.
[5] 25 Hen. VIII, c. 20.
[6] 26 Hen. VIII, c. 3.
[7] 25 Hen. VIII, c. 21.

kyng for ever, in lieu or stede of smoke pence, whiche they were wont to pay to the busshop of rome, for euery hed or house a certayne small thyng for and towardes the defense of thys Realme, whiche may be ymployed in makyng of forteresses throughout the Realme[1].' Another significant paragraph, from a letter of Chapuys to Charles V, of Dec. 19, 1534, reads as follows: 'The King, besides the 30,000 pounds which he newly obtained from the clergy, and an ordinary fifteenth from the laity, which was granted him last year, and which may amount to 28,000 pounds, has just imposed a tax by authority of Parliament, of the twentieth penny of all the goods of his subjects, and that foreigners shall pay double, which will amount to a great sum. These are devices of Cromwell, who boasts that he will make his master more wealthy than all the other princes of Christendom: and he does not consider that by this means he alienates the hearts of the subjects, who are enraged and in despair, but they are so oppressed and cast down, that without foreign assistance it is no use their complaining, and it will not be Cromwell's fault, if they are not oppressed further[2].'

The King's minister also appears to have been much occupied with the coinage. He was constantly present at 'assayes' of gold and silver, and further took active steps to stamp out the counterfeiters, of whom there appear to have been a great number[3]. He caused a proclamation to be issued 'for the false and clipped Coyne going in this Realme with a greate punyshment to euery person that is founde with any false or counterfeit moneye.' The systematic debasement of the currency that disgraced the reign of Henry VIII had begun under Wolsey, but appears to have ceased entirely during Cromwell's ministry: it began again after Cromwell's death, assuming far greater proportions than before, and continued till the end[4]. That the King did not need to resort to such costly methods of replenishing his

---

[1] Cal. ix. 725 (1).  [2] Cal. vii. 1554.
[3] Cal. vii. 1304; ix. 144, 183; x. 1170; xii. (ii), 1151.
[4] Schanz, vol. i. pp. 535-7.

treasury while Cromwell was in power, bears eloquent testimony to the wisdom and success of his minister's finance. The latter's efforts to prevent the 'conveying of coyne out of the realme' shows that he saw the importance of securing plenty of good coin for English trade, and that he did not want to create an artificial cheapness. The statutes of Henry VII forbidding the export of precious metals had been renewed by his son in an Act passed in 1511, but this law had run out in 1523, and from that time onward there was no legal hindrance to the practice, though the statutes enacted previous to Tudor times were still considered in force [1]. The result was that the earlier laws began to be transgressed, and Cromwell, in devising methods to prevent further infringements of them, hit upon the expedient of a royal proclamation, as we have already had occasion to notice.

Another most important measure passed during Cromwell's ministry, was the so-called Statute of Uses [2]. It was at the same time a legal and a financial reform. In order to evade the common law, which prohibited testamentary disposition of landed property and rendered it strictly subject to primogeniture, the custom had long been prevalent that the owner should name before or at his death certain persons to whose 'use' his lands should be held. These persons became to all intents and purposes the true devisees ; for though the trustee, or 'feoffee to uses,' alone was recognized by the common law, the beneficiary or 'cestui que use' soon began to receive strong support through the equitable jurisdiction of the Chancellor, and so was often able actually to enforce claims which originally had rested merely on moral obligation. This was the usual method of circumventing the laws of the realm, in order to make provision by will for younger children. In this particular it was perhaps legitimate, but at the same time it opened the way to a great number of abuses, which are stated at length in the preamble to the statute just mentioned. The chief of these were the extraordinary com-

---

[1] Schanz, vol. i. p. 518.
[2] 27 Hen. VIII, c. 10. Cf. also on this and the following pages

Digby, pp. 267–80, and Reeves, vol. iii. pp. 275–89.

plication of titles to land, which resulted from the secret methods of devising it, and the loss to the King and the great lords of the feudal dues on successions, wardships, and marriages. Two ineffectual attempts had been made to remedy these evils in the reigns of Richard III and Henry VII [1], and at Cromwell's accession to power, the subject was brought up again.' There is reason to think that the Statute of Uses was under consideration as early as 1531, and the main principle of it bears a close resemblance to the measure devised in the reign of Richard III. A mention of it occurs in Cromwell's 'remembrances' of the year 1535 [2], but it was not finally passed until 1536, probably on account of the popular opposition, which, according to Chapuys, was very pronounced. The upshot of the statute was, that all right to the estate was taken from the grantee to uses and vested in the beneficiary, and the distinction between legal and beneficial ownership was thus entirely destroyed. The ostensible tenant was made in every case the legal tenant ; those entitled to the use of land became the actual holders of it. The Act further was intended to abolish the right to create further uses in the future : the power of disposing of interests in land by will was thus removed, and the King was restored to the enjoyment of his ancient feudal dues.

Beyond the casual mention in his 'remembrances [3]' there is no precise record of Cromwell's connexion with this important measure. It is worthy of note, however, that the attainments needed to plan and draft such a statute were precisely those which Cromwell possessed in the very highest degree—intimate knowledge of the law, and great shrewdness in finance. The bold and effective way in which the measure struck at the root of the evil, and caused the extra-legal practice which had grown up to become its own ruin, is very characteristic of him. Furthermore, Cromwell was certainly believed to be the originator of the measure by the rebels in the Pilgrimage of Grace, which was partially

---

[1] 1 Rich. III, c. 1 ; 4 Hen. VII, c. 17.

[2] Cal. viii. 892.

[3] Cal. viii. 892 ; ix. 725.

caused by it, and as such his death was demanded. It therefore seems highly probable that it was he who devised this scheme in order to deal the death blow to a very annoying practice of evading the law, and to enrich the royal treasury. The statute, however, was not entirely successful in attaining the ends at which it aimed, for by a strained interpretation of the letter of the Act, the courts managed to evade the spirit of it, so that it failed to do away with the old distinction between beneficial and legal ownership, which it had been intended to destroy. In addition to this, the popular outburst of indignation aroused by the Statute of Uses was so strong that a few months before Cromwell's death he saw the actual right of at least partial testamentary disposition of landed property obtained by the people. The Act concerning the willing of land by testament[1], passed in the spring of 1540, gave to every tenant in fee simple the right to bequeath at his pleasure all lands which he held by socage tenure, and two-thirds of the lands which he held by knight-service. The force of usage was such that when the King and Cromwell attempted to abolish a practice, which had rendered the willing of land possible under another name, the actual right to bequeath landed property without circumventing the law was wrested from them.

The King was glad to entrust his capable adviser with the preservation of that advantageous commercial position which had been won for England through the masterful policy of Henry VII. Cromwell's varied experience in foreign markets and his intimate knowledge of all the details of the wool-trade, which was by far the most important element of English commerce, had taught him in his earlier years many lessons of which the whole nation was to reap the benefit. In general his administration witnessed but few departures from the highly successful commercial policy inaugurated by the first Tudor. His aim was rather to strengthen the advantages already gained, and to increase the security of English commerce and industry against the competition of continental rivals, than to attempt any radical

---

[1] 32 Hen. VIII, c. 1.

innovations. The monopoly of the trade in the Mediterranean which Venice had enjoyed in Lancastrian times, had been a serious menace to the interests of the English merchants ; but the Italian wars had now almost totally deprived the Republic of that prominent political position which she had occupied at the beginning of the century, and with the loss of her national greatness her commercial supremacy fell. The ancient privileges which had been granted to Venetian merchants and galleys previous to Tudor times, had been exchanged for a set of stringent enactments, which dealt a heavy blow to her trade and shipping during the reign of Henry VII. Cromwell followed the same policy, and further seized the favourable opportunity afforded by Venice's decline to foster the interests of English merchants in other parts of the Mediterranean [1]. With the towns of the Hanseatic League the case was slightly different. The extensive privileges the merchants of the North German cities had enjoyed in earlier times, had raised them to such a commanding position that the growth of English commerce in the north was rendered well-nigh impossible. Henry VII's aim had been to overthrow the supremacy of the Hanseatic League, by a gradual withdrawal of the concessions which it had wrung from his predecessors. The early part of his son's reign had witnessed a continuation of this wise policy, but during Cromwell's ministry an alliance which the threatening situation on the Continent had led England to conclude with Lübeck, necessitated a temporary cessation of the process of curtailing the privileges of the Hanse merchants [2]. But the loud outcries of the people against the destructive competition of the Germans were sufficient to prevent Cromwell from making any permanent stand in their favour. Political necessity alone had induced him to postpone the complete withdrawal of their privileges : he knew that the tendency of the times was irresistibly against the Hanseatic towns, and he was perhaps the more willing to grant them a few temporary concessions in that he realized that nothing could ever raise them again to the position of

---

[1] Schanz, vol. i. pp. 159, 160.        [2] Cf. Schanz, vol. i. pp. 224-7.

dangerous rivals to English trade. His foresight was justified
by the event; the process which Henry VII had begun was
completed by the fall of the Steelyard in the reign of
Elizabeth. A more difficult problem was presented by the
Netherlands. England and the Low Countries were com-
mercially indispensable to each other; the English wool-
market in Flanders was the centre of the mercantile interests
of both nations. The merchants of the Netherlands, however,
had contrived to get the better of their English neighbours
until the accession of the house of Tudor; but the concessions
which resulted from the temporary removals of the English
wool-mart from Antwerp to Calais by Henry VII, and the
enormously advantageous commercial treaty which that King
was able to wring from the Archduke Philip when fortune
had thrown the latter into his hands in 1506, had completely
altered the situation to England's profit[1]. The efforts of
Henry VIII and Wolsey had been directed towards preserving
the provisions of the agreement of 1506, the validity of which
the Netherlanders were of course unwilling to acknowledge.
Cromwell went further than this; his administration witnessed
not only the maintenance and increase of all the advantages
which his predecessor had secured, but also the discussion
of a plan for attaining complete commercial independence of
the Low Countries, by bringing home the English wool-mart
to London[2]. This scheme was not carried through, owing to
the unwillingness of the King to offend the Emperor; but the
news of the proposals for it was soon known in the Netherlands, and was not without its effect there. The merchants
of the Low Countries were greatly alarmed lest they should
lose the English trade, and instead of opposing every move
which their rivals made, now began to grant them all possible
concessions. The Emperor's dread of alienating Henry also
contributed to force them to adopt a more conciliatory attitude
than ever before, and it may be justly said that at the close
of Cromwell's administration the mercantile relations of
England and the Netherlands were so regulated as to secure
every advantage for the former. Cromwell's whole commercial

---

[1] Busch, vol. i. p. 149.    [2] Schanz, vol. i. pp. 76–86, 107–8.

policy was strongly influenced by his desire to increase
and improve English shipping, especially at the last, when
an invasion was threatened from the Continent[1].   His
'remembrances' are filled with items for appropriations for
building and rigging vessels of various kinds, and for making
and improving harbours[2].   He did his utmost to clear the
Channel of pirates, and was diligent in writing letters to
demand restitution of goods taken from English merchants at
sea[3].   In 1540 he caused an Act to be passed for the
'maintenance of the navy[4]': one of its provisions restricted
the privileges conferred on all foreign merchants by a proclamation in the previous year[5] to those who transported
their wares in English ships.

Throughout Cromwell's 'remembrances' occur countless
minor items dealing with miscellaneous questions of internal
reform.   Memoranda for the building and improvement of
roads and highways, for bettering the state of the coast
defences, and for the regulation of the rates of wages, are
especially numerous.   In 1538 he aided Norfolk in suppressing
a sort of strike among the Wisbech shoemakers, who had
agreed to stop work unless their wages were raised from
15$d$. to 18$d$. per dozen boots sewed[6].   It is perhaps unnecessary to state that this strike was regarded as a revolt
against authority, and that the masters gained an easy victory
over the men.   Among Cromwell's injunctions to the clergy
in 1538 is an order to keep parish registers of births, marriages,
and deaths[7].   Apparently this measure was intensely unpopular, especially in the south-west of England, where
people seem to have got the notion that 'some charges more
than hath been in time past shall grow to them by this
occasion of registering of these things[8].'   Precisely what the
immediate object of the injunction was it is difficult to say,

---

[1] Schanz, vol. i. pp. 372–4.
[2] Cal. xiv. (i) 399, 655.
[3] Letters, 74, 190, 213.
[4] 32 Hen. VIII, c. 14.
[5] This proclamation, issued Feb.
26, 1539, decreed that for seven
years 'straungers shall paye like

custome and subsidy as the king*es*
subiects.' British Museum, Titus B.
i. 572.
[6] Cal. xiii. (ii) 57, 84, 91.
[7] Letters, 273.
[8] Dixon, vol. ii. p. 83.

though there is little reason to think that the fears it aroused among the people of Cornwall and Devonshire were realized. It has been grudgingly applauded by one writer, and characterized as 'an inadequate attempt to supply the loss of the registers of various kinds which had been kept by the monks [1]'; but its inadequacy, however great, might well pass unmentioned, in the face of the many benefits which later resulted from it. However unpopular the measure may have been at the time, its author certainly deserves the thanks of posterity for preserving a vast amount of valuable information which would otherwise have been lost.

A few words remain to be added concerning Cromwell's zeal for the advancement of learning. As his political schemes had caused him incidentally to take sides with the Reformation, his object was to strengthen those who favoured the new religion and opposed Rome. Education is necessary to reform ; and Cromwell did not intend to leave to ignorant men the task of carrying on the work he had begun. He therefore took steps to see that the opportunities for learning were improved. Among the injunctions which he issued to the clergy in 1536 [2], is a clause providing for an increased number of exhibitions at the schools and the Universities, 'to thintent that lerned men maye hereafter spring the more.' His dealings with Oxford and Cambridge do not seem to have been very important, although in June, 1535, he was appointed Chancellor of the latter in place of Fisher. He appears to have been much occupied in suppressing the various quarrels that constantly took place between the students and the townspeople, and the letters which he wrote to the Magistrates of Cambridge deal for the most part with this problem [3]. In October, 1535, the King appointed him Visitor to the University, and at the same time promulgated nine injunctions in which he directed the Chancellor, Masters and Scholars of Cambridge to abandon the 'frivolous questions and obscure glosses' of the schoolmen, to read and teach the Scriptures, and to swear to the Royal Supremacy and the new

---

[1] Dixon, vol. ii. p. 83.
[2] Letters, 159.
[3] Letters, 106, 116, 124, 129, 186, 206.

Succession [1]. Henry's minister, as usual, was the instrument employed to see that the injunctions were enforced. Of Cromwell's relations to Oxford still less remains to be said. There are letters from him concerning the admission of a President of Magdalen in 1535 [2], and the election of a Master of Balliol in 1539. The latter appears to have been a most disreputable character, and Cromwell's assertion that he was chosen without 'any parcyalyte or corruptyon' was certainly false [3]. A very interesting but comparatively well-known report from the pen of Dr. Layton gives us a vivid picture of the state of the University in 1535, and tells of the foundation of several new lectures at the various colleges [4].

As a reward for his success in the management of domestic affairs, the King conferred on him the many dignities and titles which, in 1536, marked the height of his power. He had been raised to the offices of Privy Councillor, Master of the Jewels, Clerk of the Hanaper, and Master of the King's Wards in 1531 and 1532. The Chancellorship of the Exchequer had followed in 1533. He became Principal Secretary to the King in 1534, Master of the Rolls in the same year, Vicar-general and Visitor-general of the Monasteries in January, 1535, Lord Privy Seal, Vicegerent of the King in Spirituals [5] in July, 1536. He was also created Baron Crom-

---

[1] Cooper, vol. i. pp. 374, 375. In the Calendar, ix. 615, these injunctions are apparently attributed to Cromwell. But Cooper expressly states that the King promulgated them, while Strype (Ecclesiastical Memorials, vol. i. (i) p. 322, and vol. i. (ii) pp. 218, 219) seems to think that they were drawn up by Legh and Ap Rice, though he admits that they were issued in the King's name. It seems very improbable then that Cromwell wrote them, and I have not placed them among the letters.

[2] Letters, 104, and Wilson, Magdalen College, p. 80.

[3] Letters, 325, 326. The name of the Master was George Cotes or

Cootes, formerly of Magdalen. He was Proctor in 1529. Davis, Balliol College, pp. 82-86; Wood, Fasti Oxonienses, pt. i. p. 86.

[4] Cal. ix. 350.

[5] On the Commissions to Cromwell as Vicar-general and Vicegerent cf. Burnet, vol. i. pp. 292-3 n., 342-3 n.; Collier, vol. ii. p. 104; Gutch, vol. ii. p. 192; Herbert, p. 202; Dixon, vol. i. pp. 244-247; Child, Church and State, pp. 78, 79. It is probable that the last writer has confounded the two commissions: certainly there is little reason to think that the title of Vicar-general was granted later than that of Vicegerent.

well of Okeham in the same month, and Knight of the Garter in August, 1537. During the last seven years of his ministry he was granted no less than nineteen minor offices, through which his income must have been very greatly increased[1]. Just prior to the outbreak of the Pilgrimage of Grace, Cromwell's position was almost that of a despot. He was supreme in Convocation, Privy Council, and Parliament ; he enjoyed paramount authority in the direction of internal affairs, and next to the King was by far the most important man in the realm.

A letter of Chapuys in the summer of 1536[2], soon after Anne Boleyn's execution, tells us that it was even rumoured that Cromwell might marry the Princess Mary, but the Imperial ambassador himself was too shrewd to be misled by such an improbable report[3]. Had Cromwell seriously entertained the idea of a union with the daughter of the divorced Queen, he would scarcely have permitted himself to be made use of by the King as an instrument for breaking down her resolution : he could scarcely have written her such a brutal letter as that of June 10, 1536[4]. But the inequality in rank is certainly in itself sufficient proof of the absurdity of the proposition. Cromwell was about the last man in the world to become

---

[1] See vol. ii. p. 283.

[2] Cal. xi. 41.

[3] An event which took place in July, 1536, may possibly have been the source of this rumour. It appears that Cromwell had a gold ring made, with the figures of the Queen, King, and Princess carved on it, and the following Latin inscription :—

' Obedientia unitatem parit,
  Unitas animi quietem et constantiam ;
  Constans vero animi quies thesaurus inestimabilis.
  Respexit humilitatem
  Qui in Filio nobis reliquit
  Perfectum humilitatis exemplar.
  Factus est obediens Patri.
  Et ipsa etiam natura parentibus
  Et patrie obediendum docuit.'

This ring he intended to bestow on the Princess Mary, but apparently the King got wind of the plan and put a stop to it, taking the ring away from his minister, on the plea that he desired to have the honour of presenting it to his daughter himself. The episode should have been sufficient to show that even if Cromwell had any idea of marrying the Princess, the King's opposition to the plan would prove insurmountable. The inscription on the ring, moreover, surely indicates that the gift was intended rather as a reminder to the Princess of her duty towards her father, than as a preliminary to a matrimonial proposal. Cal. xi. 148.

[4] Letters, 150.

reckless with success ; he never for a moment forgot his low birth, and the imprisonment of the brother of his rival the Duke of Norfolk for presuming to wed the King's niece was a warning of the danger of such a proceeding, which could not have been lost on him [1]. If such a proposition were put forward at all, and we cannot believe that it was, it could only have been as a pretext to prevent the Princess from leaving the realm and joining with her cousin the Emperor in an attempt to dethrone the King.

Cromwell was certainly shrewd enough to see that he could never hope to marry into a reigning house himself, but he was none the less anxious that his son Gregory should wed such a wife as would enable him to found a noble family. In April, 1533, Gregory had been taken from Cambridge, and sent to live with his father's friend Dr. Rowland Lee, with whom he appears to have spent a summer in hunting [2]. In 1535 he came out into public life, and in 1539 he was summoned to Parliament as a peer of the realm. Two years earlier he had been able to contract an advantageous marriage with the widow of Sir Anthony Ughtred, sister of Jane Seymour [3]. This fortunate match must be attributed to his father's influence, for Gregory seems to have been entirely without ambition, and such an idea would never have entered his mind ; his father, on the contrary, was precisely the man to think of it. The number of grants either made jointly to Cromwell and his son, or providing for the succession of the latter at his father's death [4], corroborates the theory that the King's great minister wished Gregory to be the heir of all his possessions and emoluments as far as might be, and desired to raise his family to a permanent position among the English nobility.

Of course Cromwell was obliged in large measure to abandon his private business after he definitely entered the King's service, but his new position brought him far greater riches than he could possibly have amassed in his old occupations. The various inventories of his goods indicate great wealth

---

[1] Cal. xi. 147.
[2] Cal. vi. 913, 981, 1011, 1014.
[3] Cal. xii. (ii) 423.
[4] As Cal. viii. 571.

and prosperity. He gave costly New Year's presents at the
Court, and owned several houses, all of them magnificently
furnished[1]. After October, 1534, when he was made Master of
the Rolls, his correspondence shows him to have been constantly in residence at the Rolls House, where he held his
Court. Writing in 1535, the Prioress of Little Marlowe
complained that so great was the crowd of his visitors there,
that it was impossible to gain access to him[2].

[1] Cal. ix. 478, 862 ; xiv. (i) 5.          [2] Cal. viii. 108.

# CHAPTER VIII

## IRELAND, WALES, SCOTLAND, CALAIS

THOUGH Cromwell was so busily occupied in England itself, he was far from neglecting the adjoining countries. The subjugation of Ireland, the pacification of Scotland, and the reform of Wales and Calais, played a very important part in his political programme. He plainly saw that the English King's position could not be regarded as secure while these countries remained in the state in which they were at Wolsey's fall, and he determined as soon as possible to deal with them in such a way that they should cease to be a menace to the English Crown in the future.

When he entered the King's service he probably found little difficulty in persuading Henry that, in order firmly to establish his supremacy, he must take Ireland in hand as he had never done before. Throughout Wolsey's administration the tranquillity of the country had been continually disturbed by the feuds of two rival Anglo-Norman families, the Fitzgeralds under the Earl of Kildare, and the Butlers under the Earl of Ormond. To repress these quarrels the Cardinal had taken the office of Lord Deputy from the young Earl of Kildare, and created the Earl of Surrey Lord Lieutenant. After a year's hard service in Ireland, however, Surrey was recalled at his own request, and the Deputyship devolved on Sir Piers Butler. He in turn was forced to resign his office to his rival Kildare, who passed it on to Sir William Skeffington of Leicestershire, just at the time of Wolsey's fall [1].

The affairs of Ireland had naturally been thrown into confusion by these numerous changes, and Cromwell became convinced that subjugation by the sword was absolutely essential, before any attempt could be made to govern the

[1] Bagwell, vol. i. pp. 124-52.

country, or to draw revenues from it. This policy brought him into collision with his rival Norfolk, but he seems to have succeeded in convincing the King of the superiority of his plan to that of the Duke, whose idea had been to conciliate the Irish chieftains, and to pacify rather than subjugate the country [1].

During his first two years in the King's service, Cromwell was so busy in establishing the Royal Supremacy, that he could not pay much attention to Irish affairs. The three years of Skeffington's administration, moreover, appear to have been fairly quiet. In 1532, however, a change came. The Earl of Kildare, by craftily misrepresenting Skeffington's doings at the English Court, secured the latter's recall, and obtained for himself the post of Lord Deputy for the third time [2]. On regaining the coveted office, however, he returned to Ireland, and instead of following out the King's instructions, proceeded to stir up his adherents into open rebellion, and neglected the English at Dublin. Unmindful of his 'hole duetie to the Kingis Highnes,' he used the royal authority deputed to him, 'as a cloke or habyte to cover his cruele persecutions, mynding utterly to extynguyshe the fame and honor of any other noble man within that lande [3].' It is possible that he thus served Henry's and Cromwell's ultimate purpose of subjugation better than he knew, as he certainly weakened the power of many of the wildest clans, who hated the English rule as much as his. But his use to the Crown in this direction, if it amounted to anything, was only temporary, and things became ripe for his dismissal. Continual complaints of him reached the King and Cromwell. Dublin was almost the only place in the country, which remained perfectly loyal to England. The neighbouring tribes were so hostile, that the citizens were hard put to it for food, and its inhabitants almost perished from starvation. John Deythyke, a priest, wrote sarcastically to a friend in the autumn of 1533, that although it was the custom to refrain from meat on Wednesdays as well as Fridays, provisions were so scarce

---

[1] Cal. vii. 1141.  [2] Bagwell, vol. i. pp. 152-5.
[3] State Papers, vol. ii. p. 167.

that people had become more devout still, and abstained also on Sundays, Mondays, Tuesdays, and Thursdays. 'This is a very sore abstenaunce . . . the country is so quiett that they dare nott ryde one myle owte of the towne, to by any maner of vytteyles; and they make there complaynt to the Deputie and the wynde hath blowen hym soo in the erys that he can nott here them. But yt is a comon sayinge "whoo is so defe as he that lyst not to here[1]."' Things went on from bad to worse, and finally John Alen, Master of the Rolls in Ireland, was sent over by the Council there to report Kildare's doings at the English Court, and further to submit to the King a set of articles for the reformation of the abuses which had become prevalent in the country[2]. Alen finally succeeded in procuring Kildare's recall; and the Deputy arrived in London in April, 1534, having left his eldest son, Lord Thomas Fitzgerald, in his place. Efforts were made to induce the young man to come to England also; and when he persistently refused to put himself into the King's hands, his father was arrested and sent to the Tower. These vigorous measures, according to Chapuys, were due to Cromwell; they were the beginnings of his policy of subjugation[3].

The arrest of Kildare, coupled with a premature report of his death, set half Ireland aflame, and his son, making up a slight quarrel he had had with his kinsmen the Desmonds threw off his allegiance. All the English were ordered out of the Geraldines' land before a certain day. The Archbishop of Dublin attempted to flee the country, but encountering a storm, was driven back on the Irish coast, fell into young Thomas' hands, and was murdered with most of his following[4]. A formidable revolt against the royal authority was evidently pending. Henry and Cromwell were seriously alarmed, and the extraordinary popularity of the rebellion among the people in England, who, as Chapuys said, thought it 'a very good beginning to remedy matters at home,' greatly increased their fears[5]. Cromwell had to bear the brunt of all the blame,

---

[1] State Papers, vol. ii. p. 180.
[2] Cal. vi. 1586.
[3] Cal. vii. 957, 1141.
[4] Cal. vii. 1057.
[5] Cal. vii. 1095.

and the Duke of Norfolk seized the opportunity to speak
ill of his successful rival.   According to Chapuys, the Duke
had 'left the Court to be away when the affairs of Ireland
were discussed, and this out of disdain that the King
despised his advice, and at the suggestion of Cromwell and
Skeffington had ill-treated the earl of Kildare, and ruined the
affairs of Ireland.   On this subject the Duke and Cromwell had reproached each other with many things . . . which
shows the ill-will they have borne each other a long time,
however much they have dissembled it[1].'   But Norfolk's
efforts to undermine the influence of his rival were as yet unavailing.   The time for pacific measures had now passed ;
Henry would have been only too glad to grant Kildare peace
on any terms, but the latter refused every offer.   Skeffington,
who was Cromwell's friend, was sent over again as Deputy to
quell the rebellion.   After many delays he crossed on the
14th of October, with troops which the King had secretly
raised for him[2].

Meantime the rebels had gained a decisive victory, and
were just outside the walls of Dublin.   Piteous entreaties
from the inhabitants, begging him to come to the relief of
the beleaguered city, reached Skeffington, and after some
delay he advanced.   His arrival made the rebels retreat,
but instead of pursuing them vigorously, and striking a telling
blow, he remained at Dublin, and wasted time in trying to
get a sentence of excommunication passed against the murderers of Archbishop Alen[3].   But in spite of the Deputy's
dallying inefficiency, the superiority of Cromwell's policy to
Norfolk's was destined to be made evident by succeeding
events.   A new complication in Irish affairs arose when
young Kildare, taking advantage of Skeffington's inactivity,
sent an embassy to the Emperor, promising to hold Ireland
as a fief of the Holy See, on condition that he would offer
him protection against the English schismatics.[4].   An ambassador, Dominick Power by name, was sent by Charles to
Ireland and Scotland, but Henry soon discovered it, and

[1] Cal. vii. 1141.              [3] Cal. vii. 1418.
[2] Cal. vii. 1193, 1257, 1366, 1389.      [4] Bagwell, vol. i. p. 172.

complained[1]; Charles was not quite ready as yet to do anything active in aid of the rebels, and so the affair came to nothing.  Meantime, at the request of Cromwell, Skeffington was induced to shake off his apathy, leave Dublin and Drogheda, and move after the rebels[2].  The Lord Privy Seal's boast that the young Kildare would soon be a prisoner in the Tower, was not as empty as Chapuys thought.  Maynooth Castle, a rebel stronghold, was besieged and taken[3]; many rebels were executed, others fell away from Kildare, the young Earl finally surrendered, and was sent a prisoner to London.  Two years later he was hanged with five uncles at Tyburn[4].  With his surrender other chieftains came to terms; many districts became comparatively quiet, and by the end of 1535 Ireland seemed further on the road to tranquillity than she had been for some time.  This was a significant triumph for Cromwell's policy over that of Norfolk, and did much to increase his influence with the King.  On the last day of December, 1535, Skeffington died, and Lord Leonard Grey was made Deputy in his place[5].

Before Cromwell could hope to derive much benefit from Ireland, it was necessary to establish some sort of government in the country, as well as to subjugate it.  To this intent, Lord Grey summoned a Parliament, which met at Dublin in the spring of 1536[6].  Its first act was to pass a bill securing the succession of Anne Boleyn's issue: the report of this came to Cromwell in London in June, two weeks after Anne's execution[7].  He must have been somewhat puzzled, when he heard the news; events were moving so rapidly, that even an 'ordered' Parliament could not keep pace with them.  He finally wrote back that in case the act for the succession was not 'passed thoroughly' they were to 'staye the same tyl further knowleage of his graces pleasure[8].'  It was too late, however, to do this; but when the report came that Anne had

---

[1] Cal. vii. 1297; viii. 140.
[2] Cal. vii. 1573, and Bagwell, vol. i. p. 173.      [3] Cal. viii. 448.
[4] Bagwell, vol. i. p. 180.      [5] Cal. x. 15 *n.*
[6] Cal. x. 822.      [7] Cal. x. 897, 937.
[8] Letters, 179.

been executed, and that Jane Seymour had become Queen, the
Parliament was ready enough at once to rescind the old statute,
and pass a new one in favour of the issue of Henry's third
wife. Later there were enacted a series of measures to loosen
the bonds that held the Irish Church to Rome[1], and George
Browne, Provincial of the Austin Friars, who had already
made himself useful in forcing the oath of succession on his
brethren in the south of England, was nominated in 1535,
by Cromwell's influence, to succeed Alen as Archbishop of
Dublin. The Deputy meantime carried on the subjugation steadily and consistently in the wilder portions of the
country.

Everything in Ireland was now proceeding to the complete
satisfaction of Henry and Cromwell, except the finances.
Few could equal Cromwell's ideal, or satisfy Henry's avarice
in this respect. Ireland had never paid its expenses before;
and it was largely in the hope of deriving revenue from
a land which had hitherto been only a burden, that the King
and his minister had undertaken to subjugate it. A letter
from Henry to the Deputy and Council in 1537 blames them
for taking excessive fees, thinking only of private gain, and
not taking care of the royal income[2]. To remedy this
Cromwell appointed and sent over Commissioners, who were
ordered to try to reduce expenses and increase revenue, and,
to this end, to inquire into the conduct of every royal officer
in Ireland, learn all the particulars of the local government,
and cut down the retinue of the Deputy and Treasurer to
340 men[3]. In the list of Commissioners occurs the name of
William Brabazon (Cromwell's old friend and fellow servant
under Wolsey), who later attained a very important position in Irish affairs. The extant letters of Cromwell to
the Commissioners deal for the most part with the adjustment
of petty land claims. The most interesting of them is the
one concerning the policy to be pursued towards 'that
traytor Bryan Oconor[4].'

There are significant depositions against some of these Com-

[1] Bagwell, vol. i. pp. 196, 197.
[2] Cal. xii. (i) 503.     [3] Cal. xii. (ii) 382.
[4] Letters, 198–205, 207, 208, 211, 212, 214, 215, 232.

missioners who dared to murmur at Cromwell's notorious
accessibility to bribes, which seems to have been more notice-
able in his dealings with Ireland than anywhere else. He
appears to have received enormous sums from the rich
and powerful family of the Butlers, kinsmen of Anne Boleyn
and of the Duke of Norfolk, in return for a promise to
protect their castles from the search of the royal agents.
There was a great deal of discontent among the Commissioners on account of his rapacity, and though they openly
flattered him, they continually spoke ill of him behind his
back. 'My Lorde Pryvee Seale hathe wrought to his awne
confusion and dethe,' said one, 'and of late tyme was veray
nere the same, and escapid veray narrowly . . . noo lorde or
gentilman in Englande berith love or favor to my Lorde
Pryvee Seale by cause he is soo great a taker of money, for
he woll speke, solicite, or doo for noo man, but all for money.
. . . I wold not be in his case for all that ever he hathe,
for the King beknaveth him twice a weke, and sometyme
knocke him well aboute the pate ; and yet when he hathe
bene well pomeld about the hedde, and shaken up, as it
were a dogge, he will come out into the great chambre,
shaking of the bushe with as mery a countenaunce as thoughe
he mought rule all the roste[1].' We may well believe that
Henry was willing that Cromwell should make some private
gains, provided he brought money to the royal treasury
as well.

The subjugation of the country, however, had not yet been
thoroughly accomplished. Though 1537 was comparatively
quiet, the following year witnessed a fresh outbreak. Taking
advantage of the precarious condition of England's foreign
affairs at the time, young Gerald, brother of the late Earl
of Kildare, and heir to his power, stirred up various chieftains, and baffled all the attempts of the Deputy to lure him
into the King's hands. Letters for aid were written to the
Pope and to Cardinal Pole, and were sent by a certain monk,
as the safest means of transmitting them to their destination[2].
The monk sailed from Scotland in a French ship, which was

---

[1] State Papers, vol. ii. pp. 551, 552.      [2] Cal. xiii. (ii) 999.

blown ashore on the English coast at South Shields; the messenger was captured, and the letter intercepted[1].   In September, 1539, there were several skirmishes between the various forces of the rebels and the Deputy; but the latter was generally victorious, and another crisis was tided over[2]. Young Gerald was forced to flee into Brittany, and the rebels were left without a leader.   The Deputy, Lord Grey, appears to have become very unpopular during his term of service, however, and in the spring of 1540 he was recalled[3], on the accusations of violence to the King's Council, extortion, injustice, and maintaining the King's enemies.   Affairs were in a bad state after he left; Scotch intrigues, even an invasion of the country by James, were rumoured[4], and Sir William Brereton, who temporarily filled Grey's place, had a very hard time.   Grey was finally condemned and executed a year after Cromwell's fall, and Sir Anthony St. Leger, 'the discreet,' who had been the Chief of Commissioners of 1537, was sent over as Deputy in 1541[5].

It may be said that from 1534 until his fall, Cromwell was the virtual ruler of Ireland.   His significant triumph over Norfolk and his policy of pacification, mark the beginning of his influence.   From that time onward the King left to him the entire direction of Irish affairs; he appointed the officers, regulated the revenues, and in short managed everything connected with the country until 1540.   From the instructions which the Commissioners received in 1537, we gather that the main object of the Crown was to get a revenue from Ireland, and the plan which Cromwell pursued in order to attain this end is noteworthy, in that it differed so entirely from his policy in all the rest of England's dependencies. Realizing that the country was worse than useless to the King, while it remained in the state in which it was when he came into power, he saw that it was so wild and disorganized, that subjugation by force would be possible and profitable, if attempted vigorously, and in time.   He there-

---

[1] Letters, 297, 298.
[2] Cal. xiv. (ii) 137.
[3] Cal. xv. 441.
[4] State Papers, vol. v. p. 178.
[5] Bagwell, vol. i. p. 249.

fore pursued a most aggressive policy, which in Scotland, for instance, where the conditions were so different, he would never have dared to adopt.

In Wales he was confronted with a problem of a very different nature. What was needed there was thorough legal reform. The country was not large enough to render an insurrection there very formidable, but the wild and lawless state of the Welsh Marches, which afforded hiding-places for criminals of all kinds, was a source of much evil. One Thomas Philips wrote to Cromwell in May, 1532[1], that the whole country was in great decay, and that the King's representatives there took fines for felony and murder, and used the money for their own purposes; he begged that such a council might soon be established in Wales, that the best officer should 'quake,' if found in fault. The Bishop of Exeter, who was President of the Marches, was an inefficient ruler and took no pains to remedy the existing evils. The crimes of making and uttering counterfeit money seem to have been extremely common[2]. Cromwell saw that it was high time measures were taken to rectify this lawlessness, and his 'remembrances' are full of items for the reform of Wales. He replaced the Bishop of Exeter by his own friend Rowland Lee, Bishop of Coventry and Lichfield, who in his younger days had served with him under Wolsey[3]. Lee's energetic and business-like methods rendered him a fit man for the place, and he set about reorganizing and reforming Wales in earnest. It was probably at his instance that Cromwell devised several Acts, passed in the Parliament of 1534, to establish justice and maintain order[4]. As the King's writ did not run in Wales, it was next to impossible to get a case fairly heard there; so Royal Commissioners were sent thither, with authority to punish crimes and felonies (which were to be tried in the next English court), and to establish Justices of the Peace. Chapuys, in a letter written in December, 1535, describes the distress of the Welsh at

---

[1] Cal. v. 991.
[2] Ruding, vol. i. p. 308; Cal. vii. 1225.
[3] Cal. vi. 946; vii. 1026 (28).
[4] 26 Hen. VIII, c. 4, c. 6, c. 11, c. 12.

these measures as incredible, saying that Parliament 'has just taken away their native laws, customs, and privileges, which is the very thing they can endure least patiently[1].' He further states that the Welsh were violently in favour of the cause of Katherine and Mary, and longed for an opportunity to declare themselves. A rising was probably prevented by the fact that the King himself was of Welsh descent. Cromwell was exceedingly active in his endeavours to stamp out all sedition of this sort, and was ably seconded by Lee, who, when the clergy in 1535 were required to preach in favour of the Royal Supremacy, and against the power of the Pope, declared himself ready to ride into his diocese in his own person and carry out the decree, though, as he confessed, he had never before been in a pulpit[2]. But Lee adopted other measures to extirpate sedition, far more vigorous than preaching in favour of the Royal Supremacy; he never failed to enforce his words by deeds. He hung and beheaded offenders and criminals right and left, and sent full reports of his doings to Cromwell, who must have rejoiced to find an agent whose energy corresponded so closely to his own[3].

But in spite of Lee's good-will, the state of Wales was not satisfactory, until Cromwell's great statute of 1535 was passed[4]. By this Act, Wales was formally declared to be incorporated with England, to be entitled to the same privileges, and to be subject to the same laws. The Marches were declared to be in disorder, and were annexed or divided into shires. The King was further empowered by the Act to erect courts in Wales every five years. These fundamental reforms laid the basis for an entirely new method of administration of justice there, and the country henceforth ceased to cause anxiety to its prince.

In striking contrast to Cromwell's vigorous policy in Ireland and Wales, was his conciliatory attitude towards Scotland. The strength and proximity of this country, and the weak defences of the northern marches of England, were a con-

---

[1] Cal. vii. 1554.
[2] Cal. viii. 839.
[3] Cal. viii. 133, 195, 240, 509, 915, 1058.
[4] 27 Hen. VIII, c. 26.

stant source of alarm, which was rather increased than
diminished by Henry's strained relations with those continental
powers who were on the best of terms with James. It was
obvious that in case of a foreign invasion of England from
the Continent, the enmity of Scotland would be the only thing
lacking, to render disaster certain. It is also not improbable
that an attack from the north would have been welcomed
by some of Henry's more disaffected subjects. In his speech
in the Parliament of 1523 Cromwell had advocated a policy
of unification with Scotland: from this principle he never
departed, but he saw that it was now no time to gain his
ends by force. He therefore adopted a pacificatory attitude
towards Scotland at the opening of his ministry, and consistently followed it until the end. He began by persuading
his master to make every effort to strengthen the rather
precarious truce which, owing to French mediation, had been
concluded between the Commissioners of the two countries
upon the Borders, Oct. 1, 1533[1]. Anxious to show all possible courtesy to the Scottish delegates who were finally sent
to London to open negotiations, the King prepared for them
a house, which had been occupied by the Grand Master of
France, and, contrary to his custom with most ambassadors,
supplied it with choice wines and provisions[2]. The Scots
were not slow to realize the strength of their position, and
in proportion as Henry's desire to conclude a permanent
peace increased, their movements grew more and more de-
liberate. After long delays, which exasperated the King
greatly, an alliance was finally made, to continue during the
joint lives of the two sovereigns, and one year longer. During
the two following years Henry continued his pacific policy
by making James a Knight of the Garter, and by sending an
embassy to induce him to abandon the Pope. The latter
plan was doubtless a suggestion of Cromwell's; a mention
of the ambassadors Barlow and Howard occurs in his 'remembrances,' and Barlow later wrote him continual reports of
his progress. The mission was unsuccessful in attaining its

---

[1] Cal. vi. 1196.  Cf. also Hume Brown, vol. i. p. 381.
[2] Cal. vii. 296.

purpose; but there were no signs that James' leaning to Rome would render him an active enemy of England[1].

The year 1537 brought with it new developments of Scottish policy. James had gone abroad to marry Madeleine of Valois, an alliance highly displeasing to Henry, after all his efforts to counteract his nephew's tendency to lean upon the good-will of Francis. The King proceeded to express his vexation in an emphatic manner, and, contrary to the advice of his Council, refused to permit James to return to Scotland from France through England[2]. James' marriage and Henry's outspoken wrath stultified all Cromwell's efforts to bring about a cordial personal feeling and a lasting peace between the two sovereigns. The Scots' King was forced to travel by sea; but events took place on the voyage which filled Henry with suspicion. Twelve Englishmen boarded the Scottish ship when it touched at Scarborough for provisions, welcomed James, and promised their aid if he invaded England. This episode was repeated at another town further north, and it was even reported that the Scottish King had boasted, that if he lived a year longer, 'he would himself break a spear on one Englishman's breast[3].' Such incidents must have been unpleasant, coming as they did just after a serious northern revolt had with difficulty been quelled, and while the Borders were still in a wild and lawless state. But any thoughts James may have entertained of an invasion were interrupted by the sudden death of his young French Queen. Henry perhaps had hoped that his nephew would come to him with offers of peace and a petition for the hand of the Princess Mary, but, if so, he was rudely disappointed. In October it was announced that James was engaged to marry a second French wife, Mary of Guise[4]; and though Henry, at that time a widower, made every effort to prevent the match by putting himself forward as a rival to his nephew, his proposals were courteously set aside[5].

---

[1] Cal. ix. 178, 730; x. 75, 227, 482, 863, 944, and Pinkerton, vol. ii. pp. 327-8.

[2] Cal. xii. (i) 398, 399.

[3] Cal. xii. (i) 1286.

[4] Cal. xii. (ii) 829.

[5] Cal. xii. (ii) 1201.

That the King of France should have distinctly preferred a Scottish to an English alliance when the choice lay open, stung Henry to the quick; but he was quite aware that he could not afford just then to quarrel with Francis or James, and he may have regretted that he had not taken his minister's advice to conciliate the latter. The history of Henry's relations with his nephew from this time until Cromwell's fall, yields ample proof of the complete triumph of the English minister's pacificatory policy. Attempts made in the past to stir up Border jealousies were completely abandoned, and England seemed almost suspiciously desirous to show every courtesy to her troublesome northern neighbour. A letter of Cromwell to Sir Thomas Wharton[1], deputy Warden of the West Marches, directs him to hand over to the Scottish officers an arrant traitor who had made his escape to England, even if the Scots failed to 'doo the semblable.' Actions as gracious as this were a new thing on the Borders: the usual policy in the past had been for each nation to give shelter to the outlaws who had fled to it from the other. The news that David Beton, Abbot of Arbroath, had been raised by the Pope to the cardinalate and was working at the Scottish Court in the interests of Rome, made Henry still more anxious to preserve friendship with his nephew, and to preclude all chances of his being induced to join a continental league against England[2]. So in January, 1540, we find him sending Ralph Sadler, Cromwell's old friend, to James, to counteract, if possible, the effect of the visit of Beton[3]. By the capture of certain letters in a Scottish ship which had been wrecked on the Northumbrian coast, Henry had been furnished with the means of misrepresenting the objects of the Cardinal at his nephew's Court. Sadler was instructed to hint that Beton was plotting to usurp all the authority of the King of Scotland, and to advise James to be on his guard. The ambassador was further directed to conciliate the Scottish King by a present of six geldings, to assure him of Henry's friendship, and to suggest that James augment his revenue

---

[1] Letters, 330.     [2] Cf. Pinkerton, vol. ii. pp. 352-3.
[3] Cal. xv. 136.

by suppressing the monasteries in his kingdom as his uncle had done in England. Finally Sadler was to represent to the Scots' King the advantages of an alliance with England over one with France, and to request him to ponder on the desirability of eradicating the ancient enmity of the two peoples, especially in view of the fact that he might some day himself succeed to his uncle's crown. The result of the mission taken as a whole was satisfactory. Though James refused to accede to any of Henry's more definite requests, and would not listen to any proposals to abolish the old religion or to suppress the monasteries, he still assured Sadler that no alliance he made on the Continent would lead him to break with England, and further enlarged on the benefits that would result from a meeting with his uncle, though he puzzled the envoy by suggesting that Francis should also be present [1]. The mission of Sadler marks the last stage of the relations of England and Scotland during Cromwell's ministry; and the fact that war between the two countries broke out so soon after his fall, furnishes a final reason for believing that it was by the able and unceasing efforts of the Privy Councillor that an open rupture was so long averted.

Lastly, a few words remain to be said on the subject of the government of Calais. If the name of that town were graven on the heart of Mary Tudor at her death, from the grief which its loss during her reign caused her, it must have been also graven upon the minds of her father and his minister, from the trouble its maintenance gave them during the last seven years of the latter's power. In March, 1533, Arthur Plantagenet, Viscount Lisle, was nominated successor to that learned soldier, Lord Berners, as Deputy there, and took the oaths at the town, on the 10th of June [2]. The choice was certainly unfortunate, and Lisle's unfitness for his new position was destined soon to be made evident. He seems to have been a man completely lacking in the qualities necessary for a good ruler of such a place as Calais was in those

---

[1] Cal. xv. 248. Cf. also Hume Brown, vol. i. pp. 388-9.

[2] Cal. vi. 300 (21), 619, and Rymer, vol. xiv. p. 452.

days: he possessed small discrimination in judging what things he could deal with by his own authority, and what things it was necessary to report to head quarters. Hence there are many mild rebukes among Cromwell's letters to him [1], in some of which he chides him for bothering the King about such a trivial thing as a private quarrel between two minor officials in Calais, while in others he 'mervayles not a litel' that he should be so negligent as not to make immediate report of sacrilegious preaching. Calais was by no means an easy post to manage; Henry and Cromwell kept its officers and garrison exceedingly short of money; the soldiers wrangled and mutinied, and religious conferences amongst the townspeople sometimes took most violent forms, and not seldom resulted in dangerous riots. Placed as a sort of spy on the movements of Francis and the Emperor, in a town, the government of which on a small scale presented all the difficulties of that of a great kingdom, the Deputy was in a position which demanded resources greater than his own.

The first part of Lisle's administration seems to have been comparatively uneventful. Cromwell, always keenly alive to the necessity of having the country in an adequate state of defence, at once caused him to repair all breaches in the ramparts, a task which Lisle set about without competent men or supplies; and the immediate result of his ill-judged attempts to lay a new foundation for one of his walls was the fall of the small part of the old fortification which was yet standing [2]. Lisle was of course continually busied in preventing his neighbours, French and Flemish, from meddling with the King's Pale, especially throughout the year 1536, when the war between Francis and the Emperor broke out afresh [3]. He tried to keep the town well victualled and in good defence, and was zealous to do as he was bidden by Cromwell, though seldom successful, for he lacked ability. After 1537 he was confronted with a new and more difficult problem.

In the spring of 1538, Cranmer heard that there were seven or eight persons in Calais, who manifestly denied Christ.

---

[1] Cf. Letters, 86, 260.     [2] Cal. x. 541.

[3] Cal. xi. 183.

His Commissary there, John Butler, asserted that this report was false, but in a later epistle advised the Archbishop that there were three papists in the town, who slandered those who applied themselves to God's word ; the letter went on to suggest that Cromwell be requested to write to Lisle to have them punished [1]. The minister, however, had heard of the existence of 'certayn Sacramentaryes' or deniers of transubstantiation there, before this report arrived, and had written the Deputy a severe reproof for not informing him about them [2]. The state of foreign affairs at that moment was such as to render it indispensable for the King to preserve the appearance of being zealous for orthodoxy, and he had called on his efficient minister to aid him in his attempts to extirpate heretical doctrines. The rebuke which the latter had administered to the Deputy seems in this case to have been undeserved, for Lisle, who apparently was more on the watch than usual this time, had certainly sent home information about the Sacramentaries before he received Cromwell's epistle : the two letters perhaps crossed on the way. That of the Deputy reported the arrival in Calais of a young English priest, lately come from Germany, who had uttered opinions about the Eucharist which the King would not tolerate, and which had shocked the good people of Calais beyond measure. This young priest can have been none other than Adam Damplip, originally a strong papist, who (according to Foxe) had been chaplain to Fisher, and at the Cardinal's execution had left England and travelled in France, Germany, and Italy. His sojourn in foreign lands must have altered his opinions completely, for when he came to Calais his doctrines were so 'advanced' and heretical, that as a result of a warning of Cromwell's, in his letter to Lisle of May 14 [3], a decree was made out by the Council of the town that Butler, the Commissary who had given Damplip licence to preach, would be held responsible for any false opinions that the priest expressed [4].

Determined as he was to extirpate unlawful and treasonable

---

[1] Cal. xiii. (i) 813, 934.
[2] Letters, 260.

[3] Letters, 263.
[4] Cal. xiii. (i) 1219.

doctrines both at home and abroad, Cromwell was too much absorbed in the maintenance of his foreign policy, and the prevention of the pressing dangers which threatened the country from without, to pay much attention to Damplip at Calais during the latter part of 1538 and 1539. He was far more anxious to have the town well victualled and defended, in case of a sudden attack from France or Spain. Damplip himself, however, had gone over to England to answer to the charges brought against him before Cranmer[1]. The result of the examination seems to have been very favourable to him, and the Archbishop, in a letter to Cromwell about it, supported the position which the priest had taken up in only denying Transubstantiation while admitting the Real Presence[2]. But the accusations from Calais against the Sacramentaries did not cease. Lisle and the Council, now thoroughly roused, kept sending in depositions against Damplip, until Cromwell, in May, 1539, rebuked them for uncharitable behaviour, saying that the affair was being made too much of, and that the King was busy about other things[3]. Exhortations to 'charyte and myld handeling' were not Cromwell's usual style; and in this case at least they were superseded within ten days by instructions of a very different nature. The cause of the sudden change is doubtless to be found in the debate on the Six Articles, just then at its height. Cromwell saw the trend things were taking, and understood that as the doctrine of Transubstantiation was evidently about to be confirmed at home, it would be extremely dangerous for him to urge leniency towards those who opposed it at Calais. He consequently sent another letter to Lisle[4], in which he retreated from his former position, and ordered the Commissary and the parish priest of Our Lady Church to be sent in custody to England. The subsequent appearance of these men before the Privy Council seems to have resulted in their acquittal, and a public recantation in the Market Place at Calais was deemed sufficient to prevent a recurrence to the heresy. The recall of Lord Lisle in the

---

[1] Cal. xiii. (i) 1446, 1464.  [3] Letters, 312.
[2] Cal. xiii. (ii) 97.  [4] Letters, 314.

spring of 1540 was probably less due to his inefficiency in handling the affair of the Sacramentaries, than to the many proofs he had given of general incompetence. He was committed to the Tower, where he remained a close prisoner till January, 1542, when a message was sent to him that he was pardoned and restored to favour. The story is that his joy at hearing this news was so great, that he died of excitement that same night [1].

That Calais was not lost to England under the incompetent management of Lisle (whose actions from first to last were too much influenced by the whims of a foolish wife), was solely due to the guidance which he received from Cromwell. The brilliant success of the great minister's administration in England was fully equalled by the wisdom and skill of his dealings with her immediate neighbours and dependencies. In every case the dominant principle of his policy had been the same ; the completion of the work begun by Henry VII —the elevation of the Crown to absolute power on the ruins of every other institution which had ever been its rival. In attaining this end, which (as we must not forget) was one that commended itself to most patriotic Englishmen of the time, Cromwell had been confronted by a multitude of problems of great difficulty and infinite diversity : he handled them all with uniform success ; and the monarchy, under his guidance, passed safe through one of the gravest crises in the history of the realm, finally to emerge triumphant, absolute, supreme in Church and State.

---

[1] See Life of Arthur Lord Lisle in the Dictionary of National Biography, vol. xlv. p. 400.

# CHAPTER IX

## THE MONASTERIES

THE suppression of the English monasteries, though in one sense but a single branch of Cromwell's internal administration, still deserves to be considered in a separate chapter. Of all the changes that followed the breach with Rome, none bears as plainly as this the stamp of Cromwellian origin. The sinister genius of the King's minister particularly fitted him for this task of destruction, and his title of *malleus-monachorum* is thoroughly well deserved. Cromwell's intent in suppressing the monasteries was obviously, like that of all the rest of his internal administration, the strengthening of the Crown: how far his measures were successful in accomplishing what was expected of them must be determined not only from their immediate effects, but also from the developments which later resulted from them.

It has been pointed out in an earlier chapter that the state of the lesser monasteries was far from satisfactory in Cromwell's time ; but that in spite of this, when Wolsey's agents suppressed a few of them in order to convert their revenues to the use of the Cardinal's cherished colleges, a loud cry of indignation was immediately raised among the rural population. During his first few years in Wolsey's service Cromwell had acquired sufficient experience to master at least the elementary principles of monastic confiscation, but before he had gone half as far as he had probably intended, his master's attainder and his own consequent change of life had temporarily interrupted the work. We have seen that as soon as the King had arbitrarily assumed the Headship of the Church of England, Cromwell immediately cast about for means to secure him in his new position. To this end he had

weakened the bishops and also the lesser clergy ; the dissolution of the monasteries immediately presented itself to him as
a consistent method of following up these measures. It all
tended in the same direction of severing England's connexion
with Rome and of establishing the Royal Supremacy. The
scheme of suppressing the monasteries also promised great
things from a financial point of view ; Cromwell could have
hit upon no better plan than this to aid him to fulfil his
promise to make Henry ' the richest King that ever was in
Christendom.' If the idea of dissolving the religious houses
in order to increase the wealth of the Crown, had occurred to
Henry during Wolsey's administration, he would hardly have
dared to carry it out while there was any chance of avoiding
a breach with the Pope ; but now the course of events had
converted the only objection to the plan into an argument in
its favour. There was certainly nothing in the conscience of
the King or of his minister to deter them from such a step,
when so much advantage both political and financial promised
to result from it.

In January, 1535, two documents appeared—the first, a
royal commission to Thomas Cromwell authorizing him as
the King's Vicar-general to undertake a general visitation
of churches, monasteries, and clergy, and to depute others
to act as his agents; the second consisting of a series of
formal inquiries to be made concerning the state of the
religious houses, and royal injunctions for their reform. The
latter is written in a strange hand, copiously interlined and
corrected by that of the King's minister [1]. The decrees were
quickly put in operation. By the month of August in the
same year Cromwell's two agents, Legh and Ap-Rice, were
hard at work among the Wiltshire monasteries, and sent in
their reports to their master full of ludicrously pathetic
lamentations, when unable to trump up any plausible charges
against the monks [2]. Doctor Richard Layton, who had come
under Cromwell's notice at the time of the trials of More
and Fisher, sent him a request for employment on the same
mission, and eventually got permission to go to Gloucester-

---

[1] Cal. viii. 75, 76.     [2] Cal. ix. 139.

shire[1]. He had made a preliminary visitation at Bath and Farley, and while there had aroused the jealousy and hatred of Legh, who wrote to Cromwell complaining that he was not sufficiently severe, and urging the necessity of uniformity of action[2]. A great many grumbling letters of this kind were sent to Cromwell by his visitors. Layton and Ap-Rice were not slow to revenge themselves on Legh by reporting to the Vicar-general the pride, arrogance, 'sumptuus vsage, and roughe fasshyon' of their hated colleague[3].

The bad character of Cromwell's agents, and the devices to which they were forced to have recourse in order to extort from the monks the information they desired, furnish ample proof of the unfairness of many of the reports which they made. The 'Commissioners found means,' as it has been significantly stated, 'to make divers monasteries obnoxious[4].' Cromwell had taken special pains that the efforts of his agents should not be hindered by any external interference: it was to this end that he had issued the Prohibitory Letter to the bishops in the month of September[5]. Legh, Layton, and Ap-Rice were left a perfectly clear field, and devoted themselves to examining into the monastic discipline, and to inducing discontented monks to accuse their fellows. The arrogant Legh was especially efficient in this particular, as is shown by the letters Cromwell received from the monasteries he had visited. One monk wrote to the Vicar-general that the inmates of his house cared nothing for true religion, but came to mattins 'as dronck as myss and [played] sume at cardes, sume at dyyss[6]'—and finally imparted the significant piece of information that Cromwell's visitors had ordered

---

[1] Cal. viii. 822, 1127. The King and Cromwell were both absent on a tour in the west and south of England from the end of July until the beginning of October, 1535. Chapuys states that the object of this trip was to win the affection of the people on the Borders of Wales, and to enjoy the excellent hunting which that region afforded. It is probable that Henry and Cromwell were also desirous personally to inform themselves concerning the religious houses in the south and west counties, before permitting their agents to complete the visitation. Cal. ix. 58.

[2] Cal. ix. 138.

[3] Cal. ix. 621, 622.

[4] Herbert, p. 186.

[5] See ante, chap. vii, p. 115.

[6] Wright, p. 133. A tag of verse.

him to write these opinions to head quarters. Another, John Placett by name, sent cringing letters to the Vicegerent, begging that his zeal in advancing the new doctrines and in reporting those who opposed them, might be rewarded by official exemption from rising at midnight and from observing the customary fasts[1]. Epistles of this sort form the bulk of Cromwell's correspondence during the years 1535 and 1536. The chief reason why the Vicar-general did not protest against this flood of defamatory information, which through the efficiency of the zealous Legh continually poured in upon him, lay probably in the fact that along with these reports there came also letters of a somewhat different nature which afforded him excellent opportunities for private gain. 'I submytt myselfe,' wrote the Abbot of Rewley, 'fulle and holle to your mastershipp, as all my refuge, helpe, and socor is yn yow, glad of my voluntarye mynde to be bounde in obligacion of one hunderd powndes to be payed to your mastershipp, so that our house may be savyd[2].' We may well believe that this proposal did not fall on deaf ears. Though we do not possess the reply of Cromwell in this particular case, the letters which he sent to the Priors of St. Faith's and of Coxford in the same year, indicate that he was as willing to accept bribes from the heads of monasteries as from any one else[3].

Less crafty but scarcely less efficient than the untiring Legh was his brutal colleague Layton. The Sussex monasteries which he visited in October, 1535, were so unfortunate

---

[1] Cal. ix. 321, 322.

[2] Wright, p. 73.

[3] Letters, 163, 180. Cf. also Gasquet, English Monasteries, vol. i. pp. 413, 421. Cromwell also took good care that some of the suppressed houses also should fall to his portion. He 'appropriated to his own share the rich Priory of Lewes in Sussex (including its cell of Melton-Mowbray in Leicestershire), the Priory of Michelham in the same county, that of Modenham in Kent, of St. Osythe in Essex, Alceter in Warwickshire, Yarmouth in Norfolk, and Laund in Leicestershire. Sir Richard Cromwell, his nephew, and great-grandfather of Oliver, received Ramsey Abbey, Hinchinbrooke Nunnery, Sawtry Abbey, St. Neot's Priory, and a house of Austin canons in Huntingdonshire, with Neath Abbey in Glamorganshire, and St. Helen's Nunnery in London.' Blunt, vol. i. p. 377. See also note 4 at the bottom of the same page.

as to incur his particular displeasure. He does not appear to have troubled himself, like Legh, with devising means to make the monks accuse one another: he reported everything to head quarters on his own responsibility, and wrote to Cromwell how at one place he found the abbot the 'varaste hayne betle and buserde and the aranttes chorle' he ever saw, while at another he swore that his master would scarcely believe 'quanta sit spurcities.' He concluded with two philosophic reflections that 'sacerdotes omnes non creati ex natura angelica, sed humana,' and 'that the blake sort of dyvelisshe monkes . . . be paste amendment[1].' He possibly bore a personal grudge against these southern houses; at least this seems a likely explanation of the fact that later investigation showed them to be no worse than ordinary, and especially popular with their neighbours[2]. Layton, however, found willing listeners to his accusations in the King and Cromwell, and a commission was sent down to confiscate the property of the monasteries of Dover, Langdon, and Folkestone, and to take the surrender of these houses into the King's hands. It was the first step of the great devastation which was to ensue during the following four years.

The next scene of the visitors' operations was in the northern counties. Early in 1535 Layton had taken occasion to inform Cromwell that he and Legh were particularly competent to carry on the work there. 'Ther ys nother monasterie, selle, priorie, nor any other religiouse howse in the north,' he wrote, 'but other doctor Lee or I have familier acqwayntance within x or xii mylles of hit. . . . We knowe and have experiens bothe of the fassion off the contre and the rudenes of the pepull . . . ther is matter sufficient to detecte and opyn all coloryde sanctitie, all supersticiouse rewlles of pretensyde religion, and other abusys detestable of all sorttes[3].' Cromwell certainly had no reason to be dissatisfied with the results which his agents had already accomplished, and doubtless welcomed their zeal to continue their labours in a new field. With most astounding rapidity

---

[1] Cal. ix. 509, 632.     [2] Cal. ix. 829.     [3] Wright, p. 156.

the visitation was carried through : all the houses in the north had been reported on by the end of February. There was certainly an object in having the work completed so quickly, for Parliament had already met, and was prepared to take action on the 'comperta' or catalogue of offences sent in by Cromwell's agents. The extraordinary hurry in which the latter part of their task was accomplished, and the suspicious uniformity of the offences reported, furnish a last and most cogent reason for doubting the truth of the statements of the visitors. There must of course have been some immorality in the monasteries : the abbots and heads of houses were elected by the monks themselves, who were sure to have an eye to their own ease, and would tend to choose those whose discipline was lax. But it must be a prejudiced person indeed who will accept word for word the catalogues of the religious persons reported guilty of the lowest and most degrading forms of vice, which Legh and Layton seemed to delight in sending to their master. Parliament, however, was too completely in Cromwell's hands fairly to judge of the character of the visitors, or of the circumstances under which they drew up their 'comperta,' and the report was strong and clear ; so it was not long before the first Act for the dissolution of the smaller monasteries was passed. The statute declared that 'all Relygeous Houses of Monkes Chanons and Nonnes, whiche may not dyspend Manors, Landes, Tenementes, & Heredytamentes above the clere yerly Value of ij C li. are geven to the Kinges Highnes, his heires and successours for ever[1].' Another Act was passed at the same time establishing a Court of Augmentations of the King's revenue[2]. Power was given to this court to collect the spoils, lands, and buildings of the suppressed abbeys, and dispose of them in the way most profitable to the Crown. It consisted of a chancellor, treasurer, solicitor, and thirty subordinates. The chief persons in it were friends and hirelings of Cromwell's. In April commissions were sent to the principal men in every county[3], authorizing them to inquire further into the state of each house, to make

---

27 Hen. VIII, c. 28.　　[2] 27 Hen. VIII, c. 61.　　[3] Cal. x. 1191.

inventories and estimates of their property, and to ascertain the number of monks who desired 'capacities' for entering secular life, and the number who intended to remove to some other religious house. It is significant that the reports of these men, concerning the character and morality of the inmates, are uniformly of a more favourable description than those of Layton and Legh.

The process of the surrender immediately followed the first visit of the Commissioners. They sent in their report to the Court of Augmentations, which then issued its final orders for the dissolution of the house, and its conversion to the King's use. A 'receiver' was appointed to plunder the church, and sell the lead, bells, &c. An interesting letter, from an agent of Cromwell's to his master, sheds some light on the usual methods of these officials. 'We ar pluckyng down an hygher vaute,' writes the receiver, ' borne up by fower thicke and grose pillars xiiij fote fro syde to syde, abowt in circumference xlv fote . . . we browght from London xvij persons, 3 carpentars, 2 smythes, 2 plummars, and on that kepith the fornace. Euery of these attendith to hys own office: x of them hewed the walles abowte, amonge the whych ther were 3 carpentars: thiese made proctes to undersette wher the other cutte away, thother brake and cutte the waules ¹.' Coupled with reports like this, came curiously confused accounts of the saleable articles of the house, which had been disposed of, such as

*Item* ij brasse pottes sold to Edward Scudamor . iiijˢ
*Item* a vestment and ij tynakles of old prest
  velvet sold to Johan Savage baylyf . . xiijˢ iiijᵈ
*Item* ij pannes . . . . . . . . viᵈ
*Item* a cope of tawny damaske . . . . . xijᵈ
*Item* a image of Seynt Katerine sold to Lee . . vjᵈ
*Item* sold to John Webbe the tymber worke
  of the hyegh quyer, and a auter of alablaster
  in the body of the churche . . . . ixˢ viijᵈ ².

It will be noticed that the sums for which these articles were

¹ Wright, pp. 180-1.     ² Wright, pp. 267-9.

sold, were very small.   It is said that not more than £100,000 were obtained from the sale of the jewels, plate, lead, bells, and other valuables, which were seized in the first suppression of the monasteries.   The annual incomes of the three hundred and seventy-six houses which were suppressed, however, probably amounted to about £32,000, a sum which was quite sufficient to render the measure a successful one from a financial point of view.

In spite of the Act of Parliament, which declared that the monks were either to be pensioned, or else moved to some other religious house, there is no doubt that great misery and wretchedness invariably accompanied the dissolutions. Chapuys writes: 'It is a lamentable thing to see a legion of monks and nuns, who have been chased from their monasteries, wandering miserably hither and thither, seeking means to live, and several honest men have told me, that what with monks, nuns, and persons dependent on the monasteries suppressed, there were over 20,000, who knew not how to live[1].'   The Act for the protection of the exiled inmates cannot have been at all strictly enforced, and there were certainly many monks, to whom no homes or means of living were assigned.   Sir Henry Ellis has printed a document, concerning the dissolution of some of the monasteries, which was written in 1591 by one whose father and uncle witnessed the scenes he describes.   It tells how 'it would have made an heart of flint to have melted and wept to have seen the breaking up of the House, and their sorrowful departing; and the sudden spoil that fell the same day of their departure from the House.   And every person had everything good cheap; except the poor Monks, Friars, and Nuns, that had no money to bestow of any thing.'   The people entered the church, 'and took what they found, and filched it away. . . . . It would have pitied any heart to see what tearing up of the lead there was, and plucking up of boards, and throwing down of the sparres; . . . . and the tombs in the Church (were) all broken, . . . . . and all things of price either spoiled, carped away, or defaced to the uttermost[2].'   Nor is this tendency of the people of the neigh-

---

[1] Cal. xi. 42.     [2] Ellis, 3rd Series, vol. iii. pp. 33, 34.

bourhood to plunder in the least to be wondered at. They knew that as the monasteries were to be pulled down they would lose all the old charities, easy rents, and other advantages to which they had so long been accustomed, and they naturally wished to make good the loss. Cromwell probably did not object to this ruthless waste as much as one would expect, for he saw that if he attempted to stop it, the feeling against the suppression would be so strong, that it would be impossible to continue it. As it was, the famous rebellion of the Pilgrimage of Grace, which broke out in the northern counties, just as the first houses were being suppressed, gave him a terrible warning of the general unpopularity of the change. The insurrection, however, was soon quelled, and Cromwell's genius was able to turn it to his own advantage, and make it the pretext for carrying out the scheme which had probably been part of his original plan, namely the suppression of all the monasteries ; a step which, without some valid excuse, he would have hardly dared to take.

In 1537 the visitors began to go to the larger monasteries, and intimidate their inmates into surrender, mainly by threatening them with punishment for complicity in the rebellion which had just been put down. An excellent example of the way in which this was done, is given by the story of the suppression of the two large Cistercian abbeys in Lancashire, Whalley and Furness[1]. John Pasleu, Abbot of Whalley, had been executed in March, 1537, by the Earl of Sussex for his treason in taking part in the Pilgrimage of Grace. The Earl was commended for this action by the King, who further desired him with ' good dexteritie' to ' laye unto the charges of all the monkes there their grevous offences, . . . . . and therwith assaye their myndes, whither they woll conforme themselfes gladly for the redubbing of their former trespaces to goo to other houses of their cote . . . or rather take capacities and soo receyve seculer habite[2].' The Abbot of Furness was doubtless threatened with death if he refused to surrender his house, for a month after the execution of his brother at Whalley, he signed a document, by virtue of which

---

[1] Cal. xii. (i) 632, 668.    [2] State Papers, vol. i. p. 540.

he handed over to the King his abbey, and all its lands and possessions, 'knawyng the mysorder and evyll liff both unto God and our prynce of the bredren of the said monasterie[1].'

Another method of intimidation was to threaten punishment for superstition and image worship. Against the latter Henry's minister was particularly zealous. Some of the images were very valuable, and could be sold for a high price. Two of the most extraordinary of the venerated relics found in the 'defacement' of the monasteries have become famous to posterity, under the names of the Rood of Grace, and the Blood of Hailes. The former was a wonder-working crucifix, held in great veneration at Boxley Abbey, which Geoffrey Chambers[2], an agent of Cromwell's, found full of 'certen ingynes and olde wyer wyth olde roton stykkes in the backe of the same, that dyd cause the eyes of the same to move and stere in the hede thereof lyke unto a lyvelye thyng[3].' It was seized and exhibited, first in Kent, and then in London, and the 'abusion thereof dyvulged.' The Blood of Hailes was a phial of liquid, which a tradition of three centuries asserted to have been the blood of the Saviour[4]. The head of the monastery brought it to Cromwell in great perplexity, swearing that he was willing to suffer the most shameful death, if the phial had been meddled with in his day. A commission, appointed to inquire into it, took the liquid out of the phial, and found it to be a thick, red, sticky substance. They then gave it back to the abbot, to keep until he heard the King's pleasure concerning it. Meantime Bishop Hilsey had preached a sermon in denunciation of the fraud, in which he asserted that a former abbot had told his paramour that the phial contained only drake's blood ; but he was later compelled to take back this last statement, as a result of the Commissioners' inquiry. What ultimately became of the Blood of Hailes has remained a mystery, but it is noteworthy that Cromwell was so annoyed, at having unearthed a relic which proved value-

---

[1] Wright, p. 153.

[2] This was perhaps the man whom Cromwell years before had helped to obtain from the Pope the indulgence for the Boston Gild.

[3] Ellis, 3rd Series, vol. iii. p. 168.

[4] Introduction to vol. xiii. of the Calendar, pp. 8–14 ; Wordsworth's Cromwell, pp. 346–7 *nn*.

less from a financial point of view, that when the 'bluddy abbot,' as Latimer called him, came to consult him about it, he was forced to pay £140, his best mitre, cross, and 'another thyng or two,' to make good the amount which Cromwell had expected to obtain from the relic. The icono-clastic zeal of the Vicar-general varied in proportion to the value of the image[1].

The first Act of dissolution had only given to the King the monasteries of which the annual income was less than £200. But now that Cromwell, on the plea of com-plicity in the late rebellion, had contrived to bring in all the larger religious houses, so that a general suppression had in fact begun, a fresh Act was needed to legalize his proceedings. So in the spring of 1539, a new statute was passed for the dissolution of all monasteries and abbeys[2]. But long before this the main part of the work had been accomplished. When the monks refused to be terrorized into submission, attainder and death invariably followed. It is but justice to Cromwell's agents to say, however, that their methods of intimidation were so highly effectual that attainder was the exception, and surrender the rule. The Commissioners may well have been surprised that any of the abbots dared to stand out against them.

From 1537 to the end of 1539, the story of the suppres-sion of the monasteries is simply a catalogue of houses surrendered or confiscated, on more or less unjust pretexts. So rapidly and thoroughly did Cromwell and his Com-missioners accomplish the work, that by the end of Decem-ber no monastery in the country had been left untouched, except Westminster Abbey, and a few other larger houses. The climax of cruelty and injustice was reached in the executions of the Abbots of Glastonbury and Reading. Cromwell's famous remembrance concerning the latter was literally obeyed. There was no pretence of a fair hearing of his case. He was sent down '*to be tryed and excecutyd,*' as Cromwell had ordered it[3]. The punishment of the Abbot of

---

[1] Wriothesley's Chronicle, vol. i. pp. 76, 90. Cal. xiii. (i) 347 ; xiii. (ii) 186, 709-10.

[2] 31 Hen. VIII, c. 13.  [3] Cal. xiv. (ii) 399.

Glastonbury was, if possible, even more unjust. Though weak and broken with age and illness, he was arrested and sent up to the Tower, simply on the charge of having in his monastery a book against the King's divorce, divers pardons and bulls, and a printed life of Becket [1]. It is stated that on examination Cromwell discovered that he had lent money to the rebels in the Pilgrimage of Grace, but it mattered little whether this serious charge was proved or not. His execution was determined on long beforehand, and his rich and ancient abbey was plundered immediately after his arrest. His fate was sealed long before his mock trial at Wells took place ; the verdict of the 'worshypfull jury' was of course 'guilty,' and he was executed two days later on Glastonbury Tor [2].

Hand in hand with the suppression of the monasteries came the fall of the various houses of the friars. This had probably been a part of Cromwell's scheme from the very first ; it will be remembered that several houses suffered in the early part of his ministry, as a penalty for permitting their inmates to preach against the King's divorce. A sort of preliminary visitation had been carried on in 1534, at Cromwell's command, by his agents Browne and Hilsey [3] : but a far more energetic person was found in Richard Ingworth, Bishop of Dover, who, on the 6th of February, 1538, was commissioned by the Vicar-general to carry on a second investigation, in which he was to visit all the houses of the various orders of friars in England, to examine into and correct abuses, and to expel and punish the guilty inmates [4]. As he refers to the King's Vicegerent, as his 'synguler helper for XII yeres past [5],' there is reason to think that he had been an intimate of Cromwell's before the latter had entered the royal service : it is possible that they had worked together in the suppression of the monasteries which furnished funds for Wolsey's colleges. A greater traveller than Ingworth could scarcely

---

[1] Cal. xiv. (ii) 206.

[2] Cal. xiv. (ii) 530, 531. Cf. also Gasquet, The Last Abbot of Glastonbury, chaps. vi and vii.

[3] Cal. vii. 587 (18).

[4] Cal. xiii. (i) 225.

[5] Cal. xiii. (ii) 1021. Cf. also the Introduction to vol. xiii of the Calendar, p. 23.

have been found in those days. The number of houses he visited during the first six months of 1538 is perfectly amazing, but with all his energy, Richard of Dover was far less efficient than his terrible master. When he hesitatingly wrote to Cromwell to ask whether he should meddle with the White Friars of Winchester, he received a smart rebuke for his doubts, and was told that though he had changed his friar's habit, he had not changed his friar's heart[1]. The Vicar-general found it necessary to give him a coadjutor, and chose a singularly apt man for his purpose in Dr. John London, Warden of New College, Oxford, who received a special commission with the mayor and two others to 'loke vpon' the friars of that town[2]. The friars gave the Commissioners more trouble than the monks. They seemed to have secret ways of learning when the visitors were going to arrive, and either carefully hid, or else sold all their valuables beforehand, a fact which affords the most probable explanation of the amount of poverty reported by the visitors. Still the houses fell without ceasing; if not by voluntary surrender, by compulsion. Nor did the visitors hesitate in the case of nunneries, to resort to the most shameful devices to elicit a surrender. London's conduct was so disgraceful, that Cromwell was obliged to recognize the justice of the complaints of the Abbess of Godstow against him, and 'steye his procedinges[3].' 'Doctor Londone,' wrote the abbess to the Vicar-general, 'whiche ... was ageynste my promotyon and hathe ever since borne me greate malys and grudge like my mortall enmye, is sodenlie cummyd unto me withe a greate rowte with him, and here dothe threten me and my susters, sayeng that he hathe the kynges commyssyon to suppres the house spyte of my tethe[4].' It appears that London himself wrote to Cromwell the day after to beg him to favour the abbess and her sisters[5]. Did he perhaps feel that he had gone too far, or are we to infer that his usual methods were even more brutal than this?

---

[1] Wright, pp. 195, 197.
[2] Cal. xiii. (i) 1335.
[3] Cal. xiii. (ii) 758, 911.

[4] Wright, p. 230.
[5] Cal. xiii. (ii) 767.

And thus the work was finished. Within five years of the time that the first visitation of the monasteries had begun, a complete devastation of all the religious houses had been accomplished, and a torrent of wealth had been poured in upon the Crown, 'such,' says Hallam, 'as has seldom been equalled in any country, by the confiscations following a subdued rebellion[1].' The suppression which included the larger houses was evidently a far greater financial success than the first. A new device for gaining revenue had been invented, and put in operation during the last few years. It consisted in imposing a fine on every place in which a religious house had existed, 'for the toleracyon and contynuaunce of the monastery ther[2]'; an ingenious device, which yielded a most substantial income. 'The King had then in his hand,' says Burnet, 'the greatest opportunity of making royal and noble foundations that ever King of England had. But whether out of policy, to give a general content to the gentry by selling to them at low rates, or out of easiness to his courtiers, or out of an unmeasured lavishness of expense, it came far short of what he had given out he would do. . . . He designed to convert £18,000 into a revenue for eighteen bishoprics and cathedrals. But of these he only erected six. . . . Great sums were indeed laid out on building and fortifying many ports in the Channel, and other parts of England[3].'

Lacking any evidence from the sources on the subject of the use to which the revenues from the suppression of the monasteries were put, one must judge from this passage, and from subsequent events. An Act giving Henry the power to erect bishoprics by letters patent, was passed in Parliament, May 23, 1539[4]. It was by the authority of this statute, that the King founded the six new bishops' sees above mentioned, and also converted some of the old houses, such as Beverley, Ripon, and Manchester, into collegiate churches. But the passage in Burnet also hints at other methods of employing the money gained from the suppression of the monasteries, which it seems likely that Cromwell suggested. The use

---

[1] Hallam, vol. i. p. 76.
[2] Cal. xiii. (ii) 457 (3).
[3] Burnet, vol. i. p. 431.
[4] 31 Hen. VIII, c. 9.

of the funds to strengthen the coast defences along the
Channel was always one of his favourite schemes; it is
probable that he found no difficulty in persuading the King
how necessary such a precaution was, in view of the danger
of foreign invasion, which threatened England at the close of
1539. But the plan of selling the lands of the confiscated
houses to the nobles at low prices, is even more Cromwellian.
It immediately reminds the reader of the course which
Wolsey, ten years before, had pursued at his servant's advice,
when he bought off the popular hatred by grants out of his
own lands and revenues. Cromwell plainly saw that after the
suppression, steps must be taken to ensure the permanence
of the reform he had effected. By judicious grants he turned
aside the hatred of some of the rural gentry, who were at first
opposed to the destruction of the monasteries, and thus,
by rendering the work popular at home, he secured himself
and it from the attacks of Catholic potentates abroad. But
his action at this juncture had another more subtle and more
important result. For by the grants which he made to the
rural gentry, he laid the basis for the foundation of a territorial
aristocracy, destined at a later day to wrest from the Crown
the power which he had wrung from the older nobility, lay
and clerical. This after-effect of Cromwell's policy, which was
in direct opposition to the aims of his government, did not take
place till long after his fall. It was rendered possible solely
by the movement of events over which he had no control,
and he could have scarcely anticipated it. But it is only
fair to mention it here, in order that we may be able to look
on the suppression of the monasteries and its after-effects as
a connected whole. If we do this, the cruelty and treachery
of Cromwell and his agents in gaining their ends will not
make us blind to the fact, that in the end the destruction of
the religious houses in England certainly accomplished
other and better results than those it was originally intended
to compass.

# CHAPTER X

WHEN Cromwell entered the King's service, it was inevitable that the policy he adopted should force him to abandon all hope of popularity with the people at large, as soon as his real position became generally known. The efforts Henry and his minister made to conceal the identity of the true author of the sweeping changes of the years 1530–34, bear testimony to the fact that they were both perfectly well aware of the opposition the new measures must arouse in the minds of those who were outside the Court circle and consequently could not see the reason of them. For a long time these efforts were crowned with success. We have seen that it was not until the year 1535 that those who were in close proximity to the King discovered what a power Cromwell had become in Church and State. It was even longer before the country people began to realize the true state of affairs. News of the extraordinary revolution in ecclesiastical matters, of the King's divorce and second marriage, of the packed Parliaments, and of the ruthless execution of so-called heretics, slowly spread among the rural population. The changes were certainly unwelcome, but they were universally thought to be the work of the King alone, and traditional English respect for royalty was sufficient to check any serious outbreak. The common people contented themselves with vague murmurings and disloyal speeches which were soon suppressed through the efficiency of Cromwell's agents; and by the opening of the year 1535 the King and his minister began to hope that the crisis had been tided over.

But they were destined to be disappointed. At the very moment when he began to think himself secure in his almost exclusive enjoyment of his master's favour, Cromwell took a measure which was destined to conduce directly to the formid-

able rising that nearly hurled him from his hard-won place.
The moment the Vicar-general sent out his agents to visit the
monasteries, the Englishman of the country began to realize
that the puzzling changes, of which he had hitherto understood so little, were going to have an important and also a
disagreeable effect on his own life. Up to this time he had
been unwilling actively to express his dissatisfaction at the
new measures, because they had seemed but remotely
connected with his own fortunes: but now there came an
evidence to the contrary which he did not fail to appreciate.
The army of outcast monks and nuns, from whom in old days
he had been accustomed to receive every sort of kindness,
now passed his door, begging for food and shelter. The spoil
which he had perhaps filched from the monastery suppressed
near by, had not been sufficient to repay him for the injury
to the inmates whom he had been taught to love and respect.
His griefs are vividly described in the following verses of a
song written for the Yorkshire rebels in the autumn of 1536:

1.

Crist crucifyd
for thy woundes wide
vs commons guyde
　which pilgrames be
thrughe godes grace
for to purchache
olde welth & peax
　of the spiritualtie.

2.

Gret godes fame
doith church proclame
now to be lame
　and fast in boundes
robbyd spoled & shorne
from catell & corne
and clene furth borne
　of howsez & landes.

3.

alacke alacke
for the church sake
pore comons wake
　& no mervell

for clere it is
the decay of this
how the pore shall mys
　no tong can tell.

4.

for ther they hade
boith ale & breyde
at tyme of nede
　and succur grete
in alle distresse
and hevynes
*　*　*　*
　and wel intrete.

5.

In troubil & care
where that we were
in maner all bere
　of our substance
we founde good bate
at churche men gate
without checkmate
　or varyaunce[1].

[1] Cal. xi. 786 (3).

Such were the complaints which arose among the country
folk as a result of the suppression of the monasteries. And
just at the moment that this intensely unpopular measure
began to be carried out in earnest, and largely as a result
of it, the veil which had hitherto prevented the people from
recognizing the true author of the hated innovations was torn
away, and a pretext was offered for a revolt, which had it
been directed against the King, would have been no better
than treason. The people fastened on Cromwell as the author
of all their troubles; and the thought that a man whom they
knew to be low-born, of no better or more noble origin than
themselves, had been able to cause them such misery, was
enough to kindle a smouldering fire of discontent into
a brilliant blaze. A crusade against Cromwell, they argued,
could not be regarded as a revolt against the royal authority.
They had no complaint against the King, or even against any
of the nobles, but they were determined to rid themselves
at one blow of the plebeian minister whom they thoroughly
detested and whom they had no cause to respect: with the
destruction of Cromwell and his agents, they were certain
that the good old days would return. The last verse of their
war-song contained a frank avowal of their object:

> 'Crim[1] crame[2] & riche[3]
> with thre Ill[4] and the liche'[5]
> as sum men teache
>     god theym amend
> And that aske may
> without delay
> here make A stay
>     and well to end[6].'

The reasons why the rising against the authority of Cromwell, known to posterity by the suggestive name of the Pilgrimage of Grace, was organized, and set afoot in the northern
counties, are not far to seek. In the first place devotion to
the Old Faith, and to the cause of Queen Katherine, was
far stronger in the north than in the south of England.

---

[1] Cromwell.                [2] Cranmer.              [3] Richard Riche.
[4] The Bishop of Lincoln, Dr. Legh, and Dr. Layton.
[5] The Bishop of Lichfield.                [6] Cal. xi. 786 (3).

A comparison of the 'comperta' of the northern and southern monasteries, or of the details of the different visitations, will easily convince the reader of this discrepancy. In the south occur constant complaints by the monks that their superiors failed to observe the canons of religious asceticism; and on the other hand, whenever an abbot refused to acknowledge the Royal Supremacy, his subordinates were always sure to report him to head quarters, in the hope of gaining favour with the King or Cromwell[1]. The letters of Dr. Legh from the south of England contain frequent reports of 'towardness' among the inmates, and willingness to adopt the New Faith[2]. In the north one finds none of this. The reports concerning the monasteries there are of a very different sort: immorality and unnatural crimes are the principal charges against the inmates[3]. There is scarcely a record of apostasy; scarcely a case of mutual accusation among the monks. The abbots and their subordinates almost invariably supported each other, and their loyalty to the Old Faith and their hatred of those who tried to disestablish it, gave the Commissioners a far harder task in the north than in the south. There is also reason to think that Cromwell's spy system operated less perfectly there, partly owing to this spirit of conservatism and love of the old usages permeating every sort and condition of life, and partly owing to the great spaces of wild, uninhabited land.

This is only the religious side. But there were other almost equally valid reasons for the localization of the revolt in the north. The south was thickly populated, and to a certain extent commercial; the north sparsely populated, and for the most part pastoral and agricultural. Cromwell had done everything that he could to facilitate trade, and his efforts in this direction had been rewarded by comparative popularity in the commercial counties. The discontent in the agricultural north, however, was most pronounced. The Statute of Uses had not been in all cases correctly interpreted. It was said that the King made such laws that when a man died his wife and

---

[1] Cal. ix. 314, 321, 322.     [2] Cal. ix. 694.
[3] Cal. x. 364.

children had to go a-begging [1]. Lastly, the proximity of the
Scottish Borders, which were in a continual state of disorder,
offered great encouragement for undertaking a rebellion in
the north. Cromwell was constantly occupied with the
suppression of minor disturbances there [2], owing to the very
lax administration of the Courts and Wardens of the three
Marches, while across the Tweed an attitude of more or less
active hostility to the English government was always
maintained. There was every probability that a revolt in the
northern counties of the realm would receive substantial aid
from Scotland.

But though the Pilgrimage of Grace was locally restricted
to the northern counties, it embraced all classes, animated
by the most varied interests [3]. The objects of the insurgents
were secular and religious, their mottoes conservative and
progressive. On their banners were borne the emblems of
the five wounds of Christ, a chalice and a host, a plough, and
a horn. The first of these symbols indicated that the
insurrection had been undertaken for the defence of the
faith ; the second was to remind the commons of the spoils
of the Church. The plough was to encourage the husband-
men, and 'the horn was in token of Horncastle': for the
banner 'was brought among the rebels by the commons of
Horncastle [4].' The watchwords of the rebels were of the
very most diverse nature. Some of them cried out for the
restoration of the suppressed monasteries ; others for the renewal of guarantees against exorbitant taxation, for remedies
for the agrarian discontent, or for legal permission to leave
land by will to daughters and younger sons. All of them
united in demanding the destruction of Cromwell, whom the
people regarded as the cause of all their woes [5]. The leaders
and participants in the revolt were not of any one rank or
station in life ; the popular and aristocratic elements were
almost equally mixed. It is no wonder that a rising,

---

[1] Cal. xi. 705, 780 (2) ; xii. (i) 70 ;     also A. L. Smith in Social England,
xiii. (ii) 307.                                vol. iii. pp. 21 ff.
[2] Letters, 105.                              [4] Cal. xii. (i) 70 (13).
[3] Cal. xii. (i) 138, 786, 900. Cf.           [5] Cal. xii. (i) 163.

supported by men of such various classes, which aimed at
the extirpation of abuses of so many different sorts, and
which yet was united by the feeling that all these abuses
were due to one man alone, was regarded as 'the daungerest
insurrection that haith ben seen[1].'

On September 29, 1536, when the Commissioners for the
suppression of the monasteries came to Hexham in Northumberland, they were rudely surprised by finding the house
there fortified, and prepared to defend itself to the last.
The Commissioners left the town and reported the affair to
the King, who ordered them to assemble all the forces they
could muster, and if the monastery did not yield, to treat
the monks like arrant traitors[2].  But scarcely was this danger
past when news came that the Commissioners for levying the
lay subsidy, the collection of which was superintended by
Cromwell, had met with a similar experience at Caistor in
Lincolnshire.  It seems they had feared some disturbance
at their arrival, and had invited several country gentlemen
to join them in case of any danger.  A large force had
meantime assembled to resist the payment of the subsidy.
The country gentlemen were pursued, taken, and forced to
write to Lord Hussey at Sleaford, to summon him to join
the rebel commons, unless he wished to be treated as an
enemy, and also to send to the King to seek a general
pardon[3].  Hussey promptly reported the state of affairs to
Cromwell, and though he put a bold face on the matter in
presence of the rebels, it is evident that he was seriously
alarmed[4].  The King meantime himself received the letter
the captured gentlemen had been forced to send him, caused
the bearers of it to reveal the names of the ringleaders, and
wrote to the Commissioners for levying the subsidy, expressing his distress at the 'vnnatural vnkyndness' of his subjects,
and marvelling 'that he that is worth xx li sholde rebell for
the payment of x s[5].'  But this sort of letter of mild surprise,
with which Henry had sometimes successfully warded off

---

[1] Cal. xi. 585.

[2] Cal. xi. 504, 544.

[3] Cal. xi. 533–4, 536–9, 552–3, 567–8.

[4] Cal. xi. 547.

[5] Cal. xi. 569.

pressing danger, did not prove to be sufficient in this case.
He was relieved from any apprehension on his own account ;
the rebels had expressly denied any desire to be disloyal to
the King : they only wished that the Church of England
should have its old privileges, 'without any exaction,' that
the suppressed houses of religion be restored, and that they
should not be taxed, except for defence of the realm in time
of war.   Again and again did they repeat their demands for
the surrender or banishment of Cromwell, Audley, Cranmer,
Riche, and others of the Privy Council.   That the King did
not throw over his ministers in their hour of need, surely
shows that Henry was committed to them and to their policy,
and believed in it.

The situation was certainly alarming.   It was very fortunate
that at the time of the outbreak the position of the King was
otherwise so strong, and England's foreign affairs in such
good condition, that every effort could be centred on the
suppression of the revolt.   The insurgents evidently meant
business.   Sir Christopher Ascugh, gentleman usher to the
King, wrote to Cromwell, October 6, ' The rebels ar in nombre
of men of armys well harnesyd x or xii m spars and bows ; &
xxx m other sum harnesyd and sum not harnesyd . . . . . . and
all the contrey Rysys holly as they goo before them. . . . . . .
Mellessent your seruaunt they have hanged & Baytyd Bellowe
to deth wyth Dogges wyth a bull skyn vpon his bake wyth
many Regorous wordes agaynst your lordeshepp [1].'   Letters
were sent to the principal men in the county, asking them to
use all their efforts to check the revolt, and the King later
declared his intention to take the field himself [2].   Cromwell's
nephew Richard [3] got all the arrows and implements of war
out of the Tower, and dispatched a number of men to
Lincolnshire, among them sixty or eighty masons and
carpenters, who were at work on his uncle's house.   Cromwell
himself was in great fear.   The Imperial ambassador informs
us [4] that the whole blame for the insurrection was laid

---

[1] Cal. xi. 567.
[2] Cal. xi. 579-80.
[3] The son of Morgan Williams

and Katherine Cromwell. Cf. chap.
iii. pp. 54-5.
[4] Cal. xi. 576.

on him. Norfolk was recalled to the Court, whence he had been banished at Cromwell's suggestion, and the Duke arrived at London, happy as he had never been before in the thought that the first step towards the ruin of his rival had been taken. But in this he was doomed to disappointment, for Cromwell retained his ascendancy; the King, according to Chapuys, had been very reluctant to send for the Duke, and when the latter was dispatched again to raise men and prevent the spreading of the revolt, he was overtaken by a most 'discomfortable' message from the Court, ordering him to send his son in his place while he himself remained at home[1]. Cromwell had not only succeeded in getting him away from the Court, but had also prevented his having a hand in the suppression of the rebellion. The Lord Privy Seal himself was content with maintaining his position at the King's side. It would have been sheer madness for him to have marched against the rebels in person. If the Lincolnshire men could have murdered him, they probably would have been induced to return quietly to their homes. Nor did Cromwell even dare to give orders at arm's length, or in any way to undertake the management of the royal forces. He kept himself consistently in the background; almost all our information concerning the rebellion is contained in the correspondence of the King with Norfolk and Suffolk. The few letters which Cromwell did write in connexion with the Pilgrimage of Grace are quite unimportant[2]. They consist for the most part of messages of profuse and almost hysterical thanks to the leaders of the King's party for their loyal service. It was not until the revolt had been thoroughly suppressed that Cromwell ventured again to assume the general direction of public affairs.

Meantime the Duke of Suffolk and the Earl of Shrewsbury had been sent against the rebels, who were waiting in Lincolnshire for the King's answer to their first letter. Richard Cromwell had found great difficulty in conveying to the scene the arms and artillery he had got out of the Tower, because the people were at first unwilling to furnish the

---

[1] Cal. xi. 601-2.        [2] Letters, 165, 167, 169.

requisite number of horses, owing to sympathy with the insurgents, if one may believe the report of Chapuys' nephew[1]. Finally, however, he succeeded in overtaking the Duke of Suffolk, who was marching with an army against the rebels from the south, at Stamford on October 10. The Earl of Shrewsbury, according to the King's orders, was advancing at the same time from Nottingham. Caught between two armies supplied with the ordnance which the insurgents so much dreaded, the Lincolnshire men, further frightened by a proclamation from the Earl of Shrewsbury transmitted to them by one Thomas Miller, Lancaster Herald, began to lose heart and finally consented to surrender, on condition that they should receive assurance of merciful treatment. The King was pleased, ordered the rebels to deliver up their arms, and commanded Shrewsbury and Suffolk to examine the country gentlemen who had aided them, and report to him[2]. He further wrote an answer to the insurgents, calling them the 'rude commons of one shire, and that one of the most brute and beestelie of the hole realme[3],' expatiating on the trouble he had given himself in their defence, and assuring them that they had no grounds to complain of any of the new measures, either secular or religious. He was just thinking that the worst part of the danger was over, when suddenly news came from Lord Darcy, who was the chief person in the north, that all Yorkshire had risen in a similar way[4].

The news of this outbreak was even more disquieting than that of the first. Besides being much further from London, where the King's armies could only reach them with great difficulty, the Yorkshire rebels were nearer the lawless and hostile Scottish borders. They had from the very first been in sympathy with their neighbours in the south, and had communicated with them by means of beacons burned on the banks of the Humber[5]. The same motives had prompted them to rise in arms. They elected as captain a young

---

[1] Cal. xi. 714.
[2] Cal. xi. 674, 694, 706, 715, 717.
[3] State Papers, vol. i. p. 463.
[4] Cal. xi. 611.
[5] Cal. xi. 563, 622.

barrister named Aske, who issued a proclamation for all men
to assemble on Skipworth Moor, and take oath to be faithful
to the King's issue and noble blood, to preserve the Church
from spoil, and be true to the commonwealth—a clever
euphemism for demanding the death of Cromwell and his
adherents. The Yorkshiremen had gone about their revolt
with far more method and system than the Lincolnshire
rebels. The latter had been easily conquered, mainly because
they lacked a head; but the Yorkshiremen promised to
give far more trouble. They made musters by scrolls and
bills nailed to the door of every church in the county, and
proclaimed that any one who refused to take their oaths
and rise with them should be put to death, whether he
was lord or peasant. It was even rumoured that they intended to send an embassy to Flanders, to ask for aid in
money and armed men, and to petition the Pope for abso-
lution for all offences committed in the course of their holy
pilgrimage [1].

The King replied at once to Darcy's letter, commanding
him to arrest all seditious persons, and promising so to treat
the originators of the revolt in Lincolnshire that all York
should soon learn that they had got their deserts [2]. Darcy
wrote to the Lord Mayor of York, warning him to be
prepared to resist the insurgents, while he himself proceeded
to Pomfret Castle to hold it against the rebels, and there
awaited further instructions from the King [3]. He succeeded
in maintaining his position at Pomfret for only ten days
however, for on October 20 he surrendered the town to
the rebel army under the leadership of Aske, and together
with the Archbishop of York, who had sought refuge there,
swore to take part with the insurgents [4]. At his trial in the
following year he pleaded that he was unable to hold out
any longer because the provisions had run short, and further
stated that he had been compelled to side with the rebels
under pain of death. He also alleged as an excuse for his
conduct that he thought that if he got in touch with the

[1] Cal. xii. (i) 163, 259, 1080.    [3] Cal. xi. 627.
[2] Cal. xi. 611.    [4] Cal. xii. (i) 900, 944.

insurgents, he could the more easily induce them to lay down their arms. How loyal he really was to the King must remain a matter of conjecture, but there is strong reason to think that he had much sympathy with the revolt [1].

For a time the rebels seemed to carry all before them. Shrewsbury had been ordered to go to Yorkshire and engage the insurgents there, now that Lincolnshire was regarded as safe. Meantime Thomas Miller, Lancaster Herald, who had been so successful in obtaining the submission of the Lincolnshire men, was sent by the King from Scrooby, on October 21, to read a royal proclamation to the rebels at Pomfret, upbraiding them for their conduct, but promising them pardon on condition that they should immediately disperse. When he arrived at his destination the town had been surrendered. Aske, although he treated the royal envoy with all due respect, entirely refused to let him read his proclamation in public, and sent him away with two crowns and his errand unaccomplished [2].

Meantime the Duke of Norfolk, who two weeks before had returned sadly to Kenninghall with all his hopes of regaining the royal favour blighted, had been hurried to and fro in the south of England by a continued stream of conflicting orders from Cromwell and the King, until he finally heard of the disturbances in Yorkshire from Shrewsbury [3]. He immediately turned his steps with a small company of men towards Doncaster, in the hope of regaining the King's favour by a prompt suppression of the new outbreak. So anxious was he to recommend himself to Henry, that he spent £1,500 of his own in paying the wages of the King's soldiers ; and when this was not sufficient, and Henry refused to advance any money, he asked for a loan to meet the expenses, and took the responsibility for its payment upon himself [4]. Norfolk's whole proceeding in this crisis was eminently characteristic. He never hesitated to spend money or to tell lies, if he thought that by so doing there was any possibility of gaining

[1] Cal. xii. (i) 853, 1087.
[2] Cal. xi. 826.
[3] Cal. xi. 626, 671, 758.
[4] Cal. xi. 793, 800.

the royal favour. He assured the King that, in treating with rebels, he would pay no respect to what others might call his 'honour distayned,' for he considered it perfectly permissible to break promises in order to serve the Crown [1]. Henry, it would seem, did not take Norfolk's treacherous proposals to sacrifice his own honour in the royal service in as good part as the Duke had hoped, and wrote back hinting that if Norfolk made promises to the rebels that he could not keep, he must make them on his own responsibility, and take great care that the King's name remained unsullied.

When the Duke arrived in the rebel country he issued a proclamation to the insurgents, commanding them in proud and haughty terms to submit, and promising to be an intercessor for them with the King. This was on October 27. But the very next day he wrote to Henry that he had been forced to declare to the insurgents the royal pardon, in order to 'sparple' them, and get them to return to their homes [2]. It is evident that in the meantime a meeting must have taken place between the Duke and the rebels, in which the latter succeeded in convincing their enemy that they, and not he, were in the position to dictate terms. A general truce was arranged, and Lord Darcy was ordered to cease to molest the insurgents [3]. The dread with which Norfolk awaited his first interview with the King is vividly described in the letter in which he announced to the Council his prospective return to the Court. ' I come,' wrote the Duke, 'with my hert nere bresten . . . . inforced to appoynt with the rebelles . . . . and fearing how his maieste shall take the dispeachyng of our bande [4].'

Norfolk finally arrived at Windsor with two emissaries from the insurgents, who were to report their grievances and receive the King's answer. Henry was just composing his reply when news came that Aske had attempted to stir up the rebels in the other northern counties. Norfolk wrote to Darcy that the King suspected him of treachery in delivering up Pomfret to Aske, and advised him to do his best to

---

[1] Cal. xi. 864.      [3] Cal. xi. 901.

[2] Cal. xi. 887, 902.      [4] Cal. xi. 909.

' extinct the ill bruit,' by taking the rebel leader dead or alive [1]. Meantime the King detained Ellerker and Bowes, the two rebel envoys, as hostages, while Darcy attempted to allay any fears of a third outbreak. The King in fact was so seriously alarmed at the danger in the north, that he dreaded that his letter to the Lincolnshire men in early October might not prove sufficient to prevent their joining a new revolt, if such occurred. So seeing their ' maner, im-plieng a great repentance,' and contrasting it with the rebel-lious attitude of the Yorkshiremen, he sent them on the 14th of November a full pardon [2]. Meantime the report of the probability of a fresh insurrection passed by, and Ellerker and Bowes returned with the King's answer, with which Henry had taken much trouble, and had endeavoured to disguise the fact that he was really suing for peace, by pro-mising to pardon those who were truly penitent. A conference for discussion of terms was arranged to assemble at Doncaster on the 5th of December, in which Lords Scrope, Latimer, Lumley, Darcy, and others were to represent the rebels, and Norfolk, Suffolk, Shrewsbury, Rutland, and their subordinates the King [3].

Henry laid his plans carefully in preparation for this meeting. He instructed Shrewsbury to do his utmost to prevail upon Aske and Darcy to betray the rebels, upon promise of a free pardon for themselves. He also ordered the Duke of Suffolk to hold himself in readiness with a large force in case of another outbreak [4]. There was probably far less danger that the truce would be broken by the rebels than by the King ; but the former certainly had no intention of returning to their homes without at least an assurance of a general amnesty. Henry soon realized that they were in earnest, and reluctantly instructed Suffolk, in a second letter, to yield to their demands for a free pardon and a Parliament as a last resort, if all other expedients to induce them to disperse should fail [5]. The conference at Doncaster lasted

---

[1] Cal. xi. 995.
[2] Cal. xi. 1061.
[3] Cal. xi. 957, 995, 1115, 1206.

[4] Cal. xi. 1224, 1225.
[5] Cal. xi. 1236.

four days, but in the end the rebels were successful in gaining their wishes, and the desired pardon was proclaimed on the 9th of December [1]. Henry had never before been forced to acknowledge such a complete check at the hands of his subjects, and the sensations of the proud King must have been as disagreeable as they were novel. Still it was impossible for him to give vent to his rage until he had once more obtained the upper hand.

So he wrote to Aske requesting an interview with him in London. The tone of the letter is noteworthy. Though evidently beaten, Henry spoke as if he were master of the situation, and began by stating that he had learned that Aske was sorry for his offences in the late rebellion. The King also did his utmost to stop any rumours on the Continent which might give the impression that the rebels had come off victorious. He instructed Cromwell to write a full account of the revolt to Gardiner and Wallop at the French Court, ordering them to tell all people that though at first the insurgents 'made peticion to haue obteyned certain articles, . . . . in thende they went from all and remytted all to the kinges highnes pleasure only in moost humble and reuerent sorte desiring their pardon, with the greatest repentance that could be deuised [2].' But Henry was a little premature with his boasts that peace had been concluded on terms so favourable to himself. Aske indeed came up to London, had what certainly appeared to be a most successful interview with the King, and returned to the North, January 5, 1537, to confirm the royal pardon, and to promise that all reasonable petitions should be heard by Parliament [3]. But the other rebels did not seem by any means as sure of Henry's good faith. Aske wrote to the King a letter containing six 'marvilus congectures' of the people, among which were the dread with which they regarded the fortifying of strongholds, and their distrust that Cromwell and his adherents were as high in favour as ever [4]. Henry of course paid no attention to these complaints, with the result that many of the insurgents,

[1] Cal. xi. 1276.
[2] Letters, 174.
[3] Cal. xii. (i) 44.
[4] Cal. xii. (i) 67.

who 'saw plainly,' as the Court historian writes, 'that the King did constantly follow the reformation of the abominable Church . . . incontinently renewed the old practice of rebelling again[1].' A plan was evolved by Sir Francis Bigod and a certain John Hallam, to attack and take both Hull and Scarborough : the whole country was ready to rise again, and they anticipated an easy victory[2]. But the success of this last outbreak was very short-lived. The attempt which Hallam made against Hull failed, owing to the fact that the plot had been reported to the mayor there, and Hallam himself was captured[3]. At Scarborough Bigod was scarcely more fortunate. He had succeeded in calling out the people of the East Riding, and had harangued them ; 'Ye are deceaued by a colour of a pardon,' he said, 'for it is called a pardon that ye haue, and it is none But a proclamacion.' The commons responded to his words with a great shout, and he marched off with a large following to repair his comrade's disaster at Hull, leaving the son of Lord Lumley with a handful of men to attack Scarborough[4]. But Lumley deserted his post, abandoning the command to two subordinates, who attempted to lay siege to the castle of Scarborough in the absence of its keeper, Sir Ralph Evers ; the latter, however, soon returned, and they gave up the enterprise, only to be captured and imprisoned. Bigod's second attempt on Hull had meantime also failed, and Bigod himself fled[5].

Meantime the Duke of Norfolk had returned into the north, no longer as a peace commissioner, but as a messenger of death and destruction[6]. Now that the tide of affairs had turned and the rebels were weakened, the King thought it at last safe to inflict the long-deferred punishment on the leaders of the revolt. It is true that Norfolk was accompanied by a few persons, who together with certain gentlemen in the north were to compose a council to aid him in carrying out a general pacification : this arrangement, however, was obviously temporary, and it was soon to be replaced by a more stable form

---

[1] Thomas, The Pilgrim, p. 53.
[2] Cal. xii. (i) 201, 370.
[3] Cal. xii. (i) 104.
[4] Cal. xii. (i) 369.
[5] Cal. xii. (i) 234, 369 (p. 166).
[6] Cal. xii. (i) 86, 98.

of government. The true mission of the Duke was to do
'dreadful execution.' Before a permanent reorganization of
the north could be attempted, it was absolutely essential
that the chief rebels should be dealt with in such a way
as would deter others from attempting a fresh insurrection. The situation demanded severity, and there can be
no doubt that the inclination of the King tallied closely
with the dictates of political expediency. Norfolk justified
to the full the confidence that Henry reposed in his
ruthlessness. He reported that he thought that so great
a number had never before been put to death at one time,
and confessed that had he proceeded by jury, not one in five
would have suffered [1]. All the rebel leaders were taken and
sent up to London, and by the end of July, 1537, Aske,
Darcy, Hussey, Bigod, and many others had been condemned
to death as traitors. Darcy at his mock trial had dared to
tell Cromwell: ' It is thow that art the verey originall and
chif causer of all thies rebellyon and myschif . . . and dust
ernestly travell to bring vs to owr end and to strik of our
hedd*es* and I trust that . . . thought thow woldest procure
all the nobell mens hedd*es* within the Realme to be striken
of, yet shall ther one hedde remayn that shall strike of thy
hede [2].' But the Lord Privy Seal was still in too secure
a position to be harmed by any such words as these. He
seemed in higher favour than ever. If Norfolk had entertained the notion that he had begun to supplant his rival
in the royal favour, when the King chose him rather than
Cromwell to carry out the 'dreadful execution,' he was
again doomed to disappointment. The reason why the
King had not been willing to employ his favourite instrument of destruction in this case, lay for the most part in
the fact that he needed his aid in a far more important
task, to which Norfolk's proceedings were merely
a necessary preliminary. For the moment had now arrived
for the long-contemplated reform of the government of the
north, a matter in which the Duke vainly attempted to
give advice. His proffered counsel was consistently rejected:

[1] Cal. xii. (i) 498.          [2] Cal. xii. (i) 976.

in dealing with this problem the King preferred to consult Cromwell.

The Border Counties of England had never been governed like the rest of the kingdom [1]. The institution of the three Scottish Marches, which at first included the greater part of Northumberland and Cumberland, took its rise as early as the middle of the thirteenth century. Each of these three Marches was placed in charge of a Warden, who, aided by a special court, exercised general authority, judicial, military, and administrative, according to his commission. There appears also at a very early date a kind of informal conference or Council of the Marches, composed of the ordinary March authorities, sitting in conjunction with local magnates. When the war with Scotland broke out at the end of the thirteenth century, the King attempted through the Privy Council to increase his personal influence in the north. He did not disturb the existing organization however. By special commissions he strengthened the power of the Wardens, and later gave the government of the Marches a definite head in an officer called the Lieutenant of the North, who represented the King's interest, and derived his authority from the Crown and Council and not from Parliament. The Border Counties were thus placed under a special jurisdiction and outside the ordinary administration of the kingdom. The tendency of the Privy Council to mingle in the affairs of the north increased during the fourteenth and fifteenth centuries, and (as a result of the strained relations between England and Scotland in the early part of the reign of Henry VIII) reached its culmination under Wolsey. The Lieutenant's control had meantime been extended southward into Yorkshire.

It may perhaps seem strange that the Tudors, with their special genius for centralization and conciliar government, had not yet succeeded in rendering the condition of the north more satisfactory, when its administration lay so completely in their own hands. But the ever-threatening danger of a

---

[1] On this and the succeeding pages, cf. G. T. Lapsley, 'The Problem of the North,' in the American Historical Review for April, 1900, pp. 440-66.

raid from the Scots, coupled with the bitter feuds of the local baronage, tended so far to disorganize the region that the problem of the north had remained unsolved. The attempt of Wolsey to reform the government of the Border Counties had consisted in a thorough rehabilitation of the old Council of the Marches. He replaced the ill-defined, loosely-constructed body which had hitherto done service by a secret, permanent organization, composed principally of northern gentlemen, but still entirely dependent on the Privy Council. His reluctance to grant the local organ a sufficient degree of autonomy was the cause of the failure of his plan. The renovated Council of the Marches was forced to confess itself incompetent to deal with even the simplest problems which presented themselves for solution, and the old unsatisfactory state of affairs continued with little change, until after the Pilgrimage of Grace.

The problem of the reorganization of the north was now vigorously attacked by Henry and Cromwell during the absence of Norfolk. The question which presented itself after the suppression of the revolt was whether it would be better to create an entirely new form of government for the north, or to reconstruct, readapt, and strengthen the old. The principle of control by a permanent local council, first definitely established by Wolsey, was essentially characteristic of the Tudor policy, and Henry and Cromwell saw no reason to depart from it. It had been one of the chief sources of the strength of their rule, that though they never shrank from any change, however radical, which the demands of a royal despotism in Church and State rendered necessary, they carefully avoided any gratuitous innovations which they knew would be unwelcome to the people at large. An entirely fresh organization of the north would have been exceedingly unpopular, especially in that most conservative portion of England: it was far less obnoxious, and equally effective, to infuse new life into the old régime, by granting the Council of the Marches a sufficient degree of independence, and above all by changing its composition. The problem was in many respects similar to that with which Cromwell had been confronted in connexion with the election of bishops. No radical innovation was needed in either case; the *status quo*, when fortified by official sanction, was perfectly satisfactory, save for a few trifling readaptations. It was on this basis accordingly, that Henry and Cromwell resolved to reconstruct the government of the Border Counties. The old forms were retained though under different names. The jurisdiction of the Council of the North (merely a new version of the old Council of the Marches) was extended so as to include the counties of Northumberland, Cumberland, Westmoreland, York, and Durham. It was given wider competence in general administration, and its judicial authority in certain cases was so strengthened as to exclude that of the ordinary courts in the districts in which it exercised its functions[1].

Far more interesting for our purpose than the jurisdiction of the newly-organized Council, is its composition, especially as revealing the identity of its originator. It seems that the new body was largely composed of men of low birth, a certain indication that Cromwell's was the guiding hand in its organization[2]. The 'base-born knave' at whose feet England lay had succeeded in proving to the King, that he and others of humble origin had as much power and willingness to serve the Crown as any nobleman in the land. Moreover the personal character of many of the members of the new Council was not above reproach, and though this fact does not seem to have disturbed the King, a bitter protest was evoked from Cromwell's rival, the Duke of Norfolk, who, from his isolated position in the north, had watched with increasing impatience the success of the Lord Privy Seal in maintaining his influence at Court, and in organizing a body obviously intended to supplant the temporary council composed in the previous January. Norfolk's anxiety to recommend himself to the King had alone induced him to take upon himself the task of punishing the revolt; now that he discovered that with all his subserviency Cromwell had again stepped into the place which he had coveted for himself, his enthusiasm for executing rebels gave place to

---

[1] Cal. xii. (i) 595.          [2] Cal. xii. (ii) 914.

petitions to be permitted to return to Court. But Cromwell
was strong enough to keep him in the north till September,
and the Duke was forced to content himself with writing
letters to the King and Council, to complain of the new
arrangements for the government of the Borders which had
been made in his absence[1]. He and Cromwell came into
collision here, just as they had done before over Irish affairs:
each had his own idea as to the best method of government
in both cases, and the antagonism of the two men was the
sharper in that each knew that his favour with the King
depended on the success of his plan of administration. The
Duke from the very first was convinced that ' the wylde
peple of all the Marches wolde not be kept in order vnles
one of good estimacion and nobilitie have the ordering
therof,' while Cromwell and the Council asserted that the
King had already been ill served on the Borders ' by the
reason of controversy & variaunce depending between the
great men that ly upon the same ' ; but, they continued, ' if
it shal please his Majesty to appoynt the meanest man . . .
to rule & govern in that place ; is not his Graces aucthoritie
sufficient to cause al men to serve his Grace under him without respect of the very estate of the personage ?[2] ' The
dispute on this point began in early February, when Norfolk
wrote to protest against certain names in a list of officers
for the north which the Privy Council had sent him.
' More arraunt theves and murderers be not in no Realme,'
asserted the Duke, ' then they haue of Long tyme been
and yet ar . . . and the same shall not only cause Light
persounes to saye and beleve that the Kinges Highnes
is fayne to Hire with Fees the moost malefactors ⟨in
order⟩ to syt in rest, but also not to Loke vppon theire
most detestable offences[3].' An animated correspondence
on this topic continued for several months, the dispute
finally centering about the Presidency of the new Council
and the Wardenships of the three Marches ; Norfolk insisted
that only noblemen were fitted to hold these offices[4]. In

[1] Cal. xii. (i) 318, 319, 321,     [3] Cal. xii. (i) 319.
594, 651.                            [4] Cal. xii. (i) 651, 667, 916,
    [2] Cal. xii. (i) 594, 636.           919.

May the discussion was finally closed by the King, who had steadily supported the position adopted by Cromwell and the Council. Henry now took the matter into his own hands, and sent a peremptory letter to the Duke. 'We doo accept in good parte,' wrote the King, 'the declaracion of your opinion for the Marches. Neuertheles we doubt not but you woll both conforme your owne mynde to fynde out the good order whiche we haue therin determyned and cause other by your good meane to perceyve the same For surely we woll not be bounde of a necessitie to be serued there with lordes, But we wolbe serued with such men what degre soeuer they be of as we shall appointe to the same [1].' The Presidency of the Council was finally conferred on Cuthbert Tunstall, Bishop of Durham. The death of the Earl of Northumberland in June, 1537, served as a convenient pretext for the suppression of the Lord Wardenship of the East and Middle Marches, which that nobleman had previously enjoyed; and the Earl of Cumberland, who had hitherto held a similar office on the West Marches, was not permitted long to retain it. Three Deputy Wardens, Sir William Evers, Sir John Witherington, and Sir Thomas Wharton, were appointed in their places by the King and Cromwell [2]; the three March Courts were revived, and exercised concurrent jurisdiction with the new Council [3], which was also composed as Henry and his minister had originally planned it [2]. In every point the advice of Cromwell had been taken in preference to that of Norfolk, and when the Duke finally obtained leave to return to Court in September, it must have been with the feeling that he had again suffered defeat at the hands of his plebeian rival. The rebellion, which eleven months before had threatened to hurl Cromwell from his place, had been completely quelled, and the country had been again reduced to internal quiet. The danger while it lasted had indeed been pressing, but so firmly had Cromwell been established as the King's chief minister by the events of the years 1530 to 1536, that the storm passed over him and left him scath-

[1] Cal. xii. (i) 1118.    [2] Cal. xii. (ii) 254, 914.
[3] Cf. Gneist, pp. 513-4.

less.   The failure of the Pilgrimage of Grace and the process of reconstruction which followed it, bore witness to the thoroughness with which he had carried out his main aim in internal government, and to the security of the position to which he had elevated himself by his temporary success in establishing a royal despotism.

# CHAPTER XI

## CARDINAL POLE

THE story of the life of Reginald Pole and of the destruction of his illustrious family will always be inseparably bound up with the history of Thomas Cromwell. It affords the most striking example of the unscrupulous policy of the King's minister towards those who stood in the way of the royal despotism in Church and State. It forms moreover a valuable connecting link between the internal and foreign administration of the time, as it concerns itself with nearly all the great problems which Cromwell had to face.

To turn for a moment to the earlier history of Pole; he was born in March, 1500, the fourth son of Sir Richard Pole, and his wife Margaret, Countess of Salisbury[1]. In his youth Henry had helped him forward in his education, paying twelve pounds for his maintenance at school, and later obtaining for him a pension from the Prior of St. Frideswide's, while he was an undergraduate at Magdalen College[2]. Subsequently, by the royal munificence Pole was enabled to go to Italy, where he worked with the foremost scholars of the time[3]. He returned to England in 1527 and there received many marks of distinction, but wishing to continue his studies, he soon removed to Paris. Henry was particularly anxious that the University there should pronounce in favour of the divorce, and with some difficulty induced Pole to carry on negotiations with it to that intent. When the University finally came to the decision that the King desired, Pole received a hearty letter of commendation and was subsequently induced to return to England[4].

---

[1] Phillips, Pole, p. 3. Cf. also the genealogy at the beginning of the book.

[2] Cal. i. 4190.
[3] Cal. iii. p. 1544.
[4] Cal. iv. 6252.

Henry now urged him openly to support the divorce, and offered him as an inducement the archbishopric of York, which had been left vacant at Wolsey's death, but in vain. Pole firmly refused to approve of the King's new measures, saying that to do so would be inconsistent with his principles[1]. A little later he witnessed the concessions wrung from the clergy concerning the Royal Supremacy, and was not slow to perceive that it was by Cromwell's agency that the entire ecclesiastical system of the country had been overthrown. He called to mind the conversation he had held years before with the 'Satanae Nuncius,' when the latter had dared to uphold the superiority of Machiavelli's doctrines to the scholastic learning, and soon became convinced that England was not a safe place for a man of his ideas, while such a person as Cromwell was in power. He accordingly requested leave to continue his study of theology abroad, and obtained Henry's consent[2].

He settled down at Padua, and there lived the quiet life of a scholar until 1535, when the King determined to find out about him. He sought information concerning Pole and his beliefs from one Thomas Starkey, who had long been an intimate of the future Cardinal. In answer to the King's inquiries Starkey sent back an imaginary dialogue between Pole and his companion Lupset, in which the former was represented as opposed on principle to a royal despotism, but still personally faithful to Henry VIII. The King, however, was not contented with this vague and half-contradictory reply, and caused Starkey to write again to Pole and ask him honestly to express his views about the divorce and the Royal Supremacy[3]. To this Pole responded in May, 1536, with a letter enclosing his famous treatise, 'De Unitate Ecclesiae,' which he sent by his faithful servant Michael Throgmorton[4]. This work fulfilled all too perfectly Henry's request for a candid opinion; so plain were its expressions of disapproval, that even Starkey himself felt obliged to write to the King to say how much he had been shocked by its

---

[1] Poli Epistolae, i. 251–62.      [3] Cal. viii. 217–9.
[2] Cal. v. 737.                    [4] Cal. x. 974–5.

violence[1]. Henry dissembled his anger, and sent Throgmorton back to Pole with a message urging him to come home in order that he might talk with him more fully. The King took good care to make Throgmorton himself promise to return in any case[2]. Coupled with the King's message came a letter of reproof from Pole's mother, which had evidently been written at Henry's command[3]. This letter aroused Pole's suspicions and he refused to return, alleging as his excuse the fact that the King enforced with 'sore severitie' a law by which any man who would not consent to his supremacy was declared a traitor. It appears from Pole's reply that Cromwell had also written to him, 'to styrr hym the more vehemently.' If the letter of the King's minister was half as savage and threatening as those which he later wrote, it is no wonder that Pole was alarmed.

On the 22nd of December, 1536, Pole much against his will was created Cardinal at Rome, and two months later was appointed Papal legate to England[4]. It appears that in spite of the Ten Articles the Pope had not yet given up all hope of re-establishing his power in Henry's dominions, and had determined to make use of Pole as the most likely means of accomplishing this end. The news of the latter's new dignity and of the Papal intentions against England was received with dread at the King's Court. It was remembered that as far back as 1512 a prophecy had been made to the effect, 'that one with a Red Cap brought up from low degree to high estate should rule all the land under the King, . . . . and afterwards procure the King to take another wife, divorce his lawful wife, Queen Catherina, and involve the land in misery'; and that further 'that divorce should lead to the utter fall of the said Red Cap . . . and after much misery the land should by another Red Cap be reconciled, or else brought to utter destruction[5].' We are told that Cromwell knew this prophecy well, and that he often discussed it, and sought to learn whether the last part of it should some day come to pass, as he had seen the first fulfilled in his own time. Had

---

[1] Cal. xi. 156.　　[2] Cal. xi. 229.　　[4] Cal. xi. 1353; xii. (i) 779.
[3] Cal. xi. 93.　　　　　　　　　　　　[5] Cal. xiv. (i) 186.

Pole been able to arrive in England promptly, so that he could have taken advantage of the disturbance caused by Bigod's rebellion, it is possible that Cromwell's fears might have been realized before his death, and that a reconciliation with Rome might have taken place in 1537 instead of in 1554. But the bull of legation was unaccountably delayed till the 31st of March[1]. Meantime the northern revolt had been crushed, Francis and Charles were still at war, and Pole's chance had gone. By this time Henry had doubtless perceived that the new-made Cardinal could never be induced to support his cause, but would certainly oppose it as long as he lived. As reconciliation seemed impossible, the King turned his thoughts to arrest or execution. The foreign affairs of England at that juncture were in such a favourable condition that Henry felt strong enough to dictate both to the Emperor and to the King of France. Informed by the latter (who was just then in terror of losing England's friendship because of his war with Charles) that Pole was coming through France with money to help the northern rebels, Henry was bold enough to demand in answer that he should not be received as a legate, and also that he should be extradited as a traitor ; he also wrote to Gardiner at Paris to keep 'good espyall' on his movements[2]. A letter from Sir Thomas Palmer, a somewhat quarrelsome knight at Calais, would seem to indicate that a plot to apprehend or assassinate Pole had been set on foot as early as the spring of 1537, and Cromwell in a letter to Gardiner of May 18 further discusses the matter[3]. Pole, however, had been advised of these treacherous schemes, and had escaped first to Cambray and later to the palace of the Cardinal of Liège, where he remained, grieved and mortified at the failure of his mission, but perfectly safe from Cromwell's assassins[4]. Returning thence to Rome at the Pope's command, he reported the unsuccessful result of his journey in October.

Meantime in January, 1537, Michael Throgmorton had

[1] Cal. xii. (i) 779.
[2] Cal. xii. (i) 625, 939.
[3] Cal. xii. (i) 1219; Letters, 187.

[4] Life of Pole, Dictionary of National Biography, vol. xlvi. p. 38.

fulfilled his promise and returned to England[1]. If Henry
had once thought that Pole's servant would put his loyalty
to the Crown before his faithfulness to his master[2], he must
have been convinced of his mistake by this time; but
Throgmorton was saved from punishment for the present by
Henry's temporary failure to subdue the Pilgrimage of Grace,
and anxiety lest fresh hostility should be aroused abroad; and
was soon sent back to carry to his master a final warning
to desist from attacking the Royal Supremacy[3]. From this
errand Throgmorton did not return; it would have been the
act of a madman to do so, considering the way in which
events were moving. Instead, he wrote two long and conciliatory letters to Cromwell, one from Rome on February 15,
the other from Liège on August 20[4]. In the first he
attempted to appease the anger of the King, which had
been aroused by Pole's acceptance of the Cardinalate. In the
second he insisted that Pole had always done his utmost for
the advancement of the King's honour and good name, except
in matters which concerned the unity of the Church. Furthermore he pointed out that though Henry had treated him as
a rebel and put a price upon his head, the Cardinal had shown
great forbearance in not leaving his book against the King
in the hands of the Pope, who would infallibly have published
it, and in refusing the exercise of certain censures which had
been prepared against Henry in Rome. Throgmorton added,
moreover, that the Pope had just called Pole back to Italy to
take part in the General Council appointed for the following
November, at which it was inevitable that strong measures
would be taken against England. He assured Cromwell that
if the King desired to avoid this danger it would be indispensable for him to become reconciled to Pole, on whose attitude
at the Council so much depended. Throgmorton appears to
have supplemented this letter with a verbal suggestion that
a conference should be arranged between the King's chaplain
Dr. Wilson and the Cardinal, before the latter's departure for

---

[1] Cal. xii. (i) 34, 249.

[2] There is reason to think that
Throgmorton had promised to be
a spy on Pole's movements for

the King. Cf. Letters, 218.

[3] Cal. xii. (i) 249, 296, 313.

[4] Cal. xii. (i) 429; xii. (ii)
552.

Rome, in the hope that some final agreement might be reached. He promised to use his own efforts to induce Pole to do his part, and seized the opportunity to excuse himself for not returning to England, by observing in this connexion that he could best further the King's interests by tarrying with his master.    At first the plan which Throgmorton proposed seems to have found acceptance with Henry.    A favourable reply was drawn up by Cromwell, and Dr. Wilson and his companion, Dr. Nicholas Heath, received instructions preparatory to a conference with Pole[1].    But though Henry, discouraged as he was by his failures to kill or capture the Cardinal, appears to have been momentarily persuaded that Throgmorton's suggestion was feasible, his minister from the first was strongly opposed to it.    The first draft of the reply to the letter of Pole's servant bears every evidence of having been written under compulsion, and Cromwell must have succeeded, before it was actually sent, in persuading the King that a mission which was to meet the Cardinal on his own ground could only result in failure, and that the sole thing to do was openly to menace Pole and his family with assassination.    Such at least seems the most probable explanation of the fact that Wilson and Heath never started on their errand, and of the singularly abusive and malevolent letter with which Cromwell finally replied to that of Throgmorton[2].    The last hope of reconciliation with the Cardinal had vanished ; not he alone, but also his aged mother and brother in England, had been threatened with destruction.    Another obstacle to Henry's despotism was to be annihilated, as every attempt to surmount it had failed.

Pole meanwhile remained in Italy, assured of his personal safety but grieved to the heart that his mother and brother were still in England, where the King could take vengeance on them for his own alleged treason.    In August, 1538, his brother, Sir Geoffrey Pole, was arrested and placed in the Tower, where he was examined on the charge of having had treacherous correspondence with his brother Reginald, and

[1] Letters, 216-7.                    [2] Letters, 218.

having interfered with the King's endeavours to arrest him [1]. His replies to the questions put to him implicated many others, and before the close of the year the heads of the powerful families of Montague, Courtenay, Delawarr, and Nevill had been arrested and sent to the Tower [2]. There is reason to believe that the confessions of Sir Geoffrey Pole were extorted from him by threats of torture, to serve as an excuse for the arrest of these noblemen, and a letter of Castillon to Montmorency asserts that their destruction had been decided on long before, on account of their connexion with the Yorkist dynasty [3]. Cromwell's activity in procuring matter for the various indictments is sufficiently attested by an enormous number of notes of evidence and memoranda for prosecution in the hand of his chief clerk. The apparent difficulty which he had in trumping up any plausible charges against his victims, would seem to show that no adequate proof of any really disloyal intent could be found. Indeed, in order to have any sort of excuse for the arrests of the Marquis and Marchioness of Exeter, Cromwell had to exhume a long forgotten episode, and accuse the latter of having ridden in disguise three years before to confer with the Holy Maid ; while it was remembered that the Marquis had been put in the Tower in 1531 on the charge of assembling the commons of Cornwall for an insurrection, with intent to depose the King. An unfortunate remark of Courtenay's that ' Knavys rule about the Kyng,' and that he hoped 'to gyue them a buffet oone day,' was brought up against him as a treasonable sentence ; it certainly could not have been pleasing to Cromwell, who was doubtless the arch-' knave ' referred to [4]. But it is very unlikely that any of the un-

---

[1] Cal. xiii. (ii) 232 (p. 91).

[2] Cal. xiii. (ii) 695, 770, 771.

[3] Cal. xiii. (ii) 804, 805, 954-60.

[4] Cal. xiii. (ii) 802, 979 (7). It is said that Cromwell, in the course of these prosecutions, contrived to deprive the victims of all chance of escape by inquiring of the judges whether, if a man were condemned to death for treason in Parliament without a hearing, the attainder could ever be disputed. He finally succeeded in obtaining the reluctant but correct reply that ' an attainder in Parliament, whether or not the party had been heard in his own defence, could never be reversed in a court of law.' Cf. Hallam,

fortunate noblemen had been guilty of crimes which could fairly be interpreted as treason. The French ambassador had hit upon the real secret of their offences when he remarked that they all were adherents of the White Rose[1]. In fact the whole plot against Pole may in one sense be regarded as preparatory to a final attack on the Yorkist nobles, whose position had never been secure since the accession of the House of Tudor. Blow after blow had been struck against them by Henry VIII and his father, but still some vestige of them seemed always to remain, to threaten the King's position and endanger his succession. There can be no doubt that Cromwell, whose action in the case was certainly influenced more than usual by personal animosity, found little difficulty in persuading the King that the existence of Courtenay was a serious menace to the security of the reigning dynasty, on account of the claim that he had to the throne as grandson of Edward IV. At any rate, Henry seemed resolved on a wholesale destruction of all nobles who could possibly be regarded as rivals of the Crown, and the relationship of most of his victims to the family of the persecuted Cardinal afforded him a pretext of which he did not fail to take advantage. Exeter, Montague, and Nevill were beheaded in December, on Tower Hill, while Sir Geoffrey Pole, who had been tried and condemned with them, was spared, mainly, as Cromwell frankly told Castillon at the end of December, because the King expected to get something more out of him[2]. He was ultimately pardoned, but passed the rest of his life in musing, 'going about,' says a contemporary writer, 'like one terror-stricken all his days[3].'

The Marchioness of Exeter and the Countess of Salisbury were meantime held prisoners in the Tower. On May 12,

vol. i. pp. 29-30. Coke, Fourth Institute, p. 38, adds, 'The party against whom this was intended was never called in question, but the first man after the said resolution, that was so attainted, and never called to answer, was the said Earl of Essex (Thomas Cromwell): whereupon that erroneous and vulgar opinion amongst our historians grew, that he died by the same law which he himself had made.'

[1] Cal. xiii. (ii) 753.
[2] Cal. xiii. (ii) 986, 1163.
[3] Wriothesley's Chronicle, vol. i. p. 92.

1539, 'the moste tractable parlament' that Henry ever had passed a sweeping bill of attainder, to legalize the wanton massacres of the preceding year and to destroy the victims who still remained[1]. The Marchioness of Exeter was subsequently pardoned, but the Countess dragged on a miserable existence in prison for more than two years after her attainder. The only evidence of her treason was a cloth which had been found in her house, embroidered on one side with the arms of England and on the other with the five wounds of Christ, the emblem carried by the rebels in the Pilgrimage of Grace. Still execution was delayed, and it was not until the spring of 1541, almost a year after the death of Cromwell, that an insurrection in Yorkshire under Sir John Nevill sealed her fate, and she was barbarously beheaded by a clumsy executioner on May 28[2].

Meantime the Cardinal at Rome, powerless as he was to prevent the ruin of his family, was contriving in some way to humble the arrogant King and the ruthless minister who had caused him so much woe. The Pope saw that what Henry dreaded most of all was a coalition of Francis and Charles, and as there was a good prospect of this event at the close of 1538, he sent Pole to each of these two sovereigns to urge them to agree to stop all trade with England and lay the foundation for a continental league against her. Pole gladly accepted the task, and careless of his own safety, though he knew that his path would be full of Henry's hired assassins, he set out for Spain and reached the Emperor's Court at Toledo in safety in February, 1539. When the King heard of his arrival there, he wrote to Charles in very much the same way that he had addressed Francis two years before, accusing Pole as a traitor, and demanding his extradition as such, or at least insisting that Charles should not grant him an audience[3]. But unfortunately Henry was now no longer in a position to dictate, and the Emperor, realizing this, saw no reason to accede to his request, and answered, as Cromwell later wrote to Wriothesley, that if

---

[1] Cal. xiv. (i) 867, c. 15.     [2] Cal. xvi. 868.
[3] Cal. xiv. (i) 279-280.

Pole 'were his owne traytour, commyng from that holy
father' he could not refuse him audience[1]. But in spite
of all this, the Cardinal's mission was a failure. Charles for
the present was content with the slight rebuke that he had
given Henry for his bullying ways ; cautious as ever, he did
not propose to put himself in a position from which he could
not retreat until he was sure of his ground, and intimated
to the legate that the Pope had made a great mistake in
publishing censures which he could not enforce. Pole could
not obtain his consent to the Papal proposals and left Toledo
much discouraged[2]. He was also exceedingly suspicious
of some design of Sir Thomas Wyatt's to cause his assassination, and mentioned it in a later letter to Cardinal Contarini[3].
That his fears were not entirely groundless is shown by
a cipher letter from Wyatt to Cromwell containing many
passages pregnant with hidden meaning which can only be
explained if such a design is premised[4]. Pole soon betook
himself to his friend Sadolet at Carpentras, whence he sent
a messenger to Francis on the same errand as that on which
he himself had gone to Charles. The French King's reply was
as unsatisfactory as the Emperor's had been, and in 1540 the
Cardinal returned to Rome with his mission unaccomplished,
and deriving only small consolation from the thought that he
had been successful in baffling the attempts of Henry's and
Cromwell's assassins.

The story of Pole's life between 1535 and 1540 is the
thread which binds together the foreign and domestic, secular
and religious history of Cromwell's administration. The
Cardinal's attempts to make the King renounce his title
of Supreme Head and the other insignia of the despotism
to which Cromwell had raised him at home were an absolute
failure, and were punished with the shockingly unjust and
cruel destruction of his family. Still his efforts to thwart
the main aim of the foreign policy of the time, namely the
separation of the interests of France and Spain, though not
directly successful, were instrumental in bringing about the

<hr>

[1] Letters, 301.
[2] Cal. xiv. (i) 603.
[3] Cal. xiv. (ii) 212.
[4] Cal. xiv. (i) 560.

fall of his arch-enemy Cromwell. For the endeavours of the Cardinal were one of a number of things which combined to persuade the minister that the catastrophe which seemed imminent throughout the year 1539 could not be averted without external aid, and thus to induce him to take a step on his own responsibility which soon led him into disastrous conflict with the King.

# CHAPTER XII

## THE FOREIGN POLICY

DURING the ten years of Cromwell's ministry, the relations of England with the great continental powers presented a problem fully as difficult as that afforded by the course of events at home. Cromwell's efforts to cope with the dangers which threatened England from without were far less successful than his internal administration: in the latter he never failed to render invaluable service to the Crown, while in the former he made the mistake which finally lost him the royal favour and brought him to the block. As the results of the minister's external policy thus led directly to his fall, we may now return to the chronological order of events, which was abandoned while the various phases of his home government were under consideration.

Cromwell had entered the King's service in 1530 with training and talents which rendered him far more competent to undertake the domestic administration of the country than to guide its foreign affairs. His acquaintance with different trades, his legal ability, and his experience in the suppression of the smaller monasteries for Wolsey's purposes were of inestimable value to him throughout his ministry in dealing with problems at home. But in the management of affairs abroad he was still very inexperienced. He had borne no part in the great schemes of external policy which had occupied the Cardinal, and though his speech in the Parliament of 1523 showed a very just appreciation of the situation of England abroad, he had had no opportunity to put his ideas into practice. Thus at the outset we find him cautiously remaining in the background and awaiting the development of the King's foreign policy. In this he was wise, for at Wolsey's fall Henry had resolved to take the external administration of England into his own hands. We have seen that the Cardinal's failure had taught him the danger of concluding any definite alliance with either France or Spain, while the two great continental rivals remained at war. He had learned that England's best security lay in maintaining a position of neutrality between Charles and Francis, and in balancing one against the other, while all disputes between them were encouraged under cover of offers of mediation. It was along these lines that Henry had determined to guide the foreign affairs of England, as soon as order could be brought out of the chaos caused by the divorce. How correct his decision was is proved by the utter collapse of the Imperial alliance of 1543, the only really permanent departure from the policy of neutrality which Henry ever made after the death of Wolsey. A complete change of the political horizon led him into it, only to be left in the lurch by the Emperor at the peace of Crêpy[1] in the same way that he had been abandoned before by Francis at the treaty of Cambray. But during the life of Cromwell the King made no such blunder as this. Though he sometimes wavered, he never definitely renounced the policy of neutrality, although his minister, who sometimes doubted its efficacy, made several efforts to induce him to abandon it. There can be no doubt that, from the very first, Cromwell over-estimated the danger of a foreign invasion and failed to appreciate the real strength of England's isolated position : he was deceived by constant menaces which never really bore fruit. A more intimate acquaintance with the practical and calculating nature of Charles V would certainly have convinced the King's minister that however much the Emperor threatened, he would never actually embark on the somewhat remote project of a crusade against England, until a great many affairs in his own scattered dominions on the Continent had first been settled to his satisfaction. But Cromwell's inexperience in the management of foreign affairs blinded him to this important fact : and his over-eagerness to seek means for England's defence proved his ultimate ruin. After successfully co-operating with Henry for seven years on

[1] Cf. Robertson, vol. ii. p. 135.

the basis of maintaining strict neutrality between France and
Spain, and of encouraging all disputes between them, he
abandoned the wise policy of his master in favour of an
alliance in Germany which, in one form or another, had been
under consideration on several occasions before, but which
had been abandoned every time as unnecessary. This new
alliance turned out disastrously. At the moment of its
completion, the situation on the Continent which had called
it into existence suddenly changed; it was thrown over,
together with the minister who had originated it. Such
is the outline of the history of England's foreign affairs
from 1530 till Cromwell's fall. We can now take up the very
complicated story in detail.

Although Henry ardently desired at once to put in practice
the policy of neutrality which he had learned from Wolsey's
failure, the affair of the divorce had thrown everything into
such confusion that an immediate application of the new
principle was impossible. In fact it was not until the
beginning of the year 1536 that the King was able to assume
the position he desired in his relations with France and Spain.
The alliance with France which Wolsey had bequeathed to
Henry was so close that the King saw that he must at least
partially withdraw from it, before he could hope to come
to such terms with the Emperor as would enable him to act
the part of a neutral and benevolent mediator between the
foreign powers. But at this juncture the King's anxiety
to obtain a legal justification for his second marriage was
paramount in his mind. In fact it almost seems to have
blinded him temporarily to the policy that he doubtless
intended ultimately to pursue. His energies were all bent
towards securing the aid of Francis in his 'grete matier';
and for the moment he postponed his policy of conciliating
the Emperor, who was of course at that time in league with
the Pope. Each pair of allies had interviews and counter-
interviews, but with very different results. While Henry and
Francis were at first most cordial, Clement counted Charles'
proffered friendship as of slight weight, against the prospect
of losing the support of the two most powerful kings of

Christendom, and of being forced to submit to the summoning of the General Council by which the Emperor proposed to rectify the abuses which had crept into the Holy Church [1]. The visit at Bologna of Francis' ambassadors, Cardinals Tournon and Grammont, undid all that Charles' threats had accomplished [2], and Clement, although he feebly menaced Henry with excommunication in case he proceeded with his second marriage [3], refused to accede to the Emperor's wishes that he should take more active measures against England. Meantime Henry had endeavoured to come to an understanding with the See of Rome concerning the hearing of his case before a Council, in the hope that by giving the Pope fair words, he might still obtain a favourable decision [4]. The King's confidence in the ultimate success of his efforts was so high at the opening of the year 1533, that he dared to give it expression by increasingly harsh treatment of Katherine. She was moved further away from the Court than ever before, and hardly a day passed without seeing her subjected to some new indignity. Every effort which her friends made on her behalf seemed unavailing. As petitions to Henry himself were unanswered, Chapuys in despair turned to Cromwell, whom he had by this time recognized as the man who managed all the King's affairs [5]. But Cromwell succeeded in evading the demands of the Imperial ambassador also; in fact he displayed such ability in 'beknaving' Chapuys that Henry always employed him in future to answer the perfectly justifiable complaints of the Spanish representative. Cromwell delayed the interview which the ambassador had requested until he had had time to consult with the King [6]: and when he finally met Chapuys, he spent much time in applauding all the efforts that had been made to maintain friendly

[1] Ranke, Popes, vol. i. p. 77.
[2] Cal. vi. 64, 92.
[3] Cal. v. 1545.
[4] Cal. vi. 110.
[5] Cal. vi. 465.
[6] Cal. vi. 508. Cromwell often begged to be excused from a promised interview on the plea of illness. Cf. Cal. vii. 959. Though it is certain that he suffered at times from violent attacks of ague, it is doubtful if it was always his ill-health which prevented him from fulfilling his engagements to the Imperial ambassador.

relations between Spain and England. But when urged to do
his best to protect the Queen and Princess from the ignominies
to which they were subjected, Cromwell's replies were evasive,
if not absolutely untruthful. Chapuys was so exasperated at
the cool way in which his claims to justice had been set aside,
that he took occasion to hint that Charles and Francis might
some day join forces against England, to 'which Cromwell
assented, but showed no great joy thereat.' The threat,
however, had no lasting effect. The treatment of the Queen
went on from bad to worse, and two months later the same
conversation took place all over again, with the same
unsatisfactory result[1]. As long as Cromwell consented to
obey his master's commands implicitly, and to devote himself
solely to finding means to carry out the plans which the
King's riper experience told him were feasible, without trying
to take the lead himself, the two were an almost invincible
combination.

But the time was soon to come when Chapuys' prophecy
of a coalition of France and Spain seemed more likely to be
fulfilled. Henry's impatience to conclude his matrimonial
troubles finally led him to throw caution to the winds. He
had, as we have already seen, postponed the application of
his wise policy of neutrality in the hope of obtaining aid from
France. But the French King did not move quickly enough
to suit him, and in the summer of 1533 he committed such
a breach of diplomatic courtesy that he completely alienated
his 'nere and dere brother.' He had overtaxed his friendship
with the King of France by requiring him to support every
move he made, and to threaten the Pope, if his Holiness
refused to do the same. Francis only partially acceded to
Henry's wishes. Meantime all hope of obtaining the divorce
from Rome had been abandoned owing to Cromwell's advice ;
the affair was tried in England, and Anne Boleyn was
publicly proclaimed Queen. A provisional sentence of excommunication was passed on Henry in July, giving him
till September to decide whether he would take Katherine
back or not. A few months before, Francis and Henry had

---

[1] Cal. vi. 918; viii. 263, 327, 355, 948; ix. 594.

together endeavoured to win over the Pope against the Emperor: now that the bull of excommunication had come, Francis continued his good offices by offering to mediate for Henry with the Holy See. Henry, however, blusteringly assured him that he was not in need of any mediation—he hoped that Francis would not trouble himself[1]. But the latter would not take the hint that England's policy towards the See of Rome had changed from conciliation to open hostility, and invited Clement to meet him at Marseilles, to see if he could not bring about an agreement. The Pope, who needed Francis' aid in the furtherance of his own plans for the prevention of the dreaded Council, readily accepted the opportunity which had been offered[2]. Henry was of course unable to prevent an interview between the two potentates, but he attempted to throw cold water on the whole affair by sending an embassy to Clement while the latter was the guest of the King of France, to announce to his Holiness that he intended to appeal against his sentence to the very General Council which the Pope was attempting to forestall. The chief result of this extraordinary proceeding was simply to deprive the King of the only ally that he had. Francis was naturally exceedingly angry, and flatly refused to fight Henry's battles for him any more[3]. Such was the reward reaped from the alliance which Wolsey six years before had been at such pains to bring about, in the hope of obtaining much-needed support in the matter of the divorce[4]!

So far it certainly seemed as if Henry's foreign policy,

---

[1] Cal. vi. 614, 641.

[2] Ranke, Popes, vol. i. p. 77.

[3] Cal. vi. 1426, 1427.

[4] Mr. Friedmann (Anne Boleyn, vol. i. pp. 225, 250 ff.) believes that this break with France was due to the influence of Cromwell, who had urged the King to strike out an independent policy as regards the Pope. M. Bapst (Deux Gentils-hommes, pp. 97, 113), on the other hand, thinks that the King's minister originally favoured the French alli-ance, and adhered to it until 1535.

Neither writer produces any very conclusive evidence in support of his theory: but Mr. Friedmann's view is certainly, on the face of it, the more plausible. It may be too much to say that it was by Crom-well's advice that Francis was in-sulted at Marseilles, but it is certain that the King's minister evinced a decided preference for an Imperial alliance long before the year 1535. Cf. Froude, The Divorce of Cathe-rine of Aragon, p. 308.

instead of gaining him his desired position as neutral and pretended mediator between France and Spain, had only served to alienate both. As his cruel treatment of Katherine and Mary had not improved his position with Charles, he had to cast about for other allies to counterbalance the effect of his tiff with Francis. It is at this juncture that Cromwell first steps into prominence in connexion with foreign affairs. There can be little doubt that the negotiations with the Lutheran princes, which began in July, 1533, were planned by him. It is of course natural to look to the man, whose name six years later became inseparably associated with a German alliance, as the originator of the scheme; in addition to this there is documentary evidence. A letter which Chapuys wrote to the Emperor, July 30, 1533, informs us that two of Cromwell's men (one of whom later turned out to be his trusty Stephen Vaughan) had been sent to Germany presumably 'to embroil' all they could [1]; and on August 3, a letter reporting the progress of the ambassadors was written by them to Cromwell from Antwerp [2]. Vaughan and his companion, a certain Christopher Mont, arrived in Nürnberg on the 22nd, whence they sent home minute accounts of the state of religion in Germany; the one observing, with apparent regret, that the country was not nearly as disturbed as had been thought, while the other assured Cromwell that he had never seen a land whose towns were so much divided [3]. Some time in the autumn Cromwell sent a reply to Mont, praising his diligence, and urging him above all things to discover the state of feeling in Germany towards the King of England and the Emperor [4]. The envoy appears to have returned from his preliminary tour of investigation before the close of the year, for in January, 1534, he was sent back again to Germany, this time accompanied by Nicholas Heath, with instructions to convey to the Lutheran princes the sympathy of the King of England, as being also an enemy of the Pope, and to express his willingness to unite with them for the extirpation of false doctrines [5]. England's overtures,

[1] Cal. vi. 918.　　　[2] Cal. vi. 934.　　　[3] Cal. vi. 1039-40.
[4] Letters, 64.　　　[5] Cal. vii. 21.

however, were not received with as much enthusiasm as Henry perhaps had expected, and nothing definite resulted from the mission of Heath and Mont for a long time. The Germans probably had serious misgivings about the genuineness of Henry's Protestantism, and their suspicions of his sincerity were confirmed by a new development of England's foreign policy in the same year.

As one of the consequences of an unwarrantable act of piracy near the English coast in the autumn of 1533, Henry had been able to get hold of a prominent young man of the violently Protestant town of Lübeck, by name Mark Meyer. At London he was treated with the greatest courtesy by the King and Cromwell, and returned to his native city invested with the honour of knighthood [1]. Such bounty was seldom showered on anybody by Henry VIII without some ulterior purpose, and Meyer's case was no exception to the general rule. It soon transpired that proposals had been made for a close alliance between England and Lübeck [2]. Ever since the peace of Stralsund in 1370, the cities of the Hanseatic League had claimed a decisive voice in the affairs of the neighbouring realm of Denmark [3]: the death of the king of that country in April, 1533, had left the throne vacant, and Lübeck was at this moment bent on obtaining the disposal of it. Henry signified his willingness to aid the Lübeckers in this enterprise, on condition that they would promise that if they were successful they would be guided by him in the final bestowal of the Danish crown. In May, 1534, the Lübeckers sent an embassy to England [4], and the proposals of the previous year were accepted.

The new alliance had a very important bearing on the larger issues of Henry's foreign policy. The social and political revolution which had been in progress in Lübeck since 1530 had placed the power in the hands of a party whose anti-papal tendencies were fully as violent as those of the Wittenberg theologians, and whose conscientious scruples were of less weight, when thrown into the scales of political

---

[1] Cal. vi. 1510.  
[2] B. M. Nero B. iii, 105.  
[3] Schäfer, p. 512.  
[4] Rymer, vol. xiv. p. 539.

expediency[1]. The treaty concluded with England contained certain doctrinal statements which lay suspiciously close to the needs of Henry's immediate position[2], and the King must have been at least temporarily convinced that he had obtained a valuable ally against the See of Rome. The treaty with Lübeck was also a very distinct move against the Emperor, for an Imperial candidate had been proposed for the vacant throne of Denmark, and by supporting the Lübeckers Henry necessarily opposed Charles. But the new alliance failed to accomplish what was expected of it: in fact it actually worked to England's disadvantage. Before its conclusion, George Wullenwever, the demagogue whom the recent upheaval had rendered temporarily supreme in Lübeck, had offered to support the claims of the Lutheran Duke of Holstein to the Danish throne; but when Holstein, unwilling to gain his ends by force, prudently refused the proffered aid, the friendship of the Lübeckers was converted into bitter enmity. They soon invaded his lands, but were repulsed and besieged in turn in their own city: a peace of a most extraordinary nature finally resulted, by which an agreement was reached in regard to the affairs of Holstein, though both parties reserved the right of continuing the war for the disposal of the crown of Denmark. That country in the meantime, seeing that its sole chance of safety lay in obtaining a strong and capable leader, elected the Duke of Holstein to the vacant throne, under the title of Christian III —a severe blow to the pretensions of the Lübeckers, who were now robbed of their best excuse for interference in Danish affairs, namely their professed desire to introduce pure religion there[3]. Lübeck, however, had now gone too far to draw back, and prepared to attack the new King in

---

[1] Waitz, vol. i. p. 83.

[2] One of the provisions of the proposed agreement was: 'Ducere uxorem fratris mortui sine liberis est jure divino et naturali prohibitum. Contra prohibitiones divinas invalida ac prorsus nulla est Romani pontificis vel cujuscumque alterius dispensatio.' Entwurf eines Vertrags zwischen König Heinrich und Lübeck; Sommer, 1534. Transcribed from the original in the Archives at Weimar; Waitz, vol. ii. pp. 319-25.

[3] Ranke, vol. iii. pp. 406-425.

connexion with England. Henry must have been much annoyed at the complication into which his new alliance had led him—it seemed doubly foolish, in view of his attempts to conciliate the German Protestants, that he should get himself entangled with the enemies of those whom he wished to make his friends. But though the King was advised by Dr. Barnes, the English ambassador at Hamburg, to drop Lübeck and conciliate Christian[1], he was as usual too proud to acknowledge that he had made a mistake. He soon reaped the reward of his obstinacy, as the Lübeckers, in their new attempt to overthrow Christian, were again completely defeated. Henry had aided them with the services of two skilled engineers, and the Danish King sent an embassy to demand an explanation of his conduct[2]. Christian's envoy was treated with scant courtesy by the King and Cromwell, the latter vainly attempting to conceal his master's anxiety by several preposterous lies[3]. But still the King was unwilling to consent to a complete reversal of his Lübeck policy, and finally sent the ambassador home with an answer which Chapuys characterizes as 'obscure and ambiguous.' Several subsequent victories of Christian, in which certain English ships which had been sent to aid the Lübeckers were captured, were sufficient however to convince Henry that he had unduly despised the power of the new Danish King; and though his relations with Lübeck continued to be friendly, he carefully abstained from any further active measures on her behalf. But he had already done enough at least temporarily to alienate his Lutheran friends, who were shocked at the way in which the King of England attached himself to people whose religious principles were as extreme as those of the Lübeckers, and who had dared to attack one of their own number.

Thus each of the two alliances with which Henry had sought to fortify himself against France and Spain had rendered the other worthless. The King probably bitterly regretted that his matrimonial difficulties had led him to stray so far from the policy which he originally intended to pursue.

---

[1] Cal. vii. 970.    [2] Cal. viii. 72, 327.    [3] Cal. viii. 556, 1178.

Had he been able to secure his desired position as neutral and pretended mediator between France and Spain, he could have relied on this eminently advantageous situation alone to secure safety for England abroad, without troubling himself about any outside alliance. But to attain this position was impossible, as we have seen, until he became reconciled to Charles, and reconciliation with Charles was out of the question as long as Katherine remained subjected to such indignity. Here lay the key to the whole situation. The treatment of the divorced Queen was the sole hindrance to a cordial relation between Spain and England, and consequently to the final application of the policy which Henry so ardently desired. But there could be no hope of an alleviation of her sufferings, for the King and Cromwell were by this time irrevocably committed to a brutal attitude towards Katherine and her daughter by the course of events since the first trial of the divorce. The inference was obvious. As long as Katherine lived, a reconciliation with Charles, with all its attendant benefits, was impossible: her death alone could pave the way for it. That these thoughts had already taken shape at least in Cromwell's mind is proved by a hint which the King's minister dropped in Chapuys' presence in August, 1534, to the effect that the death of the Queen and Princess would remove all occasion for a quarrel between their masters [1].

But the autumn of 1534 saw several events which served to encourage the King and his minister, and seemed temporarily to postpone the necessity of coming to terms with the Emperor. The first of these events was the death of the Pope in September, an occurrence which, according to Chapuys, caused Henry and Cromwell such joy that the latter was 'unable to refrain from saying several times in public that this great devil was dead, and it seemed as if he was very sorry that he could find no worse name for him than devil [2].' Francis moreover, solely on account of his very strained relations with Charles, had slowly begun to recover from the effects of Henry's discourtesy at Marseilles, and had made fresh efforts to come to terms with England again ;

[1] Cal. vii. 1095.          [2] Cal. vii. 1257.

while Henry, unwilling as yet to proceed to extremities in order to gain the friendship of Charles, welcomed the prospect of a renewal of amity with France. But the satisfaction which the King derived from the attitude of Francis was rudely dispelled in a few months. Several interviews which had been arranged between the two sovereigns had failed, for various reasons, to take place, but the Emperor meantime had not been idle. Imbued with the idea of vindicating the rights of the Princess Mary by some decisive stroke, he had actually sent the Count of Nassau to the French Court to suggest that Francis should ask Henry to give her to the Duke of Angoulême[1]. Francis considered the Emperor's plan worth a trial, and in October sent over an embassy under Admiral de Brion to propose it to the King of England. Henry had little idea of the unpleasant surprise that was in store for him, and made great preparations for the reception of the Frenchmen, and Cromwell sent for a number of beautiful young ladies to come to the Court to entertain them[2]. There seems to be some doubt whether de Brion first proposed that Mary should be given to the Duke of Angoulême or to the Dauphin[3], but both suggestions were equally disagreeable to Henry. An acceptance of either proposal would of course involve retracting his declaration that Mary was illegitimate, and annulling his hard-earned invalidation of his first marriage, and yet he dared not insult Francis a second time. His first reply, according to Chapuys, was that he would agree to give Mary to Angoulême if both would make a solemn renunciation of all claims that they could bring forward to the English throne[4]. But the Spanish ambassador seemed to think that this proposal would not prove satisfactory, and we gather from the official report of Henry's answer that the suggestion was dropped. Instead, however, the King finally replied that if Francis could obtain from the new Pope a decision that the sentence of Clement was void, he might be induced to renounce his claim to the French throne in exchange for certain lands

---

[1] Cal. vii. 1060, and Baumgarten, vol. iii. pp. 145-6.
[2] Cal. vii. 1437.
[3] Cal. vii. 1483, 1554.
[4] Cal. vii. 1554.

and titles in the Netherlands, and further hinted that it might
be possible to arrange a match between Elizabeth and the
Duke of Angoulême[1]. But this proposal amounted to little
more than a diplomatic refusal of Francis' request. De Brion
went away disappointed, and forgetting his usual caution, and
the fact that England was still in a stronger position than
France, determined to avenge himself for the failure of his
mission by parading before the eyes of Cromwell and his
master the probability of the dreaded alliance of France and
Spain, in much the same way that Chapuys had done in the
previous year. When Cromwell appeared in the great hall
to make the farewell present, the Admiral disengaged himself
from the crowd, and came to the Imperial ambassador with
the greatest civility, expressing his regret at not having seen
the Princess Mary, 'the principal gem of the kingdom,' and
finally declaring that if he and Chapuys could only bring their
masters to accord, all would go well[2].

In spite of Cromwell's boasting, we may well believe that
de Brion had succeeded in making Henry feel very uncomfortable. The inferences which the King must have drawn from
the conduct of the ambassador at his departure were further
confirmed by the ominous silence from France which followed
the Admiral's return. But Francis himself was in too precarious a position to afford to throw away any chances, so
after a couple of months' delay, he pocketed his pride and sent
over another embassy under Palamedes Gontier, Treasurer of
Brittany, to continue negotiations on the basis of a marriage
between Elizabeth and the Duke of Angoulême. Henry was all
the more annoyed that Francis should take him at his word,
and entertain seriously the somewhat chimerical proposal
with which he had dismissed de Brion ; and the mission of
Gontier failed as signally as its predecessor had done, in
coming to any definite conclusion[3]. But Henry had chosen
a very poor moment to administer this final rebuff; for the
Emperor had departed on an expedition against Tunis, and
thus left Francis a comparatively free hand on the Continent.
The advantage of position had hitherto lain with England,

---

[1] Cal. vii. 1483.        [2] Cal. vii. 1507.        [3] Cal. viii. 174, 557.

but the absence of Charles totally altered the aspect of affairs. The French King felt himself once more master of the situation, and was not slow to inform Henry that he did not propose to be dallied with any longer. The reconquest of Milan was at this moment his heart's desire ; to accomplish it he needed English aid. So he commissioned the Bailly of Troyes to convey to Henry a Papal brief which had been sent to the French Court, and which required all Christian princes to cease to hold intercourse with the heretical King of England ; he further instructed his ambassador to make it clear that the sole consideration which would induce the King of France to disregard the brief, would be a liberal contribution of English gold, whenever he saw fit to make war on the Emperor. This announcement, which was practically an ultimatum, took Henry completely by surprise : angry words passed between him and the French envoy, but there was no use disguising the fact that Francis had the upper hand [1]. The King finally sent Gardiner to Paris to answer the French claims ; the instructions which the ambassador received reveal a much more conciliatory attitude than Henry had yet adopted towards France [2]. The gravity of the situation was further confirmed by the seizure and detention at Bordeaux of several English ships, for the recovery of which Cromwell kept writing urgent letters to the Bishop of Winchester [3]. It was at this juncture that the King and his minister made a feeble effort to reap some reward from the mission of Heath and Mont to the Lutherans in the preceding year. Attempts were made to bring the reformer Melancthon to England, or at least to prevent his going to Francis, who had sent for him in order to obtain the support of his followers against Charles [4]. The latter effort was superfluous ; the former failed. Melancthon had no intention of going to France, but the King and Cromwell could not persuade him to come to England either. Henry's agent, Dr. Barnes, however, informed the Lutherans that the King would not refuse to join in an alliance with them for the defence of the Gospel, provided they would

[1] Cal. ix. 148, 205, 594, 595.
[2] Cal. ix. 443.
[3] Letters, 126, 128, 135.
[4] Letters, 113.

support him against the Pope, and he promised them that another ambassador, the Bishop of Hereford, would come and talk further with them[1]. At the close of the year the envoy was received in Germany. Long negotiations followed, at first with some hope of success. A request by the English ambassador that the Germans would unite with his master in a refusal to recognize a General Council convoked by the Pope, was favourably received ; and the plenipotentiaries of the Lutherans drew up a response in which they expressed themselves as entirely in accord with Henry in regard to the See of Rome, and offered the King of England the proud title of Defender and Protector of their league. As long as the Bishop of Hereford restricted himself to theological discussion and abuse of the Pope all went well, but when he made the more practical demand for aid to his master in money and ships in case of an invasion, the Germans drew back : they were not prepared to go as far as this until a more complete agreement had been reached in matters of religion. Trouble arose also over the question of the King's divorce : the Lutherans acknowledged that marriage with a brother's widow was wrong, but they refused to admit, if such a union had taken place, that it was right to break it[2]. The news of the executions of More and Fisher, moreover, had caused great consternation in Germany, where every effort was being made to introduce the new doctrines without bloodshed ; and the Bishop of Hereford was finally sent away empty-handed, the negotiations having resulted in a failure which plainly foreshadowed the events of 1538 and 1539. Taken as a whole, the year 1535 had simply been occupied in playing over again the game of 1534. Twice had the French alliance been tested, and it had failed. Twice had Henry and Cromwell sought security in a league with the Lutherans—without success. Two proofs had been afforded that a reconciliation with Charles was the surest road to England's safety ; and this time the alternative of a closer alliance with France, which, in 1534, had offered the King and his minister

---

[1] Cal. ix. 390, 1016.       Reformatorum, vol. ii. pp. 1028 ff.; iii.
[2] Cal. x. 771. Cf. also Corpus    pp. 46-50.

a temporary escape from an ultimately inevitable conclusion, was out of the question. But a reconciliation with the Emperor, as we have already seen, was impossible during the lifetime of Katherine.

Under these circumstances then, we can scarcely wonder that the Imperial ambassador reported to his master that the death of the Queen, which occurred on January 7, 1536, was due to foul play[1]. Chapuys also possessed other evidence, which tended to strengthen him in this conclusion. He had not forgotten the sinister hint which Cromwell had let fall in his presence in August, 1534; and he had apparently discovered that in November, 1535, the King had plainly told his most trusted counsellors that he must be rid of the Queen and Princess at the next Parliament[2]. Nor did Henry's unseemly conduct when he received the news of the death of his first wife escape the notice of the Imperial ambassador. Chapuys wrote to Charles how the King clothed himself in yellow from head to foot, and spent the day in mirth and revelry. 'God be praised,' had Henry exclaimed, 'that we are free from all suspicion of war[3].' The ambassador also dwelt at length on the suspicious secrecy and almost indecent haste with which the body of the Queen was opened, embalmed, and enclosed in lead; on the very significant testimony extracted from the chandler of the house who did the work, and on the statements of the doctor and of the Queen's confessor. The verdict of the best modern medical authorities on the post-mortem examination as reported by the chandler strongly favours the conclusion that Katherine was not poisoned[4], but died of a disease called melanotic sarcoma, or, more popularly, cancer of the heart: the testimony of a sixteenth-century artisan, however, is but a poor basis for a modern scientific investigation. If the Queen was murdered, there is every reason to think that Cromwell was chiefly responsible for the crime. To a man

[1] Cal. x. 59.
[2] Cal. ix. 776, and Friedmann, vol. ii. pp. 169-73.
[3] Cal. x. 141. Cf. also Friedmann, vol. ii. p. 176.
[4] Cf. Dr. Norman Moore, on the Death of Katherine of Aragon, in the Athenaeum for Jan. 31 and Feb. 28, 1885.

of his character and training such a step would have been far less repugnant than to Henry, had he once assured himself that it was indispensable to his purposes. He had had sufficient experience of the Italy of Alexander VI and Caesar Borgia to render him quite callous to the ordinary sentiments of humanity in such matters. He had never fully realized the innate strength of England's isolated position; he was always alarmed by the danger of foreign invasion far more than his master, and consequently was more ready to adopt desperate measures to avert it. It does not seem likely that the more experienced Henry would have originated the plan of murdering his wife, until the crisis in foreign affairs had become far more acute. Though he fully comprehended the many advantages of a closer alliance with Charles, he must have been reasonably certain that he had little cause to fear a direct attack in the immediate future, especially as the death of the Duke of Milan in the end of October had opened glorious possibilities for a renewal of the quarrel between Francis and Charles. Of course it is mere folly to suppose that Cromwell would have attempted to murder the Queen without the King's full consent. It is more than probable however that—if poison it was—it was he who put the idea into Henry's mind, and took the responsibility for its execution upon himself.

In any event the death of Katherine, whether due to natural causes or 'advancé sinistrement' as Chapuys expressed it, was the means by which Henry was at last enabled to attain the position in foreign affairs that he had aimed at since the fall of Wolsey, and to put in practice a policy which, combined with a fortunate turn of events abroad, was destined, for two years, to lead to the most glorious results. It removed the chief cause of jealousy between England and the Emperor[1], and enabled Henry to point out to Francis, who as we have seen had of late been taking a very haughty tone with him, that the situation of the two countries had again been reversed, and that France was no longer in a position to dictate. This task Cromwell

---

[1] Robertson, vol. ii. pp. 40–1.

performed for him three days after the Queen's death, with his usual directness and efficiency. The King's minister wrote to Gardiner and Wallop on January 8, indicating that the death of Katherine had removed 'the onelie matier of the vnkyndenes' between his master and the Emperor, and instructing the ambassadors in their 'conferenc*es* and procedyng*es* w*it*h the frensh kyng and his counsaile' to keep themselves 'the more aloof and be the more Froyt and colde in relentyng to any their oue*r*tur*es* or request*es*[1].' A comparison of this letter with one which Cromwell had written to the Bishop of Winchester two months earlier[2] reveals a very striking change of tone, which nothing else than the death of Katherine could have rendered possible.

The King's secretary was no less prompt in pointing out to the Imperial ambassador the bearing of the decease of the divorced Queen on England's relations with Spain. He was not ashamed to remark to one of Chapuys' men that the Emperor had the greatest cause to be thankful for the death of Katherine, which in his judgement was the very best thing that could have happened for the preservation of the amity between Henry and Charles, as it completely removed the sole cause of jealousy between them[3]. The Emperor was too hard-headed a politician not to see the force of Cromwell's words. We cannot doubt that he was exceedingly angry at the death of his aunt, which he certainly believed was due to foul play ; but his situation was such that revenge was impossible, and with characteristic calmness and self-control he determined to conceal his resentment and conciliate Henry. It was doubtless with his full sanction that Chapuys welcomed all Cromwell's proposals, which looked towards a more cordial relation between England and Spain. Meantime Francis had not been slow to take the hint which Gardiner, at Cromwell's command, had given him, and was again using every effort to regain Henry's favour. The breach between the two continental sovereigns was, to the King's intense joy, becoming wider every day, with the result that each was making frantic attempts to outbid the other for

[1] Letters, 136.    [2] Letters, 126.    [3] Cal. x. 141.

England's friendship. Henry's position was for the moment almost ideal. All he needed to do was to keep the two rivals just evenly balanced. But precisely at this critical juncture, Cromwell for the first time in his ministry made a move without the King's leave, which, had it not been instantly forestalled, would have completely upset the beautiful equilibrium which Henry had laboured so hard to establish. The King had doubtless ordered him to be cordial to Chapuys, in order to counterbalance the effects of the warmth of Francis; but he had not the least idea of entering into any definite agreement, which might lose him his precious position of neutrality. But Cromwell did not see this. He exceeded his instructions, was voluble in his disparagement of the French in Chapuys' presence, and finally brought matters to such a point that he went with Chapuys to the King to propose an Imperial alliance [1]. It was the most open avowal he had yet made of a leaning towards Spain, that he had doubtless cherished for a long time. Born among the common people, Cromwell's early life had been spent in that atmosphere of bitter hatred of France, which for generations had been one of the most predominant characteristics of the lower classes in England. In the first half of the sixteenth century, hatred of France meant friendship with Spain, and from the first years of the reign of Henry VIII one encounters at every turn evidences of the devotion of the common people to the Imperial cause. Wolsey's policy of peace with France had won him almost as many enemies among the lower classes as his reputation as originator of oppressive financial measures. Cromwell had determined not to make the same mistake that his predecessor had, but he was foolish enough to err on the opposite side. During the year 1535 he had given hints that he was no friend of France [2]. His rudeness to the French ambassadors on more than one occasion had convinced Chapuys that he favoured the Emperor, but as yet he had not gone far enough to bring himself into collision with the King. But this time he had forgotten his previous caution, and his rashness resulted in

[1] Cal. x. 351.  [2] Cal. viii. 948, 1018.

his first serious quarrel with his master.  Henry may well have been furious that his minister's recklessness had threatened to destroy the whole fabric of a policy which he had been at such pains to put in operation.  The Imperial ambassador gives us an amusing account of a scene which ensued in the Privy Chamber when he came with Cromwell to propose an alliance between England and Spain.  After Chapuys had propounded the terms of a possible treaty, Henry called Cromwell and Audeley to him and retired to another part of the room.  'They talked together,' writes Chapuys, who kept a vigilant eye upon the gestures of the King and those with him.  'There seemed to be some dispute and considerable anger, as I thought, between the King and Cromwell; and after a considerable time Cromwell grumbling left the conference in the window where the King was, excusing himself that he was so very thirsty that he was quite exhausted, as he really was with pure vexation, and sat down upon a coffer out of sight of the King, where he sent for something to drink.'  Henry soon came to Chapuys, and after being as rude as possible, reproaching the Emperor with past ingratitude, and asserting that Milan rightfully belonged to the French, waived the point at issue entirely, and was with difficulty persuaded to look over the treaties at a later time.  'At this slender and provoking answer,' writes Chapuys, 'I left the Court, and went to wait on Cromwell,' whose regret was so great 'that he was hardly able to speak for sorrow, and had never been more mortified in his life, than with the said reply [1].'

---

[1] Cal. x. 699.  Mr. Friedmann points out that this quarrel of Henry and Cromwell about the Spanish alliance was intimately connected with the fate of Anne Boleyn.  The Emperor, too cautious to express any indignation at the news of his aunt's death, was still planning for the safety and, if possible, the succession of his cousin the Princess Mary.  On hearing from Chapuys of the possibility of a renewal of cordial relations with England, he wrote back on March 28, 1536, a most diplomatic reply, in which he pointed out that it would be certainly for the interest of the Princess that Anne Boleyn should continue to be Henry's wife; for should the King marry again, he might have male issue, which would succeed to the prejudice of Mary:

Ample justification was soon afforded for Henry's strict adherence to the policy of neutrality, for events on the Continent had moved rapidly forward, and Charles and Francis were at last at open war.  By restraining Cromwell from making the mistake of cementing an alliance with the Emperor, and by guarding himself against a too close intimacy with Francis, the King had succeeded in placing England in such a position that the two great continental powers were forced to grovel at her feet.  From the beginning of 1536 until the autumn of 1537, when the truce between France and Flanders (forerunner of the peace of Nice in the summer of 1538) was concluded, the history of the foreign policy of England is as simple as it is glorious and triumphant.  Henry, constantly pretending to be desirous of arbitrating between France and Spain, 'for the peax and weale of Christendome,' as he elegantly put it, was in reality solely occupied with the endeavour to embroil them the more.  Alternately encouraging and repelling advances from both sovereigns, by judiciously proposing and then retreating from alliances with each of them, he succeeded admirably in keeping Charles and Francis in a constant state of anxiety, as regarded his true position.  Cromwell's letters tell the story of the time very clearly.  'An answer soo general that it doth neither refuse their alliance, ne moche encorage them, to conceyue that they maye without difficultie obteyn their desire' was the reply which the

---

there was, on the other hand, little probability that Anne would bear Henry another child, and the Emperor knew well that in the eyes of the nation his cousin's right was far superior to that of Elizabeth. So, by a very extraordinary turn of affairs, the interests of Charles and of Anne had at least temporarily become identical. Cromwell probably had not perceived that this was the true state of affairs when he had his conversation with Chapuys ; but the failure of his attempts to bring about a Spanish alliance must have opened his eyes to the fact that he had been working in the interests of one whose ruin had been certainly resolved on by this time.  ' He took to his bed out of pure sorrow ' for a few days as we are told ; and when he returned to the Court, it was to labour with all his might for the ruin of Anne, which he saw was necessary to save his own credit with the King.  Friedmann, Anne Boleyn, chapter xvi; Cal. x. 575, 700 ; also W. H. Dixon, History of Two Queens, vol. iv. pp. 262, 263.

English ambassadors were ordered to give at the French and Spanish Courts[1]. So secure did Henry feel himself abroad that he dared to issue a manifesto in contempt of the General Council[2], which the Pope had summoned to meet at Mantua, and to publish the Ten Articles of 1536, which, while primarily intended to serve another purpose, were politically useful as a formal refusal to respect it. It was very fortunate for England that her affairs abroad were so prosperous at this juncture, as the end of 1536 and the beginning of 1537 were full of anxiety at home, owing to the outbreak of the rebellion in the North.

This happy state of affairs however was not destined to endure, for Francis and Charles soon tired of their strife, and in the autumn of 1537 there were signs of a reconciliation. Francis, moreover, had strengthened his position by a league with the Turk, and began to feel powerful enough to make a move without Henry's leave. The first intimation of this unpleasant fact came to Henry in the shape of a refusal of a matrimonial offer. The death of Queen Jane had left him free to marry again, and so gave him an excellent opportunity once more to mix in continental affairs, which he did not permit to escape him. Cromwell wrote a letter for him to Lord William Howard and Gardiner, artfully instructing them to feel the way for a possible alliance with Mme. de Longueville, who had just been affianced to James of Scotland. It was too much of a favour to ask Francis to put aside the claims of a sovereign who had always been his true friend, to make way for those of the more powerful but perfidious King of England, and Henry's offers were, after some negotiations, politely but firmly declined, to the latter's intense chagrin[3]. An almost equally ominous note of warning came from Spain at the same time. Sir John Dudley, ambassador to announce the death of the Queen at the Spanish Court, had expressed to the Emperor the King's sorrow that his repeated offers of mediation with France had been set aside, whereupon Charles turned on him, and informed him that negotiations with France were already set on foot, though he relieved Henry's anxiety a little by assuring him that no actual treaty should

---

[1] Letters, 170.     [2] Cal. xii. (i) 1310.     [3] Cal. xii. (ii) 1201.

be made without the King of England's being included as a 'premier contrahent,' a promise which Cromwell was continually harping upon a year later, when the situation had entirely changed [1].

Thus the year 1538 opened rather darkly for England. The dread with which Henry watched the increasing signs of good-feeling between Charles and Francis led him into ridiculous and undignified action. As soon as it was settled that Mary of Guise was to become James' wife, Henry literally scoured the continent of Europe in search of an alliance for himself or his daughters, which would strengthen his position and avert the impending crisis. A somewhat confusing set of double instructions from Cromwell to his friend Philip Hoby, instructing him to negotiate for possible marriages with the younger sister of James' wife, with the daughter of the Duke of Lorraine, and also with the Duchess of Milan, and to obtain their portraits, is not without interest as revealing Henry's state of mind [2]. The first two of these unions, if accomplished, would of course have rendered him safe from France ; the other would have put him on friendly terms with Spain ; but none of them was destined to succeed. The King even went so far as to permit Sir Francis Brian, his agent at the French Court, to suggest that various suitable ladies should be brought to Calais for his inspection, that he might be sure that he made no mistake. Henry's proceedings evoked such ridicule and derision in continental Europe, that Castillon, the French ambassador, contrived to convey to him the general feeling with such directness and force that he actually drew a blush from the King himself [3]. Finding that his endeavours to obtain a suitable wife for himself were abortive, Henry looked about for an advantageous marriage for his daughter Mary. By alternately holding out to the Emperor a prospect of a match for her with the Infant of Portugal, and pretending to accept a proposition of the French representative, Castillon, that she

---

[1] Cal. xii. (ii) 1053, 1285.

[2] Letters, 243. Cf. also Preface to vol. xiii. pt. i. of the Calendar, pp. 37-8.

[3] Cal. xiii. (i) 1355, 1405, 1451, 1496 ; xiii. (ii) 77, 232, 277.

should marry the Duke of Orleans, he contrived to lay the basis for a continental quarrel. But his success in this scheme was very short-lived. The only person that he could deceive at all was Castillon. It seems that Cromwell, who again at this crisis took the opportunity to show his decided leaning towards Spain, had openly disapproved of the proposed French alliance, and when Castillon complained of this, Henry turned fiercely upon his minister and reprimanded him, saying that he was a good manager, but not fit to intermeddle in the affairs of kings, and finally Norfolk was sent for. Cromwell's ' great Spanish passion,' as Castillon called it, had got him into trouble again, and the French ambassador was delighted, thinking that he had at last obtained the upper hand. But Castillon's delusions were rudely dispelled three weeks later, when he learned that the King and Council were resolved ' to withdraw from the French match,' on account of offers which the Emperor had made, and when Francis wrote that the King's proceedings only proved that he was jealous of the negotiations for peace[1]. It is needless to state that neither of the proposed unions ever took place, and Henry's frantic endeavours to frustrate the steadily increasing amity of France and Spain were entirely unavailing.

Matrimonial agitations being found useless to serve his purpose, Henry had recourse to other methods to stir up suspicions between Charles and Francis, and to prevent the dreaded peace. Whatever malicious tale-bearing and false representations could accomplish was used to the full by the King and his minister. Cromwell wrote to Sir Thomas Wyatt at the Spanish Court, directing him to ' declare how the frenche men show themselfes so ernest to put al in the kinges hand that they offer vpon any significacion that themperour woll make . . . . . . . . to condescende to the same,' and telling how the French ambassador had promised that Henry ' shuld for the French kinges parte haue the hole and entier manyeng of the Peax betwen him and Themperor[2].' If Henry could not obtain the ' hole and entier manyeng of the Peax,' he did his best to convince Charles and Francis separately

---

[1] Cal. xiii. (i) 995, 1147, 1355.     [2] Letters, 244.

that his own friendship was more valuable to each of them than that of the other. Furthermore he took pains to assure each one of the two rivals apart, that the other prized England's amity so much that great concessions would be necessary to regain it.

But in spite of all Henry's efforts to avert it, the news of the truce between Charles and Francis and of their subsequent interview at Aigues Mortes reached England in July, 1538 [1]. Still so confident was the King in the wisdom of his original policy of strengthening England solely by attempts to embroil these two powerful sovereigns under cover of offers of mediation, that he refused definitely to abandon it, in spite of the threatening outlook on the Continent. He remembered that the situation there had often changed before, and saw that it would probably do so again. He encouraged himself with hopes that in spite of the failure of his attempts to contract a marriage in France, he might still gain the hand of the Duchess of Milan, and with the reflection that the inroads of the Turk into the Emperor's dominions would be a serious hindrance to any direct attack upon England. He was unwilling to seek security in an outside alliance, for fear of imperilling his hard-won position as a neutral between France and Spain. He wished still to rely solely on judicious interference in the affairs of Charles and Francis for England's safety.

But with Cromwell the case was very different. The closing months of the year 1538 were the turning-point in his career, for they saw him take a step which was destined to bring him into collision with the King, and later to lead him to his death. The original difference of opinion between King and minister, which first came to the fore in the quarrel of 1536, now broke forth again under a slightly altered form, which it was destined to maintain till the end. At first we saw that Cromwell vented his distrust of the policy of neutrality in favouring a definite alliance with Spain. The changed situation on the Continent rendered a league with Charles impossible now, so that the only refuge that remained

---

[1] Cal. xiii. (i) 1486.

for England, if the policy which had been so successful in 1536 and 1537 really broke down, was to court an alliance with some power outside the two great continental rivals. And Cromwell, inexperienced, and overestimating the danger of foreign invasion, certainly believed that Henry's efforts to maintain his old position between France and Spain were now doomed to inevitable failure. He did not see, as the King did, that the friendship of Charles and Francis was but temporary, and that the old quarrels were ultimately certain to break forth afresh. He looked the situation as it was squarely in the face, abandoned once and for all the policy of seeking safety by playing on the mutual jealousies of Charles and Francis ; he frankly recognized the probability of war, and deliberately courted an outside league for England's defence. As he had always considered the friendship of the Emperor more valuable than that of Francis, so he considered his enmity, which he now regarded as inevitable, as more to be feared. Consequently, in looking about for an alliance to fortify England, he sought one which could be most effectively directed against Charles.

It will be remembered that in order to guard against the danger of a possible coalition of the Emperor and the King of France in 1533 and 1534, some proposals had been made for a league with the Protestant princes of Germany ; but that owing to theological differences, the Lübeck affair, and the death of Katherine and its results, the scheme had been abandoned as useless. As long as the interests of France and Spain were separated, the value of the German alliance as a defensive measure was of course lost, and England thought no more of it. But now that the news of the interview of Aigues Mortes had persuaded Cromwell that mere meddling in the affairs of France and Spain was not sufficient to prevent a coalition against England, he turned to his forsaken friends in Germany once more. Cromwell must have had great difficulty in bringing Henry to sanction a move to seek friendship with the Lutherans, but so hopeless did the King's efforts to prevent a cordial relation between Charles and Francis appear, that he was at last induced to consent to the experiment, though, as we shall soon see, his acquiescence was only temporary. The opportunity for an alliance with the Germans was in many respects most favourable. The proclamation which Henry had put forth to show his contempt of the Papal authority to convoke a General Council, coupled with the Ten Articles of 1536, had called forth the most hearty approbation of the Lutheran princes. An elaborate set of instructions in the hand of one of the King's secretaries directed Christopher Mont to go to the Germans again, and tell them how nearly Henry's theological views coincided with their own, and to request them to send representatives to discuss with him points of faith [1]. The fact that the proposals for the German alliance ostensibly emanated from the King, is no sign that Cromwell was not the real originator of it. An invitation to send ambassadors could scarcely proceed from any other source than the Crown, so that the evidence afforded by the authorship of the instructions to Mont is of small weight ; whereas the course of events in 1539 and 1540 leaves little doubt that the guiding hand throughout was that of the King's minister. Henry's name really appeared as little as possible in connexion with the Lutheran alliance from first to last, and only in the most formal manner. Cromwell's was the moving spirit in it throughout, and Henry really never cordially supported him, but regarded the measure in the light of a disagreeable necessity, temporarily forced upon him by the apparent failure of his own plans.

But the outside world of course knew nothing of the difference of opinion between King and minister, and had no suspicion that the foundations were being laid here for the quarrel which was later to bring Cromwell to disaster. The Lutherans were greatly flattered by the proposals that had been made to them, and in May an embassy, headed by Franz Burckhard, Vice-Chancellor of Saxony, arrived in England. But in spite of all the trouble that had been taken, the plans of the King's minister were not destined to bear fruit, for the only result of the Lutheran embassy was procrastination which seemed little better than failure.

---

[1] Cal. xiii. (i) 367.

Theological differences were the ostensible reason for inability
to conclude an agreement, but not the real one. The
Protestantism of the Lutherans differed from that of Henry
and Cromwell in much the same way as that of Tyndale,
years before : they cared for their theology for its own sake,
and not, like Henry, as a means to an end, as a stepping-stone
to political greatness. A theological *entente*, however, would
have been possible, had Cromwell and Henry united to bring it
about ; but they did not. The true reason for the failure to
conclude an agreement was the obstinacy of the King, which
asserted itself at the very moment that his minister had hoped
to gain his complete consent to the proposed alliance. In
the midst of the negotiations with the Lutherans, Henry's
faith in his old policy had been suddenly revived by
the news that the extensive preparations of the Emperor,
which he at first had feared were to be aimed at England,
were in reality directed against the Turk [1] : the King was at
least persuaded that he had no cause to fear an attack in the
immediate future. Gardiner in Paris, moreover, had been
steadily working to defeat the plans of Cromwell [2], and at the
crucial moment his efforts appear to have borne fruit. The
King refused to commit himself any further to the policy to
which he had given his temporary sanction, but which, if
definitely adopted, would have seriously hampered his own
schemes. The most that Cromwell could do was to persuade
the King to keep up the appearance of amity, and not to cut
himself off from all chances of returning to his Lutheran
friends at a later date. So the envoys were sent home in
October, with a letter to the Elector of Saxony, telling him
that his representatives had given assurance of such sound
erudition and Christian piety, as would certainly lead to the
best results; but as the matter of the negotiations concerned
the glory of Christ and the discipline of religion, it required
much more mature deliberation, and that a second embassy
would have to be sent over before matters could be concluded [3].
For Cromwell, the dismissal of the Lutherans amounted to

---

[1] Baumgarten, vol. iii. pp. 343 ff.  [2] Burnet, vol. i. pp. 316, 409, 435.
[3] Cal. xiii. (ii) 165, 298, 497.

a second rebuke from the King, for meddling in foreign affairs; but this time the minister did not humbly accept the rebuff as he had done before, but continued to oppose his schemes to those of his master.

Thus at the close of the year 1538, England was trembling at the prospect of a coalition of France and Spain against her. The outlook was certainly alarming, and demanded united action at home. But at this very moment the King and his minister could not agree on the best method of averting the peril which was threatening. Each adopted his own way of meeting it, and the history of the year 1539 is the story of the varying success of the two methods when brought into conflict. We shall see that fortune twice inclined to favour Cromwell, only to desert him, after he had become so hopelessly committed to the policy which he had adopted in face of the opposition of the King, that there was no drawing back, and he paid the penalty for his rashness with his life.

# CHAPTER XIII

## THE CATHOLIC REACTION AND THE ALLIANCE
## WITH CLEVES

THE first few months of the new year brought no improvement in the state of England's foreign affairs. Having postponed the Lutheran alliance which Cromwell had so strongly advocated in the end of 1538, for fear of losing his position of neutrality between France and Spain, Henry was driven back on his own policy of seeking safety for England in direct negotiations with Charles and Francis. Matrimonial agitations had failed—malicious tale-bearing had not borne fruit, so the King took the more straightforward course of making direct complaints that he was spoken of with too little respect in foreign parts. He sent grumbling letters to his neighbours, accusing them of permitting evil reports to be circulated about him. He caused the President of the Council of the North to request James of Scotland to suppress and punish the authors of several ' spyttfull ballades,' which had been published about the wrongfully usurped authority of the King of England, and also wrote to Wyatt in Spain, commanding him to protest against the malicious and unreasonable lies of the ' barking prechers ther' who slandered him behind his back[1]. But these petty remonstrances had no effect in diminishing the growing cordiality of Francis and Charles, or their hatred of England: in fact the two continental sovereigns seemed better friends than ever. On January 12, representatives of both monarchs met at Toledo and concluded an agreement not to make any new alliances, either political or matrimonial, with the King of England, without each other's consent[2]. The news of this treaty was a deathblow to Henry's hopes; and the King was reluctantly forced to

---

[1] Cal. xiv. (i) 92, 147.        [2] Cal. xiv. (i) 62.

admit that his minister's scheme of a German alliance offered better chances of safety for England than any other. So he again gave his consent to a renewal of negotiations for an outside league, though, as we shall soon see, it was on a basis somewhat different from that of the previous ones.

Disappointed by the King's refusal definitely to accept the alliance for which he had laboured so hard, Cromwell had meantime been amusing himself with a very feeble plan for gaining friends against the Pope, the chimerical nature of which was quite at variance with the direct and practical character of most of his schemes. He had proposed a league of England with the Dukes of Ferrara, Mantua, and Urbino against his Holiness, who had just challenged the title of the latter to the dukedom of Camerino. An interesting set of instructions to Cromwell's friend Edmund Harvell at Venice tells the story of this negotiation very vividly [1]. But the princes of northern Italy were too weak and the scheme itself was too remote and far-fetched to promise any real advantage, and Cromwell doubtless lost all interest in it as soon as the King again consented to approach the Germans. The fact that three months had been suffered to elapse since the return of the envoys in 1538, without an acceptance of the King's invitation to send other representatives to discuss theological points, simply proves that Henry's treatment of the first embassy had not been such as to encourage the Lutherans to persevere [2]. But now that the King had again veered round to Cromwell's policy, he 'mervayled not a litel' at the slowness of the Germans, and sent Christopher Mont over to the Court of the Elector of Saxony on January 25 to discover the feelings of John Frederic and the Land-grave of Hesse, the leaders of the Schmalkaldic League, towards the Emperor, to inquire further into their attitude on the tenets about which they had so fruitlessly disputed with

---

[1] Letters, 286.

[2] John Lambert, moreover, had been tried and burnt, for denying the Real Presence, in November, 1538. The doctrines of the Luther-ans in this matter were probably almost identical with those of the King at this time, but the Germans certainly disapproved of the violence of Henry's measures for enforcing them.

the English bishops in the preceding summer, and finally to learn whether the Duke of Cleves and his son were of the 'old popisshe fasshyon' or no[1]. Appended to these very non-committal injunctions are certain others from Cromwell himself of quite a different nature[2]. Completely dodging the theological issue, which he wisely left entirely in the King's hands, Cromwell took up the question of the German alliance from a new and far more practical side, the matrimonial. He instructed Mont to suggest to the Vice-Chancellor Burckhard the possibility of two marriages; one between the young Duke of Cleves and the Princess Mary, and the other between Anne, the elder of the two unmarried daughters of the old Duke, and the King himself[3]. It appears that Cromwell had already discussed the feasibility of the first of these two matches with the Vice-Chancellor, when the latter had been in England in the previous summer, and John Frederic had subsequently written to the King's minister that the plan met with his entire approval. The proposal for Henry's marriage, on the contrary, was now brought forward for the first time. We shall soon see why it was that Mont was sent to the Elector of Saxony, rather than to the Duke of Cleves himself, to feel the way for these two alliances.

In order to understand the precise bearing on the foreign affairs of England of the two marriages which Cromwell proposed, and of the political league which would naturally go with them, we must make a slight digression here and examine the very peculiar position in which the Duke of Cleves found himself at this juncture. Various political

---

[1] Cal. xiv. (i) 103.

[2] Letters, 287.

[3] Throughout the negotiations for the Cleves marriages Cromwell made desperate efforts to assert the dignity of the King, which he could not help feeling was a little lowered by approaching vassals of the Emperor with matrimonial offers. Mont was especially directed to confer with Burckhard about the sister of the Duke of Cleves, 'not as demaunding her, but as geving them a prick to stirr them to offre her, as the noblest and highest honour that could come into that noble house of Cleves, if they could bring it to passe.' Of course nothing could induce the mighty King of England to demean himself by asking any favours of the petty princes of Germany; it was their place, not his, to be the suitor.

considerations, above all an increasing jealousy of the power
of the House of Saxony, had led the Emperor Maximilian
in 1496 to declare Maria, the only child of the Duke of
Juliers and Berg, to be the lawful heiress of these two
provinces; a step which was in direct contravention of a
grant which Maximilian, at his election as King of the
Romans, had made to Frederic the Wise of the reversion of
Juliers and Berg in case of failure of male heirs in the ducal
line there.  This grant was definitely revoked in various
documents of the years 1508 and 1509; and Duke John of
Cleves, who in the meantime had married the heiress Maria
of Juliers and Berg, was permitted to unite these three rich
provinces in his own hand, and to establish a strong power
on the Lower Rhine which prevented undue preponderance
of the House of Wettin, and furnished a useful support for
the Hapsburgs in the western part of the Empire[1].  The
peace-loving Duke John lived and died in friendship with
Maximilian and his grandson, although his desire to see
a reform in the Church had prevented his definite acceptance
of the Imperial invitation to join a Catholic League against
the Schmalkaldner in 1537.  Instead he devoted himself to
strengthening his power in his own possessions by a series
of wise and prudent measures, through which he welded the
three component parts of his dominions into one[2].  But
during the last year of his life (which ended on February 6,
1539, while Mont was on his way to the Saxon Court)
affairs took a turn which was destined to bring his son and
heir William into direct conflict with the Empire.  In June,
1538, the warlike Duke Charles of Gelderland, whose possessions lay next to the province of Cleves on the north, died
leaving no children.  His life had been spent in a struggle
against the pretensions to his hereditary dominions brought
forward by the Emperor as heir of Charles the Bold, and
in order to prevent the substantiation of the Imperial claims
at his death he had planned to leave his lands to the King

---

[1] Cf. Ulmann, vol. i. pp. 579, 580;
Ranke, vol. i. pp. 226–9.

[2] Life of Duke John of Cleves

in the Allgemeine Deutsche Biographie, vol. xiv. p. 214.

of France [1]. This scheme however had encountered strong opposition from the estates of Gelderland, who regarded with little favour a proposal so threatening to their comparatively independent position, and Duke Charles was finally forced, much against his will, to designate young William of Cleves as his successor. The latter, though by nature weak and irresolute, was not in a position to refuse the chance which fortune had thrown in his way: he accepted the proffered inheritance, and the death of his father soon after left him in full possession of the four rich provinces [2].

The result was that he immediately became involved in a serious quarrel with the Emperor, who realizing how dangerous a rival to his own power had been created by the events just recounted, reasserted his claims to Gelderland even more strongly than before. In looking for allies against Charles, Duke William naturally turned to the Elector of Saxony, whose rights to Juliers and Berg, once rudely revoked by Maximilian, had not been forgotten, but who seems to have preserved sufficiently friendly relations with the family in favour of which his claims had been set aside, to marry Sibylla, one of the sisters of the Duke [3]. Common enmity to Charles V now drew them very close together, and at the Imperial Court it was actually thought that Cleves had been formally admitted to the Schmalkaldic League [4]. This however was a mistake. Though Duke William was certainly not opposed to the Lutheran doctrines, he had not as yet made open confession of the Protestant faith; and for that reason the Elector and the Landgrave had steadily refused to make a political alliance with him [5]. Still he was on very intimate

---

[1] Ranke, vol. iv. p. 128; Heidrich, 1, 2.

[2] Heidrich, 21.

[3] Heidrich, 4.

[4] Ranke, vol. iv. p. 129.

[5] Heidrich, 34, 35. Driven by political necessity, William in 1543 finally took the decisive step, and declared himself ready to introduce the new religion into his dominions, in the hope of gaining aid from his brother-in-law against the Emperor. But the offer came too late. The political situation had changed once more, and the over-cautious Elector now definitely and unconditionally refused the aid which he had before made dependent on William's acceptance of Lutheranism. The lands of the Duke were invaded by the Imperial forces, and William was forced, at the

terms with John Frederic, who had promised, when he wedded Sibylla of Cleves, to advance money for the marriage of her sisters, and thus had a certain right to be consulted when husbands were to be chosen for them.   Henry was doubtless well aware of all this, and it was consequently at the Saxon Court that Mont was instructed to obtain information about the Duke of Cleves, and if possible to pave the way for the two matrimonial alliances from which Cromwell hoped so much.

Having completed this preliminary survey of the position of the Duke of Cleves, we are enabled to make some interesting observations on the instructions to the English ambassador. It is very significant that the inquiries which Mont was ordered to make concerning the religious tendencies of Duke William were concerned only with his attitude towards the Pope.   Of course the King could not consistently ally himself with firm adherents of the Holy See after the events of the past ten years; but it is also of the utmost importance to notice that he apparently preferred a league with powers which he knew had not definitely committed themselves to the New Faith to an alliance with the Schmalkaldner.   Else why did he rather seek to unite with Cleves than with Saxony?  Both were politically valuable, as enemies of the Emperor; the only difference was that Cleves was not as yet avowedly Protestant, and Saxony was.   It is possible that the idea which bore fruit five months later in the Six Articles had already taken shape in Henry's mind; at least it seems certain that he was determined to keep a perfectly free hand in religious affairs, so as not to be hampered in his political relations with France and Spain.   Thus when

treaty of Venlo, Sept. 7, 1543, to renounce all claims to Gelderland and Zutphen, to return to the Church of Rome, and to permit no religious innovations in Juliers and Berg. Subsequently, however, encouraged by the milder attitude of the Emperor Ferdinand towards the Reformers, he devoted himself with partial success to an attempt to effect a sort of compromise between the two faiths in his own possessions, and to establish there a purified and enlightened Catholic Church, 'Erasmian' in its tendencies, and in many respects approaching very closely to the tenets of the Augsburg Confession.   Cf. Heidrich, 91–4, and the Life of William of Cleves in the Allgemeine Deutsche Biographie, vol. xliii. pp. 107–13.

Cromwell at last succeeded in persuading him reluctantly to return to a German alliance, it was really only half a victory for the minister. There was this great difference between the league with the Lutherans which Cromwell had proposed and which never succeeded, and the Cleves alliance which was now sought. The one would have been necessarily both political and religious (for we have seen that the Lutherans had always refused to join with England until a satisfactory theological agreement could be made), while the other was solely political. It was simply another expression of the old disagreement between Henry and Cromwell. The King, always looking for a chance of reconciliation with Charles and Francis, refused to enter an alliance the religious conditions of which would greatly enhance the difficulty of a return to his favourite scheme. He was only induced to enter a purely political league, which he doubtless felt he could throw over at any moment if he wished to do so ; an agreement both political and religious he might have found it more difficult to escape from. Cromwell on the other hand, having definitely given up all ideas of direct negotiations with France and Spain, wished to plunge headlong into the Lutheran alliance, caring little what he was committed to provided he gained solid support. But, as we have seen, the King would not agree to this, and the alliance with Cleves can thus only be regarded as a compromise between the royal and Cromwellian policies, which the King could abandon whenever affairs in France and Spain took a more favourable turn. Later events in the same year furnish further proofs of this most important fact.

Furthermore the King had contrived that the responsibility for the proposed league with Cleves should fall almost entirely on his minister's shoulders, in order that he himself might the more easily renounce it if occasion served. The fact that the new alliance, if accomplished, would from its very nature commit him to far less than the Lutheran league which he had put off in 1538, was not enough for Henry ; he must needs have other safeguards, and determined to make Cromwell his scapegoat. All the practical and important parts of the instructions to Mont were given by the King's minister. The conciliatory expressions with which Henry had directed the ambassador to sound the Elector of Saxony and the Landgrave of Hesse on the question of theology were merely empty words, as is proved by the utter failure of an attempted agreement four months later. Their sole object was to induce John Frederic more favourably to receive the practical proposals which followed. But the King purposely left to Cromwell the task of framing the vital part of the message, and it is evident that he gave his consent to the proposals it contained only in the most guarded and non-committal manner. We are merely told that as regards the match proposed for the Princess Mary, Cromwell perceived 'the king*es* hieghnes . . . by his grac*es* counten*au*nce and exterior Visage . . . to be of good Inclinac*io*n[1].' On the more vital question of the King's attitude concerning his own marriage, the instructions of Cromwell to Mont give us even vaguer information. The fact was that the King was willing definitely to bind Cromwell, but not himself, to a plan which he had resolved to abandon the moment that any favourable alteration should take place in his relations with France and Spain. From the day that Mont departed on his mission, the fate of the alliance with Cleves and the fate of Thomas Cromwell were joined together beyond the possibility of separation.

We unfortunately do not possess the letter in which Mont and his companion, a certain Thomas Paynell, reported their first reception at the Saxon Court, but the reply of Cromwell on March 10 gives us considerable information about the success of the ambassadors[2]. John Frederic had apparently welcomed the prospect of the two marriages by which Henry proposed to bind himself to Cleves, and had promised, through Burckhard, to do his best to bring them about. Cromwell's letter goes on to direct Mont to follow up the advantage already gained by telling bad stories about Charles, and to 'inculcate and p*er*suade vnto the said duke and landisgrave the moment & i*m*porta*n*ce of that grudge, which the*m*pero*ur*

<hr />

[1] Letters, 287.          [2] Letters, 295.

doth beire, for the Bishop of Rome*s* pleas*ure* against them and other of the avangelik sorte, which they may nowe easely per*c*eive by that he worketh and goeth aboute.' At the same time, another embassy, headed by a certain Dr. Nicholas Wotton, was sent to Cleves to obtain confirmation of the promises of Burckhard, and further to carry on negotiations for a supply of gunners and artillerymen to be furnished to Henry in case he should need them ; and finally to signify the King's willingness to make an offensive and defensive league with Duke William[1]. The latter was at first less eager to accept the alliance which England offered than his brother-in-law was to promote it : he wanted to postpone a definite answer in the hope that he might yet come to a peaceful solution of his difficulty with the Emperor[2]. But as this prospect daily grew more and more remote, he became correspondingly willing to entertain Henry's proposals, and the outlook for the accomplishment of the practical part of Cromwell's plan seemed very favourable. The comparatively unimportant overtures for theological reconciliation with the Elector and the Landgrave were apparently at first received with less enthusiasm by the Lutherans, who had already had some experience of the King's vacillating policy and evidently thought it a little suspicious that Henry had suddenly become so very urgent. We have seen that the King's proposals for a religious agreement were chiefly intended as a blind to cover the more practical matrimonial proposals which had followed, but Cromwell evidently thought it worth while to keep up the deception as a precaution. A second letter from the King's minister directs Mont and Paynell to continue to urge on the Elector and Landgrave the importance of theological unity, and to ' conduce to haue them somw[hat reproved for] ou*er*sight & slakenes, in shewing [so little] gratuite, and by that for to pryk th[em to] redubb the same and give you more f[avourable] a*n*swer.'

And at first Cromwell's eagerness for the alliance with Cleves seemed to have every justification, for Henry's policy in other parts of Europe appeared to have failed even more

---

[1] Cal. xiv. (i) 489.                    [2] Heidrich, 32.

completely than before. Ominous letters were received from Wriothesley, the ambassador in the Netherlands, who did not hesitate to express his fear that war would soon come and that his retreat to England would be cut off[1]. At the same time Chapuys received orders to return to the Court of the Queen Regent, and Cromwell consequently instructed Wriothesley to demand leave to depart[2]. The exchange was finally effected, but that there was deep distrust on both sides is proved by Cromwell's orders for the detention of Chapuys at Calais, until the safety of Wriothesley was assured, and by the instructions of the Queen Regent to the Provost of Mons to follow the English ambassador to Gravelines[3]. But fortunately these precautions were unnecessary; no open act of hostility took place, and the crisis seemed at least temporarily tided over by the arrival of the Dean of Cambray in London to replace Chapuys, and by the reception of Stephen Vaughan at Brussels in Wriothesley's stead[4]. But the attitude of France was more disquieting. On February 5 Castillon was recalled, and though he made a vague promise at his departure that another should be sent in his place, the anxiety at the Court was but little relieved thereby. The most that Cromwell could do, was to take care that the French ambassador should carry back to his master full accounts of the excellence of England's defences, and her readiness for war. So he took him, as he later wrote to the King, to his armoury, showing him a 'store of harneys and wepens . . . . . . the whiche he semed to esteme moche,' and telling him that there were twenty more armouries in the realm as well or better equipped; 'wherat he woundred and sayd that he thought your grace the prince best furnished thereof in Christendom[5].'

But though Cromwell may have exaggerated the security of England's fortifications, his words to Castillon were by no means empty. Though the King and his minister may have had differences of opinion in regard to the conduct of foreign affairs, in the internal management of the kingdom

[1] Cal. xiv. (i) 433, 440.      [2] Letters, 291, 301.
[3] Letters, 297; and Cal. xiv. (i) 584.      [4] Cal. xiv. (i) 570.
[5] Letters, 288.

they were, as always, united. Here Henry suffered himself to be guided at all points by Cromwell. And at no time is the masterfulness of the latter's domestic administration better exhibited, than by his action at home the moment the first rumours of an invasion reached England. Countless memoranda, lists of men fit for military service, arms, ammunition, provisions, and other necessaries of warfare, all in his hand, or in that of one of his clerks, attest his industry and ability in preparing the country to repel the dreaded invasion. All reports of the state of the coast defences at various places were sent to him. General musters were ordered throughout the realm; every precaution was taken to fortify all vulnerable points. Beacons were placed upon all the hills, and no detail that could add to the strength and efficiency of the defences was left out[1].

But just at this very moment, when everything seemed to point to an open rupture with Charles and Francis, when the schemes which Cromwell had opposed to those of the King seemed to have every justification, an event occurred which totally changed the aspect of affairs, and restored Henry's badly shaken confidence in his own ability to stave off the threatened crisis without the aid of outside alliances or an appeal to arms. This event was the arrival in England on March 28 of a new French ambassador, Charles de Marillac, who had come to replace Castillon. So long a time had elapsed since the departure of the latter that Henry had probably given up all hope of the fulfilment of the vague prospects that had been held out that a successor might be appointed. But the unexpected appearance of Marillac at once revived the King's drooping spirits. The letters in which the ambassador reported his reception at the English Court to Francis and Montmorency give us a vivid picture of the universal joy with which this apparent reassurance of friendship with France was hailed[2]. Henry was delighted, and his satisfaction was increased when Marillac, at his master's command, followed up the advantage already gained

---

[1] Cal. xiv. (i) 398-400, 529, 564, 615, 652-5.
[2] Cal. xiv. (i) 669-70.

by renewed assertions of the cordiality of France.   The whole
Court seemed 'to wear a new aspect and to be quite delighted[1].'   Had Henry seen the letter of instructions which
Marillac received from the French Court, he would have
realized that Francis was only endeavouring 'to keep him
in good humour[2],' while making a little more certain of his
own relations with Charles; and he might have been less
encouraged.   But Marillac's cordiality seems to have put him
off his guard, and he was led, in his exultation, to welcome
the apparent friendship of Francis in ways which very nearly
resulted in the permanent stultification of all the laborious
efforts of Cromwell to maintain amicable relations in Germany.
The events which took place in England in the three months
following the arrival of the French ambassador furnish ample
proof of this new departure in the royal policy.

On April 28 Parliament had met, its assembling being
indispensable to carrying on the 'Kinges busynes.'   Cromwell
had practically appointed every member, in order that Henry
might have a 'tractable' House.   His usual methods of 'ordering' the elections of members have already been described;
suffice it to say that in this case he had completely outdone
himself; the Parliament of 1539 was undoubtedly his master-
piece[3].   It will be remembered that it was in this session
that he first succeeded in forcing the Lords and Commons to
sanction the statute by which royal proclamations were given
the force of laws.   Cromwell's 'remembrance' for other Acts to
be passed in the Parliament of 1539 is also noteworthy.   It
makes casual mention of the attainders of Exeter, Salisbury,
and Pole, of plans for the fortification of the coast, and then
designates the scheme out of which the Six Articles were
later evolved as 'A devise in the parliament for the vnitie in
religion[4].'   It is very improbable that Cromwell had any
really accurate information concerning the King's real intentions in connexion with this last item.   Henry had purposely
concealed them under a very non-committal statement.
Doubtless the King had long cherished the idea of making

---

[1] Cal. xiv. (i) 908.                   [3] Cal. xiv. (i) 520, 573.
[2] Cal. xiv. (i) 804.                   [4] Cal. xiv. (i) 655.

use of a declaration that in matters of doctrine England still adhered to the Old Faith, to facilitate a reconciliation with Charles and Francis; for such a statement would remove the main pretext of the Emperor and the French King for an attack on him, namely that they were undertaking a crusade to suppress heresy. But so hopeless had been the outlook in the early part of the year, that Henry had not had the courage to try this experiment. He was rather led to shun all moves which would imperil his friendly relations with Germany, so that he had scrupulously avoided any direct statement which could lead to the belief that a Catholic reaction was possible. But the assurances of Marillac had revived all his enthusiasm for his old policy. He now abandoned all caution, and promptly proceeded to disclose his real ideas in regard to the 'vnitie in religion.' When Cromwell discovered the true state of affairs he must have been dismayed; he probably already felt how deeply he had become involved in the German alliance, and saw that the new trend which things had taken boded no good to him. His position was now a very uncomfortable one, and the fact that a committee of bishops under his superintendence was utterly unable to cope with the difficulties of the newly presented religious problem, is very significant. Henry was not to be balked however. He quickly took the matter out of the hands of the incompetent bishops, and placed it before the Lords; finally, to make assurance doubly sure, he came to them in person, 'and confounded them all with Goddes Lerning[1].' Henry's theology was of course as unimpeachable as it was confounding, and his energy was rewarded before the middle of June by the definite passage in Parliament of the Statute of the Six Articles. The doctrine of Transubstantiation was confirmed, communion in both kinds was pronounced unnecessary, the marriage of priests was forbidden, all vows of chastity were to be strictly observed, and private masses and auricular confession were adjudged meet and expedient[2].

In spite of the radically Catholic nature of the doctrines

---

[1] Burnet, vol. iv. p. 499.　　　[2] 31 Hen. VIII, c. 14.

proclaimed in this Act, however, Henry took good care that there should be no mistake about his attitude towards the Pope. He was committed to hostility to the See of Rome beyond the possibility of escape, and he knew it. Though political expediency, internal and foreign, had led him to proclaim the catholicity of the Church of England in matters of doctrine, no consideration whatever could induce him to make the least concession to the Papacy. In fact he took measures to show, simultaneously with the passage of the Six Articles, that his contempt of the See of Rome was stronger than ever. Marillac wrote that on June 15 there was played on the river in the King's presence 'a game of poor grace, much less invention, of two galleys, one carrying the King's arms, the other the Pope's, with several Cardinals' hats (so he was told, for he would have deemed it contrary to duty to be a spectator). The galleys fought a long time, and ultimately those of the King were victorious, and threw the Pope and Cardinals and their arms into the water, to show people that this King will entirely confound and abolish the power of the Holy Father[1].' Demonstrations like this were of course mainly intended to impress people at home. Let us now examine the effect of the Six Articles abroad, first in Germany, and then in France and Spain.

---

[1] Cal. xiv. (i) 1137. The martyrologist Foxe tells an amusing and characteristic story of Cromwell's saving Cranmer from punishment for a book which he had written against the Six Articles. There appears to have been a bear-baiting on the Thames before the King, which Mr. Ralph Morice, Cranmer's secretary, was watching from a small boat: and the secretary, it seems, had the Archbishop's book in his girdle for safe-keeping. The bear broke loose from the dogs and upset the wherry in which Morice was; in the tumult which ensued he lost the precious book. It was subsequently picked up by the 'bearward,' who perceiving what it was, and being himself a violent papist, gave it to a priest of his religion, who told the bearward that whosoever wrote it would be hanged if the King should see it. The bearward endeavoured to give it to some influential Catholic at the Court, utterly refusing to listen to Morice's entreaties that he should return it to Cranmer. At this juncture Cromwell appeared upon the scene, and so 'shaked up the bearward for his over-much malapertness' that the latter was glad to return the book to the secretary, and so escape without further punishment. Foxe, vol. ii. p. 428.

The rather large hopes of a religious agreement which Henry had held out to the leaders of the Schmalkaldic League early in the year, merely as a bait to induce them to favour the political alliance with Cleves, had finally, owing to Cromwell's representations, been accepted in all seriousness by John Frederic of Saxony and Philip of Hesse. They soon sent over another embassy under the leadership of Burckhard and Ludwig von Baumbach, a councillor of the Landgrave, which arrived in London on April 23. Henry was not yet quite sure of his ground with Marillac, and had not fully decided what note should be struck in the 'devise in the parliament for the vnitie in religion,' so at first he received the Germans cordially [1]. On April 29 they were granted an audience, in which Henry, though he carefully avoided committing himself to any definite promises of an alliance, spoke in the warmest terms of the Elector and Landgrave, cautioned the Lutherans against the treachery of the Emperor, and boasted long and loud because of the recent collapse of an expedition against England which, according to Wriothesley's report, had been preparing in Flanders since the previous February [2]. A subsequent interview of the ambassadors with Cromwell and other members of the Privy Council was equally satisfactory, and Burckhard and Baumbach were convinced that their mission would ultimately be crowned with success. Had they understood the meaning of the many excuses which were offered for the failure to begin definite negotiations at once, the opening of Parliament and the difficulty of gaining access to the King, they might have been less encouraged. Henry merely wished to detain them until he had made perfectly sure that they could be of no more use to him. His relations with France were improving every day, but he had not yet made sure of the state of affairs in the dominions of the Emperor. On February 24, at Frankfort, the Electors of Brandenburg and the Palatinate had opened negotiations with the Imperial plenipotentiary, the Archbishop of Lund, in the hope of mediating between Charles and the princes of the Schmal-

---

[1] Appendix I at the end of this chapter.    [2] Cal. xiv. (i) 208, 440.

kaldic League[1]; Henry had determined to learn the result of this meeting before giving the ambassadors a definite answer. The news of the truce concluded between the Emperor and the Lutherans on the 19th of April was finally announced in London towards the middle of May: it at once decided the King to send the envoys home empty-handed again, for it was obviously useless to continue negotiations for an alliance, which was primarily to have been directed against the very power with which the Schmalkaldner had just made a temporary peace. So much had Henry been encouraged by the favourable signs of the past few weeks, that he would probably have succeeded in finding an excuse for dismissing Burckhard and Baumbach, even if the result of the negotiations between the Emperor and the Schmalkaldner had been reversed; as it was he was spared the trouble of exercising much ingenuity, for, most unfortunately for the ambassadors, one of the clauses in the Frankfort agreement contained a provision which in itself was quite sufficient to stultify all their efforts. In the seventh article of their treaty with the Emperor, the Schmalkaldner had agreed not to admit any new members into their league during the period of the truce. There is every reason to think that this provision was especially directed against the English negotiations, for both Brandenburg and the Count Palatine had always looked with disfavour on the attempts of Saxony and Hesse to gain the alliance of Henry, and doubtless availed themselves of this opportunity to persuade the Schmalkaldner to put an end to them. In any case the King lost no time in acting upon the intelligence he had received, and at once complained to Burckhard and Baumbach, whose excuses and explanations were of no avail. Wearisome disputes and attempts at a compromise ensued: the question of reciprocity was discussed at length; the envoys insisting that England was sure to derive quite as much benefit from the proposed alliance as the Lutherans, the King and his ministers in turn demanding concessions which they knew that the ambassadors were not authorized

---

[1] Bezold, p. 686.

to grant. So reluctant were the latter to return without having accomplished anything however, that it was only with the utmost difficulty that Henry finally succeeded in getting rid of them. To a blunt request that they depart the envoys only replied with continued petitions for a more favourable answer to their demands: finally, with pleasing frankness, they begged that His Majesty would let himself be guided by the truth alone in directing the religious controversies then in progress in Parliament. Henry made no effort to conceal from Burckhard and Baumbach the anger which this ill-timed and incautious request aroused in him, for he probably realized that his best chance of hastening the departure of the Lutherans lay in involving himself in some sort of an altercation with them. We are not surprised to read that both parties immediately became engaged in a violent discussion concerning the celibacy of the clergy—in the midst of which the ambassadors apparently beat a somewhat precipitate retreat: they seem at last to have had the wit to realize that they had to do with a theologian, with whom it was extremely dangerous to disagree. A fruitless interview with Cromwell followed, and on May 31 the envoys finally departed[1]. In the meantime the Elector and the Landgrave had continued to show touching but unwarranted confidence in the sincerity of Henry's professions, and had remained in utter ignorance of the true state of affairs in England. Their hopes of a speedy settlement of religious differences had doubtless received considerable encouragement through the efforts of Dr. Barnes, who had been earnestly labouring to remove the disagreeable impression which Henry had made on Christian III by his blundering Lübeck policy in 1534. Barnes had been sent to Hamburg for this purpose early in the year. He was himself an ardent Protestant who never once suspected the possibility of a Catholic reaction in England ; and as his zeal more than supplied the lack of diplomatic skill, his efforts seem to have met with great success[2]. The King of Denmark was now in close

---

[1] Cf. Appendix I at the end of this chapter.

[2] Cal. xiv. (i) 441, 442, 955-958.

alliance with John Frederic, and Barnes was soon enabled to persuade them to arrange to send a joint embassy to the King of England to treat of the political league which was to follow a theological agreement [1]. But at this juncture Burckhard and Baumbach returned with a very discouraging report, which obtained full confirmation by the news which arrived a week later, that the Six Articles had actually been passed [2]. The enthusiasm of the Lutherans was of course considerably dampened, and they wrote to Henry that if a league was to be treated of at all, he would have to be the one to send ambassadors ; they could not themselves venture to visit England because of the machinations against the Evangelical cause there [3]. Even in Cleves, where Henry and Cromwell had sought an alliance of a purely political nature, unhampered by religious restrictions, the news of the passage of the Six Articles created profound distrust, and we may well believe that John Frederic discouraged his brother-in-law from continuing negotiations with England, after the proof of Henry's perfidy that he had just received. We are not surprised to find that the matrimonial projects which formed the basis of the alliance with Cleves came to a complete standstill during the month of July. The proposals for a match between Duke William and the Princess Mary had apparently never been very popular : they were now definitely abandoned and never revived. To the other plan, for a marriage of Henry and the Duchess Anne, an unexpected objection had arisen. It appears that ever since 1527 a plan for a marriage between the King's intended bride and the son of Duke Anthony of Lorraine had been under discussion. For twelve years the form of continuing the negotiations for this union had been kept up on both sides, with the idea of bringing pressure on the Emperor, though all hope of an actual completion of the match must have been abandoned long before this time. But now that the union with England seemed less desirable, the Duke of Cleves of course made the most of the opportunity of evading the requests of Henry that was afforded by the Lorraine affair. The claims of

---

[1] Cal. xiv. (i) 1273.    [2] Cal. xiv. (i) 1278.    [3] Cal. xiv. (ii) 59.

Duke Anthony and his son would have to be satisfied, he said, before his sister could be offered to Henry[1].

Altogether it looked as if the German alliance would be abandoned, and Cromwell, who of all people was most deeply involved in it, must have been roused to a sense of his danger. But the threatened reversal of his policy was destined to be postponed once more. For it soon appeared that the exultation of the King at the apparent success of his own plans was premature. We have seen that it was largely in the hope of conciliating Francis and Charles by removing their main pretext for an attack on England that Henry had caused the Six Articles to be passed. But the Act did not accomplish what was expected of it. The courtesy of Marillac had given Henry a very exaggerated idea of the cordiality of France. He did not see that Francis was merely dallying with him, and had no idea of a permanent friendship. The fact that Charles had refused to listen to the proposals of Cardinal Pole had also been regarded as a good omen[2]. But when it appeared that dread of the Turks, who had advanced up the Adriatic, was the sole cause of the Emperor's apparent unwillingness to offend England, and it was rumoured that there was immediate prospect of another interview between him and Francis, Henry discovered his mistake[3]. All the fair hopes he had entertained of preventing the dreaded coalition against England were apparently blasted. The doctrinal statement from which he had expected so much had proved but a feeble weapon with which to arrest the current of continental politics. He could consider himself fortunate if the Six Articles and his own personal rudeness to the German ambassadors had not been sufficient to preclude all hope of a return to the alliance, which a few months before he had abandoned as useless, but which now seemed to offer the one chance for England's safety. Once more the policy of Cromwell seemed justified, and Henry was forced to acknowledge it.

Fortunately for England, the situation, alarming as it was, had even more terrors for the Duke of Cleves than for Henry.

---

[1] Cal. xiv. (i) 920 ; Heidrich, pp. 17, 18.

[2] Cal. xiv. (i) 603.

[3] Cal. xiv. (ii) 218, 300, 545.

Charles' refusal to ratify the treaty of Frankfort had once more blighted the hopes of a peaceful solution of the difficulties in Germany [1]; in May the outbreak of a serious rebellion in Ghent made it imperative for the Emperor to appear in person in the Netherlands, and in early August Francis sent him an invitation to pass through France on his way to the Low Countries. The prospect that Charles, in close alliance with his former rival, would soon be brought within striking distance of Gelderland, was by no means agreeable to Duke William. It was fairly obvious that Charles would bend his energies to punishing the Duke of Cleves for his contempt of the Imperial authority, before attempting to chastise the King of England for the general weal of Christendom. The Duke of Cleves was much more practical than his brother-in-law: like Henry he never let religious considerations or conscientious scruples weigh against the dictates of political expediency. As soon as the news of the Emperor's invitation from Francis was confirmed, Duke William's doubts concerning the pre-contract of his sister Anne and the son of the Duke of Lorraine were cleared up with gratifying celerity. He probably had some difficulty in obtaining the consent of the more scrupulous John Frederic to a renewal of the negotiations with England, but his urgency was such that he triumphed over every obstacle. A messenger from Burckhard to Cromwell in the end of August was followed in early September by four ambassadors from Cleves and Saxony who were authorized to conclude the match [2]. The King must have been greatly relieved at the arrival of the envoys. Since May 3 he had heard nothing from his friends in Cleves except for the famous description of his intended bride, which his ambassador Wotton had sent him, for lack of other news. Anne appears to have been of very 'lowly and gentle conditions. . . . . She occupieth her time most with the needle, wherwithall she . . . . She canne reede and wryte her [own tongue but of] Frenche Latyn or other langaige she [knows no]ne, nor yet she canne not synge nor pleye . . . . . enye instrument, for they take it heere in

Bezold, p. 686.                    [2] Cal. xiv. (ii) 63, 127, 128.

Germanye for a rebuke and an occasion of lightenesse, that great ladyes shuld be lernyd or have enye knowledge of musike .... your Graces servant Hanze Albein hathe taken theffigies of my lady Anne and the ladye Amelye and hath expressyd theyr imaiges verye lyvelye [1].' In the end it proved unfortunate for Cromwell that this letter, and the portrait which Holbein made [2] were not sufficient to turn the King against her, without the need of further confirmation. But even if Wotton's description had been far less flattering, it is doubtful if he could have persuaded Henry to abandon the Cleves marriage at this crisis. The King was now as reckless in accepting the alliance as he had been a few months before in refusing it. He perhaps forgot that though his zeal for the national welfare had never been hampered by religion or conscience, he had not yet put his patriotism to the more practical test of a sacrifice of matrimonial bliss. So the preliminaries of the match were hurried through with a speed quite as remarkable as the delays in the previous negotiations with the Lutherans. The ambassadors departed on October 6 to return to Cleves and conduct Anne to Calais, where a noble company assembled to welcome her, Gregory Cromwell being among the number [3]. Such were the delays of travelling in those times (Wotton wrote to Cromwell that the lady's party could only make five miles a day [4]) that Anne of Cleves did not arrive at Calais until December 11, and there she waited till the 27th, for weather sufficiently favourable for her crossing [5].

Having landed, she proceeded to Canterbury, where

---

[1] Cal. xiv. (ii) 33. Minute inquiries and sometimes indelicately full replies concerning the appearance and bearing of intended brides seem to have been authorized by all Tudor traditions. The report of Wotton is but meagre in details when compared to that of the ambassadors of Henry VII concerning Joanna of Naples, whom the English King had once thought of marrying in 1505. Anne of Cleves was certainly considered beautiful in Germany. Sleidan, vol. ii. p. 150, refers to her as 'eleganti forma virginem.'

[2] Now in the Louvre.

[3] Cal. xiv. (ii) 664. Cf. also the Chronicle of Calais, pp. 167–179. In the latter, Gregory Cromwell's name is erroneously written 'George Crombwell.'

[4] Cal. xiv. (ii) 634, 677.

[5] Cal. xv. 14.

Cranmer welcomed her with due pomp and ceremony. He had received from Cromwell fifty sovereigns to be presented to her on her arrival, and promised to do his best to induce the townspeople to give her fifty angels more[1]. From Canterbury Anne journeyed on to Sittingbourne and Rochester, where she was received on December 31 by the Duke of Norfolk, with a great company of nobles[2]. When Henry heard of her arrival there he determined to visit her in disguise, and, accompanied by eight persons of his Privy Chamber, he rode down to Rochester on New Year's Day and saw for the first time his intended bride[3]. It is unfortunate that we possess no trustworthy information concerning the impression which Anne made on Henry at this first meeting. A letter which Cromwell wrote to the King, six months later, from the Tower states that when Henry, on his return from Rochester, was asked how he liked the Queen, he had answered ' hevelye And not plesantlye " nothing so well as She was spokyn of ",' and had added that had he known as much as he then knew 'she shold not haue Commen within this Realme[4].' It will be seen in a later chapter, however, that Cromwell wrote this letter under circumstances which rendered it very improbable that he told the exact truth: there is every reason to think that he greatly exaggerated the aversion which Henry first conceived for Anne of Cleves. In any case if Henry felt any such disgust as Cromwell described, he succeeded admirably in dissembling his feelings. Two days after the meeting at Rochester, he rode in state to meet his bride at Greenwich, and on January 6 he married her. ' The sonday after,' Hall adds, ' there were kepte solempne Justes, . . . . . on whiche daie she was appareiled after the Englishe fassion, with a Frenche whode, whiche so set furth her beautie and good visage, that euery creature reioysed to behold her[5].'

---

[1] Cal. xiv. (ii) 753.
[2] Cal. xv. 14.
[3] Hall, pp. 832 ff.
[4] Letters, 349-50.
[5] Hall, p. 837. It appears that the fashion changed in England at the time of the arrival of Anne. In telling of her wedding, the Chronicle of the Grey Friars of London (p. 43) informs us that 'thene beganne alle the gentyl women of Yngland to were Frenche whooddes with bellementtes of golde.'

It is important to notice that even in this hour of national peril, Henry did not make any overtures to the Elector of Saxony or the Landgrave of Hesse. Not even the immediate prospect of war with France and Spain could induce him to go as far as this and to bind himself by ties religious as well as political. Even Cromwell had by this time discovered the uselessness of endeavouring to persuade the King to return to an alliance of which he had never really approved ; more than this, he at last seemed to realize, that as advocate of a policy which his master had definitely abandoned, he ran great danger of losing his influence if not his life. It was rather late for him to attempt to break away from a plan with which his name had become identified ; but he saw that he must purchase safety at the cost of consistency, and he took care in future to discourage all efforts of the Lutherans to come to an agreement. The reception accorded to an embassy which the firm but persistent Schmalkaldner sent to England in January 1540, and the words which Cromwell spoke to the ambassador on that occasion give us a very clear insight into the attitude of the King's minister [1]. It was the last attempt which the Lutherans made to treat with England during Cromwell's ministry, and its failure marks the end of the negotiations which had begun with the mission of Vaughan and Mont in 1533. Philip of Hesse had sent his councillor, Ludwig von Baumbach, to Henry's Court once more, with instructions to express to the King his sorrow at the passage of the Six Articles, and his hope that they would not lead to any action contrary to the word of God and the truth of the Gospels. The Landgrave also trusted that the King would not suffer the negotiations with the Lutherans to drop, but the ambassador was to make it clear that a political alliance would be conditional, as always, on religious agreement [2].

Baumbach arrived early in January and immediately betook himself to Cromwell, whom he evidently considered the best friend the Lutherans had at the English Court. But this

---

[1] Cf. Appendix II at the end of this chapter.

[2] Lenz, vol. i. pp. 409-10, 420-21.

time he met with a cold reception[1]. The minister kept asking him if he had power to conclude a political alliance —a perfectly safe question, for no one knew better than Cromwell that the Lutherans would insist on doctrinal reconciliation in the first place. Baumbach tried to give an evasive answer, but was soon summoned to Henry, who repeated his minister's demand with still greater directness. The ambassador could only reply that he must consult with Burckhard, who having returned with Anne of Cleves to England, was still in London. On January 12 the two Lutherans had a conversation with Cromwell, in which the latter defined his position with absolute clearness. He told the ambassadors that the King desired a political alliance with them, but that this must come first; the religious question could be settled later. Baumbach and Burckhard answered that this was impossible; nothing could be done until a theological agreement had been concluded. At this Cromwell could contain himself no longer. With almost pathetic frankness he turned to the Lutherans and told them that he plainly saw what they wanted in regard to religion; but, as the world stood then, that he must hold to the same belief as his master, even if it cost him his life[2]. Such was the faith of the man who six months later was brought to

---

[1] Cf. Appendix II at the end of this chapter.

[2] The truth of Baumbach's statements is confirmed by Seckendorff, who obtained his information from the report of Burckhard on this same interview. Speaking of Cromwell Seckendorff says:—

'Lutheranum fuisse Burnetus pro certo habet, nec dissentiunt Saxonicorum Legatorum de eo relationes. Ex iisdem tamen et historiarum documentis constat, hominem fuisse non saltem solida doctrina minime imbutum sed eius ingenii ut Regis favorem omnibus rebus anteponeret. Ultima sane Burcardi ex Anglia relatione de 11 Jan. scripta . . .

diserte dicitur, illum de religione ita disseruisse ut se cum Evangelicis in Germania consentire non negaret, necessarium tamen sibi esse diceret ut Regis voluntati sese conformaret, etiam cum vitae suae periculo, id quod eventus paulo post comprobavit. Non est itaque, ut hunc pro martyre Evangelicae religionis habeamus, et ipse in loco supplicii mori se professus est in religione Catholica. Hoc, etsi ex D. Burneti sententia de Romana minime intellexerit, indicat tamen animum infirmum et aequivocationes sectantem.' Seckendorff, s. lxxviii, p. 261; liber iii, sect. 21.

the block on the charge of counter-working the King in matters of religion! There is little need to dwell on the rest of Baumbach's stay in England. He had another interview with Henry, who, angered at the firmness of the Lutherans on the religious question, now took occasion to throw contempt on their usefulness as political allies. He told some preposterous lies to Baumbach, informing him that he had heard nothing of the danger of the coalition of Charles and Francis of which the envoy talked so much, although he had faithful ambassadors at both Courts. Even if he were attacked, he said, he was fully able to defend himself, owing to England's insular position and strong navy, which was well manned by his own subjects. German soldiers, on the contrary, would be of little use to him as sailors, for they would certainly be always seasick. After making a few counter-proposals which he knew would never be accepted, he dismissed Baumbach with a polite but non-committal message to the Landgrave, and Cromwell, who bade the envoy farewell on January 21, followed suit. But though the minister had used this last mission of the Lutherans mainly as an opportunity to break away from the policy which he had hitherto advocated, but which he now realized the danger of being connected with, his efforts to save himself were too late. We shall see in the next chapter that the events of the previous years had so thoroughly identified him with the Lutheran alliance in the minds of the people, that his enemies were enabled to make use of his supposed adherence to it, as a pretext for conspiring his ruin.

The Lutherans did not send another embassy to England for a long time. Negotiations were not resumed until more than four years later, when the situation had entirely changed, and even then they failed as signally as before. But though Henry had thus dealt the death blow to the hopes of the Schmalkaldner, he did not suffer the year 1539 to close without attempting to form an alliance of a very different sort with another prince of the Empire. As soon as he had heard of the failure of the plan for the marriage of the Princess Mary and the Duke of Cleves, Henry began to look about for another German husband for his daughter. It was doubtless with the royal authority that Christopher Mont had let fall a casual hint in conversation with a certain Nürnberg merchant named Gundelfynger, that Henry would gladly see Mary wedded to a prince of the Empire. The merchant responded by proposing Duke Philip of Bavaria as a suitable candidate for her hand. This prince was a member of the Palatinate branch of the Wittelsbach family, and a nephew of the Elector Louis. He had been a faithful servant of the Emperor and his brother Ferdinand in the first outbreaks of the religious strife after the formation of the Schmalkaldic League, and had been severely wounded in a brave attempt to oppose the Hessian lanzknechts at the battle of Laufen [1]. In spite of the fact that he belonged to a notoriously wavering family, he appears to have been a firm adherent of the Old Faith, at least at the time of which we are speaking. But on the other hand he was certainly loyal to every tradition of Wittelsbach impecuniosity. He had sacrificed all his property in the Emperor's service, and Charles had characteristically refused to make good his losses, and had also insulted him by opposing his suit for the hand of the Duchess of Milan. A financially successful marriage seemed to offer Philip the only chance of recovering his lost fortunes, and it was at this juncture that the possibility of a match with the daughter of the rich King of England was opened to him. The proposal of Gundelfynger seems to have met with Henry's approval, and he soon signified to Philip his desire that the latter should visit him in England. The Duke jumped at the chance to conclude a marriage which promised so many pecuniary advantages, and his anger at the ingratitude of Charles certainly did not make him any less anxious to listen to Henry's proposals. He arrived in London on December 8 [2], and at first the negotiations for the match proceeded with unexpected rapidity. Against two points on which Henry insisted, however, Philip raised strong objections [3]: the first

---

[1] Von Freyberg, vol. iv. p. 264. Cf. also Life of Philip of Bavaria in the Allgemeine Deutsche Biographie, vol. xxvi. pp. 16 ff.

[2] Cal. xiv. (ii) 657.

[3] Life of Philip of Bavaria in the Allgemeine Deutsche Biographie, vol. xxvi. p. 18.

was that he should take Mary as a bastard, 'incapable by the laws and statutes of the realm of claiming any succession or title by right of inheritance.' The second was the King's refusal to except the name of the Pope from the list of those against whom the financial and political agreement which was to accompany the marriage was to be concluded: Philip, as a faithful Catholic, was apparently at first unwilling to enter a league which might bring him into conflict with the See of Rome. But the firmness of the King, coupled with the great financial profits which the match promised to Philip, finally triumphed over the religious scruples of the Wittelsbacher, and on January 24 he signed a treaty in which he accepted the marriage and the compact under the conditions on which Henry insisted: the agreement, however, was not to be considered binding unless Philip could get it ratified by his relatives in Germany before Whitsuntide, 1540. He left England, January 27, for this purpose, but his attempts were unsuccessful, and the proposal came to nothing. It was taken up a second time at a later date, and again abandoned. But though the scheme finally fell through there are a few interesting things to be noticed in connexion with the negotiations for it, which serve to make clear the trend things were taking at the time of Philip's visit in London.

The whole affair was carried on so secretly, and we have so little documentary evidence, that it is very difficult to form any certain conclusions concerning this attempted compact. The name of Cromwell figures prominently in connexion with it; we find Duke Philip consulting with the minister at his house, and visiting the Princess Mary in his company[1]; but it is pretty obvious that all the negotiations were conducted throughout with the full approval of the King, and not, as was the case with the Lutheran affair, partially in opposition to the royal wishes. For the scheme was radically different from the proposed Lutheran alliance which had failed, and not exactly similar to the union with Cleves which had just been completed. It was far more cautious and non-committal than either of them, and it was for this reason that

---

[1] Cal. xiv. (ii) 719; xv. 76.

Henry liked it. In the first place, Philip was a Catholic, so that an agreement with him involved no contradiction to the doctrines proclaimed in the Six Articles. In the second place, he was ostensibly a close ally of the Emperor's and a member of the Imperial Order of the Golden Fleece[1], though, as we have seen, the ingratitude of Charles after his services in Germany must necessarily have tended to make their relations less cordial. Henry was doubtless accurately informed of all this, and saw in an agreement with a member of this powerful though vacillating Wittelsbach family, an opportunity to gain valuable aid in case he were really attacked, without ostensibly committing himself to a policy which would at any time prevent a return to cordial relations with France and Spain. In the next chapter we shall see that it was precisely during Philip's visit at the English Court that Henry's hopes of staving off the dreaded coalition of Charles and Francis against him were once more revived in a most unexpected way. The terms of the agreement which he attempted to conclude with the Duke may thus be regarded as the first intimation of the complete reversal of England's foreign policy which was witnessed by the first six months of the year 1540. According to the draft of a treaty drawn up in England to be presented to Philip for his approval, the Duke was to send to the King's assistance the number of — horse and foot if Henry was attacked by any prince or private person, and was further to aid the King if he made war for the recovery of any right of which he was defrauded[2]. We unfortunately do not possess the original copy of the treaty signed on January 24, but in an account of Philip's life by his brother Ottheinrich, it appears that the final agreement was that the Duke should furnish the King with 1,000 horsemen and 4,000 foot-soldiers against every one except the Roman Empire[3]. The exception of the 'Roman Empire,' which was probably introduced at Philip's request,

[1] Cal. xv. 177.

[2] Cal. xiv. (ii) 733, 737.

[3] The words, as given in the life by Ottheinrich, are : 'Herzog Philipp soll dem khönig wider menigklich, ausgenommen wider das Römisch Reich, 1000 wohl geriste Pferdt Und 4000 wohl geriste fuesknecht zufiehren.' Von Freyberg, vol. iv. p. 266.

was a provision of so vague a nature that it could not bind either party very strictly; it certainly could not have applied to a coalition of Charles and Francis, which was all that Henry wanted, and it had the additional advantage that it made it appear that the compact was not especially directed against the Emperor, and so could not be resented by him. On the subject of the Pope and the illegitimacy of Mary, the King, as we have seen, had remained firm: to yield to Philip on these two points would simply have been to stultify all the work of the previous ten years, a step which Henry, even in the gravest peril, was not prepared to take. But the other terms of the agreement were precisely to his taste. The new treaty could be very useful if the crisis came, and yet it was so arranged that with his well-known ability for quibbling, the King could easily throw it over, if his hopes of a change for the better in his relations with France and Spain were actually fulfilled. It thus stands out in sharp contrast to the Lutheran alliance which Cromwell had advocated, and which, if it had been accomplished, would have irrevocably committed England to permanent hostility to Charles. The terms of the treaty with Philip were cautious, carefully guarded, and strictly non-committal; the Lutheran alliance, had it been carried through, would have been rash, definite, and irrevocable. The contrast between the two schemes is the contrast between the policies of Henry and Cromwell. Though the treaty with Philip was never ratified and the agreement which it proposed was thus never destined to succeed, the fact that so many efforts were made to accomplish it at the very moment that the negotiations with the Lutherans, of which Cromwell had been the chief supporter, were finally abandoned, is very significant in revealing the relative positions of King and minister at the opening of the year 1540.

Briefly to review the state of affairs at this critical juncture. The dread of an attack by the joint forces of France and Spain, which had hung over England for more than a year, seemed to call for a defensive league with some outside power. But even in this hour of national peril the King did not forget the lesson that he had learned at Wolsey's fall : he remembered that the situation on the Continent had often changed before and was likely to do so again, and therefore in his search for a foreign alliance he took the greatest pains to keep his hand free. Cromwell, on the contrary, was now too far advanced in the policy he had followed since the summer of 1538 to be able to retreat from it, though the warning conveyed by the reaction of June, 1539 had certainly opened his eyes to the dangers of the course he pursued. But it was in vain that he attempted to persuade his master to sanction an alliance with the Lutherans. Henry refused to consent to any move which would bind him as permanently as this. Instead the King directed his efforts towards concluding an agreement of a very different nature with Duke Philip of Bavaria, but his demands were so great that this scheme also failed, owing to the unwillingness of the other members of the Wittelsbach family to ratify the treaty. The only alliance which did materialize was that with Cleves. It was a sort of compromise between the Lutheran and the Bavarian plans ; it committed England less definitely than the one, though more so than the other. But the responsibility for it had been made to rest entirely on Cromwell's shoulders, and the minister must have realized that his safety depended on its success. While it was under negotiation, the danger from France and Spain seemed so threatening that the policy of Cromwell was apparently justified. Almost at the moment of its completion, however, events took place which totally changed the aspect of affairs, called for the abandonment of the alliance with Cleves, and led to the ruin of the man whose fortunes were identified with it. What these events were will be seen in the succeeding chapter.

# APPENDIX TO CHAPTER XIII

## I

### THE REPORT OF THE LUTHERAN AMBASSADORS TO ENGLAND IN APRIL AND MAY, 1539, ENTITLED

' *Sum*marie bericht vnd verzeichnisz der gepflog*en* handelu*n*ge in Engelant anno d*omi*ni 1539 [1].'

Nachdem die gesant*en* desz churf. zu Saxsen *etc* vnd la*n*tgraue*n* zu Hesse*n* vnser g. vnd g. hern rethte den viij tag aprilisz zu Franckfort abgeraist sint sie den 23 deszselbig*en* monatz zu Lond*on* anko*mme*n vnd nachdem die ko*nigliche* may*est*ät dazumal nicht dess orczt sondern auff eynem schloisz Riczmu*n*t genant nicht fast verne von Lunden gewest haben sie sich nichtsz destowinger biem hern Crumello, ko*niglichen* may*est*ät zu engelant obersten vnd gehey*m*bsten raidt anczaig*en* lassen. Als hat derselbige ob er wol etwas die cziet myt schwachait belad*en* solchsz ko*niglichen* may*est*ät von stond*en* an zu erke*n*nen geben hat auch den gesant*en* vo*n* wege*n* ko*niglichen* may*est*ät eyn*e* herberge vorordent vnd inen ko*niglichen* may*est*ät forderliche zukunff vormeld*en* lassen mit anczaigu*n*gen dasz sie ko*niglichen* may*est*ät gancz wilcku*mme*n were*n* vnd dasz die ko*nigliche* may*est*ät auff den neste*n* sontag wilcher der 25 aprilisz gewest der gesant*en* werbu*n*ge genedicklich zu horen erpottick. Esz ist auch der ko*nig* myt den 26 aprilisz obgemeltz monatz geg*en* Lond*on* in ir*en* pallast zu Westmo*n*ster kome*n* und nachdem eyn parlame*n*t beschriben gewest wilchesz auff de*n* 28 aprilisz angefang*en* hat sich die ko*nigliche* may*est*ät desz vorczoigksz halben entschuldig*en* lassen vnd den 29 tag aprilisz der gesant*en* werbu*n*ge anzuhoren besty*m*met wie dan geschehen. Vnd hat die ko*nigliche* may*est*ät denselbig*en* tag der gesant*en* werbu*n*ge gehort die sie vormoge irer entpfa*n*en instrucion gethan. Alsz hat sich die ko*nigliche* may*est*ät genedicklich*en* darauff vornem*m*en lassen mit f. [2] dangsagu*n*gen gege*n* den churf. zu Saxsen vnd lantgraue*n* zu Hessen mit dem anhangk dasz ire may*est*ät hern

---

[1] Transcribed from the original document in the Archives at Marburg.
[2] *sic*, for ' freundlichen.'

Crumello vnd eczlich anderen vnd vornemmisten vnd geheimsten
ir maiestät rethte befelich thon wolten mit den gesanten von eyner
erlichen trostlichen vorstennisse zu handeln haben sich auch hoich
gegen vnsere g.g. hern erpotten vnd von der franckfordissen fridsz-
handellungen allerlii gefragk auch v.g.h. von Gulich vnd Geldern
gedacht, vnd in latinisser vnd franczosser sprach sich mit den
gesanten in gespreche ingelassen darauff die gesanten siner maiestät
allenthalben nach gelegenheit nottorfftigen bericht gethan. Es hat
konigliche maiestät in sondernhait erinnerunge gethan dasz sich
obgemelte vnsere g.g. hern mit guten worten nicht wolten vorfueren
lassen dan sine maiestät wuste dasz man allerley wider ir ch. vnd
f. g. vnd der vorsten vorwanten vorhette allein dasz inen bys anhere
an forteil gemangeldt, darauff sie dan tag vnd nacht traichten vnd
bedorfften vlissigesz auffsehensz etc.

Es were auch gewisz dasz man sine maiestät hette mit den schiffen
in Selant vberfallen wollen aber Got lobp sine maiestät hette ire prachticke vornommen vnd weren durch gute frunde vorwarnnet worden
hatten sich auch alszo zur gegenwere gestellet vnd die vorsehunge
in irer mayestät kon⟨ig⟩rich thon lassen dasz sie vor innen vner-
schrocken weren vnd wolte gerne dasz sie sich etwasz tetlichesz
vnderstanden dan sie alszo entpfanen wurden dasz sie den schimp
gerucht solte haben etc. Item es hat sine konigliche maiestät angeczaigk dasz sie gewisz kunschafft hette wie dasz der kayser driemal-
hundert thusent gulden iczt oistern vorschienen in Duczlant etliche
krigsvolck domit anzunemmen vorordent darumb solte man nicht
zu vil vortruen vnd die dinge in guter achtunge haben vnd nachdem
here Crumello duezumall etwasz schwach gewest hat die konigliche
maiestät begerdt eyne kleynne cziet gedult zu tragen dan s. maiestät
wolten die saiche szo mogelich zu fordern beuelen vnd sindt alszo
daszmal die gesanten von koniglicher mayestät abgeschaiden.

Den andern tag desz monacz maij sindt die gesanten in hern
Crummello hausz zu London erfordert do dan konigliche mayestät
rethte alsz nemmelich die bayde herczogen Norfoick vnd Soyffoick
desz richsz engelant cantzeller der oberste ammerall her Crumellus
vnd der bisschoff von Derm Tunstallius genant Wilche erstlichen
desz mandatetsz halben allerley disputacionesz inngefort darauff
innen vorlegunge vnd bericht darmit sie dozumall zufrieden gewest
von den gesanten geschehen vnd zum andern haben sie sich mit
den gesanten der condicion halben vnd wilcher gestaldt die confederacion auffzurichten auch wasz konigliche mayestät vor gegenhulff zu gewarten vntteredet denen die gesanten inhalcz irer in-

strucion nach der lenge bericht vnd anczaigunge vorgewant dasz dan die rethte mit flissz angehort vnd der ding allenthalben koniglicher mayestät zu berichten auff sich gennommen vnd ist gebetten die saichen so vil mogelich zu fordern domit kein vorczoigk erfolge.

Nach disser vnderredunge vnd handelunge haben sich die dinge etliche tage vorczugen ausz vrsach dasz koniglicher mayestät rethte obgemelt teglich insz parlament haben sin mossen vnd auff den xvi tag maij sindt koniglicher mayestät rethte vnd die gesanten yn koniglicher mayestät pallast zu sent Jocop beim hern Crummello zum andern male bie eynnander gewest, vnd haben die konnigliche rethte angeczaigk wie dasz der koniglichen mayestät vor gewissz ausz Franckrich vnd Flandern geschriben dasz der churf. zu Saxsen vnd lantgraue zu Hessen sampt irer chf. vnd f. g. relionszvorwanten sich in der gepflogen fridez handellunge zu Franckfort vorpflicht forder in cziet desz anstansz nimancz in buntnissz zu nemmen wilchsz der koniglichen mayestät fast befromdlich vnd beschwerlich ⟨wird⟩ vnd darauff bericht begerdt etc.   Alsz haben die gesantten vormoge irer bieinstrucion dissesz puncktsz halben vnd sonderlichen auch auff dasz schriben szo inen vom churf. ⟨zu⟩ Saxsen irem g. h. desz fordern tagesz zukommen war den bericht vorgewant dasz die kon⟨ig⟩lichen rethte daran guten genugen gehaipt vnd sich erpotten der koniglichen mayestät solchsz zum forderlichesten zu vormelden auch die saichen irsz vormogensz zu fordern helffen vnd darbie esz daszmalsz blieben vnd haben die gesanten angehalten domit sie nicht lenger auffgehalten mochten werden.

Den xviij tag maij sindt die koniklichen rethte vnd die gsanten zum dritten male in obgemelten koniglicher mayestät pallast zu sent Jocop zusamen komen vnd haben die kongissen rethte nach lenge erczelet dasz sie koniglicher mayestät alle handelunge mit vlisz bericht gethan esz wusten sich auch koniglicher mayestät der gesanten werbunge selbst zu erinnern weren auch geneigk sich in eyn erlich glichmessig vnd trostlich vorstentnissz mit iren hern sampt derselbigen relionszvorwanten irem vorigen erbitten nach inzulassen aber die koniglich mayestät kont nicht befinden dasz sulchesz vorstentnisz der gegen hulff halben deren sich die chur vnd fursten sampt iren relionszvorwantten erbiten theten die glichait oder reciprocum mit sich breichte derhalben were der koniglichen mayestät genedigesz begeren ob die gesanten nach ferner befelich hetten der gegenhulff oder reciproci halben dasz sie sich desz wolten vnbeschwerdt vornemmen lassen.

Item die *konigliche* may*estä*t vormyrck dasz dasz ma*n*dat sere enge
vnd restringirt were wilchsz auch allerlij nachdencken hette bie siner
*koniglichen* may*estä*t vnd ob die gesant*en* vmb ferner befelich vnd
volkommener mandat schriben wolten.

Darauff ist den konigissen rethten geantwortt dasz esz die chur
vnd fursten dar aichten die *konigliche* may*estä*t alsz eyn vortrefflicher
berumpter richer konig wurde esz in solchen erlichen cristlichen
saichen wider desz romissen bisschoff prachticke vnd tiranni an
eyner tapffern su*m*ma geldesz zur defension nicht mangeln lassen
ob sich auch ire ch. vnd f. g. der gege*n*hulff halben nichtsz sonder-
lichesz erbiten tedten v*nd* aber nichtsz desto winger hetten sich ire
ch. vnd f.g. vorne*m*men lassen siner *koniglichen* may*estä*t im fall der
nottorfft do solchsz sin*e* *konigliche* may*estä*t begeren worde eczliche
thuse*n*t zu fuessz vnd etliche hundert zu rosz *etc* zu zu schicken
wilchsz kriegsvolck ire ch. vnd f. g. anne tappern vnkosten nicht
word*en* vorgadern vnd auff eynn monsterplacz bringe*n* lassen moge*n*.
V*nd* domit sulchsz do da*n*nen forder s. may*estä*t zugeschickt wurde
vnd im fall dasz esz die *konigliche* may*estä*t darvor aichte dasz
solchsz gege*n* der su*m*ma geldesz szo die *konigliche* may*estä*t erlege*n*
solte nicht szo gancz glich ader re*ci*procu*m* were szo hetten doch sine
*konigliche* may*estä*t zu bedencke*n* dasz esz siner *koniglichen* may*estä*t
selbst zu*m* besten gereichte allesz waisz ire *konigliche* may*estä*t den
chur. vnd f. sampt ire*n* vorwanten gucz erczaigt dan der romisz
bisschoff vbete sine prachtike nicht winger wider sine *konigliche*
may*estä*t dan ire ch. vnd f. g. vnd ier ch. vnd f. g. mitvorwante*n* vnd
do innen etwasz widerwertigsz wilchsz der almechtige wende*n* wolt
begegen solte worde darnach s. kon*igliche* may*estä*t solchsz auch zu
gewarte*n* haben etc. Desz mandacz halb*en* ist inne*n* die anczeige
geschehen dasz sie desz puncksz zufriede*n* gewest vnd die ding
*koniglicher* may*estä*t zu berichten auff sich geno*m*men alsz ist
deszmalsz nicht witter gehandelt vnd auff den 26 tag maij habe*n*
die *konigliche* may*estä*t die gesant*en* wiedervmb erforder*n* lassen vnd
inne*n* selbst angeczeigt desz [1] sie allenthalben vorno*m*men wasz sich
vor handelu*n*ge czuissen siner m*aiestä*t rethten vnd den gesant*en*
zugetrage*n* vnd wiewole sine m*aiestä*t gancz geneigk sich in buntnisse
mit den churf. zu Saxsen vnd lantgraue*n* zu Hessen sampt ire*n*
relionszvorwant*en* ainzulassen szo vormirck doch ir*e* *konigliche*
m*aiestä*t dasz die vorgeschlagene condicion der gege*n*hulff nicht der·
gestaldt reciproce were wie sich ire *konigliche* may*estä*t vorsehen
hetten vnd esz auch billich in confederacio*n* sin solt dan seine

[1] *sic*, for ' dasz.'

konigliche mayestät begert eyn rumelich erlich vnd baidersicz
trostlich vorstentnisse vnd confederacion myt iren chur vnd f. g. vnd
iren relionsz vorwanten auffzurichten vnd diewil die gesanten keinen
wittern oder fernern befelich hetten dan wie sie hie zuvor angeczeig[t]
szo muste esz seine konigliche maiestät dasz malsz auch darbie
wenden lassen vnd wusten witer darauff mit inen nicht zu handeln,
sondern wolten inen hiemit genedicklich wiedervmb erlaubt haben.
Auch wolte sine konigliche maiestät iren chur vnd f. g. schrifflich ire
gemut anczaigen vnd do sie iren chur und f. g. sunsten fruntlichen
willen erczaigen konte wolten ire konigliche mayestät alleczeit willig
befonden werden wie sie sich auch in glichnisse herwider vorsehen
theten. Alsz haben die gesanten irer koniglichen mayestät hinwider
angeczaigk dasz sie sich von wegen irer g. vnd genedigen hern nicht
vorsehen hetten seine konigliche mayestät worde sie nicht gancz vor-
gebelich abschaiden lassen wil ire mayestät wmb disse schickunge
bei iren g. vnd genedigen hern ansuchung auch trostlich erbitunge
gethan esz worden sich auch ire chur vnd f. g. vile winger solchsz
abschaidsz vorsehen vnd were disse kegenhulff nicht szo geringe wie
sie ire konigliche mayestät achten etc Aber wie denn szo musten sie
esz darbie wenden lassen vnd wolten ire g. vnd genedige hern aller
handelunge zum vnderthenigsten vnd truelichesten wilsz Got zu irer
widerkumpfft berichten vnd worden sich demnach ire ch. vnd f. g.
gegen seiner koniglichen mayestät irer nottorfft nach zu halten vnd zu
vornemmen lassen wissen vnd nachdem vil reden gewest dasz die
konigliche mayestät etczliche artikel der relion im parlament handeln
lassen alsz nemmelich von dem hoichwurdigen sacrament desz liebesz
vnd bludez unsersz hern Cristi item von der prister ehe haben die
gesanten gebetten seine konigliche mayestät alsz die die warhait
liebte wolte in dissen groswichtigen saichen alleyne die warhait
fordern vnd hanthaben etc Darauff dan die konigliche mayestät in
eyne hefftige disputacion desz artikelsz die pristerehe belangend mit
den gesanten komen die seiner mayestät nottorfftigen bericht vnd
anczaige gethan vnd darnach iren abschaidt von irer mayestät
genommen etc. Vnd nachdem konigliche mayestät schrifften an
hoichgemelte vnsere g. vnd g. hern vorfertiget vnd den gesanten
durch hern Crummello zugesteldt haben sie gebetten sich zu
berichten wesz doch konigliche mayestät maynunge sie der confederacion halben vnd wesz seine konigliche mayestät vor condicion
ader gegenhulff oder reciprocum begerte darauff der here Crum-
mellus angeczaigt dasz die konigliche mayestät eyne tapffere summa
geldesz zu erlegen willig aber der gestalt dasz solche geldt bayden

teilen alsz seyner ko*niglichen* may*estä*t vnd vnsern g. vnd g. hern vnd
iren relionszvorwant*en* zuglich zum besten kome vnd wilchsz tail
eher angriffen ⟨wurde⟩ dasz daszselbige solche geldt zu gebrauchen
haben solte etc. Vnd do iren ch. vnd f. g. sulchesz a*n*nemlich
⟨wäre⟩ woste eher [1] dasz die ko*nigliche* m*aies*tä*t* an eyner tapffern
su*m*ma geldesz niederzulege*n* nicht erwinde*n* lassen etc. Alsz haben
die gesant*en* diewil sie dissesz artickelsz halben zu handeln ader zu
schlissen kein*en* befelich gehaipt sich erbotten daszselbige iren chur.
vnd f. g. zu irer widerkunfft mit gotlicher hulff vnderthenichliche*n*
auch zu berichte*n* vnd alszo irn abschaidt den leczten tag maij
geno*m*men anno vt supra.

Franciscus Burchart
vicecanczler
s*ub*scri*p*si*t*.

Ludowic*us* de Baumbach
s*ub*scri*p*si*t*.

*Endd.* 'Relation Ludwigs von Baumbach vnd Mgr. Frantz Burg-
hardi von weg*en* der sendung in Engellandt.'

## II

ACCOUNT BY LUDWIG VON BAUMBACH OF HIS JOURNEY
TO ENGLAND. DECEMBER, 1539 TO JANUARY, 1540 [2].

Auff donstag nach triu*m* regu*m* byn ich myt gottesz holff zu
Lond*on* ankomen vnd mich bye dem Hern Crumello ansagen
Lassen hat er mich auff den freitag morge*n* frue alszo balde gefordert
vnd holen Lassen vnd mich allerleii gefraugk wie esz im thucze*n*lant
stehe vnd ab ich nicht macht ader befelich habe dasz buntnisz myt
ko. may*estä*t zu schlissen etc.

Dar auff ich geantwort ich habe eyn credencz an die ko. may*estä*t
vnd eyne werbunge im geheym vnd vortruen syn*er* may*estä*t anzu-
sage*n* vnd derhalp dem h. crumello gebetten myr forderlich zu sin
dasz ich auff dasz erst szo mogelich von sin*er* may*estä*t gehort moge
werd*en*.

Dar auff der H. Crumellu*s* geantwort er werde esz der ko. may*estä*t
zu forderlichesten ken grunewicz zu wyssen thon vnd vorsehe sich

---

[1] *sic*, for 'er.'
[2] Transcribed from the original document in the Archives at Marburg.

ir mayestät werde mich zu forderlichesten horen diewil ir mayestät
mich kennen.

Auff den sonnobent byn ich von Cristoffel mont beschick vnd
bericht die ko. mayestät habe befolen ich solt auff den sonntag
morgen frue zu ix vren zu grunewicz sin do wolle ir mayestät mich
ghoren vnd ir mayestät sie mynner ankonfft wole zufrieden.

Die ko. mayestät hat mich auff den sontag durch den hern
Crumellum in s. mayestät innerst gemach fordern vnd fueren Lassen
vor der messen da habe ich nach dem die ko. mayestät die credencz
erbrochen vnd vorlesen allesz waisz myr befolen ist gewest nach der
lenge myt besten flissze erczalet vnd bericht dar auff ir mayestät
myt flisse gehort vnd alle wort zweygefraugk vnd alsz balde ich
auszgeredt Hat s. mayestät geantwort ich habe lange desz ko vom
franckrichsz gemudt gesport vnd vornommen vnd er wolde eyne
botschaffe sich der dinge zu erkonnen thon vnd mich gefraugk ab
ich solchsz auch lieden moge sonst wolle s. mayestät niemancz
nicht melden dar auff ich s. mayestät geantwort dasz moge ich wole
lieden szo verne niemancz genent von wem s. mayestät disze dinge
vorstanden vnd mich gefraugk ab ich keine befelich habe die buntnisz
myt s. mayestät zu schlyssen habe ich geantwort nein sondern s.
mayestät zu raiden dasz sich ir mayestät irsz gemucz entlichen vornemmen Lasse vnd zum forderlichesten die bontnisz schlisse ehe esz
zu kriege komme dar auff ir mayestät gesag m. h. habe im geschriben
ich solde eyne zcitlangk bie s. mayestät blieben dar auff ich geantwort
desz habe ich von m. g. h. keynen befelich.

Dar nach ir mayestät allerleii gemeine rede gehaipt vnd alsz balde
in die kirchen gangen vnd alsz balde ir mayestät in ir. kapellen
komen vnd mich gesehen haben ir mayestät myr gewinckt vnd
angesprochen vor allen heren vnd gsaugk er habe mynem g. g. hern
geschriben vnd sie haben im keyne antwort dar auff ggeben, vnd
alsz witter gefraugk ab ich keynen befelich habe witter myt s.
mayestät der buntnisz halber zu reden dar auff ich geantwort von
dem schriben habe ich keine wisse der bontnisz halber wolle ich
mich eyn kleinsz bedencken vnd mych myt dem Sexsissen vice
canczeller vnderreden vnd sine mayestät beantworten.

Auff den dienstag darnach hat der H. Crumellus den vice canczeler
vnd mich gefordert vnd allerleii myt vnsz bayden geredt vnd gesaugk
s. h. der konnig sie geneigk sich myt vnsren h. zu vorbinden vnd
darnach von der relionsz saichen zu reden angefangen dar auff myr [1]
baide der vice canczeller auff latin vnd ich auff franczossiscz

---

[1] *sic*, for 'wyr.'

geantwort esz were gotelichen vnd erlichen dasz s. may*est*ät sich zu
vor vnd ehe die pontnisz geschlossen myt vnsren g. h. desz gottlichen
worcz vorgliche dar nach worde got genade vorliehen dasz alle saichen
gudt word*en* dar auff der. h. Crumellu*s* gesaugkt er siehe vnser
maynu*n*ge den glauben betreffen aber wie die weldt iczt stehet wesz
sich sin her der ko*n*nig halte desz wolle er sich auch halt*en* vnd solte
er darumb sterben er rade aber dasz die pontnisz beschlossen vnd
dar nach von bayderseicz gelarten zusam*en* komen lasze vnd sich
der schrifft vnd gotlichesz worcz vorglichen lasse wilche teil dan
recht behalt dasz dem dan dasz ander teile folge vnd szo wyr myt
s. h. dem ko. der saichen halber zu red*en* kem*en* szo wolt er vnsz
geraid*en* haben dasz wyr sidick vnd nicht zu hart myt s. may*est*ät
reden wolt*en* etc. da myt s. may*est*ät nicht zue vngenad*en* vnd
vngeduld*en* erregt werde.

Dar nach von stonde an ist der H. crumellu*s* zu dem ko*n*nige
gang*en* vnd alsz balde mich allein zu*m* konnige zu kom*en* gefordert
vnd hat s. may*est*ät angefang*en* vnd gesaugk die dinge die ich
s. may*est*ät erczaldt habe nem*en* s. may*est*ät wonder dasz dasz
vorhand*en* sin solte vnd solte im szo lange vorschwig*en* blieben sin
in ansehu*n*ge dasz er syne am*m*asatten an bayd*en* ort*en* habe, zu dem
szo ko*n*nen sie sich in ile szo starck nicht rusten er koncz in ile
erfar*en* vnd szo sie den kreigk myt ime anfahen szo sollen sie
entpfanen werd*en* dan s. konrich sie nicht eyn lant wie die lande in
thuczlant dan esz sie myt wasser vmbethom*m*e beflossen vnd konnt
niemancz zu im kom*en* dan zu schiff.

Da habe ich die sachen der massen myt ploichehausern vnd
polwercken auch myt schiffen bestaldt vnd vor wart dasz sie
entpfanen sollen werd*en* szo habe ich gudte schucze*n* vnd habe
die von Lond*on* hart bie myr vnd sonsten ey*n*e stedt ist myr zu
ne*n*ne*n* vorgessen da kan ich in ile eyn czemelich volck auff bring*en*
auch szo habe ich die vorretter gemeinklichen richten vnd die
koppe abschlag*en* Lassen dasz myr niemancz lichlich eyn*en* auffrure
wirdt anrichten dasz magestu dyne*m* hern sag*en* aber ich bedanck
mich kegen din*en* h. wie gehort vnd ich vorstehe die sache nicht
anderst dan dasz er die saichen trueliche vnd gudt myt myr
maynt.

Vnd szo vile den ko*n*nig von dennemarck betrifft da habe ich
nicht myt zu schaffen ich waiss auch kein bontnisz myt im zu
machen dan er hat den alten konig nach gefang*en* dasz isst wieder
den pfalzgraue*n* vnd myt ⟨welchem⟩ byn ich in willensz eyn
fruntschaffe eynsz hiracz zu machen etc.

T

Auch szo dynen myr die lanczknecht nicht dan alsz balde sie auff dasz mere komen szo werden sie krancg vnd sint desz mersz nicht gewont wie myne luede sint aber dasz wil ich raden dasz dyne hern der chur f. zu saxsen myn brueder der herzoig von klefa vnd gelderln vnd die andern fursten in der bontnisz sampt hanburgk vnd bremen vnd nicht vile vberlendisse stedt eyn erlichs bontnisz in allen gemeynen sachen beschlossen, were von den selbigen vberzogen worde dasz im die andern alle holffen mosten vnd eynsz sachen aller andern sachen sin most szo wil ich pfalcz auch dar zu bringen dasz sie vnsersz teilsz sin sollen.

Dan die Vberlendisse stedt haben sich nit witter dan wasz die relion betrifft keigen eubere hern vorbonden vnd ab der kaiser eyn ander vrsach zu eubern h. suchen ⟨werde⟩ szo worden sie in keinen biestandt thon. gedenck an mich vnd due magest dym h. solchesz wolle sagen dar auff ich s. mayestät geantwort ich habe die vorschribunge der bontnisz wie weidt sie sich streckt nicht gelesen der halp ich s. mayestät keynen bericht dar von thon konde dar auff ir mayestät gesaugk esz ist gudt vnd genugk darvonn geredt vnd myr die hant gebotten vnd myn abschaidt ggeben vnd der bontnisz nach malsz wie vor begerdt dar auff ich siner mayestät geantwort Ich wolle die dinge mynem g. f. vnd h. szo verne mich got gesunt frist zu myner wieder ankonff myt flissz berichten vnd zwifel nicht vnd zwifel nicht[1] s. f. g. werden sich gancz frundelich alsz siner mayestät frundt vnd der s. mayestät ere vnd gucz gunne von vor wisslichen vornemmen Lassen vnd byn do myt von s. mayestät abgeschaiden.

Auff dinstag nach sebastians vnd fabianes hat myr der H. crumellus myne abschaidt der massen ggeben dasz im s. h. der konnig befolen myr an zu sagen mynem g. h. sonderlichen dangk zu sagen vnd sien ir mayestät mynem g. h. myt allem fruntlichen willen auch allesz dasz zu thon dasz mynem h. zu eren vnd guttem kome zu willefaren hoich geneigk vnd ir. mayestät habe die saichen nicht anderst dan truelichen von myr vorstanden vnd ir. mayestät sie myr vor myne person myt allen genaden geneigk dar auff gancz mynen abschaidt genommen. geschechen auff die tage wie ob stehet anno etc. xl in vrkunt myne hant

D

Luodewig von baumbach
zu bynsfort sst.

*Endd.* ' Relation Ludove. von baumbachs aus Engelland vff d. gesheene verwarnung.'

[1] *sic.*

# CHAPTER XIV

## THE FALL OF THOMAS CROMWELL

WHILE Henry and Cromwell had been occupied in negotiations with various German princes, the Emperor and the French King had not been idle. Every day seemed to bring some fresh confirmation of the unwelcome news that the two monarchs were again on the most friendly terms. By the middle of December the anxiety of England reached the highest pitch, for the report came that Francis and Charles had actually met at Loches, and that their first interview had been marked by every demonstration of cordiality [1]. The French King accompanied the Emperor on his journey northward, and on New Year's Day they entered Paris together amid great rejoicing. For eight days the Louvre saw a succession of balls, fêtes, and jousts. It is said that Jean Cousin was ordered to make a bust of the Emperor [2].

But if the meeting of Charles and Francis and their apparently perfect amity were the cause of profound alarm in England, the proximity of the two rivals furnished at the same time an admirable opportunity for a last attempt to stir up jealousy between them. The King, who as we have seen had never even in his most anxious moments abandoned the hope of fomenting discord between the two sovereigns, was not the man to permit this chance to escape him. Sir Thomas Wyatt, who had been recalled from Spain a short time before, was now sent back to Paris to co-operate with Bonner, the ambassador to France, in the endeavour to make use of the situation for Henry's purposes [3]. His instructions to express the King's joy at the prospect of a renewal of amity between Francis and Charles were of course merely

---

[1] Cal. xiv. (ii) 717.
[2] Martin, vol. viii. p. 260.   Cf. also Guiffrey, pp. 276–318.
[3] Cal. xiv. (ii) 524.

a blind to cover his real intentions. It was not long before the character of the latter was made plainly evident. Wyatt wrote a full account of his proceedings to Henry on January 7, 1540[1]. In his letter he did not say whether he paid any attention to the written instructions which the King had previously given him or not, but reported his endeavours to obtain the arrest of one Brancetour, an Englishman in the Emperor's train, whom the Act of Attainder of 1539 had condemned. From Wyatt's account, however, it appears that the actual taking of Brancetour was a matter of secondary importance, compared to the possibility it opened of stirring up a quarrel between Francis and Charles. The two ambassadors had waited upon the French King, and had readily obtained his consent to the arrest. Brancetour was taken, but insisted that he acknowledged no master except the Emperor, and was consequently not amenable to English law. He applied to Charles, who of course refused to give his servant up; the matter was again brought before the French King, who, being far more anxious to secure the good will of the Emperor than that of Henry, gave orders for the prisoner's release. At first it seemed as if the efforts of the two ambassadors had merely resulted in drawing Charles and Francis closer together. Chagrined at the failure of his efforts, Bonner had made matters worse by rudely remonstrating with the French King for permitting Brancetour to be restored to liberty. The chief result of this proceeding was that the English ambassador became so generally hated at the French Court on account of his bluntness and discourtesy, that Henry felt obliged to recall him in favour of Sir John Wallop[2].

With the ground cleared by the retirement of his unpopular colleague, Sir Thomas Wyatt was able to display to far greater advantage that wealth of tact and diplomatic talent, which had rendered him such an invaluable servant to Henry

---

[1] Cal. xv. 38.

[2] Cal. xv. 186. Bonner and Wyatt moreover were on very bad terms at this time, owing to mutual jealousy. It would have been impossible for Henry to carry his intrigues very far, as long as the two rivals remained together at the French Court. Cf. Nott's Wyatt, vol. ii. pp. 44–52.

at the Emperor's Court. He immediately saw that it was useless to blame Francis, as Bonner had done, for an act which the situation had forced upon him, and he forbore to mention the affair of Brancetour again in the presence of the French King. Instead he addressed himself to Charles, and in the most careful and guarded phrases insinuated that the Emperor had shown ingratitude to Henry, in obtaining the Englishman's release[1]. Wyatt's action throughout was characterized by an external courtesy quite as remarkable as the previous rudeness of Bonner, and his efforts were finally rewarded in a manner which exceeded the King's highest expectations. He had caught the Emperor off his guard, and the first result of his representations was to cause the usually imperturbable Charles completely to lose his temper. The Emperor in his vexation let several words escape him, of which Wyatt was prompt to take advantage. When reproached with ingratitude, Charles had turned sharply on the ambassador with a few angry words, which implied that it was impossible for him to be 'ingrate' to Henry, on account of the superiority of his own Imperial rank. The Emperor confessed that 'the inferyour' might be 'ingrate to the greter,' though the term was 'skant sufferable bytwene lyke[2],' but hinted that an accusation of ingratitude from the petty King of England against himself, the acknowledged head of Christendom, was entirely out of place. All this was reported at the English Court in early February. The use which Henry made of the information is remarkable. As a result of Wyatt's communications, the Duke of Norfolk was sent with a special message to Francis[3]. He was ordered to quote all the conversation between Charles and Wyatt, but so to distort the meaning of the Emperor's angry words as to make it appear that Charles was using Francis' friendship merely as a stepping-stone to an ulterior purpose, and perhaps to a plan for the domination of Europe. Charles' unfortunate slip about superiors and inferiors lent itself well to such an interpretation. On February 15 the Duke arrived

---

[1] Cal. xv. 161.     [2] State Papers, vol. viii. p. 241.
[3] Cal. xv. 145, 202.

at the French Court, of which Charles had already taken leave, and was immediately received by Francis[1]. From Norfolk's own report it is evident that he had at last succeeded in creating serious distrust of the Emperor in the mind of the French King, and he reported to Henry that by Francis' countenance he 'dyd conjecte He was not content with thEmperours wordes[2].'

Of course the intrigues of Norfolk and Wyatt were only one of a number of things which contributed to cause the quarrel between Charles and Francis to break out afresh. The ground had been pretty well prepared for it by a series of petty but annoying occurrences, which had taken place during the Emperor's visit[3], and the efforts of the English ambassadors were substantially aided by Charles' flat refusal to fulfil his promises to Francis about the Low Countries and Milan, after the subjugation of the revolt in Ghent had once more left him a free hand. But the part which England played in accelerating the rupture was in itself by no means inconsiderable, and it is of the most vital importance for our purposes here, to notice that the name of Cromwell scarcely appears once in connexion with it. It is true that after Norfolk had succeeded in driving in the first wedge which started the breach between Charles and Francis, the King's minister wrote two letters to Wallop[4], directing him to follow up the advantage already gained, but they were evidently dictated by Henry, and seem to have been a necessity forced upon Cromwell by the action of his rival. The fact was that Cromwell's identification with the German alliance had cut him off from bearing a hand in any other part of the foreign policy, and that his place as a negotiator with France and Spain had been usurped by his bitterest enemy, the Duke of Norfolk. The latter's success at the French Court had proved that the policy to which the King had always pinned his faith, in opposition to Cromwell's advocacy of an outside alliance, had not lost all its efficacy, and the rapidly widening breach between Charles and Francis

---

[1] Cal. xv. 222.
[2] State Papers, vol. viii. p. 257.
[3] Cf. Gaillard, vol. iii. pp. 77, 78.
[4] Letters, 338, 340.

showed that the league with Cleves was not indispensable
for England's safety.  More than this, it now looked as if
the treaty with Duke William, far from being an advantage,
would become a positive burden.  Cromwell had sought the
alliance in the hope of gaining valuable aid in case England
was attacked : it had not occurred to him that some day the
positions might be reversed, and that England might be
expected to give aid, rather than to receive it.  The fact that
Charles, instead of planning an invasion of England with
Francis, had gone straight from Paris to the Low Countries [1]
and did not disguise his intention of regaining Gelderland,
rendered this disagreeable turn of affairs distinctly probable.
Worst of all, the King's disgust for Anne of Cleves had
increased so rapidly, that it was useless to attempt to conceal
it.  Henry might pardon a political blunder alone, but when
combined with a matrimonial misfortune, it was more difficult
to forgive.  Everything seemed to unite to call for a reversal
of the Cromwellian policy.  The King's minister had abandoned as hopeless a scheme which his rival had been able
to show was still feasible ; he had sought a cure before he
was certain that prevention was impossible : the cure he had
prescribed, besides being unnecessary, had actually proved
dangerous, and lastly, the matrimonial alliance which formed
the basis of it had turned out a complete failure.

It was certainly the most favourable opportunity that had
yet presented itself for Cromwell's enemies to compass his
ruin, and Norfolk and Gardiner, the most inveterate of his
foes, were not slow to realize it.  The latter, ever since
his recall from France in 1538, had used every effort to
undermine the influence of the man who had stepped into
the place which he had coveted for himself at Wolsey's fall.
In alliance with Norfolk, who returned from his errand to
the French King in March, 1540, he now succeeded in gather-
ing to himself all the influential persons at the English Court
who desired the downfall of their plebeian rival.  It did
not take very long to discover that Henry was ready to
abandon Cromwell, and as soon as his enemies were certain

[1] Bradford, pp. 515 ff.

of this fact, they saw that all that was necessary for the accomplishment of their designs was to devise a pretext for the minister's destruction, more plausible than an accusation of advocating a useless alliance and an unfortunate marriage. So faithfully had Cromwell served the King's interests, however, that at first it seemed almost impossible to find such a pretext, but the astute Gardiner was soon able to discover the one weak spot in his rival's armour. It is hardly necessary to state what this was. The only occasions on which Henry and Cromwell had been brought into collision were disputes over questions of foreign policy, and the Bishop of Winchester saw that the minister's reputation as advocate of an alliance with the Lutherans in opposition to the King's wishes, furnished the basis for a charge of supporting their religious principles in defiance of the doctrines proclaimed in the Six Articles. No accusation against Cromwell could have been more unjust than this. We have seen that the minister himself had abandoned the Lutherans by this time; moreover even in the days when he had urged an alliance with them, he had never made the least concession to their religious tendencies. We call to mind at once the significant words that he had spoken to Baumbach in the previous January, when he had declared that his theological beliefs were identical with those of the King. Cromwell's religion had always been dictated by political expediency; he certainly had no sympathy for Protestant theology in itself, or indeed for theology of any kind which did not lead to practical results. But unfortunately the mass of the people were totally unable to see this fact, and he was commonly looked upon as the greatest friend and helper that the Protestants had. As opposition to the Pope had given him his political greatness, the Reformers had flocked to him for protection when the Six Articles were passed, and their trust in him was further strengthened by the inferences which they drew from his foreign policy. The Bishop of Winchester was perfectly well aware of the actual state of affairs, and also of the gross misconception of Cromwell's true theological position which

existed in the minds of the people.   If he could only catch
his rival in some definite act which would justify a distinct
accusation of opposing the King in matters of religion, he
saw that the ground was already well prepared for the
success of his plot.   The opportunity which he sought was
soon to present itself.

It will be remembered that in the early part of the year
1539 Henry had sent Dr. Barnes to Germany to conciliate
the King of Denmark and the Elector of Saxony.   At the
news of the passage of the Six Articles, which of course
stultified all his efforts, Barnes had come back to England,
profoundly disgusted at the King's vacillating policy.   Henry
felt so certain of his ground at the time of his ambassador's
return, that in spite of the requests of Cromwell, he con-
temptuously refused to grant him a hearing[1].   The King's
minister was either unable or unwilling to take the hint, which
his master had given him, that Barnes was no longer in
favour, and he was rash enough to attempt to console the
envoy for the ill-success of his mission, by promoting him
to the prebend of Lanbedye[2].   Cromwell had thus played
into his enemy's hand by an action which lent itself to the
precise interpretation which Gardiner was seeking.   It was
now an easy matter to hold the minister responsible for any
rash act which his protégé might commit, and Barnes, who
was one of the very extreme Lutherans, did not take long
to fulfil the hopes which the Bishop of Winchester had
entertained of his recklessness.   He was foolish enough to
take violent exception to a sermon which Gardiner had
preached at Paul's Cross, in which the latter had denounced
certain Protestant doctrines.   Preaching in the same pulpit
two weeks later on the same text, Barnes denied all that
Gardiner had said, insulted him openly, and finally threw
down his glove to the people, as a defiance against the
Bishop[3].   Barnes had doubtless presumed on Cromwell's
protection to support him in this tirade, for it seems that the
year before, when his position had been much stronger,
the King's minister had successfully defended his friend

---

[1] Cal. xiv. (ii) 400.        [2] Cal. xiv. (ii) 688.        [3] Cal. xv. 306.

against a charge of heresy by Gardiner, and had actually
been able to remove the latter from the Privy Council in
revenge for his attack on the Lutheran[1]. But this time
Barnes had gone too far, and Cromwell, whose influence was
by no means what it had been, was unable to save him again.
The Bishop of Winchester complained to the King, who was
scandalized, and ordered Barnes to be examined before him ;
the Lutheran was utterly worsted in a theological discussion ;
he was forced to recant and beg Gardiner's pardon. This he
did with such ill grace and so many contradictions that he
was arrested and placed in the Tower with the others who
had supported him.

All this happened in the last week of March. It was
perfectly obvious to those who had any real knowledge of
the trend things were taking, that Gardiner had made his
complaint far more with the idea of harming Cromwell, than
of injuring Barnes himself, and the fact that the minister had
not been able to rescue his friend a second time led many
to predict his speedy downfall[2]. But Cromwell managed to
stave off the ultimately inevitable catastrophe for two months
more, and to maintain his ascendancy until the end of May.
He certainly had no delusions as to the gravity of the
situation in which he found himself, and he fully realized that
his best chance of safety lay in making a humble acknow-
ledgement of his error in favouring the Lutheran preacher.
Though there is no actual record that he apologized to the
Bishop of Winchester, there is every internal evidence of it.
That at least a temporary reconciliation took place between
him and Gardiner is proved by a letter of Sir John Wallop
which informs us that on March 30 the Bishop of Winchester
dined at London with the Lord Privy Seal, and that they
' were more than iiij hour*es* and opened theyre hart*es* and so
concluded that and therbe truthe or honesty in them not only
all displeasures be forgotton, but also in thayre hert*es* be
now perfight intier frend*es*[3].' It would have been hardly
possible to bring about even a temporary truce between these
two men without an apology on one side or the other, and

---

[1] Cal. xiv. (ii) 750 (p. 279).     [2] Cal. xv. 486.     [3] Cal. xv. 429.

it is not likely that Gardiner, backed as he was by the King, would have been the one to make it. In order to maintain his very precarious position, Cromwell had been forced to grovel before a man, whom two years before he could have ordered about to his heart's content.

But it had been one of the greatest secrets of Cromwell's success that he had never been too proud to take any step, however humiliating, which he deemed necessary for his profit or safety. Nevertheless it is doubtful if his apology to the Bishop of Winchester, unaided by any outside occurrence, would have been sufficient to prevent his immediate over-throw. The month of April, however, saw two events, one at home and the other abroad, which further raised his hopes and encouraged him to renewed efforts to regain his influence. The first of these was the assemblage of Parliament, an occasion on which Cromwell had always been able to make himself particularly useful to the King. He was not slow to realize the opportunity that was offered him, and he laboured with all his might for the passage of the measures which he knew his master desired. He made an opening speech in the House of Lords, in which he said that the King wished concord above all things and desired to suppress all dissension concerning religious doctrines ; and he emphasized his words by providing for the appointment of a commission to correct all abuses and enforce respect for the Scriptures[1]. What was accomplished in this direct endeavour to extirpate heresy is less important than a move of a more practical nature, which bears every evidence of being planned by Cromwell. The ancient military and religious order of the Knights of St. John of Jerusalem was the sole remaining stronghold of monasticism in England that had been suffered to escape the onslaught of the King's minister. To complete the work of destruction which he had begun their downfall was essential, and an Act to abolish them and confiscate their property finally passed both Houses after a prolonged debate[2]. A complicated Taxation Bill, which was carried through at the same time, seemed also to bear the stamp

---

[1] Lords' Journal, vol. i. p. 129.          [2] 32 Hen. VIII, c. 24.

of Cromwellian genius. Such services to the Crown had not been suffered to go unrewarded, for on April 18 those who had prophesied the ruin of the King's minister were amazed by his being created Earl of Essex and Great Chamberlain of England [1]. The French ambassador, who only seven days before had reported to Francis that Cromwell was tottering to his fall, now confessed that the new-made Earl ' was in as much credit with the King as ever he was, from which he was near being shaken by the Bishop of Winchester and others.'

The other event which gave Cromwell a momentary ray of hope was the arrival of a piece of news from France, which at first looked like a vindication of his foreign policy as against that of the King. Early in April it was rumoured in London that the French were fortifying Ardres, and the King's minister wrote a letter to Wallop on the twelfth instructing him to demand an explanation from Francis [2], who (according to the ambassador's report) replied that ' He knewe not but that He myght aswell buyld there or fortefye uppon his borders as the Kinges Highnes dothe at Callais, Guysnes, and other his fortresses [3].' These words, though spoken ' very gently and nothing in collour,' appear to have caused profound anxiety at the English Court, and Henry's faith in the success of his plans of fomenting discord between Charles and Francis received a rude shock. Everything which tended to justify the alliance with Cleves as a defensive measure was of course welcome news to Cromwell, who privately must have been as much encouraged by the messages from France as others were dismayed by them. But the satisfaction which he derived from the report of the fortifications at Ardres was only of short duration. There were no further hostile developments for the present, and an announcement was soon received from the Netherlands which offered reasons for the abandonment of the alliance with Cleves far more cogent than those which the news from France furnished for its continuance. It was reported that the Emperor, immediately after

---

[1] Cal. xv. 540, 541.  [2] Cal. xv. 543.
[3] State Papers, vol. viii. p. 323.

the subjugation of the revolt of Ghent, had repeated his
demands for the cession of Gelderland[1] by Duke William,
and there seemed every probability that in case of refusal
he would enforce them by the sword. The bearing of this
move on the alliance of England with Cleves has been
already indicated. We have seen that when Charles first
turned his steps from Paris to the Low Countries, Cromwell
probably realized for the first time that the league on which
he had based all his hopes might actually work to England's
disadvantage, and that Cleves might be the sole gainer from
it. The news from the Netherlands was virtually a confirmation of the minister's gravest fears. The prospect that he
would soon be called upon to defend an ally whom he had
expected to defend him, and for whom he had no real regard,
must have been intolerable to Henry, and the state of his
relations to Anne of Cleves at the time tended of course
to increase rather than to diminish his vexation. Add to this
the fact that tidings of a somewhat disquieting nature kept
coming in from Scotland and Ireland, the blame for which
could easily be made to fall on Cromwell, and one can well
believe that any gains the King's minister may have made in
the Parliament which had met in April were more than
counterbalanced by the losses he had sustained in the course
of affairs abroad. Norfolk and Gardiner probably siezed this
favourable opportunity to weave further plots against their
hated rival, and to devise fresh measures to poison the King's
ear against him[2]. But even had the enmity of these men
been turned into friendship, Cromwell's political blunders had
got him into a position from which nothing could extricate
him. He had incurred the enmity of a master who never
forgave, and his ultimate ruin could only be a question of
time.

The events of the month of May were but foreshadowings
of the end. On the ninth the King summoned Cromwell

[1] Heidrich, p. 43.

[2] Soames, vol. ii. p. 408, informs
us that 'in order to fan the rising
flame Gardiner invited the King
to an entertainment at Winchester
House. Katherine Howard was
among the company assembled on
this occasion, and she then achieved
the conquest of her amorous sovereign's heart.'

to a council, at which the definite abandonment of the minister's policy must have been openly discussed[1]. Records of the conference are not preserved to us, but the result of it was that two days later Cromwell was forced much against his will to write a letter to Pate, the new ambassador to the Emperor, directing him to take steps to conciliate Charles and hinting that the alliance with Cleves might be thrown over at any moment[2]. The latter part of the month brought with it further confirmation of the minister's impending fate. Duke William had sent ambassadors to the English Court, to ask the advice of his powerful ally in regard to the answer he should give to the Emperor's demands for the cession of Gelderland. Henry treated the envoys with marked coldness, and replied to their requests in the most non-committal manner: he could do nothing for the Duke of Cleves, he said, until he had more explicit information concerning the rights and wrongs of the case[3]. The ground on which Cromwell's feet rested was being cut away on all sides, and yet Marillac, in a letter of the first of June, seemed to think that the arrest of Dr. Wilson for having 'Popish leanings' was an indication that the minister and his few remaining adherents still retained some influence. He acknowledged, however, that things changed so rapidly that no person could tell what was going to happen, only he was certain that one party or the other must presently succumb[4].

The catastrophe came like a thunderbolt, less than two weeks after Marillac had written this letter. An entry in the Journal of the House of Lords on June 10 reads: 'Hodie Vicegerens Regius .... Comes Essex in hora pomeridiana per Dominum Cancellarium et alios Dominos in Arcano Domini Nostri Regis Consilio, ex Palatio Regio Domini Regis *Westm.* hora tertia pomeridiana super Accusationem Criminis lese Majestatis missus est in Arcem *Londinens.*[5]' This bald statement is confirmed by letters from Marillac to Francis and Montmorency at the time[6], but a much more

---

[1] Cal. xv. 658.
[2] Letters, 345.
[3] Cal. xv. 735.

[4] Cal. xv. 736, 737.
[5] Lords' Journal, vol. i. p. 143.
[6] Cal. xv. 766, 767.

striking account of the arrest is contained in another letter from the French ambassador to the Constable, written two weeks later. It tells us that 'as soon as the Captain of the Guard declared his charge to make him prisoner, Cromwell in a rage cast his bonnet on the ground, saying to the Duke of Norfolk and others of the Privy Council assembled there, that this was the reward of his services, and that he appealed to their consciences as to whether he was a traitor : but since he was treated thus he renounced all pardon, as he had never thought to have offended, and only asked the King not to make him languish long. Thereupon some said he was a traitor, others that he should be judged according to the laws he had made, which were so sanguinary that often words spoken inadvertently with good intention had been constituted high treason. The Duke of Norfolk, having reproached him with some " villennyes " done by him, snatched off the order of St. George, which he bore on his neck, and the Admiral, to show himself as great an enemy in adversity as he had been thought a friend in prosperity, untied the Garter. Then by a door which opens upon the water, he was put in a boat and taken to the Tower, without the people of this town suspecting it, until they saw all the King's archers under Mr. Cheyney at the door of the suspected prisoner's house, where they made an inventory of his goods which were not of such value as people thought, although too much for a "compaignon de telle estoffe." The money was £7,000, equal to 28,000 crs., and the silver plate, including crosses, chalices, and other spoils of the Church, might be as much more. These moveables were before night taken to the King's treasury, a sign that they will not be restored [1].'

On the day of the arrest, a royal messenger was sent to the French ambassador, to tell him that he must not be amazed at what had happened, for though common ignorant people spoke of it 'variously,' the King said that he was determined that Marillac should know the truth. Henry stated that while he was trying 'by all possible means to lead back religion to the way of truth, Cromwell, as attached to the

---

[1] Cal. xv. 804, and Kaulek, pp. 193, 194.

German Lutherans, had always favoured the doctors who
preached such erroneous opinions, and hindered those who
preached the contrary, and that recently warned by some of
his principal servants to reflect that he was working against
the intention of the King and of the Acts of Parliament, he
had betrayed himself and said he hoped to suppress the old
preachers and have only the new, adding that the affair would
soon be brought to such a pass that the King with all his
power could not prevent it, but rather his own party would
be so strong that he would make the King descend to the
new doctrines even if he had to take arms against him[1].'
From this and from another letter written by the council to
Wallop at the same time[2] it appears that the King had been
able to devise no more plausible pretext for the destruction of
his minister than that which had been suggested by the
Bishop of Winchester, a pretext which as we have seen was
false and unjust in every respect, but convenient in many
ways, especially as it was sure to win the approval of the mass
of the people, who looked upon Cromwell as a true Protestant
and hated him as such, not being able to see that it was
solely owing to political motives, that he had been connected
with the Reformers[3].   But the fact that the charge on which

[1] Cal. xv. 766, and Kaulek, p.
189.

[2] This letter stated that Cromwell being put in great trust by
the King in matters of religion
had 'not only of his sensual
appetite, wrought clene contrary to
this His Graces most godly entent,
secretly and indirectly advauncing
thone of thextremes and leaving the
meane indifferent true and vertuous
waye, which His Majestie sought
and soo entierly desired; but also
hathe shewed himself soo fervently
bent to the mayntenaunce of that
his oultrage, that he hath not
spared most prively, most traitor-
ously, to divise howe to contynue
the same and plainly in termes to
saye, as it hathe been justified to

his face by good wittenes, that, if
the King and all his Realme wold
turne and vary from his opinions,
he wold fight in the feld in his
oune personne, with his sworde in
his hande against Him and all
other; adding that if he lyved a
yere or two, he trusted to bring
thinges to that frame, that it shuld
not lye in the Kinges power to
resist or let it, if He wold; bynding
his wordes with such othes, and
making suche gesture and demonstration with his armes, that it
might wel appere that he had no
lesse fyxed in his harte, thenne
was uttered with his mouth.' State
Papers, vol. viii. pp. 349, 350.

[3] Henry, however, used every
means in his power to support the

he was convicted was totally unjustifiable does not in any way imply that Cromwell was wrongly condemned. There were other perfectly valid reasons for his punishment, which, however, it was quite impossible to bring forward against him, simply because the King had shared his guilt. If the number of innocent persons, whom the minister's influence had brought to the block, be not a sufficient warrant for his conviction and execution, it would be difficult to find a character in English history who merited the death penalty. But all these crimes could not be laid to his charge because the King had supported him in them, and he was arrested instead on the false accusation of opposition to the master to whose service he had devoted his life.

Cranmer was the only man who dared to say a word to the King on Cromwell's behalf. He wrote a pathetic letter to Henry the day after the arrest, expressing his wonder and distress that one whom he had deemed so good and so faithful, should be accused of treason, but in vain[1]. The fallen minister was not even permitted a trial in which he could be heard in his own defence. That terrible engine of extra-legal destruction, the attainder, by which so many of his own enemies had been annihilated, was used as a swifter and surer means to bring him to the block. The Act of Parliament which attainted him was read in the House of Lords just one week after his arrest[2]: it simply enumerated various acts and speeches which had been laid to his charge, as indicating that he had plotted to make himself more powerful than the King in matters both religious and political, and stated that he had thus incurred the charge of high treason, for which he was condemned to die. He was to suffer as a heretic or a traitor at the King's pleasure, and forfeit all property held since

main accusation, with other charges of a different nature, which if possible were even more unjustifiable. The King was not ashamed to write to Wallop in France to try and get confirmation of the old rumour (circulated on the Continent by a certain Portuguese ambassador two years before, and probably as a result of the letters of Chapuys) that Cromwell had intended to marry the Princess Mary and to make himself King. Cal. xv. 792, 801, 842.

[1] Cal. xv. 770.

[2] Lords' Journal, vol. i. p. 145.

March 31, 1538. That Cromwell was deprived of all titles and prerogatives on the day of his arrest, and was called only 'Thomas Cromwell, shearman,' and that his servants were forbidden to wear his livery, led Marillac to think that he would not be beheaded, as befitted a lord, but would be 'dragged up as an ignoble person, and afterwards hanged and quartered[1].' This impression was current two weeks later, for Norfolk told Marillac on July 6, that Cromwell's end would be 'the most ignominious in use in the country[2].' It was not until the day of his execution that 'grace was made to him upon the method of his death,' and beheading was substituted for a more painful and ignominious penalty[3]. For though his arrest had been immediately followed by his attainder, execution was delayed for six weeks more, in order that the King might make use of him for a last time, to gain an end which Cromwell had successfully secured for him once before, namely a divorce from a hated Queen.

From the day of his arrest, his execution had been a foregone conclusion; there was no chance of ultimate salvation for the fallen minister. But as a drowning man clutches at a straw to save himself from death, so Cromwell, at Henry's request, wrote a letter, which he must have known would be useless, to say what he could on his own behalf[4]. The letter speaks for itself: its denials of the charges are not as frequent as the acknowledgements of guilt and pleas for mercy, but it produced no effect on the angry King. What the injudicious words spoken before Throgmorton and Riche were, it is impossible to tell; they were probably simply sentences into which a treasonable intent was read, as into those mentioned in the attainder; the 'secrete matier' which Cromwell was accused of revealing without leave may well have been a project of Henry's to get rid of Anne, which for many reasons it was expedient for him to keep secret, until he was certain that he could free himself by one blow from the marriage which by this time had become intolerable to him.

---

[1] Cal. xv. 804.    [2] Cal. xv. 847.    [3] Cal. xv. 926.
[4] Letters, 348.

To this purpose all the King's energies were now bent, and conscious that his fallen minister had known more of his relations with Anne than any other, he sent him in the end of June a list of questions on the subject, couched in such judicious language, that if Cromwell gave the replies he confidently looked for, they would supply cogent reasons for his divorce [1]. He was sure, he said, that now that Cromwell was condemned to die, he would tell the truth and not damn his soul also, by bearing false witness at the last [2]. Whether Henry's assumption here was correct or not, it is impossible to tell. Cromwell knew of course that his chance of pardon was almost nothing, but he was not so foolish as to throw it away absolutely; he also knew that the King's heart's desire was a divorce from Anne, and he saw that his only hope lay in aiding Henry to his utmost to free himself from her. Nor was Cromwell the sort of man to whom dying with a lie on his lips would mean very much; his whole interest was absorbed in the endeavour to make the most of the one very faint chance of escape that was offered to him. Hence it is possible that the testimony he bore in this case may not have been strictly true. He appears to have written two letters in answer to the King's interrogatories; one of them is in the library of the Marquis of Salisbury at Hatfield House; the other, badly mutilated, in the British Museum [3]. Both of them are filled with abject pleas for mercy, and one of them, which was carried to the King by Cromwell's faithful Ralph Sadler, moved Henry so much, that it is said that he commanded it to be read to him thrice [4]. The two letters tell the same story in slightly different words: they give a full account of everything that Cromwell had seen of Henry's relation to Anne, since they first met at Rochester. They dilate on the

---

[1] Cal. xv. 822.

[2] Cal. xv. 825.

[3] Letters, 349, 350.

[4] Foxe, vol. ii. p. 433. If this story be true, the interest which the King evinced in Cromwell's letter is to be explained rather by his anxiety concerning his divorce, than by his sympathy for his fallen minister. Certainly there is no reason to think the closing scene of the 'Life and Death of Thomas Lord Cromwell,' in which a reprieve is brought from the King by Ralph Sadler after Cromwell's head had fallen, has any foundation in fact.

King's disgust at the first sight of the 'great Flanders mare,' tell how he endeavoured to put off the wedding, alleging as his excuse the previous engagement of Anne and the Duke of Lorraine's son, and finally quote a conversation of Henry and Cromwell, the day after the marriage, in which the King appears to have informed his minister that consummation had not followed. The truth of this last statement is apparently corroborated by a letter which Anne sent to her brother a few days later[1]. Experience of the very unscrupulous methods of Henry VIII, especially when matrimonial issues were at stake, leads the reader, however, at least to recognize the possibility that Anne may have written this letter under compulsion and the threat of death if she refused. The testimony with which the King had armed himself for the struggle he anticipated over gaining a divorce from his fourth wife, was thus all of it obtained under circumstances that certainly cast grave suspicions on its veracity; and the modern student may well be excused for refusing to accept it with that pleasingly implicit faith which the Convocations and Parliaments of this period almost invariably placed in the statements of the sovereign[2].

Certainly there was little cause for Henry to doubt his own ability to wrest a decision of the nullity of his marriage from clergy, Lords, and Commons. Ten years of Cromwell's masterfulness had been enough to convince them of the absolute futility of opposing the King in any matter on which he had set his heart. The evidence wrung from the fallen minister almost under the shadow of the scaffold, and the confirmatory letter elicited from Anne, coupled with a 'breve trew and parfaict declaracion' from the King himself[3], were quite sufficient to cause Convocation after

---

[1] Cal. xv. 898.

[2] It is somewhat significant to note that in this case Henry had practically acknowledged facts considered by the canonists as 'sufficient proof' of consummation in the case of Arthur and Katherine, and that the King had been glad to accept as such at the time of the trial of his first divorce. This is merely one of those suspiciously convenient changes of opinion one encounters so often in dealing with the personal history of Henry VIII. Cf. Burnet, vol. i. pp. 163-4.

[3] Cal. xv. 825.

three days of debate finally to agree on the judgement that
the union was unlawful, and to send their decision to Parliament on July 12. An Act to proclaim the marriage null
and void from the beginning was hurried through the Houses
with all possible speed, and on the 14th it was passed [1]. From
that time onward the 'lady Anne was treated as a sister by
the King'; she was suffered to live in retirement, adequate
lands and money were apportioned to her, and she remained
in England, contented and happy that execution had not been
substituted for divorce [2]. The Duke of Cleves was naturally
enraged at the treatment of his sister, and resolutely refused
to acknowledge that she had been honourably dealt with ; but
he knew that he was too weak to avenge the insult, and
coldly promised that the nullification of the marriage would
not cause him to 'departe from his devotion leage and
amytie' with the King of England [3].

The story of Cromwell's arrest, followed by the report of
the divorce of Anne of Cleves, was also immediately communicated to France and Spain. Francis appears to have
received the news of the first with unfeigned joy, and was
not slow to signify to Henry his satisfaction at the unexpected turn of affairs [4]. He wrote again to the King a little
later, asserting that Cromwell had adjusted a dispute over
some prizes taken by the ships of the governor of Picardy,
the Sieur de Rochepot, in such a way that he had derived personal gain from the transaction ; this complaint was sent to
Cromwell in the Tower, and drew from him the reply contained in the last existing letter which he wrote [5]. Francis'
enthusiasm at the ruin of a minister whom he had such reason
to hate, seems to have been somewhat diminished when he
learned that Anne's marriage had been dissolved, as he naturally
saw that this step would immediately put England and Spain
on a better footing. An interesting account of the ambassador
Carne's breaking the news to Francis, is given in a letter of

---

[1] Lords' Journal, pp. 154, 155.
[2] Cal. xv. 899, 901, 953. Part of
Anne's income was derived from
the manor of Canbery, previously
owned by Cromwell, and at his
attainder confiscated to the use of
the Crown. Rymer, vol. xiv. p. 713.
[3] State Papers, vol. viii. p. 421.
[4] Cal. xv. 765, 792, 794, 841.
[5] Letters, 351.

Wallop's to Henry of July 10. Francis, as it appears, ' fett
a gret sighte,' as if reflecting on the vacillating methods of his
' nere and dere brother,' but finally assented that Henry's
' owne conscience shuld be judge therein[1].' The French
King, though he greatly rejoiced in Cromwell's fall, was
evidently somewhat taken aback by the first result of the
consummation of his hopes. Charles showed none of the
same outward enthusiasm, when Pate declared to him the news
of Cromwell's arrest ; he did not even send a message, but
left the ambassador in a later letter to the King to supple-
ment his silence with his own approval. His replies to the
news of the divorce of Anne were likewise calm, but he certainly was much relieved by what he had heard[2]. The
common opinion which the sudden reversal of Cromwell's
policy had caused on the Continent seems to have been, as
Pate wrote to Norfolk on July 31, that Henry had ' lost the
hartes of the Electors of thEmpire ' but had ' contravailed
thEmprour or the Frenche King in there places[3].'

On July 27 the Parliament closed, having finished the
work that the King had mapped out for it. Since Cromwell's arrest it had practically undone all that his foreign
policy of the two past years had accomplished, by nullifying
the marriage of Henry and Anne. The rest of its proceedings are unimportant, except perhaps the attainder of Barnes,
Garret, and Jerome, the Lutheran preachers, who were
convicted of heresy and sentenced to die at the stake[4].
With the divorce from Anne secured, and those whom the
minister had favoured at home condemned, there was now no
longer any impediment to the completion of the final act of
the tragedy, and on July 28 ' Thomas Cromwell, shearman,'
was led forth to execution. In a letter to Francis, Marillac
simply mentions the fact of his death[5], but a more complete
account of the end of the great minister is fortunately preserved to us in the chronicles of Holinshed and Hall, and the
history of Foxe[6].

---

[1] State Papers, vol. viii. p. 392.
[2] Cal. xv. 794, 811.
[3] State Papers, vol. viii. p. 412.
[4] Cal. xv. 498, p. 217.
[5] Cal. xv. 926.
[6] Holinshed, p. 817; Hall, p. 839; Foxe, p. 433.

From the stories of all these chroniclers it appears that Cromwell on the scaffold made an address to the people, declaring the faith in which he died. That his speech was printed and publicly circulated is attested by Pole ; and the fact that Holinshed, Hall, and Foxe give it in almost exactly the same words corroborates the truth of the Cardinal's statement. Pole, however, goes on to say that though at first he accepted the printed speech as a true version of Cromwell's words, he later learned from trustworthy persons that what Cromwell had actually said was something very different [1]. The words of the speech certainly have the appearance of being composed beforehand and forced upon Cromwell's dying lips. He confessed that he had done wrong, asked forgiveness of his King, and finally asserted that he died in the Catholic Faith, not doubting in any article of his faith, ' no nor doubting in any Sacrament of the Church [2].' This last statement was certainly untrue ; nor would it have been in any way less false, if Cromwell had said that he died a true Protestant [3]. His religious beliefs were, as far as can be discovered, absolutely nothing when disconnected from practical ends, and he probably made his last speech at the King's command, either to save himself from a more shameful death than beheading, or else, as is quite probable, to avert the ruin of his son Gregory, who he perhaps feared would fall with him. On this point, however, he need not have had any apprehension ; Gregory Cromwell, perhaps on account of his fortunate marriage with the aunt of Prince Edward, appeared to be in as high favour as ever [4], and the title of Baron Cromwell, which his father forfeited at his attainder, was regranted to the young man by patent, Dec. 18, 1540 [5].

---

[1] Cal. xvi. 40.

[2] Cf. Appendix at the end of this chapter.

[3] Cf. Collier, vol. ii. p. 181. ' I readily grant Cromwell was no Papist at his Death. But then, it is pretty plain he was no Protestant neither.'

[4] Cal. xv. 940.

[5] Cal. xvi. 379 (34). Gregory Cromwell died in 1557, and was succeeded by his eldest son Henry. The latter's grandson Thomas, fourth Baron Cromwell, was created Earl Ardglass in the Irish peerage, April 15, 1645. The earldom of Ardglass expired in 1687, and the barony of Cromwell became

Besides this speech, which has given historians so much trouble, Hall makes mention of the fact that Cromwell ' made his praier, which was long, but not so long as both Godly and learned [1].' This prayer is given in full in Foxe, and, as it reads there, it certainly justifies the use of the epithets that Hall applied to it [2]. Whether Foxe's words were Cromwell's words, or whether Cromwell's words were his own, and not those of the King which were given him to speak, is however entirely another matter. It is unfortunate that we have no more credible authority than the martyrologist on this point. Cromwell's prayer, as he gives it, was certainly that of a man who humbly acknowledged his faults, and threw himself solely on the mercy of God ; but the words which he spoke are suspiciously devout, for those of a man to whom religion mattered so little.

'And thus,' says Foxe, ' his Prayer made, after he had godly and lovingly exhorted them that were about him on the Scaffold, he quietly committed his Soul into the hands of God, and so patiently suffered the stroke of the Ax, by a ragged and butcherly Miser, which very ungodly performed his Office [3].'

---

dormant in 1709. Life of Thomas Cromwell, in the Dictionary of National Biography,vol. xiii. p. 202.

[1] Hall, p. 839.

[2] Cf. Appendix at the end of this chapter.

[3] Foxe, vol. ii. p. 434. Cf. Mendes Silva, pp. 34, 35 : 'Acabadas de pronunciar estas palabras, se di-spuso a morir, pidiendo al verdugo, llamado Gurrea, para no sentir dilatada pena, le cortasse la cabeça de vn golpe. Tendiose, pues sobre el madero, y recibiòle terrible, muriendo aquel que nunca deuiera nacer, por quien Inglaterra desde entonces se abrasa en infernal incendio de heregias.'

# APPENDIX TO CHAPTER XIV

PASSAGES FROM FOXE'S ECCLESIASTICAL HISTORY
Vol. ii. p. 433.

' A true Christian confession of the L. Cromwel at his death.'

' I am come hither to die, and not to purge my self, as some think peradventure that I will. For if I should so do, I were a very wretch and a Miser. I am by the Law condemned to die, and thank my Lord God, that hath appointed me this death for mine Offence. For sithence the time that I have had years of discretion, I have lived a sinner, and offended my Lord God, for the which I ask him heartily forgiveness. And it is not unknown to many of you, that I have been a great Traveller in this World, and being but of a base degree, was called to high estate, and sithence the time I came thereunto I have offended my Prince, for the which I ask him heartily forgiveness, and beseech you all to pray to God with me, that he will forgive me. And now I pray you that be here, to bear me record, I die in the Catholick Faith, not doubting in any Article of my Faith, no nor doubting in any Sacrament of the Church. Many have slandered me and reported that I have been a bearer of such as have maintained evil Opinions, which is untrue. But I confess, that like as God by his holy Spirit doth instruct us in the Truth, so the Devil is ready to seduce us, and I have been seduced; but bear me witness that I die in the Catholick Faith of the holy Church; and I heartily desire you to pray for the Kings Grace, that he may long live with you in health and prosperity; and that after him his Son Prince Edward that goodly Impe may long Reign over you. And once again I desire you to pray for me, that so long as life remaineth in this flesh, I waver nothing in my Faith.'

' The Prayer of the Lord Cromwel at his Death.'

' O Lord Jesus, which art the only health of all men living, and the everlasting life of them which die in thee; I wretched sinner do submit my self wholly unto thy most blessed will, and being sure that the thing cannot Perish which is committed unto thy mercy, willingly now I leave this frail and wicked flesh, in sure hope that thou wilt in better wise restore it to me again at the last day in the resurrection of the just.   I beseech thee most merciful Lord Jesus Christ, that thou wilt by thy grace make strong my Soul against all temptations, and defend me with the Buckler of thy mercy against all the assaults of the Devil.   I see and knowledge that there is in my self no hope of Salvation, but all my confidence, hope and trust is in thy most merciful goodness.   I have no merits nor good works which I may alledge before thee.   Of sins and evil works (alas) I see a great heap ;  but yet through thy mercy I trust to be in the number of them to whom thou wilt not impute their sins ;  but wilt take and accept me for righteous and just, and to be the inheritor of everlasting life.   Thou merciful Lord wert born for my sake, thou didst suffer both hunger and thirst for my sake ; thou didst teach, pray, and fast for my sake ; all thy holy Actions and Works thou wroughtest for my sake ; thou sufferedst most grievous Pains and Torments for my sake ;  finally, thou gavest thy most precious Body and thy Blood to be shed on the Cross for my sake.   Now most merciful Saviour, let all these things profit me, which hast given thy self also for me.   Let thy Blood cleanse and wash away the spots and fulness of my sins.   Let thy righteousness hide and cover my unrighteousness.   Let the merit of thy Passion and blood shedding be satisfaction for my sins.   Give me, Lord, thy grace, that the Faith of my salvation in thy Blood waver not in me, but may ever be firm and constant.   That the hope of thy mercy and life everlasting never decay in me, that love wax not cold in me. Finally, that the weakness of my flesh be not overcome with the fear of death.   Grant me, merciful Saviour, that when death hath shut up the eyes of my Body, yet the eyes of my Soul may still behold and look upon thee, and when death hath taken away the use of my Tongue, yet my heart may cry and say unto thee, Lord into thy hands I commend my Soul, Lord Jesus receive my spirit, Amen.'

# CHAPTER XV

## THE WORK OF THOMAS CROMWELL

IT is inevitable that there should be the widest divergence of opinion concerning every great figure in Reformation history, and it is idle to attempt to form an estimate of the character and work of Thomas Cromwell that will satisfy those who take different views of the great struggle during which his life was lived. But Catholics and Protestants must agree on the fundamental and permanent nature of the changes which he wrought : whether his work was good or bad, no one can deny his success in fulfilling his life's aim as declared to Cavendish on the All Hallows Day when he rode forth to London 'to make or to marre.' He was the first chief minister that England had ever had, who was base-born and yet not a cleric. He stood completely outside the great religious movement of his time, and only made use of it to further his own political ends. He came at a time when things were in an unsettled state and ready for a change : his personality, emotionless, practical, stern, impressed itself on every phase of the national life. It was not alone in Parliament, Convocation, or Privy Council that he reigned supreme ; on every department of the government service the stamp of his individual genius remains indelibly fixed. The permanence of his work was largely due to the way in which he clinched every reform which he introduced. He followed up the separation from Rome by attacking in turn the bishops, clergy, and friars, and by suppressing the monasteries. He obtained the support of the King in almost every measure which he invented, and then forced Parliament formally to legalize it. His action was in no case ineffective ; the immediate result of it was almost always the attainment of the goal at which he aimed.

To the student of the present day, however, who is enabled to survey the decade of Cromwell's rule after a lapse of more than three and a half centuries, the immediate effects of his measures fade into the background and lose their importance, in the face of later and far greater developments. The latter were not always the results Cromwell wished to attain; in many cases they were ends which, if he could have foreseen, Cromwell would have been the last person to promote. They came years later, indirectly, as it were, and were rendered possible only by the lapse of time, the influence of other statesmen, and the growth and progress of civil and religious liberty, but none the less were they due to the impulse of Thomas Cromwell. By following out the effect of a few of the more important steps of his policy, it will not be difficult to see what some of these later developments were.

Let us take in the first place his action in rejecting the authority of the See of Rome. Cromwell advised the King to shake off his allegiance to the Pope, solely because he saw that a divorce from Katherine of Aragon could never be obtained from Clement VII, as long as the latter was in the power of Charles V. His aim was to please the King by enabling him to divorce Katherine, so that he might marry Anne Boleyn; he realized that his desire could not be accomplished while the country remained true to the Old Faith; he cut the bonds that held England to Rome, and gained what Henry wished. The direct result, the only thing he cared about, was accomplished; but far more important than that, it was by Cromwell's means that Protestantism gained a footing in England, which even the Six Articles and the terrible persecution under Mary could not shake. To guard against the return of the Papal power, and the annulling of the divorce, Cromwell attacked and subdued the clergy, and negotiated with the Protestants on the Continent. His immediate object was solely political safety; the ultimate result was the loosening of some of the strongest bonds of Romanism, and the opening of the road for the incoming of the new religion. Thus out of moves first made to attain and ensure a questionable end, grew consequences so great and so far-reaching that it is only with difficulty that one can trace their origin.

The same remark will be found to hold true of the results of the suppression of the monasteries[1]. The main object of the King's Vicegerent in destroying them was undoubtedly to fill the royal treasury with the spoils of the Church, and to clinch the advantages gained by the separation from Rome. But the later result of his measures was actually to undo much of the work which they were first intended to perform. For though they had weakened religious opposition to the Crown, they strengthened the secular element in its later struggle against the royal autocracy which Cromwell had laboured to establish. We have seen that the lands of the suppressed houses had been either given away, or else sold at exceedingly low prices to the impoverished nobles by Cromwell's advice, in order to ward off the opposition aroused by their destruction. This measure certainly attained its immediate purpose, but it also laid the foundation for the growth of an extremely powerful territorial aristocracy, that later on was to use its influence to oppose the royal prerogative and pave the way for modern constitutionalism. While Cromwell, in his attacks on the older nobility, thought that he was removing the last impediments to absolute monarchy, he really, by enriching and strengthening this new aristocracy, was rearing an infinitely more potent enemy to the kingship for which he had sacrificed everything. It is well known that such families as the Russells, Seymours, and Cavendishes, who later figured most prominently in opposition to the Crown, owed their power to gifts out of the revenues of the suppressed monasteries. The smaller gentry also claimed a share in the general advancement to wealth and prosperity among the landed proprietors, and a sudden burst of political activity in the Lords and Commons bore witness to the fact that the Houses had once more asserted their right to govern.

This brings us to Cromwell's relations with Parliament. It is here that we find the most striking instance of the contradiction between the immediate and the permanent effects

[1] Cf. for this and the following pages, Green, vol. ii. pp. 197–202.

of the changes he wrought. We have seen how his attitude towards Parliament differed from that of his predecessor. We have seen how Wolsey had looked upon the national assembly as a great force which continually hampered his schemes, so that his dislike of it led him to summon it as infrequently as possible, and only when it was absolutely necessary. We have seen how Cromwell was destined to go one step further, and how by packed elections, fraud, and violence, he succeeded in converting it into an utterly subservient instrument of the royal will. It was now no longer a power to be feared, but one to be relied on; a firm ally that consistently obeyed the slightest hint of the wishes of the Crown. Consequently instead of rarely assembling as under Wolsey, it was being constantly summoned, as a necessary means to accomplish the designs of Henry and his minister. While the latter lived, everything worked exactly as he had intended, and the Parliament remained 'tractable.' But when after his death the idea of autocracy had passed away, and England had begun to recover from the terror Cromwell's ministry had inspired, Parliament suddenly realized that it had a power of its own. Its frequent assemblings which of course had helped the Crown, as long as under Cromwell the Houses had remained subservient, now began to work just the other way, and aided it in shaking off the fetters that bound it to the King. It had been Cromwell's plan that it should keep up the forms of constitutional liberty, as a sort of sop to the popular feeling, while in reality all its legislative vigour was lost. Now that the pressure of his hand was removed, the animating spirit revived, and finding all the old traditionary customs still intact began to infuse itself into Lords and Commons. The earlier independence of the Houses returned and increased, so that the final result of the work of Cromwell was on the one hand to thwart all efforts to compass the omnipotence of the Crown, and on the other to lay the basis for a constitutional government.

Had the English character been one that could permanently suffer any form of tyranny or absolute monarchy;

had the ends the great minister aimed at been such that when the temporary madness and terror inspired by his own personality had passed by, they could have aroused one spark of enthusiasm in the English heart, Cromwell's would have been the grandest figure in his country's history. But it was not destined to be so. The national drift was throughout bitterly opposed to him and to the ideas for which he stood, so that much of his policy was reversed in the years that followed his death. There can be, it seems to me, no doubt that Cromwell was perfectly sincere in his attempt to establish an all-powerful kingship under the forms of ostensible constitutionalism. He did it not from selfish motives, but because he believed it to be the only sure road to national greatness. The crimes that marred his career cannot be excused, but may be palliated by this consideration, and by his dauntless courage in resolutely destroying the Curial control of the English courts and English Church ; on this side of his work he was the true successor of Wyclif, the true predecessor of his own great kinsman. Cromwell lived in an age when a wave of monarchical enthusiasm swept over the entire west of Europe : a belief in the absolute power of kings was the most salient characteristic of the political atmosphere of his day. He was essentially a man of his time in his faults and in his virtues, and could scarcely have anticipated modern constitutionalism. Thus his policy perished with him, but his work remained and was permitted by change and reaction finally to attain results far more glorious and lasting than he had hoped for. The despotism of the Tudors fell with their dynasty, the liberties of the nation survived.

# LETTERS OF THOMAS CROMWELL

## PREFATORY NOTE

HERE follow a complete collection of the letters of Thomas Cromwell arranged as nearly as possible in chronological order, an itinerary, and a list of his minor preferments. The letters have been copied from the original manuscripts, save in a few cases duly noted, when transcripts have been made from the official copies at the Public Record Office, from Strype and Ribier, or from the collections of Sir Henry Ellis. The spelling follows the original, all contractions are extended but italicized: the original punctuation, paragraphing, and use of capitals are preserved.

But (1) I have disregarded 'unintelligent' or faulty marks of contraction, occurring in words in which no letter is omitted. (2) I have not italicized uncontracted letters inserted above the line. For example: the name 'Thomas' is almost always written 'Thom*a*s' in the original: I have transcribed it 'Thomas' and not 'Thom*a*s.' On the other hand, the word 'your' is usually written 'yo*r*' in the manuscript: in this case I have taken the superior 'r' as a contracted form of 'ur,' and so have transcribed it '*your*.' (3) In the originals the same script form is used for 'I' and 'J'; I have followed the modern use. (4) The bracket [     ] signifies that the words or letters enclosed would have been in the manuscript had it not been injured. The bracket ⟨     ⟩ signifies that the word or words enclosed have been inserted by me to complete the sense. The parenthesis (     ) signifies that the enclosure is bracketed in the original. (5) Sentences and words crossed out or underlined in the manuscript have been set below, except when evident mistakes of the writer. The letters '*c. o.*' signify that the passage against which they are written was crossed out or underlined in the original.

In dating letters, I have followed the modern use, and have taken the first of January and not the twenty-fifth of March as the beginning of the year. I have used the bracket ⟨ ⟩ in the headings to indicate that the name or date enclosed has not been given in the letter itself, but has been found from external or internal evidence. Letters which bear no indication of the day and month in which they were written are placed at the end of the year to which they apparently belong. The abbreviations 'R. O.' and 'B. M.' refer to the Public Record Office and British Museum respectively throughout the collection.

# LETTERS

## 1. CROMWELL TO JOHN CREKE.

R. O. Cal. iii. 3249.  Aug. 17 ⟨1523⟩.

A letter of friendship, containing an account of the proceedings of the
Parliament of 1523, in which Cromwell sat.  News concerning
Creke's friends in England.

Maister Creke as hertelye as I can I commende me and
in the same wise thanke yow [for your] gentill and louyng
letteres to me at sundrye tymys Sent and wher as I accordinglye haue not in lyke wise remembrid and rescribid
it hath bene for that I haue not hade anything to wryt of
to your aduauncement.  Whom I assure yow yf it were in
my lytyll power I coulde be well contentyd to preferre as
ferre as any one man lyuyng.  But at this present I being
at Sum layser entending to remembre and also remunerate
the olde acquayntaunces and to renew our not forgoten
Sundrye communycacions Supposing ye desyre to know the
newes curraunt in thes partyes for it is said that newes
refresshith the spy[rit] of lyffe, wherfor ye shall vnderstonde
that by long tyme I amongist other haue Indured a parlyament which contenwid by the space of xvij hole wekes wher
we communyd of warre pease Stryffe contencyon debatte
murmure grudge Riches pouerte penurye trowth falshode
Justyce equyte discayte opprescyon Magnanymyte actyuyte
force attempraunce Treason murder Felonye consyli . . .
and also how a commune welth myght be ediffyed and a[lso]
contenewid within our Realme.  Howbeyt in conclusyon we
haue d[one] as our predecessors haue been wont to doo that
ys to say, as well as we myght and lefte wher we begann.
ye shall also vnderstond the Duke of Suthffolke Furnysshyd
with a gret armye goyth ouer in all goodlye hast [whit]her
I know not, when I know I shall aduertyse yow.  Whe haue
in our parlyament grauntyd vnto the Kinges highnes a right
large Subsydye, the lyke wherof was neuer grauntyd in this
realme.  all your frendes to my knowlage be in good helth
and specially thay that ye wott of: ye know what I meane.
I thinke it best to wryt in parables becaus[e] I am In dowt.
Maister Vawhan Fareth well and so doth Maister Munkcaste[r].

Maister Woodall is merye withowt a wyffe and commendyth
hym to yow : and so ys also Nycholas longmede which hath
payd William Wilfforde.   And thus as well f[are] ye as
I woolde do my Self At london the xvij daye of August by
your Frende to all his possible power

THOMAS CRUMWELL.

*Add.*   To his [esp]ecial and entyrelye belouyd Frende
John Creke be this youyn Bylbowe in Biscaye.

## 2. CROMWELL TO ELIZABETH HIS WIFE.

Ellis' Letters, 2nd Ser. ii. 125 ; Cal. iv, App. 57.   Nov. 29 ⟨1525⟩.

Sends her a doe.  Desires that Richard Swift resort to him at Begham
   or Tonbridge.  Asks for news.

Elyzabeth I commend me unto you and have sente you
by this berer a fatt doo, the one half whereof I pray you may
be delyvered unto my gossyp mastres Smyth, and with the
rest to use your pleasure.   And further yf Richard Swifte
be cum home or fortune to cum shortly, I will that he resorte
to me at Begham or Tonbridge with all dylygence.   Such
news as ye have in those partyes I pray you sende me parte
by this berer.   At Begham the xxix^{th} day of November.
And farther I pray you sende me word in wryting who hathe
resorted unto you syns my departuer from you to speke
with me.

Per your husbend

THOMAS CRUMWELL.

*Add.*   To my well beloved wyf Elyzabeth Crumwell
agenst the Freyers Augustines in London be this given.

## 3. ⟨CROMWELL⟩ TO ——.

R. O. Cal. iv. 955 (3).   ⟨1524 or 1525.⟩

Desires that the lands of John Fleming, who has broken covenant with
   Cromwell, be put in execution.

Syr in my most herty manner I commend me vnto yow
aduertesing yow that after knowlege hade of your departure
In to the north partyes was veray sorye that my chaunce was
not so happye to haue spokyn with yow befor wheruppon
I was constrayned for the Singuler trust and conffydence
which by long contenuaunce hath Succedyd & ben approuyd

In yow towardes your Frendes and louers to wryt vnto yow[1]
Syr So hyt is that one John Flemyng of Crofton in the
Countye of Yourke in the moneth of may last passid Solde
vnto Robert Bolt Certayn landes Tenementtes & heredyta-
menttes to the Clere yerlye valew of Nyntene poundes and
xvi d. of good and lawffull monaye of Ingland to myne vse
to the Sum of ccclxxxj[li] vj[s] viij[d] wheroff the sayd John
Flemyng resayuyd In partye of payment one hundereth
fortye eight powndes nyne shelinges & Syx pence and the rest
of the sayd Sum which amountyth vnto ccxxxij[li] xvij[s] ii[d] was
put in the Saffe custodye and keping of your Frend Maister
Butrye ther to remayn vntyll Suche tyme the sayd John
Flemyng sholde haue performyd all his couenauntes according
vnto a payre of Indentures For the which Summys of
Monaye and for the non performaunce of the sayd Couenauntes the sayd John Flemyng standyth bounden to the
sayd Robert Bolt In a statute of the Staple of Westminster
in one thousand markes payable in the Fest of Saynt Ber-
tholomew the appostill last past the date wherof is the xx[th]
daye. of Maii in the xv[th] yere of our souerayng lord kyng
henrye the viii[th], and forasmoche as the said Flemyng hath
brokyn Couenauntt with me In euerye poynt I am Compellyd to take the execucyon vppon my statute which by this
bringer I haue sent vnto yow desyring and her[tely] praying
yow that ye will be so Frendlye vnto me yf it be possyble
beffore your retorn hetherwardes to make Suche Instaunce vnto
the Shereffe of Yorkeshyre that the sayd execucyon may be
taken[2] and that all suche landes as the sayd John Flemyng
hathe within Yorkshyre maye be put in execucyon and
extendyd befor your retorne owte of Yourkshyre and that
the wryt of execucyon may be retournyd and what so euer
charge shalbe For the Furnysshyng of the same I promyse
yow and bynde me by this my lettere to Satysfye and Ferther
to recompence your paynys in suche wyse I trust that ye
shalbe contentyd.  Syr I hertelye desyre and praye yow to
haue me excusyd that I sholde be so bolde to requere yow
to take Suche payn for me howbeit the experyence which
I haue in your good and gentyll approuyd humanyte makyth
me the more bolde with yow hauyng no dowbt but that ye
will accept & take vppon yow as moche payne For your
Frend as any man lyuyng Ferther Syr ye shall vnderstonde

---

[1] c. o. trustyng entyerlye In yow
that ye will witsaffe as I may euer
herafter ow vnto yow my Symple
seruyce or any pleasure that shalbe

within my lytyll power
[2] c. o. before your Retorn to
London

*On the dorse*

A fragment of a document containing indentures and agreements concerning the manor of Kexby.

The manor of Kexby—

her after shall Inswe the abredgment of certayn Indentures
evydence charters ded*es* esc[riptes] and Mynument*es* concernyng the manno*ur* of Kexbye wit*h* the appertena*n*ces wit*h*in
the Countye of Yorke Delyuery[d] . . by Iohn Aleyn Cytizen
and Altherman of London to the hand*es* of Sundrye Right
worsshypfful and discret p*er*sons Councellou*r*s vnto the most
reue[rent] Father in god Thomas lorde Cardenall legate de
latere archbusshop of Yo*ur*ke pry . . . and chaunceler of
Inglonde to the vse of the sayd most Reuerend Father in god
the datt*es* of the whiche Indentures evydenc*es* charters ded*es*
escript*es* & Mynimentt*es* cons*er*nyng the sayd Manno*ur* wit*h*
p*ar*te of the effect*es* conteynyd [in] the same mor playnlye
herafter shall appere

### 4. ⟨CROMWELL⟩ TO LADY ⟨DORSET⟩.

R. O. Cal. iv. 3053 (ii).   April ⟨1527⟩.

Reports a letter received from 'my lorde' and addressed to her ladyship, and encloses the copy of another from 'my lord George.'

Pleasyth it yo*ur* good ladyship my specyall dewtes fyrst
remembred that as vppon Wensdaye being the xvij[th] daye of
Aprell I resayuyd from my lorde a *lette*re directyd vnto yo*ur*
good ladyship wit*h* also all his honourable aduenture In to
Scotland[1] theffect wherof yo*ur* ladyship shall resayue in
yo*ur* *lette*res Ferther I resayuyd the same daye a *lette*re from
my lord George the teno*ur* and Copye wherof I haue sent
yow herin Inclosyd Madame as ye shall Thinke by yo*ur* good
and vertuese discresyon it may please to adu*er*tyse my good
lord which I thinke shalbe well takyn when he shall parsayue
that ye doo and shall contenually studye for the aduansment
of his honeur.

### 5. ⟨CROMWELL⟩ TO ⟨VISCOUNT ROCHFORD⟩.

R. O. Cal. iv. 3741.   ⟨December, 1527.⟩

Legal information and advice concerning a suit in which Cromwell has
been retained as counsel by the wife of Sir Robert Clere, the sister
of Rochford.

Pleasyth it yo*ur* good lordship to be adu*er*tysed howe that
it hath pleasyd my ladye yo*ur* sust*er* wyff to S*ir* Robe*r*te
Clere Knyght to requyre and desyre me to be of counsayll

---

[1] *c. o.* I am ascertaynyd that yo*ur* ladyship shall resayue

wit*h* the sayd S*ir* Robert her husbande in a certayn[1] Matyer
in varyaunce betwene the lady Feneux late the wyff of s*ir*
John Feneux Knyght cheffe Justyce[2] desseasyd of and For
the deffence of a wrytt of extent of late passyd out of the
Kyng*es* hygh courte of the Chauncery dyrected vnto the
Sheryff of Norffolke and Suffolke aswell for the extendyng of
the land*es* of the sayd s*ir* Rob*e*rte wit*h*in the sayd countyes
as alsoo For the puttyng in execution the bodye of the sayd
s*ir* Robert Clere for the satysfactyon and payment of Foure
hundreth pound*es* supposyd to be due to the sayd late cheff
Justice disceasyd And For asmoche as by the reporte of my
sayd lady yo*ur* sust*er* and alsoo by the syght of certayn
Indentures of Couena*u*ntt*es* & deffauntt*es* made aswell bytwene
s*ir* John Paston Knyght disceasyd and the sayd S*ir* Rob*e*rte
Clere as alsoo bytwene the sayd late cheff Justice and the
sayd s*ir* Robert yt maye appere that the sayd Statute of the
Staple of cccc[li] was made and delyu*e*red to none other intente
but onlye For the p*er*fformaunce of certayn couena*u*nt*es* of
Maryage For the assuraunce and onlye aduaunseme*n*t of
a Joynter to be made to one Elyzabeth late the wyff off one
Will*i*am Clere disceasyd so*n*ne and heyre at that tyme to the
sayd s*ir* Rob*e*rte whiche Elyzabeth ys nowe wydowe and was
lately the wyffe of the sayd late lorde Feneux cheff Justice
all whiche couena*u*nt*es* of Maryage the sayd s*ir* Robert Clere
hathe always as I am Informyd bene redye and yet ys to p*er*-
fourme notwit*h*standyng[3] that the sayd S*ir* John Paston in
hys lyffe nor s*ir* Will*i*am Paston nowe lyuyng so*n*ne and heyre
of the sayd s*ir* John wolde ne wyll not accordyng to suche
couena*u*nt*es*[4] as the ⟨same⟩ be boundyn vnto paye vnto the
sayd s*ir* Rob*e*rte Clere cc[li] Resydue of foure hundreth Mark*es*
for the sayd[5] assuraunce of the sayd Couenauntt*es* of Maryage[6]
yet dewe and vnpayd the none payment wherof ys A greate
matyer and it were gret pytye and also ayenst bothe reson
& Conscyens that the sayd s*ir* Rob*e*rte shulde haue his land*es*
extendyd and be co*m*pellyd to paye the sayd so*m*me of foure
hundreth pound*es* consyderyng the sayd bounde was made
but for the p*er*formaunce of the couena*u*nt*es* of Maryage
whiche[7] the sayd Syr Robert was and ys Redye to performe

---

[1] *c.o.* case
[2] *c.o.* vnto the kyng*es* highnes
of hys benche
[3] *c.o.* yff yt soo had ben
[4] *c.o.* as was bytwene the sayd
s*ir* John and the sayd s*ir* Roberte
payd
[5] *c. o.* aduaunsement
[6] *c. o.* one to the sayd s*ir* Roberte

Clere in full co*n*tentac*io*n & payment of cccc Mark*es* whiche cc[li] ys
yet vnpayd
[7] *c.o.* was and shulde haue ben
accomplyshyd in eu*er*y poynte
yff the sayd s*ir* John Paston had
accordyng to hys couena*u*nt*es* payd
the so*m*mes of money whiche he
was bonde to paye by hys Inden-

and good Reason it were that the Couenaunt*es* on the p*a*rtie of the sayd S*ir* John Paston also sholde be p*er*formyd and the sayd cc*li* payde.  Neuertheles the sayd Syr Robert Clere ys vtterlye w*ith*out Remedye by course of the co*m*mon lawe [1] to defende the execucyon of the sayd wrytt*es* of extent so that the sayd cccc*li* shalbe recoue*r*yd of hys land*es* and bodye onles yt may please yo*ur* good lordeshyp to moue my lorde hys grace in Conscyens to graunt a wryt of Iniu*n*ctyon [2] to be dyrectyd ⟨to⟩ the sayd lady Elyzabeth Feneux Commandyng her by the same no ferther to prosecute thexecuc*io*n of the sayd wrytt*es* of extent vppon the sayd statute of cccc*li*. And alsoo ayenst the sayd S*ir* Roberte as my sayde lord*es* grace may gyue co*m*maundement [3] that no wrytt*es* of liberata goo out of the sayd courte of Chauncerye vntyll suche tyme ⟨as⟩ the hole matyer tochyng the p*re*mysses may dulye and accordyng to conscyence be harde and examyned  And yo*ur* lordshype thus doing shall do the thing in my poore opynyon which shall ⟨stand⟩ w*ith* reason and good Conscyens as knowyth the holye Trynyte whom I most hertelye beseche to p*re*serue yo*ur* lordshyp in long lyffe good helth and moche hono*ur*

## 6. CROMWELL TO WOLSEY.

R. O. Cal. iv. 4135.  April 2, 1528.

Reports his proceedings in connexion with the monastery of Wallingford. Description of the progress of the Cardinal's colleges.  Desires the benefice of St. Florence for Mr. Birton.

Please it your grace to be aduertised how that I according to your most gracyous co*m*maundement haue repayred vnto the late monasterye of Wallingforde Where I founde aswell all the ornamentt*es* of the churche as all other ymplementt*es* of houseolde clerely conueyed awaye and nothing remayning. Sauyng only the euydences Which I sorted and conueyed vnto yo*ur* colledge at Oxforde And the same delyvered vnto yo*ur* Dean there.  And afterward*es* Mr. Croke and I surueyed amended and refourmed aswell the l*e*tteres patent*es* graunted by the king his highnes vnto yo*ur* grace as also yo*ur* gyftes and gr*a*untt*es* made vnto yo*ur* said colledge in suche wise I trust that no defaulte or omyssyon at this tyme is lefte vnrefourmed.

ture for the adu*a*uncement of hys sayd doughter.  Neu*er*theles yt may please yo*ur* lordeshypp to knowe the sayd s*ir* Robe*r*te Clere

[1] *c. o.* but that the sayd foure

hundreth poundes shalbe Reco*ue*red of hys landes

[2] *c. o.* to Inyoine

[3] *c. o.* in the courte of Chauncery

I haue also founde offyces aswell of the saide late monasterye of Wallingforde and of all the londes and tenementtes belonging to the same within the Counties of Oxforde and Berk as also of suche omyssions as were omytted within the saide counties belonging to Frediswides and Lytlemore. And now I do repayre into the Counties of Buck and Bedforde for offyces to be founde there aswell of suche londes as apperteyne to the saide late monasterye of Wallingforde as also to the late monasterye of Praye besides saincte Albons.

The buyldinges of your noble colledge most prosperouslye and magnyfycently dothe arryse in suche wise that to euery mannes iudgement the lyke thereof was neuer sene ne ymagened hauing consideracyon to the largeness beautee sumptuous Curyous and most substauncyall buylding of the same.

Your chapell within the saide colledge most deuoutely and vertuously ordered And the mynistres within the same not onely dyligent in the seruyce of god but also the seruice daylie doon within the same so deuoute solempne and full of Armonye that in myne opynyon it hathe fewe peres.

There is a benefyce voyde within the dyoces of saincte dauyes in Wales which is of your gracyous gyfte by meane of the chauncelorship of Englonde. Yf it may please your grace to gyue the same to Mr. Byrton he shoulde be the more able to do your grace seruyce. The name of the saide benefyce is called sayncte Florence. I assure your grace the saide Mr. Byrton is a right honest man And by somme reporte right well lerned and shall do your grace good seruyce.

My besyness accomplisshed I shall according to my duetie repayre vnto your grace. Most humblye beseching the holie trynytee contynuallye to preserue the prosperous astate of the same in long lif and good helth. At Oxforde the Seconde day of Aprell.

Your most humble seruaunt

THOMAS CRUMWELL.

*Add.*   To my l . . .

*Endd.*  Mr Cromewel iida Aprilis 1528


## 7. CROMWELL TO THOMAS ARONDELL.

R. O. Cal. iv. 4441.   June 30 ⟨1528⟩.

Requests him to send information concerning Wolsey's wishes about various matters in connexion with the Colleges at Ipswich and Oxford.

Right woorshipfull sir in my right hartie maner I commende me vnto youe, Aduertising the same, that I have receyued my

lorde his gracious letteres, wherin his grace commaundethe to
be diligent in thexpedicion of suche busynes as Do concerne
the perfeccion of his colledge in Gypswiche, whiche I do
intende (god willing) to put in execucion withe all spede,
howbeit certeyne thinges arn first to be knowen of my saide
lorde his gracious pleasure, or euer the same can be perfected
accordingly.   Wherof one is, that it may please his grace to
name the person that shalbe his Dean of his saide Colledge,
And also to send to me ayen the Bille assigned of the licence
graunted to his grace by the kyng his highnes to erect the
saide colledge in Gipswiche, so that the signet and pryuye
Seale may be made out vpon the same, And that we maye
examyn the boke of erection which nowe must passe by my
lorde his grace with the same bille signed in euery poynt.
His gracious pleasure must also be knowen whether that (the
Dean of his saide saide [1] colledge being Decessed, or by any
other mean Depryued or amoued from the saide Deanrie) his
grace then wille that thellection of a new Dean shalbe emonges
them of the colledge or whether his grace will remytt the
same to be ordred by his Statuttes by hym to be made
accordingly.   It maye please youe also to moue his grace
whether he wille absolutelie haue a guyfte made to his
colledge in Oxforde of the late Monasterie of Wallyngforde
the parsonage of Rudbye, and suche other londes as his grace
hathe purchased of sir Antonye and sir Roberte Ughtred
in the Counties of Yorke and Lyncoln, or that he will haue
the same Monastori and other the premisses geuyn vpon
condicion to his saide Colledge in Oxforde, to thyntent that
they shall make a lyke guyfte of the londes apperteynyng to
the late Monastoris of Snape, Dodneshe, Wyke and Horkisley
to his saide colledge in Gipswiche, whiche condicion in myn
opynyon shulde well serue for all casualties, and compelle
them of the colledge in Oxforde to make a guyfte of the
same accordingly.   One speciall thing ther is that ye must
moue his grace in which is, that he maye not in any wise
procede to therrection of his saide colledge in Gipswiche,
before the xxj. daye of Julye next comyng, for asmuche as
thoffices in the Chauncerie shall not expire, vnto the full
accomplishment of iij Monethes vntill the saide xxj Daye, nor
his grace cannot haue the Syte and circuyte of the late
Monastori of Saynct Peter suppressed, vpon the whiche the
saide colledge muste be erected by thordres of the lawe of
thie londe before the saide xxi Daye.   His gracious pleasure
knowen in the premisses I trust by thassistence of my lorde

---

[1] sic.

chief Baron vnto whome I wille resorte from tyme to tyme for
his good counsaile to perfo*ur*me fulfille and accomplisshe
euery thing according to his said gracious pleasure, in suche
wise that he shall therwithe be right well contented.  Hartely
Desiring youe to moue his grace for the signature of the
*lette*re for the poore man of Arragosco who lyeth here to his
great and importunate cost*es* and charg*es* in maner to his
vtter vndoyng,  And also for the signature of one other *lette*re
in Frenche Directed to the gouernours of the Towne of Depe
for the Delyuerie of certeyn Englisshe mennys good*es* beyng
marchaunt*tes* of London of late taken vpon the See by men
of warr of the saide toune of Diepe.  It maye also please
youe to shew my lorde his grace this *lette*re and that I maye
haue answer of his gracious pleasure withe all spede, whiche
shalbe a great furtheraunce to his busynes.  The mynute of
his erexion is all redye Drawen and shalbe p*er*fected vpon
his answer  And thus o*ur* lorde preserue youe  At London
the xxx Daye of June.

At your co*m*maundement

THOMAS CRUMWELL.

*Add.*  To the right woorshipfull maister Thomas Arondell
be this youen.

*Endd.*  From Mr. Cromwell the xxx day of Junii about
the p*er*fectinge of the Cardynalls ij Colleg*es* of Oxford and
Ipswich.

## 8. CROMWELL TO WOLSEY.

R. O. Cal. iv. 4697.  ⟨Sept. 3, 1528.⟩

*Details concerning the colleges at Oxford and Ipswich, and the revenues
from the lands and monasteries appropriated for their use.*

Please it your grace to haue in remembraunce yo*ur*
Fynours of Duresme whose contynuaunce here is not onely
to their greate cost and losse of tyme but also to the greate
hinderaunce of your werk*es* ther, and also they be veray poore,
your gracious pleasure therfore wold be knowen whether
they shall resorte to yo*ur* presence, or howe otherwise yo*ur*
grace will they shalbe ordred

I haue according to your moste gracious co*m*maundement
sent herein inclosed the clere yerely valeurs of all suche
lond*es* as ye haue purchased in the Counties of Yorke and
Buckingham, and also the clere yerely value of the late
monasterie of Wallingforde

If it may stonde with yo*ur* pleasure to appoynte in whose
name yo*ur* grace intendithe to dedicate your colledge in

Gipswiche, and by what name the maister and fellowes shalbe called, the lycence of erexion, the letteres patenttes, pryuate Seales and other thinges necessarie for the same myght be put in a redynes so that no tyme shulde be loste

I haue caused suche billes as be allredie signed to passe the pryuy signet and pryuate Seale, and shall nowe put to wryting the letteres patenttes for the brode Seale, so that after the iii monethes expired your grace may geue the londes conteyned within the same according to youre moste gracious pleasure. It shalbe well done that your grace haue in remembraunce thappropriacion of the benefices to your colledge in Oxford, and that an ende maye be takyn withe all ordynaries which I thinke is not yet done

I haue spoken with maister Babington nowe lorde of Kylmayne for the exchaunge to be made bitwene your colledge in Oxforde and his religion for Saundforde, It may therfore please your grace that your pleasure may be knowen whether this vacacion your counsaile shall farther commune withe hym and other whiche haue auctoritie in that behalf, or not, whiche in myn opynyon shulde be well done, and will sett your purpose in a great forwardnes

It may also please your grace that these instruccions herein inclosed may be sent to maister Holgill for thordering of hymself in taking possession lyueraye and season at Rudby, whiche Instruccions were deuysed by the Judges, and it shalbe necessarie that he haue them withe spede.

Your gracious pleasure knowen touching the premisses I shall most humblie indeuoir myself according to my duetie to accomplisshe your most gracious commaundement, As knowithe the holly trynytie vnto whome I shall daily during my lyfe praye for the prosperous conseruacion of your good grace

Your most humble servaunt

THOMAS CRUMWELL.

*Add.* To my lorde his grace.

*Endd.* From Mr Cromwell touching rudby

Instruccions for Maister Willyam Holgill for possession lyueraye and season to be taken in the parsonage of Rudby in Clevelonde

First to cause my lorde Conyers to serche his euydence towching thaduowson of the patronage of Rudby, and to se whether it be aduowson appendaunte, that is to saye, apperteyning to a manor or to an Acre of londe, or that it be aduowson in grosse, that is to saye, aduowsonage onely appending to no manor ne yet to none Acre of londe, And to receyue the saide Euydence of the saide lorde Conyers concernyng the said aduowson

Itm to knowe whether the saide aduowson be intailed, and whether it be intailed to theires males, or to theires generall, and to receyue the dead*es* of Intaile, or Fynes if any suche be, of the saide lorde Conyers

Itm that thattourneis named in the deade of Feoffement made to the saide Willyam Holgill and other, do enter into thacre of londe named in the saide deade of Feoffement, and delyuer season by a turfe, to the saide maister Holgill, and also to delyuer possession and season by the ryng of the churche dore

Itm after possession, lyueraye and season taken in the saide Acre of londe, and by the ryng of the churche doore as is aforsaide, that then the saide Attourneis do enter into the saide p*ar*sonage and also to delyuer possession lyueraye, and season in the p*ar*sonage vnto the saide maister Holgill, and that the deade of Feoffement be redd in all thre*e*[1] places, and to take at the leste xxx or xl witnesses, calling therto asmany yonge children as ye may

### 9. Cromwell to Gardiner.

R. O. Cal. iv. 5186.    Jan. 18 ⟨1529⟩.

Has been unable to repair to the Cardinal, on account of the press of work in connexion with his colleges. Description of the damage done by the overflowing of the Thames.

Worshipfull S*ir*, after most hartie comendacyons it may please you to aduertise my lorde his grace that the cause Why I do not repayre thither at this present ys for that I haue certen bok*es* to be don and accomplisshed concerning his colledge in Gipswich  That is to say a deade of gyfte from his grace to his saide colledge of the late monasteryes of Felixstowe Rumburgh and Bromehill  The King his l*ette*res patent*es* of assent to the Suppression of the same late monasteryes, The King his l*ette*res patent*es* of assent to the pope his bull of exempcyon of the saide colledge  The King his l*ette*res patent*es* of lycence for thimpropryac*io*n of the benefyces belongyng to the saide late monasteryes  A deade of gyft from the Duke of Norff. to my lord his grace of the saide late monasterye of Felixstowe  A relesse from the prior

---

[1] *sic*, for ' these.'

and conuent of Rochester of all theyr right tytle and
patronage of in or to the same late pryory of Felixstowe
A relesse from the abbot and conuent of Saynct Maryes in
Yorke of all their right and tytle in or to the late pryory of
Rumburgh A relesse from my lorde of Oxforde of all his
right and tytle in the late pryory of Bromehill And a
relesse from the Frenssh quene and the duke of Suffolk of
all theyr right and tytle in the manours of Sayes courte and
Byckeling and in the late pryorye of Snape. All which
bok*es* be not yet in a redynes ne parfyted vnto my mynde
Intending assone as the same shalbe fynysshed and made
parfyte, whiche I trust shalbe to morow at nyght or wenesday
by none at the Ferthest to repayre vnto my lorde his grace,
vppon his gracyous pleasure knowen for thinsealing of the
same accordingly. It may also please you to aduertise
my lorde his grace that Sythen his repayree to Rychmond
I have ben at Lyesnes Where I saw one of the most
pyteous and greuous sight*es* that ev*er* I saw which to me
before the Sight of the same was incredyble concernyng the
breche out of the Thamyse into the marsshes of Lyesnes which
be all ouerflowen and drowned And that at the last chaunge
the tyde was so high that there happened a new breche which
hathe fordon*e* asmoche worke there as will cost ccc^li the
new making of the same In so moche that if my being
there had not ben to haue incouraged the workemen and
labourers I assure you all the labo*ur* and money that
hathe ben ther spent heretofore had ben clerely lost and
cast away. And the workemen and labourers wolde haue
departed and left all at chaunce whiche shoulde haue ben
the gretest yuell that eu*er* happened to the countrey ther.
Neve*r*theles I w*ith* thaduyse of suche wyse men as ben in the
countrey there haue set suche dyrectyon in the same that
I trust all shalbe well and the work*es* there ended w*ith* good
spede god willing. For the furnyture and accomplisshment
whereof there is a new assesse made and my lorde his
colledge for theyr parte ben assessed at ccxx li which money
of necessyte must be had out of hande Prayeng you so
to solycyte my lord*es* grace that the same money may be
had incontynent Assuring you that his grace shall do as
merytoryous a deade in the delyu*er*ing of the saide money
for his colledge at this tyme as though he gaue so moche
money for godd*es* sake Considering the grete hurte myschief
losses and inconuenyenc*es* that is lyke to insue to the countrey
there and to the King his streme and also the hurte that may
insue to his colledge in the losse of suche grounde and land
as they haue there Whereunto for the quantytee thereof ys

none lyke to the same in that countrey ne few in any other countrey. Yf the saide breche be not shortly amended and spedely prouyded for I assure you suche inconuenyenc*es* may insue that yt were to grete pytee. And to thintent that ye may be the more assured of the trewth in the pr*e*mysses I haue sent you a *lette*re here inclosed which I receyued from one of the maisters of the said work*es* ymedyatly after the wrytyng of this *lett*re Intending to repayre vnto Lyesnes, wit*h* all spede for the redresse and fortheraunce of the pr*e*-misses asmoche as in me shalbe possible. Hertely beseching you to procure that I may haue answer of my lord*es* pleasure in eu*er*y thing concerning the content*es* forsaid by this berer my seru*au*nte. And thus *our* lorde pr*e*serue yo*ur* long lyf At London the xviii day of Januarye.

Yours most bounden

THOMAS CRUMWELL.

*Add.* To the right wo*r*shipfull Maister docto*ur* Gardyner be this yeuen wit*h* spede.

*Endd.* Letters from M. Cru*m*wel of the xviij daie of Januarij

10. ⟨CROMWELL⟩ TO ——.

R. O. Cal. iv. 5757 (ii).   July ⟨1529⟩.

Has written in favour of the chaplain. Requests the recipient to desire his wife to take the daughter of Cromwell's sister, and bring her up. Promises to recompense him and his wife.

. . . C . . . ert as hertelye as I can I co*m*mende me vnto you and m*er*vayle gretlye that ye haue made no better spede for yo*ur* chaplayn In whos Fauours I haue wryten vnto Mr. Chaunceler of Wynchester trustyng that he wylbc good maister vnto hym For my sake I wooldbe veray lothe that ye sholde mysse yo*ur* purpose  Syr I praye you be so good vnto me as to lett me send my systers daughter vnto the Jentylwoman yo*ur* wyff and that ye wyll on my behalf desyre her to take her and to bryng her vpp for the which her goodnes yf she wylbe content so to doo I shold rekyn my self moste bounden both to you and her*e* and besyd*es* the pay-ment For her borde I wyll so content your wyff*e* as I trust she shalbe woll pleasyd that I may know yo*ur* answer herin I hertelye praye yow and thus hartelye Fare ye well.
   At london the        daye of July.

## 11. Cromwell to Mr. Claybrook.

R. O. Cal. iv. 5812.　⟨July, 1529.⟩

Desires him to seek out all registers, and the bulls of the Cardinal's legation, so that the same may be shown to the King's attorney.

Maister Cleybroke this to aduertise yow as ever ye intend to doo my lord pleasure or seruyce that ye with all dylygens seke owt the register of Maister Tonneys and also all other registers with also the bullys of my lordes legacye to thentent the same may be shewyd this nyght to the Kynges attorney for suche Causes as I declaryd vnto yow at my last spekyng with yow of answer by thys berer I praye yow that I may haue knowlege and fare ye woll.

Your Frend

Thomas Crumwell.

## 12. Cromwell to William Brabazon.

R. O. Cal. iv. 6099.　Dec. 19 ⟨1529⟩.

Desires him to ride with Mr. Copeland to the north, and assist him with advice in his affairs there.

Willyam Brabazon I comende me vnto you And wolde if ye be at conuenyent leysour that ye do Ryde with Maister Cowplonde this berer into the North partes and to assiste him with your counsaill in suche matiers as he hathe there to do according to suche instruxions as I haue drawen and delyuered to the same Mr. Cowplande　Not doubting but he will consider your paynes accordinglye　And thus fare ye well.　At London the xix^{th} day of December.

Your louyng maister

Thomas Crumwell.

## 13. Summaries of Cromwell's Letters.

MSS. Jesus Coll. in Bibl. Bodl. Oxon. c. 74, pp. 262 ff.; Cal. iv. 6076.
⟨1530.⟩

Various items concerning the relations of Cromwell and Wolsey after the latter fell into disgrace.　Cf. Letters, 18, 19.

'Crumwell to the Cardinal, July 12, ⟨1530⟩.

'As touching the processe against your Grace out of the Exchequer and all other matters and suites brought against yow I haue pleaded *your* pardon, w*h*ich is allowed in all *th*e King's Court*es* and by the same *your* Grace discharged of all man*n*er Causes at the K**ˢ** suite.

Cromwell tells the Card[1] this solliciting his Cause hath bin very chargeable to him and he can*n*ot susteine it any Longer without oth*er* Respect then he hath had hertofore. I am 1000 l. worse than I was when *your* troubles began.

As touching *your* Colleges, the King is determined to dissolve them, and that new offices shall be found of all *th*e Lands belonging to them newly to intitle his Highnes w*h*ich be allready drawn*e* for this purpose. But wheth*er* his Highnes, after the dissolution of them meane to revive *th*em againe and founde the*m* in his owne name, I know not. Wherefore I entreat your Grace to be content, and let *your* Prince execute his pleasure.'

' Cromwell to the Cardinal, May 17, 1530.

' That the King hath received his Lett*ers* and is very sorry *th*at he is in such necessity, yet that for Releefe his Ma**ᵗʸ** hath differed it till he speak w*i*th his Counsail. The D. of Norfolk p*r*omiseth you his best ayd but he willeth you for the present to be content and not much to molest the King (concerning payment of *your* Debts etc) for, as he supposeth, the time is not meet for it. His Grace (i. e. *th*e King) shewed me how it is come to his knowlege that *your* Grace should haue cert*e*in words of him and other Noblemen vnto my L**ᵈ** of Norfolk since the time of *your* adversityes w*h*ich words should sound to make sedition betwixt him and my Lord of Norfolk.

Mr. Page received *your* Lett*ers* directed vnto my Lady Anne, and delivered *th*e same. there is yet no answer. she gaue kind words, but will not p*r*omise to speake to the K. for you.

Certein Doctors of both the Vniversityes are here for the suppression of the Lutheran opinions. The Kings H**ⁿᵉˢ** hath caused the sayd doctors at divers times to assemble, and hath com*m*oned w*i*th them. The fame is that Luther is dep*a*rted this Life. I would he had never bin borne.'

' Cromwel writes to Card[1] Wolsey, August, ⟨1530⟩.

' Intreating him to haue patience etc. that there shall be some offices sent into York and Nottinghamsh. to be found of *your* Lands, belonging to *your* ArchB*isho*prick. This will be very displeasant to you, but it is best to suffer it. for if they should not be found you could not howld *your* B*isho*prick quiet, notw*i*thstanding *your* p*a*rdon : for *your* Restitution made by *your* Pardon is cleerly Voyd, for that the King did restitute *your* Grace before He was intitled by matter of Record. When these offices shall be found, *your* p*ar*don shall be good and stand in parfait effect.

He tells him that his modest behavio*ur* and humility hath gayned him the Love and good report of the Country where he now Lives and allso in the Court, yet his Enemyes depraue all. *Sir*, some there be that do allege that *your* Grace doth keep too great a Howse and family and that you are continually a-Building—for the Love of God ther*e*fore haue a respect and refraine etc.'

'Crumwell writes to *the* Cardinal, Octob⟨er, 1530⟩.

'I am informed *your* Grace hath in me some diffidence as if I did dissemble w*i*th you or p*ro*cure anything contrary to *your* p*ro*fit and hono*ur* I much muse that *your* Grace should so think or report it secretly considering the paines I haue taken etc. Wherfor I beseech you to speak w*i*thout faining if you haue such conceit, that I may cleere myself. I reckoned that *your* Grace would haue written plainly vnto me of such thing, rather than secretly to haue misreported me etc. But I shall beare *your* Grace no Lesse good will etc. Let God judge between Vs. Trewly *your* Grace in some things over-shooteth your self; there is reg[ard] to be given what things ye vtter and to whom etc.'

'I find by these Lett*re*s that Cramwel kept certein scholers in Cambrige, for he entreats *the* Card¹. to p*re*ferre the*m* to Benefices w*hi*ch should fall in his ArchB*isho*prick.'¹

## 14. ⟨CROMWELL⟩ TO ⟨WOLSEY⟩.

### R. O. Cal. iv. 6368. May 5 ⟨1530⟩.

Information concerning the progress of the Cardinal's affairs at Court. Advises him to comply with the King's requests.

After my right hartie Co*m*mendacions to *your* grace according to *your* desire specified in *your* Lett*e*res of answer to the request made vnto youe by the King*es* maiestie for the Treasourership of York I haue so solicited the matier bothe to his hieghnes and to docto*ur* Leighton that bothe be content that your gift shall stande so as *your* grace do accomplishe the teno*ur* of his hieghnes Lett*e*res nowe eftsones directed vnto youe, whiche myn advise and counsail is that youe shall in any wise ensue, and that y*our* chauncelo*ur* shall do the sembla-

---

¹ This last sentence was added by the seventeenth-century scholar by whom the foregoing passages were transcribed, and who calls himself 'Thomas Masters, Coll. Nov.'

ble in another request made by his Maiestie vnto him without
staye tract or further stycking. And in any thing elles wherin
I maye do vnto your grace stede or pleasure I shalbe as glad
to doo thoffice of a frende as you shalbe to require the same of
me. Thus moost hartely Fare youe well. From St. James
besides Westminster the v^th of Maye.

## 15. CROMWELL TO WOLSEY.

R. O. Cal. iv. 6431.   June 3 ⟨1530⟩.

Promises to send a full answer to his letters by Ralph Sadler. Recommends the bearer.

Please it your grace to be aduertised that I haue receyued
your letteres by Thomas Rawlyns and haue perceyued the
contentes thereof and will make answer to the same parti-
culerly by my seruaunt Rafe Sadleyr, who our lorde willing
shalbe with your grace with all spede. Your grace I assure
you is moche bounde to the gentilman this berer for his good
reporte in euery place who I assure your grace hathe not lefte
in euery presence to say of you as by lykelohod ye haue
gyuen him cause. I assure your grace he and such other
haue don your grace moche good, it shalbe in myn opynion
therefore right well don to give him thankes accordingly,
for by my faith he is right worthye. And thus the holie
trynitee preserue your grace in long lyf good helth and moche
honour. At london the iii^rd daye of June.

Your most humble seruaunt

THOMAS CRUMWELL.

*Add.*   my lorde Cardinall⟨s⟩ grace.

## 16. ⟨CROMWELL⟩ TO ⟨WOLSEY⟩.

B. M. Cott. App. L. 7 ; Cal. iv. 6482.   June 30 ⟨1530⟩.

Fragment of a letter, in answer to several minor requests of the Cardinal.
Various details.

. . . as to send your grace any quayles it ys not possybyll
For ther ys non that will Carye them as For Sedes I wyll
Send yow by the next maister Stubbis Sayth he will prouyde
baudekyn for your grace I am sorye for hym he ys Swed in
a primineri by burges which was ons ellect presydent of
Maudlen Colledge   I thinke it wyll cost hym money or he
get owt[1], my lord chaunselour hath promysyd that Masteres

---

[1] *c. o.* For our lordys loue what

lacye shall bere the Cost*es* of them that shall bryng vp John lawrans and Robert Turner. I beseche yo*ur* grace to be so good lorde as to send me A gelding and I trust shortlye after to se yo*ur* grace by the assistens of o*ur* lorde whom I most hertelye beseche to p*re*serue yo*ur* grace in long lyffe good helth and moche hono*ur* at london the last daye of June

## 17. Cromwell to Wolsey.

R. O. Cal. iv. 6530.   July 24 ⟨1530⟩.

In favour of his kinsman Dr. Carbot; requests Wolsey to take him into his household and service.

After my most humble Recommenda*ci*ons wit*h* my dailie *se*ruice and contynuall praier May it pleas yo*ur* grace to call to yo*ur* good and most graceous remembraunce how that I being wit*h* yo*ur* grace in yo*ur* gallerie at the Chartrehouse at Shene most humblie supplied[1] vnto the same for the acceptac*i*on of this berer Mr. doctour Carbot my kynsman vnto yo*ur* *se*ruice   At which tyme it pleased yo*ur* grace beninglie to graunt me to accept hym promising both vnto him and me that ye wolde be his good and graceous Lorde vpon the which he hath tarried here in these p*ar*ties Contynuallye to his great cost Supposing that I sholde haue repared wit*h* him vnto yo*ur* grace by meane wherof he thought the better to be esteemed   But forasmoch as he now p*er*ceyueth that for dyuers causes I maye not he hath desired me to write vnto yo*ur* grace in his fauo*ur*s Most humblie and effectuallye beseching your grace to receyue him into yo*ur* house and *se*ruice Whome I trust yo*ur* grace shall finde apte mete discrete dilligent and honest And suchon that Willinglie Louinglie and obedientlie shall and wilbe gladde to s*er*ue yo*ur* grace in any thing that yo*ur* pleaser shalbe to commaunde him   Trusting fermlie that bye experience ye shall right well lyke him Eftsones most humblie and effectuallie beseching yo*ur* grace to be his good and graceous Lorde for my sake and at this my poure and most humble sute and contemplac*i*on to take him wit*h*owt reiection   And thus the holie trenitie p*re*ser*u*e yo*ur* grace in long lyf and good helth.   At Londe⟨n⟩ the xxiiii*th* daye of July.

Your most humble s*e*ru*a*unt and bedysman

Thomas Crumwell.

*Add.* my lord*es* grace

[1] *sic*, for 'applied.'

## 18. ⟨CROMWELL⟩ TO WOLSEY.

R. O. Cal. iv. 6571.    August 18 ⟨1530⟩.

Information concerning the progress of the Cardinal's affairs at Court and elsewhere. Begs him to cease building for a time, in order that his enemies may have no chance to accuse him of extravagance. News from England and the Continent. Cf. Letter 13.

Please it your grace to be aduertised [1] that after the Receipt of your letteres dated at Southwell on saynt Laurence Day I perceyued how that your grace remayned in som displeasure and anxietie of mynde for that I by my letteres had before certefied you of the fynding certen offices concerning your busshopriche of Yorke  The Fynding whereof as I perceyue by your letteres ye do suppose should be moche to your dishonour & detriment  For the which intent that your grace may put yourself in repose & quietacion of mynde I haue sent vnto you this berer who shall at length declare vnto you besides the demonstracion of the copies of suche offices as be drawen for that purpose that the Fynding of the said offices savyng onelie that in the preamble of the same there is touched the conuiction of your grace in the premunire which all the wourld alredie knoweth shalbe for your good onelie proffit and availe And yet your pardon and restitucion stand in good & perfite effecte So that your grace shal haue no nede nether to be in fere of losse of any your spirituall or temporall goodes or to be troubeled for the same ne also to be put to any new Sute in the obteyning of any other pardon or restitucion.  And if in case your said pardon and restitucion were in any parte insufficient I assure your grace I know that the kinges highnes wold it should be made as good as by any counsaill it could be Devised  And doubt ye not but his highnes is your gracyous and benigne Souereigne lorde and wold in no wise that ye should be greued molested or troubeled.  Wherfore it may please your grace to quiet yourself and to take the fynding of these offices pacientlie and vppon the retourne of the same there shalbe such orders taken that your grace shall not be interrupted in the receyuing of your reuenues ne otherwise be molested in any maner case for any new sute  As touching your colledges the offices shalbe founde houbeit the Deane and suche other as haue sued to the kinges highnes haue had veray good answer wherof I think they haue certefied your grace or this tyme.  As touching the m¹ markes of the reuenues of Wynchester I doubt not but it shalbe obteyned at the audite  And

---

[1] c. o. that perceyuing by

concerning Batyrsey it may please your grace that such
thinges as ye haue sent me the copies of may be sent hither
vnder seale for they woll trust no scrowes and also that
Serche may be made for Busshop Bothes will concerning the
same.   Strangwissh continually cryeth and maketh exclama-
cion in the courte of you insomoch that the lordes of the
counsaill haue determyned to wryte vnto you in that behalf
wold to our lorde your grace were rid of that man.   As
concerning the prebends of Witwang doubt ye not but in that
all thing is and shalbe ordered to your good contentacion.
Sir I assure your grace that ye be moch bounde to our lorde
god that in suche wise hath suffered you so to behaue and
order yourself in thes parties to atteyne the good myndes
and hertes of the people[1] there the reporte whereof in the
courte and elleswhere in these parties is & hathe ben[2] to the
aquyryng & augmentyng the good oppynyons of many
persons towardes your grace beseching your grace therfore
to contynue[3] in the same after Suche a Sorte and Fashyon
as ye may daylye increase not onlye in the Fauours of the
pepull ther but also here and elleswhere to the pleasure of
god & the prynce And notwithstonding your good vertuous
and charitable demeaning and vsing yourself[4] in thes parties
ys not by your enemies[5] interpretyd after the best Fashyon
yet always Folow and perseuer ye attemperatelye in suche
thinges as your woorldlye affeccyons Sett apart Shall serue
to stand best with the pleasure of god and the kyng Sir som
ther be that doth alledge in that your grace doth kepe to
grete a house & famylie and that ye are contynually buylding
for the loue of god therefore I eftesones as I often tymys haue
done most hertelye beseche your grace to haue respecte to
euery thing and consyderyng the tyme to refrangne your Self
for a Season from all manner byldingges more than mere
necessite requireth which I assure your grace[6] shall sease and
putto Sylence Som persons that moche spekyth of the same.
For the geldinges which your grace Dyd send me I do most
humblie & hertelie thank you beseching your grace to gyue
Further Credens to this berer, who shall declare vnto your
grace other thinges not wryttyn[7]   I do Relys your grace

---

[1] c. o. in the hole cuntrey
[2] c. o. your grete good
[3] c. o. after such sorte by your
approuued high wisedom as ye lose
not the wele & benefite of the same
for
[4] c. o. there I assure your grace
you haue

[5] c. o. which do & will not let
to interprete all your doings not in
the best parte Alledging that your
onelie desire
[6] c. o. shalbe grete good vnto
yourself
[7] c. o. Fynallie beseching almightie god to preserue your grace

right happye that ye be now at libertye to serue god and
to lern to experyment how ye shall banyshe and exyle the
vayn desyrys of this vnstabyll warld, which vndowtydlye
dothe nothing elles but allure euery person therin  And
specyally such as our lorde hath most endewyd with his
gyftes to desyre[1] the affeccyons of theyr mynd to be
satysfyed  In Finding and Sekyng wherof most persons
besyd the gret trauaylles and afflyccyons that men Suffer
daylye bene dryuyn to extreme Repentance and Serching for
plesure and Felycyte Fynd nothing but So trowbyll Sorow
anxyete and aduersyte  Wherfor in myn oppynyon your grace
being as ye ar I suppose ye woolde not be as ye werre to
wyn a hundreth tymys as moche as ye were possessyd off
the Busshop of Bayonne ys daylye lokyd For and my lord of
Wyltshyre ys cummyn home the Saying here is that the
emperoure hathe good obbedyence of his Subiectes in all
thing sauyng that they wyll not discent from the lutheran
sekt it ys also sayd that emprour doth mak musters for
a gret army to be preparyd agenst the turke to passe into
Hungarye for the recouerey of that Regyon And that the
seconde Son of the emperour ys departyd this present lyffe
the news here ys that the Germayns wyll medlye haue
a generall Consaylle for the reformacyon of many thinges
the Florentynys doth styll contenew and defende the power of
the pope and it ys Supposyd that they shall vynce by meane
that ther ys a gret pestylence Fallen amongst them being in
the Felde of the popis partye ther ys also a gret Carystye
in Italye of all manner of grayn in so moche A quarter of
whet ys worth generallye Fortye shelyngges. they loke daylye
for an ambassadour from the pope who at the Ferthest wilbe
here with xiij dayes the kynges highnes is this nyght at
amptell and ther wyll Contenew this xiiij dayes. it may
please your grace to pardon me that I do not repayre vnto
yow at this tyme for vndowtydlye it ys not possyble as
this berer shall Ferther Declare vnto your grace our lord
knowyth my wyll and mynde. and I trust verelye that your
grace doth perffytlye think that I woolde be glade to see yow
and vnfaynydlye I woolde haue sene your grace long er this
yf I hadde not bene lettyd by Importune busynes wherfor
I eftsones most humblye besech your grace of pardon and
though I am not with yow in person yet be ye assured I am
and duryng my lyff shalbe with your grace in hert spyryt

in long lif & good helth with the     of August
full accomplisshment of your hertes     [1] c. o. and enter into blynde to
desire  From london the xviii day     satysfye

prayer & seruyce to the vttrest of my poore and symple
power as knowyth our lorde whom I most hertelye besech
to preserue your grace in long lyff good helth with thincreace
of your hertys desyre. at london the xviij[th] daye of August.
I beseche your grace to depeche this berer whom I mygh⟨t⟩
evyll haue forbern at this tyme but onlye that I persayuyd by
your letteres that ye moche desyryd to be put in quyetacyon
and that besyd myself I Coulde not send any that Coulde
certefye your grace of the effectes of such thinges as ye desyre
to be answeryd in But onlye he eftsonys beseching your
grace spedlye to send hym home for my busynes ys such that
I cannot lake hym.

*Endd.* my lorde Cardenall.

## 19. ⟨CROMWELL⟩ TO ⟨WOLSEY⟩.

B. M. Cott. App. L. 81 ; Cal. iv. 6699. Oct. 21 ⟨1530⟩.

Begs the Cardinal's favour for Doctor Carbot, Nicholas Gifford, and
Cromwell's scholars at Cambridge. News of the Emperor's movements. Information concerning the Praemunire. Cf. Letter 13.

. . . eyen three monethis in Chaunserye, howbeit your grace
shalbe so prouydyd for that ye shalbe owt of all dowttes for
all the kynges offycers in the meane Season. I most humblye
beseche your grace to be good lorde vnto my poore kynsman
Doctour Karbott and let hym haue sum lytyll offyce vnder
your grace. I dowt not thoughe he be Sumwhat Symple in
Aparence yet he shall discharge hymself yf ye put hym in
trust and A lityll auctoryte. I beseche your grace [a]lso to be
good lorde vnto your Seruaunt Nycholas Gyfforde . . . when
Anything shall happen to Fall which may do ⟨him⟩ good to
Remembre hym for my sake your grace shall [fin]de hym in
myn oppynyon thoughe he be yong and [some]what wylde[1],
on disspossyd bothe to trewthe [hone]ste and hardynes, and
he ⟨is one⟩ that wyll loue yow [with] all his harte. yf any
thing Falle I beseche your grace [to re]membre my scolers
in Cambryge and bothe they [and I sha]ll pray to our lord
Jhesu Crist to preserue [you] in long lyff good helth with
Increase of [honour. Th]emperour wyl be at Colayn In the
Feaste of . . . without Faylle the Parlyment ys prorogyd
[vntil the] vi daye of January. The prelattes shalnot appere
[in the] premunire. Ther ys Another way deuysyd in [place
thereof] as your grace shall Ferther know. the prynces of
[Almayne] Can ne wyllnot Agree to emperowr and[I bese]che
the holy trynyte preserue your grace . . . [in] quyetnes and

---

[1] *c. o.* a you[th]

Contentacyon I beseche your . . . for this *lette*re . . . Wrytyn
for lake of . . . [in] hast the xxi of octobre

### 20. CROMWELL TO MR. BOROUGH.

R. O. Cal. iv. 6800 (i). ⟨Dec. 1530.⟩

Desires to know if Borough wishes to buy a friend's horse, which certain
Frenchmen are anxious to purchase.

Mr. Borough in my most hartie wise I co*m*mende me vnto
you And so yt ys that my frende Mr. So*m*mer may at this
tyme sell his horse right well and proffutablye but forasmoche as he before this hath promised you that ye shall
refuse him before any other he hathe desyred me to know
yo*ur* mynde So that yf ye will not medell he may do his
best. for there be certeyn Frensshe men which moche
desyreth to haue the saide horse Wherefore I hartely pray
you that I may know yo*ur* mynde by this berer in wrytyng
what ye will do And this[1] hartely fare ye well  At London
this p*re*sent Saterdaye.

Assurydlye your frende.

THOMAS CRUMWELL.

*Add.*  To the right worshipfull Mr. Henry Borough be this
yeuen.

### 21. ⟨CROMWELL⟩ TO STEPHEN VAUGHAN.

B. M. Galba B. x, 338; Cal. v. 248. ⟨May, 1531.⟩

An account of the reception of William Tyndale's book, *The Answer*, by
Henry VIII, and of his anger at the opinions it advanced.  Cromwell
urges Vaughan to cease advocating Tyndale's cause, and to request
Frith to abandon him[2].

Stephen Vaughan I co*m*mende me vnto you And haue
receyued your *lette*res dated at Andwerpe the xviii[th] day
of Aprell wit*h* also that parte of Tyndall*es* boke *Sewed and*
inclosed in lether which ye wit*h* yo*ur* *lette*res directed to the
king*es* highnes After the recept whereof I dyd repayre vnto
the courte and there presented the same vnto his royall
maiestee who *after the recept thereof* made me answer for
that tyme that his highnes at oportun leyso*ur* wolde vysite
ouersee and rede the content*es* aswell of you[r] *lette*res as also
the saide boke And at my next repayre thither it pleased his

---

[1] *sic*, for 'thus.'
[2] The number of erasures and
corrections in this letter is such that
the use of an additional bracket is
necessary, in order to render it precisely.  Words enclosed thus {...}
are inserted above the line in the
original.  Words printed in italics
are crossed out.

highnes to call for me declaring vnto me aswell the content*es*
of *your letter*es as also moche of the matier conteyned in the
saide boke of Tyndall*es*.   And albeit that I might well
perceyue that his maiestee was right well pleased and right
acceptablie considered your diligence and payn[es] taken
in the wryting and sending of the saide boke as also in the
p*er*swading and exhorting of Tyndall to repayre int[o] this
realme *in the accomplisshement of his high pleasure and
comaundement yet I might coniecture by the ferther declaracyon
of his high pleasure Which sayed vnto me that by your wryting
it manyfestlie appered how moche* {yet his highnes nothyng
lyked the sayd boke being fyllyd wit*h* Scedycyous Slaunderous
lyes and Fantastycall oppynyon⟨s⟩ Shewing therin nether
lernyng nor trewthe and ferther Co*m*munyng wit*h* his grace
I mygh⟨t⟩ well coniect that he though⟨t⟩ that ye bare moche}
affection *and zele ye bere* toward*es* the saide Tyndall whom
in his maners *modestie and Symplycytee* {& knowlage in
woordlye thing*es*} ye vndoubtedlie {in y*our* letter*es*} do
moche *more* allowe and co*m*mende *then his* {whos} work*es*
*being so replete wit*h *lyes and most* {*then the warke of hit Self
is able to deserue*} {being replete wit*h* so} abhomynable
Sclaunders {& lyes} Imagened and {onlye} fayned to infecte
*and intoxicate* {*as it semythe*} the peopull *may to indyfferent
Judgement declarethe him, for the which your fauours Supposed
to be born to the saide Tyndall* (*who assuredlie sheweth himself
in myn opynyon rather to be replete wit*h *venymous envye
rancour and malice then wit*h *any good lerning vertue knowlage
or discression*) *hathe put the kinges highnes in suspectyon
of you considering* {dothe declare hym bothe to lake grace
vertue lernyng discrecyon and all other good qualytes
[n]othing [e]ll*es* p*re*tending in all his work*es* but [to] seduce
[and d]yssayve} that *ye should* {ye} in such wise {by y*our*
l*etter*es} *lene vnto and fauo*ur *the evill doctryne of so peruerse
and malycyous a person and so moche prayse him* {prayse
Setforth and avaunse hym} {*bothe to lake lernyng*} {to be
envyous and to lake lernyng gra[ce]]} {*vertue and all good
discrecyon*} *who nothing* {whiche nothing ell*es*} {pretendyth[1]}
*goeth about or p*re*tendeth* but[1] *onelie to Seduce deceyue and
disquiet the people and comenwelth of this realme Whose*
{*Repayre thether ys to be estuyd*} *cummyng into Englonde the
king*es *highnes can right well forbere and* {and sowe sedycyon
among the peopull of this realme.   The king*es* highnes
therfor} hathe co*m*maunded me *expressely to wryte vnto you*
{to adu*er*tyse you that is plesure ys} that ye should desiste

---

[1] These words doubtless ought to have been crossed out in the MS.

and leve any ferther to persuade or attempte *him thereunto*
{the sayd tyndalle to Com into this realme} alledging that
*his maieste so euydentlie* {he} p*er*ceyuing the malycyous
perverse vncharytable {and Indurate} mynde *and disposicyon
of the saide Tyndall is rather veray glad that he is out of his
Realme then,*[1] {*Joyous to haue his realme destytute*} ... {of
the sayd Tyndalle ys in man*er* with*o*wt hope of reconsylyacyon
in hym and ys veray Joyous to haue his Realme destytute
of Such a person for hys highnes right prudentlye consyderyth}
if he were present by all lykelohod he wold shortelie (which
god defende) do as moche as in him were to infecte and
corrup[t] the hole realme {*which now ys so Indurate*} to the
grete inquietacyon and hurte of the co*m*menwelth of the
same.  Wherfore {Stephen} I hertelie pray you *that from-
hensfourth* in all your doing*es and* procedinge*s* and wryting
to the king*es* highnes ye do iustely trewlie and vnfaynedlie
*shew yo*ur *self to be no Fauto*ur *vnto the saide* {with*o*ut
dyssymulacyon Shew your self his trew louyng and obedyent
Subiect beryng no mann*er* Fauo*ur* loue or affeccyon to the
sayd} Tyndale ne to his wo*ur*k*es* in any man*er* of wise but
*rather* vtterlie to contempne and abhorre the same assuring
you that {in so} doing *the contrary* ye shall not oneli[e]
cause the king*es highnes* royall Maieste whose *highnes*
goodnes at this tyme is so benignelie and gracyouslie mynded
towardes you (²*as by your good dyligence and industrie to b*[*e*]
*vsed to. serue his highnes and extewing and avoyding* [*to*]
*favo*ur *and allow the saide Tyndale his erronyous work*es *and
opynyons*) *ye are like shortelie to atteyne* (³ *So to prouyde for
you So to aduise you* So to Sett you forwardes as all y*our*
louers & frend*es* shall haue gret consolacyon *in you* of the
same [*b*]*oth welth honestie and promocyon at his gracyous
hand*es *to the singuler ioy pleasure and comforte of all yo*ur
*Frend*es) and by the contrarie *to* {doing ye shall} acquire the
indignacyon of god *and* displeasure of y*our* Sou*er*eigne lorde
and by the same *compell* {cause} y*our* good Frend*es* which
haue ben euer glad prone and redie to *aduau*n*ce* {bryng} you
*vnto the* {into his gracyous} favours *of your prynce* to lamente
and sorow that their sute in that behalf should {be frustrate
and} not {to} take effecte according to their good intent and

---

[1] Here occur the following words
*underlined*, not crossed out : 'that
[he] should retourne into the same
there to manyfest his errours and
sedycyous opynyons, which (being
out of the Realme by his most vncharytable venemous and pestilent
bok*es* craftie and false persuasions)
he hathe partelie don all redie '

² (...) underlined, not crossed
out.

³ (...) this passage is put in the
margin.

purpose, hauing therefore firme trust that for the {*Feare ye
haue in god obedyens to yo*ur *souerayn lord*} loue ye owe to
yo*ur* self *me* and *other* your Frend*es* ye *wilbe* will beware
*from hensfourth* {and estew} to enter into any *such* opynyons
{*or to the prayse of any such p*erson} whereby any sclaunder
dishonestie *or* daungier {or Susspycyon} might insue towardes
you whereof I promyse you I wold be as sorie as yo*ur good*
{natural} father.

As touching Frith mencyoned in yo*ur* saide l*ett*eres the
king*es* highnes heryng tell of his towardenes in good l*ett*eres
and lernyng doth *Regrete and* {moche} lament that he should
in such wise as he doth Set fourth Shew and applye his
lerning and doctrine in the semynacyon and sowing such euill
seed*es* of dampnable and detestable heresies mayntening
bolstring and adua*un*cyng the venemous and pestyferous
wo*urkes* erronyous and sedycyous opynyons of the saide
Tyndale and other  Wherein his highnes *as* {lyke} a most
vertuous and benigne pr[ince] and goue*r*nour hauing charge
*commytted vnto hi*m of his people and Subiect*es* {&} being
{veraye} sorie to here tell that any of the same should
in suche wise Ronne hedling and digresse from th[e] lawes
*and precept*es {*and holsom doctryns*} of almightie god {*and
holye Fathers*} {and most holsom} *into suche dampnable* {and
most holsom doctryne of holye Fathers into suche dampnable}
heresies and sedycyous opynyons *and* being eu*er* inclyned
willi[ng] and gretelie desirous to forse and prouyde for the
same {& moche desyryng the reconsylyacyon of the sayd
Fryth} *and also* fermelie trusting that *the said Frith* {he} be
not so far as yet inrouted in the evill doctryne of the saide
Tind[all] {& oder} but that by the grace of god louyng
charitable and frend[lie] exhortacions and aduer*tisement*es
of good people he may be *revoked and* called agayne to the
ryght way *wylleth* {hath therefore} *and desireth you* {wyllyd}
{*and Co*mmaundyd} {me to wryte vnto yow that ye} accordyng
to his trust and expectacyon {will} wit*h* your frendelie
persuasions admonycyons and holsome exhortacions *to*
counsaill and aduyse the said Fryth if ye may conuenientlie
speke wit*h* the same to lev[e] his wilfull opynyons and like
a good Christien to retou*rne vnto o*ur *Saueour Christe and
also* into his natif cuntrey *So that by his procedi*ng*es as he
begynneth there be no m*[ore] [se]*dycyous infections and heresies
sowed amongst the king*es *peopull* {wher he assurydly shall
Fynde the kyng*es* highnes most m*er*cyffull and benygnlye
vppon his conversyon disposyd *towardes hy*m to accept hym
to his grace & m*er*cye}  Wherefore eftesoones I *hertelie
pray you and* {exhort you} for the loue of god *do* not onelie

*exhorte you* vtterlie to forsake leve and wit*h*draw y*ou*r affectyon
from the saide Tyndale and all his secte but also as moch as
ye can poletiquelie and charytablie to allure all {the said
Fryth and other} suche p*er*sons *as ben* {being in thes p*ar*tyes
which in any wyse ye shall know or suppose to be} Fautours
and assistent*es* to the same from all their erronyous mynd*es*
and opynyons.   In which doing ye shall not onelie highlie
merite *of* {in} Almightie god but also deserue high thank*es* of
the king*es* royall maiestee who will not forgett y*ou*r deuoyrs
and labours in that behalf   So that his maiestee may {evy-
dentlye} p*er*ceyue that ye effectuallie {do} intende the same.

And as touching y*ou*r diligent adu*er*tisement vnto the
king*es* highnes of the nombre of Shippes arryued wit*h* corne
and grayn in those p*ar*ties he hathe co*m*maunded me on his
behalf to gyue vnto you condigne thank*es* for the same And
being moche desirous to know and atteyne the trewth of that
matier his grace hathe co*m*maunded me to wryte vnto you
that by all good dexteritee polycie and meanes ye should
indeuoyr y*ou*rself to atteyne to the knowlege of the Maisters,
s*er*uau*n*t*es* owners or other that made sale of the saide grayn
brought thither to thintent that by thexamynacyon of som
his highnes might haue knowlege of the rest and that ye shall
wit*h* all diligence aduertise h[is] highnes of their names, and
in likewise of such other newes concerning themperours
affayreses the discending of the turke into Germanye the
preparacyons ayenst him the gifte of money in the low
countreys to themp*er*our the abyding of themperour in the
low p*ar*ties the agremen[t] bytwen him and the prynces of
Germanye as ye sha[ll] here by m*er*chaunt*es* or otherwise
most certeynlie to acertey[n] his grace by y*ou*r l*et*t*er*es
wit*h* as moch dyligence as ye can.   Prayeng you therefore
substauncyallie and circumspect[lye] to indeuo*ur* y*ou*rself
to serue the king*es* highnes herein effectuallie So that y*ou*r
towardenes good mynde duet[ie] of allegiaunce and seruice
toward*es* his royall maiest[ie] may be apparaunt and notoryous
vnto the same.   Which I doubt not shalbe to y*ou*r singuler
proffite and aduauncement.

## 22.  〈CROMWELL〉 TO MR. STRETE.

### R. O. Cal. v. 277.  〈May, 1531.〉

Encloses a commission to survey the lands of the bishopric of Coventry
and Lichfield, and to receive the rents for the King, and orders to
cease collecting rents in Chester. Cf. Letter 43.

Mr. Strete after most hertie co*m*mendac*ion*s these shalbe to
adu*er*tise you that by the berers hereof ye shall receyue the

king*es* comission and warraunte yeuyng you auctoryte to
S*ur*uey the lond*es* of the bisshopriche of Couentre and Lich-
feld and to receyue the rent*es* and p*ro*fites of the same to the
king*es* vse.　And also ye shall receyue his grac*i*ous *lette*res
directed to the Eschetor of the Countie palentyne of Chester
vppon the sight whereof I doubte not but he will not onelie
Surcease to medle any Ferther w*it*h the receipt of any rentes
there but also in case he haue receyued any, will repay the
same vnto y*ou*r hand*es* accordinglie.　Not dowbting but ye
will diligentlie effectuallie and trewly put in execuc*i*on the
teano*ur* and effecte of your saide Co*m*myssion in suche wise
as shalbe most for your honestie & to the Kinges most p*ro*fite
and adu*a*untage.　And for y*ou*r paynes and diligence alredy
taken and susteyned aboute his affayres there his highnes
hathe co*m*ma*u*nded me to yeve vnto you his most hertie
thankes.　And trustith that ye will so indeuo*ur* y*ou*r self in the
receipt of the said rent*es* and reuenues as before the feaste of
the Natyuyte of Saynt John Baptist next ye will bryng or
send vp the hole half-yeres rent or the most p*ar*te of the same
and that ye will have good awayte and regarde to his hauk*es*
in the Cauke there wherein ye shall do and admynister vnto
his highnes right good and acceptable s*er*uyce.

　　And as touching the Catell at the pryorie of Calliche the
king*es* grac*i*ous pleasure is that ye shall suffer the berers
hereof named Fyndern and Curson to haue the p*re*ferrement
in the byeng of the same vppon suche reasonable prises as
they may conuenyently lyve on taking of them som money in
hande and such sufficient bonde and suertie for the residue as
the king may be trewly answered of the same.　And so Fare
ye well &c.

　　　　　　　　　　　　　　　　　Your mastership.

### 23.　Cromwell to ⟨Gardiner⟩.

B. M. Vesp. F. xiii, f. 154 ; Cal. v. 302.　June 18 ⟨1531⟩.

Requests him to examine and correct the enclosed 'Mynewte' before
　　presenting it to the King.　Excuses himself for not coming in person.

Right honerable after due reco*m*mendac*i*ons may it please
the same to be adu*er*tysed that I haue sent herein Inclosed
the Mynewte with your Instruccions Beseching you to Survey
the same and if ye shall fynde any erroure to order and
correcte hit according to your wysdo*m*me and goodnes
or eu*er* ye shall p*re*sente the sight thereof vnto the King*es*
highnes which ons do*n*ne and his highe pleasure knowne
I shall w*it*h dylygence cause it to be engrossed and sent I wold

myself haue co*mm*yn therew*ith* if other of the King*es* Busines
had not Lettid me, Beseching you to make myne excuse and
to depeche this Berar And this the holy trenyte p*r*eserue you
in Long lief & good helth w*ith* thencrease of muche hono*ur*
at London this xviij day of June.

Yours most bounden

THOMAS CRUMWELL.

**24. ⟨CROMWELL⟩ TO ——.**

R. O. Cal. v. 458 (i).  Oct. 1 ⟨1531⟩.

Requests, on the King's behalf, the preferment of Thomas Beryer,
warden of the Grey Friars of Blois, to be warden of the Grey Friars
of Paris.

Right worshypffull after most hertye co*mm*endacyons this
shalbe to adu*er*tyse you that the king*es* plesure ys that ye on
his gracyous behalf shall effectuallye move the Frenche kynge
for [1] the p*reff*er*ment of on Frere Thomas Beryer which ys
now gardyen of the grey Freers of Bloyse so that he at the
co*n*templacyon of his highnes may be now elect to be gardyen
of the grey Freers in parys for assurydlye his highnes desyrethe
moche the adu*a*uncement of the sayd Freer and wooll that
ye in most effectuous wyse do solycyt the same vnto ⟨the⟩
Frenche king*es* [2] requyryng the same on the his [3] graces behalf
to move the gen*er*all of the sayd relygyon now being at parys
in the effectuall prefferment of the aboue sayde Freer and that
ye Fayle not therof the kynges highnes requirythe yow.  His
Highnes also woll that ye shall moue the gret maister in that
behalf For I assure you his maiestye moche tenderyth the
adu*a*unc*e*ment & p*r*efferment of this Freer  and thus hertelye
Fare ye well.

At london the Fyrst daye of octobre.

**25. ⟨CROMWELL⟩ TO MR. HERON.**

R. O. Cal. v. 458 (ii).  Oct. 3 ⟨1531⟩.

Advises him to permit the bearer, Richard Johnson, to retain the farm
granted him by Heron's parents, as Heron's interest in it comes from
the King.

Maister Heron in my right [4] hertye wyse I co*mm*ende ⟨me⟩
vnto youe and so it is that this berer whos name is Rychard
Johnson hathe Supplyed [5] vnto the kyng*es* highnes alledgyng

---

[1] *c. o.* on the behalf of  
[2] *c. o.* highnes          [3] *sic.*  
[4] *c. o.* most  
[5] *sic,* for ' applied.'

that he being possessyd of a certayn Ferme being parcell of
the mannour of Highe Hall [1] of the dymyse and graunte
aswell of your Father as also of [2] your mother late disceasyd
whose sowlys our lord pardon owt of the which as he affer-
myth ye wooll expel hym  Syr my aduyse shalbe that ye
according to Justyce do Suffr the sayd Johnson to occupye
his Ferme, consyderyng that your Interest In the same Cum-
myth of the kynges graunt for assurydlye his grace wyll
thinke straunge yf ye sholde expell his seruaunt hauyng a
lawfful grante aswell of your Father as mother [3] as he affer-
myth.  Wherffor methinkyth ye shall do well to let hym
occupye his Ferme withowt your Interrupcyon, he paying For
the same as to right appartaynyth For I woolde ye sholde not
be notyd extreme in your proceedinges and specyallye agaynst
your Felowes the Kynges seruaunttes and thus hertelye Fare
ye well at london the thyrde daye of Octobre

### 26. ⟨CROMWELL⟩ TO ——.

R. O. Cal. v. 458 (ii).  ⟨Oct. 1531.⟩

Advises him not to receive any of the King's 'courser men' in his
monastery.

My lord aftr right hertye recommendacyons this shalbe to
Certiffye yow of the receipt of your lettere and being veray
Sorye of molestacyon doo aduyse yow not to suffr anye of the
kynges Courser men to lye with yow.  For your monasterye
vndowtydlye ys moche to small to Resayue the kynges
Coursers.

### 27. ⟨CROMWELL⟩ TO ⟨SIR RALPH ELLERCAR⟩.

R. O. Cal. v. 671.  ⟨1531.⟩

Thanks him for advice concerning a bargain that Cromwell is about to
make for the manor of Belthrop in Yorkshire.

Woorshipfull Sir in my most hertye manner I commend
me vnto yow and In the same wise thanke yow for your
good and kynd chere made vnto my seruaunt which that
of late was with yow [4] my Sayd Seruaunt Informyd yow how

---

[1] c. o. which he helde For terme
of yeres of his highnes and hauyng
good and Suffycyent graunt In the
same

[2] c. o. my ladye

[3] c. o. and hauing no Just Cause
so to do

[4] c. o. and as concernyng the

bargayn betwene me and John
Ardren of and for the manour of
Belthrop with the apportenaunces
which, as I am Informyd ye wer in
mynde to haue bought Sir I woold
I hadde bene made preuey to your
mynd at whych tyme

that I hadde concludyd a bargayn with John Ardren of and
For the Mano*ur* of Belthrop and ye then aduysyd my said
Seru*a*unt to Adue*r*tyse me Substancyallye to loke vppon the
sayd bargayn which aduertysment hath Sumwhat put me in
dowt wherfor Syr I hertelye desyre and also pray yow that
yff ye know anye manner dowt ambygwyte or Any acte done
by the sayd John Ardren or anye other Wherby I myght
Sustayn Any manner displeasure danger or losse conc*er*nyng
the sayd Manno*ur* or the purchasing of the same that I may
be certeffye⟨d⟩ by this berer in evere poynt concernyng the
same as my specyall trust is in yow and ye so doing shall
bynd me

*The letter ends abruptly here, the bottom of the sheet being
cut off.*

On the dorse is the draft of part of a letter from the King concerning an
intended invasion from Scotland by the Duke of Albany, aided by
the King of France.

## 28. ⟨CROMWELL⟩ TO ⟨GARDINER⟩.

### R. O. Cal. v. 723. ⟨Jan. 1532.⟩

Sends news of the first reading of the Bill of Annates in the Lords. Has
asked for money for Gardiner from the King, who grieves at Gardiner's
absence.

My lorde after myn humble and most hertie reco*m*mendac*i*ons these shalbe to adue*r*tise yo*ur* lordeship how that
I haue receyued your gentill *lette*re to me dely*ue*red by
thandes of Mr. Wrythesley And whereas I do p*er*ceyue
by my kynnesman this berer that ye moche desire to here
newes from hens I assure you that here be non but such as
vndoubtedlie by a multytude of *your* Frend*es* (which are
Farre more secret and nerer the knowlege of the same then
I am) be to yo*ur* lordeship all redie related and knowen but
yet to adue*r*tise of som parte that I know, as thys day was
Redd in the higher house a bill touching the Annates of
busshopriches fo*r* what ende or effecte it will succede suerlie
I know not. And as yesterday because I knew yo*ur* lordeship not to be Furnisshed of all thing*es* necessarie for yo*ur*
being there I moued the King*es* highnes aswell for money
to be defrayed in and aboutes the furnyture of yo*ur* purpose
and affayres as also for yo*ur* Reto*ur*ne hither sayeng that
vppon myn owne coniecture yo*ur* lordeship was wery of

being there whereunto his highness answered me that you were not so wery of yo*ur* being there but he was as sorie Sayeng by these word*es* exp*r*esselie. (His absence is the lacke of my right hand for I am now so moche pestred wit*h* busynes and haue nobodie to rydde ne depeche the same) So that yo*ur* lordeship may well know that yo*ur* absence is not to you so moche paynefull and greuous as yo*ur* p*r*esence here should be pleasaunt and comfortable to the King*es* highnes and all other yo*ur* poure Frend*es* beseching therefore yo*ur* lordeship to Fynde som meanes on yo*ur* p*ar*te as moche as in you is that yo*ur* Reto*ur*ne hither may be shortelie which is long loked and wisshed for As o*ur* lorde knoweth etc.

*Endd.* A mynute of my mr.'s le*tt*re.

## 29. ⟨CROMWELL⟩ TO HENRY VIII.

R. O. Cal. v. 1055. ⟨May, 1532.⟩

Has had the news from Ratisbon translated into English. The English ambassadors are going to meet those of the Emperor at Dunkirk.

May hit please yo*ur* most r*o*yall magestye to be adu*er*tysyd that of suche news as hathe Cum from Ratyspone I haue causyd the same to be translatyd owt of Italyon into Inglysshe and according to yo*ur* high co*m*mawndment to me youyn yesterdaye haue Inclosyd them in this my le*tt*ere, wherby yo*ur* highnes shall and may woll p*er*sayue of what Importaunce they be of. I haue also resayuyd a le*tt*ere from Stephyn Vawhan which ys of no gret weight but that he wrytythe that yo*ur* gracyous ambasadours do now repayre to the emperours ambassadours to Dunkyrke affermyng them to be Suffycyentlye Furnysshyd to answer all thing*es* layd by the co*n*trarye parte and nothing dowtyth but that they shall haue veray gud Successe in all yo*ur* gracyous affayres and thys o*ur* lord Jesu Crist preserue and continew the most Royall estate of yo*ur* most Ryoyall magestye in long lyffe & good helthe

## 30. ⟨CROMWELL⟩ TO HENRY VIII.

R. O. Cal. v. 1092. June 13 ⟨1532⟩.

Sends the book that the Friar Carmelite brought him. Cannot yet inform the King of the conclusion of Ap Howell's matter. News from Rome that the Turk is to invade Italy with a great army.

Pleasythit yo*ur* most Royall mageste to be adu*er*tysyd how the Freer carmelyte browght vnto me this mornyng a

boke willing me on your gracyous behalf with all spede to send
the same vnto your highnes.   Which I haue done accordinglye I cannot yet certeffye your grace touching the Conclusyon of Jamys Gyrffyth ap Howelles matyer for asmoche
as yet I haue not spokyn with mayster Thesaurer of your
most honorable howshold who vndowtydly this daye wilbe
at Westm.   Strange news haue arryuyd here aswell from
Rome as Venyse of the turkes Repayre vnto and towardes
Italye with a mervelous puisauntt Armye what shalbe the
Successe thereof our lorde knoweth  it ys Suppossyd that gret
afflyccyon will Insew not onelye to the pope & the See of
Rome but also to the emprour and his conffederattes wherfor
it may please the holye trynytie in whos Inffinyte goodnes
power & wyll Restyth the the[1] order and traunquylyte of all
thinges to bryng peax good oppynyon and quyetacyon
amongyst Cristen pryncys and euer conserue preserue & kepe
your highnes in long lyff good helthe with quyetacyon of
your most vertuous most noble and most charytable mynde
At london the xiii[th] of June


## 31. ⟨CROMWELL⟩ TO THE MAYOR OF HAVERFORD WEST.

R. O. Cal. v. 1106.   June 19, 1532.

Notifies him that Sir William Wolff is discharged of his appearance before
the council.

Master Maier I hartely recommende me vnto you And
where for Certaine causes ye toke bounde of Sir William
Wolff clerke somtyme chapplaine vnto Rice app Griff. Esquier
disceased and of other suert[ies] with him by recognisaunce
that the saide Sir William shoulde k[epe] his personall
apparaunce here in the Sterre chamber before the kinges
most honourable counsaiell there for certayne causes to him
to be obiecte on the kinges behaulf in this present Terme as
in the Condicion of the same Recognisaunce is comprisid.
I doo you to vnderstonde that the saide Sir William Wolff
is clearly dischargyd of his saide apparaunce byfore the saide
counsaill wherefore I praie you to cause the saide Recognisaunce withe the condicion [to be] made frustrate and
Void.   And thus Jhu kepe you writen the xix[th] daie of June
at London in the xxiiii yere of the Reigne of oure Soueraien
Lorde the Kinge Henry the Eight.

*Add.*   To Maister maier of Harfford Weste this be
deliuered.

[1] *sic.*

## 32. ⟨CROMWELL⟩ TO MR. ROWLAND.

R. O. Cal. v. 1185 (i).   July 19 ⟨1532⟩.

The King desires him to pay the bearer £5, to the use of the dean
and canons of his college at Oxford, for the annual portion of his
parsonage of Garsington, due to the late suppressed monastery of
Wallingford.

Maister Rowland after my herty commendacions this
shalbe to aduertyse you that hitt is the kinges graces
pleissuire and commaundement that ye shall paye immediately
after the sight off theis my letters to the handes off Maister
Herry Williams beyrrer heiroff Fyve powndes off good and
lawfull money off Englonde to the behoiffe off the deanne
and Canons off his graces Colledge in oxford now lately
erected. The whiche saide summe off Fyve powndes was
deue to haue byn payed by yow att the Feiste off sayntte
Michell tharchangell laste paste For thannuall porcion goyng
owtt off your parsonage off Garsinton vnto the late suppressed priore off Wallingford. And theis my letters shalbe
vnto yow a sufficient warrauntt & acquyttaunce For the
payment off the Forsaide Fyve powndes. Faill you nott thys
to doo as ye tendre the kinges pleissuire and thus Faire ye
well. In haist From london the xix^th daye off July.

## 33. ⟨CROMWELL⟩ TO ——.

R. O. Cal. v. 1184.   July 19 ⟨1532⟩.

Recommends Robert Hogan, the King's chief cook.

Right worshipfull after moost hartie Recommendacions
thiese shalbe to aduertise you that my louynge felowe and
freende Robert Hogan Maister Coke to our soueraigne
Lorde the Kinges grace hathe obteyned lycence of his grace
to repaire into your parties for suche his Affaires and busynes
as he hath there to do. Whom I hartelie desire you to
entreteigne and accepte in makinge and showinge vnto hym
suche freendlie and louynge Chere and other pleasures for
my sake, as ye wolde to me, yf I were there with you
presente And in so doynge ye shall mynystre vnto me a right
singler good pleasure, not to be forgoten in tyme commynge
in suche your Requestes and Affayres as ye shall haue here
to do by the grace of god who euer kepe you. Att London
the xix^th Daie of July.

## 34. ⟨CROMWELL⟩ TO ——.

### R. O. Cal. v. 1185 (ii).    July 20 ⟨1532⟩.

Requests him to grant the farm of Myxberye in Oxfordshire to John
Welsborne, one of the gentlemen of the King's privy chamber.

My lorde after most hertye recommendacyons this shalbe
to desyre and hertelye praye ⟨you⟩ to be so good at my
poore Instaunce and request to graunte the Ferme of
Myxberye vnto my veraye Frend and Felow Mr. John
Welsborne one of the gentylmen of the Kynges preueye
chaumbre in doing wherof besydes the good wyll ye shall
obteyn of hym ye shalbynde me to ⟨do⟩ yow suche poore
pleasures as shall lye in my lytyll power as knowyth our
lorde who euer preserue your lordship wrytyn at londen the
xx^{th} daye of July

## 35. ⟨CROMWELL⟩ TO THE LORD ⟨CHIEF JUSTICE FITZ-JAMES⟩.

### R. O. Cal. v. 1340.    Sept. 24 ⟨1532⟩.

The King has directed his letters for the election to the abbacy of Bruton
    in Somersetshire of that person whom Lord Lisle and Fitz-James
    have recommended. Fitz-James may postpone the election for the
    trial of the King's title if he sees fit.

My lorde after most hertie commendacions these shalbe to
aduertise your lordeship how that I haue receyued your
letteres and according to the contents of the same moued
the Kinges highnes concerning thelection of the Abbote of
Bruton   And like as I wrote vnto your lordeship in my last
letteres that ye should stay the saide election vntill the
Kinges title might be tryed   So his high pleasure is that
ye shall do if ye see good matier to bere it.   Neuertheles
his highnes at the sute of my lorde Lisle Supposing that he
and you do both sue for the aduauncement of one person to
be Abbot of Bruton forsaid as my lorde playnlye affermyd
to his grace hathe theruppon directed his gracious letteres
for that purpose whiche notwithstanding his high pleasure
is yf ye se cause that ye shall stay thelection vppon the
tryall of his title, as is aforsaide   And in case your lordeship
will haue that person promoted for whom he hathe written
his grace is therewith right well contented So that his highnes
may ⟨haue⟩ me remembryd Sumwhat, lyke as your lordeshyp
wrot vnto me in your last whyche he onelye Remyttythe to
your wisedom and discrecyon for his highnes perfectlye
trustith that ye will substauncyallie loke thervnto, who woold

as Fayne that ye were well neyhboryd as ye woold yourself.
my lord in this and all other that shall lye in my Lytill power
I shall allwayes do as I haue promysyd and thus most hertelye
Fare ye well at london the xxiiii[th] daye off Septembre

## 36. ⟨CROMWELL⟩ TO HENRY VIII.

R. O. Cal. v. 1298. ⟨September, 1532.⟩

Reports the making of patterns for the King's collar, and the accounts of
the King's jewels. Edmund Knightley has been committed to the
Fleet for contempt of the King and his laws.

Please it your highnes to be aduertised that according to
your gracious commaundement I haue caused patrons to be
drawen after your graces Deuyse albeit I haue wyllyd your
goldsmyth not to procede to the making of any thing In
perffeccyon vntill your gracious pleasure shalbe Ferther
knowen for the which purpose both he and I shall repayre
vnto your highnes on Saterday night or Sondaye in the
morning and to the Intent your grace may determyn your
pleasure I haue Sent by this berer the patron of your Coller
of balasys and Dyamondes drawn according to your graces
fyrst deuyse  touching a certen matier in varyaunce betwixt
thexecutours of Sir[1] William Spencer disceasyd and[2] my
ladye spencer whereas informacion was made vnto your
highnes that grete Spoyle of the goodes of the saide Sir[1]
William Spencer was made by the saide executours and
how that the executours wold haue put owt my ladye late
the wyff of the sayd William from the execucyon of the
testament the matier hath ben harde here before my lorde
the keper of your grete seale Sir Willyam Poulet and me[3].
And as it appereth by thexamynacion as well of the executors
as by Edmond Knyghtley and Rychard his brother the hole
spoyle and eloyning[4] of the sayd goods & plate was made
onely by the sayd Edmond Knyghtley his brother Rychard
and the sayd ladye spencer thayr suster notwithstanding that
ther was Agrement made betwene the executors and the
ladye spencer that she sholde entyr into bargayn with your
highnes and also into the execucyon of the testament with
them as an executrix which vndowtydly she hadde done yf
Edmond Knyghtle hadde not bene Which Edmonde Knightley

---

[1] c. o. Thomas
[2] c. o. Mr. Edmonde Knightley
[3] c. o. with other of your graces
counsaill
[4] c. o. as hathe ben had & made
of the saide goodes and also such

offences as haue ben commytted
in that behalf haue ben onelie
done and executed by the saide
Edmonde Knightley his Syster and
suche other of that parte and none
otherwise

hathe not onelie trauayled asmoche as in him is to sett pyke
betwene the sayd ladye and the executors and to defeate
your grace of your title to the heire of the saide Spencer
but also Justeffyed the same befor my sayd lorde keper of
the gret Seale wher on the other partye it was openlye
prouyd that your grace hade good tytyll and all his
allegacyon vntrew yet neuertheles for the reducing of the
same his vntrew purpose to effecte and to the Intent to
slaunder your gracys tytill and others he hathe caused to be
made certen proclamacions in your Countyes of Warwyke
leycester & Northampton in dyuers of your highnes Towns
there to the high contempte of your grace and your lawes
For it hathe not ben seen nor herd that any Subiecte within
this Realme sholde presume to make proclamacion within this
your realme but onelie in your graces Name Wherefore for
his offences and other contemptes ayenst your highnes in that
behalf my lorde the keper of your grete ⟨seal⟩ takyng that
matyer to be a greuous offens ayenst your Crown & Imperyall
magestye hathe commytted the sayd Edmond Knyghtley to
your pryson of the Flete where he now remayneth vntyll
your high plesure shalbe Ferther knowen in that behalf. As
touching the Cup of golde & Corporas Case I sent your
highnes woorde by Thomas Alvard the treuthe whereof this
berer Stevyn Vawhan can Informe your grace who hathe
made perfytte bokes aswell of the sayd Cuppe & Corporas
Case as also of all other your highnes Jewelles now being in
the handes of Cornelys to be orderyd according to your
graces plesure and thys the holye trynyte preserue your most
royall estate of your most excellent magestye


### 37. ⟨CROMWELL⟩ TO THE ABBOT OF ST. EDMUNDS BURY.

R. O. Cal. v. 1573.   Nov. 24 ⟨1532⟩.

Desires the farm of Harlowberry, in Essex, near Honysdon.   Will do all
he can for the monastery.

My lorde after my hartie maner I commende me vnto you.
Aduertising you that for dyuerse consideracions I am verray
desirouse To haue some house in essex nere vnto Honysdon.
And forasmoche as your parsonage of Harlowebery shall
shortly be in your Handes and Letting, By Reason that the
lease whiche Malery and his Wyff hathe is nowe all moost
expired, I shall desire and instantly pray you to lett your
said Farme of Harlowebury vnto me by lease for terme of lx
yeres for the same stokke Rent and Ferme that haithe byn

of Olde tyme accustumyd paid and perceyuyd for the same.
In doing whereof ye shall bynde me to do you and that your
monastary suche pleasure as may ly in my Lytell power, in
tyme to com.   And what shalbe your towarde mynde herin
I pray you to Aduertise me in wrytyng by this berer my
servaunt.   And as for the yeres that malery and his wyff haithe
yitt to com ye shall vnderstaund that I haue Agred with
theym for his lease Thus fare ye hartely well from Eltham,
the xxiiii day of Nouembre.

*Add.* To my Lord Thabbot of Seynt Edmoundes Bury
geve this.

### 38. ⟨CROMWELL⟩ TO ⟨THE EARL OF NORTHUMBERLAND⟩.

R. O.; not in Cal. ⟨Dec. 1532.⟩

Congratulates him on the success of his last raid against the Scots, and
assures him of the King's favour.   Urges him to keep on his guard
against a surprise.

After myn humble commendacions please it your lordeship
to be aduertised that I haue receyued your letteres the contentes wherof I haue right well perceyued And touching your
prosperous fortune and victorie in your last rode agenst your
enemyes Shewing therby your valiaunt courage glad hert
and mynde to serue the Kinges highnes and annoye his
enemyes, I assure your lordeship there is no man lyuyng
gladder to here thereof then I am your poure Frende,
Wisshing to god that your lordeship did knowe and here
as I do how louynglie and acceptablie the Kinges highnes
doth Regarde and take the same.   which vndoubtedlie
wold double the hardynes and courage of any man lyuyng
to do his grace seruice.   And because it is to be thought that
after this rode your enemyes the scottes will invente & studie
to be reuenged to your like annoyance or more if they can,
my poure aduise shalbe that by all the wayes meanes and
polycies ye can, your lordeship do circumspectlie and with
vigilant eye make such espialles and watches and so in most
poletique and warlyke Facion will forsee studye and prepare
as in no wise by your saide enemyes ye be preuented   But
rather that your lordeship as ye alredy haue begon will so
contynue endeuouring your self to greue and annoye your
enemyes by doing of such valiant actes and exployttes to
thincrease of your high merite and worthie praise   So as the
Fame renowne and noble victorie which your lordeship hathe
now won and obteyned be in no wise hurte blemisshed or
defaced by any acte or exployte to be don hereafter for

lacke of good forsight or preuencyon  Thus I am bolde to
gyue your lordeship my poure frendely aduise beseching the
same to excuse my boldenes and to thinke I do it onelie for
that I bere unto your lordeship my hertie good mynde and
will And no man more gladder then I to here tell of any
thing which should sounde to your lordeshippes good Fame
and honour, the increase and augmentacion whereof I doubt
not but your lordeship will contynew to procure with no lesse
diligent propence glad hert and mynde to serue the king
in his affairees there then as ye haue begon to the vtter grief
displeasure and annoyaunce of your enemyes wherein I
beseche our lorde to sende you as prosperous fortune and
good successe as your noble and valyaunt herte could wisshe
or desire  At london etc

*Endd.* mynute of a lettere

### 39. ⟨CROMWELL⟩ TO THE ABBOT OF BURY.

R. O. Cal. v. 1719.  ⟨1532.⟩

Regrets to hear that he has detained several workmen in his district, in
spite of the King's need of them in London.  Urges him to send
them up at once.

My lorde after all dew recommendacyons this shalbe to
aduertise your lordshyp how that I and other hauyng charge
aswell of the Kynges Buldinges at his Towre of london as
also at Westm. haue bene for lakke of masons Carpenters and
other woorkmen compellyd to sende in to all the plases of this
Realme For prouysyon of the same by the kinges commyssyon
and albeit that the kinges mesenger by the auctoryte of his
Commyssyon hathe repayryd into dyuers partyes of Suffolke
ther to execute the same and also to Burrye Saynt Edmondes
and therabowtt For to haue taken and prestyd masons For the
accomplyshment of the kynges sayd woorkes ye lytell Regarding
the kynges auctoryte and Commyssyon have stayed dyuers
masons and woorkmen abowte yow wherof I do moche mer-
vayle my lorde I woolde be loth and also veraye sorye the
the[1] kynges highnes sholde be Informyd of your demeanure in
that behalf For I dowt not though peraduenture his highnes
woolde esteme yow to be Abbot of his Monasterye of Burye,
yet he woolde not forget that he ys your kyng and soueraynge
lorde, who percase might thinke sum vnkyndenes and also pre-
sumpcyon in yow so to handell hym or his auctoryte within
his owne Realme  Wherffor my lorde I thinke it shalbe well
done in aduoyding Further busynes to sende vpp those masons
and not to Contend with your prynce ne with his auctoryte

[1] *sic.*

I beseche your lordshyp to pardon my playne wrytyng For assurydlye I woolde be veray lothe that the kinges highnes sholde haue Anye occasyon to thinke anye vnkyndnes or disobedyence in yow   and thus the holye trynyte preserue your lordshyp in long lyffe and good helthe

## 40. ⟨CROMWELL⟩ TO ⟨THE BISHOP OF ELY⟩.

R. O. Cal. vi. 312.   April 6 ⟨1533⟩.

The King desires his presence at the next session of the Council, if his health will permit.   Recommends the bearer Mr. Jones.

My specyall good lord after my most humble recommendacyons ⟨it⟩ may please the same to be aduertysyd how that the kynges highnes hathe Commaundyd me to gyue yow knowlage that yf ye may by any possyble meanys your helth and lyffe preseruyd Repayre hether this next terme yt sholde be moche to his gracyous contentacyon and Comfort to haue your presens and Cownsayle in his affayres and his grace dowtyth not but ye wyll yf it be possyble for yow to trauayle accomplyshe all thing that maye be to the Satysfaccyon of his pleasure.   I assure your lordshyp his grace hathe not a Few tymes lamentyd in the presens of your frendes not onlye your absens but also your Infyrmyte wherfor his grace hathe bene veraye Sorye.   And my lord bycause this berer Maister Jonys dothe now repayre vnto your lordshyp for your Fauours and goodnes to hym so shewyd towardes his prefferment vnto whom yt may please you at my poore Sute & medyacyon to be specyall good lorde   Assuryng your lordeship that he ys a perffect honest gentylman and such one as ye shall neuer Repent the thing that ye shall doo For hym as knowyth the holye trynyte who euer preserue your lordshyp in long lyffe and good helthe   At londen the vi^{th} daye of Aprell.

## 41. ⟨CROMWELL⟩ TO ⟨LORD SCROPE⟩.

R. O. Cal. vi. 383.   April 25 ⟨1533⟩.

The King has received his letters, and is glad that he will let him have the manor of Pyssow in Hertfordshire.   The King will give him good lands in exchange.

My specyall goode lorde after all dew Recommendacyons this shalbe to aduertyse the same that the kyngys highnes right thankffullye dyd accept your letteres to hym dyrected & delyuered by mr. chasye and his grace ys merveylouslye well contentyd that your lordshyp wooll let his grace haue

your manour & parke of Pyssow in exchaunge. Wherfor his
Magestie hathe Commaundyd me to Inserche for landes for your
Recompens which I shall doo with all conuenyent spede and
as to the rede howsys with the other thinges mouyd to me by
this berer your seruaunt I wyll vndowtydlye doo my best so
that your lordeshyp by the next shalbe certeffyed of the kynges
Full and determynate pleasure in all thinges as knowethe our
lorde who euer preserue your lordshyp in long lyffe & good
helthe at london the xxv^{th} daye of Aprell.

## 42. ⟨CROMWELL⟩ TO ⟨THE DUKE OF SUFFOLK⟩.

### R. O. Cal. vi. 415.   April ⟨1533⟩.

The King is pleased with his willingness to surrender his patent of Earl
  Marshal, which has been granted to the Duke of Norfolk.   Suffolk
  is to have the Justiceship of the Forests on this side of the Trent for
  life, in exchange.   Advises him to come to Court at once.

After my most humble Recommendacions it maye please
your grace to Vnderstande that the Kinges highnes hath been
assuredlie aduertised howe that your grace is contente to
surrendre your patente of the office of Therle Marshall into
his handes   Whervpon his Magestie hath graunted the same
vnto my lorde of Norffolk his grace Whose Auncestors of longe
tyme hadd thesame vntill nowe of late.   And his highnes is
contente that your grace in the lewe and place therof shall
haue his letteres patentes of the Justiceshipp of his Forestes on
thisside Trente for terme of your lyfe.   Assurynge your
grace his highnes doth not onlie repute moche honour in your
grace for that ye soo kyndlie will departe with the saide office
of marshalshipp vnto my saide lorde of Norffolk but also his
magestie supposeth and perfectlie percevith that your grace
hath moche more estimacion and zele to Norisshe kyndenes
and love bytwene my saide lorde of Norffolk and you then ye
haue to thatt or any other office whiche vndubtelie is highlie
to his gracious contentacion to see and perceiue so grate and
honorhable personages his subiectes so lovynglie and Frendlie
the on to love thother.   Wherfore as he that always rekonith
hymselfe [bou]nden vnto your grace and beyng also ver[ayly]
Joyouse to persayve howe pleasauntlie the kinges highnes
taketh in gude parte and repute your honorhable and moost
gentill demeanours in this and all other your procedynges
thought I coulde no lesse doo then to aduertise you
therof to thintente that ye knowynge thesame myght and
may determyn your self therafter.   And amongest other
thinges as I can perceyue it shulde not be vnthankfullie taken
towardes the kinges highnes and your grace yf it were your

ease and pleasure to repayre to the Courte w*ith* Resonable
spede consyderyng that shortlye my lorde of Norfolke de-
p*a*rtyth toward*es* his gret Jorney in Ambassade.  Beseching
yo*ur* grace to p*ar*don my bolde & Rude wryting whiche I am
movyd vnto  For the poore good wyll I b[ear] [yo*ur*]
grace as knowyth the holye trynyte who preserue yo*ur* grace
in longue lyffe good helth w*ith* thincrease of moche hono*ur*
at London the        daye of Aprell.

### 43. ⟨Cromwell⟩ to Mr. Strete.

R. O. Cal. vi. 645.   June 14 ⟨1533⟩.

Recommends various persons to receive the land, cattle, and corn of the
late priory of Calwich in Staffordshire.  Gives directions for the
administration of Strete's office.  Cf. Letter 22.

Maister Strete as hertelye as I Can I co*m*mend me vnto
yow and wher as by my last l*ette*res I wrott vnto yow in the
Fauors of Curson and Fyndern to be p*re*fferryd vnto the Catell
and Corn of late belongyng to the pryorye of Colwyche and
Sythyn that tyme I wrotte vnto yow on the behalf of
Mr. longford for his p*re*fferment vnto the demaynes of the
sayd late pryorye so hit ys that now the sayd maister longford by his Father in law Mr. Fyzherbert moche desyryth to
haue the Tythys and also suche Corn as at this tyme ys Sown
vppon the demaynes of the sayd late pryorye for this yere whych
tythe and Corn Sown vppon the demaynes I require yow
that he may haffe at suche prysys as ye shall thinke convenyent
and in such wyse as the kyng*es* highnes may be Substaun-
cyallye answeryd of the p*ro*ffytt*es* growing of the same w*ith*out
any Fauo*ur* to be born to anye othre p*ar*tye and wher as
I wrott in myn other letter that Curson and Fyndern shold haue
the p*re*ffermentt of the Catell and Corn I dyd not wrytt for
anye Corne growing on the grownde ne yet for any tythys
which in no wyse ye shall Suffer them to haue but to order hyt
as ys afforsayd most to the kyng*es* p*ro*ffytte & aduau*n*tage.
I well p*er*sayue who grauntyth suchemen an Inche they wyll
take an ell.  I am Infformyd they avaunte them selfs to haue
Co*m*myssyons and graunt*tes* of the kyng which ys vntrew
I praye yew aduyse them to vse no suche Facyons.  Syr the
kyng*es* highnes trustyth that ye w*ith* all spede will bryng up
the half yeres Ferme and Rentt*es* of the Busshopryche which
I praye yow may be here before his gracyous dep*a*rtyng in
p*ro*gresse.  and as to the Chanon off Colwyche ye may translate hym vnto Sum good howse of that relygyon being nere
vnto yow and to gyue hym sumthing after yo*ur* discrecyo*n*
suche as may stand w*ith* the kyng*es* hono*ur* and also to his

honest Contentacyon and thus trustyng in *your* approuyd wysdom and experyence Co*m*mytt all the p*r*emysses vnto yo*ur* discrecyon trustyng eu*er* that ye wyll haue respect to yo*ur* dew[tie] and charge and also that I may haue short answer of thes and other my *lette*res and so Fare ye well   at london the xiiii<sup>th</sup> daye of June

### 44. CROMWELL TO LORD LISLE.

R. O. Cal. vi. 706.   June 26 ⟨1533⟩.

Desires him to admit Bartholomew Peters as surgeon of Calais.  Will do his best to obtain Lisle's requests for the town.

My lorde after my right hertie reco*m*mendacions these shalbe to adu*er*tise [y]o*ur* lordeship that where it hathe pleased the king*es* highnes to gyve and [g]raunte to Bartholo-mew Petres the rowme of Surgeon in his grace . . . w*ith*in the towne of Calays, as by a bill signed for that purpose . . . ye shall receyue of the saide Bartholomew more playnelie shall . . . [a]ppere I shall therefore requyre yo*ur* lordeship that insuing the teano*ur* pu*r*port and effecte of the king*es* saide g*r*aunte ye do see the saide Bartholomew admytted into the saide rowme when tyme shall requyre accordingly.   And concerning suche matiers as ye latelie haue written in for the towne of Calays, I do not ne shall not cesse to do my best to reduce and bryng the same to suche good passe and effecte as shalbe thought most requysite and expedient.   I trust to yo*ur* good contentacion.   And so o*ur* lorde p*r*eserue yo*ur* lordeship in long lif and good helth w*ith* thincrease of hono*ur*.   At London the xxvi day of June

Yo*ur* lordshyppis assuryd

THOMAS C[RUMWELL]

I wrytt to yo*ur* lordeshyp For this berer by the King*es* expresse Co*m*mandmentt.

*Add.* To the right hono*ur*able and his singuler good lorde my Lorde Lisle deputie to the King*es* highnes of his town and m*a*rches of Calays be this youen.

### 45. CROMWELL TO ⟨THOMAS BEESTON⟩.

R. O. Cal. vi. 776.   ⟨June–July, 1533.⟩

Ordering him to repair to the Emperor's Court and deliver the King's letters to Dr. Hawkins there, with directions to turn them over to the Emperor.  He is to return with the Emperor's answer.

First the king*es* highnes pleasure is that ye hauing receyued yo*ur* packet of *lette*res and instructions directed vnto Mr.

docto*ur* Hawkyns, shall ymediatelie put *your*self in aredynes to dep*ar*te toward*es* the p*ar*ties of beioynde the See, inserching by yo*ur* polycie the nerest wayes to suche place where it shall happen the Emperour to lye.

Itm when ye shall repayre to themp*rours* Courte ymmediatly to delyu*er* the saide packet vnto the saide Mr. Hawkyns w*ith* hertie greting*es* and salutacions from the king*es* highnes adu*er*tesing him ferther that the king*es* pleasure is that when tyme shall Requyre, he shall not onelie intymate declare and communycate the effect*es* of suche l*ette*res and instructions conteyned in the saide packet, w*ith* themp*rour*, always insuing the teano*ur* purpose and meanyng of the same, But also after his accustomed wisedom dexterite and good polycie shall indeuo*ur* himself so to propone handle and set fourth all thing*es* as he by his good discression shall se tyme place and occasion  So as the same may take effecte according to the King*es* high trust and expectacion in that behalf.

Itm that after declaracion of the p*re*misses and co*m*munycac*i*on had at length w*ith* themp*er*our in the same, the saide Mr. Haukyns shall then if he so thinke good, devise determyn*e* and conclude w*ith* you for·yo*ur* depeche and reto*ur*ne hither w*ith* l*ette*res and instructions purporting suche answeres articles and allegacions as by themp*er*our shalbe answered leyed and obiected to those thing*es* which the saide Mr. Hawkyns shall intymate and declare as is aforsaide on the kyng*es* behalf, which being don*e* and accomplisshed the kyng*es* gracious pleasure is that ye shall make all conuenyent haste spede and diligence to repayre hither to his grace w*ith* the same accordingly.

THOMAS CRUMWELL.

*Endd.* mynute.

### 46. ⟨CROMWELL⟩ TO ⟨THE MERCHANT TAILORS⟩.

R. O. Cal. vi. 698. ⟨June, 1533.⟩

Requests them to continue and increase the annuity granted to Nicholas Glossop, servant of the late Archbishop Warham.

Right wellbeloued Frendes I recomend me hartly vnto yowe And where I am enfourmed that at the request of my late lorde of Caunterbury, whose sowle god pardon, ye graunted to his seru*a*unt Nicholas Glossop, an olde Auncient of youre Felisship of m*er*chaunt Taillours a certeyn Annuytie of xxvi s. viii d. toward the Sustentacion of his lyvyng for terme of his Naturall life.  Wherof by his report, he hath be⟨n⟩ well

and truly Answered of a long tyme.   Howe be it nowe upon
the deceas of his said maister, as it ys said, that ye entende
to withdrawe From hym 'youre saide Benyuolence and
graunte, which shulde be to his great Discomfort and
Hyndraunce.   And forasmoche as I bere good Mynde and
Favour towardes hym And it were more charitie rather to
Augemente his lyving than to dymynysshe it or withdrawe
the same, specially nowe in his great Age, whan he hath most
nede of help and Socoure.   I hertly desire yowe that for my
sake ye wille not only contynue the payment of the said
Annuytie to hym for terme of his life according to your said
graunte, But also of youre larger Benyvolence and charitie
to encreas the same xiii s. iiii d. more by yere.   Wherby in
myne opynyon, ye shall not only do the thyng whiche may
be right meritorious to yowe, but also right honorable for
youre said Felisship, and to me right great pleasure.   and
for the same doing He may hereafter do yowe pleasure And
I shalbe glad to doo yowe pleasure or any good that I can
for your Felowship at alle tymes As knoweth god who
preserue yowe.   And Further I desire yowe of your good
Answere in this behalf the morowe Folowing your next
Courte Day by yowe to be holden at your halle

*Endd.*  A lettre for Nicholas glossop.

### 47.  Cromwell to Mr. Thomas Alen.

R. O. Cal. vi. 791.   July 9 ⟨1533⟩.

For failing to pay his debts to Cromwell, and to give sureties for the
money his brother owes the King, Alen has forfeited 1000 marks to
the Crown.   Requests an answer by the bearer.

Maister Alen after right hertie commendacions these shalbe
to aduertise you that long or this tyme I loked to haue harde
from you and trusted not onelie to haue had and receyued
from you now at Midsomer last passed my Hundreth poundes
which of gentilnes I lent you but also sufficient bondes and
suertie for your brother tharchebisshop of Duntlyn concerning the payment of vii$^c$ [1] markes which he oweth to the kinges
highnes according to suche bonde as you and other with you
stonde bounde in for the complement of the same.   For lacke
and defaulte whereof ye haue forfaited to the kinges highnes
the Somme of one thousande markes which me thinketh ye
ought substaunciallye to loke vppon for the king is no person

---

[1] i. e. 700.

to be deluded nor mocked w*it*h all. And considering that for y*ou*r sake I so gentillie departed w*it*h my money me semeth that reason and good honestie requireth ye should se me payed ayen. prayeng you that I may be adu*er*tised by this berer what ye mean and intende to do in the premisses. And so hertelie Fare ye well. At London the ix^th day of Julie.

Y*ou*r louyng Frend

THOMAS CRUMWELL.

*Add.* To his louyng Frende Mr. Thomas Alen be this yeuen at Raylegh.

## 48. CROMWELL AND AUDELEY TO HAWKINS AND RANDALL, BAILIFFS OF WEYMOUTH.

R. O. Cal. vi. 858.    July 18, 1533.

Warrant for the delivery into the nearest prison of six men taken in the ship *Trinity*, of Hull. The goods and the ship are to be delivered to William Gonson.

Wellbelouyd we grete you well, and Where as Will*i*am Gonson of london hathe shewed vnto vs an Indenture datyd the viii^th daye of June last, made betwene Edward Waters and you specyfyeng the deliu*er*auns of a Ship namyd the Trinite of Hull and lxiiii Hoggyshedes of gascon wyne w*it*h dyu*er*s other thing*es* therin conteynyd to y*ou*r Handes. We certefye yow that the Kyng his pleasure is that ye shall incontynent deliu*er* or cause to be deliu*er*ed all thing*es* conteanyd in the said Indentures to the said Will*i*am Gonson or his assignes. and as towching the sixe pryson*er*s taken in the said Ship and lykewyse deliu*er*yd into your kepyng that ye deliu*er* theim into the next pryson to you, ther to be surely kepte till the king*es* pleasure be to you Further knowne wheche deliu*er*aunce of Ship and goodes & prysoners shall be vnto you a sufficyent dyscharge at all tymes herafter   Wryton at London the xviii daye of July the xxv^th yere of the Reigne of our sou*er*aigne lorde kyng Harry the viii^tb.

THOMAS AUDELEY Kt. chauncel*our*
THOMAS CRUMWELL.

*Add.* To our Welbelouyd Will*i*am Hawkyns and Will*i*am Randall Baylyff*es* of the towne of Waymowthe.

## 49. Cromwell to Sir Anthony Fitzherbert and Walter Luke.

R. O. Cal. vi. 872.    July 19 ⟨1533⟩.

Requires him to delay the trial of a case which may be prejudicial to Cromwell, as the jury has been packed, and will be likely to give an unjust verdict.

After my right hertie commendacions Forasmoche as there is a Nisiprius passed out to be tried before you at the next assises to be holden at Lyncoln concerning the tryall of the title of Anthony Stydolffe who is my warde Which Nisiprius is secretlie sued out and passed without my knowlege so as percase the same may be moche preiudiciall vnto me in that thing whereunto I haue good iust and lawfull title as ye shall apperceyue by suche deades and writinges as my Frend this berer shall shew vnto you, I therefore considering your worshippes and good indifferencies, trusting that ye will do me none iniustice in this behalf Do most hertelie require and pray you to staye the tryall of the saide Nisiprius, Vntill ye shall haue Ferther knowlege of the matier, the rather for that I am crediblie infourmed that the enquest is alredie so parciallie impaneled that vndoubtedlie it is thought they will passe directlie ayenst the trowth. Eftesones therefore most hertelie requyring you to provyde and forsee myn indempnyte in this parte, And for the good acquytall of your gentilnes to be shewed vnto me herein if there be any thing wherein my poure powers can extende to do yow pleasure I shall not Faile godd willing to accomplisshe the same to the vtterest of my lytill power. And so most hertelie Fare ye well. At London the xix^th day of Julie.

It may please you to gyve firme credence vnto this berer in such thinges as he shall declare vnto you on my behalf

Your assuryd Freend

Thomas Crumwell.

*Add.* To the right worshipfull Mr. Anthony Fitzherberte knight one of the kinges iustices of his comen benche and to Mr. Walter Luke esquier and to either of them.

## 50. ⟨Cromwell⟩ to Mr. Mustiam.

R. O. Cal. vi. 878 (ii).    July 19 ⟨1533⟩.

Desires him to permit the bearer to enjoy a lease of the farm of Brokesley.

Master Mustiam I hartely commende me vnto you. And in the same wise beseching you at this my poure contemplacion

and request to be good master and Frende vnto . . . berar
hereof, in letting hym to opteyne, and peacably to occupie
and envoye the hole effect of a lease of the ferme or parsonage
of Brokesley, in the paroche of Detford in the Countie of
Kent to hym demysed by one Mr. Otywell of Westminster
diseased without any your further let grief or disturbauns.
Vntill suche tyme as ye shall knowe further of my will and
pleasure, and inso doyng ye shall mynyster vnto me right
singuler pleasure. And this hartely fare ye well  At London
this xix day of July

### 51. ⟨CROMWELL⟩ TO MR. MUSTIAM.

R. O. Cal. vi. 878 (ii).  July 20 ⟨1533⟩.

The bearer complains that Mustiam intends unjustly to take the tithe
    corn of Brokesley from him.  Advises Mustiam not to do this.

Maister Mvstyam I hertelye commende me vnto yow
aduertysing the same that the poore man berer herof hathe
shewyd me that ye do Intend to do hym wrong in takyng
From hym the tythe Corn of Brokleye, other wyse wyse[1]
Called west greenwyche whervnto I thinke ye haue no tytyll
nor Interest, wherfor I shall aduyse yow to stay to doo any
thing in the same vntyll suche tyme as ye shall be hable
honestlye to to[1] Clayme therin and thus Fare ye well at
london this xxth daye of July

### 52. CROMWELL TO HENRY VIII.

R. O. Cal. vi. 887.  July 23 ⟨1533⟩.

Reports the examination of certain Friars Observants, who have been
    taken by Cromwell's spies.  Two of them would certainly confess
    much if examined by torture.  Desires instructions how to proceed.
    Has inquired of Cranmer about the men, as the King desired.

Please it your highnes to be aduertised that vppon myn
arryuayle at London I receyued certen letteres out of the
North directed vnto your grace from the lorde Dacre. Which
I haue sent to your maiestee herein closed with also certen
letteres and Newes sent vnto me from my Lorde Deputie
of Calays. And touching the Freres obseruantes that were
with the prynces dowagier, being subtillie conueyed from thens
were first espied at Ware by suche espialles as I leyed for
that purpose, and hauyng good awayte leyed vppon them
were from thens dogged to London, and there (notwithstonding many wyles and cauteles by them invented to
escape) were taken and deteyned till my cummyng home. So

[1] *sic.*

as vppon my arryuayle here I called them before me and vppon examynacion of them coulde gather nothing of anye momente or grete importaunce, but entring into ferther communycacion founde the one of them a veray sedycious person, and so commytted them vnto warde where they now do remayne till your gracious pleasure knowen. Ymmedy-atelie afterwardes repayred vnto me the warden of the grey Freres of Grenewich who semeth veray desirous to haue the punycyon of the saide two Freres, being named Hugh Payne and Cornelius, and made grete intercession vnto me to haue them delyuered vnto him, Shewing unto me ferther that the mynyster and generall Commyssarie of this prouynce of Englonde had made out certeyne commaundementes vnto the said Freers willing them by vertue of obedience to repayre vnto him to Rychemont to thintent they wold haue the correction of them accordinglie. Which com-maundementes being conteyned in certen mynutes of paper I haue sent to your grace herein closed. It semeth assuredlie that the saide mynyster is a right honest and discrete person and Fayne wolde haue prevented and taken the saide Freers if he had coulde by any meanes, Beseching your grace tha[t] I may knowe your gracious pleasure Whether I shall kepe and de[t]eyne them in warde and bring them with me at my repayree to the courte, or Whether your grace will haue them sent ymmedyatelie to any other place or what other direction to be taken therein as shall and may stonde with your high pleasure. It is vndoubted that they haue intended and wolde confesse sum grete matier if they might be examyned as they ought to be that is to sey by paynes, for I perceyue the saide Hugh Payne to be a subtile Felowe and moche gyuen to sedycyon.

I haue also eftesones sent vnto my lorde of Caunterbury according to your gracious commaundement touching the dissymuled holynes and supersticious demeanures of the Ipocryte Nunne, And haue declared your gracious pleasure vnto the Staple whom in maner I do Fynde agreable to all thinges according to your graces demaunde sauyng onelie they as yet requyre lenger dayes for the payment of the some of x m¹ pounds by them now graunted, and also fermely requyre that your highnes will graunt them their house for a reasonable somme of money yerelie, which I do stycke with them in. and as to morowe they will gyve me a resolute answer in the hole.

And thus I shall daylie pray vnto almightie god for the

---

¹ i.e. 10,000.

prosperous conseruacion of yóur royall maiestee in long lif and good helth felyciouslie to indure. at London the xxiii day of Julie. Your highnes most humble subiectte and seruaunt

THOMAS CRUMWELL.

*Add.* To the kinges royall maiestee.

### 53. ⟨CROMWELL⟩ TO AUDELEY.

R. O. Cal. vi. 894. July 26 ⟨1533⟩.

Desires him to permit the annuity of £20 which has just been granted to Stephen Vaughan to bear date from a year ago this summer, as there was already £20 due to Vaughan for one year's service.

Right honourable syr after myne hartie commendacions. So it is that the kinges hieghnes hathe lately graunted Vnto a seruant of his named Stephen Vaughan a certeyne annuytie of xx li by yere to be paide from the faste of the natyuytie of saynt John Baptiste now last passed Vnto the whiche Stephen by cause there is owyng by the kynges hieghnes xx li for one yeres seruyce ended at Mydsomer now laste paste, therefore is it that by cause he hathe no waise to demaunde it of maister Tuke by patent or other sufficient warrant from his hieghnes. he hathe desyred me who vndoubtidly do know that his pleasure is that he shulde be payde the sayde xx li. to Requyre yow that when his annuytie commythe to the greate seale your pleasure maye be to suffer it to bere date from Mydsomer Was a yere and that he maye by force therof be payde the yere now passed. And doubte ye not thus to do. for the kinges pleasure is he shulde be paide the xx li due for the ycre passed. And I shall alwayse warrant yow to be sufficiently discharged and to be blameles for so doyng. The saide Stephen had obteyned the kinges warrant for the same, oneles his highnes had now sent hym into Germany for thexpedicion of certeyn his affayres there. And thus the holy trynytie preserue your lordeship in long lyfe goode healthe and much honour. from London the xxvi daye of Julye.

*Add.* To the right honourable Sir Thomas Audley knyght lord chancellour.

### 54. ⟨CROMWELL⟩ TO THE ABBOT OF WOBURN.

R. O. Cal. vi. 778. ⟨July, 1533.⟩

Requests him not to maltreat the Abbot of Vawdy in Lincolnshire ; has heard he intends to depose him. Desires him to cause Davys Edward, the monk of Vawdy, to amend his ways.

My lord after my duetie remembred, soo it is that I am credibly enformed how that ye beryng inwarde grudge &

displesure to my welbeloued Frend thAbbot of Vawdy entende studie & goo aboutes by sinistre meanes to depose hyme from his abbacye for the promocion therunto of oon of your awne monkes being the cellerer of your house.  My lord I pray you vse your selffe vnto my saide frende as accordeth to your religion, For I knowe certainly that he is a good religious man, And that his house wiche was in gret debt at the tyme of his promocion, is nowe by his good policie reduced to good & welthy state and condicion aswell in catoll as in corne furnisshed with other requisites & necessaries.  Wherfor my lord my trust ys that ye wol circumspectly loke therupon baring your good & lawfull fauour unto hyme, like as good charitie requireth.  And the rather at my disire & request ascertaynyng you that I haue at this tyme writen my sem-blable letteres in the fauour of my said frend vnto thabbot of fountayns not doubtyng but that he at my requisicion wol lovingly vse and intreate my said frend in all his busuynes. And wher as ye haue with you a monk of the said house of Vawdy oon Dauys Edward Clerke, wiche ye knowe well haith gretely mysordred hymselff.  I trust that ye woll instructe hyme soo fruteffully that he shall not nede to be further reconsiled to amend his lyvynge  Wherby ye shall doo averay good & charitable dede as knoeth god who kepe yow

*Add*. To thabbot of Woborn

*Endd*. a lettere for the abbot of Woborne

## 55. CROMWELL TO LORD LISLE.

R. O. Cal. vi. 1064.    Sept. 1 ⟨1533⟩.

The King is displeased at Lisle's desire for new arrangements for 'the restraynyng of Corne.' Lisle should not take every man's or his own wife's advice concerning things pertaining to his office.

After my right harty recommendation vnto your good lordship This shalbe to aduertise the same that I have resceyved your letteres wherein ye and the Mayer of Calays do desire to have newe provisions concernyng the restraynyng of Corne otherwise then hathe byn vsyd yn tymes past. I ensure your lordship the kinges highnes is not a litle displeased withe that your desire, but supposith your besynes to be veray small that will in any wise ymportune his highnes withe any soche matiers Sayeng that before this tyme the Towne and marches of Calays hathe ben well maynteynyd and prospered without any soche newe devises. And I assure your lordship as your frynd to my power that I have great

m*er*vayll that ye will so sone enclyne to eu*ery* man*n*ys devise
and . . . . specially in matiers of small ympor[t] . . . ye and
. . . reportyd . . . nite me on . . . causes as me semythe . . .
nothyng . . . ne gentilwymen, for although my lady be right
hono*ur*able and wise yet yn soche causes as longithe to
y*our* auctoritie her advise and discresion can litle prevayle.
Wherfore I pray y*our* lordship to consider the same, and
to ymportune the king*es* highnes w*ith* none other matiers
then of necessite ye ought to do. And thus the blessed
Trynyte preserue you. At london the first day of
September.

Your lordshyppis assuryd

THOMAS CRUMWELL.

*Add.* To my veray good lord my lord Vicount Lisley the
king*es* deputie at Calays be thus youen.

## 56. CROMWELL TO THE FRENCH AMBASSADOR.

Huth Library; Cal. vi. 1128. Sept. 15 ⟨1533⟩.

Reports the arrival of Danish and Norwegian ambassadors at the Court
of the Queen Regent of the Netherlands to conclude an alliance.

Mons*ieur* lambassad*eur* Le Roy mon maistre a este aduerty
par son agent estant en Flandres. Que puisnagueres les
ambassadeurs de Danemarche Norwege & Holst au nom du
conseil et Royaulme de Danemarche, sont arriuez a la court
de la Royne douagiere de hung*ier*ye regen*e* deflandres auec
le nombre de xxxii p*er*sonnes ou eniuron et co*m*me son d*it*
agent peult entendre avecques plain et suffisant pouuoir et
auctorite A conclure et affermer vne bonne allyance et paix
auecques l'emper*eur* et tous ses pais & dominions tant defen-
siue que offensiue, Aussy autant qu'il peult entendre Lad*ite*
Royne & son conseil sont determynez a traiter et conclure
auecques lesdits ambassad*eur*s auecques telle condition que
quiconques sera eleu Roy par dela (l'election duquel est
encore prolonge*e* & differee po*ur* l'espace dung an) Il Jurera
ratifiera & confermera la*di*te allyance & Traycte de Paix.
Desquelles choses le Roy mon d*it* M*aistr*e ma co*m*mande vous
aduertir affin que en co*n*uenient diligence vous en vuelles
rescripre au Roy Tres chr*es*tie*n* vos*t*re m*aistr*e et Ladviser
quil seroit bon de penser sur cest affaire et essayer sil Luy
semble expedient a estoupper le*ur*s propoz et aultreme*n*t y
po*ur*veoir ainsi quil Luy semblera conuenable. A tant Mon-
si*eur* Lambassad*eur* apres mestre affectueuseme*n*t Reco*m*-

mande a vous je prie nostre seigneur quil vous ait en sa
tressaincte & digne garde.  Escript a Stepney le xv jour de
Septembre

Vostre entier et parfaict amy

THOMAS CRUMWELL.

*Add.* a monsieur Lambassadeur du Roy Treschrestien
a Londres

*Endd.* de M^r. Craumeuelle

57.  CROMWELL TO LORD LISLE.

R. O. Cal. vi. 1141.   Sept. 21 ⟨1533⟩.

Requests him to permit the executors of Robert Baynham freely to
  administer his testament, notwithstanding his former letters to the
  contrary.

Aftre my right harty Commendacions to your lordshipp
Whereas heretofore I addressed my letteres vnto your lordshipp
at the sute of my seruaunt Bartholomew Bayneham concernyng
the steye of such goodes as lately apperteyned to his Father
Robert Baynam of Calaish vntil suche tyme as ye harde
Further of my mynde in that behaulf.   These shalbe most
hertely to desyer and praye youe the rather at the contemplacion hereof to suffre thexecutours of his sayd Father Robert
Baynam to execute and mynistre according to the meanyng
of the Testament and last wyll of his sayd Father in as ample
wise as heretofore they haue doon my sayd former letteres
notwithstanding.   And being enformed of your goodnes and
also of my lades of late shewed vnto my sayd seruaunt
partely as I take yt for my sake I thanke you most hertely
for the same and though my lady for her parte might haue
been better before yet I requyre you bothe for my sake ye
nowe to contynewe the goodnes which youe doo presently
extende Vnto him.   Wherein ye shall admynystre Vnto me
Veray acceptable pleasur.   And thus Fare you hertely well
From Stepney the xxi^th day of Septembre

Your lordshippis assuryd

THOMAS CRUMWELL.

*Add.* To my Veray good lorde my lorde the Viconte Lisle
Deputie of the kinges Towne of Calaysh and Marches of
the same.

## 58. CROMWELL TO RICHARD AND WILLIAM HAYBOURNE.

R. O. Cal. vi. 1332.   Oct. 24 ⟨1533⟩.

The Lord Chancellor and Cromwell will sit on the dispute between them and Elizabeth Colcoke the Friday after All Hallowday.

I co*m*mend me vnto you.  Adue*r*tising you that it is fully dete*r*mynyd betwixt my lord Chaunceler and me that we will sitt vpon the mater in variaunce betwixt E*l*izabeth Colcoke widowe and you the Friday after Alhallow day.  Wherfore I requyre you in any wise to be here the day before that ye may be redy for that purpose and that ye in no wise faill so to do vpon yo*ur* peryll.  And thus fare ye well.  At london the xxiiii^th day of October.

Y*ou*r Freend

THOMAS CRUMWELL.

*Add.*  To my frynd*es* Richard Haybourne and Will*ia*m Haybo*ur*ne be this youen.

## 59. ⟨CROMWELL⟩ TO THE ABBOTS OF FOUNTAINS AND BYLAND.

R. O. Cal. vi. 1408.   Nov. 8 ⟨1533⟩.

Is surprised that they have not yet elected a new Abbot of Rievaulx as the King wished.  Advises them to delay no longer.

After my full hertie man*er* I recommende me vnto you.  And where as it hathe pleased the king*es* highnes to directe his moste grac*i*ous *lette*res vnto you nowe at this p*rese*nte tyme for the elecc*i*on of a newe Abbote of Ryyaulx wherein his grace hathe bene adue*r*tised ye haue not heretofore inde-vored youreself*es* to thaccomplishemente of the same according to his said *lette*res and co*m*maundemente (whereof I m*er*vaile not a little) that ye wold incurre his high displeasure for the none executing of the same. therefore I hertely requyre you and neue*r*thelesse doo advise you in exchewing of further Inconvenyenc*es* and displeasures that maye thereby ensue (all affeccions sette ap*ar*te) ye doo accomplishe the said elecc*i*on according to the tenou*r* and purporte of his moste grac*i*ous *lette*res directyd vnto you and to the Convente of the same monastary in that behalf.  And thereby ye shall not oonly dese*r*ue the king*es* moste grac*i*ous thank*es*, but alsoo haue me to doo for you in all yo*ur* good causes the beste I can.  As knowethe our Lorde who kepe you.  Written at London the viii^th daye of Nouembre.

*Add.*  To the right hono*ur*able in god my Lorde Abbote of Funtaunce and Bylande and to either of theym.

## 60. CROMWELL TO LORD LISLE.

R. O. Cal. vi. 1413.　Nov. 11 ⟨1533⟩.

Has heard of the trouble that has arisen owing to the blow the knight
　porter has given to a 'lewde Felowe.' Thinks that there is no cause
　why the knight porter should be molested for his action.

My lorde after my right hertie commendacions I haue
receyued your lordeshippes letteres And haue perceyued by
the same what contencion is arrysen there by meanes of
a lewde Felowe for a stroke yeven vnto him by Sir Cristofer
Garnysshe the knight porter, Which matier hath ben debated
here by the kinges counsaile who perceyuing the saide stroke
was yeven but onelie for correction and for none entente to
breke any law statute or ordenaunce of that towne of Calays,
do thinke the same but a veray light matier to make any suche
busynes of and no cause why the saide Sir Cristofer should
be put to any molestacion for the same. Wherefore your
lordeship may let it passe and wey it as it is And so our
lorde preserue your lordeship in long lif and helth with moche
honour At London the xi day of Nouember.

[I] do also hertelie thanke your lordsship for your grete
chere made to my seruaunte [Will]yam Johnson and to this
gentilman straungier for whom I do wryte vnto your lordeship
at this tyme by myn other letteres. And for all other your
lordshippes gentilnes I do most hertelie thanke you trusting
if I lyue to requyte the same if I can.

Your lordshyppis assuryd Freend

THOMAS CRUMWELL.

Add. To the right honourable and his singuler good
lorde the lorde vicount Lisle deputie to the kinges highnes
of his towne and marcheis of Calays.

Endd. M. Cromwell the xi^{th} of novembr

## 61. CROMWELL TO THE ABBOT OF NETLEY.

R. O. Cal. vi. 1502.　Dec. 6 ⟨1533⟩.

Desires him to grant his friend John Cooke a new lease for sixty years of
　Roydon farm near Southampton, as it lies by the sea and is con-
　venient for Cooke in his office of the Admiralty there.

In my right hartie maner I commende me vnto your good
lordship. And where as my frynd John Cooke the kinges graces
seruaunt berer herof hath and holdeth a Ferme of yours
callid Roydon by lesse wherof the yeres in the same be
almost expyred And forasmoche as your said ferme lieth

nygh the see syde necessaryly for my saide frynd to serue the
king*es* highnes in his office of the admyraltie in those parties
I hartely desyre you at the contemplacion of thies my *lette*res
that ye will graunte vnto the saide John Coke a newe lesse
of the saide ferme vnder your Conventuall Seale for terme of
lx yeres paying vnto you and y*our* Successours the accus-
tumable rent therof.   And for your towardnes herin I shalbe
glad to requyte the same to your good contentacion And
farther I perceyve by the reporte of the same Cooke that ye
have shewed vnto hym and other that hathe byn w*ith* hym to
do the king*es* highnes s*er*uice at the See muche Jentylnes and
lib*er*alitie, for the whiche ye have deserved the king*es* right
harty thank*es*.   And therfore I for my parte hartylye thanke
you   And of your conformable mynde herin I pray you to
adu*er*tise me in wrytyng by this berer.   And thus fare ye
hartylye welle.   At london the vi^th day of December.

Y*our* lordshyppis Freend.

THOMAS CRUMWELL.

*Add.* To the reu*er*end father in god the Abbot of letley [1]
be this youen.

## 62.  CROMWELL TO ⟨THE OFFICERS OF THE CUSTOMS⟩.

### R. O. Cal. vi. 1625 (iii).  ⟨1533.⟩

The King wishes Robert Bonvell, merchant of Paris, to come to England
with certain jewels, of which he desires a special account to be kept,
for the payment of the duty.

In my Right harty manner I Co*m*mend me vnto you
Adu*er*tis[ing] the Same that the king*es* pleasure is that
Robert Bonvell m*er*cha*u*nt of parys sholde Repayre into this
Royalme Towarde*s* his highnes w*ith* c*er*teyn Juell*es* wherfore
his speciall Co*m*maundment is that ye seing the same Jewell*es*
do make Therof a Specyall note by byll*es* Indentyd betwyxt
you and the Seid m*er*chaunt mensyonyng eu*er*y p*ar*cell therof
and what the Custom therof maye Amounte vnto, not chargyng
hym For any Custom or other Charge due vnto his highnes
For the same for hys grac*es* pleasure ys that if he do sell any
w*ith*in this Royalm that he shall therfore paye Custom as
Reason is and for that he Cannot Sell here to carry A waye
w*ith* hym A gayne w*ith*oute paye*n*g therfore any Custom or
other dut*es* Wherfore I requyre you takyng Surety in case
he do make Sale to paye the Custom accordyngly That ye do
p*er*mytt & Suffer the same m*er*cha*u*nt w*ith* the Same

[1] *sic,* see Notes.

Juell*es* to discha*r*ge And vnlade the Same Accordyng to the Effec*tes* hereof

The coppy of Mr. Crumwell*es* *lette*re Sygned w*i*[t*h*] hys hand.

### 63. DRAFTS OF PORTIONS OF CROMWELL'S LETTERS.

R. O. Cal. vi. 1625 (i). ⟨1533.⟩

Thanks the recipient for sending news. Has presented his letters to the Duke of Norfolk as he desired.

After most hertye Salutacyons this shalbe ⟨to⟩ thanke yow of y*our* exceding louyng kyndnes shewyd in the dylygent wryting to me of y*our* newse and according to y*our* request I presentyd y*our* *lette*res vnto my lorde of Norffolk*es* grace who I assure yow ys singuler good lorde vnto yow and wher ye wryt in y*our* Fyrst le*tte*res . . .

Memorandum concerning the resignation of the chantry of Barking Church, in Essex.

M*d* that maister Kendall Chauntrye preeste of the Chauntrye Foundyd in Barkyng Churche may optayne my lorde of londons Fauo*ur* ⟨in⟩ the resignacyon of the sayd Chauntrye vnto S*ir* Willi*am* Cowplaunde my freind.

End of a letter, urging care and perseverance in reporting important matters, and promising favour.

. . . thus Fare ye hertelye well trusting that ye will p*er*seue*re* as ye haue bego*nn* I meane so Freindlye and secretlye as thes thing*es* that shall passe betwene vs may be p*ro*ffytable to vs bothe so that y*our* wryting matyers of grauytie & Importaunce wherin maye be persayued good will myxyd w*ith* wisdom and trowthe I then [1] may haue Corage as an entyre frende [2] to p*ro*secute For y*our* forderaunce & aduauncement with recuperacyon of that which I am sure ye most desyre which as I shall See opportunyte I will not undowtydlye forget and ons agayn Fare well [3] daylye lokyng For answer

### 64. ⟨CROMWELL⟩ TO CHRISTOPHER MONT.

R. O. Cal. vi. 1374. ⟨1533.⟩

Encloses two letters from the King to the Dukes of Bavaria and Landgrave of Hesse, with copies. Urges Mont to discover the state of feeling in the Empire. Sends a bill of exchange for £30.

Felowe Cristofer I co*m*mende me vnto you And albeit sythen your departure ye haue not receyued any *lette*res or instructions from the king*es* maiestee concerning the execucion

---

[1] *c.o.* be the bolder, must ned*es* be co*m*pellyd  [2] *c. o.* the more boldlye  [3] *c. o.* praying

of suche his gracious affayrees as his highnes incommended
to you at your departure Yet thinke ye not that your industrie labour travayle and diligence Vsed aswell in the setting
fourth of his graces busynes, Whereof ye were sufficiently
instructed at your saide departure as also in your diligent
wrytyng often and Frequent aduertisementes is put in any
oblyuyon or forgotten But for the same his maiestee hathe
commaunded me to gyve vnto you his graces right hertie
thankes. And in this packet ye shall receyue two Letteres
addressed from the kinges maiestee vnto the Dukes of Bauarie
and the Landegraue van Hesse, which his highnes willeth you
to delyuer accordingly. the copies of whiche letteres (to
th'intent ye shalbe the more rype to answer if any thing
shalbe obiected to you by the saide prynce) I haue sent you
hereinclosed. Not doubting in your dexterytee good polycie
and wisedom to propone and set fourth the effectes of the
same, as shall apperteyne. And forasmoche as here hathe
ben the Secretarye of the duke of Bauarie who is named
Mr. Hubertus Thomas by whom the kinges highnes hathe
knowen and perceyued moche of the mynde and intent of the
same Duke, ye shall not moche nede to travayle or enbusie
yourself to procure answer other then of their owne mocyons
they shall declare vnto you, But contynuallie indeauour
your self with all diligent Circumspection to explore enserche
and knowe the state of the hole countrey of Germany and of
their myndes intentes and inclynacions towardes the kinges
highnes and this realme. And that also ye do by all the
good meanes and polycies that ye can explore and enserche
to knowe the myndes and intentes of the prynces of Germany
and of the Germaynes how they be inclyned aswell towardes
themperour as the king of Romaynes. Being contynuallie
vigilant and diligent in wryting to the kynges maiestee of
all thinges and occurrauntes then according to his gracious
trust and expectacion And because I wolde not haue you
to lacke money ye shall receyue herewith a bill of exchaunge
for the some of xxx li.

*Endd.* A copy of a lettere to Cristofer Mount.

### 65. ⟨CROMWELL⟩ TO HENRY VIII.

R. O. Cal. vi. 1369. ⟨1533.⟩

Sends news about the Nun, and proposes to apprehend two friars who
have come into the realm with mischievous intent. Sends a receipt
for 24,000 cr., the residue of the Emperor's debt, for the King to sign.

Pleasythit your Royall magestye to be aduertysyd how
that reparyng homwardes oone of my lorde chauncelers

*seruaunttes* met wit*h* me and delyue*r*id me yo*ur* warraunt*tes*
Signyd wit*h* the hande of the prynces dowager which warrauntt
I do send to yo*ur* grace herin Inclosyd what yo*ur* plesure
shalbe to haue done therin being ons known I shall right
gladlye acco*m*plyshe I haue also Sythyn my repayre to
london spokyn wit*h* Freer Lawraunce who hathe Sethens his
Repayre to london herde dyuers thing*es* touching the holye
mayde which he wyll declare to yo*ur* hygnes and to non other
and he Shewyth me also that that[1] therbe ij° strange Freers of
the order of obs*er*uant*tes* latelye repayryd into this Realme
which ij° Freers haue exploryd here For all suche bok*es*
centencys and determynacyons as hathe passyd touching
yo*ur* hygnes Matrymonye, which they Intend wit*h* other
pryvey practysys to Convey wit*h* them, to Freer Petow who as
I am Credyblye Informyd Sent them into this yo*ur* Realme[2]
the sayd ij° Freers as I am acertaynyd haue browght wit*h*
them pryuy le*tte*res to dyuers and now bene gone to the
sayd[3] dowager. in my poore oppynyon it shalbe right well done
that thaye might be sent For by Som*e* trustye p*er*son howbeit
yt were best that theye Fyrste sholde be sufferyd to speke
wit*h* her and suche other of hers as woolde p*er*aduenture
delyu*er* to them anything wherby theyr Ferther practysys
myght be p*er*sayuyd and so thayr Cankeryd Intent*tes* myght
be therbye dyscyfferyd. I am also Infformyd that there ys
A m*er*chant of london whiche dothe practyse wit*h* them in
thes p*re*mys*ses* I shall goo veray nere to haue knowlage
therein yf it be trew he ys worthye to Suffer to make other
beware in tyme he ys of good Substaunce. I wooll thys daye
goo abowt to know the trowthe, thes thing*es* woold be met
wit*h* all in tyme and the sonner the better. I trust yo*ur*
highnes wyll by this berer adu*er*tyse me in wrytyng what
shalbe yo*ur* plesure touching as well the sayd Falls Freers
as also towching of the sayd dowager's warrant*tes*. I haue
also Sent to yo*ur* grace on*e* acquytance to be assigned for
the xxiiij*ti* thousande Crowns dew to your highnes for the
resedew of the emperowrs dett and also A warrant to yo*ur*
chanceler For the Sealyng of the same which warrantt and
acquyt*au*nce it may please yo*ur* magestye to assigne and to
send the same by this berer to the Intent Robert Fowler may
be depechyd. The rest of the acquyt*au*nces for yo*ur* ordynarye
pencyon and Sale ben allredye Signed and Sealyd. and this
the Hollye trynyte to whom I shall contenewallye praye to
p*re*serue yo*ur* highnes in long lyff and most p*ro*sperous helthe

---

[1] *sic.*
[2] *c. o.* I trust to get owt the Roote of his practyse
[3] *c. o.* prynces

and send the same the vyctorye with honour over all your Enemyes.

*Endd.* ij mynutes of my Masters letters with my lord chancelours.

## 66. CROMWELL TO ⟨CRANMER⟩.

B. M. Harl. MSS. 6148, f. 81 ; Cal. vii. 19. Jan. 5 ⟨1534⟩.

The King desires Cranmer to send to him Mr. Heath, whom his highness wishes to employ as ambassador to the German princes.

### By master Crumwell

After my moste humble commendacions yt may please your grace to be aduertised that the kynges highnes hath comanded me to write vnto your grace Requiryng the same with all conveniente celeritie to send vp hither Mr. heth, whome for his Lerning, good gravitie and circumspect[i]on the kynges highnes entendeth to send into the parties of Garmany in Ambassade to treate ther with the princes of Germany, as well in the kynges great cause of Matrymony As in other causes perteynyng to the Welth of this Realme And forasmoche as your grace knoweth the grounde, veray iustnes, and equitie of the kynges said cause, his Highnes requereth you to instructe the said Mr Hethe in the same as he may be Ryppe and perfite in the knowlege of the holle circumstaunces of the same And that for lake of inst[r]uction when tyme shall com to propone the matier it Appere not hym to be vnperfaite and remysse to do suche seruice vnto the kynges Maiestie in that behalf as shalbe to his gracious truste and expectacion which his highnes nothyng at all doubtith. Howbeit your graces aduertisement and good instruction arrected vnto the said Maister Heth shall vndoubtedly make hym more rype and perfite in the premisses to do that thing that may be moche to your honour, his prayse and merite As knoweth our Lorde, who send your grace Long Lyf and good helth at London the v. daye of January.

The kynges highnes also intendeth to practise certeyn thynges in the said parties of Germany, concernyng the Auctoryte of the Bisshop of Rome.

Your gracys Bedisman

THOMAS CRUMWELL.

## 67. ⟨CROMWELL⟩ TO HENRY VIII.

R. O. Cal. vii. 73.    January ⟨1534⟩.

Reports the passage in the Commons of the Act forbidding any man to
keep more than 2000 sheep, and requiring every farmer to put one-
eighth of his land in tillage.   If the Bill passes the Lords also it will
be the most beneficial thing done 'sythyn Brewtyse tyme.'

Pleasythyt your most Royall Mageste to be aduertysyd
how that according to your most highe pleasure and commaundement I haue made serche for suche patenttes and
grauntys as your highnes and also the most Famous kyng
your father whos Sowle our lorde pardon haue grauntyd
vnto sir Rychard Weston knyght your vndertesawrer of
your exchequer and the same haue sent to your highnes herin
closyd yt may also please your most Royall Mageste to
knowe how that yesterdaye ther passyd your Commons a byll
that no person within this your Realme shall herafter kepe
and Noryshe aboue the Nombre of twoo thousand shepe and
also that the eight parte of euerye mans lande being a Fer-
mour shall for euer herafter be put in tyllage yerlye which
byll yf by the gret wysdom vertuew goodnes and zerale[1]
that your highnes beryth towardes this your Realme might
haue good Successe and take good effect Amongyst your lordes
aboue I doo Coniecture and Suppose in my pore Symple and
vnworthye Judgement that your highnes shall do the most
noble proffyttable and most benefycyall thing that euer was
done to the Commone welthe of this your Realme and shall
therby Increase suche welthe in the same amongyst the gret
Nombre & multytude for your most louyng and obedye[nt]
Subiectys as neuer was Seane in this Realme Sythen Brewtyse
tyme most humblye prostrate at the Fete of your Magnify-
cence beseche your highnes to pardon my boldnes ⟨in⟩ this
wrytyng to your grace which onlye procedythe for the trowthe
dewtye allegaunce and loue I doo bere to your mageste and
the Common welth of this your Realme as our lorde knowyth
vnto whom I shall as I am most bounden Incessantlye praye
for the contenewans & prosperous conseruacyon of your most
excellent most Royall and Imperyall estate long to Indure

## 68. ⟨CROMWELL⟩ TO ⟨FISHER⟩.

B. M. Cleop. E. iv, f. 101 ; Cal. vii. 238.   ⟨Feb. 1534.⟩

Reproves him at length for his communications with the Nun of Kent,
and replies to seven reasons given by Fisher for not reporting her
revelations to the King.   Advises him to lay aside excuses, and beg
the King's mercy.

My lorde in my right hertie wise I commende me to your
lordship doing you to vnderstand that I haue receyued your

---

[1] *sic.*

letteres dated at Rochester the xviij^{th} of this moneth. In whiche ye declare what craft and cunnyng ye haue to persuade and to set a good countenaunce vpon an yl mater. Drawing som scriptures to your purpose whiche wel weyed acording to the places whereof they be taken. make not so muche for your purpose as ye allege thaim for. And where in the first lefe of your letters ye write that ye doubt nothing neither before god, nor befor the worlde if nede shal that require: so to declare yourself. whatsoeuer hath been said of you. that ye haue not deserued suche hevy wordes or terrible thretes as hath been sent from me vnto you by your brother [1].

How ye can declare your self affore god and the world when nede shal require I can not tell, but I think verely that your declaration made by thes letteres is far insufficient to prove that ye haue deserued no hevy wordes in this behalf and to sey playnly I sent you no hevy wordes but wordes of great comfort wylling your brother to shewe you how benigne and merciful the prince was. And that I thoug[ht] it expedient for you to write vnto his highnes and to recognise your offence and desire his pardon, whiche his grace wold not denye you now in your aige and sikkenes. Whiche my counsel I wold ye had folowed, rather than to haue writen thes letteres to me excusing your self as thoughe there were no maner of defaute in you. But my lord if it were in an other mannys caas than your owne and out of the mater whiche ye fauor I doubt not but that ye wold think him that shuld haue doen as ye have doen non only worthy hevy wordes but also hevy dedys. For where ye labor to excuse your self of your hering believing and conceling of the nunnys fals and faynid reuelations, and of your manyfold sending of your chapley[n] vnto her, by a certeyn intent whiche ye pretende yourself to haue had, to knowe by commonyng with her or by sending your chapellaine to her, whether her reuelations were of god or no. alleging diuerse scriptures. that ye were bound to prove thaim, and not to reiecte thaim affore they were proued My Lord whether ye haue vsed a due meane to trie her and her reuelations, or no. It appereth by the processe of your owne letteres. For where ye write that ye had conceyuid a greate opinion of the holines of the woman for many considerations rehersed in your letteres comprised in vi articles, whereof the first is grownde vpon the brute and fame of her, the secunde vpon her entreng into religion after her traunses and disfiguration, the third vpon rehersall that

---

[1] c. o. a marginal comment as follows: I began to marke the notable poinctes of his letteres

her gostly father being lerned and religious shuld testifie that
she was a maide of greate holines.   The fourth vpon the
report that diuerse other vertuose prestes men of good lernyng
and reputation, shuld so testifie of her, with whiche gostly
father and preestes ye never spake as ye confesse in your
letters.   The fyveth vpon the prayse of my late lord of
Canterbury, which shewed you (as ye write) that she had
many greate visions the sixt vpon this saing of the prophete
Amos, Non faciet dominus deus verbum, nisi reuelauerit
secretum suum ad seruos suos prophetas by whiche considerations ye were induced to the desire to know the very
certente of this mater, whether the reuelations whiche were
pretended to be shewed to her from god were true reuelations
or nott?   your lordship in al the sengle[1] of your letteres shewe
not that ye made no ferther trial vpo[n] the trueth of her and
her reuelation, but only in commonyng with her and sending
your chapellaine to her, with Idle questions as of the thre
mary magdalens. by whiche your commony[ng] and sending,
ye tried out nothing of her falshed, nouther (as it is credibly
supposed) entended to do, as ye myght haue doen many
weyes more easely than with commonyng with her or sending
to her ; for litel credens was to be gyven to her affirmyng her
owne fayned reuelations to be from god.

For if credence shuld be gyven to euery suche lewd person
as wold affirme himself to haue reuelations from god what
redyer wey were there to subuert al common we[l]thes and
good orders in the worlde.

Verily my lord if ye had entended to trie out the trueth of
her and of her reuelations ye wold haue taken an other wey
with you, first ye wold not haue been contented with the
vayne voyces of the peple making brutes of her traunses
& disfiguration But like a wise discrete and circumspect
prelate ye shuld haue examined (as other haue) suche sad
and credible persons as were present att her traunses &
disfigurationes, not one or two, but a good number by whoes
testimony ye shuld haue proued whether the brutes of her
traunces and disfigurations were true or not And likewise
ye shuld haue tried by what craft and persuasion she was
made a religious woman.   And if ye had been so desirous as
ye pretende to enquire out the trueth or falshed of this woman
and of her reuelations, it is to be supposed ye wold haue
spoken with her good religious and wel lerned gostly father
(as ye cal him) or this tyme : and also with the vertuose, and
wel lerned preestes (as they were estemed) of whoes reaportes

[1] *sic.*

B b

ye were informed by thaim whiche herd thaim speke[1] ye
wold also haue been mynded to se the booke of her revelations
whiche was offerd you. of whiche ye myght haue had more
trial of her and of her reuelations, than a hundred communications with her, or of as many sendings of your chapellen
vnto her.   As for the late lord of Cauntreburys seying vnto
you that she had many greate visions, it ought to move you
never a deale to gyve credence vnto her or her reuelations,
For the said lord knew no more certente of her or of her
reuelations than ye dyd by her owne reaport.   And as
towching the saing of Amos the prophete, I thinke veryly
the same moved you but a litell to herkyn vnto her, for sythe
the consummation and thende of thold testament and sythens
the passion of Christ god hathe doen many greate and notable
thinges in the worl[d]e, whereof he shewed no thing to his
prophetes that hath commen to the knowlege of men.   My
lord all thes thinges moved you not to gyve credence vnto
her, but only the very mater whereupon she made her fals
proficyes to whiche mater ye were so affected (as ye be noted
to be on al maters whiche ye enter ons into) that nothing
could com amysse that made for that purpose
     And here I appelle your conscience and instantly desire
you to aunswer.   Whether if she had shewed you as many
reuelationsf or the confirmation of the kinges graces marriage
whiche he now enjoyeth as she did to the contrary, ye wold
haue gyven as muche credence to her as ye haue doen, and
wold haue let the trial of her and of her reuelations to ouer-
passe thes many yeres, where ye dwelt not from her but
xx mylys, in the same shire, where her traunses and dis-
figuringes and prophecyes in her traunses were surmised and
countrefeyd.   And if percaas ye wol sey (as it ⟨is⟩ not
vnlike but ye wol sey mynded as ye were wont to be) that
the maters be not like, for the Law of god in your opinion
standeth with the one and not with thother.   Suerly my lord
I suppose this had been no greate cause more to reiect the
one than thother for ye know by histories of the bible that
god may by his reuelation dispense with his owne Law, as
with the[2] Israelites spoyling the egiptians and with Jacob to
haue iiij wifes, and suche other[3].
     Think you my lord that any indifferent man considering
the qualite of the mater and your affeccion, and also the
negligent passing over of suche lawful trialles as ye myght

[1] c. o. with whom ye never spake
as in your lettres [ye say]
[2] c. o. Egiptians
[3] c. o. And suerly my lord what

soeuer ye sey or write for yourself,
the begynning of your letters for
your . . . g

haue had of the said nunne and her reuelations, is so dull,
that can not perceyue and discerne, that your commonyng
and often sending to the said nun was rather to here and
know more of her reuelations, than to trie out the trueth or
falshed of thes same    And in this behalf I suppose it wol be
hard for you to purge yourself bifore god or the worle, but
that ye haue been in greate defaut hering beleuyng and conceling suche thinges as tended to the destruction of the prince
And that her reuelations were bent and purposed to that
ende . it hathe been duely proued, affore as greate assembly
and counsel of the lordes of this realme as hath been seen
many yeres heretofore out of a parliament.    And what the
said lordes demed thaim worthy to suffer, whiche had beleued
and conceled thees fals reuelations be more terrible than any
thretes spoken by me to your brother

And where ye go abought to defende that ye be not to be
blamed for conceling her reuelations concernyng the kinges
grace, bicause ye thought it not necessary to reherse thaim
to his highnes, for vij causes folowing in your letteres affore
I shewe you my mynde concernyng thees causes, I suppose
that albeit ye percaas thought it not necessary to be shewed
to the prince by you . yet that your thinking shal not be
your triall, but the Law must diffine whether ye owghted to
vtter it or not.

And as to the first of said vii causes.    Albeit[1] she told
youe that she had shewed her reuelations concernyng the
kinges grace to the king herself, yet her seyng or others discharged not you but that ye were bound by your fidelite to
shewe to the kinges grace . that thing whiche semed to concerne his grace and his reigne so nyghly . for how knew you
that she[2] shewed thes reuelations to the kinges grace but by her
owne seyng, to whiche ye shuld haue gyven no suche credence
as to forebere the utterance of so greate maters concernyng
a kinges welth And why shuld you so sinisterly iudge the
prince that if ye had shewed thees same vnto him, he wold
haue thought that ye had brought that tale vnto him more
for the strenghing and confirmation of your opinion then for
any other thing els. Veryly my lord what so euer your
iudgement bee . I se dayly suche benignite and excellent
humanite in his grace that I doubt not but his highnes . wold
haue accepted it in good part if ye had shewed the same reuelations vnto him as ye were bounden to do by your fidelite.

To the secunde cause.    Albeit she shewed you not that
any prince or other temporal lord shuld put the kinges grace

---

[1] c. o. it was told or els          [2] c. o. or any other

in dainger of his crowne yet there were weyes Inoughe, by whiche her said reuelations myght haue put the kinges grace in dainger, as the foresaid counsel of lordes . haue substancially and duely considered And therefor Albeit she shewed you not the meanes whereby the daynger shuld ensue to the kinges [grace] yet . ye were neverthelesse bounden to shewe him of the dainger.

To the third. Think you my lord, that if any person wold com vnto you and shewe youe that the kinges destruction were conspired against a certen tyme, and wold ferther shewe you, that he were sent from his maister to shewe the same to the king and wol sey ferther vnto [you] that he wold go streyct to the king, were it not yet your duety to certifie the kinges grace of the relation, but also to inquire whether the said person had doen his foresaid messaige or no, yes verely. And so were ye bound, thoughe the nunne shewed youe, it was her messaige from god to be declared by her to the kinges grace.

To the iiii[th] here ye translate the temporal duety that ye owe to your prince, to the spiritual duety of suche as be bounde to declare the worde of god to the peple, and to shewe vnto them the perill and punisshement of syn in an other worlde, the concelement whereof perteyneth to the iudgement of god, but the concelement of this mater perteyneth to other iudges of this realme.

To the v[th] ther could no blame be arrested to you if ye had shewed the nunnys reuelations to the kinges grace, albeit they were afterward found fals for no man owght to be blamed doing his duety And if a man wold shewe you secretly that there were a greate mischief entended . against the prince, were ye to be blamed if ye shewed him of it, albeit it were a fayned tale, and the said mischief were never Imagined.

To the sixt . concernyng an Imagination of master Pacy. It was knowen that he was beside himself, and therefore they were not blamed that made no report thereof, but it was not lik in this caas For ye toke not this nunne for a mad woman, for if ye had ye wold not haue gyven vnto her so greate credence as ye dyd.

To the final and vii[th] cause where ye lay [1] vnto the charge of our soueraine, that he hath vnkyndly entreacted you . with grevous wordes and terrible letters for shewing his grace trowthe in his greate mater, whereby ye were discomforted to shewe vnto him the nunnys reuelations. I beleue that I know the kinges goodnes and natural gentilnes so well, that his grace wold not so vnkyndly handle you, as you vnkyndly write of him, onles ye gave him other causes than be ex-

<hr/>

[1] c. o. muche

pressed in your letters. And what so euer the kinges grace hath sayed or writen vnto you heretofore, yet that notwith-stonden, ye were neuerthelesse bounden to vtter to him thees pernicious reuelations.

Finally Where ye desire for the passion of christ that ye be no more quykkened in this mater for if ye be put to that straite ye wyl not lose your soule, but ye wyl speke as your conscience ledeth you with many moo wordes of greate curraige. My lord if ye had taken my counsel sent vnto you by your brother and folowed the same, submitting yourself by your letters to the kinges grace for your offenses in this behalf, I wold haue trusted that ye shuld neuer be quykkened in this mater more. But now where ye take vpon you to defende the hole mater as ye were in no default. I cannot so far promise you[1]. And suerly my lord if the mater com to triall : your owne confession in thes letteres besides the wittnes whiche be against you wolbe sufficient to condemne you Wherefor my lord I wol eftsones aduise you that laying apart al suche excuses as ye haue alleged in your letters whiche in myn opinion be of smal effect as I haue declared ye beseche the kinges grace by your letters to be your graciou[s] lord, and to remitte vnto you your negligence ouersight and offence committed against his his[2] highnes in this behalf And I dare vndertake that his highenes shal benignely accepte you into his gracious fauor, al maters of displeasire past affore this tyme forgoten and forgyven.

[3]As towching the speking of your conscience, it is thought that ye haue writen and haue spoken as muche as ye can . and . many thinges (as som right probably beleaue) against your owne conscience. And men report that at the Last conuocation ye spake many thinges whiche ye could not wel defende. And therefor it is not greatly ferede what ye can sey or write in that mater. howsoeuer ye be quykkened or strayted And if ye had taken *etc.*

### 69. ⟨CROMWELL⟩ TO ⟨THE SHERIFF OF YORKSHIRE⟩.

R. O. Cal. vii. 383.   Mar. 28 ⟨1534⟩.

In order to prevent any infringement of the King's rights in the lands of Sir John Dunham, lately deceased, the council considers it expedient that those persons who dwell near the lands should be impanelled to inquire for the King.

Maister Sheryff I commend me vnto yow and being Infformyd of the dethe of syr Jhon Dunham Knyghte

---

[1] *c. o.* albeit I wol speke for
[2] *sic.*
[3] The last paragraph is written along the margin.

whyche in his lyffe helde of the king*es* grace certayne land*es*
and tenement*es* in the County of Yorke In Capite.  And by
cause that the kyng*es* righte shall not be hydde ne cloked
It is therfor considered by the kyng*es* most honorable
counsell that suche persons who hath the most knowlege
sufficient of freeholde and dwellys next vnto the Land*es* of
the saied syr John Donham be impanelled to inquyre for
the kyng*es* grace the namys of whom herein enclosyd I do
send yow who are extemyd and reputed to be men of good
worship and conscience as I am credably enformed Aduer-
tysyng yow that vpon a precept to yow dyrected by the
kyng*es* excheto*ur* ye do retourne a suffycient Inquest of
the same persons to inquyre for the kyng*es* grace of the
tenure of the saied land*es*.  And in yo*ur* so doyng ye shall
do the king*es* grace a righte acceptable seruyce to his
contentatyon  And so fare ye well  from London the xxviii^ti
daye of march.

*Endd.* mynute of a *lette*re.

## 70. Cromwell to Gardiner.

B. M. Add. MSS. 25,114, f. 348; Cal. vii. 535.  Apr. 24 〈1534〉.

Requests for a friend the advowson of the parsonage of St. John's of Sher-
borne, in Hampshire, the yearly value of which is 10 or 11 pounds.

My Lord in my right hertie wise I co*m*mende me to you.
And as I haue been, and wolbe glad and redy, to do you
suche pleasir*e* as I myght or may. so I desire you to graunt
vnto me to the behoue of a dere frende of myne. the
aduocation of the p*ar*sonaige of S. Jhons of [Shire]borne in
hampshir*e* being of yo*ur* gift . whiche is of the yerely value
of x or xj^li and not aboue (as I am informed) by the gyft
whereof ye shal shewe vnto me a right acceptable pleasir*e* .
whiche I wol not forgete when I may in reco*m*pense thereof .
do the thing that may be to your co*n*tentation.  And of
yo*ur* beniuolent mynd in this behalf, I desire you not only
to certifie me by yo*ur* next w*r*iting but also to direct yo*ur*
letters to yo*ur* vicar gen*er*all and to the prio*ur* and co*n*uent
of yo*ur* churche . for thexpedition thereof to be made in due
forme, and to be deliu*er*ed vnto me wit*h* suche spede as
shall pleace you to co*m*maunde thaim . the xxiiij^th day of
Aprile.

Yo*ur* lordshippis assuryd free*n*d

Thomas Crumwell.

*Add.* To my verey loving Lord my lord of wynchester.
*Edd.* the xxiiij of Ap*ri*l  Mr. Secretary

## 71. ⟨CROMWELL⟩ TO ⟨CRANMER⟩.

### R. O. Cal. vii. 500. ⟨Apr. 1534.⟩

The King considers it expedient that More and Fisher be compelled to swear to the preamble of the Act of Succession as well as to the Act itself: otherwise it might be taken as a confirmation of the authority of the Bishop of Rome.

My Lorde after myne humble commendacions it may please your grace to be aduertesed that I haue receyued your letteres and shewed the same to the kinges highnes who perceyuing your mynde and opynyon is that it were good that the bisshop of Rochester and Mr. More should be sworn to the acte of the kinges succession and not to the preamble of the same, thinketh that if their othe should be so taken it were an occasion to all men to refuse the hole or at the lest the lyke.　For in case they be sworn to the succession and not to the preamble it is to be thought that it might be taken not onelie as a confirmacion of the Bisshop of Rome his auctoryte but also as a reprobacion of the kinges second mariage wherefore to thintent that no such thinges should be brought into the heddes of the people by the ensample of the saide Bisshop of Rochester and Mr. More the kinges highnes in no wise willeth but that they shalbe sworn aswell to the preamble as to the acte of Succession[1] in no maner of wyse Wherfore his grace specyallye trustyth that ye wyll in no wyse Suppose attempt or move hym to the Contrarye For as hys grace Suppossyth that that maner of Sweryng yf yt sholde be sufferyd myght be an vtter destruccyon to his hole Cause and Also to the effecte of the law made For the same

*Endd. m*ynute.

## 72. CROMWELL TO THE PRIOR AND CONVENT OF WENLOCK.

### R. O. Cal. vii. 593. May 1 ⟨1534⟩.

Desires them to grant to Thomas Lowley the lease of Okinbold farm, in Shropshire, at the rent which his father paid.

In myn harty maner I commende me unto youe　And wheras ye haue nowe in your handes and disposicion again, the ferme of Oxinbold belonging to that Monastery.　These shalbe to desire and hartely pray youe, for my sake to graunte a sufficient lease therof to my Freende Thomas Lowleye

---

[1] *c. o.* For the conducing whereof to effecte the kinges highnes hath specyall trust and expectacion in your graces approved wisedom and dexteryte and thus the holie trynyte . . .

ser*ua*unt to Mr. Norreys vnder yo*ur* convent seale for the
terme of xl yeres yelding and payeng vnto yow suche rent for
the same, as his father whiche was fermo*ur* therof hertofore
paid vnto your mon*astery* at that tyme that he had it in ferme.
Desiring you in noo wise to alienate it to any man but only to
this tyl ye shal knowe further, in case ye shal not condescende
to this my request, and to adu*er*tise me by yo*ur* Le*tt*eres w*it*h
spede of yo*ur* proceding in this Behaulf  And thus Fare you
hartely well  From Stepnaye the first daye of Maye

Your Freend Thomas Crumwell.

*Add.*  To my loving freendes the prior  and Convent of
the Mon*astery* of Wenlok.

### 73. Cromwell to Dr. Sampson.

R. O. Cal. vii. 655.  May 13 〈1534〉.

Requires him to appoint a bishop to 'execute' at the Court, as the Bishop
of Chester is unable to be present.

Mr. Deane, after my right hertie co*m*mendacions Forasmoche as my lorde of Chester is not onelie destitute of Myter
Crosier and other thing*es* necessarie but also shall to morowe be
enbusied and occupied about*es* other the king*es* affaires I shall
therefore hertelie requyre you to appoynte som other Bisshop
to execute to morowe before the king*es* highnes at the Courte,
till my saide Lorde of Chester shall be better Furnysshed as
app*er*tyneth  Wherein ye shall do him moche pleasure.  And
so Fare ye well.  At Stepney the xiii day of Maye.

Your assuryd Freend

Thomas Crumwell.

*Add.*  To the right wo*r*shipfull Mr. Docto*ur* Sampson dean
of the king*es* chappell be this youen.

### 74. Cromwell to the Senate and Consuls
of Lübeck [1].

B. M. Vit. B. xxi, f. 107 ;  Cal. vii. 707.  May 24, 1534.

On behalf of William Gilbank, whose ship was captured near Sandwich
and taken to Lübeck, with goods worth 53 pounds sterling.

{Henricus Dei gra*ti*a Rex Angliae, et Franciae, fidei
defensor, ac D*omi*n*us* Hiber[niae] . . . Consulibus, et} Senator-

---

[1] This letter was evidently first
written by the King, and later
altered by Cromwell.  The passages
in brackets {...} are scored through
in the original.

{ibus}es Ciuitatis Lubicen*sis etc.* Amici{s} no*s*tri{s} Car*is*-
*s*imi{s} {sal*utem*} plur*i*ma*m* Sal*utem* et Com*men* . . .

Nuper apud {nos} . . . humilite*r* conq[uestus est] . . . s, ac
fidelis {noster potentissimi no*s*t*r*i Regis} eius subditus Willel-
mus gylbanke q*uod* quum superioribus mensibus nauis quaedam cui Hugo ship . . . [prae]erat, ex harmywe Zelandiae vico
hoc {no*s*t*r*um} inclytum Regnum uersus nauigatura soluerat,
ac varij generis merces ad u[alorem] . . . quinquaginta triu*m*
librar*um* sterlingorum in ea onerasset, commercij gra*ti*a
huc aduecturus, accidit, ut dicta nauis iam . . . [n]auiga-
tionis cursu {et no*s*tr*um*} in eiusdem sere*niss*i*mi* D*omini*
no*s*t*r*[i] Regis portu*m* Sandwic*ensem* ferme ingressa, a ve*s*t*r*a
Classe quae belli praetextu, quod aduersus hollandos . . . bat,
per hoc {nostrum} mare excurrebat capta, et una cum dicti
{no*s*t*r*i subditi} Wille*l*mi bonis, ac mercibus in ciuitate*m* istam
ve*s*t*r*am . . . abducta fuit; erit longe quidem praeter vetere*m*
mutuamq*ue* {no*s*tram} amicitiam cum Sere*niss*i*m*a hac Regia
M*aies*ta*t*e, et ingenti {eiusdem subditi no*s*tri Wille*l*mi eius sub-
di[ti]} prefati sui subditi detrimento, id q[u]od quum inscijs
vobis a ve*s*t*r*ae classis praefectis {commissum fuerit, volui-
mus} eadem Regia M*aies*tas co*m*missu*m* fuisse plane credat,
iussit ut suo no*m*i*n*e no*s*t*r*is his *litte*ris hanc causam vobis
impre*s*e*n*tia commendaremus: Vos igitur quos p*r*o intimis
amici[s] habet impense rogat, ut pro vest[ro] erga iustas quas-
q*ue* causas studio, pro mutuaq*ue* {no*s*t*r*a} secum coniunctione,
ve*s*t*r*a authoritate efficere velitis q*uod* praedicta bona sic
ablat[a] eidem {no*s*t*r*o subdito} Wille*l*mo uel eius procuratori
in integrum restitua*n*tur, id quod {ut nobis} ut [e]idem
Regie M*aies*ta*t*i maxime gratum, et iustitiae consentane[um]
erit, ita {nos} ipsam ad parem beneuolentiam erga subditos
ve*s*tros, data occasione, exhibendam propensior ardentiorque
{efficiem[ur]} reddetur. Et bene valete. Ex Regia no*s*t*r*a
Richemondiae Die xxiiij Maij MDXXXIIII.

De nobis ve*r*o possunt ve*s*t*r*ates o*m*nes in iustis suis hic
occurrentib*us* negocijs ap*u*d ha*n*[c] Regia*m* M*aies*ta*t*em omne
humanitatis officiu*m* sibi polliceri quod suo loco et t*em*pore
cumulate p*r*aestabim[u]s

Vester bonus amicus

THOMAS CRUMWELL

*Add.* Mag*n*i*f*icis D*om*i*n*is Consulibus, et Senatoribus Ciuitatis Lubicen*sis etc.* Amicis no*s*t*r*is Car*iss*imis.

## 75. CROMWELL TO MR. SAPCOTTES.

R. O. Cal. vii. 790.  June 4 ⟨1534⟩.

Desires him to repair to London as soon as possible, as he is executor of Edw. Watson, deceased, who was in danger to the King.

Mr. Sapcott*es* I co*m*mende me vnto you. And For as moche as ye were executour and admynistrato*ur* of the good*es* of Edwarde Watson decessed who was in daungier to the king*es* highnes, I shall therefore aduertise and require you that vppon the sight of these my *lette*res for that matier w*ith* other thing*es* that I haue to sey vnto you ye do put yo*ur* self in a redynes to repayre vnto me w*ith* all conuenie*nt* celeryte. And at your co*m*myng ye shall knowe Ferther of the king*es* pleasure. So Fare ye well From my house at Canbery the iiii*th* day of June

Y*our* Freend

THOMAS CRUMWELL.

*Add.* To his louing frend Mr. Henry Sapcott*es* be this youen at Lyncoln.

## 76. CROMWELL TO THE EARL OF SHREWSBURY.

Ellis Letters, 2nd Ser. ii. 135 ; Cal. vii. 973.  July 13 ⟨1534⟩.

Thanks him for his zeal in apprehending a hermit, who has been examined, and is to be tried by the justices of assize, and punished according to the law.

After my right herty commendacions to your Lordship, I have by this bearer your servaunt, bailly of Chesterfeld, receyved your Lettres and the byll therin enclosed concernyng th' Ermyte, the whiche being by me examyned, answered that he could not tell whither he spake ever the same trayterouse words or not. I have caused an Inditement to be drawen therupon whiche your Lordeship shal receyve herwith ; and also I have thought convenient to retorn the said Hermite unto you agayn, there befor the Justices of Assise to be tryed and to th'exemple of all other to be punyshed according to right and the King's lawes. I thank evermor your Lordeship for your good zele, diligence, and dexterate in repressing and apprehending suche perniciouse and detestable felons : and therof shal I not faile to make true raport to his Highnes who I am assure shal tak the sam in most thankfull part. Thus

I beseche our holy Creator to sende you prosperite and long
liffe.  From Cheleshith this xiij^th of July.

Your lordshippis assuryd

THOMAS CRUMWELL.

*Add.* To my very good Lord Therle of Shrewesbury
Lorde Stuarde to the Kings Ma^tie.

### 77. ⟨CROMWELL⟩ TO ——.

R. O. Cal. vii. 990.  July 20 ⟨1534⟩.

Orders him to arrest four murderers from Yorkshire, who first fled into
Scotland, but have now returned to Durham, where they ride about
at their pleasure.

In my Right harty maner I commend me vnto you and
where as I am enfourmed that one percyvall worme, wylliam
Corneforthe John bygott and wylliam dobson lately commytted a detestable mourdour in the Countye of Yorke and
beyng Indyttyd therof thei ther vpon flede into Scottlond
where as thei ther Remayned as yt ys thought tyll now of late,
that thei lyttyll dreadyng god nor the lawes of this Realme
arne comme into the byschopryche of Durham wher as thei
doo Ryde in all places therof at ther pleasures to the greate
boldnes and peryllous example of all other suche [ev]yll dys-
posed personnes.  And therfor my mynd ys that ye with
dylygence do attach or cause the said persons to be Attachyd,
And them to deteyne in pryson vntyll such tyme as thei
schalbe by the order of the lawes acquyted or otherwyse
dyscharged as ye wyll aunswere to the kynges highnes at
your peryll.  Wretyn at my house in london the xx^th day of
July.

### 78. ⟨CROMWELL⟩ TO THE ABBOT OF ⟨ST. AUSTIN'S IN CANTERBURY⟩.

R. O. Cal. vii. 1007.  July 25 ⟨1533 [1]⟩.

Requests him to settle his differences with the bearer, whose father could
have had many offices of the abbot and his predecessor.  As the
bearer has his brothers and sisters to support, the abbot ought to do
as much for him as he would have done for his father. . .

My Lorde Abbot I recommende me vnto you etc. and
where as George Goldwyn the brynger hereof hathe byn
A continuall sutour vnto me A great tyme to haue A Warde
made betwene you and hym [2] I shall hertelye desire & praye
you vppon the sight hereof to take some reasonable waye

---

[1] *sic*, see Notes.
[2] *c. o.* which hath byn a great charge to the parties wherfore

with hym so that I be no longer molestyd by hym and his
co*n*tynuall Sute and whereas his Father myght haue had [1] of
y*our* lordshyp & y*our* predecesso*ur* dyuers offers who alwayes
refused them yet neu*er*theles me thinkyth y*our* lordshyp now
can no lesse doo then to graunte hym so moche in consciens [2] as ye woolde have yovyn his Father For he ys moche [3]
chargyd w*ith* the dett*es* of his Father as he affirmyth and also
w*ith* the Fyndyng of his Brethern and sisterne [4]. Whereffor
in myn oppynyon it shalbe well doon that ye take an ende
w*ith* hym  Yow know his Father dyed in pryson at y*our* Sute
and thus co*m*myttyng this matyer to god & y*our* Conscyens
& thanking yow For my hawke & bydde yow hertelye Fare
well at london the xxv[ti] daye of July

*Endd.* mynute of a *lette*re.

## 79. CROMWELL TO LORD COBHAM.

B. M. Harl. MSS. 283, f. 203 ;  Cal. vii. App. 33.   July 30 ⟨1534⟩.

Directions about the administration of 'the farm of the parsonage.'
Promises to attend to the monks of which Cobham speaks, if he will
send them up.

I commend me vnto y*our* good lordship yn my right harty
maner, Adu*er*tisyng you that I have receyvyd your *lette*res and
the Inventory accordyng to your wrytyng.  And touchyng
the ferme of the parsonage I desire your lordship to cause the
corne and other dutyes to be getherd together, and as for the
rent I will order your lordship therin at our metyng.  And
your Monk*es* of whome ye write if ye send theym hither
I wil be contentyd to co*m*mon w*ith* theym and to do
therin as the case shall requyre.  I pray y*our* lordshyp to
have me co*m*mendyd vnto my good lady in my right harty
maner and so to geve hir thank*es* for the foule that she hathe
sent vnto me.  And thus our lord have you yn his kepyng.  At
Stepenhey the xxx[th] day of Julye.

Your lordshippis assuryd

THOMAS CRUMWELL

*Add.* To my very good lord my lord Cobham this be
delyu*er*yd.

[1] *c. o.* and good
[2] *c. o.* to consider the said offers
vnto his sone
[3] *c. o.* he is greatly charged w*ith*
his Fathers Dett*es* & also w*ith* his
[4] *c. o.* wh*ich* ys a great charge
vnto hym wherfore my Lorde in dis-
chargyng of y*our* consciens I p*ra*y
you at my Desire to yeve vnto hym
a c[li]. whiche youe toke of his Father
And ferder to yeve vnto hym some
other Rewarde hereafter as you
shall thynke in consciens mete for
hym

## 80. Cromwell to the Mayors and Officers of Southampton, Portsmouth, and Poole.

R. O. Cal. vii. 1132.　Sept. 4 ⟨1534⟩.

*Asks assistance for two men who are going into those parts on the King's business.*

I commend me vnto you. ⟨and⟩ Aduertise you that the kinges highnes at this tyme dothe send George Whelpeley and John Brawne about certayne besynes geven vnto theym in charge to be done in those parties, with soche spede and diligence as they convenyently may requyryng you and euery of you to permytt and suffer the same George and John to execute and do in euery thyng, as the kynges grace hath commaundyd theym without any your ympedymentes let or interupcion in and about the same.　And in case any ill disposed persone or persones will disobey or gaynsay the same, I farther requyre you yn the kynges behalf to assiste ayde and counsaill theym in and about thexecucion of their purpose.　As ye will advoyde the kinges high displeasure.　And thus fare ye well.　At london the iiii^{th} day of September.

Your Freend Thomas Crumwell.

*Add.* To the Mayres Sheriffes and Bayliffes Custumers Comptrollers and Serchours within the townes and portes of Suthampton Portesmouthe and Pole and euery of theym and the Crekes belongyng to theym and euery of theym this be youen.

*Endd.* My m^{re}. lettere for George Whelpeley

## 81. Cromwell to Sir Roger Reynolds, Robert Wolf, and John Kytch.

R. O. Cal. vii. 1134.　Sept. 6 ⟨1534⟩.

*The King desires them to repair to Cromwell to answer to the charges made against them.*

I comend me vnto you And these shalbe to aduertise you that the kinges pleasure is that ye ymmediately vppon the sight of these my letteres shall repayre hither to answer vnto suche thinges as then shalbe leyed and obiected to you on the king our saide souereigne lordes behalf.　Fayle ye not thus to do as ye will avoyde ferther perill and inconuenyence.

So Fare ye well From my house at Canbery the vi^{th} day of Septembre.

THOMAS CRUMWELL.

*Add.* To Sir Roger Reynold*es* priest M*aster* of the Hospitall of Saynt Johns in Huntingdon Robert Wolf Baylif there and John Kytche and to eu*ery* of them be this youen.

## 82. CROMWELL TO LORD LISLE AND LORD EDMUND HOWARD.

### R. O. Cal. vii. 1179. Sept. 21, 1534.

The King, hearing that the searchers of Calais are remiss, and permit things to be conveyed out of the realm contrary to law, has appointed Nicholas Caldwell and John Gough to aid them.

In my right herty man*er* I co*m*mende me vnto yo*ur* good Lordshipp*es*. So it is that the King*es* Highenes is certaynly informyd that dyuers and many thing*es* arne dayly conveyd ouit of this realme into the partyes of beyond the sees contrary to the statut*es* and provisions in suche casse ordeinyd and provided. and for as muche as the s*er*chours in the towne and M*ar*chys of Calais arne remysse and negligent in thexamynacion of their office*s* his highenes therfor well considering the same, and also p*er*ceyving that his trusty s*er*vaunt*es* Nicholas Caldwall and John Gowghe byn men of good circumspiccion meate to make s*er*che and fynde owt the same, hathe ordenyd and constitutyd them Joyntly and severallie to be attendant and vigilant abouit the serching of the same w*it*hin the saide toune and m*ar*chys and the havon Longing to the same for this tyme. Wherfor adu*er*tesing yo*ur* Lordshippes of the king*es* ples*ur* therin I requyre you in the king*es* behalff to assist and ayde the same Nicholas & John and eyther of them in execucyon of this the king*es* ples*ur* and co*m*maundement as often and as the casse shall requyre as the king*es* trust is in you. and thus the blyssed trinitie pres*er*ue yo*ur* good Lordshipp*es* at Candbery the xxi of Septembre

thus subscribyd

Yo*ur* Lordshipp*es* assuryd Frynd

THOMAS CROMWELL.

The sup*er*scripcio*n*. To the right hono*ur*able and my Veray good Lord*es* my Lord Lyssle depute of Calas and my Lorde Edmonde Howard Comptroller ther and to eyther of them be this yeven

*Endd.* Copia of Mr. Cromwell*es* L*ette*re for the s*er*che to John Gowghe and N. caldewall 22 Septembre. 1534.

83. CROMWELL TO ⟨THE LORDS OF THE PRIVY COUNCIL⟩.

R. O. (Museum) Cal. vii. 1271.   Oct. 17 ⟨1534⟩.

Asks them to give audience to the bearer, who can tell them much about the evil-disposed person apprehended on Sunday last.   Advises that the said person be not put to death till he has made full confession.

My lordes after my most affectuouse recommendacion, This present berer my lord of Yorkes seruaunt is arryved nowe to me with letteres bothe to me and to the kinges highnes.   I haue remitted hym furthwith to deliver his maiestes letteres.   And because he can fully Instructe your lordships and enfourme you of many thinges I pray you to heare hym fauourably and to geve hym full audience for ye shal here of hym sundry notable thinges and specially ayenst hym that was apprehended on Sondaye last whom I tak to be an veray evill disposed persone and the which if he be examyned according to the said berers relation ye shal knowe thinges gretely to be marked & noted Therfor I beseche you to have this mater recommended And that the said person so apprehended be not put to deth tyll we may knowe the hoole and profound bothom of his cancred hert.   I pray you to sende to me aduertissement howe ye shal fynde hym and knowlege of the veray mater And also of any suche thinges As I can do here, any expedishon for the furtheraunce of any the kinges maters   For I shal spaer no diligence. Thus our blessed creatour have you in his tuition & keping From the Rooles this xviith of Octobre.

Your lordshippis assuryd Freend

THOMAS CRUMWELL.

84. CROMWELL TO LORD LISLE.

R. O. Cal. vii. 1328.   Oct. 29, 1534.

Requests him to examine and reform the 'anoysaunces' made by Sir Robert Wingfield in the Marches of Calais.

In my right harty maner I commend me vnto your good lordship.   And wher as of late the kinges highnes hathe directed his Commyssion vnto your lordship and other for pullyng downe and reformacion of certayne anoysaunces made and done by Sir Robart Wyngfeld within the Marches of Calays, the kinges pleasure is that ye and thother Commyssioners shall circumspectly viewe and ouersee the same.   And that that of necessite ought to be refourmyd for the welthe

strengthe and commodite of the sayd Towne and marches
accordyng as it was thought at my last beyng ther to be
amendyng, and the resydue that ⟨neither⟩ damagithe ne
hurtithe the same Towne to stand still as ye see reasonable
cause after your discresion. and as ye shall seme good. And
thus the blessed Trenyte preserue your lordship At london
the xxix day of October.

Your lordshyppis assuryd Freend

THOMAS CRUMWELL.

*Add.* To the honourable and my veray good Lorde my
lord Vicount Lisle the kynges Depute of Calais be this
youen.

*Endd.* Maister Cromwell the xxix^th of Octobre 1534.

85. CROMWELL TO AUDELEY.

B. M. Vesp. F. xiii, 105 b ; Cal. vii. 1415. Nov. 11 ⟨1534⟩.

Desires him to send back by the bearer a true copy of the proclamation,
which is to be printed by Bartlett the printer to-night.

Aftre my right harty commendacions to your lordship
Forasmoche as it shalbe very necessary to haue some copies
of the proclamacion also printed this night to thintent the
same maye be sent into sundry parties with the bokes, of
answer, These shalbe to desire and pray your Lordship to
sende me by this berer a true copie of the same, and I shal
sende for bartelet the printer, and first swere him, and thenne
cause him to entende this night to the printing of the copies
therof accordingly. And thus most hartely Fare you wel.
From the Rulles the xi^th of Nouembre

I require your lordship to cause the proclamacions to be
writen and sealed with suche expedicion as you may take the
payne to be here with them tomorowe by tenne of the clock
where my lord of Norffolk and I with others wil tary dyner
tyl your cummyng.

Your lordshippis assuryd

THOMAS CRUMWELL.

*Add.* To my very good Lord my Lord Chauncellour
delyuer this with spede.

*Endd.* m^r. Lord my m^r. to my lord Chauncellour, *etc.*

## 86. CROMWELL TO LORD LISLE.

R. O. Cal. vii. 1438. Nov. 17 ⟨1534⟩.

A letter of gentle reproof for failing to discharge his office, as his duty to the King demands. Points out that his 'excess of living' has brought him into contempt.

My very good lorde aftre my right harty commendacions I am now enforced to write my mynde plainly vnto youe as to him the preseruation of whose honour I desire Bothe for the discharge of my dueuty to the kinges highnes, and for the declaration of myn hartye good will whiche I bere vnto you, and therfor I require you my lorde to take it in good parte. First I trust you consider what a charge you haue there vnder the kinges Maiestie and I woold youe should remember Both what besemeth a man to doo being in that place, and that the same conteineth in it no state of inheritaunce, ne terme for lief But vppon the good Behauiour of the personne having it. Nowe if you shuld waye the thing and the nature of it indifferently, Wold you thinke it mete that a man shuld haue that charge, which wold Bring himself to suche necessitie that he shuld be constrayned to put all thinges to sale, that be commytted vppon speciall trust to his discreation, neglecting of thone parte the kinges highnes honour to be preserued in the satisfaction of his graunttes, of thother parte as it were contempnyng all frieendeship in giving place to a litle Lucre. Surely my lorde suche a gouernour as you Be shuld not Bynde himself at any manes request to performe that shall not percase lye in him, ne by any his excesse in living make himself soo nedye, that whenne the present thing shuld happen, he shuld be forced to haue more estimacion of money thenne regarde to the tayle it Bringeth with it. If I were not determyned to contynue your lordships assured Freende I wold not worke this plainly with you, neither thinke that I doo it vppon any affection, for I wold ⟨do⟩ that I maywil honestly.   oon man I haue often tymes recommended that is the Surveyour whom the Kinges Maieste woold haue serued of foure men according to his graunte and Late commaundement made for the same.   But yet I write not this so moche for him alone as for others and chiefly for yourself, and after for the poore man that is berer herof who hathe your Bonde. Whiche your honour shalbe to performe and accomplishe, and Bothe myn aduise and desire shal concurre with the same, lest it might be taken yvel where percase you did it vppon an honest grounde.   Finally my lorde I remayne your harty Freende, and desire you to expresse your Freendeship again

towardes me in your honourable procedinges, and the helping
of such as the kinges Maieste wold shuld be there preferred,
amonges the Whiche the Surveyr is not the last, and yet
I wold he shuld haue nothing onles his seruice deserue it.
Thus most hartely Fare you wel From the Nete the xvii^th of
Nouembr

Your lordshippis assuryd

THOMAS CRUMWELL.

*Add.* To my very good Lorde the Viscounte Lisle Deputie
⟨of⟩ the kinges towne and the Marches of Calays.

*Endd. by Lisle.* Tochyng the gyft of romys

## 87. CROMWELL TO LADY LISLE.

R. O. Cal. vii. 1448.   Nov. 20 ⟨1534⟩.

Denies the report that he is displeased with her.  If she continues to act
  as she has, she will always find him a firm friend.

In my right harty maner I commend me vnto your good
ladiship.  And wheras I am infourmyd that reaport hathe
been made vnto you that I shuld be displeasid with your
ladiship . Where of  trouthe  I  knowe  no  cause  wherfore
I shuld so be, Wherfore I pray you geve no soche credence
ne beleffe to any persone, for your good ladiship vsyng your
selfe in all causes none otherwise then I here that ye do, and
as I doubte not that ye will here after contynewe, shall fynd
me as redy to do you any pleasure, that may lye in me to do
as any frynd that ye have.  And thus the blessed Trenyte
preserue your good ladiship.  At london the xx^th day of
November.

Your louyng Freend

THOMAS CRUMWELL.

*Add.*  To the right honourable and  my  very good lady
my lady lisle be this youen.

## 88. ⟨CROMWELL⟩ TO ⟨HENRY VIII⟩.

R. O. Cal. vii. 1613.  ⟨1534.⟩

Reports that Mr. Southwell is content to sell the manor beside East
  Yafford, in Yorkshire, and will show it to the King's surveyor.

Pleasythit your highnes to be aduertysyd how that Sythyn
my repayre to london I haue[1] spokyn with Mr. Sowthwell
to whom I haue declaryd your most gracyous pleasure

---

[1] *c. o.* Surveyed and I Fynd I haue

touching the purchasing of his Mannour besydes est yafford
who most humblye Submyttyth hym vnto the plesure of
your magestye and ys right well content that your grace
appoyntyng[1] Suche persons to vew the sayd mannour as
shall ⟨stand⟩ with your highe pleasure he wyll gyue his
attendaunce to shew vnto them the same to thentent your
highnes may be trewlye certeffyed vppon the vew of the
Comodytes belongyng to the same. and that ons known,
with your most gracyous plesure, Further conclusyon to be
takyn & Such as to your highnes shall Seme most mete.
Wherfor and it might please your grace that I myght know
your plesure who your highnes woolde appoynt to Survey
the sayd Manour I woolde then accordyngly[2] cause Instruccyons to be in Redynes For the same[3].

## 89. ⟨CROMWELL⟩ TO ——.

R. O. Cal. vii. 1614. ⟨1534.⟩

Desires him to give Mr. Alen a lease of the farm of Canewood and Cane-
field, in Essex, without delay, and trusts he has made no promise
which will prevent him from doing this.

My Lorde after my right hertie recommendacions where
as I haue wrytten to you in the fauours of my veraye Frend
Mr. Alen for his preferrement to the Ferme of Canewod and
Canefeldes And hauing receyued your answer thereunto
whereby I do perceyve your desire is to haue respite of
your consent and graunntes in that behalf till your commyng
to London alledging that in the meantyme ye will do your
possible to call agayn a former promise by you thereof made
to a nother person, My lorde I trust ye haue made no such
promise which in case ye haue, yet I doubt not ye will so
compase it that my purpose be not Disapoynted by that
meane. And therefore my lorde Forasmoche as I do so
ernestly meane and intende the satisfaccion of my saide
Frend in that parte, I shall eftesones most hertelie requyre
you indelayedlie to confourme your self to thaccomplissh-
ment thereof, and all excuses set a parte, to make him out
a lease of the said Ferme according to my former request,
Which be ye assured in Few wordes I shall intend so to
requyte as ye shall haue no cause to thinke the same
bestowid vppon an ingrate person

---

[1] c. o. Indifferent  [2] c. o. to procede
[3] c. o. yt may also ple

## 90. ⟨CROMWELL⟩ TO ——.

### R. O. Cal. vii. 1615. ⟨1534.⟩

On behalf of Thomas Miller, an English subject, whose goods have been
wrongly detained by James Sinclair, governor of the north of Scotland, and who cannot get redress.

After my right hertie commendacions it may lyke you to
undrestonde that where A Shẏp called the Andrewe aper-
teynyng to one Thomas Miller beyng a Subiect to my most
dreade soueraigne Lorde Kyng and maister by chaunce of
tempest or other mysfortune was ronne Aground in the north
parties of the Realme of Scotland.  And yet neuerthelesse
the most parte of alle the goodes and merchandises in the
said Shypp amountyng to the value of cclx li. sterling as
I am enformed were there and then ⟨saved⟩ by the diligens
and labours of the seruauntes of the said Thomas they beyng
taken owt and by them savely kepte to their saide maisters
vse by the space of viii or ix dayes.  Vnto suche tyme
as one James Seyntcler governer and ruler in the said North
parties of Scotland vndre the Kynges grace your maister
without any reasonable cause toke awaye the said goodes and
merchandises from the Servants of the said Thomas and so
the same euer sens hathe kept and deteyned agaynst good
equitie and consciens.  And for as moche as at your last
beyng in Englond ye gentilly promised me that if I wrote
vnto you for relief or necessitie of any the Subiectes of
Englande in cases or Justice, ye wolde the rather at my pore
contemplacion put youre good endevor to accomplysshe my
request.  At whiche tyme also of your said beyng in England
thys case was then by me and other the kyng my Maisters
Counsayle mocioned, and declared vnto you, Whereapon ye
promised vs that yf the partie damaged repayred to your
parties for Justice after your comyng home that then he
shold be restored as to reason, right, and conscience shold
apperteyne.  And thys notwithstondyng albeit the said
Thomas Miller by the late maister of the said Shipp hath
made humble sutes for Justice and Restitucion of hys said
gooddes and merchandises to hys greate costes and charges
yet neuerthelesse he hath hitherto had nor can get any
redresse.  Wherefore at the desyre of the said Thomas I at
thys tyme am bold to wryght vnto you, right hartely desiryng
you that at the repaire of the said Thomas or eny of hys
servants to you with these my letteres that he may by your
good favors and meanes so reasonably be ordered in thys
case as he shall haue no cause reasonable to compleyn for

lak of Justice, by whiche doyng*es* I shall accompt my self
bounden to reaquite *your* gentilnes w*ith* semblable pleasures
for Any Frend or Neyghbour of y*our*s.

*Endd.*   A Copie of a l*ette*re writen into Scotland in the
favo*ur* of one Thomas miller of london

### 91. CROMWELL TO ——.

#### R. O. Cal. vii. 1616.   ⟨1534.⟩

Desires him to restore the lands which he has wrongfully taken from
Reginald Williams in the West Country.

After my right hertie co*mm*endac*i*ons Forasmoche as
I haue bene sued vnto and requyred by my Freendes to
adresse thiese my l*ette*res vnto you in the fauo*ur* of one
Reignolde Williams from whom as I am crediblie info*ur*med
ye do deteyne and w*ith*olde certeyne londes in the weste
cuntrey contrary to all right and good equitie albeit the
saide Reignalde Williams as manifestly appereth by his
euydenc*es* is nexte heire vnto the same lond*es* I shall
therfore hertely desyre you the rather at this my requeste
and contemplacion that w*ith*out any further molestation or
truble in the lawe ye will calle togither yo*ur* Freendes and
after co*mmu*nication had in the mattier to conclude a Finall
ende therin accordinge to equitie and co*n*sciens so that the
saide Reignolde receyue no iniurye nor wronge at yo*ur*
hande [1], but also bynde me to shewe you lyke pleasures
accordinglie.   thus Fare ye well.   At my howse of
Stepneth

### 92. ⟨CROMWELL⟩ TO THE UNIVERSITY OF OXFORD.

#### R. O. Cal. vii. 618.   ⟨1534.⟩

The King is displeased at hearing of the ill-treatment of the inhabitants
of the town by the authorities of the University, and desires that
amends be made.

I comend me vnto yow   Aduertysing the same *tha*t wher
the king*es* hyghnes is crediblie infourmed of yo*ur* abusions
vsurpacyons & vngentill demeano*ur* vsed toward*es* the king*es*
highnes his subiect*es* & inhabita*u*nt*es* of *tha*t his towne of
Oxforthe & subberb*es* of the same I can not but mervaile
*tha*t ye being men of Lerning & in whom shoulde remayne
both wisedom & discressyon wille in suche wise demeane your

---

[1] *c. o.* And in thus doynge ye shall not oonlie do a thinge proffitable
and right meritorious for yo*ur* sowle

self[1] not onelie in making of lawes & ordynaunces Amongst
your self to their hindrance hurt and preiudice but also
contrary to the kinges lawes whiche aperethe in you to haue
proceded of nothing but mere malice Wherfor intending to
conduce & Allecte yow to som good conformyte & quyetnes
the kinges hyghnes therfore hathe commandyd me to advise
yow not onlie to restore all such persons as you haue dis-
comoned permitting them to do & occupie as they did before,
without mayntening or suffering any scoler or seruauntes
to occupie with in the toune or suburbe of the same as a bur-
gesse there dothe except he or they do agree there fore with
the sayd burgesses But also that in no wise ye do vexe
trouble or inquyete any of the saide inhabitauntes by suspen-
sion excommunycacion discomonning banysshement or otherwise, vsing suche discression that all varyaunces may ceasse &
be stayed amongst yow so as all malice and evill will being
contempned & expulsed from yow, good amyte peax & quyetnes may take place accordynglie.   And duobt ye not or it be
long the Kinges Counsaile by his gracious commaundement
will & haue determyned to set suche an ende & redresse
amongst yow as god willing shall be an establisshing of a
perpetuall peax good vnyte & accorde amongst yow for euer
fayell ye not this to do as yow wyll answre vnto the kynges
highnes & advoyde the daungier of his indingnacion & high
displessur   And so Fare ye well

*Add.* To the Chauncelour and comissarie with other the
heddes & membres of the vnyversite of Oxforde be this youen

*Endd.* A copye of a lettere to Oxforth

### 93. CROMWELL TO LORD LISLE.

R. O. Cal. viii. 187.   Feb. 8 ⟨1535⟩.

The King has written to Lisle to give Ralph Hare the next vacant
   position at 8d. a day.   Advises Lisle to follow the King's orders.

In my most harty wise I commend me vnto your good
lordship.   And persayvyng that the kinges highnes hathe
not only geven vnto Raufe Hare by sufficient writyng vnder
the privey seale, the roume of eight pence sterling by the
day whiche shall first and next fall voyde within that the
towne of Calays, but hathe also writen vnto you his letteres
vnder hys signet confermyng thesame and mencionyng therby
his pleasure and expresse commaundment in that behalfe,
these shalbe therfore as your lordshippes assured frynde to

---

[1] *c. o.* to their hindrance hurte & preiudice

my power to advise you to folowe the kyng*es* co*m*maundement therin for the satisfaction of his pleasure in that behalfe.   Wherby ye shall not only des*er*ue the Kyng*es* right
harty and condigne thank*es* but also admynyster and do vnto
me and other of his frynd*es* whiche dothe write vnto you also
in his favour, great pleasure and gratuyte, the whiche god
willyng shalbe on my part in semblable wise recompensed.
And thus the blessed Trenyte p*re*serue yo*ur* good lordship.
At the Rolles the viii^th day of February.

Yo*ur* lordshippis Freend assuryd

THOMAS CRUMWELL.

*Add.*   To the right hono*ur*able and my synguler good lord
the vicount lisle the kyng*es* depute at Calays.

*Endd.*   Mr. Secretoryes *lette*re
Mr. Sekretarye the viii^th of Febrewary cons*er*ning raff Hare.

94. CROMWELL TO THE PRIOR OF DUDLEY.

R. O. Cal. viii. 191.   Feb. 10 ⟨1535⟩.

The King desires the Prior personally to repair to Cromwell at once.

I Co*m*mende me vnto youe.   Lating youe wit that for certain causes the p*ar*ticularities wherof ye shal knowe herafter
The king*es* pleasure and co*m*maundement is ye shal Ime-
diatly vppon the sight herof all delayes and excuses set-
aparte p*er*sonally repaire vnto me wheresoeuer it shall chaunce
me to be w*it*hout faylling as ye wil answer to his grace at
yo*ur* extreme p*er*ill.   From the Rulles the x^th of Februarye.

Yo*ur* Freend THOMAS CRUMWELL

*Add.*   To my Freende the prior of Dudleye yeve this w*it*h
spede.

95. CROMWELL TO THE MAYOR AND ALDERMEN OF
LONDON.

R. O. Cal. viii. 221.   Feb. 15 ⟨1535⟩.

Desires for Robert Baxter, a clerk of the Common Bench, the next
vacancy in the clerkships of their court.

In my ryght harty wise I commend me vnto you & to eu*er*y
of you   And albeit I am many wise importune & bold apon
you for my selff & my frend*es* When cause & occasion hath

so requyred.   This shalbe to aduertise you that Robert
Backster one of the Clarkes writers with John Joyner the
kynges Preignetory of his graces comen bench at Westminster is very desyrous to be one of the Clarkes of your
Courte & hath made instant peticion to me that by myne
intercession to be made vnto youe in his fauour he myght the
rather & more effectuelly opteyne the same.   And were as
I am acerteynyd that the Rowmes of your foure Clarkes are
now furnyshyd & non of theym voide.   Wherefore I hertely
desyre & pray you at the contemplacion of these my letters
and for my sake wylbe content to graunt vnto the said Robert
the next vacacion of one of the iiii Clarkes of that your courte
And I dare will undertake for hym that he shall at all tymes
(yf he lyue to optayne the same) vse and behaue hymself like
an honest officer.   And for your goodnes herein to be shewed
vnto hym (for my sake) ye shalbe well assured to fynd me as
redy semably to requyte you of suche gratuite & pleasure as
shall lye in me to shew vnto you.   And thus fare ye well
from the Rollys the xv day of february.

*Add.*   To my veray good Lorde the Mayour of the Citie
of London and to his worshypfull Brethern thaldermen of the
same & to euery of theym.

*Endd.*   From Mr. Crumwelle.

## 96.  Cromwell to Henry Burton.

R. O. Cal. viii. 239.   Feb. 19 ⟨1535⟩.

The King is informed that Burton has disturbed Lady Carew in her
possession of a free chapel and ground, granted her by the King.
Desires him to cease troubling her.

In my hartie maner I commende me vnto you, Aduertising
the same that Whereas complaint hath nowe lately been made
vnto the Kinges Maiestie on the behalf of my Ladye Carewe
howe that you haue made a wrongfull and riotouse entree into
a certayn free chapell and a litle close grounde abowt the
same whiche chapell and grounde his hieghnes hath geven and
graunted vnto her by his graces letteres patentes during her
lief, the remayndre thereof to Fraunceys Carewe her sonne,
and to the heyres masles of his bodye begoten, So that it
seameth his maiestie hath the Reversion of the fee simple in
him, his heyres and successours.   His Hieghnes willed me to
signifie vnto you by these my letteres his graces pleasour and
commaundement is that you do not onely permitte, and suffre
the saied Ladye Carewe to enioye peaxably the possession

of the premisses, and to restore suche thinges as you haue wrongfully taken owt of the chapell and grounde aforsaied, but also to cease your suete commenced againste her at the commen lawe vnto such tyme as both your titles maye be further examined and tryed by lerned and indifferent Counsaill, Not failing hereof as you tendere His Hieghnes pleasour, Thus fare you hertely well.   From London the xix<sup>th</sup> daie of Februarye.

Your louyng Freend

THOMAS CRUMWELL.

*Add.*   To my Loving freende Henry Burton.

*Endd.*   In the bahalf of the Ladye Carewe & her sonne Fraunceys.

### 97. CROMWELL TO THE EARL OF SHREWSBURY.

Heralds' Coll. of Arms, Shrewsb. MSS. A, f. 57; Cal. viii. 247.
Feb. 20 ⟨1535⟩.

Sends him a letter from the King.   As for the farm of which the Earl wrote, Cromwell has discovered that his servant is not anxious to leave it, and he is unwilling to urge him.

After my right harty commendacions to your good lordshippe with semblable thankes for your Letteres Lately addressed Vnto me The same shall herewith receyue the Kinges highnes Lettres of answer to suche credence as yow commytted to my Freende Maister Buttes to be declared Vnto him.   And albeit his Maiestie hathe not resolutely answered to the particular pointes of your credence aforsaid yet your lordshippe maye be assured at your cummyng vppe to receyve suche answer in euery of the same as shalbe to your contentacion.   And vndoubtedly his grace woolbe as gladde to see your lordshippe as any man I suppose in his realme. Suche is his entier love and fauour towardes yowe.   Whiche I am as gladde to perceyve and see as your self could desire the same.   Touching the ferme wherof your lordshippe wrote vnto me I haue been in hande with my seruaunt and like as I wold be lothe to constrayne him if I might otherwise chuse to forgoo it Soo I perceyve he woll not leave it onles it shalbe for advoyding of my displeasure, and again the man dothe me soo good seruice that with equitie I canne presse him no further therin thenne I haue doon.   Neuertheles if your lordshippe woll haue me eftsones to travail in it I shall doo asmoche more therin as your self shall at your cummyng

thinke mete for me.  And thus moost hartely Fare yow well.
From the Rull*es* the xx<sup>th</sup> of February

Y*our* lordshippis assuryd

THOMAS CRUMWELL.

*Add.* To my veray good Lorde Therle of Shrewisbury
lord Steward of the King*es* Houshold.

## 98. CROMWELL TO ADMIRAL CHABOT, SIEUR DE BRION [1].

Bibl. Nat. de Paris, Fonds Moreau, 737, page 83 ; Cal. viii. 337.
⟨Mar.⟩ 4, 1535.

The report of the Treasurer of Brittany will assure him how desirous the
King is to remain in friendship with the King of France.  Urges de
Brion to do all he can to strengthen and increase the amity.

MONSEIGNEUR,

J'ay receu les lettres qu'il vous a pleu m'escrire ensemble
entendu vostre response, et charge de M<sup>r</sup>. le Trésorier Pala-
médes, laquelle, selon sa très bonne manière de faire, et au
très grand contentement du Roy, mon maistre, il a sceu très-
bien dire et déclarer, et pourtant que par la response qu'il
emporte, vous pourrez clairement cognoistre la bonne con-
stance et continuation d'amitié et vnion, en quoy le Roy mon
dit maistre entend persister à tout iamais tant luy que sa
postérité, sans aucunement varier, ains faire tout ce que avec
son honneur et condescentement luy sera possible, au desir du
Roy, son bon frère : pourtant aussy, que le dict Trésorier vous
sçaura faire ample rapport de toutes choses ;
Monseigneur, après vous avoir très affectueusement prié que
veuilliés persuader, et si mestier est, inculquer à la ma<sup>té</sup> du
Roy V<sup>e</sup> Maistre, la grandeur de leur amitié, et bonne intention
de la dicte response et qu'il ne veuille presser ne desyrer le
Roy de chose pourquoy l'on pense avoir suspicion ou coniecture qu'en l'amitié d'entr'eux y entre aucun respect de
lucre ou proffit particulier : car ce n'est pas assez, comme
vous sçavez trop mieux, que leur amitié soit cogneue et prinse
pour ferme et establie par entr'eux et leurs amys, qui est
à leur grand confort et encouragement : Mais aussy est très
expédient de l'entretenir et conduire en sorte que leurs
Ennemis et malveillans n'ayant cause d'y pouvoir penser, ne
suspecter aucune interruption, qui sera à leur très grand
esbahissement Confusion et desconfort : et ce faisant, comme

[1] From the official Record Office transcript.

bien gist en vous, le bien et plaisir, qui à tout le monde en adviendra, ne se sçavoir assez estimer, sans vous rescrire pour le présent plus au long, m'estre de très bon cœur recommandé à Vᵉ Seigneurie et offert tout ce en quoi vous sçauray faire honneur et plaisir Je supplie nostre benoist Créateur, que, à vous Monseigneur, il veuille donner sa saincte et digne garde.

Signé, Vostre à commandement

THOMAS CRAMWELL.

Escript à Londres,
   le iv iour de May ¹.
     1534.

*Add.* A Monseigneur
     Monseigneur l'Admiral de France.

99. CROMWELL TO LORD LISLE.

R. O. Cal. viii. 419.   Mar. 21 ⟨1535⟩.

The King marvels at his delay in granting Thomas Appowell a position as soldier at Calais. Desires Lisle to give him the next vacant place.

After my right harty commendacions vnto your good lordship, thiese shalbe for asmoche as the kinges highnes before this tyme in consideracion of the good and acceptable seruice done vnto his sayd highnes by his faythefull subgec[t] Thomas Appowell. Hathe geven and graunted vnto hym the roume of a Souldiour of the retynewe at Calays whiche first or next shuld fall and be voyde with the wages of viii d. a da[y] as by the kinges graunt therof made vnder his signet beryng date the second day of May in the xxiiiᵗʰ yere of his reigne and other his speciall letteres sithens directed vnto you for that purpose it dothe more playnly appere. And that notwithstanding, hitherto he hathe not been preferred to any suche roume, as he saythe wherat considering the kinges sayd graunt and letteres seuerally made for that purpose his highnes dothe not a litle marvaill. Wherfore I requyre and pray you for asmoche as thesayd Thomas hathe done good seruice, and is right mete for that roume. And the rather for my sake and at the contemplacion of these my letteres, to graunt vnto hym the next roume that shalbe voyde with thesayd wages, shewing vnto hym your lordshippes favour in that behalf.

---

¹ The date 'May' is obviously a mistake; it should be 'March.' The dates of the embassy of Gontier and the itinerary of the King make it quite certain that the letter was written March 4, 1535, which, of course, was 1534 O. S. Cf. Cal. viii. p. 133 *n.*

Wherby besides that ye shall do a very good dede, ye shall admynyster and do vnto me right thankfull pleasu[re] the whiche god willyng I will in semblable wise requite. thus the blessed Trenyte preserue you. At the rolles the xxi day of Marche.

Y*our* lordshippis assuryd

THOMAS CRUMWELL.

*Add.* To my veray good lord the vicount lisle the King*es* depute at Calays.

### 100. CROMWELL TO SIR GREGORY DA CASALE.

R. O. Cal. viii. 523. April 10, 1535.

The King is glad to hear that the Bishop of Rome begins to appreciate the justice of his cause. Urges that every effort be made to prevail upon the Pope to give formal sentence in favour of the divorce.

Mag*ni*fice Do*mi*ne Gregori salutem et commen*dacionem* Complures post vestru*m* hinc discessum, et uariis temporibus datas a vobis *litte*ras accepi, quarum recensiores sub die xx februarii Romae scriptae sunt, quicquid uero de occure*n*tiis istis publicis, ac priuatis Regiae Ma*iesta*tis rebus in dictis *litte*ris unquam significabatur sigillatim, ac diligenter id ipsi semper exposui, gratumq*ue* et acceptum habet sedulu*m* istud *vest*rum scribendi officium, nec ego antea ve*str*is *litte*ris respondi, q*uod* putaui, praeter istoru*m* successuu*m* cognitione*m* (quae sui nouitate grata semper est) non esse admodum multa, quibus particularius foret respondendum : Nunc autem Regia Ma*iest*as quum ve*str*as tum ad se, tum ad me *litte*ras pressius, accuratiusq*ue* perlegisset, illud inter coetera, mente adnotauit, Pontificem vobiscu*m* loqui uoluisse, sum-mam*que* praesetulisse Regiae Ma*iesta*ti gratificandi propen-sionem, et ob eam causam, duos accersisse ex hetruria iure-consultos cum primis eruditos, quorum doctrinae sanoq*ue* iudicio potissimum fidat, eorumq*ue* sententias, et opiniones pro Regiae Ma*iesta*tis causa stare, et eiusmodi esse *vest*ris vos *litte*ris affirmatis ut pontifex ex officio debeat praesens matri-monium, etiam si de ualiditate dispensationis a Iulio factae constaret, approbare, Coeterum causa*m* hanc, ut ueritatis fundamento totam innitentem, et si Regia Ma*iest*as cum Deo satis firmatam habeat, et omni ex parte stabilitam, in hunc tamen sensum *litte*ras *vest*ras interpretatur, Pontificem scilicet de eius ·rectitudine et aequitate cum sua Regia Ma*iesta*te q*uam* optime sentire, Proinde si amicum ac syncerum istud pectus erga Ser*enissi*mum Do*min*um meum Regem (quod vos scribitis) re uera habet, quin potius, ut bonum quenq*ue* virum ab omni prorsus odio, et affectu liberum, et immunem in primis

decet, si ueritati ex anima fauet, eius certe sunt partes, ut
suam hanc erga Inuictissimum Dominum meum Regem in
causa omnium iustissima bene affectam uoluntatem, suo etiam
publico testimonio, et approbatione vniuersi orbi reddat per-
quam manifestam, suaque sponte, innataque animi probitate
et solius ueritatis propagandae studio, nulla Regiae Maiestatis
intercessione expectata, ad id adducatur, ut nullius metu, seu
respectu a uero rectoque deflectens de prioris matrimonii
inualiditate, praesentisque firmitate, et robore ingenue pro-
nunciet, quem ad modum doctissimis illis viris, quos huius
rei causa ab eo accersitos, istic adesse scribitis, maxime probari
significatis, efficiet certe Pontifex rem suo munere, et officio
dignam, Serenissimo Domino meo Regi, qui suae causae
iustitiam tot uigiliis, sumptibus ac laboribus diu quaesitam,
et iam pridem cum Deo compertam habet, uehementer gratam,
sibique in primis, et pontificatui suo longe utiliorem, quam
nunc demonstratione sit opus, Vos autem si hac in re nullo
Regiae Maiestatis expectato mandato, nulloque suo iussu (non
enim firmiora suae causae quam nunc habet adiumenta
aliunde sperat) quicquid profeceritis, ac Pontificem vestra
dexteritate ex vobis ad id quod scribitis adduxeritis, eiusdem
Regiae Maiestatis expectationi quae non vana, aut victa
officia, nec infructuosos rerum euentus de vestris actionibus
sibi pollicetur, procul dubio respondebitis, et haec a Pontifice
beneuolentia et gratia ex officio proueniens eo nomine gratior,
et acceptior erit, quod ueritatis ratio, deique respectus, sanaque
conscientia ad hoc eum mortalium nemine procurante, nunc
commouerit. Et bene valete. Londini Die x Aprilis M. D. xxxv.

Vester bonus amicus

THOMAS CRUMWELL.

*Add.* Magnifico Equiti, Domino Gregorio Casalio etc.
Amico carissimo.

101. ⟨CROMWELL⟩ TO ⟨SIR GREGORY DA CASALE⟩.

R. O. Cal. vii. 268[1].  ⟨April 10, 1535.⟩

Draft in English of the preceding.

After my right ⟨hearty⟩ commendacions, Sithen your departure I haue receyued sundry of your letteres whereof the last
bere date at Rome the xx day of Februarie.  And whatsoeuer
ye haue signefied vnto me by your saide letteres aswell of the
publique occurrantes there as of the Kinges highnes pryuate

[1] This letter is obviously misplaced in the Calendar.

affairees I haue aliwayes intymated and declared the same to
the king*es* maiestie who right thankefully and acceptablie
taketh and estemeth y*our* diligence in wryting And now
having p*er*vsed and redde both y*our* *lette*res addressed to his
maieste and also to me his highnes hathe speciallie noted in
the same amongst other that the bisshop of Rome speking
w*ith* you shewed himself veray propice and desirous to
gratefie his saide highnes And that he had sent for out of
Ethrurie twoo Lawyers being singulerly well lerned in whose
doctrine and good iudgement he hathe grete trust and confidence Whose senten*ces* and opynyons do stonde hollie w*ith*
the king*es* highnes cause Affirmyng (as ye wryte) that the
saide Bisshop of Rome of his duetie and office ought to
approbate and confyrme this p*re*sent matrymonie albeit it
depended vppon the validite of the dispensacion made by
Julius. So as Notw*ith*standing that the king*es* maiestie having
his saide cause sufficientlie diffyned and being himself in that
behalf resolutely determyned and grounded as vppon the
foundacion of veryte and trowth hathe discharged his conscience therein (like a good vertuous and catholique prynce)
afore god and the worlde Yet his maieste dothe in suche
sence interpretate y*our* *lette*res that (as appereth by the same)
the saide bisshop of Rome begynneth now somwhat to sauo*ur*
and fele the iustnes and equyte of the saide cause and
p*ar*telie to stande w*ith* the King*es* maiestie in the same.
Wherefore if the saide bisshop of Rome do in dede bere so
frendelie and syncere good mynde and will toward*es* the
king*es* highnes (as ye do wryte) or rather if he love the trewth
as it beco*m*meth eu*er*y good man to do setting ap*ar*te all
hatred and affection it is his parte to shew the same now to
the vnyu*er*sall worlde in this most iust and rightcious cause
by his owne publique testymonye and approbacion. And of
his owne free will and w*ith*out any sute or intercession of the
king*es* maiestie onelie adhering to the trewth and negle*c*ting
all other respec*tes* to p*ro*nounce the invalidite of the first
mat*ri*mony and the validite of the seconde according to the
senten*ces* iudgemen*tes* and diffynytions of the saide ii° lerned
men which as ye wryte the saide bisshop of Rome called and
sent for vnto him for that purpose which if the saide Bisshop
of Rome will, surely he shall do ⟨a⟩ thing wo*ur*thie his office
and merite of god and the worlde and to the king*es* highnes
veray thankefull and acceptable pleasure, and also to him
self and his see moche more p*ro*fite and good then now
nedeth to expresse. And you for y*our* p*ar*te if in this
matier as of y*our* self ye can any thing p*ro*fite or p*re*vaile
by y*our* good policie and dexteryte toward*es* the conducyng

of the saide Bisshop of Rome to that conformyte (as ye wryte
in your saide letteres) ye shall then vndoubtedlie answer to the
kinges highnes expectacion And the same proceding of
the beneuolence of the saide Bisshop of Rome and the zele
that he hathe to the due execucion of his office and duetie
shalbe the more grate and acceptable a grete dell to the
Kinges highnes and the hole wourlde, seeing that the mere
veryte and the respecte that he hath to god and his owne
conscience shall move him thereunto without any mortall
mannes procurement

*Endd.* A Mynute of certeyn letteres responsyve to on at
Rome

A mynute of a Lettere to intymate to the Pope the Kinges
desyre to haue him condiscend to the dyvorce & to allowe
the second maryage.

## 102. ⟨CROMWELL⟩ TO MR. RICHE.

R. O. Cal. viii. 563.   Apr. 20 ⟨1535⟩.

Requests him to use his influence to induce Mr. Sinclair to cease suing
Edward Campion, clerk of the peace in Essex.

After my m[ost] hertie maner I commende me vnto you,
and evyn so I pray you at this my request and contemplacion
to be good Maister and frende vnto Edwarde Campion clerke
of the peax within the shere of Essex of and in all suche his
busynes towching the same his office and to be ameane for
hym in the same unto Mr Sayntclere hym to desire to putt
the said campion to no further vexacions and sutes for the
said office as he hath heretofore done.   In doyng whereof you
shall admynister vnto me right singuler pleasure, which god
willing . I shall not for get semblable to requyte as shall lye
in my litill power. And this hertelye fare ye well.   At
london this xx^th day of Aprill

*Add.* To my lovyng frende Master Riche.
*Endd.* Mynute of lettere.

## 103. CROMWELL TO THE PRIOR OF TREWARDRETH.

B. M. Add. MSS. 6,416, f. 8 ;  Cal. viii. 743.   May 21 ⟨1535⟩.

The King is informed that the town of Fowey is in a bad state, because
the Prior, who has the liberties of the town in his hands, administers
it so badly.   Desires him to amend his ways.

M^r priour as vnaccquanted I haue me commended vnto you,
and whereas it is comen vnto the kinges highnes knowledge
that the Towne of Fowey is sore decayed and thoccasion

therof p*ar*tlie is that in the saide Towne is no order of Justice bicause the liberties concerninge the same graunted by the king*es* highnes and his noble progenitours to your predecessours and by theime vnto the inhabitaun*tes* of the saide Towne remayne in yo*ur* handes and kepinge So that betwene you no maner good order equitie nor iustice is executed and vsed w*ith*in the saide Towne. Wherfore I require you to condiscende and agree w*ith* the inhabitaun*tes* of the saide Towne so that you hauynge yo*ur* reasonable approued duties, they may haue theire liberties to be vsed and extended amongeste theime w*ith*in the saide Towne to thincrease of good order w*ith*in the same. And as ye shall agre therin to certifie me in writinge by Thomas Treffry berer herof. For his highnes thinketh that the saide porte of Fowey oweth to be his and to be holden of hime so that his grace entendeth from hensforth to haue. it as well prouided for w*ith* good gouern*au*nce and of defence for vtter enemyes as other his townes and port*es* be w*ith*in those parties. Wherunto ye for yo*ur* partie before this tyme haue had litle or no regarde neyther to the good order rule and defence therof ne yet to the good rule and gouernaunce of yourself yo*ur* monasterie and religion as ye be bounde wherfore his highnes thinketh that ye be veray vnworthey to haue rule of any towne that cannot well rule yo*ur*self. And that I may haue aunswer as is afforesaide by this berer what ye intend to do I require you to thintente I maye certifie his highnes therof And thus fare ye well. At london the xxi[th] daie of Maie

Your Freend

Thomas Crumwell.

*Add.* To the priour of trewardreth in Cornewall be this youen.

## 104. ⟨CROMWELL⟩ TO DR. LONDON AND MR. CLAYMOND.

R. O. Cal. viii. 790. May ⟨1535⟩.

Desires them to request the fellows of Magdalen to admit Thomas Marshall as president of the college, on the resignation of the present president, who has already signified his willingness to give up his position.

In my right harty man*er* I co*m*mende me vnto you. And where the Presedent of Mawdelyn College, as well by his seu*er*all l*ette*res as by mouthe (of his mere motion) at sundry tymes, myche co*m*mending the qualities of my Lord and frende master Thomas Marshal[l] g*r*aunted vnto me, that he wulde

be contented to resigne that his Rowme to the same master
Marshall, alledging that he was a man very apte & mete for
the same, promysing further and nothing doubting, but in that
behalf be bothe coulde & wolde fynde the meanes to obteyne
the goode willes & myndes of the felowes of the said College.
Neuertheles nowe of Late (to me no litle mervaile) the saide
presedent when I desired hym to accomplishe his saide pro-
messe, alledged for his excuse that the goode willes of the
saide felowes coulde not in that behalf be opteyned.  Wherfore
I hartely desire and pray you effectually in my name to
solicite & entreate the saide felowes as by your wysdomes ye
shall thinke most conuenient that they for my sake & at
this my desire wilbe contented to conforme theym selues vpon
the resignation of the said presedent to the admission of the
saide master Marshall, or elles that contrary Wyse att the Leaste
I may knowe by your writing in whome the mater sticketh.
In doing wherof ye shall not only deserue bothe Laude &
prayse in the furderaunce of the saide master Marshall, whose
aduauncement I hartely desire, but also I wille not faile
to remembre your kyndnes in that I may doo you pleasure.
And thus hartely fare ye well, from London the —— daye
of May.

*Endd.*  The Copie of alettere Sent to Mr. doctor London
& Mr. Claymond.

## 105. CROMWELL TO THE EARL OF CUMBERLAND.

B. M. Add. MSS. 12,097, f. 1 ; Cal. viii. 893.   June 18 ⟨1535⟩.

Requests him to discover and apprehend certain evil-disposed and riotous
persons, who have unlawfully assembled in the county where the
Earl lives.

After my right harty recommendacion vnto your good
lordship, thiese shalbe taduertise the same that the kinges
highnes hathe been aduertised that diuerse riotous and ill-
disposid persones of the parties wher ye inhabite, or within
your offices and roumes (as it is sayd) hathe lately vnlawfully
assembled theymselfes together to no litle nombre in riotous
maner to somme lewde and vnthriftie intent and purpose.
Wherfor his highnes myndyng the quietenes of his subiectes,
and good rule and order to be maynteynyd and kepte within
this realme Willithe and commaundithe you and other of the
Justices of his peax, furthewith after the receyt herof to make
inquisicion and serche, who and what nombre of the sayd
persones hathe so assembled theymselfe, and for what cause
intent and purpose they hathe so done  And that ye also

enquire who hathe beene the Capitall and cheffe doers in that
partye, and further that ye cause theym to be apprehended
and taken and sent hither with all convenyent spede together
with all that ye shall fynd and knowe concernyng the premysses, and suche other offenders as ye shall not think good
to be sent vp that your lordship cause theym to be put vnder
sufficient suretyes for their good aberyng accordyng to his
lawes, prayeng your lordship to aduertise me of that ye shall
do in the premysses by the berer herof with all convenyent
spede.   And thus the blessid Trenyte preserue you   At the
rolles the xviii^th day of June.

Your lordshyppis Freend

THOMAS CRUMWELL.

*Add.* To the right honourable and my veray good lord
the Erle of Cumberland be this youen.


106.  CROMWELL AND AUDLEY TO THE MAYOR AND
COMMONALTY OF CAMBRIDGE.

Cooper's Annals of Cambridge, i. 371 ; Cal. viii. 1036.   July 14 ⟨1535⟩.

Desires them to take measures to avoid any trouble with the members of
the University at the approaching Stourbridge Fair.

After our hertye commendacions, wher variaunce debate
and strif hath long depended betweene the Vycechauncellor
of the Universite of Cambridge and the scolers of the same of
the one partie, and you and the cominaltye of the towne of
Cambridge on the ⟨other⟩ party, concernyng both your iurisdiccions and liberties.   And albeit we, wyth others of the
king's counsaile by his graces commaundment, entended to
have pacyfyed the sayd variaunce or this tyme ; yet neverthelesse, for that we have had no convenient leasure for the
same, the said variaunce as yet remaynith undetermyned.
And forasmuche as Sturbridge fair is nowe nere at hand
at whiche tyme it is thought verey like that variaunce
and breche of the kings peax may happen betwixt you, bi
reason of suche iurisdiccions as ether of you pretende to
exercise in the same faire, if remedye were not·provided for
the same, we therfore, calling to rememberaunce that for the
conservacion of the Kings peax an order was takyn the last
yere at Lambeheth, before the most Reverend father in god
the archebysshop of Canterbury and other the Kings Counsaile, what ether of you shuld exercise in the said faire without
interrupcion of other, till the variaunce betweene you were
fully determyned, Do nowe therfore advertise you that the

Kings pleasure is that as well ye for your parts, as the said
Vicechancellour and scolers for their parts, shall firmely for
this faire tyme to cume this yere, observe and kepe the same
order in every poynt without violacion therof: Signifying unto
you that we have written our letteres to the said Vycechaun-
cellour and scolers for the same cause, Putting you out of
doubt that by the due keping of the said order, ye shall take
no preiudice of eny your lawfull liberties that of right ye ought
to have, uppon examynacyon and fynall determynacyon of
ether your titles, To the proceeding in the finall order wherof,
we will with all diligence (god willing) put our effectuall
endevor this next terme, as the kings pleasure is we shuld do,
requiring you to take pacyens in the meane season. And
thus almyghtye Jhu have you in keping. Wrytten at London
the xiiij$^{th}$ daye of July.

Your frends,

THOMAS AUDELEY Knt. Chauncell.

THOM$^s$. CRUMWELL.

*Add.* To the Maier and comynaltie of the Towne of
Cambridg be this yeven.

## 107. ⟨CROMWELL⟩ TO THE ⟨DUKE OF NORFOLK⟩.

B. M. Titus B. i, 318 ; Cal. viii. 1042.  July 15 ⟨1535⟩.

Sends a royal proclamation against conveying coin out of the realm, and
a copy of the statute of 5 Richard II to the same effect. The
council gave its opinion that the King's proclamation in this case
should have the same force as a statute.

May hit please your grace to be Aduertysyd that I haue
resayuyd your letteres[1] persayuyng by the Contenttes therof
that the Kynges highnes dothe moche merveyle that I haue
not aduertysyde your grace what order my lord chauncelor
and others of his Counceyll hath[2] takyn Concernyng the
conveyaunce of Coyne owt of the realme. Syr according
to your gracyous commaundement vppon tewysdaye last
Mr. Attorney and I bothe dyd Intymate & declare the
Kinges pleasure vnto my lorde Chauncelor who Immedyatlye
Sent For My lorde cheffe Justyce of the kynges benche the
cheffe Justyce of the Common place the cheffe Barron and
Mr. Fytzeherberd Mr. Attorney Mr. Solysytor and I being
present and the Case by my sayd lord Chauncelor openyd
dyuers oppynyons ther were, but Fynally it was Concludyd

---

[1] *c. o.* this nyght at xii of the Cloke
[2] *c. o.* done and what order ys

that all the statuttes sholde be Inserchyd to See whether ther were anye Statute or lawe able to serue for the purpose and yf ther were it was thought good, that yf it sholde happen any accydent to be wherby ther myght Be any occasyon that the money sholde be conveyed owt of the realme that then proclamacyon sholde be made growndyd vppon the sayd Statute adding therunto poletyklye certayn thing*es* For the putting the Kyng*es* Subiect*es* and other in more terroure ande Feare vppon which deuyse serche was made and a goode estatute Founde which was made in the Fyfte yere of Kyng Rychard the seconde the Copye wheroff translatyd[1] into Inglyshe I do sende vnto yo*ur* grace drawne in mann*er* of A proclamacyon by the aduyse of the Kyng*es* lernyd Counsayle. But Amongyst all other thing*es* I mouyd vnto my sayd lorde chauncelor my lorde cheffe Justyce and other that yf in Case ther were no law nor statute made alredye for any suche purpose what myght the Kyng*es* hignes by the aduyse of his Counsaylle doo to wit*h*stande so greate a daunger lyke as yo*ur* grace alledgyd at my beyng wit*h* you to the which yt was answeryd by my lorde cheffe Justyce that the Kyng*es* hyghnes by the aduyse of his Cownsayll myght make pr*o*clamacyons and vse all other polecyes at his pleasure as well in this Case as in Anye other lyke  For the avoyding of any suche daungers and that the sayd pro- clamacyons and polyces so deuysyd by the King & his cownsayll for any such purpose sholde be of as good effect as Any law made by parlyament or otherwyse which oppy*ny*o*n I assure yo*ur* grace I was veray gladde to here[2] wheruppon[3] the sayd statute[4] was drawen in to a ⟨copy⟩ in forme as ⟨a⟩ pr*o*clamacyon I do now sende the same to yo*ur* grace[4] and thus the holye trynyte pr*e*serue yo*ur* grace in long lyff good ⟨health⟩ wit*h* the Increase of moche honor at london the xv^th day of July.

108. CROMWELL TO SIR JOHN RUSSELL, ROGER WYNTER, JOHN PAKYNGTON AND JOHN VAMPAGE.

Library of William Berington, Esq., of Little Malvern Court. Not in Cal.
July 18 ⟨1535⟩.

Desires them to examine the complaint of Robert Symonds, of Pershore, in Worcestershire, and see that justice is done if possible.

I co*m*mende me vnto you in my right hertie maner And by the tenure [of these letters] whiche I sende vnto you

---

[1] *c. o.* drawne
[2] *c. o.* Serche was made and
[3] *c. o.* the Copye of this

[4] *c. o.* to thentent the Kyng*es* gracyous pleasure may be known drawen according to the sayd

herin closid ye may perceue the complaynt of Robert
Symondes of pershor in the countie of worcester wherfor
I hartely desire and pray you groundly to consider and
pounder the contentes of the same and callyng the parties
before you ye be soche waies and meanes as ye can best
devise examyne the hole circumstaunce therof and sett
a fynall ende therin if ye can And if through the obstinacie
of either of the said parties ye cannot convenyently so do
then my further desire is that ye wryte vnto me the truthe
and playnes of the mater with the circumstaunces therof to
thintent I may therin cause some meanes to be founde as
the [case] rightfully shall require wherby ye shall do a very
good and meritorious dede.   And thus fare ye hartely well
at London the xviij^{th} day of July

Your Frende

THOMAS CRUMWELL.

*Add.*  To my louyng frendes Sir John Russell Knyght
Roger Wynter John Pakyngton and John Vampage Esquyres
or to thre or two of them.

## 109. CROMWELL ⟨AND AUDELEY⟩ TO SIR JOHN RUSSELL, JOHN PACKINGTON, AND JOHN RUSSELL, ESQUIRE.

Library of William Berington, Esq., of Little Malvern Court.   Not in Cal.
July 20 ⟨1535⟩.

Desires them to survey the possessions of the clergy in the Shire of
Worcester according to the King's commission, and to send an
account of their value to London.

After our right hartye commendacyons where the Kynges
Commyssion was dyrectyd vnto you & other for the surveyng
and taxacion of the clere yerely values of all the possessions
of the clergie in the Shire of Worceter accordyng to a boke
of Instruccyons assigned with the hand of the Kynges highnes
annexed vnto the said Commissyon we signyfie vnto you that
the Kynges pleasure ys that ye callyng your fellowes Joyned
with you in Commyssion shall with all possible dylygens
accomplysshe theffectes therof And to sende to vs to london
all the bokes taken by you of the vieu & value of the said
possessions by one or two suche of your fellowes whiche were
Audytours of the same before the xij^{th} day of Septembre
next commyng.   Not faylyng this to do at your perill.   And as

<table>
<tr><td>estatute made in the sayd Fyfte yere</td><td>afforsayd and that was all that was</td></tr>
<tr><td>of Kyng Richarde the second as ys</td><td>done in that matyere by</td></tr>
</table>

ye entende to advaunce the Kynges pleasure in this behalf.
And thus fare you well.   At london the xx<sup>th</sup> day of Julye

THOMAS AUDELEY K. Chauncell*our*

THOMAS CRUMWELL.

*Add.*  To their loving freend*es* S*ir* John Russell the yonger
Knight John pakington Esqu*ier* and John Russell Esquier
and to eu*ery* of theym be this yoven.
*Endd.* Wigorn.

## 110. CROMWELL TO BONNER.

Library of Lord Calthorpe.  Not in Cal.  July 23 ⟨1535⟩.

Begs him to make speed in his journey.  Bonner's commission is ready,
and Mr. Gostwick will deliver to him the Duke of Holstein's letter.

Mr. Boner I co*m*mende me vnto you.  Signefieng vnto
the same that the Kyng*es* pleasure is ye w*ith* yo*ur* college
shall w*ith* all spede and possible haste set yo*ur* selff*es* forward
toward*es* thaccomplisshement of your io*ur*ney, and cause
yo*ur* Ship also to be rigged and made redy so as ye haue
no cause of Delaye.  Yo*ur* co*m*mission I vnderstonde ye
haue alredy made and sealed, and touching the Duke of
Holst*es* *lette*re if ye haue not yet receyued it Mr. gostwike
shall delyu*er* it you or to Cauendish accordinglie.   Prayeng
you ones agayne to make all thacceleracion and hast
forward*es* that ye can possiblie as ye intende to please the
King*es* highnes.  And so Fare ye well.   At Wynchcombe
the xxiii day of Julie

Yo*ur* Freend THOMAS

CRUMWELL.

Maister Boner the King*es* highnes nothing dowtyth in yo*ur*
wysedom polyce and discrecyo*n* But that ye wooll Vse yo*ur*
Self according to his trust and expectacyo*n*.

*Add.* To his louing frende Docto*ur* Boner be this youen
w*ith* spede.

## 111. CROMWELL TO MR. RICHE.

R. O. Cal. viii. 1130.  July 29 ⟨1535⟩.

Desires him to express to the Duke of Suffolk the King's displeasure at
the 'decay' of certain places, which the Duke affirms he has repaired.
Urges him to request the Duke to part with certain reversions which
are desired by the King.

After my right hertie co*m*mendac*i*ons these shalbe to
adu*er*tise you that the king*es* highnes hauyng receyued yo*ur*
*lette*res hathe youen me in co*m*maundement to make you

answer as here insueth. First touching suche leases as it is
supposed shoulde be made by the Duke of Suffolke, the
kinges highnes seyeth that he knoweth not that the saide
Duke or his officers haue made any lease syns the communycacion had betwixt them of this bargayn, but his highnes
is certenly infourmed that the saide Duke or his officers haue
offered to make fourth certen leases syns the tyme of the
saide communycacion had. Whereof his maieste can not but
mervaile and for the same conceyueth som ingratitude and
vnkyndenes in the said Duke if it can so be proved. Secondely
touching the Decay of Ewelme and Donyngton the kinges
highnes answered that what soeuer the saide Duke hathe
spent vppon them, it may well appere in what decay they
stonde, and who soeuer shall view them shall facilly perceyue
that grete somes of money will not sufficientlie repaire them
as his highnes himself with his eye hath vewed the saide
Ewelme at his graces late being there. And for Donyngton
the house is not onelie in decay but also the keper of the
same Mr. Fetyplace hath both consumed and distroyed the
Dere and game there and also wasted the woodes in such wise
as it is thought he hathe not onelie forfaited his patent but
also right ill deserued to haue eyther fee or thanke for any
good service he hathe don there. And semblablie the kinges
highnes hauing ben at Hokenorton whiche his grace lyketh
veray well can not perceyue ne also his Surueyours sent
thither can not see how that xv⁰ li should be employed
there as it is affirmed by the saide Duke, so as it is not vnlike
but that the saide Duke hathe ben deceyued by his officers.
And whatsoeuer hath ben spent there, yet will it requyre no
small sommes of money to repare and buylde it after the
kinges mynde and pleasure whiche wilbe chargeable to his
highnes. And touching the game of the red Dere at
Hokenorton aforsaide, his maiestie Doubtith not but that the
saide Duke will iustefie his couuenaunte and agrement with
the keper for the keping of lxxx red dere there accordinglie.
Thirdely concerning the reuersions of the lady Gordon and
John Verney the kinges highnes perceyuing the conformyte
of the saide Duke in that behalf and also your travaile and
diligence in the same gyueth vnto him and you both therefore
his graces hertie and condigne thankes. Trusting that like as
his highnes hathe heretofore mynystered grete benefites and
commodytees vnto the saide Duke, who hathe atteyned this
degree honour and astate that he now is in by the meanes
and onely aduauncement of the kinges saide highnes. So the
saide Duke wilbe contented to departe with the saide reuersions
frankely and frely to his highnes of his mere lyberalite to

extende towardes him, and to permytte his maiestee to haue
the saide reuersions within his bargayn alredy made as his
grace thought he had had, onely trusting to his graces bountie
and goodnes for the recompence of the same.   Wherein the
kinges pleasure is ye shalbe playne with the saide Duke,
vttering and declaring vnto him the good opynyon which the
kinges highnes hathe conceyved in his conformyte towardes
all his gracious requestes and affairees, and how he of all men
is thereunto bounde if he do well consider the manyfold
benefites that he hath receyued at the kinges hande.   Wherefore
ye may counsaile him not to gyue any cause or occasion in
this behalf to the kynges highnes to conceyve any Jalousie or
mistrust in him but that rather he will shew herein his frankenes
and liberall herte towardes his maiestie without stycking with
his grace in so small a matier.   And so doing let him be
assured that like as the kinges highnes heretofore for lesse
cause youen on the saide Dukes parte, hathe aduaunced him
to this honour and astate that he now is at, So shall his
maiestee the rather now be Dryven to consider the frankenes
and gentill liberalite of the saide Duke in this behalf if he
frankely do com forwardes with the same.   And Fynally
I pray you on my behalf to say somwhat to the saide Duke
in this matier alledging vnto him that as I am, alwayes haue
been, and euer wilbe his graces poure frende so I requere him
not to stycke with the kinges highnes in this matier, and pray
his grace not to doubte but that the kinges highnes wilbe as
good lorde to him in recompence of the saide reuersions as if
his highnes Did now parte and couuenaunte with him for the
same aforehand.   Wherein eftesones I pray you shew him on
my behalf that my poure and frendelie aduise is that his grace
shall liberally wryte to the kinges highnes in this matier so as
his highnes may thereby perceyue the saide Dukes gentill
herte and naturall zele towardes his maieste aswell in this
as in all other thinges.   Which be ye assured in myn opynyon
shalbe more beneficyall vnto the saide Duke then x tymes
so moche lande as the saide reuersions Do amount vnto.
Requering you so to shew his grace fro me as from him that
wold be as glad of his graces welth and prosperyte as any one
of his poure frendes.   So knoweth our lorde who send you
well to fare.   From the Monastery of Tewkesbury the xxix<sup>ti</sup>
Day of Julie.

Your Freend

THOMAS CRUMWELL.

*Add.*  To his louyng Frende Mr. Ryche Solycytour to the
kinges highnes be this youen.

### 112. CROMWELL TO THE EARL OF RUTLAND.

Belvoir Castle MSS.    Not in Cal.    Aug. 9 ⟨1535⟩.

Desires him to examine a certain warden and his friars, and report the result of his investigation to the King. Requests him to apprehend Friar John Colsell, and detain him till further notice.

My lorde after my right hertie commendacions these shalbe to aduertise your lordship that having receyued your letteres and declared the effectes of the same to the kinges highnes, who for your dyligent aduertisement of suche thinges as do touche his maiestie and for your good will shewed towardes the correction of suche transgressones gyueth vnto you his graces hertie and condigne thankes, Forasmoche as the kinges highnes is aduertesed that the warden of those Freres which haue spoken those sedicious wordes, is a right honest person and that it may be that he is accused by such light persons as percase can not iustefie the same, the kinges highnes therefore requyreth your lordeship to call before you the saide warden and all other his Freers and to take som payne thoroughlie and exactely to here Debate and examyne the matier with them and their accusers, so as the trewth and the hole circumstaunces of the matier may trewlie and substaun-cyallie appere in suche wise as euery man may haue his merites and desertes according to good iustice. And of your lordeshippes procedinges in that behalf and what matier ye shall Fynde vppon the saide examynacion it may please your lordeship to signefie the same with the circumstaunces to the kinges highnes or his counsaile, vppon the which aduertisement your lordship shall knowe ferther of the kinges pleasure. Touching the other Frere named Frere John Colsell vsing the decitful arte of magike and astronomye, the kinges pleasure is that ye shall cause him to be taken and apprehended and deteyn him in warde vntill ye shall haue other knowlege and aduertisement of the kinges pleasure in that behalf, and thus the holie trynytie preserue your lordeship in long lif and helth with thincrease of honour At Barklay hoornes the ix^{th} day of August.

Your lordeshyppes assuryd

THOMAS CRUMWELL.

*Add.* To the right honourable my lorde the Erle of Rut-lande be this yeuen.

## 113. ⟨CROMWELL⟩ TO ⟨WALLOP⟩.

R. O.[1] Cal. ix. 157. August 23 ⟨1535⟩.

Instructs him to justify to Francis the King's doings, especially the executions of More and Fisher, and to request Francis to support Henry in all his actions against the Pope. The King is desirous that Melancthon should come to England.

Sir after my most hertie reco*m*mendacions these shalbe to adue*r*tise you that the xvii[th] Day of this Moneth I receyued from you a packet of le*tte*res which indelayedlie I delyuered vnto the king*es* highnes and conferred w*it*h his grace theffect*es* both of your le*tte*res and all others w*it*hin the saide packet being directed aswell to his highnes as to me. And after his highnes had w*it*h me pe*r*vsed the hole content*es* thoroughlie of your saide le*tte*res, pe*r*ceyuing not onelie the lykelyhod of the not repairee into Fraunce of Philip Melanchton, but also yo*ur* co*mmu*nicac*i*ons had w*it*h the frensh king vppon yo*ur* Demaunde made of the king*es* highnes pencions w*it*h also yo*ur* Discrete answers and replicacions made in that behalf, for the which his maiestee gyueth vnto you his hertie and condigne thank*es*, Ye shall vnderstonde that his highnes co*m*maundid me to make you answer in this wise folowing First as touching the kyng*es* money his highnes dowtith not but seeing bothe the Frensh king and also the grete Maister haue p*r*omised you it shalbe depechid ye will as the case shall requyre not cease to call vppon them till it be Depeched And ferther considering that the saide frensh king vppon yo*ur* saide Demaunde of the saide pensions so sodaynelye fell into co*m*munycacion w*it*h you aswell of his frendeship and humanyte shewed to the kyng*es* highnes, alledging that he at all tymes hathe answered for the kyng*es* highnes specyally being last at Marcell*es* w*it*h Pope Clement w*it*h other thing*es* as in your saide le*tte*res appereth, as also concernyng the execucions lately don*e* here w*it*hin this realme, The king*es* highnes not a litle me*r*vaileth thereat, and thinketh it good that as of your self ye take som occasion at conuenyent tyme and oportunyte to renovate the saide co*m*munycacyon both w*it*h the Frensh kyng or at the least w*it*h the grete Maister, sayeng vnto them, that where the saide Frensh kyng alledgeth that he hath at all tymes answered for the kyng*es* highnes in his cause and specyally to the saide Pope Clement at Marcell*es* affirmyng his p*r*ocedyng*es* to be iust and vpright concernyng the Matrymony as ye do wryte, in that albeit the kyng*es* highnes p*r*ocedinge*s* in all his affairees w*it*hin this realme being of such equyte and iustnes of themself as they be, nedeth

---

[1] A copy of this letter is also to be found in Longleat House.

not any defence or assistence ayenst Pope Clement or any
other foreyn power, having goddes worde and lawes onelie
sufficient to defende him Yet in that that [1] the said frensh kyng
hathe as he sayeth answered at all tymes on the kinges parte,
he hathe done nothing but the parte of a brother in iustefieng
and verefyeng the trewth, and so contynuyng shall Do as
aperteyneth to a prynce of honour which the kinges highnes
doubtith not he hath and will do onely in respecte to the
veryte and trewth besides the amyte betwixt them both iustlye
requyring the same. And concerning thexecucions Done
within this realme ye shall sey to the saide Frensh Kyng that
the same were not so mervelous extreme as he alledgeth, for
touching Mr. More and the Bisshop of Rochester with suche
others as were executed here, their treasons conspiracies and
practises secretely practised aswell within the realme as without to move and styrre discension and to sowe sedycyon
within the realme, intending thereby not onelye the distruction of the kyng but also the hole subuersion of his highnes
realme being explaned and declared and so manyfestly proved
afore them that they could not avoyde nor Denye it and they
thereof openly detected and lawfully convicted adiudged and
condempned of high treason by the Due order of the lawes of
this realme, it shall and may well appere to all the worlde that
they having such malice roted in their hertes ayenst their
prynce and Souereigne and the totall Distruction of the
commen weale of this realme, were well worthie if they had
had a thousande lyves to haue suffered x tymes a more terrible
Deth and execucion then any of them Did suffer. And touching
suche wordes as the saide frensh kyng spake vnto you concernyng how Mr. More dyed and what he saied to his
doughter going to his iudgement and also what exhortacions
he shoulde gyue vnto the kynges subiectes to be trew and
obedient to his grace (assuring you that there was no such
thing) whereof the gret Master promysed you a Double at
length. In that the kinges pleasure is that ye shall not onelie
procure the saide double and sende it hither but also sey vnto
the saide frensh king that the kynges highnes can not otherwise take it but veraye vnkyndely that the saide frensh king
or any of his counsaile at whose handes he hathe so moche
meryted and to whom he hathe mynystered so many grete
benefites pleasures and commodytees shoulde so lightly gyue
eare faith and credence to any such vayne brutes and fleeng
tales Not hauyng first knowlege or aduertisement from the
kinges highnes here and his counsaile of the veryte and
trewth, Affirming it to be the office of a frende hering any

[1] *sic.*

suche tales of so noble a prynce rather to haue compressed
the bruters thereof to sylence or at the leest not permytted
them to haue dyvulged the same vntill such tyme as the
kinges maiestee being so dere a frende had ben aduertesed
thereof and the trewth knowen before he shoulde so lightly
beleve or allege any suche reporte which ingrate and vnkynde
Demeanure of the saide frensh king vsed in this behalf
argueth playneleye not to remayn in his brest such integryte
of herte and syncere amyte towardes the kinges highnes and
his procedinges as his highnes alwayes heretofore hathe
expected and loked for. Which thing Ye may propone and
alledge vnto the saide frensh king and the grete Maister or to
one of them with suche modestie and sobrenes as ye thinke
they maye perceyue that the kinges highnes hathe good and
iust cause in this parte somwhat to take their light credence
vnkyndelye. And where as the saide frensh king sayeth
that touching such lawes as the kinges highnes hathe made
he will not medle withall alledging it not to be mete that one
prynce should desire a nother to chaunge his lawes sayeng that
his be to olde to be chaunged, to that ye shall sey that such
lawes as the kinges highnes hathe made here be not made
without substauncyall groundes by grete and mature aduise
counsaile and deliberacion of the hole polycie of this realme
and are indede no new lawes but of grete antiquyte and many
yeres passed were made and executed within this realme as
now they be renovate and renewed onlye in respecte to the
comen weale of the same. And it is not a litle to his highnes
mervaile that the saide frensh kyng euer wolde counsaile or
aduyse him if in case hereafter any suche like offenders should
happen to be in this realme that he should rather banyssh
them then in suche wise execute them And specyallie considering that the saide frensh king himself in commonyng
with you at that tyme not onely confessed thextreme execucyons and grete Bruyllie of late don in his realme But
also that he now intendeth to withdraw the same and to
revoke and to call home agayn such as be out of his realme
the kinges highnes therefore the more straungely taketh his
saide aduise and counsaile Supposing it to be neyther thoffice
of a frende nor of a brother that he wold Determyn himself to
call home into his realme agayn his subiectes being out of the
same for speking ayenst the Bisshop of Romes vsurped auctoryte, and counsaile the kynges highnes to banysshe his
traytours into straunge partes where they myght haue good
occasion tyme place and oportunyte to worke their feates of
treason and conspiracie the better agaynst the kinges highnes
and this his realme. In which parte ye shall somwhat

engreve the matier after such sorte as it may well appere to
the saide frensh king that not onelie the kinges highnes might
take those his counsailes and communycacions both straungely
and vnkyndely thinking the same not to procede of mere
amyte and frendship, but also vsing such polycie and austeryte
in proponyng the same with the saide frensh king and the
grete Maister taking such tyme and oportunyte as may best
serue for the same, as they may well perceyue the kinges
highnes procedinges here within this realme both concerning
the saide execucyons and all other thinges to be onely groundid
vppon iustice and the equyte of his lawes which be no new
lawes but auncyent lawes made and establisshed of many
yeres passed within this realme and now renovate and renewed
as is aforesaide for the better order weale and suretie of the
same.  And ye may ferther say that if the frensh king and
his counsaile well consyder as they ought to do that it were
moch better to aduaunce the punysshment of traitours and
rebelles for their offences then to ponysshe such as do speke
ayenst the vsurped auctoryte of the bisshop of Rome who
Daylie goth about to suppresse and subdue kynges and prynces
and their auctorytee gyuen to them by goddes worde.  All
which matiers the kynges pleasure is that ye shall take tyme
and occasion as ye talkyng agayn with the frensh king or the
grete Maister may declare your mynde as before is prescribed
vnto you.  Adding thereunto such matier with such reasons
after your accustomed dexteryte & discression as ye shall
thinke most expedyent and to serve best for the kinges
purpose, Defence of his procedinges and the profe of the frensh
kinges ingratitude shewed in this behalf.  Not Doubting in
your wisedom good industrie and discrete circumspection for
thordering and well handeling of the same accordinglye.
And touching Melanchton [1] considering there is no lyke-
lihod of his repayree into Fraunce as I haue well perceyued
by your letteres, the kynges highnes therfore hath appoyntid
Cristofer Mount indelaiedlie to take his iourney where Melanchton is and if he come to prevente Mounsieur de Langie
in suche wise as the saide Melancton his repayre into Fraunce
may be stayed and dyuertid into Englond Not doubting but
the same shall take effect accordynglie.  And as to Mr. Heynes
the kynges pleasure is that he shall go to Parys there to [2]
lerne and dissiphre the opynyons of the lernid men and their
inclynacions and affections aswell towardes the kynges highnes
procedinges as to the bisshop of Rome his vsurped power and
auctoryte, after such sorte as the kinges saide highnes hathe

---

[1] c. o. &c. the kynges high          [2] c. o. reside and demoure

now wrytten to him by his grac*i*ous *lette*res addressed both to
him and the saide Cristofer Mount[1].  Dyrecting them what
they shall do in all thing*es* comytted to their charge at this
tyme As I doubt not they will put thereunto their devoires
for the accomplisshment of the king*es* pleasure as ap*er*-
teyneth.  And thus makyng an ende prayeng you to vse
yo*ur* discression in the pr*o*poning of the pr*e*misses to the
Frensh king and the grete M*aster* or the one or both of them
vsing the same as a Medecyn and after suche sorte that as nere
as ye can it be not moch displeas*au*ntly taken  Adu*er*tesing
the king*es* highnes from tyme to tyme of the successes thereof
and of all other occur*au*nt*es* as the case shall requyre, I shall
for this tyme bid you most hertelie Fare well &c.   Thorne-
bery the xxiij day of August.

*Endd.*  Fraunce

### 114. ⟨CROMWELL⟩ TO NICHOLAS OLDISWORTHY.

R. O. Cal. ix. 241 (i).   Sept. 1 ⟨1535⟩.

Desires him to give up all the possessions of the bishopric of Hereford to
such persons as the Bishop-elect shall appoint.

In my harty wise I co*m*mend me vnto you .  Aduertising thesame that for certayne causes the king*es* highnes sp*e*cially
movyng, his graces pleasure is that ye shall surcease any
farther to yntermedle w*it*h the possessions and land*es* belongyng to the Busshopriche of Hereford but that ye suffer
suche as the Busshop elect shall appoynt to haue the doyng
of the same.   And that ye farther suffer the officers appoynted
by thesayd Busshop to resceyve aswell the next rent due at
the Fest of thannu*n*ciacion of o*ur* lady last past as all other
rentes due sithe that tyme.   And that ye fayll not thus to do
as the king*es* trust is in you .  thus fare ye well.   At Bromham
the first day of September.

for Nicholas Oldisworthye.

### 115. ⟨CROMWELL⟩ TO ⟨THE ABBESS OF WILTON⟩.

R. O. Cal. ix. 271.   Sept. 4 ⟨1535⟩.

Desires her to act kindly towards his friend William Nevill in the matter
of the lands belonging to her monastery.   Nevill does not wish to sue
her though he has good cause so to do.

Madame, after my right harty reco*m*mendations vnto you,
thiese shalbe like as here tofor*e* I have writen vnto you, to

[1] *c. o.* whereby

desire you to be good lady and frynd to my lovyng frynd
william Nevell about the Ferme of Chalke and do such
reparacions as belongithe vnto the same according to your
graunt therof made and that ye will suffer hym to have and
enioy such copy holdes as he of right shuld have and holde of
your Manour of Semley belongyng to that your Monastery, as
by sufficient writyng and copies therof it dothe more at large
appere, in suche wise as he may have no cause farther to
complayne ouer you therfore.   I cannot persayve any reason
iust cause or meanes wherby[1] ye may or shuld deny hym thesame.   he hathe been, and yet is all wayes redy to paye his
rent and do that which ought or shuld[2] apperteyne vnto hym
to do in that behalf according to his wrytyng therefore.
Which ye refuse and will not suffer hym to do[3].   I persayve
the honestie of the man to be suche, that he is veray lothe to
vexe or sewe you by the order of the common lawe or otherwise[4], although he hathe good cause even so to do, whiche
if he wold he may do right well to your inquietacion for
thadvoydyng [wher]of I desire you the rather at the contemplacion of thiese my letteres and for[5] your owne quietenes and
ease to graunt hym his right yn the premysses[6].   Wherby besides that ye shall shewe and declare your self to be one that
will do no persone wronge, and kepe yourselfe in quyetenes
and rest, ye shall admynester and do vnto me therby right
thankfull pleasure.   The whiche I will not forgete semblably
to requyte.   And thus fare ye hartely well.   At Wolfall the
fourthe day of September.

## 116. CROMWELL TO THE MAYOR AND COMMONALTY OF CAMBRIDGE.

Cooper's Annals, i. 372 ; Cal. ix. 278.   Sept. 5 ⟨1535⟩.

As Chancellor of the University desires that all differences between the
town and the scholars may cease.   Requests the Mayor to permit
the University to continue in the enjoyment of its privileges.

After my moost harty commendacions, Understanding that
the body of that the Universitie of Cambridge hath elected
and chosen me to be their hed and Chauncelor, and that there
is question at this tyme betwene you touching the exposition
and qualifieng of the Decre made the last yeer by the kings

[1] c. o. ye can haue to     right well do and
[2] c. o. shall                    [5] c. o. my sake
[3] c. o. wherfore and for asmoche     [6] c. o. in suche wise as he may
as                                haue no cause eftesones to com-
[4] c. o. whiche if he wold he may     playne one you for this matier

counsail, for an order to be had without contencion betwene
youe and the Universitee in Sturberige fayr, whiche decre ye
have already commaundement for this yere to observe and
kepe, contending on your part nothing to be comprehended
under the name of Vitaill, but that whiche shuld be presently
spent in the said faiier, and calling Salmon in barrel, musterde
sede, fishe, and suche other, with an exempcon from the terme
of vitaill by the name of merchandise, denyeing in like maner
the said Universitie to appoint two of their body to ioyne
with two of youe in the serche of merchandises there, sayeing
ther shal non other serche this yere for their parte, but those
that being of their congregacion the last yere were thenne
appointed for that purpose, whiche be nowe departed from
them and ioyned to youe in the libertie and freedom of the
towne. Bicause ye knowe that I have been ever desirous to
establish a quiet order betwene youe, and that with as moche
favour towards your parte as I might with indifferency and
justice, And that I doubt not but that ye will at my con-
templacon remembre the preservacion of the Kings peax,
and use suche a temperaunce in your procedings, as with the
saufgards thereof I may have cause to rest in your love and
kindness towards me, Being again for myn owne parte, moche
desirous nowe at the entree to the said Chauncelorship (which
office with the kings contentacion and pleasure I accepted
not so moch upon any respecte as to be the rather a meane
to set a quietnes betwene youe) to have al contencions and
controversies ceasse on eyther side, tyl direction and final
order may be taken therein, In the whiche I assure youe
I shal with such celeritee and indifferency travyll, as ye shall
not perceyve me a partie, but a personage holly bent without
al respects to the advancement of the common weal ; I have
thought good to address my letteres unto youe and by the
same to desire and praye youe, al vayne and frivolous qualifi-
cacons set aparte, to permyt and suffer the said Universitie
for this yere, according to the mynde and entent of the said
decre, to use and exersise their privileages in the things
specified, and also to use at their libertie the comen prison
of the Tolbothe as they have doon and as by their charters
they clayme to doo, soo as their procede on your part no
cause of breache of the peax, wherin ye shal serve the king
as appertayneth, and administer unto me suche thankfull
pleasure as I shall be gladde to deserve and requite towards
youe, in like maner most hartely desiring and eftsones praye-
ing youe, touching their Civile courte to be kept in the fayr
or any other thing that may com in to question, so to use
yourself as I may perceyve you remembre your dueties

towards the king in the keping of his peax, and shewe your-
selves gladde to doo unto me gratitude and pleasure. And
thus fare youe hartely wel. From Whofall the fifte day of
September.

Your lovying freend,

THOM⁸ CRUMWELL.

*Add.* To my loving Frends the Mayre and his Brethern
of the towne of Cambridge, and to every of them.

### 117. CROMWELL TO CHAPUYS¹.

Vienna Archives; Cal. ix. 326.  Sept. 10 ⟨1535⟩.

Reports the joy of the King at hearing of the success of the Emperor in
storming Tunis. Hopes on his return to give Chapuys satisfaction
in his request to visit the Princess Mary. Cf. Letter 121.

Magnifice atque observande Domine orator plurimam
salutem et commendationem. Quem admodum D. vestra,
felices et christiano cuique principi speratos cesaree ma^tis
successus non grauatur crebris suis litteris Serenissimo domino
meo regi significare ita sepe antea ab eius regia ma^te conceptam
toto pectore letitiam, suis nunc recentioribus litteris eadem
vestra D. ingeminauit et quam pulcherrime adauxit. Ex
lectione namque tum cesaree ma^tis tum domini de granuell
litterarum, que toti christiano orbi saluberrimam diuinitusque
concessam Tunisii expugnationem describebant tam solido
gaudio inuictissimus dominus meus rex affectus est, ut si sue
ipsi ma^ti gloriosa hec obuenisset victoria, maiori neutiquam
affici potuisset nec alium vllum quam qui a deo nunc concessus
est, tam sancte a cesare suscepte expeditionis euentu sibi
vnquam pollicebatur. Hanc igitur victoriam omni quidem
dignam laude, cesaree ma^ti iterum atque iterum gratulatur
salutaremque rei publice christiane precatur, cui sic ex corde
fauet, vt si vlla vnquam occasione, vllane sua opera, quicquam
addi poterit, experietur cesarea ma^tas me nihil de Serenissimi
domini mea regis in se affectu, amicoque animo meis antea
litteris vestre D. frustra, aut parum sincere totiens affirmasse.
Ad id vero quod in suarum litterarum calce vestra D. addidit,
vt scilicet, quantum intelligo, bona regia Ma^tis venia, sibi liceat
illic Dominam mariam inuisere iuxta regia pollicita impense
rogo D. vestram, vt istud suum desiderium velit in meum re-
ditum defferre, tuncque futurum spero quod tum hac in re, tum
aliis omnibus presenti meo sermone vestre do^is expectationi

¹ From the official Record Office transcript.

plurimum satisfiet siue feliciter valeat.   Ex aula regia apud
Wolfal die x. septembris.

v.    D.

Ex animo amicissimus

THOMAS CRUMUELL.

*Add.*  Magnifico atque observando domino Eustachio
Chapuysio Cesare ma<sup>tis</sup> oratori.

118. ⟨CROMWELL⟩ TO ——.

R. O. Cal. ix. 470.   Sept. 29 ⟨1535⟩.

The King desires him to pay half the last year's rent of the bishopric of
   Worcester to the Bishop, and the remainder to M. Gostwick for the
   King.

[1] I co*m*mend me vnto you.  Adue*r*tisyng thesame, that the
kyng*es* pleasure and co*m*maundement is, that ye w*ith* convenyent spede after the receyt herof, shall content and pay
vnto my lorde the Busshop of Wissetour the halfe yeres rent
of the hole Busshopriche due this last yere, and the rest
to retayne yn yo*ur* owne hand*es* to the kyng*es* vse Wherfore
I require you furthew*ith* so to do w*ith*out any delay, as the
kyng*es* trust and expectacion is yn you.  Thus fare ye hartely
well.  At Wynchester the xxix day of September.

*Postscript.*

I Co*m*mend me vnto yow aduertysing the same that the
kyng*es* highnes pleasure is that of the holle yeres Rent dew
to his highnes and levyable at this Fest of Saynt Mychell
of the yssews reuenews and p*r*offectt*es* of the Busshoprych
of Worcest*er* ye shall Content and paye or Cause to be
Contentyd ⟨and⟩ payde vnto my lorde the Busshop of
Woorcest*er* the hole half yeres proffytt*es* evynlye to be
deuydyd and the residew For the Fyrst hallffe yere to
be payd to the hand*es* of Maister gostwyke to the kyng*es*
vse and this ys expresslye the kyng*es* plesure and so Fare ye
well at Wynchest*er*

119. CROMWELL TO THE COUNTESS OF OXFORD.

R. O. Cal. ix. 485 (i).   Sept. 30 ⟨1535⟩.

Desires her to restore Mr. Tirrell to the possessions from which she has
   wrongfully expelled him.  The King wishes to have justice done in
   that cause.

In my most harty maner I co*m*mend me vnto yo*ur* good
ladishippe.  And wher as ther hathe of long tyme depended

---

[1] *c. o.* In my right harty wise

betwene you and this berer Maister Tirrell certayne con-
trauersies, aswell concernyng his clayme to the parke and
Bailliswike of Camps, as a certayne copie Holde Whiche he
bought in the same Towne, from all the whiche ye haue
expulsed hym, I shall most hartely desire and pray you at the
especiall contemplacion herof, to restore hym agayne to
thesame. Whiche request I make not only vnto you bycause
I thinke ye haue vpon displeasures conceyved agaynst hym,
parcase in some part by the mysvsyng of hymselfe towardes
you, done vnto hym, in his expulsion from the same park
Bailliwike and copie hold and your detynewe therof all
togither wronge and Iniurye, but because it should be
dishonourable to you, to haue the same in open Court of
Audience tried agaynst you, and likewise displeasaunt to be,
that way disapoynted of your will and pleasure, whiche as
I nowe frendly and frankly write vnto you, bicause that
I wold be glad, ye shuld without constraynt do as shall
apperteyne to your honour, and iustice. So I am enforced
to aduertise you, as your poore frende, that the kinges highnes
like a prynce of honour is mynded to haue iustice procede
without respect in that cause, Eftesones therfore requyryng
your good ladiship the rather for my sake without any
extremyte to be good lady vnto hym, who I dare affirme wilbe
glad to do vnto you during his liffe that seruice and pleasure
that shall lye in his litle power. As knoweth god who send
your good ladiship long liffe and well to fare. From
Wynchester the last day of September.

Your ladyshyppis assuryd

THOMAS CRUMWELL.

*Add.* To the right honourable and my good lady my
Lady Anne Countes of Oxford by this youen.

*Endd.* A lettere directed from my master to the Lady
Anne Countes of Oxford.

120. CROMWELL TO ⟨DAVYE MORGAN KEMYS⟩.

R. O. Cal. ix. 486.   Sept. 30 ⟨1535⟩.

Requests him to allow John Crede to retain possession of certain lands
in Cromwell's manor of Rumney in Monmouth to which he has a deed,
until reasonable cause can be shown for his ejection.

Datum per Copiam

I Commend me to yow. And for Asmoche As I haue
seene the Deed made ⟨to⟩ John Crede for certeyn Landes
in my mannour of Rompney called the Splottes And other

Lond*es* there. W*hich* I take to be a goode Deade. And that Notw*ith*standing the said Crede Saithe that ye entend to putt hym From the Same. Wherefore I Requyre you to p*er*mytt And Suffre hym to holde And kepe the possession thereof According to the tenno*ur* of his Deade Vntill Suche tyme as Apon youre Adu*er*tisement thereof I maie knowe A Reasonable Cause . Whie he shuld be putt from the same. Att Wynchester the Laste daie of September.

Y*our* Loving maister

THOMAS CRUMWELL.

121. CROMWELL TO CHAPUYS [1].

Vienna Archives ; Cal. ix. 484.    Sept. 30, 1535.

Reports the King's joy at the news of the Emperor's success at Tunis. Desires Chapuys to postpone a little longer his visit to the Princess Mary. Cf. Letter 117.

Magnifice et observande domine orator plurimam salutem et commendationem. Litteras quas vestra D. antea ad me dedit grato hilarique semper animo accepi, non mediocremque animi letitiam ob id presertim semper attulerunt, quod cesaree ma^tis successus vt sperandum et christiano reipublice salutiferos, vberrime nunciabant ; recentiores vero iste eo nomine gratiores acceptioresque extitere quod succinte atque distincte totius expeditionis rerum, temporum atque locorum seriem et euentum ab ipso initio in hunc vsque diem sic describunt et ob ipsos oculos ponunt vt eas legendo rebus gestis prope modum mihi videar interfuisse, tantaque Serenissimus dominus meus rex animi attentione de hiis me referentem audiebat vt fraternum eius erga cesaream ma^tem affectum et propensum quoddam erga publicam quietem studium quam facile fuerit agnovisse. Ad id porro quod per ministrum suum vestra dominatio mecum agit et de quo statuendo iniectis comperendinationibus se protrahi suspicatur, non possum pro mutue nostre coniunctionis sinceriorisque amicitie vinculo, eam non summopere rogare, et pro innata sua prudentia et animi equitate, boni consulere velit, quicquid in hoc Dominationis vestre desiderio deffertur quum nihil interim omittatur quod ex Serenissimi domini mei regis honore et dignitate, simulque illustrissime domine marie securiori salubriorique educatione esse posse videatur, quum maiori cure nemini sit quam ipsi Serenissimo patri, qui regie sue humanitatis nimis

<hr>

[1] From the official Record Office transcript.

esset oblitus nisi carissimam filiam paterno complecteretur
affectu et aliorum vigilantia sibi in mentem redigi expectaret,
quod salubritati, atque solatio filie esse posset.  Itaque quam
possum ex animo dominationem vestram obsecro, vt suum
istud illustrissimam dominam mariam inuisendi desiderium
ab amico pectore potius quam vlla necessitate profectum in
aliud commodius tempus defferre non grauetur, et enim vt fieri
facile potest de huius illustrissime domine neglecta valetudine
falso aliquid ad vos deferri, ita a dominatione vestra peto, vt
affirmanti mihi velit certam habere fidem nihil scilicet cure
studii, atque diligentie omitti quod ad illustrissime domine
Marie conseruationem expedire posse videatur.  Pestis deinde
sic londini, locisque vicinioribus seuit, vt inofficiosus videri
posset, quicunque illinc veniens dominam mariam in aere
alique temperie agentem, quam saluberrima, officii gratia
nunc temporis vellet inuisere.  Non grauetur itaque dominatio
vestra hoc meum responsum benigne amiceque, vt solet
interpretari nilque a me prospiciet pretermissum, quod ex
huius regie ma^{tis} dignitate, Cesaris honore et domine marie
conseruatione esse potuerit.  Sed de hiis in proximum con-
gressum colloquemur vberius, et felix valeat vestra dominatio
cui ex animi sententia, optima queque euenire precor . wintonie
die vltimo septembris 1535.

E. v. D.

Ex corde amicus

THOMAS CRUMUELL.

*Add.*  Magnifico Domino Eustachio Chapuysio Cesaree
ma^{tis} oratori plurimum observando.

122.  CROMWELL TO SIR GREGORY DA CASALE.

R. O. Cal. ix. 240.  Sept. 1535.

Explains, for the Pope's benefit, the reasons for the executions of More and
    Fisher, and describes them as men proved guilty of high treason
    Wonders at the Pope's indignation at their just sentence.

Mag*nifi*ce D*omi*ne Gregori plurimam salutem et commen*dacionem*.  Quae tum ex ferraria tum ex bononia ve*str*is
*lette*ris nuper ad me scripsistis, sigillatim omnia (ut mei est
officii) Serenissimae Regiae Ma*iesta*ti significaui, in quibus,
ut multa erant, publicarum rerum cognitionis gratia lectu non
iniucunda, et ve*str*i cum D*omi*no Parisiensi habiti sermones
ipsi probantur, ita non satis demirari potuit, Ep*iscop*i Roffen*sis*
et Thomae Mori mortem, pontificis, illiusq*ue* curiae animu*m*
adeo grauiter offendisse, ut ex hac re conceptam indignationem

haud facile possint concoquere, licetq*ue* Inuictissimae Regiae
Ma*iesta*ti mortalium nemini, praeterq*ue* Deo (cum quo actiones,
consiliaq*ue* sua habet q*uam* maxime coniuncta)ulla sit factorum
suorum reddenda ratio, ne tamen maleuolor*um* calumniis, ac
ueritatis obscuratione, Regium suum nomen istic traducatur,
quid ea in re actu*m* fuerit succincte ad vos perscribam : Post-
q*uam* igitur Regia Ma*ies*tas bene fauente, ac promouente Deo,
causam suam publicam eruditissimor*um*, probatissimorum*que*
totius christianitatis viror*um*, qui nullis passionibus, seu
affectibus essent obnoxii, consensu, et authoritate tandem
terminasset, et ad ipsam ueritatem omni ex parte firmasset,
coeperunt isti boni viri, quibus res praeter expectatione*m*
ceciderat, et spes moliendi noua (ut iam animo agitarant)
praecisa fuerat, in alias cogitationes, syncere parum, animum
intendere, quumq*ue* optimus Rex ex uigilantissimi principis
officio (quod a Deo acceptum sustinet in terris) sui Regni
quieti, et commodo prospicere, hominumq*ue* mores multa iam
parte collapsos in melius corrigere conaretur, istud etiam
publicum bonum, quoad fieri per eos potuit, simulatae integri-
tatis praetextu adnissi [1] sunt, sed nullo cum fructu impedire,
atq*ue* praeuertere, huius eorum sceleris indicia Rex habebat
perq*uam* manifesta, sed ut vana semper floccifecit, et nihili
habuit, sperans aliquando futurum q*uod* hac sua indulgentia,
hos viros (quos ut non penitus cognitos nonnunq*uam* antea
in precio habuisset) ad aliquam frugem, ac mentis sanitatem
reuocaret, At ipsi, quibus genuina ambitio, sui ipsius amor
et sapientia quaedam singularis diuersum persuaserat, optimi
principis benignitate, ac mansuetudine pertinaciter sunt abusi,
et ubi publicum Regni concilium (quod parliamentu*m* uocant)
pro Regni quiete stabilienda, ut ad certa tempora haberetur,
indictum foret, ceperunt undecunq*ue* sollicita cum sedulitate
clanculu*m* exquirere, qua de re tractari, quidq*ue* in hoc
parliam*en*to, ut expediens rei *publi*cae agi oporteret, quicquid
uero alior*um* delatu ex re praeterita rerum usu, uel coniectura
usq*ue* collegissent id statim communibus consiliis trutinabant,
omnia secus interpreta*n*tes, q*ue* Regni quies ac utilitas ex-
poscebat, eo quidem argumentor*um* et rationum apparatu, ut
rudi plebeculae non multo cum labore potuisset imponi,
quumq*ue* ex conscientia parum sana, Regis animum sibi
offensum suspicarentur, ueriti ne parum commode, audacterq*ue*,
quod tacite animo moliebantur, tractare possent, ex hiis non-
nullos delegerunt, quos audaculos aut linguae uelocitate
promptiores, aut sui studiosos existimarunt cum his anti-
quioris amicitiae occasione ageba*n*t familiaribusq*ue* colloquiis
excipiebant, ac si quos morbo animi laborantes suae opinionis

[1] *sic.*

reperissent, in horum sinum iam antea conceptum pectore
uenenum euomebant, suae erga claementissimum Regem fidei,
et obseruantiae, atque in ipsam patriam charitatis prorsus
obliti, Haec dum in uulgus haberentur passimque sparsa
promiscue essent, haud somnulenter solertissimus princeps
perscrutari coepit, quibus fundamentis tam impia coniuratio
niteretur, quibusque enutriretur authoribus, luce clarius per-
spexit, ab hiis integerrimis iuris tantam iniquitatem deriuari,
quam redarguebant non obscuri testes, ultro, citroque missa
chyrographa, ipsorumque oris confessio, haec et alia que multa
iustissimum principem adegerunt, ut hos rebelles, ac degeneres
subditos, in patriam ingratos, communi bono aduersos, publicae
pacis turbatores, tumultuosos, impios, seditiososque viros in
uincula carceresque coniecerit, nec id praetermittere poterat,
nisi patefacta iniquitate, sui officii consulto immemor permittere
uoluisset, huius sceleris contagionem publica cum pernicie in
quam multos transferri.    Carceribus autem mancipati tracta-
bantur humanius, atque mitius quam par fuisset, pro eorum
demeritis, per Regem illis licebat proximorum colloquio, et con-
suetudine frui, ij fuerant illis appositi, praescriptique ministri,
quos a uinclis immunes antea fidos charosque habebant, id cibi
genus eaque condimenta, et uestitus ei concedebantur, quae
eorum habitudini, ac tuendae sanitati, ipsi consanguinei, nepo-
tes atque affines, et amici iudicabant esse magis accommoda,
Coeterum tanta Regis mansuetudine, fides, obseruantia, ueritas,
amorque recti apud rebelles istos, proditoresque homines usque
adeo exoleuit, ut constanter iniqui esse maluerint, quam sui
sceleris poenitentia Regis bonitatem atque claementiam experiri,
et enim postquam certae leges, statuta, atque decreta, re prius
multa deliberatione in omnem partem discussa, publica parlia-
menti authoritate, assensu atque consensu condita prae-
scriptaque fuere, et ab omnibus nullo discrimine, repugnante
nullo, ut sancta necessaria toti Regno utilia, et cum uera
christi religione potissimum consentientia admissa, atque re-
cepta sunt, soli isti repugnabant, suae impietatis praesidium
semper aliquod fortuitum sibi ex tempore pollicentes, non-
nunquam omissa rerum humanarum cogitatione se totos
diuinarum contemplationi egregie simulabant addictos, interim
studia, uigilias, cogitatusque, suos omnes utcunque carceribus
obnoxii eo intendebant, ut quibuscunque possent fallaciis,
praestigiosisque argumentis tam sanctas Regni leges, tantaque
authoritate firmitas ac rectissime stabilitas, soli ipsi perni-
ciosissimae seditionis principes in commune malum eluderent,
refellerent, atque turbarent, huius autem tam impiae, perfidae
ac iniquae affectae uoluntatis extant manifestissima indicia
extant chyrographa ipsa eorum manu carbonibus, et creta (si

quando deerat atramentum) depicta, ultro, citroque clam ab
ipsis destinata, neque ipsi ibant inficias complures mutuo
acceptas missasque litteras, fuisse in ignem coniectas ut
tacitum, tutumque suae iniquitatis seruatorem, aliud nihil
hiis litteris conscriptum erat, quam quod ad publicam sedi-
tionem potissimum spectaret, sustinere diutius non potuit
mitissimus Rex istorum culpam tam atrocem, legumque
examini publico foro et aperto iudicio illos commisit, Laesae
Maiestatis, ac rebellionis rei reperti sunt, atque damnati,
supplicium de eis sumptum est longe quidem mitius quam
leges, ac iudicia praescribebant aut eorum culpa exegisset,
ex quorum exemplo ad sanitatem, ad fidem quam multi
rediere : Quicunque sano defecatoque est iudicio non obscure
huic perspicere potest quod praecipitanter pontifex, et curia
Romana ullam ex hac re animi offensionem conceperit, per
Regiam Maiestatem non stat, quominus pontifex in suos
Cardinales Episcopos eosque omnes, in quos ius ullum sibi
uendicat, iure suo utatur, non eorum causam suam aestimat,
nec offenditur, si pontifex, aut quiuis alius christianus princeps
ullum de male meritis subditis aut rebellibus supplicium
exigat : Iterum igitur, atque iterum miratur, pontificem ex
hac re tantum indignationis animo concepisse, sed hanc
indignationem, quam tantopere exacerbare uidetur curia, tunc
depositam iri putat, quum desierint maleuoli suggerere quae
falsa sunt, quumque mentiendi uia fuerit illis praeclusa, quibus
quum nil aeque graue, atque molestum sit, quam quod suorum
consiliorum tam strenua fundamenta deiecta fuerint, id operae
precium non exiguum esse ducunt, ut hoc uelamine suas
technas callide contegant priuatamque offensionem, si quae
sit, pontificis causam faciant.   Non grauetur itaque pontifex,
si Regia Maiestas suo Regnique sui iure, si quando expedit,
uicissim utatur :   Haec itaque omnia tum pontifici, tum
coeteris omnibus, qui ex horum rebellium suscepto supplicio
quicquid offensionis concoeperint sedulo enarrabitis, ut quam
ex falsa auditione animi molestiam imbiberunt, hanc uera
audiendo, multa mentis tranquillitate quandoque deponant,
nihilque omittetis, in eorum qua superius commemoraui
enarratione, etenim Regiae Maiestati gratissimum erit, ne
ipsa ueritas, ut se habet, maleuolorum calumniis obscuretur,
quia si tantum increbuerit mendax paucorum delatio, ut
nullus hac in re amplius apud illos sit locus ueritati relictus,
falsas eorum calumnias quantum cum Deo poterit Regia
Maiestas sustinebit, quae sic Regni sui statum, resque omnes
undequaque firmitas, stabilitasque habet, sic suorum fidem,
pectora, et obseruantiam compertam tenet, ut iniuriam omnem,
si qua alicunde inferatur, queat non multo cum labore deo

bene iuuante, refellere et propulsare.  Et bene valete.  Ex
Aula Regia apud Brumham Die     Septembr*is* MDXXXV.

Vester bonus amicus

THOMAS CRUMWELL.

*Add.*  Mag*nific*o Equiti, D*omi*no Gregorio Casalio etc.

123. ⟨CROMWELL⟩ TO ——.

R. O. Cal. ix. 241 (ii).    ⟨Sept. 1535.⟩

The King thanks the recipient for his letter, and for the articles of the
charge he has given to the inquests, and desires him to act further
according to his discretion.

After right harty co*m*mendacion, ye shall vnderstand that
I have resceyved y*our* l*ette*re of the xxvi[th] day of August w*ith*
the articles of the charge that ye haue geven to thenquestes
ther the whiche l*ette*re and articles I have at large shewed
and declared vnto the king*es* highnes who [1] consideryng y*our*
payne and travaill takyn therin right well allowithe and
acceptithe y*our* good procedyng*es* and doyng*es* in that
behalfe, yevyng vnto you therfore right harty thank*es*,
requyryng [2] the same farther like as ye have alredy begonne
So to p*r*ocede therin withe suche acceleracion and spede as ye
convenyently may do, accordyng to thexpectacion and trust
that his highnes hathe in you.   And touchyng the enquestes
that ye have charged for that purpose all though they be the
king*es* s*er*uaunt*es* and sworne for that purpose, yet for asmoche
as many of theym in some poynt*es* p*er*chaunce may be
offendo*ur*s will therfore conceyll and not fynd the truthe in
eu*er*y poynt.   Wherfore the king*es* pleasure is that ye well
consideryng the same may order and devise eu*er*y thyng after
y*our* discresion, and as ye shall se cause besid*es* theffect of
the verdictes of thesame enquestes.

124. CROMWELL TO THE MAYOR, BAILIFFS, AND
BURGESSES OF CAMBRIDGE.

Cooper's Annals, i. 373 ;  Cal. ix. 615.   Oct. 15 ⟨1535⟩.

As the King has approved his election as Chancellor of the University, he
desires them to appear at the two yearly leets held by the University,
and not to deny to the University the use of the King's prison called
the Tolbooth.

In my right harty maner I commende me unto youe.   And
whereas it hath pleased the kings highnes, uppon an election
passed by the universitie of Cambridge wherin they chose me
to be their hedde and Chaunceler, to condescende that I shuld
accepte and take the same, to the intent that all matiers

---

[1] *c. o.* for y*our*     [2] *c. o.* you even

depending betweene you and them, in contencon and variaunce, might be rather by my meane and mediacon be finished, and soo determyned, as eyther parte myght enjoye such privileages as shuld be thought conveniente for them, with the advauncement of justice, the quiet and tranquillitie of the common weale, Wherin I purpose with suche dexteritie to travayl, as *you* shall have good cause to think that all respects and affecttions laide aparte, I only mynd that which appertayneth to the office of a faithfull counsailor. Ye shall understande, that forasmoche as I am credibly advertised, that notwithstanding the said universitie hath hertefor had not only the serche of vitail and the correccon of waightes and measures there, and may by the kings Charters (as they doo and of long tyme have doon) kepe two letes in the yere, to be furnyshed with the townesmen, for the punishment and amerciament of suche as shuld be founde offenders in that behaulf, but also the use of the kings prisonne there called the Tolbothe, for the punyshment of all such other offences, as they may by their said Charters correct and punish, the rather of perverse mynd than otherwise, doo from tyme to tyme, when the said letes be summoned, as wel make slender appearance in the same, ne being theer charged, present and amerce the offenders, as by virtue of *your* othe you be bounde, wherby the good order to be observed therin is utterly confounded, to the great detryment of the publique weale of the hole towne, with the inquietacon of the kings subgiectts abiding within the same, As utterly deny them the use of the said prisonne; I have thought good, by these my lettres, to desire and praye youe, and nevertheles on the kings behaulf for the better preservacion of his graces peax, to commaunde youe, not only to mak *your* due appearance in the said letes, and their to enquire, present, and amerce the offenders, as hath been accustomed, but also bothe to permytt and suffer them to have the correction of waightes and measures, and the use of the said prisonne at their liberties, as they have had, without *your* denyal or interrupcon to the contrary, untyl suche tyme as the kings highnes shal take finall order and direction in all things depending in variaunce or question betweene youe, whiche his Majestie wil not fayle to do with al speede and celeritie. And thus fare youe hartely well. From Stepnay, the 15th daye of Octobre.

Your lovyng freend,

THOM*AS* CRUMWELL.

*Add.* To my hartely beloved Freendes the Mayre, Bailieffs, and Burgesses, of the towne of Cambridge, and to every of them.

## 125. ⟨CROMWELL⟩ TO JOHN GOSTWICK.

B. M. Titus B. iv, ff. 114–5 ; Cal. ix. 647.    Oct. 20, 1535.

Finds that Gostwick is charged with the sum of £16,032 16s. 8d. due to
the King from divers persons, for conveying corn out of the realm.
Desires him to collect as much of it as he can.

Mr Gostwyck. Where ye stande Charged in the Bookes
of Specialties Betwene you & me made at your furst entrie
into your Office subscribed with our handes for the Receipt
of Sixtene Thousande thirty & two poundes sixtene shil-
linges and eight pence, due vnto the Kinges Maiestie by
diuerse & sundry personnes, for the Conveyaunce of Corne
& other thinges out of this Realme contrary to the Kinges
Lawes, as appereth by the condicions of their obligacions,
remaynyng in your Custodye, And forasmuche as I do vnderstande and perfitely knowe that a grete parte of the said
summe of xviml xxxii li xvi s viii d ys vnlevyable, desperat
& cannot be had nor recouered by reason that certain of the
saide personnes haue certificaths, somme other fallen in vtter
decay, by occasion of the grete losses & hynderaunces that
they haue susteyned as well by See, as Lande, And somme of
theim dedde, & not knowing of whome to be aunswered
Whereby I haue Considered the same to be mattier of Conscience, not intending nor mynding to charge you further
than shall stande with the same, nor with nomore sume or
summes than hath or herafter shall comme vnto your handes
Have therfore thought it good, aswell for your Discharge, and
myne, As also for the spedy Recoueryng and Receipt of the
Rest of the Money due by the saide specialties, this to devise
& wryte, By the same in the Kinges Maiesties name Auc-
torizing you, to call all the said parties before you, with all
seleritie & spede, And by your discrescion, so to vse them,
That the kinges highnes may be aunswered of the money,
that by your saide discrescion shalbe thought of verey right
& Conscience sufficient. Further in the kinges name Auc-
torizing you by vertue herof, to take newe composicions of
suche as hath not their money in arredynesse. And also by
the same to deliuer all suche specialties vnto the parties or
ther deputies, as shalbe proved of right either to haue Cer-
tificate or other sufficient Discharge. And this Subscribed with
my hande shalbe vnto you your heires executours & deputies
sufficient Discharge at all tymes hereafter, for your so doing.
Wrytten the xxti day of Octobre the xxviiti yere of the Reigne
of our Soueraigne Lorde king Henry the eight.

*Endd.* A minute of a lettre to Mr Gostwyke, towching

a newe ordre and composicion to be taken with certayn persons standing chardged in grete sommes of monaye vnto the kinges Maiestie whiche be vnleviable and desperate by reason the parties by casualtes be brought to greate pouertie

## 126. CROMWELL TO GARDINER.

B. M. Add. MSS. 25,114, f. 110 ; Cal. ix. 848. Nov. 19 〈1535〉.

Urges him to work diligently in France for the delivery of the ships at Bordeaux. Sends a dozen of Gardiner's orations and a dozen of those of the Dean of the Chapel Royal also, for him to distribute according to his discretion.

My veray good lorde aftre my moost harty commendacions by maister brian whom the kinges highnes at this tyme sendeth vnto his good brother the frenche king sufficiently instructed to certain purposes, as by his instructions wherunto ye shalbe participant and make him again the semblable to yours, ye shal perceyve, ye shal receyve his highnes letteres, touching matiers of importaunce, whiche as his grace doubteth not but ye wil setfurth with suche dexteritie as shal best conduce his desire to effecte   Soo his pleasure is ye shal with suche stomak and courage travail with the frenche king and his counsail in that pointe touching the delyueraye of the shippes as ye maye not onely obteyne the same but also declare and shewe therwith howe ingrately his highnes is handeled therin specially being at this tyme soo secrete and freendly treatie betwene him and his good brother as there is for matiers of soo high consequence, amonges whiche thinges also his grace desireth youe to remembre the declaracion of the french king of tharticles sent by Melancton, luthers epistle in the same, with thother circumstances conteyned in the copies lately sent vnto you. Ye shall also receyve herwith a dosen of your orations and another dosen of the deanes, whiche the kinges pleasure is ye shall by thaduise of Mr. brian and Maister Wallop destribute to suche persounes there as amonges youe ye shal think convenient.  In whiche treatie to be had concernyng the shippes ye may not forget to inculce what Joye the subgiettes here conceyved for his recouerye in the procession, and howe they bee again sithens stayed vppon this staye of the shippes whiche hath indede soo contrary a countenaunce to our doinges as it is no mervayl thoughe they be abasshed at it.  And this matier the kinges highnes woll haue you chiefly prosecute, leving to Sir John Wallop only the sute for the moneye, bicause the promyse therof was made vnto him.  And thus I pray god sende your lordshipp well to fare. From the Rulles the xix<sup>th</sup> daye of Nouembre

Yo*ur* lordshippis assuryd

THOMAS CRUMWELL.

*Add.* To my veray good lorde my lorde of Winchestre the king*es* highnes Ambassado*r* at this tyme w*ith* the french king.

*Endd.* From the Roulles the xix<sup>th</sup> of Novembre. Mr. Secretary

### 127. CROMWELL TO GARDINER AND WALLOP.

B. M. Add. MSS. 25,114, f. 232 ; Cal. ix. App. 8. Dec. 7 ⟨1535⟩.

Desires them to discover the real inclination of the French King, and to ascertain whether they have any secret plans on foot. Gives a list of the sums of money due to the King.

Aftre my moost harty co*m*mendac*i*ons w*ith* like thank*es* for yo*ur* gentle l*e*tt*e*res and aduertisement*es* of the Occurrant*es* there, ye shal at this tyme receyve the king*es* highnes l*e*tt*e*res answering to yo*ur*s of the xxviii<sup>th</sup> of Nouembre The content*es* wherof as his highnes doubteth not but ye wil duely consider and accomplishe temp*e*ring neu*er*theles the same in suche sorte, as yo*ur* wisedomes shall think maye best s*er*ue to thentertaynement of thamytie betwene his grace and the frenche king, and the conducing of his graces desire to effecte. Soo his highnes spec*i*ally desireth youe to endeuo*ur* yo*ur*self*es* by all the meanes ye canne possibly deuise and excogitate to explore serche and knowe the veray inclynac*i*on of the frenche king and whither the frenchemen haue any pryvie practises in hande, and of the lightlywod of the successes of the same w*ith* suche other occurrant*es* as shall chaunce to co*m*me to yo*ur* knowleage to aduertise his highnes, as I shal for my p*ar*te desire youe to doo to me the semblable as the tyme and hast of yo*ur* dispeches wil give you leave. The treatie belli offensiui ratified at Amyans I sende vnto youe herw*ith*, And as co*n*cernyng thaccompt of the money due to the king*es* highnes First there is due to his grace lM<sup>1 1</sup> crownes lent to the duke of Bavier for the whiche the frenche king standeth bounde by obligac*i*on. Item lM<sup>1 1</sup> crownes lent at his request for the assistence of the duke of Wittenberge, for the whiche they haue non acquietance, but were bounde by promyse to repaye it in cace there ensued no good successe

¹ i. e. 50,000.

of themployment of the same whiche condition and convenaunt is without question determyned.

Item there is due vnto his grace the hole pencion and salt moneye for the last yere ended at Nouembre.

And wheras the kinges highnes in these his letteres nowe sent vnto youe hathe commaunded youe Mr. wallop to presse themperours, Ambassadour for your declaration to the denyal of thouertures, like as I writing by his graces commaundement vsed the same terme, for declaracion of yourself, to thintent ye shal not thinke that anything is further ment therby thenne to haue youe vse that worde to him to extorte what ye canne in that matier, his highnes commaunded me in this sorte to expounde the same vnto youe. And thus moost hartely fare youe well. From Richemont the vii[th] of decembre.

The kinges highnes specially desireth youe to remembre his commandement touching the delyuerance of the shippes

Your assuryd Freend

THOMAS CRUMWELL.

*Add.* To myn assured frendes My lorde of Winchestre and sir John Wallop knight the kinges Ambassadours in fraunce.

*Endd.* From Richemonde the vii[th] of decembre. Mr. Secretary.

### 128. CROMWELL TO GARDINER.

B. M. Add. MSS. 25,114, f. 234; Cal. ix. App. 9. Dec. 7 ⟨1535⟩.

Has been unable to obtain a copy of the treaty which he promised to send, and thought it better to postpone sending it than to delay the bearer. The King desires him to labour for the delivery of the ships.

Aftre my moost harty commendacions to your lordshippe Thise shalbe to aduertise youe that Albeit in myn other letteres writen ioyntly to youe and Maister Wallop I haue signified that ye shuld by this berer receyve the treaty belli offensiui whiche ye wrote for, yet having here suche busines that I could ⟨not⟩ departe to london to cause the same to be copied, I thought it more expedient to differre the sending of it vntil we shal dispeche another currour vnto youe, thenne to demore your seruaunt here tyl I might haue goon to london for that purpose. And wheras your said seruaunt hath declared vnto me your credence concernyng your necessitie of money, I shall not fayle by the next messanger to take suche direction with youe for the satisfaction of your desire in that parte as ye shall haue cause to be contented. The kinges highnes desireth youe to labour effectually ⟨for⟩ the

delyuerance of the shippes at Burdeulx according to suche
instructions as ye haue in that behaulf. And thus moost
hartely Fare youe well. From Richemonte the vii<sup>th</sup> daye of
Decembre in hast

Your lordshippis assuryd Freend

THOMAS CRUMWELL.

*Add.* To my veray good lorde my lorde of Wynchestre
the king*es* Ambassado*ur* in fraunce.

*Endd.* From Richemonde the vii<sup>th</sup> of decembre.  Mr.
Secretary.

### 129. CROMWELL TO THE MAYOR, ALDERMEN AND BAILIFFS OF CAMBRIDGE.

Cooper's Annals, i. 377 ; Cal. ix. 977.  Dec. 15 ⟨1535⟩.

Marvels that they have not complied with his requests that the University
be permitted to use the Tolbooth, and desires them to delay no
longer.  Will see that justice is done in all respects.

In my right harty maner I comende me unto youe. Lating
you wit that I cannot a little marvayle to understand that
notwithstanding my sundrey lettres hertofor addressed unto
youe, tuching the permission of the use of the Tolboth, the
furniture of the Universitie leates, the advoyding of newe
practises, usages, or imposicions, wherby might insewg debate
and contencion betweene you and the said universitie, to yo*ur*
owne disquiet, with the offence of the kings peax, ye have
both refused to doo and accomplish those things persuaded
and enioined therin unto youe, and for the contynuance and
nutryment of discorde and trouble amonge the kings subiectts,
devised newe things and meanes to augment and engrece the
same. The prysonne first is the kings, and seing his grace by
his charters and grauntes hath ioyned the universitie with
youe in the use therof, I cannot conceyve what ye meane to
denye that whiche his grace hath grauntid, and by vertue
thereof, they have so long enjoyed, which expressly your
baylie Ousburn did bothe to the procurators, and also to the
vicechancelors deputie. A sergeant of yours also lately tok
a peace of cloth from the stall of a commone minister of the
Universities for non apparance in y*our* Leate contrary to the
comandment given at the tyme of Sturberige fayr, that ye
shuld reyse no newe custome, or gather any newe exaction or
imposiccon, uppon any scoler, his servaunt or their comone
ministers ; ye have also refused alonly this yere, to make a
certain othe before the congregacion at Saint Maryes church,
for the conservacion of the peax, and the presentement to

the vicechauncelor of vagabundes and others, breakers and interrupters of the said peax. Nowe shal I, being only a Counsailor, and otherwise then honestie and justice wil no partie, whiche have not only proffessed to travayl for the quiet of both parties, but will devise and labor also to performe the same, desire youe to permytt them, first to have the free use of the tolboth as they have had: to see the cloth restored, taken violently awaye by your sergeant ; To see their leats furnished, and to tak such othe, and use all suche things and custumes as ye have doon, untyl fynal direction may be taken betweene both parties. And yet I must ever saye, whiche ye shall also fynde true, that in cace ye shall doo any wrong, or not fulfill that ye be bound unto, wherby tumult and busines shuld rise amonge the kings people, though I do indede favor your cause, as appertayneth, and will also be gladde to doo therein what I canne for your comoditie, Yet in cace prayer and gentle entreatie cannot pull and allure youe awaye from the doing of wrong and iniury, both to the king and his subjectts, I will not fayle to advaunce, to the uttermost of my power Justice and to see punished with extremytie the interrupters thereof, to the example of other. And therfor eftsones, I most hartily praye youe to conforme yourselfs to quietnes in these pointes, and therein to performe that without contencon whiche the princes grauntes, ever to be reverently obeyed, doo require of youe, Ye shal by this waye and meane, doo your dueties, first toward his grace, to me administer most thankfull pleasure, and with your honesties provyde yourselfs quiet and rest, with a good end in all suche controversies as depende between youe and the said universitie. And thus fare youe hartely well. From Stepnaye, the xv[th] daye of Decembre.

Your freend,

THOM*AS* CRUMWELL.

*Add.* To my loving freendes, the Mayre, Aldermen and bailieffs of the towne of Cambridge.

### 130. CROMWELL TO GARDINER.

B. M. Add. MSS. 25,114, f. 112 ; Cal. ix. 1010. Dec. 24 ⟨1535⟩.

Thanks him for his letters, and promises to attend to Gardiner's wants. The postscript of Cromwell's other letter will inform Gardiner of Thwaites' arrival here, and of the answers made to the letters he brought.

Aftre my moost harty co*m*mendacons to your lordshippe wit*h* like thank*es* for *your* gentle *lette*res by the post scripta in myn other *lette*res nowe writen vnto youe by the king*es* highnes co*m*maundement ye shal p*er*ceyve tharryval here of y*our* s*er*ua*u*nt Thwaytes, w*ith* the determynac*i*on for answer to be made to suche *lette*res as he brought w*ith* him.   I shall in the meane tyme so satisfie peter lark y*our* s*er*ua*u*nt touching y*our* request for money that ye shall by the next post p*er*ceyve ye be not forgotten, but sufficiently and soo furnished as ye shall haue cause to be contented.  Y*our* doing*es* be no lesse thankfully accepted, thenne y*our* wisedom travail and diligence therin do require and for my p*ar*te if there be anything ell*es* here that I may doo y*our* pleasure in, vppon y*our* aduertisement I shalbe glad w*ith* al my harte to satisfie youe in the same.   And thus most hartely fare youe wel, from the Rulles the xxiiij^{th} of Decembre

Y*our* lordshippis assuryd freend

THOMAS CRUMWELL.

*Add.*  To my veray good lord my lord of Winchestre.

*Endd.*  From the roulles the xxiiij of decemb*er* Mr. Secretary.

131. CROMWELL TO GARDINER.

B. M. Add. MSS. 25,114, f. 114 ; Cal. ix. 1039.   Dec. 30 ⟨1535⟩.

The King approves of his service, and assures him that he will be glad to welcome him on his return.  Reports the illness of Katherine.  Has arranged for his money with Peter Lark.

My veray good lord aftre my moost harty co*m*mendac*i*ons This shalbe taduertise youe that vndoubtedly the king*es* highnes doth in soo thankfull sorte accepte your s*er*uice there doon vnto his maiestie, and in euery condic*i*on soo allowe approve and co*m*mende y*our* wise substanciall and discreate proced*i*ng, as like as ye haue moche cause to reioyse therin, soo shall the same be certain meane and occasion, that ye shall assuredlye what ende soeuer y*our* busines there shall take, returne to his highnes as hartely welcom and in as great reputac*i*on as youe could y*our*self desire, wherof for my p*ar*te I am euen for many respect*es* as gladde as ye canne be y*our*self.   Touchyng his graces affayres I write nothing bicause the same be sufficiently touched in his highnes *lette*res nowe addressed vnto youe, only for newes ye shal vndrestand that the douagier is in greate daunger whiche his Maiestie also willed me to signifie vnto youe, as by the copye of a *lette*re sent from themp*er*our*s* Ambassador here touching her syknes ye shal p*er*ceyve. And as concernyng y*our* money I haue taken ordre w*ith* *yo*u*r* serva*u*nt peter lark, soo as ye shall I doubt ⟨not⟩ be shortly therin satisfied. And thus beseching god to sende youe a good newe yere, I bid youe as well to fare as I wold myself. From the Rulles the penultime of Decembre

Y*ou*r lordshippis assuryd freend

THOMAS CRUMWELL.

*Add.* To my veray good lord, My Lord of Winchestre the King*es* highnes Ambassad*our* in Fraunce.

*Endd.* From the Roulles the xxx^th of Decembre   Mr. Secretary

### 132. ⟨CROMWELL⟩ TO ⟨THE PRIOR OF MONTACUTE⟩.

R. O. Cal. ix. 1127. ⟨1535.⟩

Has received his letters saying that a young person has made suit to obtain the lease after its expiration. The King is assured that he will not recommend any one to him who will not act honourably and for the King's profit.

In my right hertie man*er* I co*m*mende me vnto you Adu*er*tesing the same that I haue receyued your l*ette*res right well p*er*ceyuing the content*es* of the same   And where as ye write vnto me that a nother p*er*son of younger yeres should make sute for thopteyning of the lease after the yeres all redie gr*a*unted in the same being expired and determyned the truth is that there is labour made aswell vnto Mr. Norres as other which is not so vehement ne hastie But that it may be right well stayed.   Neu*er*theles the king*es* highnes hauing ferme trust in y*ou*r dexteritie and wisedom must ned*es* haue regarde and expectac*i*on in y*ou*r l*ette*res.   Doubting not but ye will not p*re*ferre any other vnto his highnes but suche as shalbe right mete to do that thing which shalbe most for their own honestie and will haue good regarde and aspect to the King*es* most proffite.

### 133. ⟨CROMWELL⟩ TO ⟨POLE⟩[1].

B. M. Cleop. E. vi, 371 ; Cal. viii. 220. ⟨1535.⟩

Desires the recipient to answer the things contained in Starkey's letter to him, which was written by the King's express commandment.

Syr after my most harty reco*m*me*n*datyanys thys shalbe in few & short wordys to requyre you accordyng to the callyng

---

[1] This letter, though written in Starkey's hand and addressed to Harvell, is believed by Mr. Gairdner to be a copy of a letter written by Cromwell to Pole, transcribed by Starkey on the inside of the cover of a letter to Harvell.

that our lord Jh*e*su Chryst hath callyd & redemyd you that
ys to say as wel wyth the gyft of gud l*ette*res and vnder-
stondyng, as wyth the most excelle*n*t gyft of jugeme*n*t in the
same, ye wyl indeuur yourselfe to make answere vnto such
thyngys as be co*n*tynyd in master starkeys l*ette*res to you
wrytyn at thys tyme, by the kyng our masturys & soueraynys
expresse cu*m*ma*n*deme*n*t & that the same answer may be
such & of such gravyte, as the lyght & truthe therof may be
to the honowre of god, & the satysfactyon of hys hyghnes.
Wherof I assure you I wold be as glad as any pare*n*t or frend
ye haue lyuy*n*g not dowtyng in your approuyd wysedome &
jugeme*n*t but that ye wyl exte*n*d the gyftys gyue*n* vnto you
in such wyse as leuyng al your respectys or affectyon wole
so inserch your co*n*scyence & jugeme*n*t for the truth as ye
wole both dyscharge yourselfe agaynst god & your pry*n*ce, in
dowyng wherof you shal assurydly dow the thyng much to
thencrese of your meryte & fame, wherin as he that ys your
assuryd frend to hys lytyl power I requyre you to haue
indyffere*n*t co*n*syderatyon & so to ordur yourselfe therin
as the expectatyon of your frendys wythe the jugeme*n*t of al
me*n* that knowyth you may be satysfyd in that behalfe & thus
our lord send you no worse to fare than I wold ye dyd at
london

*Add.* To my synguler frend Mayster Edmu*n*de Herwel
marchant at Venyce

## 134. ⟨CROMWELL⟩ TO ⟨AN ABBOT⟩.

### R. O. Cal. viii. 1122. ⟨1535.⟩

In consideration of his willing mind, has obtained the King's licence for
  him to resort to his manors near his monastery, provided that by so
  doing he causes no disturbance.

Ye shall vnderstand that I haue resceyved y*our* l*ette*res [1],
and touching that ye desire among*es* other thing*es* licence for
y*our* selfe and certayn of y*our* bretherne to walke to y*our*
mano*ur*s and other places about y*our* monastery. Ye shall
understand that in considera*c*ion of the good and toward
mynd that I have found yn you toward*es* me and my s*er*-
uaunt*es* diu*er*se ways I [2] have opteynyd licence of the king*es*
highnes for y*our* selfe that ye may resorte vnto y*our* maners
and other convenyent walkes nygh vnto y*our* monastery, so

---

[1] *c. o. wit*h *the . . .* and towching the content*es* of the same ye
shall vnderstand that I haue res-

ceyued y*our* l*ette*res
[2] *c. o.* am contented

that no common brute may be reysed therby, not doubtyng but ye will vse your selfe so (as for the good will and mynd I bere toward you) it may be to the good zele of religion and as I may therby resceyve no disworship therby. so that always your bretherne must nedes use and order theymselfes accordyng to the Iniunccions in that case geven unto theym in that behalf.

END OF VOL. I.

## DATE DUE

| DEC 15 1989 | | | |
|---|---|---|---|
| | | | |
| | | | |
| | | | |
| | | | |
| | | | |
| | | | |
| | | | |
| | | | |
| | | | |
| | | | |
| | | | |
| | | | |
| | | | |
| | | | |
| | | | |
| | | | |
| | | | |